D1736453

Theatre, Opera, and Audiences in Revolutionary Paris

Recent Titles in
Contributions in Drama and Theatre Studies

Richard Wagner and Festival Theatre
Simon Williams

Playwright versus Director: Authorial Intentions and Performance Interpretations
Jeane Luere, editor; Sidney Berger, advisory editor

George Bernard Shaw and the Socialist Theatre
Tracy C. Davis

Playwrights and Acting: Acting Methodologies for Brecht, Ionesco, Pinter,
and Shepard
James H. McTeague

Israel Horovitz: A Collection of Critical Essays
Leslie Kane, editor

Jung's Advice to the Players: A Jungian Reading of Shakespeare's Problem Plays
Sally F. Porterfield

Where the Words Are Valid: T. S. Eliot's Communities of Drama
Randy Malamud

Greek Tragedy on the American Stage: Ancient Drama in the Commercial Theater,
1882–1994
Karelisa V. Hartigan

"Vast Encyclopedia": The Theatre of Thornton Wilder
Paul Lifton

Christopher Marlowe and the Renaissance of Tragedy
Douglas Cole

Menander and the Making of Comedy
J. Michael Walton and Peter D. Arnott

A History of Polish Theater, 1939–1989: Spheres of Captivity and Freedom
Kazimierz Braun

Theatre, Opera, and Audiences in Revolutionary Paris

Analysis and Repertory

Emmet Kennedy, Marie-Laurence Netter,
James P. McGregor, and Mark V. Olsen

Contributions in Drama and Theatre Studies, *Number 62*

Greenwood Press
Westport, Connecticut • London

Library of Congress Cataloging-in-Publication Data

Theatre, opera, and audiences in revolutionary Paris : analysis and
   repertory / Emmet Kennedy . . . [et al.].
       p.   cm.—(Contributions in drama and theatre studies, ISSN
   0163-3821 ; no. 62)
     Includes bibliographical references and indexes.
     ISBN 0-313-28960-3 (alk. paper)
       1. Theater—France—Paris—History—18th century.   2. Opera—
   France—Paris—18th century.   3. Theater—France—Paris—Calendars.
   I. Kennedy, Emmet.   II. Series.
   PN2633.T54   1996
   792'.0944'09033—dc20   95-5677

British Library Cataloguing in Publication Data is available.

Library of Congress Catalog Card Number: 95-5677
ISBN: 0-313-28960-3
ISSN: 0163-3821

First published in 1996

Greenwood Press, 88 Post Road West, Westport, CT 06881
An imprint of Greenwood Publishing Group, Inc.

Printed in the United States of America

The paper used in this book complies with the
Permanent Paper Standard issued by the National
Information Standards Organization (Z39.48-1984).

10 9 8 7 6 5 4 3 2 1

To the students

who made this work possible

Contents

Preface

Pondering theatrical announcements in the Bibliothèque Nationale in 1977, it appeared to me that the plays of the French Revolution which were the most frequently performed might not be those history has canonized. The thought came to mind that frequency of performances might tell something about the mentalities of people who frequented the theatres. Sampling every tenth day of the daily announcements to learn what they actually saw and heard proved unreliable because there was no regular run of performances. Daniel Roche, the leading quantitative historian of eighteenth-century French culture, urged a daily count.

This study is the result of such a count of all performances of plays and operas announced in two Parisian newspapers: *Le Journal de Paris*, from 1789 through 1794, and *Les Affiches, Annonces et Avis Divers*, known as the *Petites Affiches*, from 1795 to Bonaparte's coup on November 9, 1799. The count was made to determine what theatregoers, from among the 600,000 Parisians, were viewing while the French Revolution raged in the streets. An American Council of Learned Societies grant-in-aid in 1980 made possible the employment of several meticulous American undergraduate and graduate students, fluent in French, who recorded on cards every performance for the period 1789-1794. In Paris, Marie-Laurence Netter of the Ecole des Hautes Etudes en Sciences Sociales paralleled my efforts for the period of the Directory (1795-1799) at the Bibliothèque Nationale, where the only complete set of the *Petites Affiches* exists. Over 86,000 performances were recorded on index cards. In 1982, in the midst of the computer revolution, we decided to submit this record to an IBM mainframe, initially under the direction of Carol Johnson of the George Washington University Computer Center, and then under the patient guidance of co-author James P. McGregor, a programmer and social scientist of the United States Information Agency. Preliminary findings were divulged by me in March 1980, at the George Washington University Dilthey Society meeting; in December 1980, at the Washington meeting of the American Historical Association; in March 1982, at the Washington Area Group of Old Regime French Historians; in December 1982, at the History, Literature and Society Program at Brown University; in April 1983, in New York at the annual meeting of the Society for Eighteenth Century Studies; in October 1983, in Washington, D. C. at the annual meeting of the Social Sciences History Association; in July 1983, in Brussels at the Fifth International Congress on the Enlightenment, which resulted in a first publication; in June 1984, at the Woodrow Wilson International Center for Scholars; in July 1989, at the Sorbonne, Paris, at the Congrès Mondial pour le Bicentennaire de la Révolution Française; in October 1990, in Kingston, Ontario, at the Canadian Society of Eighteenth Century Studies; in July 1991, in Bristol, England, at the Eighth International Congress on the Enlightenment; and, finally, in August 1994, in Graz, Austria, at the Fourth Conference of the International Society for the Study of European Ideas. Some of the data and conclusions were published in the proceedings of the three international congresses.[1]

Marie-Laurence Netter presented papers titled "Le Théâtre pendant la Révolution française: Instrument et miroir du politique" (1988) and "L'Intégration de nouvelles valeurs par le théâtre," the latter as part of a Bicentennial Colloquium on Theatre and Revolution at Besançon in 1989.[2]

Special thanks go to the George Washington University for its patient subsidization of this project from 1980 to 1983, in 1991, and in 1993; to the Ecole de Hautes Etudes en Sciences Sociales for subsidies in 1983 and 1993, and to the American Philosophical Society and the French cultural attaché in New York for grants-in-aid in 1991 and 1994, respectively. These funds provided for research and clerical assistance for collecting and correcting what eventually were over 90,000 records.

We are also grateful to the George Washington University's deans; History Department heads and secretaries; its University Research Facilitating fund; its reference librarians; and its secretaries, who helped this project proceed to completion.

Ms. Stavroula Lambrakopoulos did most of the original keyboarding of the data between 1980 and 1983. Nancy Roberts continued this work with the performance records drawn from the *Petites Affiches* by M. L. Netter in Paris. Between 1983 and 1984, Ms. Roberts and Mme Netter identified many of the authors. Son Tran, Jennifer Keene, Kevin Gessler, Angela Wilkins, Catherine Pochari, Janelle Hanson, Mathew Lachesnez-Heude, Misha Yi, and Sandy Schreibel, all of George Washington University; and Margaret Jewett, of the University of Chicago, provided invaluable research and word-processing assistance in "cleaning up" and completing the original database by a laborious process of verifying and standardizing authors' names, titles, genres, premiere dates, etc. My daughter, Gaëlle Kennedy, helped check the original card entries against the computer printout. Rob Kennedy helped with some critical, last-minute proofreading. David Charlton, a musicologist from the University of East Anglia, United Kingdom, went further and combed our entire author-title list indicating composers, saving us from innumerable conflations of different works with identical titles. Our coauthor, Mark Olsen, a cliometrician and historian of France, and the assistant director of ARTFL (American Research on the Treasury of the French Language) at the University of Chicago, generously agreed to program for us after duties at USIA obliged James McGregor to terminate his work on the project in 1991.

Michèle Root-Bernstein offered valuable information before and after the publication of her pathbreaking book (1984) as did the Sorbonne theatre historian Martine de Rougemont. I am grateful to both.

In its long penultimate stage, two other persons contributed invaluably to this publication: (1) Michael Weeks, secretary to the History Department at the George Washington University, whose expertise with the personal computer saw the manuscript through its penultimate stages, and (2) Janine Maltz, who skillfully proofed and edited my translations of M. L. Netter's chapters, as well as my own chapters.

Lest one wonder why this small platoon of researchers was necessary, let me illustrate some of the problems this study encountered:

1. Authors and composers, and dates of premieres of these 3,700 plays, were usually not published in our newspaper announcements and hence needed to be searched in the bibliographies listed in our appendix, especially in the catalogs of the Bibliothèque Nationale, the Bibliothèque de l'Arsénal, the Bibliothèque du Sénat (Pixérécourt Collection), Tourneux (1900), Brunet's index to the Soleinne library (1914), Brenner (1947), Grove and Sadie (1980), Sadie (1992), and Tissier (1992). The texts of the plays were found with the help of the staff at the Library of Congress Rare Book Room, the Bibliothèque de l'Arsénal (the Rondel Theater Collection), the Bibliothèque Nationale, and the Bibliothèque du Sénat (the Pixérécourt collection).

2. Many different plays had identical titles (e.g., *Guillaume Tell, Paul et Virginie, Lodoiska, Le Sourd, La Prise de Toulon* or *Cange*). Clues had to be found to determine which author wrote which of them.

3. Any slight variation in the name of a play or author entered into the computer at different times from different sources, be it so small as a hyphen or a comma, meant the items would be listed separately by the computer. This had to be corrected.

4. Pseudonyms and compound names caused names to be listed elsewhere than one might expect.

Since we were dealing with several thousand plays, corrections took time. Students generally could work only one day a week except in the summer, and the project was put altogether on the back burner between 1983 and 1989.

Although intended as a complete record of Parisian theatre for the

Revolutionary decade (January 1, 1789 to November 9, 1799), there were numerous dates (such as the days following the overthrow of the king on August 10, 1792) when the theatre column was missing. Consultation of other journals would doubtless augment the figures by inclusion of other theatres. Allowances should be made for an undetermined number of unrecorded performances (estimated at roughly 1 percent of the total) due to human error. Attributions of plays to authors were checked and rechecked, but there are undoubtedly some errors because so many plays shared common titles. Dates and theatres of premiere were clues, but not proofs. André Tissier's work has been of great help in corroborating our attributions and figures with his for the first three and a half years of the Revolution. In spite of all this checking, there remain a large number of anonymous plays and plays without extant texts.

Although the book is accurate *en gros*, anyone studying an eighteenth-century author will want to verify his or her subject's performance record independently to be absolutely sure. Our figures should be taken as minima. The fact that the theatre lists were not *always* published in our newspapers on all the 3,965 days covered, and that some theatres (presumably performing some of the same plays) were not included in the list of spectacles, means that the real figures should be higher. But the proportionate performance of eighteenth-century authors given here is statistically accurate.

If in the twenty-first century researchers further our study—for example, in a much-needed history of provincial theatre during the Revolution—and find it as substantially accurate a count as historians of literacy have found Louis Maggiolo's inquest of marriage contract signatures from the seventeenth to the nineteenth century, we shall be satisfied.

At times this project seemed interminable. We must thank all of our collaborators and assistants for persevering through the tedium and bringing this research to the light of day.

E. K.

1

History of the Problem and the Method of Solving It

Emmet Kennedy

The theatre of the French Revolution has interested historians more than the theatre of many other periods because of its alleged political and ideological character. Although a good, up-to-date political history of this theatre remains to be written, it appears appropriate to us to question the extent to which political drama permeated the stage between 1789 and 1799. Authors C. G. Etienne and A. Martainville (1802), E. Jauffret (1869), H. Welschinger (1880), P. d'Estrée (1913), J. Hérissay (1922), M. Carlson (1966), R. Herbert (1973), D. Hamiche (1973), J. Schlanger (1979), E. Blanchard (1980), M. H. Huet (1982), M. Mili (1989), and N. Guilbert and J. Razgonnikoff (1989) have all supposed that this theatre was essentially revolutionary; that it became a political club, a school of good citizenship and republican mores, a tribune, a mirror of the assemblies and popular societies, an organ of "pure propaganda," or a reflection of the class struggle. The methodology followed by these historians has often been wanting, and histories of individual theatres such as H. Lecomte's and A. Pougin's are little more than chronicles in which the daily repertory is tediously reproduced and theatrical incidents, relations with authorities, and finances are recounted only as they occur chronologically.

Etienne and Martainville's highly readable, contemporary account contains many valuable insights and anecdotes, but covers only the Comédie Française. Carlson's treatment of all theatres of the Revolution is based almost entirely on secondary sources; moreover, there is no real order to his work other than a chronological one. Jauffret's deprecatory history of Revolutionary drama does give a summary and brief analysis of a number of significant plays on a yearly basis. Welschinger and Hérissay's histories are both excellent—the former concentrates mostly on the thematic content of the plays themselves, while the latter is a very well-researched account of all dimensions of theatre history during the Revolution. Hamiche limits himself to two plays—*Charles IX* and

Le Jugement dernier des rois—and claims to have discovered therein the script of class conflict of the Revolution. For all of these historians the most salient trait of Revolutionary theatre was its political and social relevance, its contemporaneity. Theatre had, it seems, almost ceased to feed on traditional poetic illusion and had begun to reflect everyday reality. Most of these authors (except Hamiche) see theatre more as a reflection rather than as a stimulus of Revolutionary politics. They ask what the Revolution did to theatre rather than what theatre did to the Revolution. All, except those writing after the Second World War, deplore the effect of the Revolution on the artistic and literary quality of theatre, considered a source of cultural pride during the Old Regime.

Three authors have taken a different and—in our view—more felicitous approach to the Revolutionary stage. Maurice Albert, in a marvelously written account of the boulevard stages from 1789 to 1848 (1902), has shown how *l'indécence, les grossièretés,* and *le merveilleux* continued to characterize the boulevard stage after 1789. The theatrical assault on the Old Regime emanated from the privileged rather than from the popular theatres, but by year II (1793-1794) salacious, anticlerical "convent plays" roused the boulevard as well. Michèle Root-Bernstein, in a book based on archival and rare printed texts, has reconstructed the legal, administrative, economic, literary, and performing history of the boulevard from 1780 to 1795. She maintains that the traditional boulevard fare survived or resisted the Revolution; that the distinctions between high, privileged, and low theatre were breaking down before the Revolution; and that it was not (contra Darnton 1968, 1971) the "grub street" playwrights of the boulevard who found themselves political leaders of the Revolution after 1789. Beatrice Hyslop (1945) conducted a count from the *Moniteur* of all performances during the Terror, defined chronologically as the period between January 21, 1793 and July 27, 1794. Although it covers only the Terror, her excellent article most closely resembles our methodology. During this revolutionary crisis, she argues, theatres produced mostly pleasing, agreeable comedy with political and ideological overtones.

Most recently, André Tissier (1992) has published a repertory of French theatre during the constitutional monarchy that is very complete for the period it inventories (1789-1792), but this period is limited and the 50-page introduction is quite brief, given the 500 pages of data that follow. Tissier confirms some of our conclusions (he made an independent count of performances for the period he studies), but he does not fundamentally challenge the interpretation that has dominated theatre history of this period since 1800.[1]

Our study, then, begins with a certain concern about how one can access what was actually experienced in the theatre between 1789 and 1799. Our premise has been that before one can write or speak reasonably about several thousand plays, and tens of thousands of performances, one must find some rational principle of selection.

The method we employed involved recording on cards all the performances of the 3,700-odd plays staged at some 50 theatres between 1789 and 1799. The cards were filed by theatre for the period 1789 to 1794, and by title for the period 1795 to 1799. Preliminary manual cross-referencing was necessary to establish the total number of performances of a play in all theatres in all years. Since each theatre put on anywhere from two to five plays per evening [*sic*], and since there were often as many as fifteen theatres listed for one day in our sources, thousands of cards were filled out (perhaps 9,000) for the total of 90,000 performances.

The sources used were the daily lists in the *Journal de Paris* for 1789-1793, supplemented by the *Moniteur* when the *Journal de Paris* failed to publish lists, and the *Affiches, Annonces et Avis Divers* (*Petites Affiches*) for the period 1794-1799. The latter lists more theatres but is available only to researchers in Paris. The *Journal de Paris*, although slightly less comprehensive, lists the first performance of each play, and indicates its genre, the number of acts, and occasionally the author more systematically than does the *Petites Affiches*.

These sources provide an unusual, if unintended, serial documentation of the performance history of a play, which is somewhat analogous to the publishing history of a book; the record of the number of spectators at a play—available only exceptionally for the period under consideration—would be equivalent to the record of the run or *tirage* of a book. (Excellent use has been made of such data by Henri Lagrave [1972] on the history of the privileged theatres of the mid-eighteenth century.) In both cases we are dealing not only with the history of a literary genre but also with the history of the consumption of that genre—with public taste and public opinion.

The newspaper records offer 3,811 lists for 3,963 days on which some 50 theatres at one time or another performed over 3,700 plays of both the Old Regime and the French Revolution. These entertained a theatregoing public that was almost certainly larger than that of the mid-eighteenth century, which Henri Lagrave estimated at 63,000 Parisians (out of a population of 500,000) (Lagrave 1972, 195). No entertainment of this magnitude exists for any previous period of French history. Indeed, we have a record here that is much more complete than what the Bibliothèque Bleue of Troyes—consisting of chapbooks of devotional literature, technical know-how advice on agriculture, romances of the Middle Ages—offers for Old Regime popular culture. But unlike those literary sources, we have here a record of something we know was actually seen by a sizable portion of the Paris public. Our count of frequency of performance offers a statistic from which we can infer what people actually saw.

Concerning the missing newspaper lists: on certain days, such as those following the overthrow of the king in August 1792 and those following the September massacres, there are no performance records and it is to be assumed that there were probably no performances. No other period during the Revolution has a comparable hiatus. (Needless to say, since these records are all on computer diskettes, researchers should eventually be able to obtain from us a complete calendar of the French Revolutionary stage. Unfortunately, space restrictions make it impossible to publish such a calendar in this work.)

A more troublesome problem is errors in the listings we do have. A check of listings in the *Moniteur* against those in the *Journal de Paris* shows a number of discrepancies for the same day. Contemporaries complained about changes in the billing between the time of the announcements were made in the posters or newspapers and curtain time. Such changes were often due to, say, the indisposition of an actress or the military obligations of an actor. A sample of performances in the published archives of the Comédie Italienne was compared against our *Journal de Paris* listings; the margin of discrepancy was 5 percent—a figure that is tolerable in our view and in no way threatens our conclusions. This does mean, however, that one cannot be absolutely sure that on any one night an announced play was actually performed. The *Chronique de Paris* printed the letter of an irritated theatregoer on September 8, 1789: "I broke my engagements only to find my expectations disappointed....I dined alone at home; I left at 5 in order to get a seat in the orchestra....instead of a new play, I learn that the *Ecole des femmes* was going to be performed."

Then there are the plays that would have been performed more frequently had the natural law governing spectators and directors in their determinations of repertory been left undisturbed. Chénier's *Charles IX* was taken out of the repertory after some forty performances because Chénier was incensed by the existing royalties law. Laya's *Ami des lois* would have had many more performances than it did during the trial of the king, but it caused too much commotion for the Commune de Paris to let it continue. Sylvain Maréchal's *Jugement dernier des rois* stopped after twenty-two performances even though it was well received at the Théâtre de la République in October 1793. The reason was probably that the authorities, possibly the Comité du Salut Public, were stemming radical Hébertism at the time of its performance in late 1793 and early 1794. The play may have represented too much the kind of "barbarism" that Robespierre felt was discrediting France in the European courts. *Timoléon*, Chénier's famous tyrannicide tragedy of 1794, was seen as aiming at the tyrants on the Great Committee (Comité du Salut Public), particularly Robespierre—it was not performed until after Thermidor, and then only twice. Censorship also affected the performance record of *La Chaste Suzanne,* which had nothing to do with Revolutionary politics but had two lines that were taken as a denunciation of the Jacobins. Thus, censorship cut short the life of a certain number of plays during the Terror. Unfortunately, the archives containing these records were destroyed in the Commune fires of 1871. According to one scholar who saw them before they burned, a total of thirty-three plays were banned in the last months of the Terror and another twenty-five were altered (Vivien 1844)(See Chap. 16, Table 12).

Conversely, after a decree of August 2, 1793, the government could prolong the life of patriotic plays (see Chap. 8). Finally, theatre managers' financial considerations come into play. Plays by dead authors (that is, dead for more than five years) were performed royalty-free after the 1791 Le Chapelier law. Plays by living authors had complicated royalty agreements.

A play could be sold for a lump sum, as *Nicodème dans la lune* and *Le Sourd ou L'Auberge pleine* apparently were. Otherwise, royalties depended on the number of acts of the play and the number of times it had been performed. In the cases where a play had not been performed sufficiently, or had not earned enough box office receipts (this was particularly true of the Comédie Française and the Théâtre Italien), the play fell *en règles* and became the property of the theatre society or manager. Clearly, other considerations aside, a theatre director would be more inclined to perform a play for which he had to pay no royalties. This must necessarily have favored the production of Old Regime plays, especially after the passing of the author royalty legislation of 1793, which protected authors' rights up to ten years after their deaths.

It would be tempting to come up with a mathematical formula that would explain the financial calculations a director made when he or she decided what to perform, but the existing financial arrangements were either too diverse or too obscure to allow us to do that. Let it simply be said that there *were* such considerations and that many plays may have been dropped because they were too expensive to produce or, on the contrary, were prolonged because they were not.

Common sense dictates that a theatre director's primary consideration before producing a play was box office receipts. This is where the public was allowed to speak when the ballot boxes were closed (as they were for the whole of the Terror). That theatres had this function seems clear when one reads the constant temperature checks the secret police were making in their daily reports on public opinion in theatres after 1792 (Caron 1910-1978). Even when royalties were steep as they were for a four- or five-act play at the Théâtre de la République, a director had to consider what was going to draw the crowds. And that is where the popularity of a play could override royalty considerations.

One must also recognize that the larger a theatre's repertory, the less frequently any given play would be performed. The Grand Danseurs du Roi had an enormous repertory, 188 plays in 1789, over 9,023 performances in the decade, which meant that not one of their plays ever really qualified among the top fifty. The Comédie Française had a repertory of 170 in 1789, but rarely did it perform a play more than 40 or 50 times. The Beaujolais, the Feydeau, and the Opéra had repertories of 32, 41, and 25 plays, respectively. Some theatres performed only twice a week—this was the case for the Opéra—which meant its repertory rarely reached the top of the list of most performed. In these cases it is best to take the repertory theatre by theatre—something space limitations have made impossible except for the Opéra (See Chap. 15).

The size of the theatre must also be taken into account. The Théâtre Français Comique et Lyrique was small; the Variétés Amusantes sat only 700 people;

whereas the Comédie Française sat 2,000, the Théâtre Italien upward of 2,000, and the Théâtre de l'Estrapade reportedly 3,000; the Théâtre Français de la rue Richelieu, later called the Théâtre de la République, 2,300; the Théâtre de la Cité, 1,800 to 2,000. The Académie Royale de Musique (the Opéra), had 1,650 places; the Théâtre Montansier, 1,300 places. It is impossible to calculate the size of the audience at given performances, since archives are lacking for all but the former privileged theatres. But we know 78,000 tickets were sold for Favières and Kreutzer's *Paul et Virginie* between January 15, 1791, and December 21, 1793, in 68 performances.[2] These figures appear astronomical compared with the average sales of novels recorded in the 1810 censorship records, which rarely list a printing of more than 5,000 copies (A. N. F7 3488 dept. Nord, 1810).

A perfect audience study would take into account the size of the audience as well as the number of performances. But box office records have been found only for the Théâtre Italien (See Chap. 16, Table 11). Other variables such as censorship, authors' rights, size of the repertory, and performance schedule of the theatre are needed to gauge or weight the importance of certain plays with high records of performance versus those without. This is almost always impossible with the evidence available to us. Lacking these, it does seem that a simple computation and sorting of numbers of performances is quite useful in examining the accuracy of the traditional picture of French Revolutionary theatre. Repertories remain one reliable index of audience tastes. The only other sources are isolated impressions of contemporary critics, and these we have used to corroborate or qualify our statistics.

Scholars now do pay attention to this recent counting of performances and receipts for they tell us something (see Hyslop 1945; Alasseur 1967; Lagrave 1972). More people certainly saw Beffroy de Reigny's (Cousin Jacques's) *Nicodème dans la lune* (266 performances by our count, 373 [according to H. Beaulieu 75] and 249 times according to Tissier) than any play performed at the Comédie Française between 1789 and 1793. Ignorance of the number of performances of plays can only lead to hyperbolic errors of judgment such as that of Daniel Hamiche, who claims that Pierre-Sylvain Maréchal's *Jugement dernier des rois* was a "model of Revolutionary dramatic production," viewed by no fewer than 100,000 (Hamiche 1973, 188, 176), and marked the passage from "un répertoire réactionnaire à un répertoire révolutionnaire" (Hamiche 1973, 193). Nothing could be farther from the truth. The *Jugement* never defined the repertory of any year.

Why are these records so precious, and what confidence can we have that they will provide any index of theatre tastes? Historians of the Old Regime have quantified the book trade and its readership. Every archive of a publisher, such as that of Berger-Levrault of Strasbourg (Barbier 1979) or the Société Typographique de Neuchâtel (Darnton 1982), has been viewed as a veritable gold mine. But did people read more than they went to the theatre? The total reading public of Paris during the Revolution could be estimated at approximately 60 percent of 500,000, or 300,000. But this is only a figure of those capable of reading, not of those who actually bought books, plays, and newspapers. All the editions of the *Encyclopédie* sold only approximately 20,000 sets (Darnton 1973, 1344-1345).

Performance records are for theatre what numbers of edition are for the history of the book—indispensable evidence. To complete this record, it would be necessary to go into some detail not only on the number of performances but also on box office receipts and audience size, for clearly a consistently large audience at fifty performances is a greater indication of public demand than an audience of less than half that size with double the number of performances. It seems to us that Parisian society, both high and low, gave far more importance to the theatre than to the novel, as the *Mémoires* of Grimm et al. attest (Grimm et al. 1879, X, 341) for mid-eighteenth-century Paris. Lagrave estimates the *regular* theatregoing public at 10,000-18,000 persons, and occasional spectators at another 25,000-45,000, for a total of 35,000-63,000, or approximately 7-13 percent of the population (Lagrave 1972, 192-195). Saint-Just, in his *Institutions republicaines*, written during the Terror, complains that the public is working less and going to the theatre more (Saint-Just 1984, 993). Given the fact that there were approximately five times as many theatres in Paris in 1793 as there were in 1750, his complaint may have been well-founded.

Far from becoming an instrument for the Committee of Public Safety's Terror, the theatre of the Revolution was one of the targets of that Terror by reason of its lassitude, its frivolous character, and its traditionalism. In the following pages we hope to show, through an investigation of authors, plays, audiences, and authorities, why and how we have reached this conclusion.

2

The Authors

Marie-Laurence Netter[1]

There was no dearth of theories, essays, and speeches, before and after 1789, demanding that new issues be staged—for example, that the question of education be given more recognition in the theatre. But the theorists, even those as prestigious as Rousseau or Diderot, were not great dramaturges. Thus there was always a place for authors, major or minor, who wrote essentially for the theatre, who knew its inner workings, and who knew that they must dare to innovate—but who also knew they ought not to completely baffle the spectator and above all not bore him. These considerations, as well as the personalities of the authors and the milieu in which they matured, explain the slow evolution we have been able to observe.

The lack of audacity of these authors corresponded, as has already been noted, to the more conformist taste of a public that went to the theatre to enjoy themselves and not to learn or to discuss. The authors understood this very well, and it is to this mentality, more than to censorship or to the privileges of the great theatres (abolished at the beginning of 1791), that we must attribute the conventional quality of the majority of plays. It was the mixture of genres and of stage productions that counted, rather than the development of plots. To understand this phenomenon, I have thought it useful to examine in greater detail the education and the careers of these authors, for the most part unknown today, to see what place the theatre occupied in their lives.

BRIEF SOCIOLOGY OF THE AUTHORS

As a sample, we have made a prosopography of 100 dramaturges selected on the basis of the success of their plays during the Revolution (Michaud 1854-1862; Balteau et al., 1933-).

Twenty-seven authors died before 1789, and thirteen produced their work before this date. Thus forty authors, or more than a third of our group, were exclusively men of the seventeenth or of the eighteenth century whose writings obviously did not undergo any Revolutionary influence. This figure is high, if one thinks about the pedagogical role the Revolutionary authorities meant theatre to play, but it confirms in a very logical manner the important place of seventeenth-century and especially eighteenth-century theatre on the Revolutionary stage and the undeniable influence it exercised on the production of contemporary authors.

The remaining sixty Old Regime authors—if one holds to the date of the creation of all or part of their work—had extremely different and sometimes tragic experiences during the Revolution: four were guillotined, including one woman (Fabre d'Eglantine, Ronsin, Du Buisson, and Olympe de Gouges); one was deported (Collot d'Herbois, who died in Guiana in 1796); and five were members of the Convention (Bouquier, Chénier, Collot d'Herbois, Fabre d'Eglantine, and Ronsin).

If one considers the social backgrounds of these authors, that is, their professions and those of their fathers, and the persons with whom they associated, one realizes quickly that they belonged, with very few exceptions, to the leisure classes. We know the father's professions for only sixty-five authors, but the figures speak eloquently (see Table 1). The fathers who were magistrates or who are simply identified as wealthy represent 34 percent of the total to whom can be added nobles, counsellors of Parlement and army officers or 52 percent of the total. Eleven fathers (17 percent of the total) were professionally connected with the theatre as composers, dancers, or comedians, and nineteen (29 percent) belonged to the world of trade, business, or service. None of the fathers was a peasant. Many of the authors had attended reputable secondary *collèges*, such as those of the Jesuits or of the Oratorians.

Since most of the playwrights lacked personal fortunes, their incomes as writers were insufficient to live on and they had to search elsewhere for a more certain source of revenue. What is still doubtless true today was even truer at that time, when literary property was hardly respected or protected in spite of the improvements brought about by the copyright laws of 1793.

Of the 100 authors whose careers we have studied, thirty-nine were theatre entrepreneurs and/or actors, prompters, or other employees of a theatre, and were thus ideally situated to protect their work (Table 2). Molière was clearly the archetype.

Those who were secretaries or librarians of dignitaries—princes, nobles, prelates—obtained such positions because of their literary talent and in order to allow themselves sufficient leisure to continue their work. It was a sort of sinecure. Others dedicated themselves to education, either in noble families or in *collèges*. These activities, as well as journalism, were closely associated with the world of letters and thus of the theatre. Together with those directly linked

Table 1: Fathers' Professions   Table 2: Authors' Professions*

		Number	Percentage			Number	Percentage
◆	Magistrates Lawyer Procurator Notary	18	28	◆ Theatre Professionals		39	30
◆	Rich Relatives	4	6.2	◆ Magistrates, Lawyers		15	11.4
◆	Nobles	8	12.5	◆ Administration, Business		12	9
◆	Councilors of Parliament Military Officers	4	6.2	◆ Secretaries Educators Librarians		31	23.6
◆	Theatre Professionals	11	17.7	◆ Journalists		13	10
◆	Artisans Merchants	14	21.7	◆ Clergy Army		14	10.5
◆	Diverse: Doctor, Sculptor, Architect	5	7.7	◆ Diverse: Merchant, Engineer, Doctor		7	5.5
		64				131	

* Certain Authors exercised more than one profession.

to the theatre, 60 percent of the playwrights engaged in another profession.

The other sectors of activity—40 percent of the total—appear to be divorced from the theatre world. However, one must not forget that the men of the Enlightenment had a more universal knowledge than we. For these men, who had solid classical educations, embracing a career without any apparent relationship to the theatre did not forcibly extinguish all literary ambitions. For instance, the 20 percent who had become members of the royal administration or businessmen were not compelled to renounce writing or the theatre in particular. Finally, some authors pursued a career or went into the army or the church, while a small number were at some point artisans, merchants, or doctors. Whatever the case may be, the profession of playwright was more open than it is today. Indeed, the whole eighteenth century should probably be described as a unique period in which theatrical production was less abundant and was considered to be the province of men of letters. Yet these authors were not apathetic to political life: five of them were members of the Convention, and one became a peer under Louis XVIII. As for the Académie Française, it attracted writers, as it had for a long time: ten were elected to it.

This sketchy portrait shows how the authors belonged, in loose terms, to the leisure classes but only hints at what kind of existence they had, and says nothing about the place writing held in their lives. To try to understand the nature of theatrical production, we must turn to the personalities of the authors and to their lifestyles. Although the itineraries were as numerous as the individuals, one nonetheless easily notices three distinct approaches to writing.

A first group is made up of those who managed to lead relatively peaceful existences, thanks to their fortunes or their friendships with well-placed individuals. The second group consists of authors who belonged to the "literary bohemia" so well described by Princeton historian Robert Darnton, some of whom led very dissolute lives and died in misery. Finally, the third group could be said to be those for whom theatre was everything and to which they sacrificed themselves as well as their families. For all of them theatre was a passion.

THEATRE: AVOCATION OR PROFESSION?

Some authors led rather tranquil lives while satisfying the passion that they had for the theatre, either because the theatre was only part of their activity or, conversely, it had so thoroughly invaded their lives that it became a part of them. But avocation or profession, it is evident that because of the moderation of their temperament, these men did not find an outlet in bohemia and its excesses. Socially and politically they were moderate men who knew how to procure patronage and manage their fortunes sensibly without losing their independence. Whether or not they were partisans of the new ideas, they were, above all, prudent.

The most typical example of these authors who, at peace with themselves and with those around them, consecrated all or part of their time to the theatre was without doubt Edmond Favières (1755-1837), the author of the play *Paul et Virginie*. Son of a counselor in the Parlement of Paris, he was also a counselor from 1780 until 1790, when the position was eliminated. At that time he completely changed his way of life and dedicated himself to writing comedies and librettos for operettas for the Théâtre Italien. In 1792, he retired to the château of Val d'Oise, married, became mayor of his commune under the Empire, and continued to write for the theatre. The Baron de Saint-Just (1769-1826), son of a farmer-general and author of *Selico* and of *La Famille suisse*, had a very similar lifestyle. Since they did not need to make money, the theatre represented an agreeable pastime for these two men who were attracted by witticisms and the literary life.

Marsollier des Vivetières (1750-1817), author of *Nina ou La Folle par amour*, and *Les Deux petits savoyards*, his most successful work, could have remained an enlightened amateur like Favières and Saint-Just, but the events of the Revolution obliged him to discover in his talent a means of subsistence. Financially ruined by the Revolution, theatre became for him a source of revenue before his situation improved once again. The sensibility that expresses itself in his work was not just pure form—he helped authors who came to consult him as much as he could by barraging them with advice and material assistance. Thus he communicated the passion for theatre that possessed him.

These authors, and a few others like them, had this in common: they broke with their lifestyles or their milieu only when circumstances obliged them to do so. One must add that these men, who did not pretend to be men of letters, wrote only for the stage and exercised their art as a social talent. The sum of works they produced—comedies, comic operas—corresponds to the frivolous spirit of the eighteenth century, which opened the door to the taste of the aristocracy for popular entertainment and made a fortune at the theatres of the fairs.

More numerous are the authors who, turning their backs on the way chosen for them by their families, decided to embark on a career that would secure for them a comfortable if not bourgeois existence. For them, literature was a calling, a true vocation from which they intended to be distracted as little as possible. (Theatre was, generally, only one part of their literary activity.) They were also essayists, poets, journalists, and sometimes novelists. The serious character of their works and their conduct, not exempt occasionally from a bit of subservience to the powers that were, made them typical candidates for the Académie Française, which did indeed receive some of them. Jean Marmontel, Auguste Lachabeaussière, and Jean Laya are representative of this group in which professionalism got the upper hand and strangled any drift toward bohemia. This does not mean that they had neither talent nor personal thoughts to express.

Of very modest provincial origin, Jean F. Didon Marmontel (1723-1799) had everything he needed at the outset to swell the ranks of these ambitious, penniless youths who hastened to Paris in the hope of living there by their pen and winning recognition. Nothing distinguished him except his sense of responsibility vis-à-vis his family. A brilliant student of the Jesuits, whom his parish priest had him enter, he began teaching at eighteen, after the death of his father. During the same period, he participated in some literary "jousting" and began a correspondence with Voltaire that would last thirty-five years. It was at the latter's invitation that he went up to Paris and a few years later experimented with tragedy, a genre in which he hardly shone. He wrote several articles for the *Encyclopédie* and above all made himself known by composing several poems dedicated to the glory of Louis XV. A protégé of Mme de Pompadour, he became secretary of "buildings" (the Cultural Ministry), then director of the *Mercure de France*, in which he published his famous *Contes moraux*. In 1762 he was elected to the Académie Française and continued to publish novels, articles, and essays. During the Revolution, his discretion made possible his election to the Council of Ancients in April 1797; the coup d'état of 18 Fructidor (September 4, 1797) cost him his seat. This perfect man of letters of the eighteenth century died on December 31, 1799.

For the theatre Marmontel wrote numerous comic operas, such as *Zémire et Azor ou La Fausse Magie*. Put to music by Grétry, these plays were received with great acclaim. The comedies taken from his *Contes moraux* are weaker.

It was as a librettist of operas that Marmontel established a durable reputation as playwright—always in collaboration with Grétry and Piccinni—notably with *Didon*, which was a major success in 1783 and was regularly revived. During the Revolution, this lyrical tragedy was performed ninety-one times.

Lachabeaussière (1752-1820), son of a lawyer, abandoned his ecclesiastical career, then his military career, to consecrate himself entirely to literature. Before the Revolution he composed several essays and plays that were rather well received and revived after 1789, such as *Azémia ou Les Sauvages* and *Le Sourd*, which should not be confused with the comedy by Desforges. On the political side, Lachabeaussière always supported the regime in power, which until 1820, the year of his death, gave him the opportunity for many retractions. During the Revolution he composed hymns for civic festivals and wrote a famous *Catéchisme français ou Principes de la morale républicaine*, destined for the *écoles primaires*; it gained him a monetary compensation from the Convention and a seat on the Commission of Public Instruction (the body charged with theatre censorship, among other things). He was one of the less scrupulous administrators of the opera, and does not seem to have written for the stage in this period. Subsequently, Lachabeaussière became a member of various literary societies and renewed his ties to poetry and theatre. Apparently, these two genres did not form part of his universe as militant revolutionary, which is surprising, considering the place that theatre played in the discourse on the new civic education.   ˏ

Lachabeaussière, a playwright conscious of the importance of the diffusion of republican maxims to the point of consecrating a *catéchisme* to them, did not want to mix genres and came back to theatre only when the Revolution ended. Must one conclude that for him, theatre was only diversion?

Jean L. Laya (1761-1833), the author of *L'Ami des lois*, had the opposite attitude. His plays were almost entirely political or, if one prefers, pedagogical; he wrote for the theatre only during the Revolution. As of 1790, with *Dangers de l'opinion*, he put the public on guard against excesses of all kinds; but it was with *L'Ami des lois*, performed for the first time on January 2, 1793, three weeks before the execution of the king, that he leveled a complete and unambiguous accusation against the Jacobins for having simultaneously betrayed the people and the Revolution. The play was banned in spite of the author's courageous defense. "I will never be avaricious with my ideas, once I think them useful," Laya wrote in the preface, adding later that "the true love of liberty proves itself with sacrifices"—a sentence on which he had plenty of leisure to meditate after his property was confiscated in the wave of riots provoked by his play. Under the Empire, he renounced theatre to consecrate himself to education and criticism. The stage was for him essentially a form of political action, an occasion to change the course of events or at least to reflect upon their consequences.

Whether theatre was their privileged mode of literary production or the lesser part of a life dedicated essentially to literature, all these authors had in common the fact of having kept a certain distance from the world of entertainment. The general character of their plays testifies, by its classicism, to a state of mind in which reason prevails over passion. In spite of their success, it is not among them that one must seek the forgers of new characters or new dramatic situations. They were good students of excellent playwrights and philosophes who preceded them, but they invented nothing. This is not the case with the authors whom we will examine next. Immersed in the world of the theatre, they showed a great deal more audacity than their predecessors, even if they were not geniuses.

FROM LA BOHÈME TO THE GUTTER

What is so surprising about these authors who were, for the whole or part of their lives, marginal individuals or adventurers, sometimes engaged in very different undertakings than those of the classical playwrights? One can point out that among the "classical" figures certainly Molière, who was himself an adventurer in the theatre, borrowing from minor genres like those of the fairs or the commedia dell'arte, created characters and situations that became "classics" thanks solely to his genius. The generation after his was full of minor authors who, impassioned by the theatre and strongly attached to their independence, continued to work in the direction traced by the master, and to open the stage to a more "popular" public. Some of their works survived and attracted full houses during the Revolution.

Alain-R. Lesage (1668-1747) belongs to the category of authors who chose an uncertain existence over a certain dependence. Very rigid on this point, he was extremely respectable (*honnête*); the bohemian side of his existence can be attributed to real material difficulties in his household rather than to a weakness of character. He is still known as the author of *Gil Blas*, a picaresque novel, and of *Turcaret*, a comedy in five acts. Even though the latter was performed by the Comédie Française in February 1709, Lesage, wounded by the attitude of the actors, decided to turn his back on an official theatre and devote himself to writing for the "popular" theatres.

In this way he renewed his work with the popular verve that had first inspired him in *Crispin, rival de son maître* (1707). To deflect the numerous prohibitions directed at these spectacles, he introduced satirical songs and sung dialogue in his plays, which caused him to be considered the founder of *opéra comique*. In this vein, Lesage wrote more than 100 plays, including a series with Harlequin as hero.

The example of Louis Achambault Dorvigny (1742-1812) and some of his contemporaries shows to what degree there was a sort of coherence between the private lives of the authors and the directions taken by their imaginations. Here it is a matter of the literary bohemia that promoted the staging of new personality types—popular, truculent, more or less respectable individuals—as later, in the twentieth century, totalitarianism gave birth to a *théâtre engagé*.

After having spent a few years at sea, Dorvigny returned to France and established himself as a comedian and author. Minor theatres were eager to purchase his comedies, "proverbs," and farces because they proved to be hits. An insolent bon vivant and heavy drinker, Dorvigny provoked many a scandal and did not always manage to get paid a fair price. He died in misery. His great physical resemblance to Louis XV allowed him to pass for a bastard of the king. Although the link has never been proved, this distinction appears to have helped him many times to get out of a bad situation.

It was in the cabarets in which he wrote that Dorvigny found the models of his roguish and rather stupid valets who became famous under the names of Janot and Jocrisse (Allorge 1921). These naïve and rather uncouth characters serve humble folk; they do not resemble the valets of Molière but rather are a broad cross section of the city population, that had access to theatrical productions. The public gave an enthusiastic reception to these plays. The observations of Dorvigny, like those of Rétif de la Bretonne, have the exact tone of one who has lived in contact with the world they describe. The literary and urban bohemia of the end of the eighteenth century had certainly opened the way to the staging of very differently behaved people—people until then forgotten—that is, people of the cities.

Eve *dit* Maillot (1747-1814) and Joseph Aude (1755-1841), who respectively, put on stage *Madame Angot* and *Cadet Roussel*, also belonged to this school that mixed a love of current events with observations of popular behavior in the form of caricatures. Police informer, anarchist, or pillar of the cabarets, they both knew how to profit from their knowledge of the "little people" in order to castigate the nouveaux riches and provoke laughter at the expense of the naïve. They, too, died in misery.

More extravagant than bohemian, Pigault Lebrun (1753-1835) led a very turbulent life until he was almost fifty. First, he seduced the daughter of a London businessman with whom he worked, then fled with her aboard a boat that was later shipwrecked. Back in France his father had him imprisoned, then enlisted him in a company of elite police where he led a merry life for three years. This corps having been dissolved, he returned home, fled again with another young woman, and was once again imprisoned. Rejecting the option of suicide, he became an actor and married the daughter of an artisan. It was at this time, in the early 1780s, that his father inscribed him on the civil registry (*état civil*) as having disappeared. With a petition in process, his situation became tenable only when the seizure of the Bastille saved him from a new imprisonment. It was at this time that he began to write for the theatre with some success—*Charles et Caroline ou Les Abus de l'Ancien Régime*—but the spirit of adventure had not left him, and he signed up with a regiment of dragoons. In 1794, having returned to civilian life, he wrote *Les Dragons et les bénédictines* and *Les Dragons en cantonnement*. He continued to write numerous theatrical scripts and simultaneously established himself as a novelist, becoming famous under the Empire. There is no doubt that Pigault Lebrun's own life was his principal source of inspiration, and he had a marvelous talent for exploiting its diverse sides for the public's pleasure.

For these authors who led such active lives, the small theatres for which they wrote were veritable refuges. They found there a niche where the imagination was king and innovations were well-received. The theatres also benefited, as the playwrights gave them an identity and made their fortunes, as we shall see.

LIVING FOR THE THEATRE

Besides the two types of authors discussed above, who were certainly impassioned by the theatre, but who consecrated only a part of their lives to it, there were those who lived for it alone, in a tight symbiotic relationship. These often filled all the jobs of the theatre: prompter, employee, actor, director. Nothing was unfamiliar to them; their wives were sometimes actresses and their children followed in their footsteps.

As has already been stated, the perfect model of this type is Molière. But one must again stress his genius, which set him apart from the other playwrights. Not only was Molière an excellent actor, he was also a director (in the modern sense of the word) of an unparalleled theatrical troupe. Moreover, the actors had great liberty, at the expense of the global interpretation of the play. Molière knew how to do everything, which is why he remains unique.

Among 100 authors we hav e studied, eight were also theatre directors and will be discussed at a later point in the text. Let us turn our attention to those who were actors too and for whom the theatre was a family business.

Boutet de Monvel (1745-1811), known as an actor by the name Monvel, is a perfect example of the type of author who lived only for the theatre. Son of an actor, he made his debut at the Théâtre Français (Comédie Française) where he served as Molé's double in the roles given to young beginners. As an actor Monvel gained a solid reputation and, according to contemporary testimony, could have been a star had he not been unattractive. He was short, rather puny, and had a weak voice. One can easily understand that his acting and his intelligence were enough to compensate for his handicaps. Parallel to this career, which he abandoned only after he was sixty, he wrote a large number of theatrical scripts—dramas and comedies—that were performed at the Théâtre Français or at the Théâtre des Variétés. After writing some charming comedies like *Blaise et Babet* and the sequel of *Les Trois fermiers* (which had, as soon as it was written in 1783, an immense success), Monvel served the Revolutionary cause with enthusiasm, producing in 1791 the acclaimed *Victimes cloîtrées*, a four-act drama in prose. However, during the Revolution,

Blaise et Babet, a comedy about love and jealousy, peasant wisdom, and the good rapport between seigneurs and peasants, was performed 239 times, while *Victimes* was performed only 109 times.

These figures show that Monvel was a successful author, all the more so where entertainment was valued more than politics. If he was a convinced revolutionary, playing an active role in the Festival of Reason at Notre Dame in 1793, Monvel was no less sensitive to honors. He became a member of the National Institute and professor at the Imperial Conservatory, appropriate rewards for a life dedicated entirely to the theatre. He knew how to communicate his passion to his children, among whom was the famous actress Mademoiselle Mars.

Theatre, or more precisely dance and opera, were omnipresent in the life of the Gardel family. The father and uncle had been dancers before them. Maximilien (1741-1787) and Pierre (1758-1840) were not only dancers but also composers of music and ballets, carrying off a stunning success both during and after the Revolution (though Maximilien died in 1787). Maximilien married a daughter of Nicolas Audinot, the director of the Ambigu Comique. Pierre married a dancer who was the daughter and daughter-in-law of musicians. In a word, apart from opera, nothing seemed to exist for the Gardel brothers, who knew how to make a profit from their art and live from it decently. With *Le Déserteur* and *L'Offrande à la liberté,* Maximilien Gardel is ranked among the most prolific and the most performed playwrights of the Revolution, as is Pierre, with his *Psyché* and *Télémaque dans l'île de Calypso.*

Passion for the theatre certainly animated Alexandre-Louis Robineau, known as Beaunoir (1746-1823), author of more than 200 plays. In 1777 he renounced his ecclesiastical career and changed his name so as to be able to give free rein to his libertine imagination. His dramas, farces, and comedies assured the success of Nicolet's theatre, the Grands Danseurs du Roi, from 1768 to 1780, and then of Lécluze's Théâtre des Variétés Amusantes. Beaunoir, with his *La Bourbonnaise* (1768), *L'Amour quêteur* (1770), *Jeannette, ou Les Battus ne payent pas l'amende* (1780), which was a riposte to Dorvigny's *Janot,* and finally *Jérôme Pointu* (1781), played by the famous actor Volange, gave boulevard theatre some of its greatest successes. Beaunoir became rich and famous, but after attributing his somewhat indecent plays to his wife in order to protect his honor and to appease his hostile colleagues at the Bibliothèque du Roi, he was forced to resign his position in 1784. In 1787 he became director general of the theatres of Bordeaux, an assignment in which he was unsuccessful. He returned to Paris in 1789 but left for Belgium in September. From there he traveled to Rhineland Prussia, where he published *Le Royaliste ou Lettres d'un français réfugié sur les bords du Rhin* (Neuwied 1791), declaring: "la contrerévolution se fera donc" (p. 32). He did not return to Paris until 1801. From then until his death, he wrote mainly essays and some plays of little value that had no success. Beaunoir remains one of the authors who made the boulevard fashionable and, ironically, became the most performed author of the Revolution (Chap. 16, Table 5).

The life of this type of playwright turned exclusively on the theatre. In many cases they became authors in order to give an actor a role worthy of his talent and vice versa. These men lived and wrote only for the theatre. Dramaturgy was not for them a literary talent among others, but their unique way of expressing themselves, the prism through which they saw the world. It is among these authors who knew everything about theatre that one finds those who imprinted on their genres their most worthwhile revisions. Bourgeois drama reached its zenith in 1776 with *La Brouette du vinaigrier*, written by L. S. Mercier, the famous author and theoretician of the dramatic art; and melodrama assumed its form in the last years of the Revolutionary decade in the play *Victor ou L'Enfant de la forêt* (1798) by Guilbert de Pixerécourt, a man of the theatre if ever there was one. Later we will examine the evolution of these genres and the manner in which the dramatists worked.

The different approaches to dramatic writing, as we have seen through these three categories of authors, paint a society that was extraordinarily open and avid for self-knowledge. The explosion of popular theatre during the Revolution was prepared by the host of authors who took an interest throughout the eighteenth century in depicting the transformations of the society that surrounded them and through stage characters often taken from daily life. The diversity of authors shows that theatre was at this time, and more particularly during the Revolutionary decade, a highly esteemed mode of expression that did not belong to a few specialists. More than ever, personal experience became a source of inspiration, which the authors proposed to the public as a personal dimension it knew how to recognize and appreciate. This new proximity between authors and their subjects did not yield many masterpieces, but it marked the beginning of spectacles "for everyone" (or "for the people"), if not yet for "the masses," which in itself is certainly a question of revolution.

3

The Most Performed Plays of the Decade

Emmet Kennedy

A "deaf" boor in a roadside inn, wandering urchins with a performing marmot, protective fathers marrying their daughters against their "inclinations," insolent servants who get the upper hand, brigands who carry off nubile women, a Turkish raid on an Imperial camp pitched on the Danube, the loves of Telemachus—these are the leading subjects of our fifty most frequently performed plays of the French Revolution (Chap. 16, Table 4). In this chapter, we will try to analyze briefly the characterization, plot, setting, and mood of these plays in an attempt to show how different they were from what has usually been designated as typical Revolutionary drama.

RUSTIC ROMANCE AND RICHES

How can one explain the discrepancy between our list of plays and the repertory analyzed in the dozen published accounts of Parisian Revolutionary theatre? Our most-performed selection principle, as opposed to that of the most political, the most literarily worthy, or the most tumultuously received, provides the answer. By definition, the prevailing approach has ruled out the non-Revolutionary and the Old Regime repertory; our approach will highlight that exiled repertory, to the extent that it was more performed, by considering it as the backdrop against which the more inflammatory plays were staged.

The genre of these top fifty plays of the decade is overwhelmingly comedy (thirty-three out of fifty, or two-thirds, as opposed to 37 percent for the whole repertory), continuing the preference expressed for that genre during the Enlightenment. Chapter 6 will examine this preponderance, but one can surmise that Revolutionary audiences were seeking entertainment rather than edification. Old Regime comedy is generally divided into three categories:

comedy of intrigue, comedy of character, and comedy of mores. We have found that all three overlap in our corpus. The method followed here has been to treat them according to certain themes, such as love in the bucolic setting; intrigues (usually for love); social rank and social ascension; brigandage (a side effect of the Revolutionary struggle); the exotic, including the classical heroic and the classical erotic; and Revolutionary politics.

Thirty-three of the forty-four texts we have been able to read offer love as their principal theme. Almost all of them involve some kind of courtship, and most of them feature the inevitable obstacle to a desired marriage in the form of an unsympathetic parent or tutor. Another six plays have love as a subsidiary theme and three others have sex, rather than love, as a theme. Many of these plays involve intrigue, quite likely Molièresque in origin. Only one proposes love of country as a substitute for romantic love.

An eighteenth-century mental association linked virtue to bucolic simplicity, yet Rousseau's village soothsayer (*Le Devin du village*), counsels astuteness to village youth who come to him for advice on love. They must be content with the attractions of the country over the seductions of the city but must not be so naïve as not to play hard to get with one another. Peasant guile is evidently innocent and virtuous. Listen to Colin:

> Goodbye château, fame, wealth:
> Your pomp tempts me no more...
> When one knows how to love and to please...
> Give me your heart, my shepherdess,
> Colin has given to you his flute and his shepherd's crook.

This light opera, which had been much performed before the Revolution, was number 13 on the list of the Revolution's most performed plays, the highest of any play written by a philosophe.

The two hunters of *Les Deux chasseurs et la laitière* (1763) are quite a pair of bunglers; they get their powder wet and fail to kill their bear, and ruin their chances for winning the milkmaid, who spills her milk. The moral of this little pastoral comedy is, in rough translation, that you cannot count your eggs before they hatch or, put in political terms (see the concluding satiric song), you cannot count on the successful outcome of such plans as building ports around the French coast, presumably during the just-finished Seven Years' War against England and Prussia. The passage from pastoral to political is abrupt: one wonders why Revolutionary audiences found it so compelling. One reason may have been the music of Duni, which Diderot described in *Le Neveu de Rameau* as having "feeling, by God, and plenty of melody and expression" (Diderot 1966, 117) in other words, just what Rousseau had championed in the *Guerre des bouffons* of 1753. The *Deux petits savoyards* by Marsollier des Vivetières (music by Dalayrac), had its premiere in January 1789, just at the time that the Abbé Sieyès was publishing his *Qu'est ce que le Tiers Etat*. Two little Savoyard urchins, known collectively to every Parisian as chimneysweeps and beggars, happen upon a country fair, where they resourcefully display their trick rodent. They catch the attention of the wary bailiff and then the benevolent regard of the seigneur of the château, who had made his fortune in America and had distinguished himself at the same time, serving his country by "long labor." He then returned to France with the hope of sharing his wealth with his brother (who, it seems, had died). As it turns out, the Savoyards have a locket with the portrait of the brother, who is indeed their father. The seigneur is joyous at finding heirs to his fortune, and virtuous ones at that—they refuse to accept their uncle's munificence without sharing it with their mother, whom they have left in a neighboring village. Commiseration for these poor tramps and delight in their good fortune were highly cherished emotions in this period of universal brotherhood. (The winter of 1788-1789 was a particularly severe one. Thomas Jefferson, then in Paris, compared it to Siberia.) The fact that the "seigneur" is not a feudal noble but a self-made man who acquired his fortune in the land of mythic opportunity also fits the Revolutionary ideology. However, the text is replete with pity rather than Sieyès's Revolutionary justice. As with many of these plays, success was due in no small measure to the accompanying music. The records of the Théâtre Italien reveal 104,000 spectators saw this comedy by the end of 1793 (Brenner 1961).

More typical models of noble fortune and lineage can be found in *Le Réveil du charbonnier* (1788) in which a coal merchant's daughter turns out to be related to the mistress of the château where the coal merchant is convalescing from a fall off a horse. Again we have the search for parental origins, the delightful discovery of noble lineage, which may take the place of a Revolutionary abolition of hereditary distinctions. In *La Dot* (1785) and *Blaise et Babet* (1783) by François Desfontaines and Boutet de Monvel, respectively, the nobles are portrayed as paternal matchmakers in their villages. In the first play the seigneur bestows a dowry on the worthy demoiselle; in the second, he actually conducts nuptials after patching up a misunderstanding between the betrothed.

In all these plays nobles are magnanimous and are far from being summoned to surrender their titles and privileges, even by the radical revolutionary-to-be J. M. Boutet de Monvel. And these plays that presented the nobility in a good light were performed approximately twice as often as Beaumarchais's *Mariage de Figaro* of 1784 (150 performances), in which the nobility is sullied. But not all our plays portrayed noble-commoner relations with condescension. In Destouches's *Fausse Agnès* (1759), we have a wonderful characterization of a saucy, independent woman who employs all her wits to foil her parents' plan to marry her to a pretentious fuddy-duddy who is enthralled by his aristocratic status. Only by feigning ignorance (she insists that there have been 1,736 kings of France), which baffles and horrifies him, does she get off the hook.

The problem in A. J. Bourlin, *dit* Dumaniant's *Ricco* (1789) is not love (the eternal theme) or the incompatibility of personalities, but an ancient hostility between the members of two noble families who quarreled over precedence ages ago and have not stopped killing one another ever since. Only after a maid intervenes by smuggling a disguised Ormeuil, the groom-to-be, into the castle of Germancel, where the beloved lives, does Ormeuil gain the favor of the father, who arranges the very marriage he was determined to quash. The theme of the survival of aristocratic habits from the Middle Ages to the Revolution supersedes the subtheme of equality (the maid's relationship to her master). Although this play premiered in 1789, it countenances neither abolition of titles nor any use of the familiar personal pronoun by a maid when speaking to her master. Paradoxically, it does contain the most impertinent remark made by a servant in this corpus of plays.

Other plays drew attention to a familiar problem of the Old Regime: the Church after the Council of Trent had recognized clandestine marriages of minors, which the state and most parents did not. For the latter the issue was protecting family name and fortunes through advantageous alliances. Only in 1792 would the Revolution recognize the majority of both women and men at the age of twenty-one, sanctioning unions made independently of parental consent, thus favoring personal happiness over familial rights (Traer 1980, 150; Flandrin 1979, 130 ff.).

MASTER-SERVANT RELATIONS

The rich-poor theme need not pit aristocrats against commoners; it could encompass relations among the working class itself. In Guillemain's *L'Enrôlement supposé*, we have the marriage of Fanchon, daughter of an apple tradesman, to Guillaume, son of an orange tradesman at Les Halles. Guillaume's father opposes the marriage because he believes apple tradesmen to be of lesser dignity than orange tradesmen. The obstacle is surmounted when Guillaume dresses up in an army uniform (whence the title) and forces Fanchon's mother's hand. The play closes with the observation that there are many "respectable people who are wealthy, but worth prevails over wealth." Again, as in the *Deux petits savoyards*, meritocratic ideology does not oppose wealth to worth.

Harlequin afficheur is another refreshing play about lower-class sansculottes or shopkeepers. The figure of Harlequin, imported in the seventeenth century from Italy to the fairs, boulevards, and eventually to the Opéra-Comique, was quite a familiar one. In this skit, Harlequin is a bill-sticker, affixing the announcements of the Théâtre du Vaudeville on public walls—in this instance, a notice about Molière near the window of his sweetheart, who is locked in by her father. Harlequin nevertheless carries on a conversation with her and manages to outmaneuver his rival, Gille, the lover her father prefers because he has "a profession, [and] an inheritance." The eternal theme of love over interest (rather than love and interest, which we have already noted) has a definite place in popular as well as elite entertainment.

A more familiar play (still performed at the Comédie Française) is Marivaux's *Jeu d'amour et du hasard*, a comedy of high quality involving the double role reversal of master and valet and mistress and maid. Lisette speaks to the master-servant question when she says, "I have to appear either mistress or the maid, that I obey or that I order" (II,vii). Harlequin, who has reversed roles with *his* master, mimics his master in the last scene by saying, "A respectable man [*honnête homme*] never pays attention to his chambermaid," while Dorante, an *honnête homme* says, "Merit is certainly worth birth" (III,viii). A double betrothal takes place in the denouement when Harlequin upbraids Lisette: "For joy, Madame, you have lost your rank, but you have nothing to complain about since you still have Harlequin."

This rococo boudoir play was performed 160 times during the Revolution, including 9 times during the Terror. Its relevance to Revolutionary audiences was twofold: it combined the perdurable theme of love and marriage with the almost equally popular theme of master-servant relations in which servants, at least for a while, play the exhilarating role of masters. There is no vindictiveness in this role reversal—it is, one must remember, a *jeu*, like Carnival when roles are also reversed. One can understand, nonetheless, why such themes might have been popular among audiences composed to a larger part than ever before of servants or former servants, some of whom could well have usurped their masters' or mistresses' positions.

INTRIGUE AND LOVE

A salient component of plays performed during the Revolution is intrigue—a staple of Molièresque comedy that was perhaps seen as newly relevant amid the intrigue of Revolutionary politics on the national, municipal, and neighborhood levels. Intrigue is a test of the playwrights' ingenuity as well as of the audience's wits. It enhances comedy—if it does not actually create it—by mistaking identities and by creating generally incongruous situations.

In Molière's *Le Dépit amoureux* and in Regnard's *Les Folies amoureuses*, female transvestites intrigue for love. A healthy and perceptive man pretends to be deaf in an attempt to get a room in a fully occupied inn in Desforges's *Le Sourd, ou L'Auberge pleine*. In *La Servante maîtresse*, a maid intrigues to usurp the role of mistress. The wrong person (Valère) is in the apartment where Sagnarelle goes to search for the woman he vowed he would marry in Molière's *L'Ecole des maris*.

The better-known imbroglio of Molière's *Le Médecin malgré lui* features

Lucinde's marriage of inclination, which is foiled by her father, Géronte. The stratagem she employs to get her way is to feign dumbness, which determines her father to search for a doctor. Sagnarelle, who is not really a doctor, nevertheless cures her of her illness when he introduces Léandre, her lover, as his apothecary. *Le Dépit amoureux*, adapted from a play by Niccolò Secchi, contains another imbroglio, in which Valère unintentionally marries Ascagne (who had been disguised from birth as a boy in order to conserve the family fortune), all the while thinking he was marrying Lucille, the beloved of Eraste.

Brueys's *L'Avocat Pathelin* is a superior comedy of errors in which a poor lawyer tries to defraud a rich merchant of cloth and sheep, calling him, behind his back, "un juif" (a pejorative epithet that appears in two or three of our texts). Pathelin indulges in psychological reverie and delusion, particularly at his trial in the third act. The stuff of the play is the same as that of all these dramas, namely money and marriage—the money Pathelin owes the merchant and his desire to marry his daughter to the merchant's son because he is rich.

Desforges's *Le Sourd* was the most performed play of the Revolution (463 performances). It is pure situation comedy with some sexual innuendos focusing mostly on the apparently ignorant and uninhibited *naïf*, a stock character of the Enlightenment whether it be Usbek, l'Ingénu, or Candide. The setting is a country inn, a stopover for voyagers from Paris to Marseilles. A party of travelers fills the inn. A pair of latecomers have, however, made a bet that one of them, known as "the voyager" or the "deaf one," will sleep in a room that night in the inn.

Like *Fausse Agnès*, this is a play about provincials who have been to Paris (which they found horribly expensive). Throughout the play, all the characters show preoccupation with money, from the *mille écus* one spent in Paris in two months to the dowry in land, which Doliban has bought his daughter near Vaucluse, to a tip for which the chambermaid calls the donor "the right kind of man."

Act I stages the arrival of the guests at the inn. When "the voyager" and his companion, Saint-Firmin, arrive, they are denied rooms. Act II involves "the voyager" sitting at the dinner table of the other guests in the host's place. This comical situation is heightened when the guests first try to displace him and then try to get him to pay for his meal. The climax of the comedy occurs in scenes v and vi, when the "deaf one" barricades himself in the room of one of the guests and pretends he cannot hear the banging and knocking at the door, the movement of which he attributes to a storm. (There is a bit of Condillac's and Diderot's psychology here; one is told what the "deaf one" can know, having been deprived of one of his senses.) Act III reveals that D'Orbe, "the voyager," is not really deaf, and that he disapproves of the arranged marriage of Josephine, who is being treated "like an imbecile against her will as well as against reason." He wins his bet with Saint-Firmin, and challenges Doliban to a duel for insulting him the night before, "for the infirmity that I was pretending to have!" General reconciliation ends the play.

Stock eighteenth-century themes are skillfully exploited here: marriage of love over marriage of interest, bourgeois frugality and prudence over aristocratic honor, testy master-servant relations in which money is the main factor, and the psychology of deaf-mutes. *Le Sourd* is a skilled combination of *comédie de moeurs* and *comédie d'intrigue*. It has no political message, only a few social banalities.

A more amusing case of intrigue is that of Andrieux's *Les Etourdis*, in which two students, Folleville and the nephew of D'Aiglemont, fake the death of the latter and publish his obituary in a paper, in order to receive a thousand *écus* stipulated for funeral expenses. One learns that they are heavily in debt, and the supposed death of D'Aiglemont's nephew has triggered their Jewish creditors to ask for the payment of his debts. The uncle arrives on the scene in Act II, and the remaining scenes are devoted to his efforts to unravel the conspiracy, forgive his nephew and Folleville, and permit the nephew to marry his daughter, Julie. The intrigue in this play is a little more poignant and involved than most; the resolution quite improbable.

Love and intrigue dominate Joseph Patrat's *La Résolution inutile ou Les Déguisements amoureux*, in which Julie, lacking a rich uncle to marry her off, must content herself with painting gouaches. She abandons her pastimes only for love of Monrose. In Jean Antoine Bourlin's *Guerre ouverte ou Ruse contre ruse*, a baron stops at nothing to keep his daughter away from her suitor; nonetheless, he agrees to oblige the marquis, his daughter's lover, if he can reach the room where his daughter is locked up before midnight. The marquis bribes all the servants of the house and carries off his beloved in time. Again, we have here two rather inane love comedies based on the eternal theme of paternal protection of daughters. The *Folies amoureuses* of Jean Regnard (the Molière of the eighteenth century) is also about a chaperon who keeps his tutee under lock and key. Her two suitors act as if they were going to war and seize the "fortress" containing Agathe—herself dressed up as a warrior.

Beaumarchais's *Barbier de Séville* (1775) uses the stock theme of a jealous, greedy, and somewhat sordid uncle-tutor from characters of Molière, Regnard, and others, but he introduces personalities of infinitely more verve and impertinence. Like Agathe, Rosine thinks her guardianship by Bartolo, who intends to make her his wife, is slavery: "Me his wife? Passing my days in the company of a jealous old man who offers my youth no happiness, but only an abominable slavery?" (III, xii).

The intrigue of the *Barbier* almost attains the intrigue later achieved in the *Mariage de Figaro*. Again we have a tutor, Bartolo, who keeps his protégé, Rosine, under the strictest surveillance—or so he thinks. Enter Count Almaviva, who gains the confidence of Bartolo when he shows him a letter that Rosine has written him. The count is dressed as a student so that he can tutor Rosine himself—an improbable motive that only strengthens the impression of

Bartolo's stupidity. As that rapprochement between Rosine and the count takes place unbeknownst to Bartolo, a second thread of the plot unravels. Bartolo parts with the key to Rosine's shutter, giving it to the barber, who uses it to get into the most protected room in the house: Rosine's. The two conspiracies proceed simultaneously. The denouement in Act IV, scene viii, as many will recall, occurs when Bartolo and Rosine are supposed to be married by a notary. The latter, who arrives when Bartolo is momentarily out of the house, mistakenly marries Rosine to her beloved Count Almaviva. Figaro admonishes him: "But to tell the truth, doctor, when youth and love conspire together to deceive an old man, anything he might do to stop them may well be called 'the useless precaution.'" Nature prevails over old age, meanness, suspicion, chaperoning, and unnatural customs.

Beaumarchais is indifferent to the genre of his play—a common feeling in the wake of Mercier's deliberate confusion of genres in his *Nouvel essai sur l'art dramatique* (1773). Even earlier, Voltaire refused to pigeonhole *Nanine* as a comedy. Beaumarchais goes so far as to call his play a *mélodrame* long before the word was in common use. In his preface he attacks the classic codes of decency, modesty (*bienséance*) and verisimilitude.

The fact that this play was performed twice as often (313 performances) as the *Mariage de Figaro* (150 performances) probably springs from the more trenchant, scathing attack on the high society of Old Regime that the *Mariage* represents, as well as from its more unpalatable sexual innuendos. Revolutionary audiences were probably more coarse and prim than their aristocratic predecessors on the eve of the Revolution—at least that is what the Revolutionaries believed. The *Barbier*, although replete with vigorous and feisty language, has relatively modest sexual allusions.

RESCUE PLAYS

Two other types of plays remain to be analyzed, the first of which could be described as rescue plays and the second, exotic plays. *Die Räuber* (1781), by Friedrich von Schiller, was the original robber-rescue drama—adapted for the Parisian stage by Jean H. F. La Martelière and titled *Robert, chef de brigands* (1792). The two pantomimes by Arnould-Mussot, *La Forêt noire* and *Le Maréchal des logis*, the three-act pantomime by Jean G.-A. Cuvelier de Trie, *La Fille hussard* (1796)—to which we can add two plays slightly further down on our list, namely, Dercy's *La Caverne* (1793), a lyrical drama with music by Le Sueur, and Jean Dejaure's *Lodoiska, ou Les Tartares* (1791), a comedy—comprise our sample.

Taking these five plays together, we find all feature a demoiselle in distress: Seraphine in *La Caverne* is being held against her will by bandits. Lucille, in *La Forêt noire*, is an unwed mother whose father wants to kill her child. She escapes his clutches and, in a novel twist of the plot, is rescued by robbers, one of whom takes a fancy to her and takes her, like Seraphine, to a cave. Lodoiska, the title character of a drama set in Poland, is fiancée to Lovinski. She has been confided, however, to one of the most powerful and wicked counts of Poland, Boleslas, by her father, Lapauski, who seeks revenge against Lovinski on account of a disagreement the two men had over a vote for the king of Poland. Lodoiska is held captive in a tower of what appears to be an impregnable fortress. In *La Fille hussard* two young women, Cathérine and Sophie, along with their fathers, are trapped in a German Imperial military camp on the Danube, which is being attacked by Turks (who are called "brigands"). Cathérine is taken hostage in Act I, while Sophie has a different problem: her father, the general of the army, has destined her to marry a German baron whom she reviles. Instead she would marry the Swedish sergeant in the camp, Laureto. *Le Maréchal des logis* was based on a true story in the *Mercure de France* in 1783 about an officer who, traversing the moors of Nevers, responded to the shouts of a woman about to be molested by "assassins." The fictionalized version has Gillet and Lucille leave a village festival for the woods, where she accidentally drops a piece of ribbon he has given her. She goes back later, when it is dark, is attacked by bandits, and is tied to a tree.

The rescues in four of these plays are complicated. In *La Caverne*, brigands plot to liberate Seraphine. Her husband is blind, but enters the cavern setting nonetheless. Finally her brother delivers the coup de grâce from outside. In *Forêt noire*, a pitched battle takes place between Lucille's lover (and father of her child) and the captain of the robbers. Even though Gillet's valorous rescue of Lucille is not noble, it is seen as worthy of a noble. In *Maréchal des logis*, the young woman's lover arrives in time to disperse the bandits and untie her from the tree, much to the gratification of all celebrants in the village festival. In *La Fille hussard*, after dazzling combat with the Turks, Sophie descends the walls of a feudal tower. Her father is so indebted to Laureto for his routing of the Turks that he agrees to let him marry Sophie. Marriage of love wins out again. So do the exotic cast of Turks, the setting on the Danube, and adventure.

Lodoiska features the most spectacular rescue of these plays, for the wicked Boleslas makes good on his threat to blow his castle up with Lodoiska inside. She is saved only by the bravery of Lovinski, who, accompanied by the Tartars, braves the flames to save her. At that point Lodoiska's father naturally permits her to marry him. This play, set to music by Kreutzer, possesses much local color (Polish, Tartar, medieval) and has some touching moments, especially when Lovinski and Lodoiska sing of their love while she is still imprisoned in the castle. Rescue plays lifted spectators out of their anxiety about the Revolution in the street—from the watch committees to the ward meetings, the military levees—providing them with safer, more distant, more gallant subjects.

EXOTIC PLAYS

Edmond Favières's adaptation of Bernardin de Saint-Pierre's exotic novel *Paul et Virginie*, a three-act comedy that premiered on January 5, 1791 at the Théâtre Italien, was performed 150 times at the Opéra Comique, a quarter of them during the Terror. Favières's stage direction sets the play on the Ile de France in the Indian Ocean: "The site should offer a wild, imposing and picturesque perspective: several banana trees are scattered here and there, a date tree covered with fruit is in the middle of the Theatre." The play focuses partly on the slaves of the isle toward whom the European inhabitants—Paul, Virginie, their mothers, and the pastor—have a benevolent attitude. We can find a good deal of Rousseau, of whom Bernardin was a disciple, in this depiction of innocent love and virtuous slaves. The simplicity of Virginie's life with Paul on the Ile de France contrasts sharply with the Old World, represented by the aunt of Virginie, Mme de Saint Phar, to whom Virginie is to be sent to finish her education, and whose fortune she will inherit.

As if the saccharine relations of the hero and heroine were not enough for tender-hearted audiences, Favières goes further and changes Bernardin's ending. The novel depicts Virginie returning after eighteen months, only to be caught in a violent storm as she nears the island. Virginie is seen on the poop of the ship as it goes under, while Paul swims unsuccessfully to her rescue. Favières has the ship at sea for only a matter of hours before it is caught in a storm and wrecked on reentering the port. Paul and Zabi swim to save Virginie. The curtain drops with Paul holding an unconscious Virginie in his arms and the governor, La Bourdonnais, manumitting Zabi while the chorus sings "No more sufferings, no more alarms,/May the pleasures of a better day,/ Tender lovers, follow your tears,/And may your hearts be united by love."

Revolutionary audiences, attending the Terror's daily executions, could not be counted on to endure the loss of Virginie in faraway waters, not even on stage. Napoleon himself read and reread the novel, which often brought him to the point of shedding tears.[1]

Télémaque, by Pierre Gabriel Gardel, is a ballet version of Fénelon's epic romance about the wanderings and education of Ulysses's young son and is similar to his *Psyché* of 1790. Also one of the top fifty for the decade, *Télémaque* depicts goddesses vying for man's attention—this time, Venus, Amour, the enchantress Calypso, and Eucharis. The denouement of the ballet occurs when Amour, Calypso, Mentor, and Télémaque appear saved on a rock. But then the victorious Eucharis appears on the deck of the burning boat and is also saved. Calypso tears out her hair, Télémaque stretches out his hand to Calypso, and Mentor pushes him into the sea, then dives after him.

Gardel has taken as many liberties with Fénélon's poem as Favières did with Bernardin de Saint-Pierre's novel. The ballet encapsulates only the Eucharis-Calypso episode of Télémaque's travels. Missing is the moral pedagogy of the original as well as its more serious, chaste, and adventurous Télémaque.

Instead we have a luxurious and voluptuous tableau replete with all the twittering inconstancy of amorous passion: timidity, fear, doubt, pain, abandonment, jealousy, intrigue, and revenge, counterbalanced by the wisdom and fidelity of Mentor.

Télémaque premiered on February 23, 1790, was performed roughly twice a month in that year, almost disappeared from the repertory in 1791, came back weakly in 1792 and 1793, then rebounded in 1794 with thirty-three performances, forty-nine in 1795 and twenty-three in 1797. To a large extent its performance history was strongest during the Thermidorean Reaction and the hedonistic Directory.

POLITICAL DRAMA

While none of the plays we have so far examined is primarily political in content, there are several that do have political overtones and two more—the "folie" *Nicodème dans la lune* and the opera *Offrande à la liberté*—that are explicitly political. Let us first ask whether there are not any political dimensions of our essentially nonpolitical plays.

The concluding arietta of the *Deux chasseurs et la laitière* (1763) draws a puzzling political analogy between the misfortunes of the hunters and the milkmaid on the one hand, and France on the other. "An intriguer in need devises a thousand different projects;/He wants to install seaports all around France in order to enrich her./Dead set on the affair, he borrows, finds credit, but one beautiful morning,/The jig is up, the pot of milk has spilled on the ground."

Could this be an allusion to the powerful foreign minister, Etienne François duc de Choiseul (1719-1785), who held most of the important portfolios during the Seven Years' War, which ended so disastrously for France in 1763, the year of the premiere of the *Deux chasseurs,* or does it allude to his more remote predecessor Colbert? Whatever the allusion is, this defeatist note is far removed from the intoxicating idealism of 1793! If the conclusion is undeniably political, it is hardly Revolutionary. *Paul et Virginie* can be read on one level as a political play because the hero and heroine represent the natural goodness of man and are sentimentally opposed to slavery. Moreover, they are hard pressed to tolerate other overbearing demands of European civilization—the trip back to France for an education and an inheritance. The great popularity of this play coincides with the Convention's abolition of slavery in 1794. The abolition of that heinous institution is portrayed in absolutely saccharine terms, considering the human carnage it cost in Haiti after 1791.

The village plays we have examined (*La Dot, Le Devin du village, Les Deux petits savoyards, Blaise et Babet*) also have a political dimension: that of mutual devotion of seigneur and villager. The seigneur is the villagers' father, the representative of the king, and ultimately of God. Village conflicts, marriages, and money pass through him. In all these plays we have a certain cult of helplessness on the part of the lowly, who receive benevolence from above. One is still speaking the language of grace and gifts rather than of rights and revolution.

Going beyond 1789, we have one play by Boutet de Monvel, *Philippe et Georgette*, which premiered at the end of December 1791 at the Théâtre Italien, and which dramatized the plight of a young deserter, terribly afraid of the scaffold, hiding out in a Paris apartment. This play, full of all the sentimental excesses of the age, is one of the most maudlin of our top fifty. Even though there are no explicit allusions to the Revolution, the play was performed forty-two times in 1792, the first year of the war against Austria, then twenty times each in 1793 and 1794, and much more frequently in the two years thereafter.

There were three plays entitled *Le Déserteur*: one by Maximilien Gardel, a second by Michel de Sedaine, and a third by Louis Sebastien Mercier. All three premiered before the Revolution; Gardel's drama was first performed in 1786 at Fontainebleau. It is a short ballet that tells the story of Alexis and Louise, whose wedding plans are interrupted by Alexis's arrest for desertion from the king's army. Louise flees precipitously to the camp of the king, at whose feet she falls, imploring pardon for Alexis. The "grace" of the king is given and Louise runs back to her lover; then "a general ballet of the greatest possible gaiety causes them to forget all the misfortunes which they have experienced."

This play, which had ten or fewer performances each year between 1789 and 1793, and none at all in 1794, was revived in 1795, when it had thirty-seven performances, and continued to be performed about twice a month for the rest of the decade. Again it is a political drama, but hardly Revolutionary. Its popularity, along with that of *Philippe et Georgette* during the Directory, shows, perhaps, that the problem of desertion was more on people's minds after 1795, at the very time that Bonaparte was constructing the most popular army in history.

This leads us to our last two plays. Beffroy de Reigny's *Nicodème dans la lune*, a play that Alphonse Aulard termed "royalist," is number 12 on our list (performed 266 times). It is the story of Nicodème, a French valet-astronomer who, after witnessing a moderate and beneficial revolution in France, is taken by his master in a balloon to the moon. The peasants of the moon are still laboring under feudal burdens imposed by unjust seigneurs. The Emperor is benevolent but blinded to the sufferings of his subjects by his conniving ministers. The courtiers are villainous, consumers of public funds. As a free man Nicodème refuses to kneel before a minister. The Emperor offers to let him choose one of his three women to take back to France. Eroticism mixes with an aura of *bienfaisance* and transparent political allusions to Louis XVI and "ministerial despotism." Airs are sung in argot about the risk kings run of being pushed into the "abyss" by such malevolent advisers and about the obligation to love humble villagers as well as the grandees.

The moon's state is that of France before the Revolution. The subtitle of the play, *ou La Révolution pacifique,* denotes either an idealization of the revolution that was or a yearning for a revolution that would never be. The final line informs all discontented spectators of the play that they, too, can go to the moon. Gaiety ("l'apanage des âmes farouches"; III, vi) and the peaceful harmonization of all social orders—king, clergy (there is a *bon curé* solicitous of the peasants), aristocracy, peasants (bourgeois do not appear)—express the aspirations of France in the early days of the Revolution, when Louis was serenaded as the "Régénérateur de la Liberté française." When crowds flocked to see this "folie" of Cousin Jacques (as Beffroy was known) after November 1790, at the Théâtre Comique et Lyrique, they treated themselves to a taste of nostalgia rather than to the political realities of a monarchy that was about to collapse.

Quite different was the musical creation or opera entitled *L'Offrande à la liberté.* A few months after the outbreak of war between Austria and France and the composition of the "Marseillaise" by Rouget de Lisle in Strasbourg, the ballet master of the Opéra, Pierre Gabriel Gardel, was having dinner with the composers Etienne Nicolas Méhul and François Joseph Gossec, as well as several other musicians. Patriotism ran high. An onlooker asked two singers present to sing the "Marseillaise." When they reached the second stanza, which begins "Amour sacré de la patrie," the spectators took off their caps and knelt down. Gardel allegedly leaned over and said to Gossec, "There is something in this scene for the Opéra."

Gossec arranged a short opera, or "scene," as the score sheet titles it, then put it to the music of the well-known patriotic air "Veillons au salut de l'Empire" and to the "Marseillaise." It begins: "Citizens, suspend your games/Numerous enemies threaten your country/Against the liberty of a generous people/The tyrants of Germany and the tyranny of Europe are at last united/....If despotism conspires/Let us conspire for the/downfall of kings. Liberty, Liberty,/Let every mortal render homage to you." The transcendental significance of the conflict is suggested by the words "On the welfare of our country/Depends that of the Universe." Stanzas one, four, five, and six of the "Marseillaise" are then interpolated, at which point the stage directions read: "The adorers of Liberty, children of both sexes dressed in white, carry perfumes to be burnt around the statue of Liberty..." and there follows a "religious dance of liberty" to the words of the second stanza of the "Marseillaise": "Amour sacré de la patrie..." and then the refrain: "Aux armes citoyens...!"

The opera premiered on October 2, 1792, and was performed 174 times between 1792 and 1799: reaching a peak in 1793 with fifty-seven performances, sinking to only two in 1795 (when the counterrevolutionary

"Réveil du peuple" was far more popular), reaching almost its 1793 level in 1796 with fifty-two performances, and then virtually disappearing from the repertory.   As a sacralization of the *patrie*, it is an important piece of the religion of revolution, or the religion of man (MS, Conservatoire National de Musique).

The long-term repertory of the decade was by and large oblivious to the Revolution, but was punctuated by political comedy (*Nicodème*) and the sacralization of what became the most important cultural emblem of the Revolution, the "Marseillaise."   The search for peace and harmony at the beginning of the Revolution combined with an equally universal desire to repulse the foreign invaders as the Revolution neared a climax. Moreover, so many of those comedies about love that we have examined have a definite social, if not precisely political, message: young women should have some freedom in the conduct of their lives; in particular, they should be free to choose whom they marry; they should marry for love.

If the seigneurs' lack of concern for peasants is one of the outstanding grievances of 1789, then the benevolent seigneur, beginning with the king, is one of that generation's greatest passions.   Indulgent fathers, kind masters, village harmony, money,   marriage, and social advancement are the predominant themes of not very revolutionary drama.   These plays, most of them written during the Old Regime, triggered nostalgia, it seems, in spectators disillusioned or worried about the Revolution, and who longed for a past that never was.

4

The Great Successes of Each Year

Marie-Laurence Netter

The great successes of Parisian theatre, year after year, offer an image at once close to, and very different from, the one we have just studied. If half of the most performed plays through the decade were logical inclusions in the ten most performed plays of the year, there were others, more dynamic and more political from the perspective of Revolutionary culture, that were at the top of the annual list.

The ten most performed plays in Paris each year demonstrate that the public's attachment to a theatre of diversion did not weaken. Over time, love intrigues and unexpected turns of events continued to hold center stage in spectacles that became increasingly extravagant and that caused comedy to evolve in the direction of vaudeville in the modern sense of the term. We will examine this evolution of genres in Chapter 6. At this juncture, we will focus on a content analysis of these plays, their social and political meaning, and the way in which they evolved in terms of Revolutionary relevance.

Love and social relations constitute the eternal, indeed omnipresent, themes of plays performed during the French Revolution and, in this sense, situate the period in direct continuity with the eighteenth century. The vogue that Molière, Baurans, and some others enjoyed, shows that the comic and critical legacy of their works was far from being exhausted. Even in the throes of the Revolution, the special place reserved for Molière is naively emphasized in a scene in which we find Harlequin affixing some posters for a spectacle, then drawing back in awe in front of a poster for a play by "the master." He decides not to cover it up, declaring: "By the children of the Vaudeville you will always be respected" (Barré et al. *Arlequin Afficheur* 1792).

But events followed at a vertiginous speed, and the type of conflicts put on stage in these comedies did not exhaust the public's thirst to see the vestiges of a crumbling world and the promise of the one that was about to be born. These two requirements constitute the background of a large number of contemporary plays of the Revolution and, by this count, even those that came under the rubric of "entertainment" can nevertheless be considered as political. In light of this consideration, the distinction between the theatre of diversion and political theatre is not always evident. Created during the Directory, is not the character of the fishwife, Madame Angot, the quintessential comic character? But is she not also the ferocious caricature of the nouveaux riches who made a fortune in speculating? The topicality is linked to the evolution of the principal characters on stage who were witnesses to a society confronted with new values and new conflicts.

The Revolutionary events themselves also have their part, even if this is not as important a factor as has often been suggested (Hamiche 1973; Carlson 1966). They are noticeably present in the most performed plays in 1793 and 1794, when censorship was reestablished (first in an ad hoc fashion by the Committee of Public Safety, then completely by the Commission of Public Education in April 1794). It is, however, difficult to determine whether the politics of a play are due to the public infatuation with commitment or the obligation imposed on authors to write "patriotic" scripts. The two periods that preceded and followed the Terror appear more devoted to diversion, though the later years often carried a strong connotation of social criticism. From 1789 to 1792, it was essentially a matter of provoking laughter at the expense of those who allowed themselves to be mocked for stubbornness or for attachment to false principles, but also for stupidity. After the Terror, from 1794 to 1799, the preferred target of the playwrights became the cowardice of petty potentates and the nouveaux riches. Throughout all these three periods, including 1793-1794, omnipresent love developed its intrigues and created its emotions without which the theatre would not have had its immense popular success.

1789-1792: THE TRIUMPH OF CLASSIC COMEDY

It certainly was the work of chance that put a play of Plautus among the most performed in 1789. The debt of Molière to this Latin author of the third century B.C. has often been stressed, as well as the debt of the authors of the eighteenth century to Molière himself. In linking Revolutionary theatre with ancient theatre, the Revolutionary theatre linked itself with its origins, thus clearly manifesting the tradition in which it was situated. The theatre that triumphed in the first years of the Revolution would be acknowledged by a modern audience as classical, but was not perceived as such by the popular audiences of the time, which, unlike the bourgeoisie and the aristocracy, were unfamiliar with the classics.

The expense of tickets and the privileges of exclusive performances contributed to people's ignorance of what happened on the stages of the big theatres. The subversive stock of this comic theatre, in which valets and maids help each other mock their masters one by one, had not been exhausted. The popular success of numerous plays written before 1789 testifies to it. So do the productions of the 1790s that borrow from eighteenth-century situations in which an individual—valet, child, or pupil—vociferously demands his liberty and a just salary from his superior, be he master, father, or tutor. The affirmation of equality of persons that reverberates in this theatre does not, however, go so far as to demand equality of conditions. The social hierarchies are always respected here when the exercise of power is just; only the abuses of power are condemned. Except for a few very violent plays, it was this way throughout the period from 1789 to 1799.

Theatre, during the first years of the Revolution, was the vehicle of a reformist pedagogy and was not very revolutionary at all, even in 1791 and 1792 when the censorship apparatus had been abolished. From our point of view (which consists in examining the plays that had true success and not those which momentarily caught the public's attention by the scandal they provoked), the prudence of the Parisian spectacles shows that the public was not disposed to have a radically new representation of society imposed on it. In effect, the public was master in the matter, since it alone was responsible for making or breaking a play and determining the duration of its success on stage. A spectacle that received no applause and was not demanded by the pit was not performed again and had little chance of being revived.

More than the Revolution, it was the Enlightenment which one found on stage. It ushered in such concepts as the marriage of inclination, which causes individuals of similar age and tastes to unite, the idea that intelligent women are the equal of men, and the recognition that natural sentiments govern upright and respectful dealings among people. Dissimulation and intrigue, it taught, serve only to teach those who have not understood that the time of blind obedience has passed.

The successful plays of 1789 and especially of 1790 were, rather paradoxically, more political than those of the following years. It was as if the Revolution, in speeding up, took refuge behind old verities of authors long deceased, who did not inflame public opinion by attracting the thunderbolts of the pamphleteers, writers, and journalists. It was during 1791 and 1792 that the plays of Molière, Marivaux, Brueys, Anseaume, and a few others were performed often and had their greatest success in the entire Revolutionary period. Their work is certainly not without potential subversive force, as we have already pointed out, but by this time, the social and political upheavals in progress placed them far behind the reality. Their extraordinary vogue is without doubt one of prudence.

In 1789, the play that won the favor of the public was Dorvigny's comedy *Le Père Duchesne ou La Mauvaise habitude*, which introduced the public to the instantly popular Père Duchesne, who became a symbol in 1790 with the creation of the newspaper of Hébert with the same title. In particular, Père Duchesne became famous for the violence and obscenity of his language. Based on a real person, a stove merchant by profession, Dorvigny's Père Duchesne is a sailor-turned-stove repairman who wishes to marry Lucile, the chambermaid of a marquise. The marquis and the marquise give their consent to this marriage, which pleases Lucile, but they wish to meet the Père Duchesne, whose uncouthness has been pointed out to them. He has "the bad habit" of embellishing his words with resounding and colorful profanity. To marry Lucile, he has to appear before her masters and speak to them without uttering the least obscenity. The marquis, who secretly sympathizes with him, wants nonetheless to put him to the test and asks him to recount some of his experiences for him. At the beginning everything goes well, the Père Duchesne controlling himself and avoiding by circumlocution the profanity he is about to let fly. Recounting a second exploit, however, he gets carried away by his memories and swears in his accustomed manner. The marquis laughs up his sleeve, the marquise gets angry, and Gilotin, another suitor of Lucile, thinks he has made a conquest. But this leaves out of account the good judgment of the Père Duchesne, who, in the last act, reappears before Lucile's masters and declares to them that he is a free man, and that if Lucile consents, they can marry without their permission. If, in spite of his respectability and his tenderness for her, Lucile hesitates because of the vulgarity of his language, he vows to renounce her without further importuning. In the end, everyone consents to the marriage and the marquis concludes, "Abruptness and goodness are better than politeness and a bad heart."

The play is funny because one waits at each moment for the faux pas of Père Duchesne and then, when he lets himself go, his verve carries him away with the vulgarity of his language. Moreover, the political message is clear: to each his role and his language. The man of the people is free to marry the woman of his choice, on condition that the latter consents. Père Duchesne's laughter, the truculence of his character, and his determination assured the success of the play. The play also succeeded in spreading the image of an independent *peuple*, proud of its identity. But not all the plays are so captivating. A pretext for every kind of demonstration, love is as adept at painting the faults or the quality of a character as it is at revealing the absurdity of certain situations.

An idyll that is sketched, affirmed, or revealed brutally to the protagonists is the central theme of a multitude of plays and offers an occasion to stage the character traits it reveals: hostility, benevolence, cupidity, egoism, and jealousy. These sentiments are generally linked to a well-defined social situation and constitute stereotypes. One perceives that in spite of new costuming each time, this theatre was not terribly original, and it is therefore not surprising that the majority of these productions have been consigned to oblivion. The influence of these plays on the social imagination was not negligible, however. Their numerical importance shows that the public never had enough. Moreover, through these plays, and by delicate brush strokes, audiences saw the whole spectrum of values and habits of the Old Regime criticized to the profit of a world not so much overthrown as idealized, that is, where justice, tolerance, and friendship would reign.

As we have seen, *Le Père Duchesne* featured a couple of broad-minded aristocrats whose sole intention was to assure that their maid did not commit an error in wishing to marry a churl. But there was no true conflict, since they were ready to recognize a respectable man under a vulgar appearance. Under these conditions, the weakness of his character and the affirmation—without aggression— of his condition as a free man could only be supplementary proofs of his excellent heart.

True aristocratic characters do not appear frequently in the theatre of the first years of the Revolution; when they are present, they are never depicted as evil. In the *Marquis Tulipano*, another success of 1789, the lead role is that of an enriched and ennobled peasant, who pretends to marry his son, Giorgino, to a true countess, despite the love his son feels for a rich peasant girl of his village. The latter, capable of passing herself off as a countess, marries Giorgino. When the real countess arrives, she rejoices with the new spouses and agrees to marry the father, who ends up recognizing his wrongdoing to his son.

In *Ricco*, the centuries-old conflict between the Ormeuils and the Germances cannot withstand the love of the marquis and the young countess, who meet without knowing each other's identity. The personal merits of the marquis, his good sense and heart, cause the count to drop his prohibition against their marriage.

Based on these few examples, the anti-noble rhetoric seems quite light as long as the characters are animated by good sentiments and do not evince some sort of superiority that would place them above the common sort. Much better than a title of seigneur is the trump card of the man who has made himself and who has not forgotten it. Monsieur Verseuil, in *Les Deux petits savoyards*, is the exemplum of the generous noble who uses his power to reestablish justice and do good around him. It is not the nobles themselves whom the playwrights attack, nor is it their power; rather, it is the arbitrary abuses that imperil the humble folk. The people responsible for these abuses are rarely high-placed persons but intermediaries. The most performed plays in 1790 are very revealing of this state of mind, which seems to denounce the excessive power of the "little bosses" without calling into question the established order.

Using a tried technique for escaping censorship, Guillemain's *Menuisier de Baghdad* describes how a good prince reestablishes the reign of justice among his subjects and corrects a troublemaker, under the cover of an exotic setting. The caliph of Baghdad has condemned Pasha Mohammed to become a joiner in Hali's place and has him whipped because he refuses to pay what he owes. Hali then becomes the pasha. Hali and his wife, astonished by the useless luxury that surrounds them, nevertheless maintain their simple lifestyle. They share their rich meals with the poor and give freedom to the women in the harem, two of whom wish to go to France, where they have learned liberty has triumphed. A commissioner has just pleaded the cause of Mohammed, who apologizes for his attitude without complaining about his lot. Hali then asks for mercy from the caliph, obtains it, and then seeks a peaceful retreat in the countryside for himself. As one can see, there is no true plot in this play but only a lesson of wisdom given to the nobles in the person of the pasha and formulated by the joiner, alias the people: "He will see that the humble people never ceased to hold the nobility in esteem; and that all they were against was arrogance and harshness."

Social criticism is clearly stronger in *Le Soldat prussien ou Le Bon fils*, a German comedy adapted for the French stage by Dumaniant. In this play, the bailiff profits from the absence of his seigneur by severely exploiting his peasants. Marcel and Geneviève, an aged couple, find themselves in misery and their house about to be seized. Their son George is in the army, as a result of a fraudulent drawing of lots organized by the bailiff. When the play commences, George arrives at his parents' home with other soldiers who must all be lodged with him. The parents, as true patriots, permit the soldiers to eat their last provisions, but George notices his parents' extreme vexation. He learns that since his departure, their situation has become catastrophic. To procure the money demanded by the bailiff, George formulates a plan. He pretends to desert and is denounced by a friend, who, according to their scheme, will get his reward and give it to his parents. In deserting, George condemns himself to death. His colonel, who knows him to be a good soldier, makes inquiries and learns of George's heroic sacrifice. He makes George's situation known to the king, who sees to it that the bailiff is punished and George is made captain. The king, true father of his subjects, reestablishes justice. Not only is his authority not called into question, it is portrayed as good and just.

The political character of this type of play is undeniable, but because it is not a matter of whether to reestablish the rights of humble people, the image of the great is spared, and the wicked one is always a subordinate. On the other hand, when it is a matter of princes, the worst action becomes possible, which is the mark of a certain realism and, by the same token, opens for a public little familiar with these realities an enormous space for the imagination.

Although in most of the eighteenth century, historical plays enjoyed a certain vogue in the *collèges* and in the armies (under the watchful eyes of the censors), they achieved only a moderate success during the Revolution. The celebrated *Charles IX ou L'Ecole des rois* of M. J. Chénier incited prohibition, disorder, and demonstrations in its favor but, once authorized, hardly attracted a crowd. Though it was performed some sixty times, it was in a very discontinuous fashion.

Doubtless, what was needed at the time was a more clearly contemporary staging and text than the very classical tragedy composed by Chénier. *Paris sauvé ou La Conspiration manqué* of Gabiot de Salins, performed for the first time on February 10, 1790, was more successful, because it encoded recent events in a very recognizable manner. Through the narrative of the fourteenth-century conspiracy of Etienne Marcel to deliver Paris to the king of Navarre, the theme of loyalty to the king of France is broached. Gabrielle, the daughter of Marcel, who has just revealed the treachery of her father, commends her lover, Richard, son of the faithful Maillard, who is loyal to the king, for his bravery and declares, "In a faithful lover, an adored spouse, I will still possess the model of French women." The modern quality of the language and the similitude of the situation of conflict between two factions of the aristocracy won over the public.

But it is not only the political conflicts that reveal the wickedness of the high and mighty of this world and their brutal appetite for power. Their abusiveness is revealed also, and perhaps better, by their amorous sentiments or by the rights they arrogate to themselves over the emotional life of their children. The banal side of everyday life, the type of situation lived by everyone, reveals a power that becomes misused when it is in the hands of persons who impose their will without any respect for others, and who have the extraordinary means to do so. The authors do not hesitate to have magic and the supernatural intervene to cause the innocent to triumph.

L'Homme au masque de fer ou Le Souterrain, a pantomime by Arnould, tells the story of a count and a marquise harmed by the jealous desire of a prince who wishes to be loved by the marquise. After a violent altercation between the prince and the count, the king, wishing to avenge his son, has the count imprisoned, and condemns him to wear an iron mask so that no one can recognize him. The marquise, faithful to her lover, is locked in a dungeon in the Bastille. The count finds himself in the cell above hers, whereupon they manage to communicate, and after a long pursuit led by the prince, who seeks their deaths, to recover their liberty.

When they love, the great do not countenance rejection, and they do not hesitate to put to death anyone who resists. But the success of the plays in 1789 and 1790 was much more due to the painting of mores of high society, which fascinated the public because the characters were so exotic. The discrepancy between the banality of the sentiments and the violence of the actions they trigger, reinforced the idea that the rules governing the aristocratic world were absurd and harmful.

Simultaneously, the simplicity of sentiments expressed in naïve plays is such that all intrigue is removed and is replaced by the gentility and candor of the characters. By contrast, the outbursts of hatred and passion become the property of the great, while tenderness and lack of ambition make the humble folk a model of virtue.

The heroes here are peasants. The *Deux chasseurs et la laitière* triumphs in this pastoral register. This "vaudeville" is a musical interpretation of a moral tale of history, in this case a fable of La Fontaine, the moral of which is that one must not sell the skin of a bear before having killed it. The *Devin du village* of Rousseau is the story of the lives of Colin and Colette, who are happy to find each other after a moment of jealousy. But the summit of imaginary simplicity is reached by Charles Demoustier's *Amour filial*, a short bucolic opera that triumphed in 1792 and during the first months of 1793, when the Revolution took an irreversible turn with the trial and execution of the king. Two old soldiers are found by chance on a battlefield where one has saved the life of the other. They are accompanied by their children, Louise and Felix, who have fallen in love at first glance. So as not to be separated, they decide to live all together on the mountain where they have found one another. Although written in 1792, this fable remains, because of the naïveté of its dialogue and situations, in strict line with preceding works of the eighteenth century. The time, however, has imperceptibly changed. It is the love of the *patrie* that guides the action and sentiments of these four persons throughout, simultaneously giving rise to true declamation, as if popular wisdom and patriotism henceforth would be naturally mixed.

Among the great successes at the beginning of the Revolution, only one play adopted for its theme the events of the day: *Nicodème dans la lune ou La Révolution pacifique* of Beffroy de Reigny. We have already spoken about this play, which was one of the great successes of Revolutionary theatre. We will not concern ourselves with it here except to recall the extreme moderation of the political criticism it contained.

It is thus social criticism and the depiction of mores, and not the political events themselves, that command the attention of the theatre public in the first years of the Revolution. We have already pointed out the paradoxical situation that arose in 1791-1792. For reasons of prudence, in 1791 and 1792 the oldest authors, those of the seventeenth and eighteenth centuries, were the most often staged. It was also at this time that audiences were introduced to the very popular farcical characters of the fair theatre—like Arlequin, Colombine, and Nicaise, who occasioned songs and injected a heavy dose of common sense about everyday matters, lacking any social allusions. Once censorship was abolished, it was possible for all theatre directors to take possession of these popular figures; fear doubtless led them to hide behind characters that were anything but aristocratic. Even before censorship was officially restored in an ad hoc fashion on August 2, 1793, and formally in April 1794, the criticism of patriotic spectators obliged the authors and directors to practice self-censorship in order to avoid the fulminations of the authorities. In this context, the characters of farce, both popular and without danger, became veritable sheet anchors.

1793-1794: A THEATRE UNDER SURVEILLANCE

In 1793-1794 the theatre was less free; at this time, the Terror tried to impose some exclusively patriotic plays on directors. In fact, it was only during these two years that the most-performed plays were all contemporary. But were they for that reason ultrarevolutionary, as the surveillance committees in operation since March 1793 wished, and as many accounts of this period have affirmed? In spite of the political and official success of the famous play by Sylvain Maréchal, *Le Jugement dernier des rois*, often considered to be the model of plays produced and performed during the Terror, it did not achieve the anticipated success; it never appears on the list of most performed plays. It was performed only twenty-two times at the Théâtre de la République from October 18, 1793, date of its premiere, to February 20, 1794, with a one-performance revival in 1795 at the Théâtre du Marais. This was a very average performance record.

It was not plays that provoked noise and furor that were passed down to posterity; nonetheless, at this time the Revolution was quite present on stage, notably with patriotism in all its forms. It was not political life itself that the authors staged, nor the ideology that underlay it, but the patriotism that had changed—or was believed to have changed—the mode of life and thought of all citizens, whatever their earlier condition might have been. The vogue of patriotism no doubt responded to the will of the surveillance committees, the police, and of the Committee of Public Safety to make theatre an instrument of propaganda. It also permitted authors to manifest the revolutionary spirit that these committees demanded of them, without directly putting on stage the rival factions in France, which could have been very dangerous for them while the factions were tearing each other apart. Patriotism alone served all causes—provided they were Revolutionary.

In 1793, it was Louis-Benoît Picard's comedy, *Les Visitandines* that soared to the top of the year's performances. This anticlerical comedy was one of the rare examples of its genre to obtain a success for several years. If the play seemed certainly Revolutionary by the irreverent manner in which nuns were publicly treated, it was not really so in fact. The reputed gourmandise of nuns and priests had been the subject of jokes from time immemorial, and as for hypocritical chastity, or the despair about their vocation, the sole fact of having evoked it on stage could pass for Revolutionary. Freethinking anticlericalism nourished itself on this type of argument.

The *Heureuse décade*, which triumphed in 1793 and 1794, was defined by its authors as a "patriotic entertainment." The opening vaudeville indicates it covers the most faithful depiction possible of the patriotism that henceforth will animate Frenchmen.

There is no intrigue in this picture, in which one finds some of the virtues of the ideal patriot family, but the movement is rapid thanks to the effects of announcements that follow one upon another. The play is short (one act) and interrupted by numerous vaudevilles; it was, according to one of its authors, "written, learned, and performed in five days," which, in spite of the simplicity of the dialogue, was quite an accomplishment. As was the vogue at that time, the characters carry names which define their state or rank. The father and the mother have as their patronym Socle (base), a transparent allusion to the fact that they represent the pivot of the family, the pillar of a little community. One son-in-law, mayor of a neighboring village, is called Le Juste, as one would expect the first magistrate of the region to be; the other, Labêche (the spade), as befits the good laborer. The future husbands of the younger sisters are Bonnefoi, an upright merchant, and Alerte, the young patriot, ready to defend his country.

The scene is the day of the decade, the day of rest of the Republican calendar. Father and Mother Socle rise early and rejoice that the new calendar offers fewer days of rest than the old one: "The days consecrated to the holy days were days lost to the *patrie*" (sc. I).

After that they break into a hymn to liberty, thanks to which the weather is always "superb," the children numerous, the harvest abundant. The father, as a good patriot, then unveils his great idea to occupy this day of repose. Until then he had gathered his children together and read to them the *History of France;* henceforward, they will write their own history together.

> Liberty must reject
> These monuments in which each page
> Seemed consecrated to dictate
> The maxims of slavery:
> From these errors let us not burden
> Our memory painfully
> So as to mention only virtues
> Let us write our own history. (sc. I)

And the mother approves: "It is very true; for in all that the poor people were always counted as nothing, and one would have said that there were none but kings and princes in this world" (sc. I).

The children-in-law arrive in their turn and learn that they have become heroes of a new history. The father has consigned the great deeds of each one and recalls the devotion of the daughters in the service of wounded soldiers, the sacrifice of their linens to make bandages, the law of the maximum applied by the merchant "even before it was promulgated," the voluntary provisioning of a volunteer with grain by the farmer, and the help given to the mayor by his wife in the denunciation of suspects. With each new deed, the person in the lead shouts that he has done nothing but what comes naturally, and the father takes advantage of it to denounce an impulse of jealousy or bad humor that would be ill-received because these actions are all aimed at the general welfare. The play ends with the arrival of the young volunteer, who although wounded, wears on his good arm a flag taken from the enemy and who still finds the energy to sing in vaudevilles to the glory of the sansculottes.

The skit came off well, its patriotism was moving; its naïveté could make one laugh. The success of the play two years in a row, in spite of the fact that it was very dated, can be explained only by the double reading that one could give it.

Several other plays that were performed in 1793 bear titles in manifest conformity to civic demands—*La Fête civique, Les Capucins aux frontières, L'Offrande à la liberté,* but unfortunately we have found the scripts of only the last which has been described above (pp. 33-34).

La Bonne aubaine by Radet is a comedy of mores in which clerks take revenge on the avarice of their patrons, an attorney and his wife. All the intrigue turns around a turkey sent by a defendant; Madame Griparin sells it; the clerks buy it back and discover that it contains 600 francs. After hesitating, they decide to teach the masters a lesson by inviting them to a sumptuous dinner and, before their arrival, ordering some work to be done in the shabby lodging assigned to them. Finally, they announce that all those works were done with money contained in the turkey. The Griparins are crushed, but they must remain silent under penalty of being accused of greed. The clerks, after discussing the matter between them, have drawn the lesson of this story: justice today is less complicated than before, the attorney has less work and thus less revenue; he lives better while the plaintiffs are better treated. Although the pedagogical aims of this play are as clear as they were for the *Heureuse décade,* the public, as long as it was amused, was ready to be receptive to this new genre, however didactic.

The great successes of the year 1794, and more precisely those from the middle of January to July, were *Au retour* and the several plays about the siege of Toulon (see listings under this title) such as Picard's *La Prise de Toulon,* works of circumstance which responded more to the demands of propaganda than to censorship.

While Lucette readies herself to marry Justin in *Au retour,* the mayor arrives and announces the conscription of all boys eighteen to twenty-five years of age. Justin, who will be twenty-five in three days, declares that he will enlist, to the great happiness of Lucette, who has been hoping he would not act otherwise. This very flimsy event serves as a pretext for numerous declarations and songs about the love of the *patrie* (which takes precedence over everything), while the curé of the village, who has been recently married, cries out his patriotic faith. Everyone is ready to greet with pikes the aristocrats and the upper clergy who would dream of "the return."

In Picard's *La Prise de Toulon,* the English and some representatives of the Old Regime dine together and dream about the monarchy they will soon restore. At the same moment, the cannons fire, the battle rages, and the French patriots invade the city.

These plays are all replete with stereotypes. Everyone acts and speaks exactly as he or she is supposed to in his or her position: quite imbued with their person and with the interests of their caste in the case of aristocrats; dreaming of nothing but the general interest, and the defense of the *patrie* in the case of soldiers and of the people. Never is a personal sentiment expressed except to mock it as the vestige of old habits that no longer have any justification.

This vogue subsists in the very typical characters like Arlequin, Colombine, Cadet Roussel, and Nicaise, who doubtless respond to the same desire to simplify the exposition when addressing a more and more "popular" public. Arlequin, in spite of his mysterious airs which expose him to the gossip of the wicked, thinks only of Colombine, who loves him just as much; Cadet Roussel, braggart and vain, is at heart a good and generous man of the people. As for Nicaise, her innocence and her lack of malice end by creating her happiness after having convinced her patron-godfather of the honesty of her character. These farcical characters—or those who make a semblance of farce—cause one to laugh by their extreme simplemindedness. They lend to Revolutionary theatre a dimension both quotidian and human that has no place or "rights of the city," unlike the patriotic spectacles.

The two plays of Pigault-Lebrun, *Les Dragons et les bénédictines* and the sequel, *Les Dragons en cantonnement,* are hardly more complicated, so unsurprising are the characters. In the former, a young captain breaks into a convent that his regiment is preparing to liberate. He falls in love with a young nun, Sainte-Claire, who is determined to break her vows and live as a "free" woman. This situation is complicated when the captain is forced to hide in the convent and is aided by two aged nuns, each of whom helps him in the belief that he will marry her as soon as she is free. It is, of course, Sainte-Claire who becomes his wife. This turn of events delights the colonel, who applauds his nephew's wisdom in contracting a marriage in which love and reason are united, and which promises a simple happiness and a future patriotic family. In the *Dragons en cantonnement,* the young husband, who has become a colonel, courts a younger widow, who is on the point of succumbing when Sainte-Claire arrives. Comprehending and rational, she becomes the friend of the widow, explains to her the very natural inconstancy of young men, and without the least reproach, pardons her husband. Besides this edifying fable, the sergeant major gives a lesson in good citizenship to *his* wife—Sister Gertrude in the preceding play—by threatening her with divorce if she renounces her position as sutler, under the pretext of his having been promoted captain and her desire to play the role of a lady. She yields to the wisdom of his suggestions.

All these characters submit to reason and demonstrate remarkable simplicity in whatever situation they find themselves. Only age and sex can at times lead to an instant of weakness, but the latter is easily surmounted thanks to a vigilant entourage; more than Revolutionary, these plays are naïvely militant. Given the context and the constraints imposed on the authors, they are not very violent.

As was the case with classical comedy, these "historic deeds," pantomimes or comedies are concerned with mores more than institutions. One of the few truly Revolutionary plays was the *Ami des lois,* played at the beginning of 1793 and promptly forbidden, by a power that, like its predecessors, tolerated no criticism of its methods, on the pretext that it disturbed public order.

1795-1799: THE REACTION AND REPUBLICAN THEATRE

Some months after 9 Thermidor, the end of the Terror was greeted in the theatre by plays that denounced the arbitrary arrests and welcomed the return to a legal order. The first of these was performed from October 1794 on, and had such a marked success that it was plagiarized several times. *Cange ou Le Commissionnaire de Lazare* and its several variants stage the history of a family reduced to misery by the unjustified arrest of the father, Durand, a lawyer by profession. It is the occasion of scenes—some more touching than others—in which mothers and children rival each other in courage to earn their daily bread and delicacy in dissimulating their troubles to the others. There is a villain who does everything to keep the father in prison and seems to abuse the daughter. There is a just man who works for his liberation and encourages the son: "Console yourself, my little friend, gone are the days of mourning and terror in which patriotism was a title of proscription. The system of oppression is destroyed." After an investigation, Durand is set free, and the upright representative of the people and school friend of Durand finds work for him, which he entrusts to him with the words, "Pardon this distrust on my part; I could leave my fortune to my friend, even my life; but I could never confide to him haphazardly a position important to the Republic." As for Cange, the title role, he links the prisoner and his family; moved by their misery, he divides his savings between them, making each party believe that it was the other who sent him/her the aid. He has six children in his charge, his own and three orphans of the deceased mother whose husband fights for the *patrie.* For (and this is something new) all these characters, great and small, good and wicked, are republicans and patriots, but some of them have let themselves be taken advantage of and have taken a bad fall at the hands of the now condemned tyranny.

Once more one notes that it is after the Terror that the idea of a good and bad revolution is born: that the period just ending has nothing to do with its beginnings, nor even with the Republic. It truly required putting a parenthesis around the reign of the Committee of Public Safety, under pain of seeing the entire Revolutionary edifice crumble because it did not manage to convert itself into a stable regime. The Thermidoreans well understood that not having abolished censorship, they thus allowed themselves the right to prohibit plays with an anti-Republican slant while authorizing criticism of the Terror.

This criticism provided theatre with some successful plays, performed for the most part in 1795, such as *Les Suspects* or *L'Intérieur des comités révolutionnaires*. These two plays deal with the subject of the Revolution in the comic mode by making the Jacobins look ridiculous. In *Suspects*, the entire plot turns on the ignorance and the vanity of a small town's municipal counselors who imagine that to be suspect—a word they do not understand—is a new municipal post from which one can drive profit and honor. They all compete with paltry stupidities, and when two modest peasants nominated are about to be arrested, a virtuous man fleeing the Terror announces the fall of the tyrants and the return to the order of the laws. The peasants, instructed by their error, promise each other to be less credulous in the future. In the *Intérieur des comités révolutionnaires* the members of the Jacobin municipality are not only rude, they are veritable swindlers, recidivists, and opportunists who arrest honest citizens under pretexts that they concoct from the victims' slightest statements, deforming and bending them to their design. The 9 Thermidor arrives just in time to prevent the arrest of a new family of innocents whose virtues, familiar to the whole city, have indisposed the committee.

These plays of circumstance are evidently very Manichaean and simplistic in their description of the Revolutionary tyranny. But they both make the better part of the stupidity and ignorance of men who were its instruments, avoiding thus all reflection on the nature of this power or its place in the Revolution. The Terror finds itself exorcised by the ridicule heaped on its protagonists.

The plays of this genre were not very numerous, and theatre was pressing to renew its ties with spectacles in which diversion was paramount. In 1795 and 1796, the greatest successes were once again the classics written and performed before the Revolution. The enduring popularity could be explained by the prescient illustration they offered of the new social relations. The new plays, often melodramatic in the modern sense of the term, are tinged with an egalitarian philosophy that tends to show that the inequality of conditions is only an accident which cannot prevent two beings from uniting. However, fairies and magic often mix in the action, as if to say that without their intervention, the obstacles to these natural sentiments would be insurmountable.

In keeping with the philosophy of the eighteenth century, numerous plays try to show that one must not trust appearances and that true grandeur—founded on respectable and courageous behavior and sentiments—is present in all classes of society. In this theme, one finds the underlying attitude that good blood cannot lie. This had been the plot of the *Deux petits savoyards*, and it is again the plot of the *Réveil du charbonnier*, performed for the first time in 1788 and received well in 1797. It is above all *Victor ou L'Enfant de la forêt*, a melodrama of Guilbert de Pixérécourt, that has a new twist: this time—bad heredity.

Victor, abandoned when he was very little, was taken in by a baron whose daughter Victor, now a man, loves. On account of his virtues (and in spite of his unusual birth), the marriage is to be permitted. Then Roger, a feared brigand, reappears in the region after years of absence. He is seeking his son abandoned long ago by his mother in order to remove him from his father's influence. This son is indeed Victor, who is brutally confronted by the obligation to challenge his father, who has refused to reform. Finally, Roger repents while dying in combat alongside the troops of the Emperor. This incredible adventure gives rise to a series of reflections on which family blood lines one should honor and on the education that alone can overcome negative influences.

These plays are great spectacles in which the magical and the fantastic are both a reaction to the austere virtue that the members of the Committee of Public Safety tried to impose everywhere and the culmination of a long evolution, both theoretical and practical, of the three great theatrical genres: tragedy, comedy, and drama. We will see later how melodrama was born and became the genre of the nineteenth century par excellence, but first we must show the success of this genre in the wake of traumatic political events; the coincidence certainly has something fortuitous about it, but it is not without influence on the nature of the subjects treated.

The theatre of the Directory created new stereotypical characters used to criticize the new mores of the times, albeit in a comic manner. Commerce and the rapid enrichment it procured—notably in this period when speculating and provisioning for the army went hand in hand—were particularly targeted. In *Madame Angot ou La Poissarde parvenue*, the character of Mme Angot is the object of ridicule, for she represents all those who pretend to live above their social condition, preoccupied only with appearances and forgetting their origins. The character's fortune is well-known. She rapidly escaped her creator Eve (Maillot), to be exploited by Dorvigny and above all by Joseph Aude in *Madame Angot à Constantinople*. The success of this character, undiminished through the nineteenth century, abated only in the aftermath of the First World War.

The ridiculous character of Madame Angot was not, however, new: in the pretension to culture, beautiful language, and alliance with nobles, one recognizes the peculiarities attributed by Molière to M. Jourdain. But the latter becomes rich because he is a good merchant, not a vile speculator. Besides, though he was ridiculous, he was not unattractive; and his naïveté allowed him to pass for a pedant of the culture to which he aspired. Madame Angot is not fundamentally evil at heart, but her manners are so far removed from those of the society she pretends to have joined, thanks to her money, that she has become grotesque, to the point that one is delighted to see her ridiculed. By contrast, her daughter and cousin give proof of intelligence and of good sense, showing the pointless vanity of wanting to change one's status. The caricatures are accurate and are directed as much at the nouveaux riches as at the mores of those with whom they pretend to identify, while popular wisdom becomes the correct point of reference. The immense popularity of this play, and of the series that followed, springs at once from its critical context and from the acting of the actors, who saw themselves here being offered roles which permitted them to improve. Boulevard theatre, an eminently bourgeois genre, was thus born.

Liberated from the influence of the Enlightenment and of the patriotism constantly imposed by the Committee of Public Safety, theatre of 1795-1799 can be said to have been the most innovative. In the months that followed 9 Thermidor, theatre played a political role by placing the responsibility for the Terror on the heads of a few misguided men. But it was a matter explained inductively and not deductively, in order to propagate the new institutions. On the social side, the theatre of the Directory played the same critical function as that formerly played by the "classical" comedies, but in a republican environment. The style and the staging were, however, profoundly reworked, as we will see below.

Theatre in the course of these ten years of the Revolution was not, then, as revolutionary, in the political sense of the term, as has been so often affirmed. The social criticism greatly exceeds the criticism of political institutions, and even then it is very moderate and quite unrevolutionary, in that it hardly invites great upheavals.

Theatre, which had been styled a "school of mores" in the eighteenth century, then a "school of good citizenship" during the Revolution, proved itself an imperfect instrument of education or of propaganda. The analysis of the plays year by year, shows that theatre followed the evolution of society rather than the other way around. One can no longer so easily agree with Danton's famous statement: "If *Figaro* killed the nobility, *Charles IX* will kill royalty." Theatre remained, nonetheless, an irreplaceable instrument by which to judge the state of mind of society itself.

5

Old Regime Tragedy and the Terror

Emmet Kennedy

The most revolutionary plays performed in Paris during the Revolution were written during the Old Regime. When Mirabeau recommended three plays for the first Festival of the Federation, he chose two by Voltaire—his *Brutus* of 1730 and his *Mort de César* of 1731—and Chénier's *Charles IX* (written before 1789) (Herbert 1972, 71). In the summer of 1793 the Committee of Public Safety, disturbed by the frivolous and indecent nature of much of Parisian theatre, decided to subsidize all theatres to put on republican plays.[1] They recommended three tragedies: Voltaire's *Brutus* (1730), Antoine Lemierre's *Guillaume Tell* (1766), and Marie Joseph Chénier's *Caïus Gracchus* (1792). Two of the three had premiered more than a generation earlier. Only *Gracchus* had premiered during the Revolution, and it was not explicitly[2] about the Revolution; rather, like Voltaire's *Brutus*, it dramatized a famous episode of Roman history. Of these three, Le Mierre's had the only "modern" subject—a thirteenth-century Swiss patriot.

The reason why these plays were chosen seems to have been that they spoke to contemporaries transparently about their republicanism, but not so dangerously as a play about the execution of the king might have. The whole French Revolution was saturated with an enthusiasm for the Roman and Greek republics of antiquity, and French political leaders were convinced that if they could imbue their fellow citizens with that spirit, the nation would be uplifted. Men and women would live for the "public thing" (*res publica*), and the face not only of France but also of the world would be changed for the better (Parker 1937).

Voltaire's *Brutus* was revived on November 17, 1790, at the Théâtre de la Nation (the former Comédie Française). It is quite possible that the controversial exhibition of Jacques Louis David's painting *The Lictors Returning to Brutus the Bodies of his Sons* in the Salon of 1789 had been the inspiration to revive this tragedy (Herbert 1972). The theatre critic Emile Duchosal had complained in the *Chronique de Paris* on July 17, 1790, about what the federated soldiers of France could see during the Festival of the Federation on July 14, 1790: "Why all these works, in which kings are raised up with servility at the expense of the peoples? It is *Brutus*, it is those tragedies of the great Corneille, it is the *Death of Caesar*, it is Lemierre's *Barnevelt*, it is *Charles IX*, in a word, that must be put before the eyes of French citizens."

Brutus concerns the loyalty of the consul Brutus to the recently-created Roman Republic just after the expulsion of the last Tarquin king. As in Corneille's *Cid*, love conflicts with heroic duty, for Tarquin's daughter, Tullia, is in love with Brutus's son, Titus. Tarquin will not consent to this union unless Brutus supports his efforts to reclaim his throne. Titus is at first firm, then vacillates, then conspires against the Roman Republic. The conspiracy is unmasked and Tullia commits suicide. Titus confesses his treason to his father, who after a wrenchingly tender embrace, orders his execution. The play and the painting both focus on the unthinkable sacrifice Brutus must make to remain loyal to this republic. Patriotic duty to the *patrie* must prevail over paternal love.

On the opening night of the revival, Mirabeau was present in the audience, which persuaded him to take a box of honor. When the words "It is on you alone that our eyes are fixed: for you are the first to break our chains" were recited, the audience took it as a direct allusion to Mirabeau (Herbert 1973, 74). On the second night Houdon's statue of Voltaire and one of Brutus, as well as a copy of David's painting *Brutus*, were displayed on stage, which heightened the effect. Strictly speaking, this was no regicide play.[3] Not only is no king killed (unlike the *Mort de César*), but the script occasionally suggests that love of kings is compatible with love of *patrie*—a favorite theme in 1790.

As for Voltaire, most scholars deny that he had become a republican in England[4] and see this play as perfectly compatible with his idea of an enlightened monarchy. Voltaire himself speaks of his play as "letting public liberty flourish under the sacred canopy of monarchic power" (Ridgway 1961, 71-79; Herbert 1973, 72). *Brutus* was a play that lent itself to quite different interpretations, but it is clear that in 1793 it was considered a republican play, just as earlier its monarchical and patriotic overtones prevailed. It must also be remembered that the monarchy under the Revolution had really become a republic, that the lines distinguishing the two were blurred as the credibility of Louis's attachment to the Revolution diminished (Furet 1992, 77-78).

The performance history of this play during the Revolution shows that although it was revived by the Théâtre de la Nation (the former Comédie Française) in 1790, it was soon taken up by the dissident artists who had deserted the Comédie to establish the Théâtre Français rue Richelieu for personal, political, and repertorial reasons. Although it was performed twenty-two times by the Théâtre de la Nation between 1790 and 1793, it was rarely performed at such key moments as the burial of Voltaire in the Panthéon in July 1791, the crisis of the monarchy in the summer of 1792, and, surprisingly, only twice after the August 2 decree prescribing it. The theatre was closed by decree of the Committee of Public Safety for its lack of patriotism on September 2 (Guilbert and Razgonnikoff 1989, 231). In striking contrast, the dissident theatre performed the play a total of thirty-seven times in the decade. Even Nicolet's Gaîté—a "popular" theatre in the French sense of the word, but not very revolutionary— staged *Brutus* eight times during the Thermidorean Reaction, when the "tyrant" was thought to be Robespierre. Altogether, there were 107 performances of the play in the decade at fourteen theatres. This was a lot for a five-act tragedy, but the August decrees did not increase its performance significantly (fifty performances antedated the August decree, fifty-seven postdated it) and probably resulted in fewer performances than the Convention had anticipated. One scholar has determined that *Brutus* met with a mediocre reaction when it was performed in the provinces even under the prodding of representatives on mission (McKee 1941, 100-106). Let us examine some of the rhetoric of the play—rhetoric that echoed the rhetoric of the Convention. Brutus, the hero says:

Accoutumons des rois la fierté despotique/A traiter en égale la république; (I,i)	Let us accustom the despotic pride of kings/ to treat the Republic as an equal;

Or again:

Qu'aux tyrans désormais rien ne reste en ces lieux,/Que la haine de Rome et le courroux des dieux. (I,ii)	Henceforth let nothing remain in this place,/But the hatred of Rome and the anger of the gods.

The following lines could be read as encouraging a republican "martyrdom" of *an* II:

Donne ton sang à Rome, et n'en exige rien;/Sois toujours un héros, sois plus; sois citoyen. (IV,vi)	Give your blood to Rome, and ask for nothing for yourself;/Be always a hero, better yet; be a citizen.

The supreme gift a republican could make for the *patrie* would be to sacrifice his or her loved ones (by way of denunciation) as Brutus sacrificed Titus:

Prenez garde, Romains, point de grâce aux perfides;/Fussent-ils nos amis, nos frères, nos enfans,/Ne voyez que leur crime, et gardez vos sermens./Rome, la liberté, demandent leur supplice;/Et qui pardonne au crime, en devient le complice.(V,i)	Take heed, Romans, no mercy to traitors;/Even were they our friends, our brothers, our children,/Believe only in their crime, and guard your oaths,/ Rome, liberty demands their execution;/and he who pardons their crime becomes their accomplice.

The vocabulary cluster in these speeches strongly resembles the vocabulary of Robespierre and other Jacobins of the Convention. Words like *despote* (despot), *perfide* (perfidious), *tyrans* (tyrants), *courroux* (anger), *sang* (blood), *haine* (hatred), *crime* (crime), and *supplice* (execution) all point to radical evil that must be extirpated, even by bloodshed. Much of this language can also be found in the black novels and melodramas of Ducray-Duminil and Guilbert de Pixerécourt of this decade (Descotes 1964, chap. 7). There is a circulation of vocabulary and ideas among these discourses which one can identify without being able to trace precisely. It is a language of anxiety and suspicion, of fear and projection that makes tragedy the quintessential revolutionary drama, not in the sense of the most seen drama, but of the drama that best expressed the angst of the Revolutionary elite.

The second play that the Committee of Public Safety prescribed for the theatres of Paris on the eve of the Terror was *Guillaume Tell*, a five-act tragedy by Antoine-Marin Lemierre (1723-1793), the son of an artisan. This work recounts an episode in the life of Tell, the thirteenth-century liberator of Switzerland. Melchtal, Tell's sworn conspirator, denounces Gesler, the villainous governor of the canton of Uri, for seizing his father's animals. Gesler now wants Melchtal's head after having imprisoned his father. Tell, already in chains, tells Melchtal to raise his sights to the general welfare. Tell himself vows to fight for his country rather than personal glory. In Act I, scene iii, Cleofe, Tell's wife, reproaches Tell for forgetting the rights of women and hopes that his conspiracy will not aggravate her ills. Every woman, she explains, is a free "citoyenne" sharing "your rights." Tell answers her complaint obliquely by saying that they will be victorious and sow the seeds of liberty in their cantons. In Act II, Gesler is told how dedicated Tell and his followers are to "this phantom they call liberty" (II,i), which, Gesler says, is "empty." Gesler insinuates himself, in disguise, amidst the conspirators and arrests Melchtal for seditious language. In Act III, scene ii, Tell observes that slavery is not far from freedom because the people are led to revolt out of desperation. The Swiss are a "people born for independence." Gessler arbitrarily takes Tell's son away and tells Tell that to recover him, he must shoot an apple off the top of his head. Anticlimactically (and contrary to the legend), Gesler lifts this demand. In Act V Cleofe patriotically rallies to her husband's cause. The conspirators are crossing a lake in a boat with Gesler, who orders them to man the ship. They capsize deliberately, causing Gesler to drown.

The tragedy seems defective in that the assassination of the villain is indirect. There is no dagger thrust. Tell could have shot the apple off his son's head but does not use his prodigious talent as a marksman for any purpose in the play. Could the merit of the tragedy for the *conventionnels* lie in its tyrannicide? Let us listen:

Vois l'abyme effroyable où nous sommes tombés,/ Vois sous quel joug de fer nos peuples sont courbés;/L'ambition sans frein, l'orgueil, la violence,/Pour nous persecuter armés de la puissance,/Le fardeau des impôts, les emprison-nements,/ Le pillage, le meurtre et les enlèvements,/Sur les moindres soupçons, les peines les plus dures,/La mort multipliée au milieu des tortures,/ Plus d'ordre, plus de lois, nos privilèges vains,/Le mépris ou l'oubli de tous les droits humains,/Landenberg et Gesler, ces monstres d'injustice.../Ne borne pas tes soins à venger la nature;/ Immoler de tes maux le détestable auteur,/ Ce ne seroit changer que de persecuteur.../ Osons tout, joins un bras à ceux de nos amis.../Affranchis avec nous la Suisse qu'on opprime (I, i).

Look at the frightful abyss into which we have fallen,/Look at what an iron yoke our people are bent under,/Ambition without check, pride, violence,/To persecute us armed with power./The weight of taxes, the imprisonments,/Pillage, murder and kidnappings,/On the least suspicions, the harshest punishments,/Death multiplied in the midst of tortures,/No more order, no more laws, our empty privileges,/The contempt or the forgetfulness of the human rights,/Landenberg and Gesler, these monsters of injustice.../Do not restrict yourself to avenging nature;/To immolate the detestable author of your woes/Would only be to change persecutors.../Let us dare everything, join an arm to those of our friends.../Free with us the Switzerland that is oppressed.

Lemierre speaks the coded language of political tragedy. Here and else-where in this play we register words like *fers* (irons), *barbarie* (barbarism), *trembler* (to quake, tremble), *gémir* (to groan [under oppression]), *courroux* (anger), *funeste* (dreadful), *férocité* (ferocity), *violence* (violence), and, above all, *vengeance* (vengeance). This is a language of emphasis and exaggeration, a language that hyperbolizes an ever-menacing evil.

Guillaume Tell was performed nine times between its August 6, 1790 revival and the August 1793 decree, then five more times after the decree in 1793. In 1794, it was performed fifteen times by the Théâtre de la République—a theatre that lived up to its name—and then by the Théâtre National rue Richelieu for twelve performances and by several smaller theatres for a total run of forty-nine performances in all theatres.

The third tragedy prescribed by the Committee of Public Safety and the Convention was Marie-Joseph Chénier's 1792 *Caïus Gracchus*. This play situated republicanism once again in Roman antiquity. The issue here is heroic sacrifice. Caïus, the second son of Cornelia, is asked to give his life for the plebs in its struggle against the patrician Senate. Cornelia provides Caïus with a dagger, but he refuses to use her sanguinary instrument against the enemy, crying out, "Des lois et non du sang," words that Laya had used in his *Ami des lois* and that had rocked audiences of the Théâtre de la Nation in January 1793—words that also probably made the play seem dangerous during the Terror by its allusions to the Jacobins (Bingham 1939, 60-61).

The senators try to bribe Caïus, but he is unalterably loyal to his followers, to the point of refusing escape. He wants to avoid a massacre of the plebs but realizes that only his demise could achieve this end. After warning the patricians of the vengeance of the people, commending his son to obey the gods and to love mankind, he stabs himself while uttering libertarian phrases. In I,i, he describes his cause:

La voix d'équité,/Le cri de la vertu, le cri de tout un peuple sous le joug abbatu....	The voice of equity, under the call of virtue,/the cry of a whole people, crushed under the yoke....

In I,iv, Caïus then promises:

Si vous foulez aux pieds l'orgueil patricien;/Enfin, si vous pouvez, fiers du nom plébein,/Sourds aux vains préjugés d'une antique noblesse,/Concevoir votre force et sentir leur faiblesse;/Tous ces droits éternels que vous avez perdus,/Soyez sur qu'en un jour ils vous seront rendus.	If you crush under your feet patrician pride;/Again, if you can, proud of the name plebeian,/Deaf to the vain prejudices of an ancient nobility,/Recall your force and feel their weakness;/All these eternal rights that you have lost./Will, you may be sure, be one day restored to you.

Popular sovereignty is acknowledged by Caïus when he says in act II, scene ii:

Au Peuple souverain je garderai ma foi.	To the sovereign People I will keep my faith.

The following lines in III,v, could be understood to allude to the court nobility of the Old Regime:

Les discours séduisants, les perfides caresses,/les éloges flatteurs, les bienfaits, les promesses.	Seductive speeches, perfidious caresses,/Flattering praises, favors, promises.

When the sides are drawn up, the Senate's army with mercenaries, the plebeians with citizens, the patriots' cause is clearly identified with the latter as the *type* of soldiery pitted against the armies of aristocratic Europe.

Mother and wife are shown initially divided about the merits of such violent patriotism and heroic self-sacrifice, but eventually are won over to these ideas, as the heroic Cornelia prevails over the more sensible Licinia. Caïus's suicide is quite anticlimactic:

La liberté de Rome... ne dépendra jamais de la perte d'un homme./Viens, mon fils, crains les Dieux chéris l'humanité/Sois le soutien du Peuple et de la liberté... (III,viii)	The liberty of Rome... will never depend on the loss of one man./Come, my son, fear the gods, cherish humanity./Be the support of the People and of liberty...
J'épargne du sang. Dieux protecteurs du Tibre./Voici mon dernier voeu; que le Peuple soit libre.	I spare the blood. Gods, protectors of the Tiber./Here is my last wish; that the People be free.

While tragedy was the touted Jacobin genre, it did not fare particularly well after the August decree prescribing the performance of these three plays. *Caïus Gracchus* was performed twenty-two times between its February 1792 premiere and August 2, 1793, and then only four times for the rest of 1793 (at the Théâtre de la République). It was revived there for three performances during the Directory, for a total of twenty-nine performances, close to the least-performed plays. *Guillaume Tell*'s meager performance record was further compromised by the fact that Sedaine's comic opera by the same name had 118 performances between April 1791 and the fall of 1799. The responses of the theatres did not satisfy the Jacobin authorities, who continued to complain about the repertory and the continuing presence of the Old Regime on stage. For this reason, as we have seen, they continued to call theatre directors in for interrogations.

Soon the same authorities became nervous about the potentially counter-revolutionary threat that tragedies about kings could pose. Even if kings on stage were villainous and were killed, their very appearance sullied the republican air, which could be purified only by disposing of them altogether, as indeed vandals were doing in October to the remains of the kings of France at Saint-Denis. If kings were to come on stage at all, they would have to be blown up, it would seem, as they were in Sylvain Maréchal's *Jugement dernier des rois* in October 1793. But the best or preferred solution was not to let them on stage at all. Thus Corneille's and other dramatists' *rois* were changed by the censors into *lois* (Lieby 1903, pt. 3, 511-527).

Although the state paid 188,000 livres to nineteen theatres (Welschinger 1880, 32-33) in the weeks after the August decree, it did not republicanize the stage. Indeed, the last significant tragedy proposed for performance after the reestablishment of censorship in April 1794 was Chénier's *Timoléon*. Due to the intervention of two Robespierrists, Payan and Jullien, and possibly Robespierre himself, this play was disallowed, for it painted a tyrant of Corinth who closely resembled Robespierre (Bingham 1939, 158-169). Thus a republican leader was made the villain of a tyrannicide play. The moderate republicans, who hoped to use the play to foster a republican spirit, showed the Jacobin hero in the hour of his triumph to be a tyrant himself. In fact, the play was not performed until September 11, 1794. The Old Regime genre thought by republicans to be such a good instrument of government proved to be a two-edged sword when they themselves were identified as tyrants.

6

The Most Performed Genres and Their Evolution

Marie-Laurence Netter

Tragedy, comedy, and of course opera constituted, at the end of the seventeenth and at the beginning of the eighteenth centuries, the noble genres par excellence, while farce and pantomime were popular diversions that barely belonged to the world of theatre. To this hierarchy of genres of spectacles corresponded a hierarchy of theatres: the Opéra, the Comédie Française, and the Théâtre Italien enjoyed privileges that removed them from all competition, while the boulevards and the fairs of Saint-Germain and Saint-Laurent accepted the ephemeral troupes composed more of jugglers than of true actors.

In the course of the eighteenth century the directors of these different theatres gave battle without mercy, some to conserve their privileges and what they considered to be their public, the rest in order to have a right to operate year-round and to enlarge their repertories. We have already seen that this competition gave birth to a new genre: the *opéra-comique*. The refusal of the directors of the three official theatres to allow comedy, tragedy, and opera to be performed elsewhere than on their stages, combined with the determination of the directors of the ambulatory theatres to install themselves and to put to work all the resources of which their imaginations were capable, resulted in the multiplication of the number of genres.

After 1789, Revolutionary events became the motor of imagination. As there were no longer prohibited subjects, one had to show everything, and authors soon lacked words to describe the genres of the new plays they submitted to the public. *Intermède, féerie, farce, divertissement-parade, tragédie-comédie, proverbe allégorique, opéra-bouffon, héroique, fait-historique, parodie, pastoral, prophétie*...and of course *pantomime, tragédie, opéra*, and *comédie* often mixed with *ariettes* and with *vaudevilles*. All these terms can be juxtaposed. For example, *C'est le diable ou La Bohémienne* of Cuvelier de Trie, performed for the first time on November 13, 1797, consists of a drama

mixed with *pantomime, exercices, combats, chansons,* and *danse.* These
multiple appellations do not truly correspond to new genres, but rather to
indications of the content of the play and the manner in which it is treated. Thus
the patriotic plays are distinguished from the historical plays by the fact that the
vraisemblance of the former is often poorly executed to the benefit of the
demonstration of a new state of mind. We will not try here to make an analysis
of the differences—generally little evident—that distinguish these new "genres."
We will try, rather, to see the importance of each in the totality of spectacles
shown during the Revolution: how comedy evolves and how vaudeville and
melodrama appear destined for a brilliant future in the nineteenth century. It is
not surprising to see comedy triumph during this period over all the other
genres, new or old; its preeminence has already been assumed. Of the 3,713
plays performed during the Revolution whose titles we have entered into our
database, 866 are anonymous and their genre is unknown; there remain then
2,847, of which 1,383 (36.9 percent) are comedies. In decreasing order of
incidence, we find comedy trailed by pantomime (5.6 percent), opera (6.1
percent), vaudeville and *opéra-comique* (each around 4 percent), drama,
patriotic and historical plays, and ballets (each between one and two percent).
Melodrama comprises only 0.7 percent of plays performed and identified. The
authors' imaginative characterizations of their work yield a multiplication of
terms that do not call into question the hierarchical order of ordinary genres.
The seventeenth century was the century of tragedy, and the eighteenth of
comedy—the Revolutionary period does not overthrow this classical image in
French theatre history (Lintilhac 1910).

The supremacy of comedies over all other genres is clearly demonstrated by
the number of comedic performances. We know the genre of 77 percent of the
plays. Among the fifty most performed plays during the Revolutionary decade,
there are thirty-two comedies (64 percent, a proportion that increases to 72
percent if one considers the ten most performed plays in each of these ten
years). In brief, comedy was the preferred genre of both the playwrights and the
public, which suggests that the desire to enjoy oneself at the expense of one's
fellow citizens prevailed widely over that of instruction. The infatuation with
comedy was not, however, equally intense from 1789 to 1799. Comedies
represent two thirds, indeed, three quarters of the plays performed until 1792;
in 1793 and 1794, they furnish hardly more than one third of the great
successes; resume their place at the top in the years which follow, then fall again
in 1798 and 1799. These remarks can be nuanced according to the size of the
sample (the top ten or top fifty plays of each year), but the tendency is the
same.

The dearth of comedies in 1793 and 1794 is evidently due to the obligation
imposed on theatre directors to perform patriotic plays, a genre that dominates
these two years, only to disappear subsequently. Comedy's massive comeback
among the most performed plays just after the Terror is easily attributable to the

need for relaxation and laughter that followed this particularly tense period of public life. The number of comedies put on stage tends nonetheless to diminish—notably those written before 1789, in spite of a brief revival—as if these dramatic moments marked the end of an epoch—the eighteenth century—and the birth of a new world in which the dramaturges sought to express themselves through less academic forms than the classic comedies, tragedies, and operas.

We have seen that the evolution of these classic genres and the appearance of new stage settings were closely linked to the existence of privileged theatres and to the desire of some theatre entrepreneurs to circumvent their privileges in order to obtain a stable existence. Parallel to this, the classic genres evolved and new ones appeared, this time in relation to the new theories about the pedagogical function of theatre, but also and perhaps especially in direct relation to the tastes of the public and to the violence of Revolutionary events.

The idea that theatre has an exemplary function, that the stage is a place where spectators can judge the consequences of passions and human behaviors, is not new. It was already being experimented with by Aeschylus and Sophocles in Greek theatre. In the seventeenth century the tragedies of Corneille and of Racine demonstrated that the power of the great in this world is accompanied by duties they are not free to shirk. Molière ennobled comedy by making this genre serve as the implacable mirror of the *moeurs* of his time and, still more, of the eternal foibles of man in *L'Avare* and *Tartuffe*. *L'Ecole des maris*, *Le Dépit amoureux*, and *Le Médecin malgré lui*, the plays of Molière that were most performed during the Revolution, are all comedies of *moeurs* that describe situations more factual than universal: their characters are persons in daily situations who arouse audiences passionately immersed in the Revolution. This had occurred earlier in the eighteenth century when Lesage triumphed with *Turcaret*, in which he painted as ridiculous suspicious financiers with whom he had dealings and who were one of the scourges of the period. During the Revolution, comedy is always assigned to denounce the ridiculous in characters and to make one laugh at them. But as Harlequin sings in *Arlequin afficheur*, the lesson is not always heeded, because the spectators cannot identify with these ridiculous or frankly unsympathetic characters: "Comedy is a mirror/which reflects the ridiculous.../One is inclined to flatter oneself:/In these portraits which appear before us,/one recognizes easily one's neighbor/one does not want to recognize oneself." Comedy is both socially normative and individually revealing. It is exemplary.

A little more than a year later and on a more serious subject, Laya, in his preface to *L'Ami des lois,* does not say anything different. If one compares the contents of these two comedies with those of Molière, one measures the magnitude of the evolution that has taken place in a century. In *L'Ecole des maris* and *Le Dépit amoureux* eternal jealousy is denounced—it afflicts young lovers as well as dotards of every country and insults the dignity of women. In

Le Médecin malgré lui Molière satirizes a prevalent phenomenom of his time: ignorant doctors who take themselves for savants. His play draws its force and universality from the astonished credulity that the esoteric language of these supposed doctors provokes in their patients. The abuse of scientific nomenclature with the unique aim of inflicting it upon, or of deceiving, one's audience remained very relevant and was one of Molière's key ingredients and allowed him to keep his public. This timeless dimension does not exist in the work of Barré, Radet, and Desfontaines, nor in that of Laya, in spite of the latter's patent effort to emphasize the psychological springs that animate his characters. But hypocrisy and the thirst for power, which Laya stigmatizes in the *L'Ami des lois*, remain the attributes of mediocre characters, all formed in the unique mold of personal ambition, while the defense of the general interest is incumbent upon the characters consumed by goodness and by grandeur of soul, generous to the point of wanting to sacrifice their lives as examples. This extreme Manichaean dichotomy was easily deciphered by the public in a period that identified the Jacobins and the leaders of the Terror without difficulty. The commotion accompanying this play when it premiered was immense, but after 9 Thermidor it no longer aroused such passions, and its revival was a failure. The play corresponded to a bygone situation.

The limits of comedy understood as a mirror are reached with this type of play, where the pure and simple identification replaces the accumulation of particular traits with which Molière composed an emblematic character. In using excessively precise social situations to illustrate present realities, the playwrights of the period limited the long-term survival value of their plays and the issues they represented. The birth of vaudeville as a genre is one of the consequences of the evolution of comedy.

Vaudeville, at the beginning of the eighteenth century, was a song introduced into a play whose original words, referring to current events, were set to the music of a well-known air. It was differentiated from the *ariette* in that the latter had original music. There were more and more vaudevilles in comedies with themes taken increasingly from current events, so many and so well done that the accessory soon became a new genre. It is difficult to be precise about the date of this transformation. Anseaume premiered a light play in January 1759 called *Les Epreuves d'amour* that he described as a vaudeville; however, it is during the Revolution, notably with Piis and Barré, prolific authors and founders of the Théâtre du Vaudeville at the end of 1791, that the genre takes shape, confirming the rupture that the staging of the present had de facto worked on classical comedy.

> Vaudeville—instead of attacking characters and passions, instead of studying them and of evoking laughter or tears, which theatre involves, [as] matter of profound reflection and instruction—sticks more to the little facts of everyday life. It mixes them up in the form of blunders and unravels them

> afterward as it can, without worrying too much about the *vraisemblance*, or the slight irregularities of contemporary life that it turns to ridicule with a light hand without driving too far home the stroke of mockery (Sarcey 1884, Introduction).

This definition certainly underlines the elements that led authors, in the second half of the eighteenth century, to distinguish between comedy and vaudeville. One notices on this occasion that the difference is much greater than that which we know today based on the work of Feydeau, Labiche, and others who retained only the levity of amorous behavior.

The frontiers between genres, above all when they just begin to become distinct from one another (as was the case during the Revolution), are not always very clear. Melodrama, which was destined for such a beautiful future in the nineteenth century, is a striking example.

The origin of melodrama is a sung drama, and J. J. Rousseau, on account of his *Pygmalion* (1770), is often considered the inventor of the genre (Thomasseau 1984, 8). This title is more properly given to L. S. Mercier, who, in his *La Brouette du vinaigrier* (1775), reunites practically all the elements that a few years later would constitute the classic melodrama: love, wickedness, and the triumph of virtue. Undoubtedly the Revolutionary experience, with its unleashing of passions, could not help but to modify this simple plot and give to the unpredictable a magic but very real credibility. The Revolution itself can be said to have been a veritable melodrama with its scenes of eternal love between its king and its nation, its nation and its representatives, the ensuing carnage, and the Terror, when one never knew if the denunciation of one's neighbor would not make of oneself, tomorrow, the condemned person whom the *charrette* took off to the guillotine. Elements such as persecution, the recognition of the parental tie, love, and stock characters such as the traitor, the wicked *grand seigneur*, the exemplary woman, and the abandoned child have become over time the agreed-upon vocabulary of melodrama. Melodrama gained in popularity under the Directory with *Victor ou l'Enfant de la forêt* of Guilbert de Pixerécourt, and *Le Petit poucet ou L'Orphelin de la forêt* of Cuvelier de Trie. The latter play is very interesting, for it is called a drama by its author, although in terms of its setting (cottage, chateau, and deep forest) and content it is more properly termed a melodrama. The genre is therefore perfectly identifiable before authors regularly use the term—which is characteristic of a genre that has just been born.

Contrary to what the avalanche of new terms used to designate the genre of theatrical plays could make us believe, the Revolutionary period is not the moment when classical genres are called immediately into question. Comedy conserves its predominant place in spite of condemnation by most of the political leaders, who were primarily concerned about public spirit. Its content and its workmanship, however, do not altogether correspond to the taste of the period. The triumph obtained in the last years of the Revolution by some vaudevilles and melodramas shows that spectators, at the dawn of the nineteenth century, had need of a theatre in which characters would be socially close to them yet immersed in a fantastic environment. These are the two criteria that would be fundamental to a renewal of theatre during the next century.

7

Theatres and Their Directors

Marie-Laurence Netter

The history of theatres in Paris during the Revolution is not easy to follow, in part because theatres were very numerous and often ephemeral, but even more because they changed names in response to outside political events or at the insistence of the director or the troupe.

On the eve of 1789, there were three official theatres: the Comédie Française, installed in April 1782 at the Théâtre Français (presently the Odéon); the Opéra or the Royal Academy of Music, on Boulevard Saint-Martin; and the Théâtre des Italiens, otherwise known as the Opéra-Comique, installed at Place de la Comédie Italienne (today the Place Boieldieu). These three theatres, or more precisely these three troupes, enjoyed for nearly a century exclusive privileges that authorized the first, to put on tragedy and comedy; the second, to stage dance and song; and the third, to perform Italian theatre and comic opera. By the Revolution, this third house had already had a long history, characteristic of the evolution of mores and of genres, as well as of the conflicts between the privileged troupes and the actors or jugglers of the popular spectacles, which were produced on the Boulevard du Temple.[1]

It would take too long to recount the history of these three theatres before the Revolution, which, in any event, is already well known. Their fights with the traveling shows are at the origin of the liberal, suicidal politics inaugurated in January 1791, and for this reason we will recall briefly the obstacles that the secondary theatres had to overcome in order to open before this date (Bonnassiès 1875).

Besides these three privileged houses, nine other theatres were built in these years. The construction of these theatres, which replaced the traveling shows, was the result of a double conjuncture: the fairs were in jeopardy in the second half of the eighteenth century, and, at the same time, there appeared a new type of entrepreneur of spectacles, such as Nicolas Médard Audinot and Jean

Baptiste Nicolet, who were intent on making their living with a troupe assembled each year, profiting from the infatuation of the public for these popular spectacles. In the world of the theatre, it amounted to a first revolution.

As these theatres opened, a geography of theatres in Paris was put in place that, with a few exceptions, would become even more pronounced during the Revolution. The Left Bank was largely abandoned, to the benefit of the Boulevard du Temple and the Palais Royal and its surroundings: a victory of popular culture over aristocratic culture even before power had changed hands. The Comédie Française played the role of an exile, and its actors complained of their installation at the Place de l'Odéon.

The history of these new theatres, their successes, and their difficulties were intimately mixed with the liberal politics that would prevail after 1791. We must, therefore, examine them attentively.

The theatre that took the name of Théâtre de la Gaîté in 1789 was the same one created in 1759 by Nicolet, which in 1772 became the Théâtre des Grands Danseurs du Roi on the authorization of Louis XV (Campardon 1877, vol. 2, 151-156). Jean Baptiste Nicolet (1728-1796) had had a long-standing association with the public since his father had directed a spectacle of marionettes at the fairs of Saint-Germain and Saint-Laurent for thirty years. When Nicolet began directing, he had already had a certain experience, and he did not hesitate to perform plays that were in the repertory of the Théâtre des Italiens, especially its *opéras-comiques*. From 1762 on, his success continued to grow, and he was obliged endlessly to seek the good graces of the lieutenant general of police in order to escape the vindictiveness of the Comédie Française and of the Théâtre des Italiens. In 1784 the Council of State ceded to the Académie Royale de Musique the control of the traveling theatres, which Nicolet strove to make profitable. Then two persons appear whom we will have occasion to speak of again: Gaillard and Dorfeuille,[2] who bought a right of inspection for the Grand Danseurs du Roi, the Ambigu Comique of Audinot, and the Variétés Amusantes. In contrast with Audinot, Nicolet understood immediately that he could not avoid these harassments, unjust as they were, except through buying at a high price the withdrawal of these two associates. He remained at the head of his quite prosperous enterprise, but in 1791 he had to steer between two perils in order to protect his right to exist. Although he remained an effective administrator, he and his associates had to face up to the competition of the new theatres. In 1795, a year before his death, he abandoned the management of the Théâtre de la Gaîté to one of his actors, the famous Ribié, who rebaptized it Théâtre de l'Emulation. The theatre once more became the Théâtre de la Gaîté in 1799, when a destitute Ribié left the directorship to Coffin-Rosny and Martin.

Nicolet was not a very nice person, managing his troupe with an iron hand, firing actors who did not obey the rules he laid down. The rumor circulated that he lacked an education and knew little about playwriting or music, but he was a businessman and had the theatrical instinct.

The collective mentality of theatre directors and entrepreneurs of spectacles is without doubt one of the most original phenomena of this period, which stretches from the 1750s to 1807, the date when Napoleon suppressed a good number of the so-called secondary theatres. Stimulated by their love of the stage and by their will to succeed financially, these men knew how to encourage the authors to mix genres, first to circumvent the privileges of the great theatres, then to attract the public and thereby make a fortune. Molded by the fair and the boulevards, the new directors had a nose for profit and knew how to please; more than the theoreticians or the philosophers, it was they who stirred up the world of theatre before the Revolution and contributed to the multiplication of theatres during this period.

The Boulevard du Temple was without contest the place in which the transformation took place. Nicolet installed himself there in 1759, as did Audinot in 1769, opening a marionette theatre that bore his name before becoming the Ambigu Comique the following year. Arnould, whom he knew in the troupe of the prince of Conti, assisted him and became his associate in 1775; for this theatre he wrote numerous comedies and pantomimes that assured his prosperity. Little by little, Audinot replaced the marionettes with child actors; this theatrical innovation, adorned with vaudevilles and dances, rapidly made the Ambigu Comique one of the most frequented theatres and provoked, as one might expect, the jealousy of the Opéra. At first, Audinot had to pay 12,000 livres to be able to continue his activity, but in 1784 he refused to buy back from Gaillard and Dorfeuille the privilege of which he had been arbritrarily stripped. He lost the case he had brought against the Opéra, and resigned himself to paying a new sum in order to reopen his theatre on the Boulevard du Temple, which he did in 1786. Audinot and Arnould resisted all these attacks but lost strength during the Revolution, vanquished by the new liberties. It was not one of the lesser paradoxes of this period to see the most ardent propagandists of theatrical liberties suffer subsequently from the competition they themselves had helped create. In 1795 the direction of the theatre was left to actors in the troupe. Arnould died the following year and Audinot died in 1801, a few months after the actor Corsse again took over the Ambigu Comique, which he restored to its former glory.

Associations between theatre directors and one or several authors were very common in the period. Such associations permitted one simultaneously to specialize in a genre and formally to constitute a repertory for oneself. Beyond what we have just seen, the best-known collaboration is that of Nicolet and of Alexandre L. B. Robineau, called Beaunoir. Between 1768 and 1778 Beaunoir gave exclusive rights to his productions—farces, parades, and comedies—to Nicolet, who staged 116. After that, Beaunoir collaborated with Lécluze, who had just created the Variétés Amusantes, on the famous *Jérôme Pointu*, a one-act comedy written for the actor Volange, who made it a triumph (Abbott 1936).

Apart from the Ambigu Comique and the Théâtre de la Gaîté, seven other secondary theatres were founded before 1791, of which three were on the Boulevard du Temple. These included the Théâtre des Elèves de l'Opéra, founded, as its name indicates, to train the future actors of lyric theatre and give them the habit of being on stage. The theatre was opened in January 1779, but the management soon faced major financial problems, so much so that the theatre was empty from September 1780 to the middle of 1787. At this date a spectacle of Pyrrhic Games was set up, without success. Turned out of the Palais Royal by Mlle Montansier, the Beaujolais comedians reclaimed their house, but the public did not follow them. At the end of 1790, the theatre became the property of the Lycée Dramatique; it was taken over in 1792 by Lazzari, who renamed it the Variétés Amusantes, abandoned by Gaillard and Dorfeuille. In 1793, to show his good citizenship, Lazzari renamed the theatre Théâtre Français du Boulevard. The following year he restored its former name, which corresponded more to the genre of spectacles that he proposed. On May 31, 1798, the theatre was ravaged by a fire and the ruined Lazzari committed suicide. This theatre, in less than twenty years of existence, had remained empty for nearly eight years and had had six different names: difficult conditions under which to create faithful spectators.

On the Boulevard du Temple one can still find the Délassements Comiques and the Associés. The first, opened in 1785 by Plancher Valcour, who was simultaneously author, actor, and director, was destroyed by a fire in 1787 and reconstructed the following year. The Comédie Française, envious of this new theatre, obliged Valcour to give only pantomimes—no more than three actors on stage at a time, and they were to be separated from the public by a veil of gauze. When he reopened his theatre after July 14, 1789, the director of the Délassements Comiques made himself famous by tearing the gauze at the cry of "Vive la liberté."

The Théâtre des Associés was born in 1774 from the curious association of Nicolas Vienne, called Beauvisage, and of Louis Gabriel Sallé, respectively coach crier and title actor of the role of Harlequin in Nicolet's theatre. Beauvisage was famous for his grimaces, and the two associates made a specialty of parody, taking inspiration from the classical repertory of the Comédie Française and from that of the Opéra-Comique. But they did not neglect new plays: *La Brouette du vinaigrier* of Louis Sébastien Mercier was performed there with many revivals, and Dorvigny and Cammaille Saint-Aubin gave them several of their plays. The audience was very "popular"—the place being "filled by boot-blacks and boulevard girls" (Campardon 1877, Vol 1, 27). One laughed a lot there, and the two directors rapidly made a fortune. In 1789, Sallé became the sole proprietor of the theatre, and gave it the name Théâtre Patriotique du sieur Sallé; it was renamed Théâtre sans Prétention in 1795, after his death.

There were four other theatres constructed before the law of 1791 took effect.

The Théâtre de Monsieur belongs to this category even though it did not open its doors before January 6, 1791, several days before the famous law. The establishment was directed by Aulié, the coiffeur of the queen, who had known how to obtain the protection of the brother of the king (the source of the name of the theatre). But after the flight to Varennes this appellation became compromising, and the theatre was renamed Théâtre Feydeau in July 1791, after the name of the street on which it was situated. The period of the greatest Revolutionary troubles having passed, the troupe was revived as the Opéra-Comique and in 1797 became the Théâtre Favart.

The three other establishments that remain to be examined are without doubt the most interesting, as their experiences during the Revolution typify those of theatres and theatre troupes of this period, and of the changes of position which followed one upon the other.

In 1777 an entrepreneur called "Sieur de l'Ecluse" or Delecluze (or still more frequently Lécluze), created on the Rue de Bondy a little theatre to which he gave the name Jeunes Artistes. The following year he was obliged to change the name to Variétés Amusantes (Lecomte 1908). After a period, sustained by the productions of Dorvigny and Beaunoir, Lécluze retired and left the direction to three entrepreneurs who had to deal with Gaillard and Dorfeuille. In 1784, the latter bought back for the Opéra its rights of production in the three theatres: those of Nicolet and Audinot, as we have already seen, and those of the Variétés Amusantes, which they decided to keep. After a long trial, the three entrepreneurs were evicted with the sole consolation of a very small indemnification. In 1785, the two new directors abandoned the Rue de Bondy in order to move to the Palais Royal. From that moment on, the history of the troupe of the Variétés and that of the first theatre that protected the Théâtre des Variétés Amusantes, became distinct. The latter, a theatre of wood in the Rue de Bondy, was destroyed and replaced by a new building designed by the architect Sobre; it took the name Théâtre Français Comique et Lyrique (or Théâtre Lyrique) and was opened June 21, 1790. The theatre closed in 1793 and reopened at the end of 1794, under the name of Théâtre des Jeunes Artistes.

The troupe of the Variétés Amusantes, directed by Gaillard and Dorfeuille, appeared to have a promising future. Installed at the beginning of 1785 in the court of the Palais Royal, the directors had been granted by the duc d'Orléans the theatre he was having built at the corner of the Rue de Richelieu for the use of the Opéra. The latter remained on the Boulevard Saint Martin, and the troupe of the Variétés resumed performing on May 15, 1790, in the new theatre constructed by the architect Louis, which became the Palais Royal. From this date on, the events accelerated and became considerably complicated. In 1791 the actors of the Comédie Française—which became the Théâtre de la Nation in 1789—split in two, at which time the most Revolutionary actors, including Talma, Dugazon, Mlle Vestris, and some others, abandoned their companions and joined the Palais Royal, which was more innovative and which became the

Théâtre Français de la rue Richelieu. A year later, on the morning of August 10, 1792, it became the Théâtre de la Liberté et de l'Egalité. Finally it was named the Théâtre de la République after the installation of this regime on September 22, 1792. It would keep this name until May 1799, when the actors of the Théâtre Français who had remained at the Théâtre de la Nation—Théâtre de l'Egalité under the Terror, then the Odéon once it reopened in 1797—rejoined their former companions to recreate the Comédie Française; the theatre took the name at that time of Théâtre Français de la République. This is the present Comédie Française, still located at the same place, although it has undergone considerable transformations over two centuries.

The Théâtre de la Montansier also had a tumultuous history, very much linked to the personality of its proprietor (Bouet 1934). Mlle Montansier (1730-1820) had arrived in Paris in October 1789, following the king and the queen. For nearly fifteen years it had been she who organized the balls and spectacles given at Versailles. This woman, who in 1789 was sixty years old, had behind her a long past as a coquette and as a director of theatres. She had known how to procure the favor of highly placed patrons, and in 1768 found herself at the head of six theatres: those of Nantes, Rouen, Caen, Orléans, Le Havre, and Versailles, which she administered financially as well as artistically. In 1777 she opened a new theatre at Versailles, became intimate with the queen, and found herself entrusted successively with the theatres of Saint Cloud, Marly, Fontainebleau, and Compiègne, that is, the theatres of the court. She then abandoned the provinces in order to devote herself entirely to the service of the king.

When she arrived in Paris, she immediately looked for a theatre to take over and chose the Théâtre Beaujolais, run by Delomel, who was having grave financial difficulties at the time. The matter was briskly negotiated directly with the duc d'Orléans, who owned the lease; Delomel, in spite of all his efforts, was evicted and obliged to give up his theatre in January 1790. In October 1784 the Beaujolais had been installed in the Palais Royal's Montpensier Gallery with a puppet show, rapidly replaced by a spectacle of child actors who played comedy, backed up by adults who spoke and sang in the wings. The success was prodigious, and the jealousy of the great theatres was stirred once more; they obtained the replacement of the children by adults, which was then a privilege, and Delomel's demise was sealed.

The theatre, now known as the Théâtre de la Montansier, was enlarged and reopened its doors on April 12, 1790 with an opera and above all with *Le Sourd ou L'Auberge pleine*, a comedy of J. B. Desforges (1746-1806). The play was an immense success—in fact, the most performed play of the Revolution, with more than 450 performances—of which 251 were at the Montansier. The play brought in the considerable sum of 500,000 francs (the author received only 600 francs). A businesswoman, Mlle Montansier was also a diplomat and a politician, and knowing that she was suspect because of her past service to the queen, she closed her theatre in the summer of 1792, formed a company with her actors, and caught up with the army. In the autumn she resumed her activities, all the while managing to keep on the good side of Robespierre. She succeeded in managing the construction of a second theatre on the Rue de la Loi (formerly Richelieu), which was opened on August 15, 1793, under the name of the Théâtre National. This theatre was provided with the most modern lighting and accoutrements of the period. Comedy, drama, and *opéra-comique* were performed there and people danced and sang.

Mlle Montansier's success roused the jealousy of her competitors, who saw to it that she was arrested on November 14, 1793; her Théâtre National was confiscated, assigned to the Opéra, and renamed the Théâtre des Arts. Mlle Montansier's companion, Neuville, undertook the direction of the older Théâtre Montansier of the Palais Royal, which he renamed Théâtre du Péristyle du Jardin-Egalité, then Théâtre de la Montagne in 1794. After 9 Thermidor, Mlle Montansier was released, but the loss of the Théâtre National weighed heavily upon her. The Théâtre de la Montagne, which became the Théâtre des Variétés-Montansier in 1795, was rented after April 1798 to one A. M. Foignet, who joined with four other directors, among whom was Ribié. After Volange, actors such as Brunet and Tiercelin triumphed in farces and comedies of Patrat, Aude, Dorvigny, and many others. In 1807, the theatre was obliged to close its doors and Mlle Montansier returned to work, endeavoring to convince Napoleon to accept an arrangement.

The vicissitudes of Mlle Montansier amply illustrate what being an *entrepreneur de spectacles* really meant in the eighteenth century and during the Revolution. There are many other examples that show how theatres were set up and how fortunes were made and unmade. Thus, Ribié (1755-1830) created for himself a veritable empire in the last years of the Revolution, when he was an actor in the Théâtre des Associés, and then when he worked for Nicolet, to whom he gave his first comic plays. In 1791, he embarked for the colonies; returning a year later, he organized a troupe in Le Havre and set himself up in Rouen, where he opened a theatre. After 9 Thermidor he came to Paris, where he threw himself into theatre. In 1795 he took over the management of the Gaîté, which became the Théâtre de l'Emulation; in 1798 he reopened the Théâtre Louvois (founded in 1791 and closed in 1797), and resumed the direction of the Théâtre Molière, not to mention the management of two amusement parks, the Elysée Bourbon and the Tivoli. Head of a vast enterprise, he did not renounce his professions of actor and author. In spite of his dynamism, he did not succeed in paying back the large sums which he had borrowed, and consequently was obliged in 1799 to give up his enterprises, one after the other. The Théâtre de l'Emulation became once again the Théâtre de la Gaîté, of which Ribié assumed the direction in 1806.

At the same time, during the Directory, Sageret, another individual with grandiose ambitions, took in hand the direction of the Théâtre Feydeau, the

République and the Odéon, with the intention of having each specialize: the Théâtre Feydeau in opera and *opéra-comique*, the République in drama and tragedy, and the Odéon in popular plays (Carlson 1966, 317-318). The actors were obliged to perform in these three places, and on certain days they had to run from one to the other to play their roles. In spite of everything, the formula did not cover all the expenses incurred by Sageret; like Ribié, he was obliged to abandon his theatres, first the Odéon and then the Théâtre de la République. The burning of the Odéon and the destruction of its books managed to save Sageret from the accusation of fraudulent bankruptcy. He was arrested and released shortly afterward for lack of evidence.

Another figure, Barré (1749-1832), was a man of one theatre, the Vaudeville (founded in 1792 on rue de Chartres), whose direction he assumed until 1815. This theatre, among the few that did not change their names, was faithful to the popular genre—farces, comedies, and vaudevilles—and its success did not flag. Barré, conscious no doubt of his success, was rude to those who solicited him, but he knew how to keep a cluster of faithful actors with whom he often collaborated. The association of Barré, Radet, and Desfontaines was very fruitful, and was the source of a series of plays with Harlequin as hero. He also composed with Piis and Bourgeuil. Radet, who was also his friend, practically gave him exclusive rights over his works.

For every theatre that achieved stability like the Vaudeville, there were twenty, founded after the law of 1791, that had only ephemeral existences. This was true of the Théâtres Molière, du Mont-Parnasse, de l'Estrapade, de la Concorde, de la Cité, du Marais, des Mareux, and a few more (Radicchio and d'Oria 1990, 83-114; Brazier 1838). To grasp the uncertain character of the new theatre's existence, let us turn our attention to the functioning of the Théâtre Molière.

The Théâtre Molière, opened on June 11, 1791, was the property of Boursault-Malherbe, who had it built in two months, at the corner of the Rue Saint Martin and Quincampoix (Pougin 1903). Boursault-Malherbe (1752-1842) was a curious person. Son of a businessman who was destined to become a lawyer, he abandoned this path in order to become an actor. Before the Revolution he had directed a French theatre in Sicily; in the France of 1789, he was an ardent patriot, elected acting deputy to the Convention, where he sat after the death of the king. A little later he took a concession for the cleaning of the city of Paris and became extremely rich.

The old repertory did not interest Boursault-Malherbe, who showed only new and preferably patriotic plays, which did not attract regular crowds to his theatre. At the end of August 1792, he abandoned the direction of the theatre to the actors, who reopened it on September 29 under the name of Théâtre National de Molière, which became the Théâtre des Sans Culottes in 1793. In May 1794, a new subsidy was accorded to the theatre but this could not prevent its closing a few months later. At the beginning of the year, the theatre, which once again called itself the Théâtre Molière and styled itself as reactionary, reopened its doors, only to close them again for three years. Some shows of societies—that is, of private persons—were sometimes given there. It reopened on May 16, 1798, under the name of Théâtre des Amis des Arts et des Elèves de l'Opéra-Comique, but its success was no greater. In 1799, it closed and opened several more times; the troupe of the Troubadors played there from time to time; those of the Cité and the Odéon passed through there as well.

This theatre, which closed more or less definitely in 1807, had a chaotic existence that was an ideal but not a singular example of the disorder that liberty of spectacles engendered during the Revolution. The liberty that was established in 1791 had been sought by, among others, the theatre entrepreneurs, true adventurers on the stage who sought freedom of maneuver. But they did not see that they were preparing their own ruin in this way. Through the eighteenth century, the official theatres had eagerly defended their privileges because they did not know how to innovate and because the public, dissatisfied with them, was attracted by the spectacles of the fairs and, soon, by other permanent theatres. The directors of these theatres, forced to multiply their stratagems to evade the law, showed great imagination—marionettes, children, posters, mixing genres—and their success was prodigious. They believed that the constraints of the law were a check on still greater successes, whereas it was these very laws that were at the heart of their originality and hence of their fortune.

When in 1791 the liberty became complete, these entrepreneurs and others opened some twenty new theatres, believing that the public would attend. But the end of privileges did not have the expected result; far from it: from one stage to the other one could see the same comedies, amorous and patriotic, played by actors who had often failed in their professions. The financial conditions of so many theatres quickly became very difficult, mostly because they all took it upon themselves to put on shows that were too similar to one another and that had been based on a few great successes. We shall have the opportunity to return to this facet of theatre life when we come to examine the evolution of genres.

The Directory, which did not wish to accord any subsidy to an art it deemed subversive, was ready to restore order in the theatres when Bonaparte took power on 18 Brumaire *an* VII (November 9, 1799). It fell to him, then, in 1807, to legislate in this domain, leaving no more than ten theatres. He reestablished censorship, but the theatre world hardly reacted, finding solace in the fact that regulation would put an end to a period of anarchy that economically had proved nearly fatal.

8

High Culture and Popular Culture: Paris Theatre Audiences, the Critics, and the Police

Emmet Kennedy

What can be inferred about audiences from repertories? The predominance of comedy during the Revolution would suggest a somewhat less educated, less refined audience than what critics of the Comédie Française, for whom tragedy enjoyed a privileged position, would have liked to have seen.[1] The apparent demand for the comic and the sentimental implies an appetite for entertainment and gentleness (*douceur*) rather than patriotic edification or terrorist revenge. But it is always somewhat dangerous to leap from text to audience without any supporting documentation. Fortunately we do not lack the latter: theatre criticism in pamphlets and journals, occasional memoirs, documents relating to controversies between authors and directors, reports from police commissars and secret agents of the Minister of the Interior all corroborate the statistical evidence extracted from our unintentional sources—the theatre listings of the *Petites Affiches* and the *Journal de Paris*.

What assurance do we have that audiences were treated to what they wanted during the Revolution and not to what directors or public authorities thought they should see? Considerable evidence points to obstreperous spectators either bringing down a play they did not like or vigorously demanding a play the authorities disallowed. For example, on December 6, 1790, a police commissar of the Commune agreed that the spectators had paid more than a fraudulent "automobile" show was worth, had the show closed, the poster changed, and some of the money returned to the ticket buyers. Nothing ideological was involved here—just an angry audience in search of a *merveille* (A.P.P., A.A., 239, 15).

At the other end of the social spectrum was the audience of the Comédie Française, which was informed in August 1789 that Chénier's *Charles IX*, the historical tragedy about the Saint Bartholomew Massacre, had not been given a "permission by the police," presumably because it vilified two pillars of the

Old Regime: the church and the monarchy. An orator in the crowd responded: "We do not want to hear about permission; for too long the public has suffered from the despotism of censorship. We want to be free to hear and see the works which please us, just as we are free to think" (Lacroix 1894, I, 284-285; II, 286-287). The Commune eventually reconsidered the matter and allowed the performance of *Charles IX* on November 4, 1789. The public again had its way.

A third example is that of a crowd resisting the municipality's cancellation of theatre performances in honor of the slain deputy Lepeletier-Saint-Fargeau (slain because of his regicide vote at the Convention in January 1793). The would-be spectators threatened to smash the doors of the Théâtre de l'Estrapade or to burn it down if a play were not given. "If [the play] is not performed, we will burn down the hall...the municipality has no right to close theatres" (A. P. P., A. A. 198, 134).

At the Gaîté a popular audience angered by a play favorable to divorce, according to the *Journal des Spectacles* of October 5, 1793, demanded the author, who was then said to be "in the Vendée fighting the enemies of his play." But then he *did* appear and was asked by the audience to get down on his knees (*à genoux*) for having insulted them with such a cavalier comment. Audiences, according to the *Journal des Spectacles* of July 30, 1793, were "tout puissant."

If audiences were so powerful, what were their preferences? Much evidence points to their ardent patriotism until Thermidor. Their tastes are reflected not only in the repertory record of 1794 (considerably more political than that of the decade) but also in the commentary of the press and police reports.

At a performance on December 21, 1793 of the opera *Militiade à Marathon* by Guillard and Lemoyne, and of Gossec and Gardel's opera, *Offrande à la liberté*, a secret agent of the Ministry of the Interior reported "transports inexprimables" of the audience. Five days later another agent reported the reception of the news announced between plays that the army of the Moselle had been victorious and that the rebels of the Vendée had been repulsed: "Thousands of sansculottes spectators applauded ecstatically" (Caron 1910, I, 317; II, 6).

Patriotism did not exclude *gaieté* or *sensibilité*. Sylvain Maréchal's regicide *Jugement dernier des rois* staged the sovereigns of Europe and the pope being blown up on an island volcano at the Théâtre de la République between October 1793 and February 1794. The *Journal des Spectacles* of October 22, 1793 reported that its audience was quite unlike the *ci-devants* of the *comédiens français* or the *muscadins* of the Vaudeville, composed, as it was, "of a legion of tyrannicides, ready to pounce on the leonine species known by the name of kings....the theatre was completely filled even up to the musicians' orchestra....Such is the pleasing plan of this work that it was received amid gales of laughter and sustained applause" (*J. S.*, 888).

Wild *gaieté* could greet anticlerical plays, such as *Le Prélat d'autrefois ou*

Sophie et St. Elme, fait historique performed on 28 Ventôse *an* II (March 18, 1794) and the *Capucins aux frontières*, a three-act pantomime in the top fifty for 1794 and of which the *Journal des Spectacles* praised the "folle gaieté" as well as its "esprit républicain" on October 28, 1793 (cf. Caron, V, 379-380).

But where *gaieté* and edification conflicted, it was *gaieté* that prevailed. People went to the theatre then, as now, to be entertained rather than to be edified, hence the ratio of fourteen comedies to every tragedy performed during the decade. With the exception of four or five theatres offering plays "of public utility," argued an agent of Minister Garat, all the rest presented only "frivolous diversions, while the country is in danger" (Tuetey 1890, IX, 205).

Sensibilité could be applauded with "intoxication," as was a performance of *La Famille indigente* on 4 Germinal *an* II (March 24, 1794), another play on our top fifty for 1794. The reviewer observed: "Whenever one emphasizes a somewhat romantic [*romanesque*] sentiment one is sure to succeed" (*P. A.* 1794, 6818). *Sensibilité*, it is clear, did not exclude patriotism, as Pierre Trahard showed more than half a century ago. It could even be one of its lubricants. Weeping for victims of the guillotine was not incompatible with clamoring for their execution, and women were described as having this Janus-like trait more commonly than men: crying in the theatre about a petit savoyard or other unfortunate creature while pressing forward at the Place de la Révolution to see traitors decapitated.[2]

Even before audiences got inside the theatre, they told managers how much they liked the announcements posted in the streets by buying or not buying tickets. Directors had to calculate their billings carefully. During the Terror the *Journal des Spectacles* reported on July 30, 1793 that the reputedly patriotic Théâtre de la République was praised by the police for abandoning "gay comedies and farces" in 1793 for more ambitious political plays that were subsidized in part by the government. But the directors reported losing much revenue after doing so, and one of them, Dorfeuille, wanted to take a businesslike approach and offer pure entertainment, "which would procure him *the money of the tranquil and sweet man, who needs relaxation* at the theatre, and even [the money] of the most extreme types of all parties" [emphasis added].

Two weeks earlier at the performance of *Le Sourd*, our top play of the decade, the *Journal des Spectacles* (July 14, 1793) comments: "The success of this comedy, which has already had a very large number of performances, is still continuing....The *Auberge pleine* is not nearly as good as *La Femme jalouse* by the same author; but if one likes the latter, one laughs a lot at the former, *and it is truly a good deed, at the present moment, to cheer men up*" [emphasis added].

The spectacle of the "rich" seeking their old pleasures, although not explicitly counterrevolutionary, was hardly consoling. Secret agent Perrière, in September 1793, distinguished between good (popular) and bad (formerly privileged) theatres. But this was far from correct. Perrière was closer to the mark when he continued: "As for the rest, a general reproach one can make of all the theatres is that there is hardly any in which plays are not performed that are the disgusting picture of the corruption and frivolousness [*légèreté*] spawned by despotism."[3] Another secret agent, Latour-Lamontagne, confirmed on September 11, 1793, the prevalence of our repertory list for the decade when he sighed: "Would that the marquis cede their place to the patriots, let us burn, if necessary, the masterpieces of Molière, of Regnard, the arts will lose something, but certainly *moeurs* will gain" (Caron 1910, I, 69). (See Chap. 16, Table XII.)

Frivolity and gaiety could undermine the austerity and firmness of republican virtue and reveal an insouciance to the public welfare. Such softness, wherever it might be found, was really "aristocratic," just as patriotism was sansculotte even at the Opéra: "With the exception of two or three theatres," says Lamontagne, "they are all infected by aristocracy" (Caron 1910, I, 68).

Dugas, another secret agent, reports in mid-January 1794: "We can see that the theatres are slowing up on the patriotic plays" (Caron 1910, II, 357). And in March, Le Breton writes, "The theatres are always rather well-frequented; there are some which are not very patriotic and in which the heroes of our Revolution do not play the most brilliant role" (Caron 1910, V, 50). But we must turn to Saint-Just for a lamentation about theatregoing as a manifestation of an aristocracy of the spirit.

In his *Institutions républicaines*, Saint-Just, troubled by the lethargic character of the bureaucracy and the public—the more intractable kind of counterrevolution—asks himself who goes to the theatre. Not the "nobility, it is banished." Rather, "those who used to work in the past...today one works only three days, another four and they flaunt the same extravagance" [*luxe*] as the aristocrats had before (Saint-Just 1984, 993).

Audience reactions during the Terror fell far short of the desired Republican simplicity or, in today's vocabulary, "transparency." Dissimulation could take the place of violent reaction. Latour-Lamontagne comments about the Théâtre de la République on January 4, 1794, when *Les Contre-Révolutionnaires jugés par eux-mêmes* was being performed. One actor in the play says that "civic cards" prove anything but good citizenship and the secret agent à propos the play says, "Every day they allow plays with impressive titles to be performed, yet they are sometimes very *incivique*, and one often sees there *old plays reappear which are quite immoral*" [emphasis added] (January 4, 1794; Caron II, 175). Plagiarized plays under new, hopefully satisfactory, titles were indicated regularly by the *Journal des Spectacles*. Hypocrisy was a means of survival during the Terror, as Benjamin Constant maintained, and theatres practiced it as well as individuals (Holmes 1984, 121-125). Theatres' patriotic names, like the patriotic titles of plays, were thought by one inspector to serve as covers for counterrevolution. Does a change of name satisfy the exigencies of patriotism, he asked? And then exasperatedly: "When will we manage to purify the theatres" (January 12, 1794; Caron, II, 320)?

Both actors and spectators could mask their true feelings. Leaving a performance of *Les Petits montagnards* at the Cité Variétés, one spectator commented that the actors said those patriotic things because they had to ("Oh! Combien de choses on leur fait dire là qu'ils ne pensent pas!") (23 Ventôse *an* II [March 13, 1794], Caron V, 382). Secret agent Perrière was there eavesdropping and protested—not as a prosecutor but as an educator—arguing that it was not so at all, while a bystander looked on with disbelief. Again, another agent, Béraud, comments on the boulevard theatre of the Variétés Amusantes of Lazzari, where the *Noblesse au village* was playing: "This play is a tissue of aristocracy hidden under a veil of patriotism" (Caron I, 22).

What, then, did the censors encounter? They encountered insubordination, a recalcitrant spirit addicted to "gay" humor and sweet sensibility that was a far cry from the heroic patriotism and republicanism of the five-act tragedy. They encountered theatre directors who were imprisoned in late 1793 and early 1794 for their failure to produce patriotism on stage: Monnié, Barré, Léger, and Desfontaines of the Vaudeville on September 20, 1793; Nicolet on 27 Nivôse *an* II (January 17, 1794) for having "violated all the principles of decency and honor"; Audinot of the Ambigu Comique on the same day and for the same reason ("There are plays in the repertory of the Ambigu Comique which could shock one's sense of decency"); Mlle Montansier and her codirector Neuville on 19 Ventose *an* II (March 9, 1794); Francoeur of the Opera (for refusing Fabre d'Eglantine's blasphemous *La Passion du Christ*); Dorfeuille of the République for a year, for reasons unknown to this author (Tuetey IX, 414, 300).

Imprisonments were not the only recourse. Convocations could remind directors of their duty, too. These began just before the August 2, 1793, decree calling for a purified repertory. On July 29, the Comité du Salut Public of the Department of Paris began calling in directors, in preparation for the festival of August 10 "to invite them to the committee and to play patriotic plays" (Tuetey, IX, 321). While in fact repertories were not systematically examined in advance before April 1794, these sporadic inspections did put pressure on directors. The September 1793 arrest of all the Comédiens Français and the closing of their theatre must have struck fear into the hearts of other companies. Some sort of self-censorship took place in the ensuing months, even though it may have taken the form of token, hypocritical, or intermittent compliance. On 1 Pluviôse *an* II (January 20, 1794) a new series of convocations began. Again directors were invited to "purify *moeurs* by the performance of good plays filled with morality" (Tuetey X, 316). By 6 Pluviôse (January 25, 1794) most of the theatres of Paris had been convoked. Whatever freedom remained to directors in choosing their repertories was finally suppressed by the institution of prior censorship (See Table 12) by the Commission d'Instruction Publique (not the Comité) on 12 Germinal *an* II (April 2, 1794) (Cochin 1935, III, 382; Lieby

1904, 103). Henceforth, repertories were examined fortnightly.

This censorship necessarily made repertories more revolutionary and patriotic than they would have been otherwise, and one can see the effect on the list of the top fifty for 1794. The radicalized stage of that year was clearly more the product of censorship than of a genuinely politicized audience.

But audience outbursts prove that the theatre public *could* get what it wanted and get rid of what it did not want, so that what succeeded in the repertory was a pretty good indication of what audiences wanted to see. Secret agents' and police's reports prove that theatres often resisted a completely patriotic repertory, hence the agents' frequent denunciations. The number of theatre directors who were imprisoned or convoked proves that the repertories were a far cry from what the Committee of Public Safety and the Convention wanted. Nor do we find the subsidized tragedies recommended by the Convention on the fifty most performed list of the decade nor on the lists of the ten most performed of each year. The preference for comedy over tragedy illustrates further the popular disregard of official preferences. Instead we find a play (*Cadet Roussel ou Le Café des aveugles*) ridiculing tragedy and heroic suicide high on the list of 1793. While there was a theatrical patriotism manifested by audiences in connection with the defense of national territory, particularly upon the recapture of Toulon, it was far from reaching a level sufficient to reassure the monitors of public opinion, the secret agents of the Ministry of the Interior. Their testimony, along with that of the Committee of Public Safety and our unwitting source—the theatre listings of what was actually shown between 1789 and 1799—all point to a theatre that was a good deal less "une école des moeurs républicaines" than contemporaries and historians have believed. Instead, we find more often than not an inconstant patriotism and a persistent predilection for amusement that, gleaned from different types of sources, show that *douceur* prevailed over *rigueur*.

On April 2, 1794, censorship of plays was delegated primarily to one of the *bureaux* of the Commission d'Instruction Publique, whose records were later destroyed by one of the fires of the Paris Commune in 1871. By the time of the second Directory, in late 1797, censorship was the province of the newly formed Ministry of the Police, specifically the first division of the Bureau of Police and the Bureau Central, Canton de Paris, and the records of this censorship are extant. By *an* VII (1798-1799), manuscripts of plays were being submitted in advance for authorization to be printed and performed (A. N., F[7]3491). The police of the Directory might have considered censoring a play for any of three reasons: (1) to protect public officials from calumny and disrespect; (2) to shield morality; and (3) to prevent a sympathetic portrayal of the enemy (nobles, priests, kings) on stage.

Thus, on 1 Germinal *an* VI (March 21, 1798), at the performance of the patriotic opera *Léonidas* at the Théâtre de la Cité, the police reported: "The least civic moral was immediately parodied by shouting of youth" (A. N.,

F[7]3491, Chemise I, 13). The work had only three performances.

At the Opéra, where the very civic *Horatius Cocles* was being performed, the spectators deserted en masse to the Feydeau and Vaudeville so they would not have to listen to the "political charivari" (A. N., F[7]3491, Chemise I, 18).

The line "Il est bien de Maîtres en France qui n'etaient jadis de valets" (words that might have come from Baurans's *Servante maîtresse*) was probably aimed at all the Revolutionary upstarts (*parvenus*). The police flagged it on May 5, 1798, because it undermined respect for those in power (A. N., F[7]3491, Chemise I, 20).

A play entitled *Les Anglais tels qu'ils sont* was suppressed because it showed Frenchmen leaving France because they opposed the Revolution. A similar play, *Emigrés français*, was censored because it was too dangerous to portray émigrés on stage. *Brigands de Rome ou La Mort du General Duphot* put the French invasion of Italy by Bonaparte in too bad a light to be allowed (A. N., F[7]3491, Chemise I, 54).

So great was the censorship that a large number of playwrights signed a petition addressed to Minister of Police Duval, complaining about the prior censorship of their works, which they did not think a "surveillance of theatres" warranted. Scripts, they complained, circulated at length from office to office, and came back in a "mangled, unrecognizable" state (A. N., F[7]3491, Chemise I, 4515).[4]

We have seen that there was plenty of republican drama on stage, but it was being continually challenged by politically neutral and counterrevolutionary works. French Revolutionary theatre witnessed a clash between "Red" and "Black" audiences, characterized as the ardent and excited singers of three songs before the lifting of the curtain: the patriotic "Chant du départ" or the "Marseillaise" and the counterrevolutionary "Réveil du peuple" (Schmidt 1867, III, 66, 72-75, 82, 85, 92-93, 128). Many a night in the theatre ended almost as soon as it began: with a *rixe* (brawl) triggered by the competition between sections of the audience wanting or not wanting the "Marseillaise." The battle raged at the popular theatres of Audinot and Nicolet, the Ambigu Comique, the Vaudeville, the Feydeau, the Opéra, and the République. The struggle that was taking place in the primary electoral assemblies of the Directory between royalists, Directorial republicans, and Jacobins was mirrored on stage, and it does not seem that the government was winning the battle. The coups d'état in government in years V, VI, and VII tried to do for elections what censorship attempted for stage.

REVIEWS

A typical review in one of the Paris dailies that covered theatre, such as the *Petites Affiches*, the *Chronique de Paris*, or the *Journal de Paris*, consisted of a plot summary, a short description of the play's reception, identification of the playwright(s) who had been asked by the audience to appear on stage (if it liked the play), some evaluation of the acting (usually in very stereotypical terms), and a suggestion to revise the play (usually to shorten it!). To a large degree, these newspapers—which had to look toward their own survival—were as out of touch with their audiences as the police were, that is, they were more republican than the spectators.

Let us look at a few reviews from each of these newspapers. The editor of the *Petites Affiches* was a popular writer of *romans noirs* named Ducray-Duminil. Ducray was probably the author of the numerous reviews in his patriotic paper. On the *Réunion du 10 août ou L'Inauguration de la République française* by Gabriel Bouquier, he writes: "[W]e have not seen before a more high-sounding republican play" (*P. A.*, 20 Germinal *an* II [April 9, 1794], 7065). The anticlerical *Dragons et les bénédictines* of Pigault-Lebrun was praised for its "unaffected republican morality, easy dialogue, and gaiety" (*P. A.*, January 1794, 5648). Of the *Journée d'amour*, he wrote on March 15, 1794: "The sole regret that indubitably one has in seeing this ballet is that it has no relevance to liberty, that it has nothing to say to the republican soul" (6631-6632).

Characteristic of this genre of patriotism was its moral orthodoxy: the republican mainstream was heterosexual and usually monogamous. Thus the polygamy in Jean Ducis's *Abusar ou La Famille arabe* offended "our mores and our civilization."[5]

The *Chronique de Paris* also praised patriotic as well as emotionally touching plays unconnected with the Revolution. "The patriotic plays always attract a crowd," it wrote on January 11, 1790, of a production of Voltaire's *Mort de César* "which had the greatest success" at the Comédie Française.[6]

The *Chronique* (March 15, 1791) and other newspapers did not distribute praise equally among the different novelties on stage. Flops did occur, even patriotic flops such as the play by the future general of the "revolutionary armies," Ronsin, whose *Louis XII, père du peuple* ceased to be staged after ten performances. Likewise, the author of *Nicodème dans la lune* experienced a frightful setback when his anticlerical *Capucins* was brought down before the end of the premiere performance.

But it need not have been political plays to which the *Chronique* warmed. It, too, was quite susceptible to the appeal of feeling and sentiment, as can be seen in its review of Jean Ducis's adaptation of *Macbeth*, which premiered at the Théâtre de la Nation on January 6, 1790. The reviewer comments, "Some new scenes, some very beautiful things, some truly poetic details, [all of] which obtained some much merited applause."

Indeed, on July 6, 1793, in reviewing the *Corsaire*, a three-act opera by Marsollier des Vivetières with music by Dalayrac, the *Chronique* opined quite frankly that "The second reason for the decided success of this revival merits the attention of authors and directors of spectacles: It is the fine gaiety that prevails in all the appropriate scenes. *The more our political horizon darkens, the more the mind is in need of finding an illusion of pleasure at the theatre that the interior situation cannot offer.* Instruct or amuse, that is what ought to be the sole purpose of playwrights, and one can be sure that the reality of black scenes has turned us away from their theatrical performances" [emphasis added]. One could not ask for a more explicit explanation of the preference on the part of playwrights, theatre directors, and ultimately audiences for light, "gay," "sweet" drama. It met both a psychological and a commercial demand.

The *Journal des Spectacles* was, unlike the *Petites Affiches*, the *Chronique de Paris*, and the *Journal de Paris*, what we could call a dedicated theatre paper as opposed to a daily that printed reviews. Its publication commenced on July 1, 1793, after the elimination of the Girondins from the Convention and two months before the formal beginning of the Terror. Its editor was Pascal Boyer, who was one of several journalists to be guillotined. His newspaper too met a premature death on January 8, 1794, six months before his own demise on 19 Messidor *an* II (July 7, 1794) which was three weeks before the death of Robespierre.

Boyer's *Journal*, however, was not outspokenly critical of the Republic or of the Jacobins, but its republicanism was subtler than that of the *Petites Affiches*. We read in the issue of 21 Brumaire (November 11, 1793) that "since the example of *Pamela* and the actors of the Comédie Française [who had been imprisoned because of it in September], the theatres have put together new repertories; they have removed from the stage everything that could reproduce, under dangerous and seductive forms, that tone, that spirit, those mores, those prejudices of our former slavery. [But] the authors of these new plays, experimenting in a new manner, have not produced any masterpieces." The observation on the one hand substantiates our depiction of the non-Revolutionary character of Parisian theatre at the outset of the Terror, but it overestimates the success of the theatrical establishment in changing that repertory, at least during the first months of the Terror. Otherwise the secret agents would have had little cause to complain.

This mildly pro-Revolutionary critique of counterrevolutionary stage dovetails with a sense of literary superiority or outright snobbery toward the new audiences who did not know the first thing about theatre. But Boyer's genre of survivalism did not work. A partisan of high theatre, he was disdainful of the sansculotte audiences. We have been unable to find out anything about his arrest and execution, but it is quite possible that his journal had something to do with it. Boyer launched his paper to counteract the vulgarization of theatre. Thus Boyer in his prospectus speaks of the "barbarian incursion into the republic of letters....what do we find in most [theatres]? Farces instead of comedies, [melodrama] instead of tragedy, antitheses instead of eloquence, plays on words instead of witticisms, gibes instead of epigrams...balderdash instead of refinement." (*J. S.*, July 1, 1793).

Two more theatre journals, both of them from the Directory, and both manifesting acute disgust with the character of the theatregoing public were *Le Censeur Dramatique* of Grimod de la Reynière and the *Journal des Théâtres et des Fêtes Nationales* of Duchosal.

The *Journal des Théâtres*, a very republican paper, began publishing on August 18, 1794, and lasted until February 21, 1795, about the same span of time as the *Journal des Spectacles* a year earlier. Although short-lived, it endured long enough to print several thousand pages of criticism. It approved Chénier's very popular tyrannicidal play *Timoléon*, welcomed the revival of the *Sourd ou L'Auberge pleine*, which once again "aroused the avid curiosity of numerous spectators." The review of *Le Devin du village* at the Théâtre des Arts (Opéra) reveals greater attention to acting than one finds in most reviews: "The citizen [actress] Ponteuil forgot that Colette, abandoned and betrayed by an ingrate whom she still loves, ought to show an expression of pain and sensitivity" (*J. T.*, 12 Brumaire *an* III [November 2, 1794], 613-614).

In general, this review is more prolix than those we have examined, and more inclined to moralize in a republican vein. But again, it has a real taste for high theatre, as can be seen in its comment on a verse in act IV of a performance of Molière's *Misanthrope*: "Redoutes tout après un tel outrage./Je ne suis plus à moi, je suis tout à la rage." The editor extols the passage: "We do not know anything in theatre so perfect as this scene, played by Molé and the citizeness Contat; they are worthy of one another, worthy both of this masterpiece" (*J. T.*, 21 Brumaire *an* III [November 11, 1794], 689). He is referring to two of the most famous French actors (formerly of the Comédie Française). But the success of farcical comedies like *Le Sourd* threatened to totally dispirit our good editor, who writes about the juxtaposition of the two: "Who will henceforward spend years on the creation of an important work, if the lowest buffoonery is preferred to the masterpieces of Molière?" (*Journal de l'Instruction publique*, quoted in *J. T.*, 16 Brumaire *an* III [November 6, 1794], 644-645). Popular theatre was a threat to the survival of high theatre.

The *Censeur Dramatique* was another specialized periodical of the Directory, that was devoted, as its title indicates, entirely to the theatre. It tended to publish much longer reviews than the publications analyzed above, extending to as many as twenty pages. Favorable to the established actors of the former Comédie, Grimod is merciless in dealing with incompetent *débutants*. Commenting on the famous Molé playing Alceste in the *Misanthope* he writes: "[S]uccessively an angry, weak, passionate, and jealous lover, M. Molé has grasped all the nuances of this admirable scene with a skill above any kind of praise. His acting was truly sublime, and we lack the words to praise him adequately" (I, 360).

But examining the performance of M. Michot in Molière's *L'Avare* at the Feydeau, Grimod writes:

> We will not speak of his revolutionary roles, which he
> fulfilled with great celebrity, as everyone knows; this part of
> his life is irrelevant to our purpose: we will be content just to
> say that at the Théâtre de la République he enacted some
> peasants, some lock pickers, some character studies, above
> all in new plays, for his talent and his memory both appeared
> to exclude the roles of the old repertory.
>
> Unfortunately, this actor has proved, by the manner in
> which he acted Maître Jacques, that he was absolutely
> incapable of playing a role of the former Comédie. There
> wasn't the least spark of real gaiety, of finesse, of comedy.
> He thought that this grimacing manner...this natural [style] of
> the boulevard which has won so many partisans in this
> permanent class of idiots [*sots*], could replace the talent that
> he learned, and yet the lack of success that he has gained
> ought to have proved to him the contrary...It is despicable to
> play [the role] Maître Jacques badly and to play it with such
> an emphatic pretentiousness; on any other day than Sunday
> [the day "le peuple" went to the theatre in droves], we doubt
> whether he could pull off this role without merited and
> violent murmurs (*C. D.*, III, 286-289).

We know not a better text to illustrate the bitter conflict between
Revolutionary and Old Regime theatre, between boulevard vulgarity and
Revolutionary opportunism, on the one side, and highbrow connoisseurship and
snobbery, disdainful of the revolution and *le peuple,* on the other. Although the
boulevard was vulgar by all accounts, it was not particularly revolutionary in its
repertory, but the editor clearly linked the two. These reviews tended to
reinforce what the secret agents and Saint-Just had said during the Terror.
Theatres had become major distractions for the people, who flowed to them for
sheer entertainment rather than to acquire *moeurs républicaines*.

The *Décade Philosophique* was, like the *Censeur Dramatique*, definitely
highbrow, and attached to the rules of classical dramaturgy but, unlike the
Censeur, staunchly republican and "philosophe." It felt that Molière was better
than the dramas with ariettas of Marsollier (e.g., *Les Deux petits savoyards*).
It disliked the moralizing tendencies of Revolutionary playwrights who tried to
make sermons out of their scripts, yet it, too, condemned immoral subjects such
as that of the *Double divorce*. Rejecting stock characters of the Old Regime
from which vice exuded, they favored republican tragedies like those of
Lemierre, Corneille, Legouvé, Ducis, and Chénier; the comedies of Collin
d'Harleville, Andrieux, and Picard; and even the dramas of Baculard d'Arnaud
(Regaldo 1976, III, 1324-1511).

In its 2,000 pages of theatre criticism published between 1794 and 1807 (thoroughly and insightfully studied by Marc Regaldo), the *Décade Philosophique* preferred the great repertory of France's classical dramaturges to the scribblers of the Revolutionary period. Like many playwrights (Chénier, for example), it felt that the regime of unrestricted freedom and competition had been harmful, if not disastrous, to theatres, and therefore it supported the idea of a National Dramaturgical Institute or Jury of the Arts that would regulate the number and quality of theatres and their productions. (Regaldo 1976, III, 1358-1370.) Perhaps this is part of the organizing impulse that led post-Thermidorean France to found the National Institute, which regrouped and reformed the old academies. It was this spirit that ultimately allowed the Brumairians to reorganize the government of France in 1799 into a powerful consular dictatorship—a dictatorship that in 1807 would reduce the number of Parisian theatres to eight, thus ending the experiment in free market drama that began with the Le Chapelier Law in 1791.

9

Conclusion

Emmet Kennedy and Marie-Laurence Netter

The Revolution had a theatrical agenda as it had a pedagogical one. Indeed, they were one and the same in most respects: to create a republican "school" and to regenerate *moeurs*. Theatre's role, according to the dramatic theory of a pre-Revolutionary Diderot or a L. S. Mercier, was to moralize the domestic, to dignify the quotidian, and not to worry about the classical genres or unities. To this formula the leaders of the Revolution added the Revolution itself, which could be opened like a sacred book to inspire and guide the "new man."

French men, women, and children went to the fifty newly-opened theatres in droves during the 1790s. Compared with the monopoly exercised by the three privileged theatres of the Old Regime, this multiplication of stages provided undreamed-of possibilities for entertaining the Parisian masses.

But for the most part, these audiences were not edified in the manner the revolutionaries intended. The latter wanted patriotism and heroic republican tragedy to be staged. The Committee of Public Safety intervened on the Convention floor on August 2, 1793, to prescribe precisely this and to ban the "indecent" drama then playing in many theatres like the Vaudeville. Moreover, it agreed to subsidize specific republican tragedies in theatres that would agree to stage them.

We have shown at length the type of drama that *did* prevail during the Revolution. It was not tragedy, which was outperformed by comedy by a ratio of fourteen to one. Most of these plays—indeed, almost all of the top fifty for the decade—had nothing to do with the Revolution. They dealt uncritically with peasants and lords and the seignorial regime, naïve bucolic lovers, masters and maids, deaf-mutes in country inns, nuns disturbed by a male intruder—and only occasionally with an idealized 1789 or with an operatic consecration of liberty.

The Committee of Public Safety did not achieve its goals and had to resort to formal censorship on April 2, 1794. Before that, it had closed down the

Comédie Française and imprisoned its actors and actresses. There had been other acts of censorship even earlier, such as the interdiction of Laya's *Amis des lois*. In the winter of 1794, the directors of theatres were convoked before the great Committee to explain why their repertories were not more revolutionary. Some of these directors were subsequently imprisoned.

A Revolutionary stage *did* exist and has been written about repeatedly since the days of the Consulate. Although many of the Revolutionary productions did not overtly question the socio-political hierarchy, plays like *Le Convalescent de qualité, Les Rigueurs du cloître, Charles IX, Le Jugement dernier des rois*, and *L'Intérieur des comités révolutionnaires* did.

Indeed, some scholars believe that the most important innovation of the theatre in the Revolution was precisely the dramatization of the Revolution in the *theatres*. If politics can be said to have been largely absent from the pre-Revolutionary stage, then a politicization of theatre was the most important novelty of Revolutionary theatre. The thesis of the present work is that although politics may have been the most important *innovation*, it was not the most telling characteristic of that theatre, nor the most revealing of its audiences.

In view of the plays performed during the period between the monarchy and the Terror, when censorship existed—that is between 1791 and 1793—it is evident that political life itself—in its most concrete dimensions, the debates, and the new press—hardly inspired the authors at all. The triumph of the epoch, *Nicodème dans la lune*, is only a succession of naïve allegories, an idealized presentation of the Revolution, in truth the opposite of the historical and heroic scenes that sought to awaken and regenerate minds. As for plays that brandish relevance, like *L'Ami des lois* or *L'Intérieur des comités révolutionnaires*, their success was very short.

It is clear, as we have already stressed, that the *social* critique put on stage in the comedies simultaneously captured the imagination of the authors and the approval of the spectators. But if the situations are often new, as in the *faits-historiques* or *faits-patriotiques* like *L'Heureuse décade*, the substance of the intrigues is hardly revolutionary. Indeed, it is even rather conservative, in the sense that the hierarchies, familial or social, are always respected and good sentiments are always recompensed. It is, moreover, this constant theatrical morality, mixed with dramatic and confused situations, to which the Revolution gave birth, that results in the *melodrama*.

The Le Chapelier Law of January 1791 broke the old monopolies of repertories and made it possible for any entrepreneur to open a theatre when and where he or she pleased. This law resulted in the proliferation of theatres detailed above. Supply seems to have created demand: genre restrictions broke down, and repertories spread from theatre to theatre (and not always in the trickle-down fashion). Chaos ensued and entrepreneurs went bankrupt. Like newspapers under the Directory, theatres disappeared and resurfaced with new names, only to go under again.

Theatre during the Revolution obeyed the rules that were proper to it, like any art. There can exist a certain complementarity between a genre and an epoch, and even a certain osmosis, but an overly precise staging of actuality removes from the scene its magic and its power. It is this without doubt that explains the weakness of the Revolutionary theatre and also in part explains the success of plays prior to 1789.

As for the multiplication of theatres from 1791 on, far from creating emulation among spectacles, it resulted in competition in stage productions among actors, who were not very professional and provoked repeated bankruptcies. The true theatre professionals, after this cruel experience, were the first to rejoice at the return to discipline under the Consulate and the Empire.

New genres did appear: the political vaudeville at the Vaudeville and the melodrama on the boulevard. The comic opera enjoyed a new lease on life. The decade was not without its contributions to Thalia. But the overall effect was minor compared with, say, the epoch of classical theatre under Louis XIV, which the cultural moguls of the Revolution never forgot. The dramatic arts had to struggle to survive and, it seemed, could not flourish without energetic support from the state. One could say it was a matter of Colbertism vs. Chapelierism! Liberty, it seems, did not work out to the advantage of theatre during the Revolution any more than it had for publishing firms; the parallels are striking (see Hesse 1991).

Nonetheless, freedom was found in the very defiance of the Revolutionary project. Reading the texts—*Le Sourd, Le Barbier de Séville, L'Enrôlement supposé, Le Déserteur* (and other plays about military desertion), *La Fausse Agnès* (which ridicules Parisian snobbishness and aristocratic pretensions), the comedies of Beaunoir (with their working-class grumbling)—one gets the sense that these plays and many more like them enabled spectators to survive the Revolution through laughter, and pity.

There are two plays with which we would like to conclude. The first is one by J. B. Radet, written during the Terror for the Vaudeville. It is an inversion of Molière's *Bourgeois gentilhomme* and is called *Le Noble roturier*. It depicts a marquis who is trying to procure a genealogical proof that he is of common descent. Why? Because that was supposedly the preferred lineage during the Terror. The genealogist declares that he used to have great difficulty producing noble genealogies before the Revolution, but that he would have no trouble proving the marquis's descent from a weaver or a fruit merchant! The sansculotte Revolution stood Molière on his head with a social typing not unlike that of the great *comédien*.

The second play is J. Aude and L. Tissot's *Cadet Roussel au café des aveugles*, a play within a play. The popular hero Roussel is staging a drama that is a comedy-opera in the first act and a tragedy in verse in the second. Theatrical genres are ridiculed as are tragic conventions like heroic suicide, when Cadet drinks the poisonous phial with his father protesting in the audience.

Comedy prevailed over tragedy, laughter over rhetoric, in the 1790s. What else could account for the odd assortment of characters—a royalist astronaut, a bumbling deaf-mute, two hunters and a milkmaid, two little Savoyards with a performing rodent, a marquis qua fruit merchant—who became the most popular heroes of the most performed plays of the Revolution? The new theatrical ethos was comedy—sweet and sentimental. Is it really that deplorable? To the twentieth century, perhaps, but evidently not to the Revolutionary generation.

We hope that we have proved that despite the theatrical innovations of Revolutionary theatre—*faits-historiques, pièces-patriotiques, vaudevilles, mélodrames*—the main Revolutionary thrust was continuity with the Old Regime and resistance to Revolutionary politicization. Nothing proves this better than the list of the fifty most performed plays of the 1790s and the similar list of top authors. For some reason, difficult to identify, a substantial segment of theatregoers, most likely the majority, remained attached to the pre-Revolutionary repertory or to that part of the new repertory that mimicked the old. Was this public counterrevolutionary like its first author, Beaunoir, eager to escape the "black scenes" in the street, as the observer for the *Chronique de Paris* claimed? If the high rankings of *Le Sourd* and *Les Deux chasseurs* signify their broad popularity among Parisians, the question is, which ones? Saint-Just opined that it was not the old theatregoing class; La Harpe said the same thing somewhat earlier. This points to two possible interpretations: (1) many sansculottes (taken here in a social rather than a political sense) were disaffected by the Revolution and sought solace in the theatre; (2) many sansculottes (in the radical political sense) sought diversion in the evening from taxing political commitments of the day.[1]

The secret agents of the Ministry of the Interior in *an* II (1793-1794) worried most about the first of these possibilities. For them, theatres were oracles of public opinion, and public opinion was one source of political power. To lose public opinion was to lose the Revolution. Hence, their denunciations of the frivolities, nonsense, or critical opposition on stage.

Had the theatres, along with the newspapers, the clubs, and the political factions, been wholly supportive of the government, no Terror would have occurred. The theatre represented, for the Jacobins, a part of the unregenerate world of diversion and pleasure that the Revolutionary will had to purge if it were to pass to a civil existence. The French Revolution sought to remold the French people according to Republican precepts of virtue. That same people resisted. Its entertainment world proved more Rabelaisian than Robespierrist.

10

Abbreviations

A. P. P., A. A.	Archives de la Préfecture de la Police (Paris)
A. N.	Archives Nationales
B. N.	Bibliothèque Nationale
P. A.	*Petites Affiches (Affiches, Annonces et Avis Divers)*
J. S.	*Journal des Spectacles*
J. T.	*Journal des Théâtres*
C. D.	*Censeur Dramatique*

11

Repertory of French Revolutionary Theatre

Sorted by author and title with number of performances by theatre. For works with multiple authors, a period followed by a comma is used to separate one name from the next.

Adolphe, D. *Lettre de cachet, La* [*Comédie* in 1 act, Prem. on 13-5-1791].
 Th. de l'Ambigu Comique (**66**); **Total: 66**.
Alain, Robert., Legrand, Marc-A. *Epreuve réciproque, L'* [*Comédie* in 1 act, Prem. on 16-10-1711, Pub. in 1711].
 Th. de l'Odéon (**6**); Th. de la Liberté (**1**); Th. de la Nation (Comédie Française) (**4**); Th. de Molière (**5**); Th. Français (de la rue Richelieu) (de la République) (**10**); Th. Lyrique des Amis de la Patrie (**3**); **Total: 29**.
Alainval, Abbé-L.-J.-C.-S. D'. *Ecole des bourgeois, L'* [*Comédie* in 3 acts, Pub. in 1728].
 Th. de la Nation (Comédie Française) (**29**); Th. du Feydeau (de Monsieur) (**3**); Th. du Marais (**6**); Th. Français (de la rue Richelieu) (de la République) (**2**); **Total: 40**.
_____. *Mari curieux, Le* [*Comédie* in 1 act, Prem. on 17-7-1731, Pub. in 1731].
 Th. Patriotique et de Momus (**9**); **Total: 9**.
 Total Performances, Alainval, Abbé-L.-J.-C.-S. D'.: **49**
Allaire, Henri-A. *Hommes du jour, Les* [*Vaudeville*, Prem. on 8-5-1797].
 Th. des Jeunes Artistes (**7**); **Total: 7**.
Andrault de Langeron. *Duel supposé, Le* [*Comédie* in 1 act, Prem. on 5-2-1789, Pub. in 1789].
 Th. de l'Ambigu Comique (**41**); **Total: 41**.
André-Murville, Pierre-N. *Abdélazis et Zuleïma* [*Tragédie* in 5 acts, Prem. on 3-10-1791, Pub. in 1791].
 Th. Français (de la rue Richelieu) (de la République) (**18**); **Total: 18**.
Andrieux, François-G.-J.-S., Berton, Henri-M. (comp). *Deux sentinelles, Les* [*Opéra* in 1 act, Prem. on 27-3-1791, Pub. in 1788].
 Th. des Italiens (Opéra-comique) (**6**); **Total: 6**.

_____., Dalayrac, Nicolas (comp). *Enfance de Jean-Jacques Rousseau, L'* [*Comédie* in 1 act, Prem. on 23-5-1794, Pub. in 1794].
> Th. des Italiens (Opéra-comique) (**20**); **Total: 20.**

_____. *Etourdis, Les, ou Le Mort supposé* [*Comédie* in 3 acts, Prem. on 14-12-1787, Pub. in 1788].
> n/a (**4**); Th. de l'Ambigu Comique (**12**); Th. de l'Emulation (Gaîté) (**7**); Th. de l'Odéon (**4**); Th. de la Bienfaisance (**2**); Th. de la Rue Martin (**16**); Th. de Molière (**3**); Th. des Délassements Comiques (**5**); Th. des Elèves Dramatiques (**1**); Th. des Grands Danseurs (Gaîté) (**1**); Th. des Italiens (Opéra-Comique) (**26**); Th. des Variétés Amusantes (Lazzari) (**7**); Th. des Variétés Amusantes, Comiques et Lyriques (**11**); Th. des Victoires (**2**); Th. du Marais (**3**); Th. du Palais (Cité)-Variétés (**1**); Th. du Vaudeville (**5**); Th. Français (de la rue Richelieu) (de la République) (**69**); Th. Français, Comique et Lyrique (**1**); Th. Patriotique et de Momus (**6**); **Total: 186.**

_____. *Manteau, Le* [*Comédie* in 2 acts].
> Th. de l'Ambigu Comique (**23**); **Total: 23.**

_____. *Trésor, Le* [*Comédie* in 5 acts, Prem. on 25-6-1797].
> Th. des Délassements Comiques (**10**); Th. des Grands Danseurs (Gaîté) (**15**); Th. des Jeunes Artistes (**17**); Th. des Variétés Amusantes (Lazzari) (**15**); Th. du Feydeau (de Monsieur) (**2**); Th. du Vaudeville (**10**); **Total: 69.**
> **Total Performances**, Andrieux, François-G.-J.-S.: **304**

Année, Antoine. *Arlequin décorateur* [*Vaudeville* in 1 act, Prem. on 24-8-1798, Pub. in 1798].
> Th. du Vaudeville (**21**); **Total: 21.**

Ansart, Jean-B. *Ressorts amoureux d'Arlequin, Les* [*Farce* in 2 acts, Prem. on 22-10-1768, Pub. in 1769].
> Th. des Grands Danseurs (Gaîté) (**5**); **Total: 5.**

Anseaume, Louis., Duni, Egidio-R. (comp). *Clochette, La* [*Comédie mêlée d'ariettes* in 1 act, Prem. on 24-7-1766, Pub. in 1766].
> Th. de l'Ambigu Comique (**44**); Th. de l'Estrapade au Panthéon (**4**); Th. de la Citoyenne Montansier (**13**); Th. de la Concorde (**1**); Th. de Molière (**1**); Th. des Jeunes Artistes (**43**); Th. des Variétés Amusantes, Comiques et Lyriques (**4**); Th. du Marais (**6**); **Total: 116.**

_____., Duni, Egidio-R. (comp). *Deux chasseurs et la laitière, Les* [*Comédie mêlée d'ariettes* in 1 act, Prem. on 23-7-1763, Pub. in 1766].
> Th. de l'Ambigu Comique (**123**); Th. de l'Emulation (Gaîté) (**3**); Th. de l'Estrapade au Panthéon (**2**); Th. de la Citoyenne Montansier (**26**); Th. de la Concorde (**1**); Th. de la Liberté (**1**); Th. de la Montagne (**1**); Th. de Molière (**16**); Th. des Délassements Comiques (**18**); Th. des Italiens (Opéra-Comique) (**51**); Th. des Jeunes Artistes (**17**); Th. des Variétés Amusantes (Lazzari) (**24**); Th. des Variétés Amusantes, Comiques et Lyriques (**20**); Th. du Lycée des Arts (**16**); Th. du Lycée Dramatique (**1**); Th. du Marais (**9**); Th. du Mareux (**1**); Th. du Palais (Cité)-Variétés (**1**); Th. du Vaudeville (**1**); Th. Français, Comique et Lyrique (**20**); Th. Patriotique et de Momus (**3**); **Total: 355.**

_____., Pannard. *Ecosseuse, L'* [*Comédie* in 1 act, Prem. on 4-9-1760, Pub. in 1761].
> Th. des Grands Danseurs (Gaîté) (**32**); **Total: 32.**

_____. *Epreuves de l'amour, Les* [*Vaudeville* in 1 act, Prem. on 1-10-1759, Pub. in 1759].
> Th. Français, Comique et Lyrique (**5**); **Total: 5.**

_____., Marcouville, P.A. Lefèbvre de., Duni, Egidio-R. (comp). *Isle des foux, L'* [*Comédie* in 2 acts, Prem. on 29-12-1760, Pub. in 1764].
>   Th. de l'Ambigu Comique (6); **Total: 6.**

_____., Duni, Egidio-R. (comp). *Mazet* [*Comédie mêlée d'ariettes* in 2 acts, Prem. on 24-9-1761, Pub. in 1761].
>   Th. de l'Ambigu Comique (107); Th. de Molière (1); Th. du Vaudeville (7); **Total: 115.**

_____., Duni, Egidio-R. (comp). *Milicien, Le* [*Comédie mêlée d'ariettes* in 1 act, Prem. on 29-12-1762, Pub. in 1763].
>   Th. de l'Estrapade au Panthéon (2); Th. de la Citoyenne Montansier (24); Th. de la Cité (4); Th. de Molière (2); Th. des Variétés Amusantes, Comiques et Lyriques (8); Th. du Marais (8); Th. du Palais (Cité)-Variétés (3); Th. Francais, Comique et Lyrique (41); **Total: 92.**

_____., Duni, Egidio-R. (comp). *Peintre amoureux de son modèle, Le* [*Opéra-Comique* in 2 acts, Prem. on 26-7-1757, Pub. in 1757].
>   Th. de l'Ambigu Comique (11); **Total: 11.**

_____., Philidor, François-A. Danican (comp). *Soldat magicien, Le* [*Opéra-Comique* in 1 act, Prem. on 14-8-1760, Pub. in 1760].
>   Th. de Molière (1); Th. des Italiens (Opéra-Comique) (13); **Total: 14.**

_____., Grétry, André-E.-M. (comp). *Tableau parlant, Le* [*Comédie* in 1 act, Prem. on 20-9-1769, Pub. in 1769].
>   Th. de l'Ambigu Comique (2); Th. de l'Emulation (Gaîté) (5); Th. de la Citoyenne Montansier (9); Th. de la Cité (1); Th. de la Rue Martin (3); Th. des Italiens (Opéra-Comique) (49); Th. des Variétés Amusantes, Comiques et Lyriques (4); Th. du Lycée des Arts (13); Th. du Marais (2); **Total: 88.**
>   **Total Performances**, Anseaume, Louis: **834**

Arde, Hélolïse. *Nouvelle fête civique, La* [*Comédie* in 3 acts].
>   Th. National (de la rue Richelieu) (1); **Total: 1.**

Arnaud, François-T.-M. de B. D'. *Amants malheureux, Les, ou Le Comte de Comminges* [*Drame* in 3 acts, Prem. in 1765, Pub. in 1764].
>   Th. de l'Ambigu Comique (25); Th. de la Nation (Comédie Française) (28); **Total: 53.**

_____. *Coligny ou La Saint-Barthélemy* [*Tragédie* in 3 acts].
>   Th. de Molière (11); **Total: 11.**

_____. *Euphémie ou Le Triomphe de la religion* [*Drame* in 3 acts, Prem. on 24-12-1791, Pub. in 1768].
>   Th. de la Citoyenne Montansier (3); **Total: 3.**
>   **Total Performances**, Arnaud, François-T.-M. de B. D'.: **67**

Arnault, Antoine-V. *Blanche et Montcassin ou Les Vénitiens* [*Tragédie* in 5 acts, Prem. on 16-10-1798, Pub. in 1798].
>   Th. Français (de la rue Richelieu) (de la République) (15); **Total: 15.**

_____., Méhul, Etienne-N. (comp). *Horatius Coclès* [*Opéra-Vaudeville* in 1 act].
>   Académie de la Musique (Opéra) (24); **Total: 24.**

_____. *Lucrèce* [*Tragédie* in 5 acts, Prem. on 4-5-1792, Pub. in 1792].
>   Th. de la Nation (Comédie Française) (4); **Total: 4.**

_____. *Marius à Minturnes* [*Tragédie* in 3 acts, Prem. on 19-5-1791, Pub. in 1791].
>   Th. de la Nation (Comédie Française) (22); Th. Français (de la rue Richelieu) (de la République) (16); **Total: 38.**

_____., Méhul, Etienne-N. (comp). *Melidore et Phrosine* [*Drame-Lyrique* in 3 acts, Prem. on 4-5-1794, Pub. in 1794].
   Th. des Italiens (Opéra-Comique) (22); **Total: 22.**

_____. *Oscar, fils d'Ossian* [*Tragédie* in 5 acts, Prem. on 2-6-1796].
   Th. Français (de la rue Richelieu) (de la République) (11); **Total: 11.**

_____. *Quintius Cincinnatus* [*Tragédie* in 3 acts, Prem. on 31-12-1794, Pub. in 1794].
   Th. Français (de la rue Richelieu) (de la République) (5); **Total: 5.**
                               Total Performances, Arnault, Antoine-V.: 119

Arnould, Jean-F. Mussot, dit. *Bascule, La* [*Pièce* in 1 act, Prem. on 12-2-1791, Pub. in 1791].
   Th. de l'Ambigu Comique (138); Th. du Lycée des Arts (28); Th. du Vaudeville (1); **Total: 167.**

_____. *Braconnier anglais, Le* [*Pantomime* in 2 acts, Prem. on 6-10-1773, Pub. in 1773].
   Th. de l'Ambigu Comique (31); **Total: 31.**

_____. *Dénicheur de merles, Le* [*Pantomime* in 1 act, Prem. in 1770, Pub. in 1770].
   Th. de l'Ambigu Comique (18); **Total: 18.**

_____. *Forêt noire, La, ou Le Fils naturel* [*Pantomime* in 3 acts, Prem. on 12-9-1791].
   Th. de l'Ambigu Comique (310); Th. du Palais (Cité)-Variétés (1); **Total: 311.**

_____. *Fourberies de Sganarelle, Les* [*Pièce* in 3 acts, Prem. in 1773].
   n/a (44); **Total: 44.**

_____., Ribié, César. *Hérolhe américaine, L'* [*Pantomime* in 3 acts, Prem. on 16-3-1786, Pub. in 1786].
   Th. de l'Ambigu Comique (140); Th. du Palais (Cité)-Variétés (1); **Total: 141.**

_____. *Homme au masque de fer, L', ou Le Souterrain* [*Pantomime* in 4 acts, Prem. on 7-1-1790, Pub. in 1790].
   Th. de l'Ambigu Comique (145); **Total: 145.**

_____. *Maréchal des logis, Le* [*Pantomime* in 1 act, Prem. on 24-7-1783, Pub. in 1783].
   Th. de l'Ambigu Comique (160); Th. des Grands Danseurs (Gaîté) (1); Th. du Marais (1); **Total: 162.**

_____. *Mort du capitaine Cook à son troisième voyage au nouveau monde* [*Pantomime* in 4 acts, Prem. in 10-1788, Pub. in 1788].
   Th. de l'Ambigu Comique (59); **Total: 59.**

_____. *Pierre de Provence* [*Pantomime* in 4 acts, Prem. in 8-1779, Pub. in 1779].
   Th. de l'Ambigu Comique (87); **Total: 87.**

_____. *Quatre fils Aymon, Les* [*Pantomime* in 3 acts, Prem. in 8-1779, Pub. in 1779].
   n/a (1); Th. de l'Ambigu Comique (58); **Total: 59.**

_____. *Vétéran, Le, ou Le Bûcheron déserteur* [*Pantomime* in 3 acts, Prem. on 27-6-1786, Pub. in 1786].
   Th. des Grands Danseurs (Gaîté) (2); **Total: 2.**

_____. *Villageois clairvoyant, Le* [*Pantomime* in 1 act, Prem. in 1771, Pub. in 1771].
    Th. de l'Ambigu Comique (**18**); **Total: 18.**
            Total Performances, Arnould, Jean-F. Mussot, dit: **1244**

Aubrier, Xavier. *Mariage nocturne, Le, ou Les Deux locataires* [*Comédie* in 3 acts, Prem. on 31-5-1787, Pub. in 1787].
    Th. du Palais Royal (**4**); **Total: 4.**

Aude, Joseph. *Acteur embarrassé, L', ou L'Amour et les arts* [*Comédie* in 3 acts, Prem. on 16-2-1792].
    Th. de la Citoyenne Montansier (**4**); **Total: 4.**

_____., Tissot, Charles-L. *Bruits de paix, Les, ou L'Heureuse espérance* [*Comédie* in 1 act, Prem. on 21-8-1796].
    Th. de la Cité (**11**); **Total: 11.**

_____., Mirabrunet. *Cadet Roussel barbier à la fontaine des innocents* [*Comédie* in 1 act, Prem. on 20-5-1799, Pub. in 1802].
    Th. de la Citoyenne Montansier (**114**); Th. de la Cité (**1**); **Total: 115.**

_____., Flan, Alexandre., Hapdé, Jean-B.-A. *Cadet Roussel misanthrope et Manon repentante* [*Comédie* in 1 act, Prem. on 23-4-1799, Pub. in 1799].
    Th. de la Citoyenne Montansier (**48**); **Total: 48.**

_____., Tissot, Charles-L. *Cadet Roussel ou Le Café des aveugles* [*Pièce* in 2 acts, Prem. on 13-2-1793, Pub. in 1793].
    Maison Egalité (**12**); Th. du Palais (Cité)-Variétés (**57**); **Total: 69.**

_____. *Ecole tragique, L', ou Cadet Roussel maître de déclamation* [*Comédie* in 1 act, Prem. on 27-8-1799, Pub. in 1819].
    Th. de la Citoyenne Montansier (**41**); **Total: 41.**

_____. *Gertrude ou Le Suicide du 28 décembre* [*Drame* in 2 acts, Prem. on 25-1-1792].
    Th. de la Citoyenne Montansier (**11**); **Total: 11.**

_____. *Journaliste des ombres, Le, ou Momus aux Champs-Elysées* [*Héroique* in 1 act, Prem. on 14-7-1790].
    Th. de la Nation (Comédie Française) (**6**); **Total: 6.**

_____. *Paix, La* [*Vaudeville* in 2 acts, Prem. on 3-11-1797, Pub. in 1797].
    Th. des Jeunes Artistes (**6**); **Total: 6.**

_____. *Relâche au petit théâtre de Cadet Roussel ou Le Déluge universel* [Prem. on 4-2-1798].
    Th. de la Cité (**6**); **Total: 6.**
            Total Performances, Aude, Joseph: **317**

Audinot, Nicolas-M. *Bons et des méchants, Des, ou Philémon et Baucis* [*Pantomime* in 2 acts, Prem. on 1-1-1783, Pub. in 1783].
    Th. de l'Ambigu Comique (**40**); **Total: 40.**

_____. *Déguisements, Les* [*Comédie* in 1 act, Pub. in 1784].
    Th. de l'Ambigu Comique (**37**); **Total: 37.**

_____., Arnould, Jean-F. Mussot, dit. *Dorothée* [*Pantomime* in 3 acts, Prem. on 13-2-1782, Pub. in 1782].
    Th. de l'Ambigu Comique (**75**); **Total: 75.**

_____. *Hercule et Omphale* [*Pantomime* in 3 acts, Prem. on 9-10-1790, Pub. in 1790].
    Th. de l'Ambigu Comique (**36**); **Total: 36.**

_____. *Musicomanie, La* [*Comédie* in 1 act, Prem. on 19-12-1778, Pub. in 1779].
Th. de l'Ambigu Comique (**81**); **Total: 81.**

_____., Arnould, Jean-F. Mussot, dit. *Portefeuille, Le, ou La Fille comme il y en a peu* [*Comédie* in 1 act, Prem. on 25-5-1785, Pub. in 1785].
Th. de l'Ambigu Comique (**56**); **Total: 56.**

_____., Arnould, Jean-F. Mussot, dit. *Preux chevaliers, Les* [*Pantomime*, Prem. on 13-2-1782, Pub. in 1782].
Th. de l'Ambigu Comique (**46**); **Total: 46.**

_____., Arnould, Jean-F. Mussot, dit. *Prince noir et blanc, Le* [*Pantomime* in 2 acts, Prem. on 11-12-1780, Pub. in 1780].
Th. de l'Ambigu Comique (**40**); **Total: 40.**

_____., Quêtant, François-A., Gossec, François-J. (comp). *Tonnelier, Le* [*Opéra-Comique* in 1 act, Prem. on 16-3-1765, Pub. in 1765].
n/a (**1**); Th. de la Citoyenne Montansier (**12**); Th. de la Cité (**2**); Th. de la Rue Martin (**3**); Th. des Grands Danseurs (Gaîté) (**2**); Th. des Italiens (Opéra-Comique) (**36**); Th. des Variétés Amusantes, Comiques et Lyriques (**1**); Th. Français, Comique et Lyrique (**1**); **Total: 58.**

Total Performances, Audinot, Nicolas-M.: **469**

Audriette. *Matinée du comédien, La* [*Comédie* in 1 act, Prem. on 14-9-1784, Pub. in 1785].
Th. de l'Ambigu Comique (**13**); **Total: 13.**

Aumale de Corsenville., Beck, Franz (comp). *Pandore* [*Mélodrame* in 1 act, Prem. on 2-7-1789, Pub. in 1789].
Th. du Feydeau (de Monsieur) (**16**); **Total: 16.**

_____. *Retour de Camille à Rome* [*Comédie* in 1 act, Prem. on 2-8-1789].
Th. du Feydeau (de Monsieur) (**9**); **Total: 9.**

Total Performances, Aumale de Corsenville: **25**

Aunay, Hector D'. *Blonde et la brune, La* [*Comédie* in 1 act, Prem. on 30-7-1798, Pub. in 1803].
Th. des Jeunes Artistes (**2**); Th. du Marais (**1**); **Total: 3.**

Avisse, Etienne-F., Grandval, Nicolas-R. de (comp). *Divorce, Le, ou Les époux mécontents* [*Comédie* in 3 acts, Prem. on 29-4-1730, Pub. in 1730].
Th. de la Citoyenne Montansier (**38**); **Total: 38.**

Avisse, J.-B. *Ruse d'aveugle, La* [*Comédie* in 1 act, Prem. on 22-12-1796, Pub. in 1797].
Th. de la Bienfaisance (**7**); **Total: 7.**

Balisson de Rougemont, Michel-N. *Deux soeurs, Les* [*Comédie* in 1 act, Prem. on 26-12-1796].
n/a (**1**); Th. de l'Emulation (Gaîté) (**2**); Th. de la Nation (Comédie Française) (**1**); Th. des Délassements Comiques (**3**); **Total: 7.**

Barban, C. *Ridicules du jour, Les, ou Les Deux parisiens en province* [*Comédie* in 5 acts].
Th. du Palais (Cité)-Variétés (**3**); **Total: 3.**

Barbier, Nicolas. *Heureux naufrage, L'* [*Comédie* in 3 acts, Prem. on 18-8-1710, Pub. in 1710].
Cirque National (**1**); **Total: 1.**

Baron, Michel Boyron, dit. *Adelphes, Les, ou L'Ecole des pères* [*Comédie* in 5 acts, Prem. on 3-1-1705, Pub. in 1736].
Th. du Feydeau (de Monsieur) (**13**); **Total: 13.**

_____. *Coquette et la fausse prude, La* [*Comédie* in 5 acts, Prem. on 27-5-1793, Pub. in 1687].

Th. de la Nation (Comédie Française) (**3**); Th. Français (de la rue Richelieu) (de la République) (**2**); **Total: 5.**

_____. *Homme à bonnes fortunes, L'* [*Comédie* in 5 acts, Pub. in 1686].

Th. de la Citoyenne Montansier (**3**); Th. de la Nation (Comédie Française) (**11**); Th. du Feydeau (de Monsieur) (**13**); Th. Français (de la rue Richelieu) (de la République) (**2**); **Total: 29.**

Total Performances, Baron, Michel Boyron, dit: **47**

Barré, Pierre-Y., Radet, Jean-B., Desfontaines, François-G. Fouques, dit. *Abuzar ou La Famille extravagante* [*Parodie* in 1 act, Prem. on 15-5-1795, Pub. in 1795].

Th. du Vaudeville (**65**); **Total: 65.**

_____. *Amours d'été, Les* [*Divertissement/parade* in 1 act, Prem. on 20-9-1781, Pub. in 1781].

Th. des Italiens (Opéra-Comique) (**9**); Th. du Vaudeville (**44**); **Total: 53.**

_____., Piis, Chevalier P.-A.-A. de. *Aristote amoureux ou Le Philosophe bridé* [*Opéra-Comique* in 1 act, Prem. on 11-8-1780, Pub. in 1780].

Th. des Italiens (Opéra-Comique) (**3**); Th. du Vaudeville (**12**); **Total: 15.**

_____., Radet, Jean-B., Desfontaines, François-G. Fouques, dit. *Arlequin afficheur* [*Comédie* in 1 act, Prem. on 9-4-1792, Pub. in 1792].

Th. du Marais (**1**); Th. du Vaudeville (**180**); **Total: 181.**

_____., Radet, Jean-B., Desfontaines, François-G. Fouques, dit. *Arlequin cruello* [*Pantomime* in 2 acts, Prem. on 13-12-1792, Pub. in 1792].

Th. du Vaudeville (**74**); **Total: 74.**

_____., Radet, Jean-B. *Candide marié ou Il faut cultiver son jardin* [*Comédie* in 2 acts, Prem. on 20-7-1788, Pub. in 1788].

Th. des Italiens (Opéra-Comique) (**10**); **Total: 10.**

_____., Radet, Jean-B., Gouffé, Armand Alexandre Duval., Desfontaines, François-G. Fouques, dit. *Cassandre Agamemnon et Colombine Cassandre* [*Parodie* in 1 act, Prem. on 20-4-1798, Pub. in 1804].

Th. de la Citoyenne Montansier (**2**); **Total: 2.**

_____., Piis, Chevalier P.-A.-A. de. *Cassandre oculiste ou L'Oculiste dupe de son art* [*Comédie* in 1 act, Prem. on 30-5-1780, Pub. in 1780].

Th. des Italiens (Opéra-Comique) (**3**); Th. du Vaudeville (**42**); **Total: 45.**

_____., Radet, Jean-B., Desfontaines, François-G. Fouques, dit. *Chaste Suzanne, La* [*Comédie* in 2 acts, Prem. on 5-1-1793, Pub. in 1793].

Th. du Palais (Cité)-Variétés (**1**); Th. du Vaudeville (**61**); **Total: 62.**

_____., Radet, Jean-B., Desfontaines, François-G. Fouques, dit. *Colombine mannequin* [*Comédie* in 1 act, Prem. on 15-2-1793, Pub. in 1793].

Th. des Variétés Amusantes, Comiques et Lyriques (**1**); Th. du Vaudeville (**148**); **Total: 149.**

_____., Ourry, E.-T.-Maurice. *Danse interrompue, La* [*Vaudeville* in 1 act, Prem. on 4-9-1795, Pub. in 1795].

Th. du Marais (**2**); Th. du Vaudeville (**122**); Th. Français (de la rue Richelieu) (de la République) (**1**); **Total: 125.**

_____., Radet, Jean-B. *Docteurs modernes, Les* [*Comédie* in 1 act, Prem. on 16-11-1784, Pub. in 1784].

Th. des Italiens (Opéra-Comique) (**1**); **Total: 1.**

_____., Piis, Chevalier P.-A.-A. de. *Etrennes de mercure, Les, ou Le Bonnet magique* [*Opéra-Comique* in 3 acts, Prem. on 1-1-1781, Pub. in 1781].
 Th. du Vaudeville (4); **Total: 4.**

_____., Radet, Jean-B., Piccinni, Luigi (comp). *Fat en bonne fortune, Le* [*Opéra-Bouffe* in 2 acts, Prem. on 30-4-1787].
 Th. des Beaujolais (50); Th. du Lycée au Palais Egalité (1); Th. du Lycée des Arts (14); **Total: 65.**

_____., Radet, Jean-B., Desfontaines, François-G. Fouques, dit. *Favart aux Champs-Elysées ou L'Apothéose* [*Vaudeville* in 1 act, Prem. on 26-6-1793, Pub. in 1793].
 Th. du Vaudeville (36); **Total: 36.**

_____., Léger, François-P.-A., Lesouppey de la Rosière, J.-R. dit R. *Heureuse décade, L'* [*Divertissement/parade* in 1 act, Prem. on 26-10-1793, Pub. in 1793].
 Th. de l'Ambigu Comique (42); Th. de la Montagne (19); Th. de la Rue Martin (4); Th. des Délassements Comiques (3); Th. des Variétés Amusantes, Comiques et Lyriques (3); Th. du Feydeau (de Monsieur) (3); Th. du Vaudeville (44); Th. National (de la rue Richelieu) (4); **Total: 122.**

_____., Piis, Chevalier P.-A.-A. de., Desfontaines, François-G. Fouques, dit., Radet, Jean-B. *Hommage du petit Vaudeville au grand Racine, L'* [*Vaudeville* in 1 act, Prem. on 21-5-1798, Pub. in 1798].
 Th. du Vaudeville (28); **Total: 28.**

_____., Radet, Jean-B., Lesouppey de la Rosière, J.-R. dit R. *Léandre candide* [*Comédie* in 2 acts, Prem. on 27-7-1784, Pub. in 1784].
 Th. de la Nation (Comédie Française) (1); Th. des Italiens (Opéra-Comique) (7); **Total: 8.**

_____., Piis, Chevalier P.-A.-A. de., Desfontaines, François-G. Fouques, dit., Radet, Jean-B. *Mariage de Scarron, Le* [*Comédie* in 1 act, Prem. on 8-5-1797, Pub. in 1797].
 Th. du Marais (1); Th. du Vaudeville (87); **Total: 88.**

_____., Piis, Chevalier P.-A.-A. de. *Mariage du vaudeville et de la morale, Le* [*Comédie* in 1 act, Prem. on 16-1-1796, Pub. in 1794].
 Th. du Vaudeville (22); **Total: 22.**

_____., Piis, Chevalier P.-A.-A. de. *Matinée et la veillée villageoises, La, ou Le Sabot perdu* [*Divertissement/parade* in 2 acts, Prem. on 27-3-1781, Pub. in 1781].
 Th. des Italiens (Opéra-Comique) (14); Th. du Vaudeville (53); **Total: 67.**

_____., Radet, Jean-B., Desfontaines, François-G. Fouques, dit. *Monet, directeur de l'Opéra comique* [*Comédie* in 1 act, Prem. on 22-7-1799, Pub. in 1802].
 Th. du Vaudeville (23); **Total: 23.**

_____., Bourgeuil. *Mur mitoyen, Le, ou Le Divorce manqué* [*Comédie* in 1 act, Prem. on 21-2-1795, Pub. in 1802].
 Th. du Vaudeville (105); **Total: 105.**

_____., Radet, Jean-B. *Négresse, La* [*Comédie* in 1 act, Prem. on 15-7-1787, Pub. in 1787].
 Th. des Italiens (Opéra-Comique) (4); Th. du Vaudeville (6); **Total: 10.**

_____., Piis, Chevalier P.-A.-A. de. *Oiseau perdu et retrouvé, L'* [*Opéra-Comique* in 1 act, Prem. on 5-11-1782, Pub. in 1782].
Th. du Vaudeville (7); **Total: 7.**

_____., Desprez, Jean-B.-D., Desfontaines, François-G. Fouques, dit., Radet, Jean-B. *Pari, Le* [*Divertissement/parade* in 1 act, Prem. on 28-10-1797, Pub. in 1797].
Th. des Italiens (Opéra-Comique) (3); Th. du Vaudeville (33); Th. Patriotique et de Momus (8); **Total: 44.**

_____., Piis, Chevalier P.-A.-A. de. *Printemps, Le* [*Divertissement/parade* in 1 act, Prem. on 19-5-1781, Pub. in 1781].
Th. des Enfans Comiques (2); Th. du Vaudeville (14); **Total: 16.**

_____., Piis, Chevalier P.-A.-A. de., Desfontaines, François-G. Fouques, dit., Radet, Jean-B. *Projet manqué, Le, ou Arlequin taquin* [*Parodie* in 1 act, Prem. on 18-5-1792].
Th. des Grands Danseurs (Gaîté) (1); Th. du Vaudeville (34); **Total: 35.**

_____., Piis, Chevalier P.-A.-A. de. *Quatre coins, Les* [*Opéra-Comique* in 1 act, Prem. on 31-10-1783, Pub. in 1783].
Th. du Vaudeville (27); **Total: 27.**

_____., Piis, Chevalier P.-A.-A. de. *Santeuil et Dominique* [*Anecdotique* in 3 acts, Prem. on 11-11-1796, Pub. in 1797].
Th. des Jeunes Artistes (1); Th. du Marais (1); Th. du Vaudeville (84); **Total: 86.**

_____., Piis, Chevalier P.-A.-A. de. *Vendangeurs, Les, ou Les Deux baillis* [*Divertissement/parade* in 1 act, Prem. on 7-11-1780, Pub. in 1780].
Th. de l'Emulation (Gaîté) (6); Th. des Grands Danseurs (Gaîté) (8); Th. des Italiens (Opéra-Comique) (10); Th. du Vaudeville (56); **Total: 80.**

_____., Piis, Chevalier P.-A.-A. de. *Voyages de Rosine, Les* [*Opéra-Comique* in 2 acts, Prem. on 20-5-1783, Pub. in 1783].
Th. du Vaudeville (7); **Total: 7.**

Total Performances, Barré, Pierre-Y.: **1662**

Barthe, Nicolas-T. *Fausses infidélités, Les* [*Comédie* in 1 act, Prem. on 25-1-1768, Pub. in 1768].
Th. de l'Ambigu Comique (1); Th. de l'Emulation (Gaîté) (12); Th. de l'Estrapade au Panthéon (4); Th. de l'Odéon (4); Th. de la Citoyenne Montansier (4); Th. de la Montagne (1); Th. de la Nation (Comédie Française) (9); Th. de la Rue Martin (2); Th. de Molière (8); Th. des Beaujolais (1); Th. des Délassements Comiques (6); Th. des Grands Danseurs (Gaîté) (14); Th. des Jeunes Artistes (1); Th. des Variétés Amusantes, Comiques et Lyriques (14); Th. des Victoires (1); Th. des Victoires Nationales (2); Th. du Feydeau (de Monsieur) (1); Th. du Lycée des Arts (7); Th. du Lycée Dramatique (8); Th. du Marais (17); Th. du Vaudeville (4); Th. Français (de la rue Richelieu) (de la République) (24); Th. Français, Comique et Lyrique (4); Th. Lyrique des Amis de la Patrie (7); Th. National (de la rue Richelieu) (4); Th. Patriotique et de Momus (11); **Total: 171.**

_____. *Mère jalouse, La* [*Comédie* in 3 acts, Prem. on 23-12-1771, Pub. in 1772].
Th. de la Citoyenne Montansier (4); Th. du Lycée Dramatique (7); Th. du Marais (2); **Total: 13.**

Total Performances, Barthe, Nicolas-T.: **184**

Bastide, Jean-F. de. *Jeune homme, Le* [*Comédie* in 5 acts, Prem. in 1764, Pub. in 1766].
Th. de la Citoyenne Montansier (2); **Total: 2.**

_____. *Soldat par amour, Le* [*Opéra-Comique* in 2 acts, Prem. on 4-11-1766].
Th. des Italiens (Opéra-Comique) (1); **Total: 1.**
                                        Total Performances, Bastide, Jean-F. de: **3**
Baurans, Pierre., Pergolesi, Giovanni-B. et Auletta, Pietro (comp).
Maître de musique, Le [*Pasticcio* in 2 acts, Prem. on 28-5-1755, Pub. in
1755].
Th. Lyrique des Amis de la Patrie (18); **Total: 18.**
_____., Pergolesi, Giovanni-B. (comp). *Servante maîtresse, La*
[*Comédie* in 2 acts, Prem. on 14-8-1754, Pub. in 1754].
Cirque National (1); Maison Egalité (2); n/a (5); Th. de l'Ambigu Comique
(49); Th. de l'Estrapade au Panthéon (1); Th. de l'Odéon (1); Th. de la Ci-
toyenne Montansier (49); Th. de la Cité (1); Th. de la Concorde (1); Th. de
la Liberté (3); Th. de la Montagne (3); Th. de Molière (11); Th. des Beau-
jolais (3); Th. des Délassements Comiques (6); Th. des Grands Danseurs
(Gaîté) (1); Th. des Italiens (Opéra-Comique) (8); Th. des Jeunes Artistes
(76); Th. des Variétés Amusantes (Lazzari) (14); Th. des Variétés
Amusantes, Comiques et Lyriques (18); Th. du Lycée au Palais Egalité (1);
Th. du Lycée des Arts (3); Th. du Lycée Dramatique (7); Th. du Marais
(4); Th. du Vaudeville (3); Th. Français (de la rue Richelieu) (de la
République) (1); Th. Français, Comique et Lyrique (23); Th. Lyrique des
Amis de la Patrie (17); Th. Lyrique du Foire St. Germain (5); Th. National
(de la rue Richelieu) (3); Th. Patriotique et de Momus (14); Veillée de
Thalie (1); **Total: 335.**
                                        Total Performances, Baurans, Pierre: **353**
Beauchamps, Pierre-F.-G. de. *Amants réunis, Les* [*Comédie* in 3 acts, Prem.
on 26-11-1727, Pub. in 1728].
Th. de la Cité (7); Th. des Beaujolais (1); Th. des Grands Danseurs (Gaîté)
(4); Th. des Jeunes Artistes (9); **Total: 21.**
_____. *Fausse inconstance, La* [*Comédie* in 3 acts, Prem. on 14-2-1731, Pub. in
1731].
Th. de la Citoyenne Montansier (26); Th. de la Cité (1); **Total: 27.**
_____. *Portrait, Le* [*Comédie* in 1 act, Prem. on 9-1-1727, Pub. in 1728].
Th. des Italiens (Opéra-Comique) (3); **Total: 3.**
                                        Total Performances, Beauchamps, Pierre-F.-G. de: **51**
Beaugeard, Jean-S.-F. *Oncle et le neveu, L'* [*Comédie* in 2 acts, Prem. on
29-1-1789, Pub. in 1789].
Th. de l'Emulation (Gaîté) (13); Th. du Feydeau (de Monsieur) (18); Th.
du Vaudeville (4); **Total: 35.**
Beaumarchais, Pierre-A.C. de. *Autre Tartuffe, L', ou La Mère coupa-
ble* [*Drame* in 5 acts, Prem. on 6-6-1792, Pub. in 1794].
Th. de la Cité (5); Th. du Feydeau (de Monsieur) (30); Th. du Marais (45);
Th. Français (de la rue Richelieu) (de la République) (4); **Total: 84.**
_____. *Barbier de Séville, Le, ou La Précaution inutile* [*Comédie* in 4
acts, Prem. on 23-2-1775, Pub. in 1775].
Th. de l'Emulation (Gaîté) (5); Th. de l'Estrapade au Panthéon (4); Th. de
l'Odéon (17); Th. de la Citoyenne Montansier (32); Th. de la Cité (2); Th.
de la Nation (Comédie Française) (19); Th. de la Rue Martin (16); Th. de
Molière (15); Th. des Délassements Comiques (10); Th. des Grands Danseurs (Gaîté) (8); Th. des Italiens (Opéra-Comique) (18); Th. du Feydeau
(de Monsieur) (81); Th. du Marais (21); Th. du Palais (Cité)-Variétés (15);
Th. du Vaudeville (2); Th. Français (de la rue Richelieu) (de la
République) (40); Th. Lyrique des Amis de la Patrie (1); Th. Patriotique et
de Momus (7); **Total: 313.**

_____. *Deux amis, Les, ou Le Négociant de Lyon* [*Drame* in 5 acts, Prem. on 13-1-1770, Pub. in 1770].

Th. de l'Estrapade au Panthéon (**2**); Th. de l'Odéon (**3**); Th. de la Citoyenne Montansier (**1**); Th. de la Rue Antoine (**1**); Th. de la Rue Martin (**9**); Th. de Molière (**7**); Th. du Marais (**13**); Th. Français (de la rue Richelieu) (de la République) (**6**); Th. Lyrique des Amis de la Patrie (**4**); **Total: 46.**

_____. *Eugénie* [*Drame* in 5 acts, Prem. on 29-1-1767, Pub. in 1767].

n/a (**3**); Th. de l'Emulation (Gaîté) (**21**); Th. de l'Estrapade au Panthéon (**1**); Th. de l'Odéon (**4**); Th. de la Citoyenne Montansier (**9**); Th. de la Nation (Comédie Française) (**8**); Th. de la Rue Martin (**15**); Th. de Molière (**3**); Th. des Victoires (**1**); Th. des Victoires Nationales (**1**); Th. du Feydeau (de Monsieur) (**10**); Th. du Marais (**18**); Th. Français (de la rue Richelieu) (de la République) (**27**); Th. Lyrique des Amis de la Patrie (**4**); **Total: 125.**

_____. *Folle journée, La, ou Le Mariage de Figaro* [*Comédie* in 5 acts, Prem. on 27-4-1784, Pub. in 1785].

Académie de la Musique (Opéra) (**7**); n/a (**1**); Th. de l'Odéon (**9**); Th. de la Citoyenne Montansier (**30**); Th. de la Nation (Comédie Française) (**5**); Th. de la Rue Martin (**24**); Th. de Molière (**12**); Th. des Délassements Comiques (**6**); Th. du Feydeau (de Monsieur) (**19**); Th. du Marais (**29**); Th. du Palais (Cité)-Variétés (**1**); Th. Français (de la rue Richelieu) (de la République) (**7**); **Total: 150.**

_____. *Jean bête à la foire ou Les Deux niais* [*Pantomime* in 1 act, Prem. on 23-6-1790].

Th. des Grands Danseurs (Gaîté) (**29**); **Total: 29.**

_____., Salieri, Antonio (comp). *Tarare* [*Opéra* in 5 acts, Prem. on 8-6-1787, Pub. in 1787].

Académie de la Musique (Opéra) (**64**); **Total: 64.**

Total Performances, Beaumarchais, Pierre-A.C. de: **811**

Beaunoir, Alexandre-L.-B. Robineau dit. *Amis du jour, Les* [*Comédie* in 1 act, Prem. on 1-9-1786, Pub. in 1786].

Th. des Italiens (Opéra-Comique) (**19**); Th. du Marais (**1**); **Total: 20.**

_____. *Amour est de tout âge, L', ou Le Pédant amoureux* [*Comédie* in 1 act, Prem. in 1773, Pub. in 1772].

Th. des Grands Danseurs (Gaîté) (**106**); Th. des Ombres Chinoises (**1**); **Total: 107.**

_____. *Amour quêteur, L'* [*Comédie* in 2 acts, Prem. in 9-1777, Pub. in 1785].

Th. de l'Emulation (Gaîté) (**7**); Th. des Grands Danseurs (Gaîté) (**11**); **Total: 18.**

_____. *Amours de Colombine, Les* [*Pantomime* in 1 act, Prem. in 1771, Pub. in 1771].

Th. des Grands Danseurs (Gaîté) (**1**); **Total: 1.**

_____. *Amours de l'étalier boucher, Les* [*Comédie* in 1 act, Prem. on 25-11-1782].

Th. des Grands Danseurs (Gaîté) (**17**); **Total: 17.**

_____. *Barbier de village, Le, ou L'Officieux désobligeant* [*Comédie* in 3 acts, Prem. on 15-2-1780, Pub. in 1776].

Th. des Grands Danseurs (Gaîté) (**60**); **Total: 60.**

_____. *Batelier de Catalogne, Le* [*Comédie* in 3 acts].

Th. du Feydeau (de Monsieur) (**13**); **Total: 13.**

_____. *Brave poltron, Le, ou Trois contre un* [*Pantomime* in 3 acts, Prem. on 17-1-1778].

Th. des Grands Danseurs (Gaîté) (**1**); **Total: 1.**

_____., Renout, Jean-J.-C. *Cacophonie, La* [*Comédie* in 1 act, Prem. on 31-7-1779, Pub. in 1782].
> Th. de l'Emulation (Gaîté) (**17**); Th. de la Cité (**4**); Th. des Grands Danseurs (Gaîté) (**31**); Th. Lyrique des Amis de la Patrie (**2**); **Total: 54.**

_____. *Ce qui vient de la flûte s'en retourne au tambour* [*Opéra-Comique* in 2 acts, Prem. in 1774, Pub. in 1774].
> Th. des Grands Danseurs (Gaîté) (**40**); **Total: 40.**

_____. *Ceinture merveilleuse, La* [*Comédie* in 1 act, Prem. in 1772, Pub. in 1772].
> Th. des Grands Danseurs (Gaîté) (**9**); **Total: 9.**

_____. *Colinette ou La Vigne d'amour* [*Pastoral* in 1 act, Prem. on 4-4-1780, Pub. in 1783].
> Th. de l'Emulation (Gaîté) (**6**); Th. des Grands Danseurs (Gaîté) (**15**); **Total: 21.**

_____. *Commissionnaire et le jockey, Le* [*Comédie* in 2 acts, Prem. on 4-10-1791].
> Th. du Marais (**11**); **Total: 11.**

_____. *Comtoise à Paris, La, ou Le Vieillard dupe* [*Farce* in 1 act, Prem. on 18-6-1783, Pub. in 1776].
> Th. des Beaujolais (**1**); Th. des Grands Danseurs (Gaîté) (**2**); **Total: 3.**

_____. *Contentement passe richesse* [*Pantomime* in 1 act, Prem. in 1776, Pub. in 1776].
> Th. de l'Emulation (Gaîté) (**1**); Th. de Molière (**1**); Th. des Grands Danseurs (Gaîté) (**126**); **Total: 128.**

_____. *Corne de vérité, La, ou L'Honnête homme dupe de sa bonne foi* [*Comédie* in 2 acts, Prem. in 1776, Pub. in 1776].
> Th. des Grands Danseurs (Gaîté) (**49**); **Total: 49.**

_____. *Danger des liaisons, Le* [*Comédie* in 1 act, Prem. on 9-12-1783, Pub. in 1786].
> Maison Egalité (**2**); Th. de l'Emulation (Gaîté) (**22**); Th. de la Cité (**40**); Th. de Molière (**2**); Th. des Victoires (**4**); Th. des Victoires Nationales (**6**); Th. du Palais (Cité)-Variétés (**29**); Th. du Palais Royal (**25**); Th. Lyrique des Amis de la Patrie (**2**); **Total: 132.**

_____. *Danse des sans-culottes républicains, La* [*Tableau-Patriotique*].
> Th. des Grands Danseurs (Gaîté) (**4**); **Total: 4.**

_____. *Déménagement du peintre, Le* [*Comédie* in 1 act, Pub. in 1770].
> Th. des Grands Danseurs (Gaîté) (**44**); **Total: 44.**

_____. *Diable boiteux, Le* [*Pantomime* in 3 acts, Prem. on 2-6-1781].
> Th. des Grands Danseurs (Gaîté) (**87**); **Total: 87.**

_____. *Ecouteur aux portes, L'* [*Comédie* in 1 act, Prem. on 1-5-1784, Pub. in 1784].
> Th. du Palais Royal (**9**); **Total: 9.**

_____. *Epoux à la mode, Les* [*Comédie*, Pub. in 1771].
> Th. des Grands Danseurs (Gaîté) (**1**); **Total: 1.**

_____. *Eustache pointu chez lui ou Qui a bu boira* [*Comédie* in 1 act, Prem. on 21-7-1784, Pub. in 1785].
> Th. de la Citoyenne Montansier (**39**); **Total: 39.**

_____. *Famille des pointus, La* [*Pantomime*].
> Th. de l'Emulation (Gaîté) (**14**); **Total: 14.**

_____. *Fanfan et Colas ou Les Frères de lait* [*Comédie* in 1 act, Prem. on 7-9-1784, Pub. in 1784].
n/a (**4**); Th. de l'Estrapade au Panthéon (**1**); Th. de la Rue Martin (**1**); Th. des Italiens (Opéra-Comique) (**60**); Th. du Mareux (**1**); **Total: 67.**

_____. *Frères amis, Les* [*Comédie* in 2 acts, Prem. on 21-5-1788, Pub. in 1788].
Th. du Palais Royal (**1**); **Total: 1.**

_____. *Glicère et Aléxis* [*Pantomime* in 1 act, Prem. on 7-1-1781, Pub. in 1781].
Th. des Grands Danseurs (Gaîté) (**9**); **Total: 9.**

_____. *Gribouille* [Prem. in 1777].
Th. de l'Emulation (Gaîté) (**6**); **Total: 6.**

_____. *Habit fait l'homme, L'* [*Comédie* in 1 act, Prem. on 23-8-1783, Pub. in 1772].
Th. des Grands Danseurs (Gaîté) (**41**); **Total: 41.**

_____. *Habit ne fait pas l'homme, L', ou La Valise perdue et retrouvée* [*Pièce* in 3 acts, Prem. in 1772, Pub. in 1772].
Th. de l'Emulation (Gaîté) (**1**); Th. des Grands Danseurs (Gaîté) (**60**); **Total: 61.**

_____. *Homme et la femme comme il n'y en a point, L', ou Le Double travestissement* [*Comédie* in 2 acts, Prem. on 29-5-1784, Pub. in 1784].
Th. des Grands Danseurs (Gaîté) (**12**); **Total: 12.**

_____. *Jeannette ou Les Battus ne payent pas l'amende* [*Comédie* in 1 act, Prem. in 5-1780, Pub. in 1782].
Th. de la Citoyenne Montansier (**2**); Th. des Grands Danseurs (Gaîté) (**93**); **Total: 95.**

_____. *Jérôme pointu* [*Comédie* in 1 act, Prem. on 23-6-1781, Pub. in 1781].
Th. de l'Emulation (Gaîté) (**1**); Th. de l'Estrapade au Panthéon (**1**); Th. de la Citoyenne Montansier (**76**); Th. de Molière (**29**); Th. du Marais (**3**); Th. du Palais Royal (**2**); Th. Lyrique des Amis de la Patrie (**1**); **Total: 113.**

_____. *Madame Miroton* [Prem. in 1771].
Th. de l'Emulation (Gaîté) (**7**); **Total: 7.**

_____. *Madame Tintamarre* [*Farce* in 2 acts, Prem. in 1772, Pub. in 1772].
Th. des Grands Danseurs (Gaîté) (**20**); Th. des Troubadours (**1**); **Total: 21.**

_____. *Madelon Friquet et Monsieur Vacarmini* [*Pièce* in 1 act, Pub. in 1776].
Th. de la Citoyenne Montansier (**1**); Th. des Grands Danseurs (Gaîté) (**54**); **Total: 55.**

_____. *Manon Ferlue au cabaret de l'écu* [*Pièce* in 2 acts, Prem. in 1773, Pub. in 1773].
Th. des Grands Danseurs (Gaîté) (**4**); **Total: 4.**

_____. *Manteau, Le, ou Les Deux nièces rivales* [*Opéra-Bouffe* in 1 act, Prem. on 2-9-1786, Pub. in 1786].
Th. de la Rue Martin (**1**); Th. des Beaujolais (**7**); **Total: 8.**

_____., Grétry, Lucile (comp). *Mariage d'Antonio, Le* [*Comédie mêlée d'ariettes* in 1 act, Prem. on 29-7-1786, Pub. in 1786].
Th. des Italiens (Opéra-Comique) (**18**); **Total: 18.**

_____. *Ménage du savetier, Le* [Prem. on 9-1-1799].
Th. de la Citoyenne Montansier (**1**); Th. des Grands Danseurs (Gaîté) (**44**); Th. des Ombres Chinoises (**2**); **Total: 47.**

_____. *Mère nitouche, La* [*Pièce* in 1 act, Prem. in 1771, Pub. in 1773].
Th. des Grands Danseurs (Gaîté) (**28**); **Total: 28.**

_____. *Mère ragot, La* [*Pièce* in 1 act, Prem. in 1771, Pub. in 1771].
     Th. des Grands Danseurs (Gaîté) (**22**); **Total: 22**.

_____. *Monnaie ne fait rien en amour* [*Pièce* in 1 act, Prem. in 1770, Pub. in 1776].
     Th. des Grands Danseurs (Gaîté) (**6**); **Total: 6**.

_____. *Mort vivant, Le* [*Pièce* in 2 acts, Prem. on 9-6-1782].
     Th. des Grands Danseurs (Gaîté) (**22**); **Total: 22**.

_____. *Nuit espagnol, La, ou Le Frère jaloux et barbare* [*Comédie* in 3 acts, Prem. in 1771, Pub. in 1773].
     Th. des Grands Danseurs (Gaîté) (**2**); **Total: 2**.

_____. *Qui paye les violons ne danse pas toujours* [*Divertissement/parade* in 2 acts, Prem. in 1773, Pub. in 1773].
     Th. de Molière (**2**); **Total: 2**.

_____. *Rose et le bouton, La, ou Le Temple de l'hymen* [*Pantomime* in 2 acts, Prem. in 1782, Pub. in 1782].
     Th. de l'Ambigu Comique (**1**); Th. de l'Emulation (Gaîté) (**2**); Th. des Grands Danseurs (Gaîté) (**44**); **Total: 47**.

_____. *Rose ou La Suite de Fanfan et Colas* [*Comédie* in 3 acts, Prem. on 13-9-1785, Pub. in 1806].
     Th. de l'Ambigu Comique (**1**); **Total: 1**.

_____. *Sculpteur, Le, ou La Femme comme il y en a peu* [*Comédie* in 2 acts, Prem. on 14-1-1784, Pub. in 1784].
     Maison Egalité (**7**); Th. de l'Ambigu Comique (**6**); Th. de la Citoyenne Montansier (**51**); Th. de la Cité (**13**); Th. de la Montagne (**4**); Th. de Molière (**8**); Th. des Variétés Amusantes, Comiques et Lyriques (**4**); Th. du Palais (Cité)-Variétés (**2**); Th. du Palais Royal (**22**); Th. Lyrique des Amis de la Patrie (**8**); **Total: 125**.

_____. *Souper des dupes, Le* [*Farce* in 1 act, Prem. in 1769, Pub. in 1769].
     Th. des Grands Danseurs (Gaîté) (**32**); **Total: 32**.

_____. *Triste journée, La, ou Le Lendemain de noces* [*Comédie* in 1 act, Prem. on 14-7-1784, Pub. in 1785].
     Th. des Grands Danseurs (Gaîté) (**2**); **Total: 2**.

_____., Pannard, Charles-F. (comp)., Boizard de Ponteau, Claude-F. *Trousseau d'Agnès, Le, ou La Veuve à marier* [*Divertissement/parade* in 1 act, Pub. in 1772].
     Th. des Grands Danseurs (Gaîté) (**15**); **Total: 15**.

_____. *Vendanges de la vigne d'amour, Les* [*Pantomime* in 1 act, Prem. on 4-4-1780].
     Th. des Grands Danseurs (Gaîté) (**19**); **Total: 19**.

_____. *Vénus pèlerine* [*Comédie* in 1 act, Prem. in 11-1777, Pub. in 1782].
     Th. de l'Emulation (Gaîté) (**27**); Th. des Grands Danseurs (Gaîté) (**119**); **Total: 146**.

_____. *Visites du jour de l'an, Les* [*Divertissement/parade* in 1 act, Prem. on 1-1-1776].
     Th. des Grands Danseurs (Gaîté) (**25**); **Total: 25**.

_____. *Zing-zing ou La Relique* [*Divertissement/parade* in 1 act].
     Th. de l'Emulation (Gaîté) (**9**); Th. des Grands Danseurs (Gaîté) (**3**); Th. Lyrique des Amis de la Patrie (**9**); **Total: 21**.
     Total Performances, Beaunoir, Alexandre-L.-B. Robineau, dit: **1968**

Beaupré-Larigaudière. *Annette et Jacques ou Les Semestriers alsaciens* [*Ballet* in 1 act, Pub. in 1792].
Th. du Palais (Cité)-Variétés (**3**); **Total: 3**.

_____. *Fête d'amour* [N/A].
Th. du Lycée des Arts (**2**); **Total: 2**.

_____. *Sabotiers, Les* [*Ballet*, Prem. on 26-10-1791, Pub. in 1796].
Th. des Grands Danseurs (Gaîté) (**143**); Th. des Variétés Amusantes, Comiques et Lyriques (**1**); **Total: 144**.

_____. *Sabotiers, Les* [*Pantomime*, Pub. in 1792].
Cirque National (**10**); Th. du Palais (Cité)-Variétés (**18**); **Total: 28**.
Total Performances, Beaupré-Larigaudière: **177**

Beffroy de Reigny, Louis-A. *Allons, ça va ou Les Quakers en France* [*Tableau-Patriotique* in 1 act, Prem. on 28-10-1793, Pub. in 1793].
Th. du Feydeau (de Monsieur) (**22**); **Total: 22**.

_____. *Club des bonnes gens, Le, ou Le Curé français* [*Vaudeville* in 2 acts, Prem. on 24-9-1791, Pub. in 1797].
Th. du Feydeau (de Monsieur) (**112**); Th. du Marais (**2**); **Total: 114**.

_____. *Confédération du Parnasse, La* [In 1 act, Prem. on 11-7-1790].
Th. des Beaujolais (**28**); **Total: 28**.

_____. *Cousin Jacques hors du salon* [*Folie*, Pub. in 1787].
Th. de l'Ambigu Comique (**1**); **Total: 1**.

_____. *Deux charbonniers ou Les Contrastes* [*Comédie* in 2 acts, Prem. on 24-8-1799, Pub. in 1800].
Th. de la Citoyenne Montansier (**31**); **Total: 31**.

_____. *Emilie ou Les Caprices* [*Comédie* in 3 acts, Prem. on 9-7-1799].
Th. de l'Ambigu Comique (**1**); Th. des Jeunes Artistes (**29**); Th. du Marais (**1**); **Total: 31**.

_____., Gaveaux, Pierre et Martini, J.P.E. (comp). *Histoire universelle, L'* [*Comédie* in 2 acts, Prem. on 16-12-1790, Pub. in 1791].
Th. du Feydeau (de Monsieur) (**78**); **Total: 78**.

_____. *Jean Baptiste* [*Opéra-Comique* in 1 act, Prem. on 1-6-1798, Pub. in 1798].
Th. de l'Odéon (**1**); Th. du Feydeau (de Monsieur) (**29**); **Total: 30**.

_____. *Magdelon* [*Comédie* in 1 act, Prem. on 4-6-1799, Pub. in 1800].
Th. de la Citoyenne Montansier (**40**); **Total: 40**.

_____., Leblanc (comp). *Nicodème dans la lune ou La Révolution pacifique* [*Folie* in 3 acts, Prem. on 7-11-1790, Pub. in 1791].
Th. de la Cité (**20**); Th. Français, Comique et Lyrique (**246**); **Total: 266**.

_____. *Petite Nanette, La* [*Opéra-Comique* in 2 acts, Prem. on 9-12-1796, Pub. in 1796].
Th. du Feydeau (de Monsieur) (**30**); **Total: 30**.

_____. *Retour du champ du mars, Le* [*Fait Historique* in 1 act, Prem. on 25-7-1790].
Th. des Beaujolais (**9**); **Total: 9**.

_____., Lemoyne, Jean-B. (comp). *Toute la Grèce ou Ce que peut la Liberté* [*Tableau-Patriotique* in 1 act, Prem. on 5-1-1794, Pub. in 1794].
Académie de la Musique (Opéra) (**32**); **Total: 32**.

_____. *Turlututu, Empereur de l'île verte* [*Comédie* in 3 acts, Prem. on 3-7-1797, Pub. in 1796].
Th. de la Cité (**13**); **Total: 13**.

_____. *Un rien ou L'Habit des noces* [*Episodique* in 1 act, Prem. on 7-6-1798, Pub. in 1798].
>   Th. de l'Ambigu Comique (**28**); Th. Lyrique des Amis de la Patrie (**1**); **Total: 29.**
>   **Total Performances,** Beffroy de Reigny, Louis-A.: **754**

Belat-Bonneille, J.-B. *Coquette généreuse, La* [*Comédie* in 2 acts, Prem. on 22-5-1797, Pub. in 1793].
>   Th. de l'Emulation (Gaîté) (**4**); Th. Lyrique des Amis de la Patrie (**8**); **Total: 12.**

Bellement, André-P., Jadin, Louis-E. (comp). *Cange ou Le Commissionnaire de Lazare* [*Fait Historique* in 1 act, Prem. on 21-11-1794, Pub. in 1794].
>   Th. Lyrique des Amis de la Patrie (**15**); **Total: 15.**

_____. *Hospitalier, L'* [Pub. in 1794].
>   Th. de l'Emulation (Gaîté) (**3**); Th. des Grands Danseurs (Gaîté) (**16**); **Total: 19.**

_____. *Reprise de Toulon, La, ou Les Patriotes provinciaux* [*Fait Historique* in 2 acts, Prem. on 3-12-1797].
>   Th. des Italiens (Opéra-Comique) (**6**); **Total: 6.**
>   **Total Performances,** Bellement, André-P.: **40**

Belloy, Pierre-L. B. de. *Gabrielle de Vergy* [*Tragédie* in 5 acts, Prem. on 12-7-1777, Pub. in 1770].
>   Th. de l'Odéon (**2**); Th. de la Citoyenne Montansier (**2**); Th. de la Nation (Comédie Française) (**12**); Th. des Variétés Amusantes (Lazzari) (**1**); Th. du Feydeau (de Monsieur) (**1**); Th. du Marais (**5**); Th. Français (de la rue Richelieu) (de la République) (**16**); Th. Lyrique des Amis de la Patrie (**1**); **Total: 40.**

_____. *Gaston et Bayard* [*Tragédie* in 5 acts, Prem. on 24-4-1771, Pub. in 1770].
>   Th. de l'Emulation (Gaîté) (**2**); Th. de l'Odéon (**8**); Th. de la Nation (Comédie Française) (**24**); Th. des Délassements Comiques (**6**); Th. du Lycée Dramatique (**3**); Th. du Marais (**4**); **Total: 47.**

_____. *Pierre le cruel* [*Tragédie* in 5 acts, Pub. in 1772].
>   Th. de la Citoyenne Montansier (**4**); Th. de la Nation (Comédie Française) (**2**); **Total: 6.**

_____. *Siège de Calais, Le* [*Tragédie*, Prem. on 13-2-1765, Pub. in 1765].
>   Th. de la Nation (Comédie Française) (**10**); **Total: 10.**

_____. *Zelmire* [*Tragédie* in 5 acts, Prem. on 6-5-1762, Pub. in 1762].
>   n/a (**7**); Th. de la Citoyenne Montansier (**7**); Th. de la Nation (Comédie Française) (**3**); Th. de Molière (**1**); Th. des Délassements Comiques (**7**); Th. du Lycée Dramatique (**1**); Th. du Marais (**2**); Th. Lyrique des Amis de la Patrie (**2**); **Total: 30.**
>   **Total Performances,** Belloy, Pierre-L.B. de: **133**

Benoist-Lamothe, François-N. *Laurent de Médicis* [*Héroique* in 5 acts, Prem. on 20-1-1799, Pub. in 1799].
>   Th. de l'Odéon (**12**); **Total: 12.**

Bérard, Jean-A. *Verseuil ou L'Heureuse extravagance* [*Comédie* in 3 acts, Prem. on 7-7-1787, Pub. in 1787].
>   Th. de la Cité (**3**); Th. du Palais (Cité)-Variétés (**24**); Th. du Palais Royal (**26**); Th. Français (de la rue Richelieu) (de la République) (**6**); **Total: 59.**

Béraud, Louis-F.-G. *Adonis ou Le Bon nègre* [*Mélodrame* in 4 acts, Pub. in 1798].
>   Th. de l'Ambigu Comique (**6**); **Total: 6.**

_____. *Coraline ou L'Ecole du théâtre* [*Comédie*, Pub. in 1797].
Th. de l'Ambigu Comique (3); **Total: 3.**
Total Performances, Béraud, Louis-F.-G.: **9**

Bernard, Pierre-Joseph., Candeille, Amélie (comp). *Castor et Pollux*
[*Tragédie-lyrique* in 5 acts, Prem. on 24-10-1737, Pub. in 1737].
Académie de la Musique (Opéra) (**134**); Th. du Lycée des Arts (3); Th.
Français (de la rue Richelieu) (de la République) (5); **Total: 142.**
_____. *Cérémonie, La* [*Tragédie* in 5 acts, Prem. on 24-10-1737, Pub. in 1737].
Th. Français (de la rue Richelieu) (de la République) (1); **Total: 1.**
Total Performances, Bernard, Pierre-Joseph: **9**

Bernouilly, L.P. de. *Philosophe soi-disant, Le* [*Comédie* in 3 acts, Pub. in
1785].
Th. du Palais Royal (**10**); **Total: 10.**
_____. *Point d'honneur, Le* [*Comédie* in 5 acts, Prem. on 11-12-1790, Pub. in
1702].
Th. du Palais Royal (**2**); **Total: 2.**
Total Performances, Bernouilly, L.P. de: **12**

Berquin, Arnaud. *Page, Le* [*Drame* in 1 act, Pub. in 1782].
Th. de l'Ambigu Comique (3); **Total: 3.**

Bertati, Giovanni. *Convitato di pietra, Il* [*Opéra* in 4 acts, Prem. on 5-2-1787,
Pub. in 1790].
Th. des Variétés Amusantes, Comiques et Lyriques (9); Th. du Feydeau
(de Monsieur) (2); **Total: 11.**
_____., Anfossi, Pasquale et Cambini, Giovanni-G. (comp). *Geloso in
cimento, Il* [*Dramma Giocoso* in 3 acts, Prem. on 14-5-1790].
Th. du Feydeau (de Monsieur) (7); **Total: 7.**
_____., Bianchi, Francesco (comp). *Villanella rapita, La* [*Opéra* in 3 acts,
Pub. in 1802].
Th. du Feydeau (de Monsieur) (**45**); **Total: 45.**
_____. *Vendemmia, La, ou Les Vendanges* [*Opéra* in 2 acts, Prem. on 12-5-
1778, Pub. in 1791].
Th. du Feydeau (de Monsieur) (11); **Total: 11.**
Total Performances, Bertati, Giovanni: **74**

Berthe, F.-L. *Trois frères, Les* [*Opéra-Comique* in 2 acts, Pub. in 1793].
Th. du Palais (Cité)-Variétés (1); **Total: 1.**

Berthevin, Jules-J., Châteauvieux, Armand-F.-R.-C.-L. *Assemblée
électorale à Cythère, L'* [*Intermède* in 1 act, Prem. on 22-4-1797, Pub. in
1797].
Th. de la Cité (3); **Total: 3.**

Bertin D'Antilly, Auguste-L., Philidor, François-A. Danican et Berton,
Henri-M. (comp). *Bélisaire* [*Opéra* in 3 acts, Pub. in 1796].
Th. des Italiens (Opéra-Comique) (1); **Total: 1.**
_____. *Ecole de l'adolescence, L'* [*Comédie* in 2 acts, Prem. on 30-6-1789,
Pub. in 1789].
Th. des Italiens (Opéra-Comique) (**26**); **Total: 26.**
_____., Kreutzer, Rodolpho (comp). *Encore une victoire ou Les
Déserteurs liègeois et les prisonniers français* [In 1 act, Prem. on 30-
10-1794].
Th. des Italiens (Opéra-Comique) (1); **Total: 1.**

_____., Kreutzer, Rodolpho (comp). *Lendemain de la bataille de Fleurus, Le* [*Impromptu* in 1 act, Prem. on 15-10-1794].
   Maison Egalité (2); **Total: 2.**

_____., Blasius, Mathieu-F. (comp). *Le Pelletier de Saint-Fargeau* [*Trait Historique* in 2 acts, Prem. on 23-2-1793].
   Th. des Italiens (Opéra-Comique) (4); **Total: 4.**

_____., Kreutzer, Rodolpho (comp). *Siège de Lille, Le* [*Fait Historique* in 1 act, Prem. on 14-11-1792, Pub. in 1792].
   Th. du Feydeau (de Monsieur) (45); **Total: 45.**

_____., Chapelle, Pierre-D.-A. (comp). *Vieillesse d'Annette et Lubin, La* [*Comédie* in 1 act, Prem. on 1-8-1789, Pub. in 1790].
   Th. des Italiens (Opéra-Comique) (19); **Total: 19.**
                   Total Performances, Bertin D'Antilly, Auguste-L.: **98**

Berton, Henri-M., Berton, Henri-M. (comp). *Ponce de Léon* [*Opéra-Bouffe* in 3 acts, Prem. on 4-3-1797, Pub. in 1797].
   Th. des Italiens (Opéra-Comique) (33); **Total: 33.**

Biancolelli, Pierre-F., dit Dominique., Renault (comp). *Amours d'Arlequin, Les* [*Comédie* in 1 act, Prem. on 4-11-1704, Pub. in 1704].
   Th. des Grands Danseurs (Gaîté) (7); **Total: 7.**

_____., Romagnesi, Jean-A., Riccoboni, Antoine-F. *Arlequin Hulla* [*Comédie* in 1 act, Prem. on 1-3-1728, Pub. in 1731].
   Th. des Grands Danseurs (Gaîté) (50); Th. du Vaudeville (54); **Total: 104.**

_____., Romagnesi, Jean-A., Riccoboni, Antoine-F. *Arlequin toujours Arlequin* [*Comédie* in 1 act, Prem. on 10-8-1726].
   Th. de l'Ambigu Comique (1); **Total: 1.**

_____., Romagnesi, Jean-A. *Débuts d'Arlequin, Les* [*Comédie* in 1 act, Prem. on 14-7-1729, Pub. in 1729].
   Th. de l'Ambigu Comique (29); **Total: 29.**

_____., Romagnesi, Jean-A., Riccoboni, Antoine-F. *Enfants trouvés, Les, ou Le Sultan poli par l'amour* [*Pantomime* in 1 act, Prem. on 9-2-1732, Pub. in 1732].
   Th. des Grands Danseurs (Gaîté) (1); Th. des Variétés Amusantes, Comiques et Lyriques (4); **Total: 5.**

_____. *Folie raisonnable, La* [*Comédie* in 1 act, Prem. on 9-1-1725].
   Th. du Vaudeville (9); **Total: 9.**

_____., Romagnesi, Jean-A., Riccoboni, Antoine-F. *Mariage d'Arlequin et de Silvia, Le* [*Comédie* in 1 act, Prem. on 18-1-1724, Pub. in 1731].
   Th. des Grands Danseurs (Gaîté) (4); **Total: 4.**

_____. *Méchante femme, La, ou L'Hôtesse* [Prem. on 9-9-1791].
   Th. des Grands Danseurs (Gaîté) (5); **Total: 5.**

_____., Romagnesi, Jean-A. *Paysans de qualité, Les, ou Les Débuts* [*Comédie* in 1 act, Prem. on 14-7-1729, Pub. in 1729].
   Th. de l'Ambigu Comique (2); Th. des Grands Danseurs (Gaîté) (28); **Total: 30.**
                   Total Performances, Biancolelli, Pierre-F.: **194**

Bièvre, François-G.-M. Marquis de. *Séducteur, Le* [*Comédie* in 5 acts, Prem. on 4-11-1783, Pub. in 1783].
   Th. de la Nation (Comédie Française) (7); **Total: 7.**

Bilderbeck, Ludwig B. F. Von. *Amour délicat, L'* [*Drame* in 1 act, Pub. in 1788].
    Th. de l'Ambigu Comique (**1**); Th. du Vaudeville (**1**); Th. Patriotique et de Momus (**6**); **Total: 8.**

Billard-Dumonceau, Edme. *Suborneur, Le* [*Comédie* in 5 acts, Prem. on 5-3-1792, Pub. in 1782].
    Th. des Italiens (Opéra-Comique) (**1**); **Total: 1.**

Billardon de Sauvigny, Louis-E. *Courtisan devenu citoyen, Le* [*Comédie* in 3 acts, Prem. on 21-7-1790].
    Th. du Palais Royal (**7**); **Total: 7.**

_____. *Hirza ou Les Illinois* [*Tragédie* in 5 acts, Prem. on 27-5-1767, Pub. in 1767].
    Th. de la Nation (Comédie Française) (**2**); **Total: 2.**

_____. *Mort de Socrate, La* [*Tragédie* in 3 acts, Prem. in 5-1763, Pub. in 1763].
    Th. de Molière (**3**); Th. des Ombres Chinoises (**2**); Th. des Ombres de J.-J. Rousseau (**16**); **Total: 21.**

_____. *Nègres, Les* [*Comédie* in 1 act].
    Th. de l'Ambigu Comique (**2**); Th. du Palais (Cité)-Variétés (**2**); **Total: 4.**

_____. *Washington ou La Liberté du nouveau monde* [*Tragédie* in 4 acts, Prem. on 13-7-1791, Pub. in 1791].
    Th. de la Nation (Comédie Française) (**2**); **Total: 2.**
    Total Performances, Billardon de Sauvigny, Louis-E.: **36**

Bizet. *Boîtes, Les, ou La Conspiration des mouchoirs* [*Divertissement/parade* in 1 act, Prem. on 5-9-1796, Pub. in 1796].
    Th. de la Cité (**1**); **Total: 1.**

Blanchard, Pierre. *Bons enfants, Les, ou La Cabane dans les bois* [*Vaudeville* in 3 acts, Prem. on 31-12-1798].
    Th. des Jeunes Artistes (**19**); Th. du Marais (**1**); **Total: 20.**

Bodard de Tézay, Nicolas-M.-F. *Arlequin roi dans la lune* [*Comédie* in 3 acts, Prem. on 17-12-1785, Pub. in 1786].
    Th. du Palais Royal (**13**); **Total: 13.**

_____. *Duc de Monmouth, Le* [*Comédie* in 3 acts, Prem. on 4-11-1788, Pub. in 1789].
    Th. du Palais Royal (**31**); **Total: 31.**

_____., Bruni, Antonio-B. (comp). *Spinette et Marini ou La Leçon conjugale* [*Comédie* in 1 act, Prem. on 21-6-1790].
    Th. de la Citoyenne Montansier (**20**); **Total: 20.**
    Total Performances, Bodard de Tézay, Nicolas-M.-F.: **64**

Boindin, Nicolas., Grandval, Nicolas-R. de (comp). *Port de mer, Le* [*Comédie* in 1 act, Prem. on 27-5-1704, Pub. in 1704].
    Th. des Beaujolais (**3**); **Total: 3.**

_____., Grandval, Nicolas-R. de (comp). *Trois Gascons, Les* [*Comédie* in 1 act, Prem. on 4-6-1701, Pub. in 1702].
    Th. Lyrique des Amis de la Patrie (**6**); **Total: 6.**
    Total Performances, Boindin, Nicolas: **9**

Boissel de Monville, Thomas-C.-G., Champein, Stanislas (comp). *Nouveau don Quichotte, Le* [*Opéra* in 2 acts, Prem. on 25-5-1789, Pub. in 1792].
    Ampithéâtre National (**2**); Th. de Molière (**17**); Th. des Italiens (Opéra-Comique) (**21**); Th. du Feydeau (de Monsieur) (**92**); **Total: 132.**

Boissy, Louis de. *Babillard, Le* [*Comédie* in 1 act, Prem. in 6-1725, Pub. in 1725].
> Maison Egalité (1); Th. de l'Ambigu Comique (8); Th. de l'Odéon (2); Th. de la Nation (Comédie Française) (18); Th. de la Rue Martin (2); Th. de Molière (9); Th. des Variétés Amusantes, Comiques et Lyriques (8); Th. du Feydeau (de Monsieur) (9); Th. du Marais (1); Th. du Palais (Cité)-Variétés (1); Th. Français (de la rue Richelieu) (de la République) (7); Th. Lyrique des Amis de la Patrie (3); Th. National (de la rue Richelieu) (4); **Total: 73.**

_____. *Dangers de l'inconséquence, Les* [*Comédie* in 1 act].
> Th. du Palais (Cité)-Variétés (1); **Total: 1.**

_____. *Dehors trompeurs, Les, ou L'Homme du jour* [*Comédie* in 5 acts, Prem. on 18-2-1740, Pub. in 1740].
> Th. de la Nation (Comédie Française) (5); Th. de Molière (3); Th. du Feydeau (de Monsieur) (8); Th. du Marais (3); Th. Français (de la rue Richelieu) (de la République) (15); Th. Lyrique des Amis de la Patrie (1); **Total: 35.**

_____. *Embarras du choix, L'* [*Comédie* in 5 acts, Prem. on 11-12-1741, Pub. in 1742].
> Th. du Vaudeville (3); Th. Lyrique des Amis de la Patrie (15); **Total: 18.**

_____. *Epoux par supercherie, L'* [*Comédie* in 2 acts, Prem. on 9-3-1744, Pub. in 1744].
> Th. de la Nation (Comédie Française) (4); Th. de la Rue Martin (4); Th. des Délassements Comiques (1); Th. des Variétés Amusantes, Comiques et Lyriques (6); Th. du Lycée Dramatique (7); Th. du Marais (1); Th. Français (de la rue Richelieu) (de la République) (5); Th. Lyrique des Amis de la Patrie (8); Th. Patriotique et de Momus (17); **Total: 53.**

_____. *Fête d'Auteuil, La, ou La Fausse méprise* [*Comédie* in 3 acts, Prem. in 8-1743, Pub. in 1745].
> Th. de la Rue Martin (3); **Total: 3.**

_____. *Français à Londres, Le* [*Comédie* in 1 act, Prem. on 19-7-1727, Pub. in 1727].
> Th. de l'Estrapade au Panthéon (3); Th. de la Citoyenne Montansier (1); Th. de la Liberté (3); Th. de la Nation (Comédie Française) (3); Th. de Molière (5); Th. des Variétés Amusantes, Comiques et Lyriques (6); Th. du Feydeau (de Monsieur) (9); Th. du Lycée Dramatique (7); Th. du Marais (11); Th. Français (de la rue Richelieu) (de la République) (6); Th. Lyrique des Amis de la Patrie (1); **Total: 55.**

_____. *Maire de village, Le* [*Opéra*, Prem. on 22-2-1793, Pub. in 1793].
> Th. de l'Ambigu Comique (45); Th. de la Nation (Comédie Française) (1); **Total: 46.**

_____. *Sage étourdi, Le* [*Comédie* in 3 acts, Prem. on 5-7-1745, Pub. in 1745].
> Th. du Marais (3); Th. Français (de la rue Richelieu) (de la République) (10); **Total: 13.**

_____. *Vie est un songe, La* [*Comédie* in 3 acts, Prem. on 12-11-1732].
> Th. des Grands Danseurs (Gaîté) (7); **Total: 7.**

> **Total Performances**, Boissy, Louis de: **304**

Bombarde. *Faux serment, Le* [*Comédie* in 2 acts, Prem. in 1738, Pub. in 1738].
> Th. des Beaujolais (52); Th. des Jeunes Artistes (39); **Total: 91.**

Bonnefoy de Bouyon, Abbé., Mengozzi, Bernardo (comp).
Aujourd'hui ou Les Fous supposés [*Opéra* in 3 acts, Prem. on 3-2-1791].
> Th. de la Citoyenne Montansier (1); **Total: 1.**

_____. *Coquette surannée, La* [*Comédie* in 1 act, Prem. on 14-6-1790].
Th. de la Citoyenne Montansier (**21**); **Total: 21.**
Total Performances, Bonnefoy de Bouyon, Abbé: **22**

Bosquier-Gavaudan, Jean-S.-F., Langle, Honoré-F.-M. (comp). *Claudinet ou Le Dernier venu en graine* [*Comédie* in 1 act, Prem. on 23-8-1796].
Th. des Jeunes Artistes (**26**); **Total: 26.**

Bouchard, Armand de. *Arts et l'amitié, Les* [*Comédie* in 1 act, Prem. on 5-8-1788, Pub. in 1788].
Th. de la Rue Martin (**1**); Th. des Italiens (Opéra-Comique) (**35**); Th. des Variétés Amusantes, Comiques et Lyriques (**1**); **Total: 37.**

Bouilly, Jean-N. *Famille américaine, La* [*Comédie*, Prem. on 17-2-1796].
Th. des Italiens (Opéra-Comique) (**29**); **Total: 29.**

_____. *J.-J. Rousseau à ses derniers moments* [*Fait Historique* in 1 act, Prem. on 31-12-1790, Pub. in 1791].
Th. des Italiens (Opéra-Comique) (**21**); **Total: 21.**

_____., Gaveaux, Pierre (comp). *Léonore ou L'Amour conjugal* [*Fait Historique* in 2 acts, Prem. on 19-2-1798, Pub. in 1797].
Th. des Grands Danseurs (Gaîté) (**5**); Th. du Feydeau (de Monsieur) (**47**); **Total: 52.**

_____., Grétry, André-E.-M. (comp). *Pierre le grand* [*Comédie* in 4 acts, Prem. on 13-1-1790, Pub. in 1790].
Th. des Italiens (Opéra-Comique) (**52**); **Total: 52.**

_____. *René Descartes* [*Fait Historique* in 2 acts, Prem. on 20-9-1796, Pub. in 1796].
Th. Français (de la rue Richelieu) (de la République) (**13**); **Total: 13.**

_____. *Tombeau de Turenne, Le, ou L'Armée du Rhin à Sasbach* [*Fait Historique* in 1 act, Prem. on 8-1-1799, Pub. in 1809].
Th. du Palais (Cité)-Variétés (**7**); **Total: 7.**
Total Performances, Bouilly, Jean-N.: **174**

Boullault, Mathurin-J. *Acteur dans son ménage, L'* [*Anecdotique*, Prem. on 22-9-1799, Pub. in 1799].
Th. de l'Ambigu Comique (**12**); Th. du Feydeau (de Monsieur) (**2**); **Total: 14.**

_____. *Brigands de la Vendée, Les* [*Opéra-Bouffe* in 2 acts, Prem. on 3-10-1793, Pub. in 1793].
Th. des Grands Danseurs (Gaîté) (**2**); Th. des Variétés Amusantes, Comiques et Lyriques (**3**); **Total: 5.**

_____. *Déjeuner anglais, Le, ou Le Bombardement d'Ostende* [*Comédie* in 1 act, Prem. on 3-6-1798].
Th. du Palais (Cité)-Variétés (**4**); **Total: 4.**

_____. *Mort de Cadet Roussel, La* [*Comédie* in 1 act, Prem. on 11-10-1798, Pub. in 1798].
Th. du Mareux (**1**); Th. du Palais (Cité)-Variétés (**4**); **Total: 5.**

_____. *Tabagie, La* [*Prologue*, Pub. in 1798].
Th. du Palais (Cité)-Variétés (**3**); **Total: 3.**
Total Performances, Boullault, Mathurin-J.: **31**

Boullot. *Hôtellerie républicaine, L'* [*Comédie* in 2 acts].
Th. de l'Ambigu Comique (**1**); Th. des Grands Danseurs (Gaîté) (**15**); **Total: 16.**

Bouquier, Gabriel., Moline, Pierre-L., Porta, Bernado (comp). *Réunion du Dix août, La, ou L'Inauguration de la république française* [*Sans-Culottide Dramatique* in 5 acts, Prem. on 5-4-1794, Pub. in 1794].
  Académie de la Musique (Opéra) (**40**); **Total: 40.**
Bourgeuil. *Pour et le contre, Le* [*Vaudeville*, Prem. on 5-5-1798, Pub. in 1798].
  Th. du Vaudeville (**47**); **Total: 47.**
Bourlin, Antoine-J., Pseud. Dumaniant. *Alonse et Cora* [*Tragédie* in 3 acts, Prem. on 28-11-1792, Pub. in 1794].
  Th. Français (de la rue Richelieu) (de la République) (**2**); **Total: 2.**
_____. *Amant femme-de-chambre, L'* [*Comédie* in 1 act, Prem. on 8-11-1787, Pub. in 1788].
  Th. du Palais (Cité)-Variétés (**3**); Th. du Palais Royal (**33**); Th. Français (de la rue Richelieu) (de la République) (**7**); **Total: 43.**
_____. *Beaucoup de bruit pour rien* [*Comédie* in 3 acts, Pub. in 1793].
  Th. du Palais (Cité)-Variétés (**3**); **Total: 3.**
_____., Philidor, François-A. Danican (comp). *Belle esclave, La, ou Valcour et Zeila* [*Comédie* in 1 act, Prem. on 18-9-1787, Pub. in 1787].
  Th. des Beaujolais (**55**); Th. Lyrique des Amis de la Patrie (**7**); **Total: 62.**
_____. *Bon fils, Le* [*Comédie*, Pub. in 1795].
  Th. du Feydeau (de Monsieur) (**3**); **Total: 3.**
_____. *Deux cousins, Les, ou Les Français à Séville* [*Comédie* in 3 acts, Prem. on 22-7-1788, Pub. in 1788].
  Th. de la Cité (**7**); Th. du Palais Royal (**23**); **Total: 30.**
_____. *Double intrigue, La, ou L'Aventure embarrassante* [*Comédie* in 2 acts, Prem. on 10-7-1790, Pub. in 1790].
  Th. du Palais Royal (**18**); **Total: 18.**
_____. *Dragon de Thionville, Le* [*Fait Historique* in 1 act, Prem. on 26-7-1786, Pub. in 1786].
  Maison Egalité (**1**); Th. des Variétés Amusantes, Comiques et Lyriques (**1**); Th. du Palais (Cité)-Variétés (**5**); Th. du Palais Royal (**47**); Th. Français (de la rue Richelieu) (de la République) (**3**); **Total: 57.**
_____. *Eléonore de Gonzagues ou Les Rivaux sans le savoir* [*Comédie* in 2 acts, Prem. on 28-7-1789].
  Th. du Feydeau (de Monsieur) (**1**); **Total: 1.**
_____. *Ellinore ou Les Deux épouses* [*Comédie* in 3 acts, Prem. on 7-9-1789].
  Th. du Palais Royal (**4**); **Total: 4.**
_____. *Français en Huronie, Le* [*Comédie* in 1 act, Prem. on 30-4-1787, Pub. in 1787].
  Th. du Palais Royal (**2**); **Total: 2.**
_____. *Georges ou Le Bon fils* [*Comédie* in 3 acts, Prem. on 1-12-1789, Pub. in 1790].
  Maison Egalité (**10**); Th. de la Citoyenne Montansier (**1**); Th. de la Cité (**2**); Th. des Variétés Amusantes, Comiques et Lyriques (**3**); Th. du Feydeau (de Monsieur) (**8**); Th. du Palais (Cité)-Variétés (**37**); **Total: 61.**
_____., Jadin, Louis-E. (comp). *Guerre ouverte ou ruse contre ruse* [*Comédie* in 3 acts, Prem. on 4-10-1786, Pub. in 1787].
  Maison Egalité (**16**); Th. de la Cité (**23**); Th. des Variétés Amusantes, Comiques et Lyriques (**24**); Th. du Marais (**1**); Th. du Palais (Cité)-Variétés (**61**); Th. du Palais Royal (**45**); Th. Français (de la rue Richelieu) (de la République) (**6**); **Total: 176.**

_____. *Honnête homme, L', ou Le Rival généreux* [*Comédie* in 3 acts, Prem. on 4-2-1789, Pub. in 1789].
  Th. du Palais Royal (**8**); **Total: 8.**

_____. *Intrigants, Les, ou Assauts de fourberies* [*Comédie* in 3 acts, Prem. on 6-8-1787, Pub. in 1787].
  Maison Egalité (**11**); Th. de la Citoyenne Montansier (**3**); Th. de la Cité (**38**); Th. des Variétés Amusantes, Comiques et Lyriques (**4**); Th. du Palais (Cité)-Variétés (**42**); Th. du Palais Royal (**47**); **Total: 145.**

_____. *Isaure et Gernance ou Les Réfugiés* [*Comédie* in 3 acts, Prem. on 6-11-1794, Pub. in 1794].
  Th. du Palais (Cité)-Variétés (**2**); **Total: 2.**

_____. *Jodelet* [*Comédie* in 1 act, Prem. on 27-10-1798, Pub. in 1798].
  Th. de la Citoyenne Montansier (**19**); **Total: 19.**

_____. *Journée difficile, La, ou Les Femmes rusées* [*Comédie* in 3 acts, Prem. on 19-11-1792, Pub. in 1792].
  Th. des Enfans Comiques (**1**); Th. du Palais (Cité)-Variétés (**9**); **Total: 10.**

_____. *Loi de Jatab, Le, ou Le Turc à Paris* [*Comédie* in 1 act, Prem. on 22-1-1787, Pub. in 1787].
  Th. du Palais Royal (**13**); **Total: 13.**

_____. *Médecin malgré tout le monde, Le* [*Comédie* in 3 acts, Prem. on 20-2-1786, Pub. in 1786].
  Th. de la Citoyenne Montansier (**1**); Th. du Palais (Cité)-Variétés (**11**); Th. du Palais Royal (**33**); **Total: 45.**

_____. *Mort de Beaurepaire, La, ou Les Héros français* [*Fait Historique* in 1 act, Pub. in 1792].
  Th. du Palais (Cité)-Variétés (**11**); **Total: 11.**

_____. *Nuit aux aventures, La* [*Comédie* in 3 acts, Prem. on 7-2-1787, Pub. in 1787].
  Maison Egalité (**8**); Th. de la Citoyenne Montansier (**3**); Th. de la Cité (**27**); Th. des Variétés Amusantes, Comiques et Lyriques (**1**); Th. du Palais (Cité)-Variétés (**20**); Th. du Palais Royal (**24**); **Total: 83.**

_____. *Prodigue par bienfaisance et le chevalier d'industrie, Le* [*Comédie* in 4 acts, Prem. on 22-11-1790].
  Th. du Palais Royal (**7**); **Total: 7.**

_____. *Ricco* [*Comédie* in 2 acts, Prem. on 30-9-1789, Pub. in 1789].
  Maison Egalité (**12**); Th. de l'Ambigu Comique (**1**); Th. de la Citoyenne Montansier (**9**); Th. de la Cité (**20**); Th. des Variétés Amusantes, Comiques et Lyriques (**11**); Th. du Palais (Cité)-Variétés (**62**); Th. du Palais Royal (**80**); **Total: 195.**

_____. *Ruses déjouées, Les* [*Comédie* in 3 acts, Prem. on 14-11-1798, Pub. in 1798].
  Th. du Palais (Cité)-Variétés (**18**); **Total: 18.**

_____. *Secret découvert, Le, ou L'Arrivée du maître* [*Comédie*, Prem. on 24-2-1798].
  Th. de la Citoyenne Montansier (**3**); **Total: 3.**

_____. *Soixante mille francs, Les* [In 1 act, Prem. on 9-11-1790].
  Th. du Palais Royal (**1**); **Total: 1.**

_____. *Soldat prussien, Le, ou Le Bon fils* [*Comédie* in 3 acts, Prem. on 1-12-1789, Pub. in 1790].
> Maison Egalité (**1**); Th. de la Citoyenne Montansier (**1**); Th. de la Cité (**3**); Th. du Palais (Cité)-Variétés (**4**); Th. du Palais Royal (**55**); Th. Français (de la rue Richelieu) (de la République) (**10**); **Total: 74.**

_____. *Tour aux douze portes, La* [*Comédie* in 1 act, Prem. on 22-8-1789].
> Th. du Palais Royal (**3**); **Total: 3.**

_____. *Urbélise et Lanval ou La Journée aux aventures* [*Comédie* in 3 acts, Prem. on 30-4-1788, Pub. in 1788].
> Th. du Palais (Cité)-Variétés (**5**); Th. du Palais Royal (**3**); **Total: 8.**

_____. *Vengeance, La* [*Tragédie* in 5 acts, Prem. on 26-11-1791].
> Th. Français (de la rue Richelieu) (de la République) (**3**); **Total: 3.**

_____. *Voyages de Cadet Roussel, Les* [*Comédie* in 2 acts, Pub. in 1793].
> Th. du Palais (Cité)-Variétés (**8**); **Total: 8.**
>
> **Total Performances**, Bourlin, Antoine-J.: **1118**

Boursault, Edmonde. *Esope à la cour* [*Comédie* in 5 acts, Prem. on 16-12-1701, Pub. in 1702].
> Th. de la Citoyenne Montansier (**1**); Th. de la Nation (Comédie Française) (**8**); Th. de Molière (**1**); Th. du Palais Royal (**2**); Th. Français (de la rue Richelieu) (de la République) (**2**); **Total: 14.**

_____., Salieri, Antonio (comp). *Mercure galant, Le, ou La Comédie sans titre* [*Comédie* in 4 acts, Prem. in 1679, Pub. in 1687].
> Maison Egalité (**3**); Th. de l'Estrapade au Panthéon (**1**); Th. de la Citoyenne Montansier (**5**); Th. de la Liberté (**1**); Th. de la Nation (Comédie Française) (**17**); Th. de la Rue Martin (**3**); Th. de Molière (**7**); Th. des Grands Danseurs (Gaîté) (**7**); Th. des Variétés Amusantes, Comiques et Lyriques (**1**); Th. du Feydeau (de Monsieur) (**4**); Th. du Marais (**2**); Th. du Vaudeville (**2**); Th. Français (de la rue Richelieu) (de la République) (**35**); Th. Lyrique des Amis de la Patrie (**1**); Th. National (de la rue Richelieu) (**1**); Th. Patriotique et de Momus (**5**); **Total: 100.**

_____. *Mort vivant, Le* [*Comédie* in 3 acts, Prem. in 1662].
> Th. de l'Emulation (Gaîté) (**3**); Th. des Variétés Amusantes (Lazzari) (**1**); **Total: 4.**
>
> **Total Performances**, Boursault, Edmonde: **118**

Boussenard de Soubreville. *Réveil du charbonnier, Le* [*Comédie* in 3 acts, Pub. in 1788].
> Th. de l'Emulation (Gaîté) (**116**); Th. de la Citoyenne Montansier (**1**); Th. de la Rue Martin (**1**); Th. des Grands Danseurs (Gaîté) (**55**); **Total: 173.**

Boutet de Monvel, Jacques-M., Dalayrac, Nicolas (comp). *Agnès et Olivier* [*Opéra* in 3 acts, Prem. on 10-10-1791].
> Th. des Italiens (Opéra-Comique) (**8**); **Total: 8.**

_____., Dezède, Nicolas (comp). *Alexis et Justine* [*Comédie* in 2 acts, Prem. on 14-1-1785, Pub. in 1785].
> Th. de l'Ambigu Comique (**2**); Th. de la Citoyenne Montansier (**28**); Th. de Molière (**8**); Th. des Beaujolais (**1**); Th. des Italiens (Opéra-Comique) (**42**); Th. du Marais (**1**); **Total: 82.**

_____. *Amant bourru, L'* [*Comédie* in 3 acts, Prem. on 14-8-1777, Pub. in 1777].
> Th. de l'Odéon (**5**); Th. de la Bienfaisance (**2**); Th. de la Citoyenne Montansier (**6**); Th. de la Cité (**2**); Th. de la Nation (Comédie Française) (**24**); Th. de Molière (**5**); Th. des Victoires Nationales (**1**); Th. du Feydeau (de Monsieur) (**8**); Th. du Marais (**9**); Th. du Palais (Cité)-Variétés (**2**); Th. Français (de la rue Richelieu) (de la République) (**19**); **Total: 83.**

_____., Dalayrac, Nicolas (comp). *Ambroise ou Voilà ma journée* [*Comédie* in 1 act, Prem. on 12-1-1793, Pub. in 1796].
>   Th. des Italiens (Opéra-Comique) (71); **Total: 71.**

_____. *Amours de Bayard, Les* [*Héroique* in 3 acts, Pub. in 1786].
>   Th. de l'Emulation (Gaîté) (23); Th. de la Nation (Comédie Française) (8); Th. du Marais (2); **Total: 33.**

_____., Dezède, Nicolas (comp). *Blaise et Babet ou La Suite des trois fermiers* [*Comédie* in 2 acts, Prem. on 4-4-1783, Pub. in 1783].
>   n/a (9); Th. de l'Ambigu Comique (16); Th. de la Citoyenne Montansier (44); Th. de la Cité (1); Th. de la Rue Martin (2); Th. de Molière (2); Th. des Italiens (Opéra-Comique) (133); Th. des Variétés Amusantes, Comiques et Lyriques (4); Th. du Marais (25); Th. du Palais (Cité)-Variétés (1); Th. Français, Comique et Lyrique (2); **Total: 239.**

_____., Dalayrac, Nicolas (comp). *Chêne patriotique, Le, ou La Matinée du 14 juillet 1790* [*Tableau-Patriotique* in 2 acts, Prem. on 10-7-1790].
>   Th. des Italiens (Opéra-Comique) (7); **Total: 7.**

_____. *Clémentine et Desormes* [*Drame* in 5 acts, Prem. on 14-12-1780, Pub. in 1780].
>   Th. Français (de la rue Richelieu) (de la République) (33); **Total: 33.**

_____. *Deuil prématuré, Le* [*Comédie* in 1 act, Prem. on 17-5-1793, Pub. in 1793].
>   Th. Français (de la rue Richelieu) (de la République) (15); Th. Lyrique des Amis de la Patrie (1); **Total: 16.**

_____. *Heureuse indiscrétion, L'* [*Comédie* in 3 acts, Prem. on 11-8-1790].
>   Th. du Palais Royal (16); **Total: 16.**

_____., Dezède, Nicolas (comp). *Julie* [*Comédie* in 3 acts, Prem. on 28-9-1772, Pub. in 1772].
>   Th. des Italiens (Opéra-Comique) (3); **Total: 3.**

_____. *Junius ou Le Proscrit* [*Tragédie* in 5 acts, Prem. on 3-4-1797, Pub. in 1797].
>   Th. Français (de la rue Richelieu) (de la République) (9); **Total: 9.**

_____., Duval, Alexandre-V.-P. *Lovelace français, Le* [*Drame* in 5 acts, Prem. on 26-12-1796, Pub. in 1796].
>   Th. du Feydeau (de Monsieur) (5); Th. du Marais (1); Th. du Palais (Cité)-Variétés (1); Th. Français (de la rue Richelieu) (de la République) (12); **Total: 19.**

_____. *Mathilde* [*Drame* in 5 acts, Pub. in 1799].
>   Th. Français (de la rue Richelieu) (de la République) (18); **Total: 18.**

_____., Dalayrac, Nicolas (comp). *Philippe et Georgette* [*Comédie* in 1 act, Prem. on 28-12-1791].
>   Th. de la Rue Martin (2); Th. des Italiens (Opéra-Comique) (197); Th. des Variétés Amusantes, Comiques et Lyriques (1); Th. du Marais (1); **Total: 201.**

_____. *Poule aux oeufs d'or, La* [N/A].
>   Th. du Vaudeville (2); **Total: 2.**

_____., Dalayrac, Nicolas (comp). *Raoul, sire de Créqui* [*Opéra-Comique* in 3 acts, Prem. on 31-10-1789, Pub. in 1789].
>   Th. des Italiens (Opéra-Comique) (112); **Total: 112.**

_____., Dalayrac, Nicolas (comp). *Sargines ou L'Elève de l'amour*
[*Comédie* in 4 acts, Prem. on 14-5-1788, Pub. in 1790].
   n/a (1); Th. des Italiens (Opéra-Comique) (71); **Total: 72.**
_____., Dalayrac, Nicolas (comp). *Tout pour l'amour ou Roméo et Ju-
liette* [*Drame-Lyrique* in 4 acts, Prem. on 7-7-1792].
   Th. des Italiens (Opéra-Comique) (16); **Total: 16.**
_____. *Trois fermiers, Les* [*Comédie* in 2 acts, Prem. on 24-5-1777, Pub. in
1777].
   Th. de la Citoyenne Montansier (20); Th. des Italiens (Opéra-Comique)
   (29); **Total: 49.**
_____., Dalayrac, Nicolas (comp). *Urgande et Merlin* [*Comédie* in 3 acts,
Prem. on 14-10-1793].
   Th. des Italiens (Opéra-Comique) (1); **Total: 1.**
_____. *Victimes cloîtrées, Les* [*Drame* in 4 acts, Prem. on 28-3-1791, Pub. in
1792].
   n/a (1); Th. de l'Emulation (Gaîté) (7); Th. de la Cité (2); Th. de la Nation
   (Comédie Française) (46); Th. de la Rue Antoine (3); Th. de la Rue Martin
   (1); Th. des Variétés Amusantes, Comiques et Lyriques (1); Th. du Fey-
   deau (de Monsieur) (16); Th. du Marais (3); Th. du Palais (Cité)-Variétés
   (5); Th. Français (de la rue Richelieu) (de la République) (24); **Total: 109.**
_____. *Visite des mariés, La* [*Comédie* in 3 acts, Prem. on 23-6-1796].
   Th. de la Citoyenne Montansier (7); **Total: 7.**
                  Total Performances, Boutet de Monvel, Jacques-M.: **1206**
Boutillier, Maximilien-J., Deshayes, Prosper-D. (comp). *Adèle et Di-
dier* [*Opéra-Comique* in 1 act, Prem. on 5-11-1790].
   Th. des Italiens (Opéra-Comique) (1); **Total: 1.**
_____., Rigel, Henri-J. (comp). *Alix de Beaucaire* [*Opéra* in 3 acts, Prem.
on 10-11-1791, Pub. in 1791].
   Th. de la Citoyenne Montansier (55); **Total: 55.**
_____. *Elise ou L'Ami comme il y en a peu* [*Drame* in 3 acts, Prem. in 1776,
Pub. in 1776].
   Th. du Palais Royal (2); **Total: 2.**
_____. *Héritage, L'* [*Fait Historique* in 1 act, Prem. on 21-5-1798].
   Th. de la Rue Antoine (1); Th. des Variétés Amusantes, Comiques et
   Lyriques (5); Th. du Vaudeville (8); **Total: 14.**
_____. *Laurence et Bonval* [*Comédie* in 1 act].
   Th. Français, Comique et Lyrique (2); **Total: 2.**
_____., Rigel, Henri-J. (comp). *Pauline et Henri* [*Comédie* in 1 act, Prem.
on 9-11-1793, Pub. in 1793].
   Th. du Feydeau (de Monsieur) (13); **Total: 13.**
_____. *Souper de Henri IV, Le, ou Le Laboureur devenu gentilhomme*
[*Fait Historique* in 1 act, Prem. on 12-10-1789, Pub. in 1789].
   Th. du Feydeau (de Monsieur) (40); **Total: 40.**
                  Total Performances, Boutillier, Maximilien-J.: **127**
Brazier, Nicolas. *Alain et Suzette ou Le Fils adoptif* [*Tableau-Patriotique*
in 2 acts, Pub. in 1793].
   Th. des Grands Danseurs (Gaîté) (69); **Total: 69.**
Bré d'Olivet, A., Rochefort, Jean-B. (comp). *Toulon soumis* [*Fait His-
torique* in 1 act, Prem. on 4-3-1794].
   Académie de la Musique (Opéra) (13); **Total: 13.**

Bret, Antoine. *Deux Julies, Les, ou Le Père crédule* [*Farce* in 3 acts, Prem.
on 10-12-1790, Pub. in 1778].
> Th. du Palais Royal (**1**); **Total: 1**.

_____. *Ecole amoureuse, L'* [*Comédie* in 1 act, Prem. on 11-9-1747, Pub. in
1748].
> Th. de la Nation (Comédie Française) (**1**); **Total: 1**.

_____. *Humeur à l'épreuve, L'* [*Comédie* in 1 act, Prem. on 17-6-1790, Pub. in
1778].
> Th. du Palais Royal (**6**); **Total: 6**.
> **Total Performances**, Bret, Antoine: **8**

Brazier, Nicolas., Villeneuve, Ferdinand Vallon de., Charles de Livry.
Santeuil, ou Le Chanoine au cabaret [N/A].
> Th. du Vaudeville (**12**); **Total: 12**.

Briois, Belle-Roche, dit de. *Cent Louis, Les* [*Comédie* in 1 act, Prem. in 11-
1786, Pub. in 1787].
> Maison Egalité (**11**); Th. de la Cité (**3**); Th. du Palais (Cité)-Variétés (**26**);
> Th. du Palais Royal (**41**); **Total: 81**.

_____. *Fermier d'Issoire, Le* [*Comédie*, Pub. in 1795].
> Th. de l'Ambigu Comique (**19**); **Total: 19**.

_____. *Journée de la Vendée, Une* [*Fait Historique*].
> Th. des Grands Danseurs (Gaîté) (**28**); **Total: 28**.

_____. *Prise de Toulon, La* [*Drame* in 2 acts, Prem. on 22-2-1794, Pub. in
1794].
> Th. des Grands Danseurs (Gaîté) (**39**); **Total: 39**.
> **Total Performances**, Briois, Belle-Roche, dit de: **167**

Brousse-Desfaucherets, Jean-L. *Dangers de la présomption, Les*
[*Comédie*].
> Th. du Feydeau (de Monsieur) (**6**); **Total: 6**.

_____. *Mariage secret, Le* [*Comédie* in 3 acts, Prem. on 4-11-1785, Pub. in
1786].
> Th. de la Nation (Comédie Française) (**22**); Th. du Feydeau (de Monsieur)
> (**14**); Th. du Marais (**3**); Th. Français (de la rue Richelieu) (de la
> République) (**1**); **Total: 40**.
> **Total Performances**, Brousse-Desfaucherets, Jean-L.: **46**

Brueys, David-A. de., Palaprat, Joseph. *Avocat Patelin, L'* [*Comédie* in 3
acts, Prem. on 4-6-1706, Pub. in 1715].
> n/a (**1**); Th. de l'Odéon (**7**); Th. de la Citoyenne Montansier (**42**); Th. de la
> Liberté (**2**); Th. de la Nation (Comédie Française) (**27**); Th. de la Rue Mar-
> tin (**5**); Th. de Molière (**9**); Th. des Variétés Amusantes (Lazzari) (**4**); Th.
> des Variétés Amusantes, Comiques et Lyriques (**5**); Th. des Victoires Na-
> tionales (**4**); Th. du Feydeau (de Monsieur) (**13**); Th. du Lycée Dramatique
> (**8**); Th. du Marais (**12**); Th. du Palais (Cité)-Variétés (**12**); Th. Français
> (de la rue Richelieu) (de la République) (**30**); Th. Lyrique des Amis de la
> Patrie (**15**); Th. National (de la rue Richelieu) (**3**); **Total: 199**.

_____., Palaprat, Joseph. *Grondeur, Le* [*Comédie* in 3 acts, Prem. in 1-1691,
Pub. in 1693].
> Th. de la Citoyenne Montansier (**2**); Th. des Victoires Nationales (**5**); Th.
> du Feydeau (de Monsieur) (**7**); Th. du Marais (**1**); Th. Français (de la rue
> Richelieu) (de la République) (**28**); Th. Lyrique des Amis de la Patrie (**11**);
> **Total: 54**.

_____., Palaprat, Joseph. *Muet, Le* [*Comédie* in 5 acts, Pub. in 1691].
Th. du Palais (Cité)-Variétés (1); Th. Français (de la rue Richelieu) (de la République) (8); **Total: 9.**
Total Performances, Brueys, David-A. de: **262**

Buhan, Joseph-M.-P., Gouffé, Armand Alexandre Duval., Desfougerais, P.F. Aubin, dit. *Gilles aéronaute ou L'Amérique n'est pas loin* [*Comédie* in 1 act, Prem. on 24-7-1799].
Th. du Vaudeville (14); **Total: 14.**

Bulle., Anfossi, Pasquale (comp). *Feinte jardinière, La* [*Opéra-Comique* in 3 acts, Prem. in 1774].
Th. du Feydeau (de Monsieur) (1); **Total: 1.**

Cadet de Gassicourt, Charles-L. *Souper de Molière, Le, ou La Soirée d'Auteuil* [*Fait Historique* in 1 act, Prem. on 23-1-1794].
Th. du Vaudeville (46); **Total: 46.**

Cadoret. *Arlequin invisible* [*Comédie* in 3 acts, Prem. on 29-10-1741, Pub. in 1741].
Th. des Grands Danseurs (Gaîté) (20); **Total: 20.**

Caffaut. *Arlequin au tombeau ou Le Tombeau magique* [*Comédie* in 3 acts, Prem. in 1766].
Th. des Grands Danseurs (Gaîté) (55); **Total: 55.**

Cahusac, Louis de. *Zénéide* [*Comédie* in 1 act, Prem. on 13-5-1743, Pub. in 1744].
Th. de la Nation (Comédie Française) (5); Th. Français (de la rue Richelieu) (de la République) (2); **Total: 7.**

_____., Rameau, Jean-P. (comp). *Zoroastre* [*Tragédie lyrique* in 5 acts, Prem. on 5-12-1749, Pub. in 1749].
Th. des Variétés Amusantes (Lazzari) (24); Th. des Variétés Amusantes, Comiques et Lyriques (30); **Total: 54.**
Total Performances, Cahusac, Louis de: **61**

Cailhava de L'Estendoux, Jean-F. *Ménechmes grecs, Les* [*Comédie* in 4 acts, Prem. on 13-1-1791, Pub. in 1791].
Th. de la Rue Martin (1); Th. de Molière (6); Th. du Palais Royal (24); Th. du Vaudeville (3); Th. Français (de la rue Richelieu) (de la République) (36); Th. Patriotique et de Momus (5); **Total: 75.**

_____. *Tuteur dupé, Le, ou La Maison a deux portes* [*Comédie* in 5 acts, Prem. on 30-9-1765, Pub. in 1765].
Th. de la Citoyenne Montansier (4); Th. de la Cité (1); Th. des Variétés Amusantes (Lazzari) (1); Th. des Variétés Amusantes, Comiques et Lyriques (2); Th. du Feydeau (de Monsieur) (2); Th. du Vaudeville (13); **Total: 23.**

_____., Léger, François-P.-A. *Ziste et zeste ou Les Importuns* [*Comédie* in 1 act, Prem. on 27-8-1796].
Th. de Molière (3); Th. des Troubadours (10); Th. du Marais (1); Th. du Vaudeville (62); **Total: 76.**
Total Performances, Cailhava de L'Estendoux, Jean-F.: **174**

Cailleau, André-C. *Soubrette rusée, La* [*Comédie* in 1 act, Prem. in 1776, Pub. in 1776].
Th. des Beaujolais (6); **Total: 6.**

Cammaille-Saint-Aubin, M.-C. *Ami du peuple, L', ou Les Intrigants démasqués* [*Comédie* in 3 acts, Prem. on 6-9-1793, Pub. in 1793].
Th. du Palais (Cité)-Variétés (18); **Total: 18.**

_____. *Elève de la nature, L', ou Le Nouveau peuple* [*Pantomime* in 3 acts, Prem. on 8-3-1795, Pub. in 1801].
　Th. des Italiens (Opéra-Comique) (**18**); **Total: 18.**

_____. *Hochets, Les* [*Vaudeville* in 2 acts, Pub. in 1790].
　Th. des Variétés Amusantes, Comiques et Lyriques (**2**); **Total: 2.**

_____. *Louise ou Le Théâtre* [*Comédie*, Pub. in 1799].
　Th. des Grands Danseurs (Gaîté) (**4**); **Total: 4.**

_____., Ribié, César. *Moine, Le* [*Comédie* in 5 acts, Pub. in 1797].
　Th. de l'Emulation (Gaîté) (**80**); Th. des Grands Danseurs (Gaîté) (**14**); Th. Lyrique des Amis de la Patrie (**22**); **Total: 116.**

_____. *Werther* [*Drame*, Prem. on 6-2-1798].
　Th. des Italiens (Opéra-Comique) (**1**); **Total: 1.**
　　　　Total Performances, Cammaille-Saint-Aubin, M.-C.: **159**

Campistron, Jean-G. de. *Jaloux désabusé, Le* [*Comédie* in 5 acts, Prem. on 13-12-1709, Pub. in 1710].
　Th. de la Nation (Comédie Française) (**3**); Th. du Feydeau (de Monsieur) (**2**); Th. du Marais (**1**); Th. Français (de la rue Richelieu) (de la République) (**11**); **Total: 17.**

Candeille, Amélie-Julie. *Bathilde, La, ou Le Duo* [*Comédie*, Prem. on 16-9-1793].
　Th. Français (de la rue Richelieu) (de la République) (**4**); **Total: 4.**

_____. *Bayadère, La, ou Le Français à Surate* [*Comédie* in 5 acts, Prem. on 25-1-1795, Pub. in 1793].
　Th. Français (de la rue Richelieu) (de la République) (**2**); **Total: 2.**

_____. *Catherine ou La Belle fermière* [*Comédie* in 3 acts, Prem. on 27-11-1792, Pub. in 1793].
　Th. de la Cité (**1**); Th. de Molière (**17**); Th. des Variétés Amusantes, Comiques et Lyriques (**1**); Th. des Victoires (**9**); Th. du Marais (**3**); Th. Français (de la rue Richelieu) (de la République) (**82**); **Total: 113.**

_____. *Commissionnaire, Le* [*Comédie* in 2 acts, Prem. on 18-11-1794, Pub. in 1794].
　Maison Egalité (**20**); Th. des Italiens (Opéra-Comique) (**1**); **Total: 21.**

_____. *Louise ou La Réconciliation* [*Drame* in 4 acts].
　Th. des Grands Danseurs (Gaîté) (**12**); **Total: 12.**
　　　　Total Performances, Candeille, Amélie-Julie: **152**

Capinaud., Chevalier-Seguenot. *Bataille de Jemmapes, La, ou La Prise de Mons* [*Tableau-Patriotique* in 2 acts, Pub. in 1792].
　Th. du Feydeau (de Monsieur) (**1**); **Total: 1.**

Carbon de Flins des Oliviers, Claude-M. *Jeune hôtesse, La* [*Comédie* in 3 acts, Prem. on 24-12-1791, Pub. in 1792].
　Th. du Palais (Cité)-Variétés (**1**); Th. Français (de la rue Richelieu) (de la République) (**65**); **Total: 66.**

_____. *Mari directeur, Le, ou Le Déménagement du couvent* [*Comédie* in 1 act, Prem. on 25-2-1791, Pub. in 1791].
　Th. de la Nation (Comédie Française) (**6**); **Total: 6.**

_____. *Réveil d'Epiménide à Paris, Le* [*Comédie* in 1 act, Prem. on 1-1-1790, Pub. in 1790].
　Th. de la Nation (Comédie Française) (**31**); **Total: 31.**
　　　　Total Performances, Carbon de Flins des Oliviers, Claude-M.: **103**

Carmontelle, Louis-C. *Abbé de court-dîner, L'* [*Proverbe/allégorique* in 1 act, Prem. on 11-10-1790, Pub. in 1768].
    Th. des Grands Danseurs (Gaîté) (**19**); **Total: 19.**
_____. *Billet perdu, Le* [*Comédie* in 1 act, Pub. in 1771].
    Th. des Enfans Comiques (**1**); **Total: 1.**
_____. *Enragé, L', ou Madame Thomas* [*Proverbe/allégorique* in 1 act, Pub. in 1786].
    Th. de l'Ambigu Comique (**92**); **Total: 92.**
                    Total Performances, Carmontelle, Louis-C.: **112**
Carolet, Denis. *Capitaine notaire, Le, ou L'Engagement imprévu* [*Comédie* in 1 act, Prem. on 23-1-1794, Pub. in 1736].
    Th. de l'Ambigu Comique (**2**); **Total: 2.**
_____. *Mariage en l'air, Le* [*Parodie* in 1 act, Prem. on 13-3-1737, Pub. in 1737].
    Th. des Jeunes Artistes (**4**); **Total: 4.**
                    Total Performances, Carolet, Denis: **6**
Carpani, Giuseppe., Paisiello, Giovanni (comp). *Nina, o sia la pazza per amore, La* [*Opéra*].
    Th. du Feydeau (de Monsieur) (**25**); **Total: 25.**
Carrière-Doisin, A. *Ambigu-comique, L', ou L'Audience de Minerve* [*Comédie* in 1 act, Pub. in 1789].
    Th. de l'Ambigu Comique (**25**); **Total: 25.**
Castaing, J. *Femmes curieuses, Les, ou Les Francs-maçons* [*Comédie* in 3 acts, Pub. in 1793].
    Th. Patriotique et de Momus (**17**); **Total: 17.**
Casti, Giambattista., Salieri, Antonio (comp). *Grotta di Trifonio, La* [*Opéra*].
    Th. du Feydeau (de Monsieur) (**3**); **Total: 3.**
Caux de Montlebert, Gilles de. *Marius* [*Tragédie* in 5 acts, Prem. on 15-11-1715, Pub. in 1716].
    Th. de la Nation (Comédie Française) (**10**); **Total: 10.**
Cérou, Chevalier de. *Amant auteur et valet, L'* [*Comédie* in 1 act, Prem. on 8-2-1740, Pub. in 1740].
    Th. de l'Emulation (Gaîté) (**3**); Th. de l'Estrapade au Panthéon (**3**); Th. de la Bienfaisance (**1**); Th. de la Citoyenne Montansier (**8**); Th. de la Nation (Comédie Française) (**1**); Th. de la Rue Martin (**7**); Th. de Molière (**9**); Th. des Délassements Comiques (**2**); Th. des Grands Danseurs (Gaîté) (**22**); Th. des Italiens (Opéra-Comique) (**3**); Th. des Variétés Amusantes (Lazzari) (**1**); Th. des Variétés Amusantes, Comiques et Lyriques (**19**); Th. du Lycée des Arts (**1**); Th. du Lycée Dramatique (**10**); Th. du Marais (**12**); Th. du Vaudeville (**3**); Th. Français (de la rue Richelieu) (de la République) (**8**); Th. Lyrique des Amis de la Patrie (**6**); Th. Patriotique et de Momus (**12**); **Total: 131.**
Chabanon, Michel-P.-G. de., Gossec, François-J. (comp). *Sabinus* [*Tragédie-Lyrique* in 5 acts, Prem. on 4-12-1773, Pub. in 1773].
    Th. Lyrique des Amis de la Patrie (**4**); **Total: 4.**

Chamfort, Sébastien-R.-N. *Jeune indienne, La* [*Comédie* in 1 act, Prem. on 30-4-1764, Pub. in 1764].
> n/a (2); Th. de l'Ambigu Comique (3); Th. de l'Emulation (Gaîté) (9); Th. de l'Odéon (2); Th. de la Nation (Comédie Française) (11); Th. de la Rue Martin (12); Th. des Grands Danseurs (Gaîté) (30); Th. du Feydeau (de Monsieur) (2); Th. du Lycée des Arts (9); Th. du Vaudeville (4); Th. Français (de la rue Richelieu) (de la République) (3); Th. Patriotique et de Momus (11); **Total: 98.**

_____. *Marchand de Smyrne, Le* [*Comédie* in 1 act, Prem. on 26-1-1770, Pub. in 1770].
> Th. de la Nation (Comédie Française) (17); Th. de Molière (1); Th. du Marais (1); Th. Français (de la rue Richelieu) (de la République) (37); Th. National (de la rue Richelieu) (1); **Total: 57.**
> **Total Performances**, Chamfort, Sébastien-R.-N.: **155**

Charlemagne, Armand. *Adoption villageoise, L', ou L'Ecouteur aux portes* [*Comédie* in 1 act, Prem. on 17-5-1794, Pub. in 1794].
> Th. du Palais (Cité)-Variétés (12); **Total: 12.**

_____. *Agioteur, L'* [*Comédie* in 1 act, Prem. on 30-10-1795, Pub. in 1796].
> Th. Français (de la rue Richelieu) (de la République) (8); **Total: 8.**

_____. *Arlequin riche impromptu* [*Pantomime*, Prem. on 8-7-1797].
> Th. des Jeunes Artistes (4); **Total: 4.**

_____. *Ecoliers, Les* [*Comédie* in 1 act, Prem. on 22-12-1792, Pub. in 1793].
> Th. du Palais (Cité)-Variétés (4); **Total: 4.**

_____. *Fille à marier, La* [*Comédie* in 1 act, Prem. on 22-2-1793, Pub. in 1793].
> Th. du Palais (Cité)-Variétés (16); **Total: 16.**

_____. *Homme de lettres et l'homme d'affaires, L'* [*Comédie* in 1 act, Prem. on 3-5-1795, Pub. in 1793].
> Th. de la Citoyenne Montansier (2); Th. de la Rue Martin (18); Th. des Jeunes Artistes (2); Th. du Lycée des Arts (1); **Total: 23.**

_____. *Insouciant, L'* [*Comédie* in 1 act, Prem. on 16-11-1792, Pub. in 1792].
> Th. du Palais (Cité)-Variétés (1); **Total: 1.**

_____. *Monsieur de Crac à Paris* [N/A].
> Maison Egalité (4); Th. des Variétés Amusantes, Comiques et Lyriques (7); Th. du Feydeau (de Monsieur) (10); Th. du Palais (Cité)-Variétés (36); Th. Français (de la rue Richelieu) (de la République) (1); **Total: 58.**

_____. *Paroles et la musique, Les* [*Comédie* in 1 act, Prem. on 19-6-1799, Pub. in 1799].
> Th. des Troubadours (25); **Total: 25.**

_____. *Père aveugle, Le* [*Comédie* in 2 acts].
> Th. de l'Ambigu Comique (1); Th. des Jeunes Artistes (21); Th. du Palais (Cité)-Variétés (5); **Total: 27.**

_____. *Soirée de Vaugirard, La* [*Anecdotique* in 1 act, Pub. in 1796].
> Th. de la Rue Martin (7); **Total: 7.**

_____. *Souper des Jacobins, Le* [*Comédie* in 1 act, Prem. on 15-3-1795, Pub. in 1795].
> Th. de l'Ambigu Comique (1); Th. de la Citoyenne Montansier (2); Th. de la Rue Martin (52); Th. des Variétés Amusantes, Comiques et Lyriques (1); Th. du Lycée des Arts (4); **Total: 60.**
> **Total Performances**, Charlemagne, Armand: **245**

Charrin, Pierre-J., Lapotre, le P. Arthur. *Lion parlant, Le* [*Opéra-Comique* in 3 acts, Prem. on 16-11-1792].
> Th. de la Citoyenne Montansier (2); **Total: 2.**

Chaussard, Pierre-J., Scio, Etienne (comp). *France régénérée, La* [*Comédie* in 1 act, Prem. on 14-9-1791].
Th. de Molière (17); **Total: 17.**

Chaussier, Hector., Bizet. *Anacréon à Suresnes* [*Parodie* in 3 acts, Prem. on 13-3-1797, Pub. in 1797].
Th. de l'Ambigu Comique (8); **Total: 8.**

_____. *Bientôt* [*Vaudeville* in 1 act, Prem. on 7-5-1795, Pub. in 1795].
Maison Egalité (3); **Total: 3.**

_____., Martainville, Alphonse. *Concert de la rue Feydeau, Le, ou L'Agrément du jour* [*Vaudeville* in 1 act, Prem. on 19-2-1795, Pub. in 1795].
Maison Egalité (18); Th. de la Citoyenne Montansier (1); Th. de la Cité (6); Th. des Variétés Amusantes, Comiques et Lyriques (1); Th. du Palais (Cité)-Variétés (5); **Total: 31.**

_____. *Despotisme et la liberté, Le* [*Pantomime* in 3 acts, Pub. in 1794].
Th. des Variétés Amusantes, Comiques et Lyriques (8); **Total: 8.**

_____., Bizet. *Diableries, Les, ou Gilles hermite* [*Comédie* in 3 acts, Pub. in 1797].
Th. de l'Ambigu Comique (17); **Total: 17.**

_____. *Jacobins aux enfers, Les* [*Vaudeville* in 1 act, Prem. on 22-3-1795, Pub. in 1795].
Th. des Variétés Amusantes, Comiques et Lyriques (29); **Total: 29.**

_____., Bizet. *Oiseaux d'Idalie, Les* [*Vaudeville* in 1 act, Prem. on 21-8-1798].
Th. Lyrique des Amis de la Patrie (3); **Total: 3.**

_____., Hapdé, Jean-B.-A. *Parachute, Le* [*Comédie* in 1 act, Prem. on 11-11-1797, Pub. in 1798].
Th. des Jeunes Artistes (47); **Total: 47.**
Total Performances, Chaussier, Hector: **146**

Chazel, Père. *Auberge allemande, L', ou Le Traître démasqué* [*Comédie* in 5 acts, Prem. on 20-1-1799, Pub. in 1801].
Th. de Molière (11); **Total: 11.**

Chazet, René-A.-P. de. *Champagnac et Suzette ou Fait comme lui* [*Vaudeville* in 1 act, Prem. on 16-10-1799].
Th. du Vaudeville (14); **Total: 14.**

_____., Ourry, E.-T.-Maurice. *Commissionnaires, Les, ou La Récompense honnête* [*Comédie* in 1 act].
Th. du Feydeau (de Monsieur) (1); Th. du Lycée des Arts (16); **Total: 17.**

_____., Léger, François-P.-A., Dupaty, Louis-E., Desfougerais, P.F. Aubin, dit. *Déménagement du salon, Le, ou Le Portrait de Gilles* [*Vaudeville*, Prem. on 16-10-1798, Pub. in 1798].
Th. du Vaudeville (2); **Total: 2.**

_____. *Il faut un état ou La Revue de l'an six* [*Proverbe/allégorique* in 1 act].
Th. des Troubadours (16); Th. du Vaudeville (59); **Total: 75.**

_____. *Monsieur de Bièvre ou L'Abus de l'esprit* [*Vaudeville*].
Th. des Troubadours (9); **Total: 9.**

_____. *Petite métromanie, La, ou La Pièce nouvelle* [*Comédie* in 1 act, Prem. on 9-9-1797].
Th. du Vaudeville (44); **Total: 44.**

_____., Léger, François-P.-A. *Troubadours en voyage, Les* [*Comédie* in 2 acts, Prem. on 23-10-1799].
Th. des Troubadours (**9**); **Total: 9.**
Total Performances, Chazet, René-A.-P. de: **170**

Chénier, Marie-J. *Caïus Gracchus* [*Tragédie* in 3 acts, Prem. on 9-2-1792, Pub. in 1793].
n/a (**2**); Th. du Marais (**1**); Th. Français (de la rue Richelieu) (de la République) (**26**); **Total: 29.**

_____. *Camp de grand-pré, Le, ou Le Triomphe de la République* [*Divertissement/parade* in 1 act, Prem. on 27-1-1793].
Académie de la Musique (Opéra) (**10**); **Total: 10.**

_____. *Charles IX ou L'Ecole des rois* [*Tragédie* in 5 acts, Prem. on 4-11-1789, Pub. in 1790].
Th. de la Nation (Comédie Française) (**29**); Th. des Délassements Comiques (**5**); Th. du Lycée Dramatique (**2**); Th. Français (de la rue Richelieu) (de la République) (**26**); **Total: 62.**

_____. *Fénelon ou Les Religieuses de Cambrai* [*Tragédie* in 5 acts, Prem. on 9-2-1793, Pub. in 1793].
Académie de la Musique (Opéra) (**1**); Th. de l'Ambigu Comique (**3**); Th. de l'Emulation (Gaîté) (**28**); Th. de Molière (**1**); Th. des Grands Danseurs (Gaîté) (**17**); Th. du Feydeau (de Monsieur) (**4**); Th. du Marais (**9**); Th. du Palais (Cité)-Variétés (**1**); Th. Français (de la rue Richelieu) (de la République) (**77**); **Total: 141.**

_____. *Henri VIII* [*Tragédie* in 5 acts, Prem. on 27-4-1791, Pub. in 1791].
Th. Français (de la rue Richelieu) (de la République) (**21**); **Total: 21.**

_____. *Jean Calas* [In 5 acts, Prem. on 6-7-1791, Pub. in 1793].
Th. de Molière (**1**); Th. du Marais (**2**); Th. Français (de la rue Richelieu) (de la République) (**15**); **Total: 18.**

_____., Méhul, Etienne-N. (comp). *Timoléon* [*Tragédie* in 3 acts, Prem. on 11-9-1794, Pub. in 1795].
Académie de la Musique (Opéra) (**1**); Th. du Feydeau (de Monsieur) (**1**); **Total: 2.**
Total Performances, Chénier, Marie-J.: **283**

Chéron de la Bruyère, Louis-C. *Homme à sentiments, L', ou Le Tartuffe des moeurs* [*Comédie* in 5 acts, Prem. on 10-3-1789, Pub. in 1801].
Th. de la Nation (Comédie Française) (**1**); Th. des Italiens (Opéra-Comique) (**5**); **Total: 6.**

Chevalier de Mont-Rémy. *Heureuse vengeance, L'* [*Comédie* in 1 act].
Th. de l'Odéon (**2**); **Total: 2.**

Chiavacchi, Andrea G., dit. *Journée du vatican, La, ou Le Mariage du pape* [*Comédie* in 3 acts, Prem. on 2-2-1790, Pub. in 1790].
Th. Lyrique des Amis de la Patrie (**27**); **Total: 27.**

Cizos-Duplessis, François. *Deux contrats, Les, ou Le Mariage inattendu* [*Comédie* in 1 act, Pub. in 1781].
Th. Français, Comique et Lyrique (**41**); **Total: 41.**

_____. *Mari coupable, Le* [*Comédie* in 3 acts, Prem. on 20-9-1794, Pub. in 1794].
Th. de la Cité (**6**); Th. du Palais (Cité)-Variétés (**1**); **Total: 7.**

_____. *Mère de famille, La* [*Comédie*, Prem. on 14-3-1791, Pub. in 1791].
Th. du Palais Royal (**5**); **Total: 5.**

_____. *Peuples et les rois, Les, ou Le Tribunal de la raison* [*Proverbe/allégorique* in 5 acts, Prem. on 12-4-1794, Pub. in 1794]. Th. du Palais (Cité)-Variétés (13); **Total: 13.**

_____. *Plan de comédie, Le* [*Comédie* in 3 acts, Pub. in 1634]. Th. Français, Comique et Lyrique (30); **Total: 30.**

_____. *Plus de bâtards en France* [*Comédie* in 3 acts, Prem. on 23-4-1795, Pub. in 1794]. Th. du Palais (Cité)-Variétés (10); **Total: 10.**

Total Performances, Cizos-Duplessis, François: **106**

Coffin-Rosny, André-J. *Affrico et Menzola* [*Mélodrame* in 3 acts, Prem. on 10-3-1798, Pub. in 1798]. Th. de l'Ambigu Comique (28); **Total: 28.**

Collé, Charles. *Amants déguisés, Les* [*Opéra-Comique* in 1 act, Prem. on 19-11-1754, Pub. in 1754]. Th. des Grands Danseurs (Gaîté) (2); **Total: 2.**

_____., Monsigny, Pierre-A. (comp). *Bouquet de Thalie, Le* [*Prologue*, Prem. on 25-12-1764, Pub. in 1768]. n/a (2); **Total: 2.**

_____. *Dupuis et Desronais* [*Comédie* in 3 acts, Prem. on 17-1-1763, Pub. in 1763]. Maison Egalité (1); Th. de l'Emulation (Gaîté) (5); Th. de l'Estrapade au Panthéon (3); Th. de l'Odéon (8); Th. de la Citoyenne Montansier (4); Th. de la Liberté (2); Th. de la Nation (Comédie Française) (8); Th. de la Rue Martin (5); Th. de Molière (1); Th. des Beaujolais (1); Th. des Victoires Nationales (1); Th. du Feydeau (de Monsieur) (6); Th. du Lycée des Arts (1); Th. du Lycée Dramatique (4); Th. du Marais (8); Th. du Palais Royal (2); Th. du Vaudeville (2); Th. Français (de la rue Richelieu) (de la République) (17); Th. Lyrique des Amis de la Patrie (8); Th. Lyrique du Foire St. Germain (1); Th. National (de la rue Richelieu) (3); Th. Patriotique et de Momus (10); **Total: 101.**

_____. *Partie de chasse d'Henri IV, La* [*Comédie* in 3 acts, Pub. in 1766]. Th. de la Citoyenne Montansier (23); Th. de la Liberté (7); Th. de la Nation (Comédie Française) (37); Th. de Molière (11); Th. des Beaujolais (1); Th. des Grands Danseurs (Gaîté) (4); Th. des Variétés Amusantes, Comiques et Lyriques (11); Th. du Marais (1); Th. Lyrique du Foire St. Germain (1); **Total: 96.**

_____. *Veuve, La* [*Comédie* in 1 act, Prem. in 4-1767, Pub. in 1764]. Th. du Palais Royal (33); Th. Français (de la rue Richelieu) (de la République) (7); Th. Français, Comique et Lyrique (6); **Total: 46.**

Total Performances, Collé, Charles: **247**

Collet de Messine, Jean-B. *Ile déserte, L'* [*Comédie* in 1 act, Prem. on 23-8-1758, Pub. in 1758]. Th. de la Nation (Comédie Française) (1); **Total: 1.**

Colleville, Anne-H. de Saint-Léger, Dame de. *Deux soeurs, Les* [*Comédie* in 1 act, Prem. on 14-6-1783, Pub. in 1783]. Th. de la Citoyenne Montansier (19); Th. des Grands Danseurs (Gaîté) (4); **Total: 23.**

_____. *Sophie et Derville* [*Comédie* in 1 act, Prem. on 8-1-1788, Pub. in 1788]. Th. des Italiens (Opéra-Comique) (20); **Total: 20.**

Total Performances, Colleville, Anne-H.de Saint-Léger, Dame de: **43**

Collin d'Harleville, Jean-F. *Artistes, Les* [*Pantomime* in 4 acts, Prem. on 9-11-1796, Pub. in 1797].
Th. Français (de la rue Richelieu) (de la République) (**11**); **Total: 11.**

———. *Châteaux en Espagne, Les* [*Comédie* in 5 acts, Prem. on 20-2-1789, Pub. in 1790].
Th. de la Nation (Comédie Française) (**18**); Th. du Marais (**6**); Th. Français (de la rue Richelieu) (de la République) (**35**); **Total: 59.**

———. *Etre et paraître* [*Comédie* in 5 acts, Prem. on 22-11-1796, Pub. in 1837].
Th. du Feydeau (de Monsieur) (**1**); **Total: 1.**

———. *Inconstant, L'* [*Comédie* in 5 acts, Prem. on 13-6-1786, Pub. in 1786].
Th. de la Nation (Comédie Française) (**7**); Th. du Feydeau (de Monsieur) (**8**); **Total: 15.**

———. *Moeurs du jour, Les, ou L'Ecole des jeunes femmes* [*Comédie* in 5 acts, Prem. on 26-7-1800, Pub. in 1800].
Th. des Jeunes Artistes (**10**); **Total: 10.**

———. *Monsieur de Crac dans son petit castel ou Les Gascons* [*Comédie* in 1 act, Prem. on 4-3-1791, Pub. in 1796].
Th. de la Nation (Comédie Française) (**26**); Th. du Feydeau (de Monsieur) (**7**); Th. Français (de la rue Richelieu) (de la République) (**1**); **Total: 34.**

———. *Optimiste, L', ou L'Homme content de tout* [*Comédie* in 5 acts, Prem. on 22-2-1788, Pub. in 1788].
Th. de la Nation (Comédie Française) (**29**); Th. du Feydeau (de Monsieur) (**14**); Th. Français (de la rue Richelieu) (de la République) (**4**); **Total: 47.**

———. *Rose et Picard ou La Suite de l'optimiste* [*Comédie* in 1 act, Prem. on 16-6-1794, Pub. in 1795].
Th. Français (de la rue Richelieu) (de la République) (**8**); **Total: 8.**

———. *Vieux célibataire, Le* [*Comédie* in 5 acts, Prem. on 24-2-1792, Pub. in 1793].
Maison Egalité (**3**); Th. de l'Emulation (Gaîté) (**9**); Th. de la Nation (Comédie Française) (**28**); Th. du Feydeau (de Monsieur) (**16**); Th. du Marais (**1**); Th. Français (de la rue Richelieu) (de la République) (**3**); Th. National (de la rue Richelieu) (**2**); **Total: 62.**

Total Performances, Collin d'Harleville, Jean-F.: **247**

Collot d'Herbois, J.-M. *Adrienne ou Le Secret de famille* [*Comédie* in 3 acts, Prem. on 12-4-1790, Pub. in 1790].
Th. du Palais Royal (**9**); Th. Français (de la rue Richelieu) (de la République) (**1**); **Total: 10.**

———. *Aîné et le cadet, L'* [In 2 acts, Prem. on 17-1-1792].
Th. du Feydeau (de Monsieur) (**8**); **Total: 8.**

———. *Amant loup-garou, L', ou M. Rodomont* [*Comédie* in 4 acts, Prem. in 1780, Pub. in 1780].
Th. de l'Emulation (Gaîté) (**2**); **Total: 2.**

———. *Famille patriote, La, ou La Fédération* [*Tableau-Patriotique* in 2 acts, Prem. on 17-7-1790, Pub. in 1790].
Th. du Feydeau (de Monsieur) (**17**); **Total: 17.**

———. *Il y a bonne justice ou Le Paysan magistrat* [*Drame* in 5 acts, Prem. on 7-12-1789, Pub. in 1778].
Th. de la Nation (Comédie Française) (**2**); Th. de la Rue Martin (**8**); **Total: 10.**

_____. *Inconnu, L', ou Le Préjugé nouvellement vaincu* [*Comédie* in 3 acts, Prem. on 17-11-1789, Pub. in 1790].
> Th. du Palais Royal (**13**); Th. Français (de la rue Richelieu) (de la République) (**3**); **Total: 16**.

_____. *Journée de Louis XII, La* [*Héroique* in 3 acts, Prem. on 14-9-1790].
> Th. du Palais Royal (**21**); **Total: 21**.

_____. *Portefeuilles, Les* [*Comédie* in 2 acts, Prem. on 10-2-1791, Pub. in 1791].
> Th. du Feydeau (de Monsieur) (**53**); Th. du Marais (**8**); **Total: 61**.

_____. *Procès de Socrate, Le, ou Le Régime des anciens temps* [*Comédie* in 3 acts, Prem. on 9-11-1790, Pub. in 1791].
> Th. du Feydeau (de Monsieur) (**27**); **Total: 27**.
>
> **Total Performances**, Collot d'Herbois, J.-M.: **172**

Cordier de Saint-Firmin, Edmond. *Galant savetier, Le* [*Comédie* in 1 act, Prem. on 9-3-1799, Pub. in 1779].
> Th. des Grands Danseurs (Gaîté) (**39**); **Total: 39**.

_____. *Mariage par les petites affiches, Le* [*Comédie* in 1 act, Pub. in 1797].
> Th. des Jeunes Artistes (**20**); **Total: 20**.

_____., **St. Amand, J. Gassier dit.** *Mort de Madame Angot, La* [*Tragi-Comédie* in 1 act, Prem. on 30-10-1797].
> Th. des Variétés Amusantes, Comiques et Lyriques (**28**); **Total: 28**.
>
> **Total Performances**, Cordier de Saint-Firmin, Edmond: **87**

Corneille, Pierre. *Cid, Le* [*Tragédie* in 5 acts, Prem. in 1637, Pub. in 1637].
> Th. de l'Odéon (**3**); Th. de la Citoyenne Montansier (**2**); Th. de la Nation (Comédie Française) (**24**); Th. de Molière (**8**); Th. du Marais (**3**); Th. Français (de la rue Richelieu) (de la République) (**9**); **Total: 49**.

_____. *Cinna ou La Clémence d'Auguste* [*Tragédie* in 5 acts, Prem. in 1640, Pub. in 1643].
> Th. de la Citoyenne Montansier (**1**); Th. de la Nation (Comédie Française) (**8**); Th. du Marais (**2**); Th. Lyrique des Amis de la Patrie (**1**); **Total: 12**.

_____. *Héraclius, Empereur d'Orient* [*Tragédie* in 5 acts, Prem. in 1647, Pub. in 1647].
> Th. de la Nation (Comédie Française) (**8**); **Total: 8**.

_____. *Horace* [*Tragédie* in 5 acts, Prem. in 1640, Pub. in 1641].
> Académie de la Musique (Opéra) (**1**); Maison Egalité (**2**); Th. de l'Odéon (**6**); Th. de la Nation (Comédie Française) (**7**); Th. Français (de la rue Richelieu) (de la République) (**3**); **Total: 19**.

_____. *Médée* [*Tragédie* in 5 acts, Pub. in 1639].
> Th. de l'Odéon (**6**); Th. de la Citoyenne Montansier (**11**); **Total: 17**.

_____. *Menteur, Le* [*Comédie* in 5 acts, Prem. in 1642, Pub. in 1644].
> n/a (**1**); Th. de la Citoyenne Montansier (**4**); Th. de la Nation (Comédie Française) (**8**); Th. de Molière (**1**); Th. du Feydeau (de Monsieur) (**3**); Th. du Marais (**4**); Th. Français (de la rue Richelieu) (de la République) (**22**); **Total: 43**.

_____. *Polyeucte* [*Tragédie* in 5 acts, Prem. in 1643, Pub. in 1643].
> Th. de la Nation (Comédie Française) (**2**); **Total: 2**.

_____. *Pulchérie* [*Comédie* in 5 acts, Prem. in 1672, Pub. in 1673].
> Petits Comédiens de Palais Royal (**14**); Th. Français, Comique et Lyrique (**1**); **Total: 15**.

_____. *Rodogune, princesse des Parthes* [*Tragédie* in 5 acts, Prem. in 1644, Pub. in 1647].
> Académie de la Musique (Opéra) (**1**); Th. de l'Odéon (**3**); Th. de la Citoyenne Montansier (**8**); Th. de la Nation (Comédie Française) (**13**); Th. du Marais (**1**); Th. Français (de la rue Richelieu) (de la République) (**5**); **Total: 31**.

_____. *Sertorius* [*Tragédie* in 5 acts, Prem. in 1662, Pub. in 1662].
> Th. de la Nation (Comédie Française) (**1**); **Total: 1**.
>
> **Total Performances**, Corneille, Pierre: **197**

Corneille, Thomas. *Ariane* [*Tragédie* in 5 acts, Prem. on 4-3-1672, Pub. in 1672].
> Th. de la Citoyenne Montansier (**3**); Th. de la Nation (Comédie Française) (**1**); **Total: 4**.

_____. *Baron d'Albikrac, Le* [*Comédie* in 5 acts, Pub. in 1669].
> Th. Français (de la rue Richelieu) (de la République) (**4**); **Total: 4**.

_____. *Comte d'Essex, Le* [*Tragédie*, Prem. in 1678, Pub. in 1691].
> Th. de la Citoyenne Montansier (**1**); Th. de la Nation (Comédie Française) (**3**); **Total: 4**.

_____. *Festin de Pierre, Le* [*Comédie* in 5 acts, Prem. in 1642, Pub. in 1677].
> Th. de l'Estrapade au Panthéon (**3**); Th. de la Citoyenne Montansier (**1**); Th. de la Liberté (**2**); Th. de la Nation (Comédie Française) (**3**); Th. de la Rue Martin (**1**); Th. des Variétés Amusantes, Comiques et Lyriques (**9**); Th. du Feydeau (de Monsieur) (**4**); Th. du Marais (**7**); Th. Français (de la rue Richelieu) (de la République) (**14**); **Total: 44**.
>
> **Total Performances**, Corneille, Thomas: **56**

Corsange de la Plante, Jean-F.-J. *Augustin et Babet ou Le Fils naturel* [*Comédie* in 1 act, Prem. on 8-11-1791, Pub. in 1792].
> Cirque National (**9**); Th. des Jeunes Artistes (**54**); Th. du Marais (**1**); **Total: 64**.

_____., Hapdé, Jean-B.-A. *Dernier couvent de France, Le, ou L'Hospice* [*Comédie* in 2 acts, Prem. on 13-8-1796, Pub. in 1796].
> Th. des Jeunes Artistes (**98**); Th. du Marais (**1**); **Total: 99**.
>
> **Total Performances**, Corsange de la Plante, Jean-F.-J.: **163**

Cottereau., Jadin, Louis-E. (comp). *Amélie de Montfort* [*Opéra* in 3 acts, Prem. on 13-2-1792].
> Th. du Feydeau (de Monsieur) (**3**); **Total: 3**.

Courtial. *Piété filiale, La, ou La Jambe de bois* [*Pièce* in 5 acts, Pub. in 1769].
> Th. de l'Emulation (Gaîté) (**2**); Th. du Feydeau (de Monsieur) (**1**); Th. du Marais (**3**); **Total: 6**.

Coypel, Charles-A. *Don Quichotte* [*Pantomime*, Prem. on 29-8-1799].
> Ampithéâtre National (**5**); Th. de l'Ambigu Comique (**1**); Th. de la Cité (**4**); Th. de Molière (**1**); Th. des Italiens (Opéra-Comique) (**1**); Th. du Palais (Cité)-Variétés (**8**); Th. Lyrique des Amis de la Patrie (**1**); **Total: 21**.

Crébillon, Prosper Jolyot de. *Atrée et Thyeste* [*Tragédie* in 5 acts, Prem. on 14-3-1707, Pub. in 1716].
> n/a (**1**); Th. du Lycée Dramatique (**2**); **Total: 3**.

_____. *Electre* [*Tragédie* in 5 acts, Prem. on 14-12-1708, Pub. in 1702].
> Th. de la Nation (Comédie Française) (**2**); **Total: 2**.

_____. *Rhadamisthe et Zénobie* [*Tragédie* in 5 acts, Prem. on 23-1-1711, Pub. in 1711].
>Th. de l'Odéon (**2**); Th. de la Citoyenne Montansier (**2**); Th. de la Nation (Comédie Française) (**6**); Th. du Feydeau (de Monsieur) (**1**); Th. du Marais (**2**); **Total: 13**.
>**Total Performances**, Crébillon, Prosper Jolyot de: **18**

Crêton de Villeneuve. *Entêté, L', ou On ne connaît jamais son enfant* [*Pièce* in 2 acts, Prem. on 19-1-1789].
>Th. des Grands Danseurs (Gaîté) (**31**); **Total: 31**.

_____. *Gusman d'Alfarache ou Le Mariage nocturne* [*Pièce* in 2 acts, Prem. on 31-8-1789].
>Th. des Grands Danseurs (Gaîté) (**59**); **Total: 59**.

_____. *Pardon imprévu de la nièce malheureuse, Le* [*Pièce* in 2 acts, Prem. on 18-6-1788].
>Th. des Grands Danseurs (Gaîté) (**19**); **Total: 19**.

_____. *Pari imprudent, Le, ou Plus heureux que sage* [*Proverbe/allégorique* in 1 act, Prem. on 23-4-1789].
>Th. des Grands Danseurs (Gaîté) (**91**); **Total: 91**.

_____. *Rivaux congédiés, Les, ou Le Duel sans danger* [*Comédie* in 2 acts, Pub. in 1788].
>Th. de l'Emulation (Gaîté) (**1**); Th. des Grands Danseurs (Gaîté) (**41**); **Total: 42**.

_____. *Valet favorable, Le, ou Le Mariage par enlèvement* [*Pièce* in 1 act, Prem. on 1-3-1788].
>Th. des Grands Danseurs (Gaîté) (**9**); **Total: 9**.
>**Total Performances**, Crêton de Villeneuve: **251**

Creuze de Lesser, Auguste. *Ninon de Lenclos ou L'Epicuréisme* [*Comédie* in 1 act, Pub. in 1800].
>Th. des Troubadours (**30**); **Total: 30**.

Cubières-Palmezeaux, Michel de. *Baronne de Chantal, fondatrice de l'ordre de la visitation, La* [*Fait Historique* in 3 acts, Prem. on 3-2-1797, Pub. in 1795].
>Th. de la Rue Martin (**5**); **Total: 5**.

_____. *Epreuve singulière, L', ou La Jambe de bois* [*Comédie* in 3 acts, Prem. on 10-9-1787].
>Th. du Palais Royal (**8**); **Total: 8**.

_____. *Mort de Molière, La* [*Pièce* in 3 acts, Prem. on 19-11-1789, Pub. in 1802].
>Th. de la Nation (Comédie Française) (**1**); **Total: 1**.
>**Total Performances**, Cubières-Palmezeaux, Michel de: **14**

Curmer, F.-Alexandre. *Laitière polonaise, La, ou Le Coupable par amour* [*Pantomime* in 3 acts, Prem. on 17-2-1798, Pub. in 1798].
>Th. de la Citoyenne Montansier (**1**); Th. de la Cité (**23**); Th. du Palais (Cité)-Variétés (**18**); **Total: 42**.

Cuvelier de Trie, Jean G.-A. *Akancas, Les* [*Prologue* in 1 act, Prem. on 30-17-1797, Pub. in 1797].
>Maison Egalité (**1**); Th. de la Cité (**18**); Th. des Variétés Amusantes, Comiques et Lyriques (**1**); Th. du Palais (Cité)-Variétés (**21**); **Total: 41**.

_____., Vandenbroeck, Othon (comp)., Mittié, Jean-C. *Anniversaire, L', ou La Fête de la souveraineté* [*Mélodrame*, Prem. on 20-3-1798, Pub. in 1798].
> Th. de l'Ambigu Comique (2); **Total: 2.**

_____. *C'est le diable ou La Bohémienne* [*Drame* in 5 acts, Prem. on 13-11-1797].
> Th. de l'Ambigu Comique (96); **Total: 96.**

_____., Vandenbroeck, Othon (comp). *Codicille, Le, ou Les Deux héritiers* [*Comédie* in 1 act, Prem. on 10-6-1793, Pub. in 1793].
> Th. de la Citoyenne Montansier (16); Th. de la Montagne (3); **Total: 19.**

_____. *Conseil de Lucifer, Le* [*Prologue* in 1 act, Prem. on 15-12-1796].
> Th. de la Cité (10); Th. du Palais (Cité)-Variétés (12); **Total: 22.**

_____. *Damoisel et la bergerette, La, ou La Femme vindicative* [*Pantomime* in 3 acts, Prem. on 3-2-1799, Pub. in 1814].
> Th. de la Cité (31); Th. de Molière (1); Th. des Variétés Amusantes, Comiques et Lyriques (2); Th. du Palais (Cité)-Variétés (74); **Total: 108.**

_____., Navoigille, Julien (comp). *Empire de la folie, L', ou La Mort et l'apothéose de Don Quichotte* [*Pantomime* in 3 acts, Prem. on 6-6-1799].
> Th. du Palais (Cité)-Variétés (6); **Total: 6.**

_____. *Enfant du malheur, L', ou Les Amants muets* [*Féerie*, Prem. on 29-3-1797].
> Th. de l'Ambigu Comique (110); **Total: 110.**

_____. *Enlèvement, L', ou La Caverne dans les Pyrénées* [*Pantomime* in 3 acts, Prem. on 29-12-1792, Pub. in 1793].
> Th. de la Cité (1); Th. du Palais (Cité)-Variétés (47); **Total: 48.**

_____. *Espagnols dans la Floride, Les* [In 1 act].
> Th. du Palais (Cité)-Variétés (6); **Total: 6.**

_____., Gresnick, Antoine (comp). *Faux monnayeurs, Les, ou La Vengeance* [*Drame* in 3 acts, Prem. on 1-5-1797, Pub. in 1797].
> Académie de la Musique (Opéra) (1); Th. de la Citoyenne Montansier (29); **Total: 30.**

_____., Vandenbroeck, Othon (comp). *Fête de l'Etre suprême, La* [*Tableau-Patriotique*, Prem. on 10-6-1794, Pub. in 1794].
> Th. du Palais (Cité)-Variétés (4); **Total: 4.**

_____., Vandenbroeck, Othon (comp). *Fille hermite, La* [*Opéra* in 1 act, Prem. on 21-9-1797, Pub. in 1796].
> Th. de l'Ambigu Comique (4); Th. du Lycée des Arts (46); **Total: 50.**

_____. *Fille hussard, La, ou Le Sergent suédois* [*Pantomime* in 3 acts, Prem. on 19-3-1796, Pub. in 1797].
> Th. de la Citoyenne Montansier (4); Th. de la Cité (91); Th. des Grands Danseurs (Gaîté) (1); Th. des Variétés Amusantes, Comiques et Lyriques (1); Th. du Palais (Cité)-Variétés (86); **Total: 183.**

_____. *Frédégilde ou Le Démon familier* [*Drame* in 4 acts, Prem. on 22-10-1798].
> Th. du Palais (Cité)-Variétés (21); **Total: 21.**

_____., Vandenbroeck, Othon (comp). *Génie Asouf, Le, ou Les Deux coffrets* [*Féerie* in 2 acts, Prem. on 25-12-1795, Pub. in 1797].
> Th. de la Cité (2); **Total: 2.**

_____., Navoigille, Julien (comp)., Hapdé, Jean-B.-A. *Hérolhe Suisse, L', ou Amour et courage* [*Pantomime*, Pub. in 1794].
    Th. du Palais (Cité)-Variétés (**28**); **Total: 28.**

_____. *Menuisier de Vierzon, Le* [*Fait Historique* in 1 act, Prem. on 10-17-94].
    Th. de l'Ambigu Comique (**13**); Th. de la Rue Martin (**1**); **Total: 14.**

_____. *Mort du Maréchal de Turenne, La* [*Fait Historique* in 3 acts, Prem. on 17-6-1797].
    Th. de la Cité (**12**); Th. des Grands Danseurs (Gaîté) (**1**); Th. du Palais (Cité)-Variétés (**35**); **Total: 48.**

_____., Navoigille, Julien (comp)., Hapdé, Jean-B.-A. *Naissance de la pantomime, La* [*Mélodrame*, Prem. on 21-4-1798, Pub. in 1797].
    Th. du Palais (Cité)-Variétés (**8**); **Total: 8.**

_____., Hapdé, Jean-B.-A. *Petit poucet, Le, ou L'Orphelin de la forêt* [*Drame* in 5 acts, Prem. on 14-3-1798, Pub. in 1798].
    Th. des Jeunes Artistes (**156**); Th. du Marais (**7**); **Total: 163.**

_____. *Phénix, Le, ou L'Isle des vieilles* [*Féerie* in 4 acts, Prem. on 4-11-1797].
    Th. de la Cité (**15**); Th. des Jeunes Artistes (**82**); Th. du Marais (**2**); **Total: 99.**

_____., Morange (comp). *Quiproco nocturnes* [*Opéra*, Prem. on 13-12-1797, Pub. in 1798].
    Th. de la Citoyenne Montansier (**6**); **Total: 6.**

_____. *Royalistes de la Vendée, Les, ou Les Epoux républicains* [*Pantomime* in 3 acts, Prem. on 10-9-1794, Pub. in 1794].
    Th. du Palais (Cité)-Variétés (**25**); **Total: 25.**

_____. *Tentations, Les, ou Tous les diables* [*Pantomime* in 3 acts, Prem. on 17-12-1796, Pub. in 1800].
    Th. de la Cité (**45**); Th. du Palais (Cité)-Variétés (**39**); **Total: 84.**
             Total Performances, Cuvelier de Trie, Jean G.-A.: **1223**

Da Ponte, Lorenzo., Martini, Vincente (comp). *Burbero di buon cuore, Il* [*Opéra-Comique* in 2 acts, Prem. on 4-1-1786].
    Th. du Feydeau (de Monsieur) (**8**); **Total: 8.**

_____., Gazzaniga, Giuseppe (comp). *Finto cieco, Il* [*Opéra* in 2 acts, Prem. on 20-12-1786].
    Th. du Feydeau (de Monsieur) (**5**); **Total: 5.**
             Total Performances, Da Ponte, Lorenzo: **13**

Dabaytua, Joachim-E. *Eléonore de Rosalba ou Le Confessionnal des pénitents noirs* [*Drame* in 4 acts, Prem. on 5-6-1798, Pub. in 1798].
    Th. du Palais (Cité)-Variétés (**34**); **Total: 34.**

Daine. *Barbe bleue* [*Comédie* in 2 acts, Prem. on 28-9-1795].
    Th. des Italiens (Opéra-Comique) (**2**); **Total: 2.**

_____., Porta, Bernado (comp). *Blanche haquenée* [*Opéra-Comique* in 3 acts, Prem. on 22-5-1793].
    Th. des Italiens (Opéra-Comique) (**1**); **Total: 1.**
             Total Performances, Daine: **3**

Danchet, Antoine. *Alcine* [*Tragédie lyrique* in 5 acts, Prem. on 15-1-1705, Pub. in 1705].
    Th. des Variétés Amusantes, Comiques et Lyriques (**23**); **Total: 23.**

_____. *Muses, Les* [*Ballet* in 4 acts, Prem. on 28-10-1703, Pub. in 1703].
    Th. des Grands Danseurs (Gaîté) (**7**); **Total: 7.**
             Total Performances, Danchet, Antoine: **30**

Dancourt, Florent C. *Bourgeoises de qualité, Les* [*Comédie* in 5 acts, Prem. on 25-9-1724, Pub. in 1690].
    Th. de la Nation (Comédie Française) (**12**); Th. Français (de la rue Richelieu) (de la République) (**23**); **Total: 35.**
_____. *Chevalier à la mode, Le* [*Comédie* in 5 acts, Pub. in 1687].
    Th. de la Citoyenne Montansier (**2**); Th. de la Nation (Comédie Française) (**6**); Th. de la Rue Martin (**7**); Th. du Marais (**4**); Th. Français (de la rue Richelieu) (de la République) (**1**); Th. Lyrique des Amis de la Patrie (**2**); **Total: 22.**
_____. *Colin-Maillard* [*Comédie* in 1 act, Prem. on 28-10-1701, Pub. in 1701].
    Th. de la Citoyenne Montansier (**1**); Th. de la Nation (Comédie Française) (**5**); Th. des Grands Danseurs (Gaîté) (**47**); Th. des Troubadours (**16**); **Total: 69.**
_____. *Curieux de Compiègne, Les* [*Comédie* in 1 act, Pub. in 1698].
    Th. de la Nation (Comédie Française) (**1**); **Total: 1.**
_____. *Fête de village, La* [*Comédie* in 3 acts, Prem. on 13-7-1700, Pub. in 1700].
    Th. du Feydeau (de Monsieur) (**3**); **Total: 3.**
_____. *Fonds perdus, Les* [*Comédie*, Prem. on 8-6-1686].
    Th. des Variétés Amusantes, Comiques et Lyriques (**1**); Th. du Palais (Cité)-Variétés (**1**); **Total: 2.**
_____. *Galant jardinier, Le* [*Comédie* in 1 act, Prem. on 22-10-1704, Pub. in 1705].
    Th. de la Nation (Comédie Française) (**22**); **Total: 22.**
_____. *Loterie, La* [*Comédie* in 1 act, Pub. in 1697].
    Th. des Délassements Comiques (**1**); Th. des Jeunes Artistes (**18**); **Total: 19.**
_____. *Maison de campagne, La* [*Comédie* in 1 act, Pub. in 1688].
    Th. de la Nation (Comédie Française) (**5**); Th. des Grands Danseurs (Gaîté) (**4**); **Total: 9.**
_____. *Mari retrouvé, Le* [*Comédie* in 1 act, Prem. on 25-10-1698, Pub. in 1698].
    n/a (**2**); Th. de l'Estrapade au Panthéon (**2**); Th. de l'Odéon (**8**); Th. de la Citoyenne Montansier (**2**); Th. de la Liberté (**3**); Th. de la Montagne (**7**); Th. de la Nation (Comédie Française) (**25**); Th. de la Rue Martin (**7**); Th. des Grands Danseurs (Gaîté) (**10**); Th. des Victoires Nationales (**2**); Th. du Lycée Dramatique (**2**); Th. du Marais (**8**); Th. du Vaudeville (**7**); Th. Français (de la rue Richelieu) (de la République) (**15**); Th. Français, Comique et Lyrique (**3**); Th. Lyrique des Amis de la Patrie (**4**); **Total: 107.**
_____. *Parisienne, La* [*Comédie* in 1 act, Prem. on 14-12-1791, Pub. in 1691].
    Th. des Grands Danseurs (Gaîté) (**10**); **Total: 10.**
_____. *Trois cousines, Les* [*Comédie* in 3 acts, Prem. on 18-10-1700, Pub. in 1725].
    Th. de la Nation (Comédie Française) (**15**); Th. des Grands Danseurs (Gaîté) (**38**); **Total: 53.**
_____. *Tuteur, Le* [*Comédie* in 1 act, Pub. in 1695].
    Th. de l'Ambigu Comique (**1**); Th. de la Citoyenne Montansier (**20**); Th. de la Liberté (**3**); Th. de la Montagne (**1**); Th. de la Nation (Comédie Française) (**12**); Th. de la Rue Martin (**6**); Th. du Feydeau (de Monsieur) (**3**); Th. du Marais (**5**); Th. Lyrique des Amis de la Patrie (**2**); Th. National (de la rue Richelieu) (**1**); **Total: 54.**

_____. *Vacances, Les* [*Comédie* in 1 act, Pub. in 1696].
  Th. de l'Ambigu Comique (**32**); Th. de la Nation (Comédie Française) (**19**); Th. du Feydeau (de Monsieur) (**7**); Th. du Marais (**3**); **Total: 61**.

_____. *Vendanges de Suresne, Les* [*Comédie* in 1 act, Pub. in 1695].
  Th. de l'Odéon (**8**); Th. de la Nation (Comédie Française) (**3**); Th. des Grands Danseurs (Gaîté) (**49**); Th. des Victoires (**6**); Th. du Marais (**1**); Th. du Palais (Cité)-Variétés (**1**); Th. Français (de la rue Richelieu) (de la République) (**10**); **Total: 78**.

Total Performances, Dancourt, Florent C.: **545**

Dancourt, L.-H., Lebrun, Louis-S. (comp). *Art d'aimer au village, L', ou L'Enchère amoureuse* [*Comédie mêlée d'ariettes* in 1 act, Prem. on 16-6-1790, Pub. in 1764].
  Th. de la Citoyenne Montansier (**42**); **Total: 42**.

_____., Rigel, Henri-J. (comp). *Atine et Zamorin ou L'Amour turc* [*Opéra-Bouffe* in 3 acts, Prem. on 26-9-1786, Pub. in 1787].
  Th. des Beaujolais (**2**); **Total: 2**.

_____. *Diogène fabuliste* [*Comédie* in 1 act, Prem. on 12-9-1782, Pub. in 1783].
  Th. de l'Ambigu Comique (**32**); **Total: 32**.

_____. *Eté des coquettes, L'* [*Comédie* in 1 act, Pub. in 1690].
  Th. de la Nation (Comédie Française) (**1**); **Total: 1**.

_____. *Folle enchère, La* [*Comédie* in 1 act, Pub. in 1690].
  Th. de l'Ambigu Comique (**17**); **Total: 17**.

Total Performances, Dancourt, L.-H.: **94**

Danzel de Malzéville., Méreaux, Nicolas-J. (comp). *Laurette* [*Opéra* in 1 act, Prem. on 23-7-1777, Pub. in 1777].
  Th. de Molière (**1**); **Total: 1**.

Dard d'Aucourt de Saint-Just, Claude., Marmontel, Jean-F., Longchamps., Boïeldieu, François-A. (comp). *Heureuse nouvelle, L'* [*Opéra-Comique* in 1 act, Prem. on 7-11-1797].
  Th. des Délassements Comiques (**1**); Th. du Feydeau (de Monsieur) (**10**); **Total: 11**.

_____., Boïeldieu, François-A. (comp). *Méprises espagnoles, Les* [*Opéra-Comique* in 1 act, Prem. on 18-4-1799].
  Th. du Feydeau (de Monsieur) (**6**); **Total: 6**.

Total Performances, Dard d'Aucourt de Saint-Just, Claude: **17**

Darhilly. *Bagnaudière, La, ou Le Fou malgré lui* [*Comédie* in 3 acts, Prem. on 8-8-1793].
  Th. du Palais (Cité)-Variétés (**8**); **Total: 8**.

Dauberval, Jean Bercher, dit. *Fille mal gardée, La* [*Ballet* in 2 acts, Prem. in 1785, Pub. in 1785].
  Th. Patriotique et de Momus (**12**); **Total: 12**.

De Lille, B. Dupont. *Double réconciliation, La* [*Vaudeville* in 1 act, Prem. on 23-7-1796].
  Th. de la Rue Martin (**1**); Th. des Jeunes Artistes (**47**); **Total: 48**.

_____. *Mariage de Justine, Le, ou La Suite de la double réconciliation* [*Comédie* in 2 acts, Prem. on 23-7-1796, Pub. in 1799].
  Th. des Jeunes Artistes (**39**); **Total: 39**.

_____. *Montre, La, ou Les Effets du repentir* [*Comédie*, Prem. on 20-2-1798].
  Th. des Jeunes Artistes (**21**); **Total: 21**.

Total Performances, De Lille, B. Dupont: **108**

De Senne., Bonnay, Franco (comp). *Curieux punis, Les* [*Comédie* in 1 act, Prem. on 20-11-1786, Pub. in 1787].
    Th. des Beaujolais (**46**); Th. du Lycée des Arts (**29**); **Total: 75.**

_____., Bonnay, Franco (comp). *Fête de l'arquebuse, La* [*Opéra-Comique* in 2 acts, Prem. on -11-1787].
    Th. du Lycée des Arts (**9**); **Total: 9.**

_____. *Revenant, Le, ou Les Deux grenadiers* [*Comédie* in 2 acts, Prem. on 1-7-1786, Pub. in 1786].
    Maison Egalité (**2**); Th. de la Citoyenne Montansier (**16**); Th. de la Cité (**4**); Th. des Variétés Amusantes, Comiques et Lyriques (**7**); Th. du Palais (Cité)-Variétés (**27**); Th. du Palais Royal (**49**); **Total: 105.**
    Total Performances, De Senne: 189

De Vasse, Corneille W. *Mari soupçonneux, Le* [*Comédie* in 5 acts, Prem. on 16-8-1791, Pub. in 1786].
    Th. Lyrique des Amis de la Patrie (**10**); **Total: 10.**

Dehesse, Jean-F. Deshayes, dit. *Mariée de village, La* [*Ballet* in 1 act, Prem. on 12-10-1757, Pub. in 1757].
    Th. des Grands Danseurs (Gaîté) (**1**); **Total: 1.**

_____. *Montagnards, Les* [*Ballet*, Prem. on 14-8-1754].
    Th. de la Cité (**3**); **Total: 3.**

_____. *Noce villageoise, La* [*Ballet* in 1 act, Prem. on 3-7-1755, Pub. in 1755].
    Th. des Grands Danseurs (Gaîté) (**2**); **Total: 2.**

_____. *Villageois, Les* [*Ballet* in 1 act, Prem. on 3-9-1755, Pub. in 1755].
    Th. des Grands Danseurs (Gaîté) (**4**); **Total: 4.**
    Total Performances, Dehesse, Jean-F. Deshayes, dit: 10

Dejaure, Jean-E. Bédéno., Kreutzer, Rodolpho (comp). *Déserteur de la montagne du Hamm, Le* [*Fait Historique* in 1 act, Prem. on 6-2-1793].
    Th. des Italiens (Opéra-Comique) (**11**); **Total: 11.**

_____. *Dot de Suzette, La* [*Comédie* in 1 act, Prem. on 5-9-1798, Pub. in 1798].
    Th. des Italiens (Opéra-Comique) (**40**); **Total: 40.**

_____. *Epoux généreux, L', ou Le Pouvoir des procédés* [*Comédie* in 1 act, Prem. on 15-2-1790, Pub. in 1804].
    Th. de l'Ambigu Comique (**16**); Th. des Italiens (Opéra-Comique) (**21**); **Total: 37.**

_____. *Epoux réunis, Les* [*Comédie* in 1 act, Prem. on 31-7-1789, Pub. in 1790].
    Th. des Italiens (Opéra-Comique) (**25**); Th. Français, Comique et Lyrique (**6**); **Total: 31.**

_____. *Fille naturelle, La* [*Comédie* in 1 act, Prem. on 11-1-1792, Pub. in 1792].
    Th. des Italiens (Opéra-Comique) (**16**); Th. du Feydeau (de Monsieur) (**4**); Th. du Vaudeville (**3**); **Total: 23.**

_____., Kreutzer, Rodolpho (comp). *Franc Breton, Le, ou Le Négociant de Nantes* [*Comédie* in 1 act, Prem. on 15-2-1791, Pub. in 1791].
    Th. des Italiens (Opéra-Comique) (**48**); **Total: 48.**

_____., Kreutzer, Rodolpho (comp). *Imogène ou La Gageure indiscrète* [*Comédie* in 3 acts, Prem. on 27-4-1796].
    Th. des Italiens (Opéra-Comique) (**4**); **Total: 4.**

_____. *Incertitude maternelle, L', ou Le Choix impossible* [*Comédie* in 1 act, Prem. on 5-6-1790, Pub. in 1790].
    Th. des Italiens (Opéra-Comique) (**45**); **Total: 45.**

_____., Kreutzer, Rodolpho (comp). *Lodoiska ou Les Tartares* [*Comédie* in 3 acts, Prem. on 1-8-1791, Pub. in 1798].
   n/a (41); Th. des Italiens (Opéra-Comique) (84); **Total: 130.**

_____. *Louise et Volsan* [*Comédie* in 3 acts, Prem. on 2-8-1790, Pub. in 1790].
   Th. des Italiens (Opéra-Comique) (11); **Total: 11.**

_____., Berton, Henri-M. (comp). *Montano et Stéphanie* [*Opéra-Vaudeville* in 3 acts, Prem. on 15-4-1799, Pub. in 1802].
   Th. des Italiens (Opéra-Comique) (25); **Total: 25.**

_____., Berton, Henri-M. (comp). *Nouveau d'Assas, Le* [*Tragédie* in 1 act, Prem. on 15-10-1790, Pub. in 1790].
   Th. des Italiens (Opéra-Comique) (17); **Total: 17.**

_____. *Ombre de Mirabeau, L'* [*Episodique* in 1 act, Prem. on 7-5-1791, Pub. in 1791].
   Th. des Italiens (Opéra-Comique) (7); **Total: 7.**

_____., Kreutzer, Rodolpho (comp). *Werther et Charlotte* [*Drame* in 1 act, Prem. on 1-2-1792, Pub. in 1792].
   Th. des Italiens (Opéra-Comique) (19); **Total: 19.**
   Total Performances, Dejaure, Jean-E. Bédéno: **448**

Delaporte, Pierre-M. *Télémaque cadet* [*Parodie*].
   Th. de la Cité (15); **Total: 15.**

Delautel, G. *Forgeron, Le* [*Opéra-Bouffe* in 1 act, Prem. in 4-1762, Pub. in 1762].
   Th. de l'Ambigu Comique (51); **Total: 51.**

_____. *Naufrage d'Arlequin, Le* [*Comédie* in 2 acts, Prem. in 1766, Pub. in 1766].
   Th. de la Citoyenne Montansier (1); **Total: 1.**
   Total Performances, Delautel, G.: **52**

Delon, M.-N. *Mariage de Chérubin, Le* [*Comédie* in 3 acts, Prem. on 22-8-1791, Pub. in 1785].
   Th. de l'Ambigu Comique (6); **Total: 6.**

Delrieu, Etienne-J.-B. *Adèle et Paulin ou La Prévention paternelle* [*Comédie* in 3 acts, Prem. on 15-8-1793, Pub. in 1792].
   Th. de la Citoyenne Montansier (18); Th. de la Montagne (2); Th. National (de la rue Richelieu) (1); **Total: 21.**

_____. *Amélia ou Les Deux jumeaux espagnols* [*Drame* in 5 acts, Prem. on 14-7-1798, Pub. in 1798].
   Th. du Palais (Cité)-Variétés (9); **Total: 9.**

_____., Rigel, Henri-J. (comp). *Bon fermier, Le* [*Comédie* in 1 act, Prem. on 18-5-1789, Pub. in 1789].
   Th. de la Rue Martin (4); Th. des Beaujolais (16); Th. du Lycée des Arts (4); **Total: 24.**

_____., Jadin, Louis-E. (comp). *Défi des sauteurs, Le, ou Le Défi hasardeux* [*Opéra-Comique* in 2 acts, Prem. on 8-8-1796].
   Th. des Variétés Amusantes (Lazzari) (1); Th. du Lycée des Arts (14); **Total: 15.**

_____., Gaveaux, Pierre (comp). *Delmon et Nadine* [In 2 acts, Prem. on 13-7-1795].
   Th. du Feydeau (de Monsieur) (9); **Total: 9.**

_____., Jadin, Louis-E. (comp). *Deux lettres, Les* [*Comédie* in 1 act, Prem. on 4-8-1796].
>Th. des Italiens (Opéra-Comique) (**2**); **Total: 2.**

_____. *Jaloux malgré lui, Le* [*Comédie* in 1 act, Prem. on 3-4-1793, Pub. in 1803].
>Th. de l'Odéon (**12**); Th. de la Nation (Comédie Française) (**11**); Th. des Italiens (Opéra-Comique) (**1**); Th. du Feydeau (de Monsieur) (**1**); Th. du Marais (**6**); Th. du Palais (Cité)-Variétés (**3**); **Total: 34.**

_____. *Père supposé, Le, ou Les époux dès le berceau* [*Comédie* in 3 acts, Prem. on 14-12-1798].
>Th. du Palais (Cité)-Variétés (**14**); **Total: 14.**

_____., Méhul, Etienne-N. (comp). *Pont de Lodi, Le* [*Fait Historique* in 1 act, Prem. on 15-12-1797].
>Th. du Feydeau (de Monsieur) (**4**); **Total: 4.**

_____. *Ruses du mari, Les* [*Comédie* in 3 acts, Prem. on 29-8-1799].
>Th. de la Cité (**12**); Th. du Palais (Cité)-Variétés (**5**); **Total: 17.**
>>**Total Performances**, Delrieu, Etienne-J.-B.: **149**

Demautort, Jacques-B. *Arlequin Joseph* [*Comédie* in 1 act, Prem. on 26-12-1793, Pub. in 1794].
>Th. du Vaudeville (**42**); **Total: 42.**

_____. *Marchandes de la halle, Les* [*Comédie* in 1 act, Prem. on 23-10-1794, Pub. in 1794].
>Th. des Variétés Amusantes, Comiques et Lyriques (**1**); Th. du Vaudeville (**33**); **Total: 34.**

_____., Chardiny, Louis-A. (comp). *Petit Sacristain, Le, ou Le Départ des novices* [*Comédie* in 2 acts, Prem. on 13-3-1792, Pub. in 1792].
>Th. du Vaudeville (**77**); **Total: 77.**
>>**Total Performances**, Demautort, Jacques-B.: **153**

Demoustier, Charles-A., Devienne, François (comp). *Agnès et Felix ou Les Deux espiègles* [*Opéra* in 3 acts, Prem. on 22-8-1795].
>Th. du Feydeau (de Monsieur) (**6**); **Total: 6.**

_____. *Alceste à la campagne ou Le Misanthrope corrigé* [*Comédie* in 3 acts, Prem. in 1790, Pub. in 1798].
>Académie de la Musique (Opéra) (**15**); Th. de l'Emulation (Gaîté) (**10**); Th. des Grands Danseurs (Gaîté) (**7**); Th. des Variétés Amusantes, Comiques et Lyriques (**22**); Th. du Feydeau (de Monsieur) (**18**); Th. du Marais (**6**); Th. Français, Comique et Lyrique (**1**); Th. Lyrique des Amis de la Patrie (**6**); **Total: 85.**

_____., Gaveaux, Pierre (comp). *Amour filial, L', ou Les Deux suisses* [*Opéra* in 1 act, Prem. on 6-3-1792, Pub. in 1794].
>Th. de l'Ambigu Comique (**1**); Th. de Molière (**20**); Th. du Feydeau (de Monsieur) (**166**); Th. du Marais (**3**); Th. du Palais (Cité)-Variétés (**2**); Th. Français, Comique et Lyrique (**1**); Th. Lyrique des Amis de la Patric (**1**); **Total: 194.**

_____., Gaveaux, Pierre (comp). *Apelle et Campaspe* [*Opéra* in 1 act, Prem. on 12-7-1798, Pub. in 1798].
>Académie de la Musique (Opéra) (**6**); **Total: 6.**

_____. *Conciliateur, Le, ou L'Homme aimable* [*Comédie* in 5 acts, Prem. on 29-9-1791, Pub. in 1794].
>Maison Egalité (**1**); Th. de la Nation (Comédie Française) (**31**); Th. du Feydeau (de Monsieur) (**25**); Th. Français (de la rue Richelieu) (de la République) (**5**); Th. National (de la rue Richelieu) (**4**); **Total: 66.**

_____. *Constance* [*Comédie* in 2 acts, Pub. in 1792].
   Th. des Italiens (Opéra-Comique) (**7**); **Total: 7**.

_____. *Divorce, Le* [*Comédie* in 2 acts, Prem. on 10-7-1791, Pub. in 1795].
   Maison Egalité (**4**); Th. du Feydeau (de Monsieur) (**23**); Th. du Palais
   (Cité)-Variétés (**24**); Th. du Vaudeville (**13**); **Total: 64**.

_____. *Femmes, Les* [*Comédie* in 3 acts, Prem. on 19-4-1793, Pub. in 1795].
   Th. de la Nation (Comédie Française) (**16**); Th. du Feydeau (de Monsieur)
   (**25**); Th. Français (de la rue Richelieu) (de la République) (**3**); **Total: 44**.

_____., Gaveaux, Pierre (comp). *Sic paria, Le, ou La Chaumière indi-
enne* [*Opéra* in 2 acts, Prem. on 8-10-1792].
   Th. du Feydeau (de Monsieur) (**12**); **Total: 12**.

_____., Gaveaux, Pierre (comp). *Sophronime ou La Reconnaisance*
[*Opéra* in 1 act, Prem. on 13-2-1795, Pub. in 1795].
   Th. du Feydeau (de Monsieur) (**3**); **Total: 3**.

_____. *Toilette de Julie, La* [*Comédie* in 1 act, Prem. on 18-2-1791].
   Th. du Feydeau (de Monsieur) (**16**); **Total: 16**.

_____. *Tolérant, Le, ou La Tolérance morale et religieuse* [*Comédie* in 5
acts, Prem. on 23-4-1795, Pub. in 1796].
   Th. du Feydeau (de Monsieur) (**2**); **Total: 2**.

                              Total Performances, Demoustier, Charles-A.: **505**

Dercy, P., Le Sueur, Jean-F. (comp). *Caverne, La* [*Opéra* in 3 acts, Prem.
   on 16-2-1793, Pub. in 1793].
   Th. de l'Emulation (Gaîté) (**1**); Th. de l'Odéon (**3**); Th. de la Citoyenne
   Montansier (**1**); Th. de la Cité (**15**); Th. de la Rue Martin (**1**); Th. des
   Délassements Comiques (**9**); Th. du Feydeau (de Monsieur) (**107**); Th. du
   Palais (Cité)-Variétés (**16**); **Total: 153**.

_____., Le Sueur, Jean-F. (comp). *Télémaque dans l'îsle de Calypso
ou Le Triomphe de la sagesse* [*Opéra* in 3 acts, Prem. on 10-5-1796, Pub.
in 1796].
   Th. de l'Emulation (Gaîté) (**15**); Th. du Feydeau (de Monsieur) (**41**); **Total: 56**.

                              Total Performances, Dercy, P.: **209**

Desaudrais, Charles Emmanuel Gaulard de. *Amants ridicules, Les, ou
   Les Deux jaloux* [*Comédie* in 1 act, Prem. on 3-9-1790, Pub. in 1711].
   Th. des Beaujolais (**11**); **Total: 11**.

Desaudras. *Hôtellerie de Worms, L'* [*Comédie* in 1 act, Prem. on 11-8-1791].
   Th. Français (de la rue Richelieu) (de la République) (**3**); **Total: 3**.

_____. *Minuit* [*Comédie* in 1 act, Prem. on 31-12-1791, Pub. in 1798].
   Th. de l'Ambigu Comique (**2**); Th. de l'Emulation (Gaîté) (**1**); Th. de la
   Cité (**1**); Th. de la Nation (Comédie Française) (**20**); Th. des Italiens
   (Opéra-Comique) (**1**); Th. du Feydeau (de Monsieur) (**11**); Th. du Marais
   (**5**); Th. du Palais (Cité)-Variétés (**3**); Th. Français (de la rue Richelieu) (de
   la République) (**9**); **Total: 53**.

                              Total Performances, Desaudras: **56**

Desaugiers, Marc-A. *Amour et la peur, L'* [*Comédie* in 1 act].
   Th. des Jeunes Artistes (**23**); **Total: 23**.

_____. *Testament de Carlin, Le* [*Vaudeville*, Prem. on 29-3-1799, Pub. in
   1798].
   Th. de la Cité (**1**); Th. des Jeunes Artistes (**14**); **Total: 15**.

                              Total Performances, Desaugiers, Marc-A.: **38**

Deschamps, Jacques-M. *Charles Rivière Dufresny ou Le Mariage impromptu* [*Comédie* in 1 act, Prem. on 31-3-1798, Pub. in 1798].
  Th. du Vaudeville (**36**); **Total: 36.**

_____., Bruni, Antonio-B. (comp). *Claudine ou Le Petit commissionnaire* [*Comédie* in 1 act, Prem. on 6-3-1794, Pub. in 1794].
  Th. de l'Ambigu Comique (**20**); Th. de la Citoyenne Montansier (**12**); Th. de la Cité (**3**); Th. du Feydeau (de Monsieur) (**58**); Th. Lyrique des Amis de la Patrie (**53**); **Total: 146.**

_____. *Loi d'accord avec la nature, La* [*Comédie* in 1 act, Prem. on 5-10-1794].
  Th. Français (de la rue Richelieu) (de la République) (**3**); **Total: 3.**

_____., Desprez, Jean-B.-D. *Nouveau magasin des modernes, Le* [*Comédie* in 1 act, Prem. on 8-12-1798, Pub. in 1799].
  Th. du Marais (**1**); Th. du Vaudeville (**33**); **Total: 34.**

_____. *Piron avec ses amis ou Les Moeurs du temps passé* [*Comédie* in 1 act, Prem. on 19-6-1792, Pub. in 1793].
  Th. du Marais (**1**); Th. du Vaudeville (**178**); **Total: 179.**

_____. *Poste évacué, Le* [*Comédie* in 1 act, Prem. on 30-1-1794, Pub. in 1794].
  Th. du Vaudeville (**27**); **Total: 27.**

_____. *Revanche forcée, La* [*Comédie* in 1 act, Prem. on 10-2-1792, Pub. in 1792].
  Th. des Beaujolais (**11**); Th. du Vaudeville (**140**); **Total: 151.**

_____., Desprez, Jean-B.-D. *Succession, La* [*Opéra-Comique* in 1 act, Prem. on 4-5-1796, Pub. in 1796].
  Th. du Vaudeville (**73**); **Total: 73.**
  Total Performances, Deschamps, Jacques-M.: **649**

Desfaucherets, J.-L.-B., Lebrun, Louis-S. (comp). *Astronome, L'* [*Opéra-Comique*, Prem. on 10-9-1799].
  Th. du Feydeau (de Monsieur) (**28**); **Total: 28.**

_____., Chérubini, Luigi (comp). *Punition, La* [*Opéra* in 1 act, Prem. on 23-2-1799].
  Th. du Feydeau (de Monsieur) (**11**); **Total: 11.**
  Total Performances, Desfaucherets, J.-L.-B.: **39**

Desfontaines, François-G. Fouques, dit., Dalayrac, Nicolas (comp). *Amant statue, L'* [*Comédie* in 1 act, Prem. on 4-8-1785, Pub. in 1785].
  Th. des Italiens (Opéra-Comique) (**92**); **Total: 92.**

_____. *Amour et la folie, L'* [*Opéra-Comique* in 3 acts, Prem. on 5-3-1782, Pub. in 1782].
  Th. du Vaudeville (**18**); **Total: 18.**

_____. *Chasse, La* [*Comédie* in 3 acts, Prem. on 12-10-1778, Pub. in 1778].
  Th. de l'Ambigu Comique (**8**); Th. du Lycée Dramatique (**4**); Th. du Palais (Cité)-Variétés (**2**); **Total: 14.**

_____. *Chouans de Vitré, Les* [*Fait Historique* in 1 act, Prem. on 12-6-1794].
  Th. du Vaudeville (**19**); **Total: 19.**

_____., La Borde, Jean-B. de (comp). *Cinquantaine, La* [*Pastoral* in 3 acts, Prem. on 13-8-1771, Pub. in 1771].
  Th. de la Citoyenne Montansier (**6**); Th. du Lycée des Arts (**14**); **Total: 20.**

_____. *Destin et les parques, Le* [*Vaudeville* in 1 act, Prem. on 5-5-1788].
  Th. des Italiens (Opéra-Comique) (**6**); **Total: 6.**

_____. *Dîner imprévu, Le* [*Opéra-Comique* in 2 acts, Prem. on 28-4-1792].
  Th. du Vaudeville (**18**); **Total: 18.**

_____. *District de village, Le* [*Vaudeville* in 1 act, Prem. on 15-3-1790, Pub. in 1790].
      Th. des Italiens (Opéra-Comique) (**15**); **Total: 15.**

_____. *Divorce, Le* [*Comédie* in 1 act, Prem. on 18-5-1793, Pub. in 1794].
      n/a (**1**); Th. du Palais (Cité)-Variétés (**8**); Th. du Vaudeville (**121**); **Total: 130.**

_____., Dalayrac, Nicolas (comp). *Dot, La* [*Comédie* in 3 acts, Prem. on 8-11-1785, Pub. in 1785].
      Th. de l'Ambigu Comique (**129**); Th. des Italiens (Opéra-Comique) (**90**); Th. du Vaudeville (**1**); **Total: 220.**

_____., Martini, Jean.-P.-E. (comp). *Droit du seigneur, Le* [*Comédie* in 3 acts, Prem. on 17-10-1783, Pub. in 1783].
      Th. des Italiens (Opéra-Comique) (**42**); **Total: 42.**

_____. *Ecole des mères, L'* [*Comédie* in 3 acts, Prem. on 3-12-1795].
      Th. du Vaudeville (**48**); **Total: 48.**

_____., Dalayrac, Nicolas (comp). *Fanchette* [*Comédie* in 2 acts, Prem. on 13-10-1788].
      Th. des Italiens (Opéra-Comique) (**39**); **Total: 39.**

_____. *Fille soldat, La* [*Fait Historique* in 1 act, Prem. on 13-12-1794].
      Th. du Vaudeville (**46**); **Total: 46.**

_____. *Imprimeur, L', ou La Fête de Franklin* [*Comédie* in 2 acts, Prem. on 8-4-1791].
      Th. du Feydeau (de Monsieur) (**9**); **Total: 9.**

_____. *Mille et un théâtres, Les* [*Opéra-Comique* in 1 act, Prem. on 14-2-1792, Pub. in 1792].
      Th. du Vaudeville (**19**); **Total: 19.**

_____. *Tombeau de Desilles, Le* [*Anecdotique* in 1 act, Prem. on 3-12-1790].
      Th. de la Nation (Comédie Française) (**5**); **Total: 5.**

_____. *Union villageoise, L'* [*Tableau-Patriotique*, Prem. on 9-8-1793, Pub. in 1794].
      Th. du Vaudeville (**42**); **Total: 42.**

_____., Dalayrac, Nicolas (comp). *Vert-vert* [Prem. on 11-10-1790].
      Th. des Italiens (Opéra-Comique) (**1**); **Total: 1.**

_____. *Vieux époux, Les* [*Comédie* in 1 act, Prem. on 22-4-1794, Pub. in 1795].
      Th. du Vaudeville (**31**); **Total: 31.**

                Total Performances, Desfontaines, François-G. Fouques, dit: **834**

Desforges, Pierre-J.-B. Choudard de., Jadin, Louis-E. (comp). *Alisbelle ou Les Crimes de la féodalité* [*Opéra* in 3 acts, Prem. on 2-3-1794, Pub. in 1794].
      Maison Egalité (**2**); Th. de la Citoyenne Montansier (**1**); Th. National (de la rue Richelieu) (**29**); **Total: 32.**

_____., Mengozzi, Bernardo (comp). *Deux vizirs, Les* [*Opéra* in 3 acts, Prem. on 10-3-1792].
      Th. de la Citoyenne Montansier (**11**); **Total: 11.**

_____. *Epouse imprudente, L'* [*Comédie* in 5 acts, Prem. on 13-9-1791].
      Th. de la Citoyenne Montansier (**10**); **Total: 10.**

_____., Grétry, André-E.-M. (comp). *Epreuve villageoise, L'* [*Opéra-Comique* in 2 acts, Prem. on 24-6-1784, Pub. in 1784].
> n/a (**2**); Th. de l'Emulation (Gaîté) (**2**); Th. de la Rue Martin (**1**); Th. des Délassements Comiques (**2**); Th. des Italiens (Opéra-Comique) (**132**); Th. des Variétés Amusantes, Comiques et Lyriques (**5**); Th. du Marais (**3**); **Total: 147.**

_____. *Femme jalouse, La* [*Comédie* in 5 acts, Prem. on 15-2-1785, Pub. in 1785].
> Académie de la Musique (Opéra) (**2**); Th. de l'Odéon (**4**); Th. de la Citoyenne Montansier (**25**); Th. de la Montagne (**3**); Th. de la Rue Martin (**4**); Th. de Molière (**8**); Th. des Italiens (Opéra-Comique) (**6**); Th. des Victoires Nationales (**4**); Th. du Feydeau (de Monsieur) (**14**); Th. du Marais (**7**); Th. du Palais (Cité)-Variétés (**2**); Th. Français (de la rue Richelieu) (de la République) (**31**); Th. Lyrique des Amis de la Patrie (**1**); Th. National (de la rue Richelieu) (**1**); **Total: 112.**

_____. *Féodor et Lisinka ou Novogorod sauvée* [*Drame* in 3 acts, Prem. on 3-10-1786, Pub. in 1787].
> Th. du Marais (**4**); **Total: 4.**

_____., Méreaux, Nicolas-J. (comp). *Grisélide ou La Vertu à l'épreuve* [*Opéra* in 3 acts, Prem. on 8-1-1791].
> Th. des Italiens (Opéra-Comique) (**3**); **Total: 3.**

_____. *Hymne éducative, L'* [N/A].
> Th. National (de la rue Richelieu) (**1**); **Total: 1.**

_____., Kreutzer, Rodolpho (comp). *Jeanne d'Arc à Orléans* [*Comédie* in 3 acts, Prem. on 10-5-1790].
> Th. des Italiens (Opéra-Comique) (**9**); **Total: 9.**

_____., Jadin, Louis-E. (comp). *Joconde, La* [*Opéra* in 3 acts, Prem. on 14-9-1790].
> Th. du Feydeau (de Monsieur) (**22**); **Total: 22.**

_____. *Perruque de laine ou L'Entêté* [*Comédie* in 3 acts].
> Th. de la Citoyenne Montansier (**2**); **Total: 2.**

_____., Berton, Henri-M. (comp). *Promesses de mariage, Les* [*Opéra-Bouffe* in 2 acts, Prem. on 4-7-1787, Pub. in 1788].
> Th. des Italiens (Opéra-Comique) (**1**); **Total: 1.**

_____. *Sourd, Le, ou L'Auberge pleine* [*Comédie* in 3 acts, Prem. on 30-9-1790, Pub. in 1793].
> n/a (**16**); Th. de l'Ambigu Comique (**17**); Th. de l'Emulation (Gaîté) (**1**); Th. de la Citoyenne Montansier (**251**); Th. de la Cité (**4**); Th. de la Montagne (**23**); Th. de la Rue Martin (**6**); Th. de Molière (**3**); Th. des Délassements Comiques (**28**); Th. des Victoires (**3**); Th. des Victoires Nationales (**2**); Th. du Marais (**10**); Th. du Palais (Cité)-Variétés (**9**); Th. du Vaudeville (**1**); Th. Français (de la rue Richelieu) (de la République) (**89**); **Total: 463.**

_____. *Tom Jones à Londres* [*Comédie* in 5 acts, Prem. on 22-10-1782, Pub. in 1782].
> Th. de l'Odéon (**11**); Th. de la Citoyenne Montansier (**13**); Th. de la Rue Martin (**4**); Th. des Italiens (Opéra-Comique) (**10**); Th. des Variétés Amusantes, Comiques et Lyriques (**1**); Th. du Feydeau (de Monsieur) (**16**); Th. Français (de la rue Richelieu) (de la République) (**1**); **Total: 56.**

_____. *Tom Jones et Fellamar* [*Comédie* in 5 acts, Prem. on 4-7-787, Pub. in 1788].
> Th. des Italiens (Opéra-Comique) (**2**); **Total: 2.**

_____. *Tuteur célibataire, Le* [*Comédie* in 1 act, Prem. on 17-11-1789, Pub. in 1786].
> Th. de la Citoyenne Montansier (**18**); Th. des Italiens (Opéra-Comique) (**6**); Th. National (de la rue Richelieu) (**1**); **Total: 25.**
> > **Total Performances,** Desforges, Pierre-J.-B. Choudard de: **900**

Desfougerais, P.F. Aubin, dit. *Aveugle et le muet, L' ou Les Nez cassés* [*Opéra-Comique* in 1 act, Prem. on 17-4-1797, Pub. in 1797].
> Th. de la Cité (**12**); **Total: 12.**

Desgagniers de B. *Fanny ou L'Heureux repentir* [*Drame* in 1 act, Prem. on 6-5-1790, Pub. in 1774].
> Th. du Feydeau (de Monsieur) (**7**); **Total: 7.**

Desportes, Claude-F. *Veuve coquette, La* [*Comédie* in 1 act, Prem. on 28-10-1721, Pub. in 1732].
> Th. des Grands Danseurs (Gaîté) (**24**); **Total: 24.**

Desportes, Philippe. *Chasseurs, Les* [N/A].
> Th. de l'Emulation (Gaîté) (**1**); Th. de la Citoyenne Montansier (**2**); Th. des Italiens (Opéra-Comique) (**2**); Th. des Jeunes Artistes (**1**); Th. des Variétés Amusantes (Lazzari) (**4**); Th. Patriotique et de Momus (**1**); **Total: 11.**

Desprès, Jean-B.-D. *Alarmiste, L'* [*Tableau-Patriotique* in 1 act, Prem. on 21-7-1794, Pub. in 1794].
> Th. du Vaudeville (**18**); **Total: 18.**

_____., Rouget de Lisle., Della-Maria, Dominique (comp). *Jacquot ou L'Ecole des mères* [*Opéra-Comique*, Prem. on 28-5-1798].
> Th. des Italiens (Opéra-Comique) (**5**); **Total: 5.**

_____. *Retour à Bruxelles, Le* [*Opéra-Comique* in 1 act, Prem. on 11-9-1794, Pub. in 1794].
> Th. du Vaudeville (**6**); **Total: 6.**
> > **Total Performances,** Desprès, Jean-B.-D.: **29**

Desriaux, Philippe., Blasius, Mathieu-F. (comp). *Amour Ermite, L'* [*Opéra-Bouffe* in 1 act, Prem. on 31-1-1789, Pub. in 1789].
> Th. des Beaujolais (**38**); Th. du Lycée des Arts (**2**); **Total: 40.**

_____. *Constance et Colignan* [*Drame* in 4 acts, Prem. on 2-3-1792].
> Th. de Molière (**1**); **Total: 1.**

_____., Jadin, Louis-E. (comp). *Constance et Gernand* [*Comédie* in 1 act, Prem. on 15-7-1790].
> Th. Français, Comique et Lyrique (**12**); **Total: 12.**

_____., Vogel, Johann-C. (comp). *Démophon* [*Opéra* in 3 acts, Prem. on 15-9-1789, Pub. in 1789].
> Académie de la Musique (Opéra) (**14**); **Total: 14.**

_____. *Ombre de Jean-Jacques Rousseau, L'* [*Comédie* in 2 acts, Pub. in 1787].
> Th. de l'Estrapade au Panthéon (**1**); Th. des Variétés Amusantes, Comiques et Lyriques (**7**); **Total: 8.**
> > **Total Performances,** Desriaux, Philippe: **75**

Destival de Braban, Jean N., dit. *Artiste infortuné, L', ou La Famille vertueuse* [*Comédie* in 2 acts, Prem. on 2-7-1788, Pub. in 1788].
> Th. des Grands Danseurs (Gaîté) (**36**); **Total: 36.**

_____. *Chercheuses d'esprit, Les* [*Opéra-Comique* in 1 act, Pub. in 1792].
> Th. des Grands Danseurs (Gaîté) (**20**); Th. des Troubadours (**8**); Th. du Vaudeville (**2**); **Total: 30.**

_____. *Egyptiens de qualité et les diseurs de bonne aventure, Les*
[*Comédie* in 2 acts, Prem. on 23-2-1786].
  Th. des Grands Danseurs (Gaîté) (**15**); **Total: 15.**
_____. *Enfant prodigue, L'* [*Pantomime* in 4 acts, Pub. in 1769].
  Th. des Grands Danseurs (Gaîté) (**45**); Th. du Lycée des Arts (**3**); **Total: 48.**
_____. *Enlèvement de Proserpine, L', ou Arlequin bouffon des enfers*
[*Comédie* in 3 acts, Prem. on 23-10-1786].
  Th. des Grands Danseurs (Gaîté) (**19**); **Total: 19.**
_____., Cammaille-St.-Aubin, M.-C. *Fausse mère, La, ou Une Faute
de l'amour* [*Drame* in 5 acts, Prem. on 5-5-1798, Pub. in 1798].
  Th. de l'Ambigu Comique (**21**); Th. du Feydeau (de Monsieur) (**20**); **Total: 41.**
_____., Valcour, Aristide. *Gâteau des rois, Le* [*Opéra* in 1 act, Pub. in
1792].
  Th. des Grands Danseurs (Gaîté) (**1**); **Total: 1.**
_____. *Nouveau calendrier, Le, ou Il n'y a plus de prêtres* [*Tableau-
Patriotique* in 3 acts, Pub. in 1793].
  Th. des Grands Danseurs (Gaîté) (**47**); **Total: 47.**
_____. *Nuit de Henri IV, La, ou Le Charbonnier est maître chez lui*
[*Pantomime* in 3 acts, Prem. on 12-12-1789].
  Th. des Grands Danseurs (Gaîté) (**45**); **Total: 45.**
_____. *Pêche aux huîtres de Bayeux, La* [*Comédie* in 3 acts, Prem. on 13-10-
1785].
  Th. des Grands Danseurs (Gaîté) (**23**); **Total: 23.**
_____. *Philosophe soi-disant, Le* [*Comédie* in 2 acts, Prem. on 24-5-1785].
  Th. des Grands Danseurs (Gaîté) (**8**); **Total: 8.**
_____. *Polichinelle protégé par la fortune* [*Pantomime* in 3 acts, Prem. on
17-3-1786].
  Th. des Grands Danseurs (Gaîté) (**33**); **Total: 33.**
_____. *Politique et l'homme franc, Le* [*Comédie* in 2 acts, Prem. on 3-9-
1789].
  Th. des Grands Danseurs (Gaîté) (**76**); **Total: 76.**
_____. *Retour de Figaro à Madrid, Le* [*Comédie* in 1 act, Prem. on 17-8-
1784].
  Th. des Grands Danseurs (Gaîté) (**5**); **Total: 5.**
_____. *Verrou, Le, ou Jeannot dupe de son amour* [*Comédie* in 1 act, Prem.
on 28-12-1784, Pub. in 1785].
  Th. des Grands Danseurs (Gaîté) (**5**); **Total: 5.**
_____. *Voyage de Figaro esclave à Alger, Le* [*Pantomime*].
  Th. des Grands Danseurs (Gaîté) (**1**); **Total: 1.**
  Total Performances, Destival de Braban, Jean N., dit: **433**
Destouches, Philippe-N. *Ambitieux et l'indiscrète, L'* [*Tragi-Comédie* in 5
acts, Prem. on 14-6-1737, Pub. in 1737].
  Th. de la Nation (Comédie Française) (**5**); **Total: 5.**

_____. *Dissipateur, Le, ou L'Honnête Friponne* [*Comédie* in 5 acts, Prem. on 23-3-1753, Pub. in 1736].

Maison Egalité (**1**); Th. de l'Estrapade au Panthéon (**3**); Th. de l'Odéon (**13**); Th. de la Citoyenne Montansier (**4**); Th. de la Cité (**2**); Th. de la Nation (Comédie Française) (**9**); Th. de la Rue Martin (**3**); Th. de Molière (**4**); Th. du Feydeau (de Monsieur) (**8**); Th. du Marais (**8**); Th. du Mareux (**2**); Th. Français (de la rue Richelieu) (de la République) (**34**); Th. Lyrique des Amis de la Patrie (**2**); Th. National (de la rue Richelieu) (**6**); **Total: 99**.

_____. *Fausse Agnès, La, ou Le Poète campagnard* [*Comédie* in 3 acts, Prem. on 12-3-1759, Pub. in 1736].

Académie de la Musique (Opéra) (**1**); Th. de l'Ambigu Comique (**4**); Th. de l'Emulation (Gaîté) (**12**); Th. de l'Estrapade au Panthéon (**1**); Th. de l'Odéon (**13**); Th. de la Citoyenne Montansier (**4**); Th. de la Nation (Comédie Française) (**26**); Th. de la Rue Martin (**13**); Th. de Molière (**15**); Th. des Grands Danseurs (Gaîté) (**36**); Th. des Italiens (Opéra-Comique) (**2**); Th. des Variétés Amusantes, Comiques et Lyriques (**1**); Th. des Victoires (**8**); Th. du Feydeau (de Monsieur) (**24**); Th. du Marais (**18**); Th. du Palais (Cité)-Variétés (**1**); Th. du Palais Royal (**3**); Th. Français (de la rue Richelieu) (de la République) (**50**); Th. Lyrique des Amis de la Patrie (**7**); Th. Lyrique du Foire St. Germain (**1**); **Total: 240**.

_____. *Fausse veuve, La* [*Comédie* in 1 act, Prem. on 21-12-1790, Pub. in 1715].
Th. Français, Comique et Lyrique (**1**); **Total: 1**.

_____. *Glorieux, Le* [*Comédie* in 5 acts, Prem. on 18-1-1732, Pub. in 1732].
Académie de la Musique (Opéra) (**1**); Th. de l'Ambigu Comique (**1**); Th. de l'Estrapade au Panthéon (**3**); Th. de l'Odéon (**3**); Th. de la Citoyenne Montansier (**3**); Th. de la Nation (Comédie Française) (**18**); Th. de la Rue Antoine (**1**); Th. de Molière (**8**); Th. du Feydeau (de Monsieur) (**13**); Th. du Lycée Dramatique (**5**); Th. du Marais (**19**); Th. Français (de la rue Richelieu) (de la République) (**25**); Th. Lyrique des Amis de la Patrie (**1**); Th. Lyrique du Foire St. Germain (**1**); **Total: 102**.

_____. *Homme singulier, L'* [*Comédie* in 5 acts, Prem. on 5-11-1764, Pub. in 1765].
Th. de la Citoyenne Montansier (**4**); Th. de Molière (**1**); Th. du Marais (**2**); Th. Français (de la rue Richelieu) (de la République) (**21**); **Total: 28**.

_____. *Jeune homme à l'épreuve, Le* [*Comédie* in 5 acts, Pub. in 1751].
Th. de l'Emulation (Gaîté) (**14**); Th. Lyrique des Amis de la Patrie (**3**); **Total: 17**.

_____. *Obstacle imprévu, L', ou L'Obstacle sans obstacle* [*Comédie* in 5 acts, Prem. on 18-10-1717, Pub. in 1718].
Th. de la Citoyenne Montansier (**3**); Th. du Marais (**3**); Th. National (de la rue Richelieu) (**1**); **Total: 7**.

_____. *Philosophe marié, Le, ou Le Mari honteux de l'être* [*Comédie* in 5 acts, Prem. on 15-2-1727, Pub. in 1727].
Th. de l'Estrapade au Panthéon (**2**); Th. de l'Odéon (**5**); Th. de la Citoyenne Montansier (**4**); Th. de la Rue Antoine (**3**); Th. de Molière (**12**); Th. des Variétés Amusantes, Comiques et Lyriques (**1**); Th. du Marais (**4**); Th. Français (de la rue Richelieu) (de la République) (**16**); Th. Lyrique des Amis de la Patrie (**2**); **Total: 49**.

_____. *Tambour nocturne, Le, ou Le Mari devin* [*Comédie* in 5 acts, Prem. on 16-10-1762, Pub. in 1736].
Th. de la Citoyenne Montansier (**3**); Th. de la Nation (Comédie Française) (**4**); Th. de la Rue Martin (**1**); Th. de Molière (**1**); Th. du Feydeau (de Monsieur) (**4**); Th. du Marais (**3**); Th. Français (de la rue Richelieu) (de la République) (**4**); **Total: 20**.

_____. *Triple mariage, Le* [*Comédie* in 1 act, Prem. on 7-7-1716, Pub. in 1716].
Th. de la Citoyenne Montansier (**3**); Th. de la Nation (Comédie Française) (**18**); Th. des Victoires (**5**); Th. du Feydeau (de Monsieur) (**10**); Th. du Marais (**1**); Th. Français (de la rue Richelieu) (de la République) (**8**); **Total: 45.**
Total Performances, Destouches, Philippe-N.: **613**

Deville, Jean-B.-L. *Pierre Bagnolet et Claude Bagnolet, son fils* [*Comédie* in 1 act, Prem. on 27-7-1782, Pub. in 1782].
Th. de l'Emulation (Gaîté) (**20**); Th. de la Cité (**10**); Th. des Grands Danseurs (Gaîté) (**60**); **Total: 90.**

Dezède, Nicolas. *Ferdinand ou La Suite des deux pages* [*Comédie* in 3 acts, Prem. on 19-6-1790].
Th. des Italiens (Opéra-Comique) (**16**); **Total: 16.**

_____. *Paulin et Clairette ou Les Deux espiègles* [*Comédie* in 2 acts, Prem. on 5-1-1792].
Th. de la Nation (Comédie Française) (**8**); **Total: 8.**

_____. *Trois noces, Les* [*Comédie* in 1 act, Prem. on 23-2-1790].
Th. de la Nation (Comédie Française) (**4**); **Total: 4.**
Total Performances, Dezède, Nicolas: **28**

Didelot, Nicolas. *Métamorphose, La* [*Ballet*].
Th. Français (de la rue Richelieu) (de la République) (**3**); **Total: 3.**

Diderot, Denis. *Fils naturel, Le, ou Les Epreuves de la vertu* [*Comédie* in 5 acts, Prem. on 26-9-1771, Pub. in 1757].
Th. de l'Ambigu Comique (**1**); **Total: 1.**

_____. *Père de famille, Le* [*Comédie* in 5 acts, Prem. in 9-1760, Pub. in 1758].
Maison Egalité (**4**); Th. de l'Emulation (Gaîté) (**4**); Th. de l'Estrapade au Panthéon (**3**); Th. de l'Odéon (**3**); Th. de la Citoyenne Montansier (**10**); Th. de la Liberté (**2**); Th. de la Nation (Comédie Française) (**21**); Th. de la Rue Martin (**10**); Th. de Molière (**11**); Th. des Délassements Comiques (**8**); Th. du Feydeau (de Monsieur) (**10**); Th. du Lycée Dramatique (**1**); Th. du Marais (**6**); Th. du Palais Royal (**1**); Th. Français (de la rue Richelieu) (de la République) (**31**); Th. Français, Comique et Lyrique (**7**); Th. Lyrique des Amis de la Patrie (**4**); Th. Lyrique du Foire St. Germain (**1**); Th. National (de la rue Richelieu) (**2**); **Total: 139.**
Total Performances, Diderot, Denis: **140**

Dieulafoy, Michel. *Moulin de sans souci, Le* [*Fait Historique* in 1 act, Prem. on 6-7-1798, Pub. in 1798].
Th. du Vaudeville (**52**); **Total: 52.**

_____. *Quart d'heure de Rabelais, Le* [*Comédie* in 1 act, Prem. on 14-1-1799, Pub. in 1799].
Th. du Vaudeville (**15**); **Total: 15.**
Total Performances, Dieulafoy, Michel: **67**

Diodati, G.-M., Cimarosa, Domenico (comp). *Impresario en Angustie, L'* [*Opéra* in 2 acts, Prem. on 6-5-1789].
Th. du Feydeau (de Monsieur) (**25**); **Total: 25.**

_____., Cimarosa, Domenico (comp). *Trame deluse, Le* [*Comedia Per Musica* in 3 acts, Prem. on 7-12-1786].
Th. du Feydeau (de Monsieur) (**6**); **Total: 6.**
Total Performances, Diodati, G.-M.: **31**

Dognon, Jean-F., Foignet, Charles-G. (comp)., Rebory. *Prisonniers français en Angleterre, Les* [*Opéra* in 2 acts, Prem. on 8-4-1798, Pub. in 1798].
>   Th. de la Citoyenne Montansier (13); **Total: 13.**

Dorat, Claude-J. *Feinte par amour, La* [*Comédie* in 3 acts, Prem. on 31-7-1773, Pub. in 1774].
>   Académie de la Musique (Opéra) (1); Th. de l'Ambigu Comique (1); Th. de l'Estrapade au Panthéon (1); Th. de l'Odéon (7); Th. de la Citoyenne Montansier (7); Th. de la Nation (Comédie Française) (30); Th. de la Rue Antoine (1); Th. de la Rue Martin (7); Th. de Molière (10); Th. des Variétés Amusantes, Comiques et Lyriques (10); Th. des Victoires (1); Th. des Victoires Nationales (4); Th. du Feydeau (de Monsieur) (12); Th. du Lycée Dramatique (3); Th. du Marais (9); Th. du Mareux (1); Th. du Palais (Cité)-Variétés (1); Th. du Vaudeville (1); Th. Français (de la rue Richelieu) (de la République) (23); Th. Français, Comique et Lyrique (4); Th. Lyrique des Amis de la Patrie (4); Th. Lyrique du Foire St. Germain (1); Th. Patriotique et de Momus (9); **Total: 148.**

Dorcey, Mlle. *Niza et Békir* [*Comédie* in 2 acts, Prem. on 26-12-1770, Pub. in 1770].
>   Th. de l'Ambigu Comique (13); **Total: 13.**

Dorvigny, Louis-A. *Arlequin corsaire* [N/A].
>   Th. des Ombres Chinoises (13); Th. des Ombres de J.-J. Rousseau (13); **Total: 26.**

_____. *Bataille d'Arlequin, La* [N/A].
>   Th. des Ombres Chinoises (7); Th. des Ombres de J.-J. Rousseau (9); **Total: 16.**

_____. *Bernique ou Le Mariage par comédie* [*Comédie* in 1 act, Pub. in 1787].
>   Th. de l'Ambigu Comique (46); **Total: 46.**

_____. *Blaise le Hargneux* [*Comédie* in 1 act, Prem. on 7-11-1782, Pub. in 1783].
>   Th. de l'Emulation (Gaîté) (6); Th. des Grands Danseurs (Gaîté) (80); **Total: 86.**

_____. *Bon coeur récompensé, Le* [*Comédie* in 1 act, Prem. on 12-11-1787].
>   Th. des Grands Danseurs (Gaîté) (34); **Total: 34.**

_____. *Bons amis, Les, ou Il était temps* [*Pantomime* in 1 act, Prem. on 2-7-1779, Pub. in 1779].
>   Th. des Grands Danseurs (Gaîté) (6); **Total: 6.**

_____. *Ca ira ou Le Retour des fédérés* [*Ballet*, Pub. in 1791].
>   Th. des Grands Danseurs (Gaîté) (35); **Total: 35.**

_____. *Ca n'en est pas ou Tout ce qui reluit n'est pas or* [*Proverbe/allégorique* in 1 act, Prem. on 23-12-1779, Pub. in 1781].
>   Th. de Molière (11); **Total: 11.**

_____. *Caquets du matin, Les* [N/A].
>   Th. des Ombres Chinoises (1); Th. des Ombres de J.-J. Rousseau (21); **Total: 22.**

_____., Dancourt, L.-J.-H. *Carmagnole et Guillot Gorju* [*Comédie* in 1 act, Prem. on 24-1-1782, Pub. in 1782].
>   Th. de l'Ambigu Comique (40); **Total: 40.**

_____. *Chacun son métier* [*Proverbe/allégorique* in 1 act, Prem. on 4-9-1779, Pub. in 1780].
>   Th. de la Citoyenne Montansier (3); **Total: 3.**

_____. *Christophe le Rond* [*Comédie* in 1 act, Prem. on 2-1-1782, Pub. in 1782].
Th. de l'Emulation (Gaîté) (**12**); Th. des Grands Danseurs (Gaîté) (**13**); Th. du Palais Royal (**32**); Th. Lyrique des Amis de la Patrie (**5**); **Total: 62**.

_____. *Désespoir de Jocrisse, Le* [*Comédie* in 2 acts, Prem. on 22-11-1791, Pub. in 1793].
Th. de la Citoyenne Montansier (**137**); Th. de la Cité (**50**); Th. de la Montagne (**14**); Th. des Variétés Amusantes, Comiques et Lyriques (**7**); Th. du Marais (**2**); Th. du Palais (Cité)-Variétés (**1**); **Total: 211**.

_____. *Extravagance amoureuse, L', ou La Boiteuse* [*Comédie* in 1 act, Prem. on 8-4-1784, Pub. in 1784].
Th. de la Citoyenne Montansier (**20**); Th. des Grands Danseurs (Gaîté) (**16**); **Total: 36**.

_____. *Fausses consultations, Les* [*Comédie* in 1 act, Prem. on 27-11-1780, Pub. in 1781].
Th. de la Citoyenne Montansier (**46**); Th. de Molière (**10**); **Total: 56**.

_____. *Fête de campagne, La, ou L'Intendant comédien malgré lui* [*Comédie* in 1 act, Prem. on 1-1-1784, Pub. in 1784].
Th. de l'Emulation (Gaîté) (**5**); Th. de la Bienfaisance (**1**); Th. de la Citoyenne Montansier (**43**); Th. de la Cité (**3**); Th. de la Montagne (**6**); Th. de Molière (**22**); Th. des Délassements Comiques (**7**); Th. des Jeunes Artistes (**2**); Th. des Variétés Amusantes, Comiques et Lyriques (**4**); Th. du Lycée des Arts (**3**); Th. du Marais (**2**); Th. du Palais (Cité)-Variétés (**8**); Th. du Palais Royal (**5**); Th. du Vaudeville (**4**); Th. Français (de la rue Richelieu) (de la République) (**1**); Th. Lyrique des Amis de la Patrie (**12**); **Total: 128**.

_____., Desorméry, Leopold.-B. (comp). *Fête de village, La* [*Comédie* in 2 acts, Prem. on 29-6-1775, Pub. in 1784].
Th. des Grands Danseurs (Gaîté) (**11**); **Total: 11**.

_____. *Fourbisseur patriote, Le* [*Tableau-Patriotique*, Prem. in 1794].
Th. des Grands Danseurs (Gaîté) (**2**); **Total: 2**.

_____. *Hospitalité, L', ou Le Bonheur du vieux père* [*Opéra-Comique*, Pub. in 1794].
Maison Egalité (**1**); Th. des Variétés Amusantes, Comiques et Lyriques (**18**); Th. du Vaudeville (**2**); **Total: 21**.

_____. *Janot chez le dégraisseur ou A quelque chose malheur est bon* [*Proverbe/allégorique* in 1 act, Prem. on 18-10-1779, Pub. in 1779].
Th. de Molière (**10**); **Total: 10**.

_____. *Janot ou Les Battus paient l'amende* [*Comédie* in 1 act, Prem. on 11-6-1779, Pub. in 1779].
Th. de la Citoyenne Montansier (**41**); Th. de la Cité (**1**); Th. de la Montagne (**11**); Th. de Molière (**19**); Th. des Jeunes Artistes (**2**); Th. du Marais (**1**); **Total: 75**.

_____. *Jean Gilles ou Le Frère de Jocrisse* [*Vaudeville* in 2 acts].
Th. de la Citoyenne Montansier (**6**); **Total: 6**.

_____. *Jocrisse change de condition* [*Comédie* in 2 acts, Prem. on 17-5-1798, Pub. in 1795].
Maison Egalité (**12**); Th. de la Citoyenne Montansier (**63**); Th. de la Montagne (**7**); Th. des Variétés Amusantes (Lazzari) (**1**); Th. des Variétés Amusantes, Comiques et Lyriques (**13**); Th. du Palais (Cité)-Variétés (**13**); **Total: 109**.

_____. *Jocrisse congédié* [*Comédie* in 2 acts, Prem. on 27-6-1799, Pub. in 1803].
Th. de la Citoyenne Montansier (**19**); **Total: 19**.

_____. *Méprise innocente, La* [*Comédie* in 1 act, Prem. on 22-5-1783, Pub. in 1783].
Th. de l'Ambigu Comique (**2**); **Total: 2**.

_____. *Moment dangereux, Le* [*Comédie* in 1 act, Prem. on 17-5-1790].
Th. des Grands Danseurs (Gaîté) (**21**); **Total: 21**.

_____. *Noces du Père Duchesne, Les* [*Comédie* in 2 acts, Prem. on 26-12-1789, Pub. in 1789].
Th. de l'Ambigu Comique (**4**); **Total: 4**.

_____. *Omelette miraculeuse, L'* [*Comédie* in 1 act, Prem. on 8-12-1793].
Th. de la Montagne (**3**); Th. du Palais (Cité)-Variétés (**4**); **Total: 7**.

_____. *On fait ce qu'on peut et non pas ce qu'on veut* [*Proverbe/allégorique* in 1 act, Prem. on 8-11-1779, Pub. in 1780].
Th. de l'Emulation (Gaîté) (**7**); Th. de la Citoyenne Montansier (**33**); Th. de la Cité (**2**); Th. de Molière (**14**); Th. des Variétés Amusantes, Comiques et Lyriques (**5**); Th. du Palais Royal (**1**); Th. du Vaudeville (**7**); **Total: 69**.

_____. *Orphée aux enfers* [N/A].
Th. des Ombres Chinoises (**1**); Th. des Ombres de J.-J. Rousseau (**10**); **Total: 11**.

_____. *Oui ou non* [*Comédie* in 1 act, Prem. in 1780, Pub. in 1786].
Th. de la Citoyenne Montansier (**8**); Th. des Grands Danseurs (Gaîté) (**3**); **Total: 11**.

_____. *Parfaite égalité, La, ou Les Tu et les toi* [*Comédie* in 3 acts, Prem. on 23-12-1793].
Maison Egalité (**4**); Th. de la Montagne (**1**); Th. National (de la rue Richelieu) (**28**); **Total: 33**.

_____. *Père Duchesne, Le, ou La Mauvaise habitude* [*Comédie* in 2 acts, Prem. on 3-2-1789, Pub. in 1789].
Th. de l'Emulation (Gaîté) (**4**); Th. des Grands Danseurs (Gaîté) (**133**); **Total: 137**.

_____. *Place Maubert, La* [N/A].
Th. des Ombres Chinoises (**5**); Th. des Ombres de J.-J. Rousseau (**17**); **Total: 22**.

_____. *Poissardes ambassadrices, Les* [N/A].
Th. des Ombres de J.-J. Rousseau (**8**); **Total: 8**.

_____. *Prix de la vertu, Le, ou Le Désespéré* [*Comédie* in 2 acts, Prem. on 2-12-1788].
Th. des Grands Danseurs (Gaîté) (**8**); **Total: 8**.

_____. *Proverbes, Les* [N/A].
Th. des Ombres de J.-J. Rousseau (**5**); **Total: 5**.

_____. *Qui court deux lièvres n'en attrape aucun* [*Comédie* in 1 act, Prem. on 30-11-1782].
Th. des Grands Danseurs (Gaîté) (**4**); **Total: 4**.

_____. *Réclamations contre l'emprunt forcé, Les* [*Comédie* in 1 act, Prem. on 9-1-1796, Pub. in 1796].
Th. de l'Emulation (Gaîté) (**12**); Th. des Variétés Amusantes, Comiques et Lyriques (**1**); Th. du Feydeau (de Monsieur) (**1**); **Total: 14**.

_____. *Suisses de Châteauvieux, Les* [*Fait Historique* in 2 acts, Prem. on 5-12-1791].
Th. de Molière (**52**); Th. des Variétés Amusantes, Comiques et Lyriques (**5**); **Total: 57**.

_____. *Sultan généreux, Le* [*Comédie* in 3 acts, Prem. on 10-3-1784, Pub. in 1784].
    Th. de l'Ambigu Comique (**43**); **Total: 43**.
                        Total Performances, Dorvigny, Louis-A.: **1528**
Dorville. *Marché Saint-Martin, Le* [*Pièce* in 2 acts, Prem. in 1773].
    Th. de la Cité (**2**); **Total: 2**.

_____. *Paysan parvenu, Le, ou Les Coups de la fortune* [*Comédie* in 1 act].
    Th. du Vaudeville (**2**); **Total: 2**.
                        Total Performances, Dorville: **4**
Dorvo, Hyacinthe. *Faux député, Le* [*Comédie* in 3 acts, Prem. on 17-2-1795, Pub. in 1793].
    Th. de la Rue Martin (**17**); Th. du Lycée des Arts (**3**); **Total: 20**.

_____. *Figaro de retour à Paris* [*Comédie* in 1 act, Prem. on 19-5-1795].
    Th. de la Rue Martin (**14**); Th. des Jeunes Artistes (**1**); Th. du Lycée des Arts (**3**); Th. Français, Comique et Lyrique (**4**); **Total: 22**.

_____. *Je cherche mon père* [*Comédie* in 3 acts, Prem. on 8-5-1797].
    Th. de la Cité (**8**); **Total: 8**.

_____. *Trois héritiers, Les* [*Comédie* in 3 acts].
    Th. du Palais (Cité)-Variétés (**5**); **Total: 5**.

_____. *Veille des noces, La, ou L'Après souper de misanthropie et repentir* [*Comédie* in 1 act, Prem. on 15-4-1799, Pub. in 1798].
    Th. de Molière (**5**); Th. du Marais (**1**); **Total: 6**.
                      Total Performances, Dorvo, Hyacinthe: **61**
Dossion, Etienne-A. *Arlequin Pygmalion ou La Bague enchantée* [*Pantomime* in 1 act, Prem. on 11-2-1794, Pub. in 1794].
    Th. des Jeunes Artistes (**31**); Th. du Vaudeville (**73**); **Total: 104**.
Dourde. *Fête villageoise, La* [*Pantomime* in 1 act, Prem. on 10-6-1754].
    Th. de l'Emulation (Gaîté) (**2**); Th. Lyrique des Amis de la Patrie (**1**); **Total: 3**.
Du Berry. *Isle des femmes, L'* [*Comédie*, Prem. in 1733, Pub. in 1737].
    Th. de l'Emulation (Gaîté) (**14**); Th. du Vaudeville (**3**); **Total: 17**.
Du Boccage, Anne-M.-L. *Amazones, Les* [*Tragédie* in 5 acts, Prem. in 7-1749, Pub. in 1749].
    Th. de l'Ambigu Comique (**43**); **Total: 43**.
Du Buisson, Paul-U., Anfossi, Pasquale (comp). *Curieux indiscret, Le* [*Opéra* in 3 acts, Pub. in 1778].
    Th. de la Citoyenne Montansier (**7**); **Total: 7**.

_____., Cimarosa, Domenico (comp). *Directeur dans l'embarras, Le* [*Opéra-Bouffe* in 2 acts1786, Pub. in 1792].
    Th. des Beaujolais (**7**); Th. Lyrique des Amis de la Patrie (**5**); **Total: 12**.

_____. *Epoux mécontents, Les, ou Le Divorce* [*Opéra* in 4 acts, Pub. in 1793].
    Th. National (de la rue Richelieu) (**5**); **Total: 5**.

_____., Fay, Etienne (comp). *Flora* [*Opéra* in 3 acts, Prem. on 4-2-1792].
    Th. du Lycée des Arts (**8**); Th. Lyrique des Amis de la Patrie (**78**); **Total: 86**.

_____., Sarti, Giuseppi (comp). *Hélène et Francisque* [*Opéra-Comique* in 4 acts, Prem. in 1782, Pub. in 1786].
    Th. de la Citoyenne Montansier (**47**); Th. National (de la rue Richelieu) (**4**); **Total: 51**.

_____., Haydn, Joseph (comp). *Laurette* [*Opéra* in 3 acts, Prem. in 1779].
>   Th. du Feydeau (de Monsieur) (**5**); **Total: 5.**

_____., Paisiello, Giovanni (comp). *Maître généreux, Le* [*Opéra* in 1 act,
Prem. in 1786, Pub. in 1788].
>   Th. de la Citoyenne Montansier (**31**); Th. Français (de la rue Richelieu) (de
>   la République) (**1**); Th. National (de la rue Richelieu) (**5**); **Total: 37.**

_____. *Nadir ou Thamas Kouli-kan* [*Tragédie* in 5 acts, Prem. on 31-8-1780,
Pub. in 1780].
>   n/a (**1**); Th. des Délassements Comiques (**5**); Th. du Marais (**1**); **Total: 7.**

_____., Paris, Guillaume-A. (comp). *Nouveau sorcier, Le* [*Comédie* in 3
acts, Prem. on 29-1-1785, Pub. in 1787].
>   Th. des Beaujolais (**6**); **Total: 6.**

_____., Paisiello, Giovanni (comp). *Philosophe imaginaire, Le* [*Opéra-
Bouffe* in 1 act, Prem. in 1779, Pub. in 1789].
>   Th. de la Citoyenne Montansier (**1**); Th. des Beaujolais (**89**); Th. du Fey-
>   deau (de Monsieur) (**15**); Th. Lyrique des Amis de la Patrie (**6**); **Total:
>   111.**

_____., Cambini, Giuseppe-M. (comp). *Révanche, La, ou Les Deux
frères* [*Comédie* in 3 acts, Prem. on 12-7-1790].
>   Th. des Variétés Amusantes (Lazzari) (**2**); Th. du Lycée des Arts (**36**); Th.
>   Lyrique des Amis de la Patrie (**76**); **Total: 114.**

_____., Paisiello, Giovanni (comp). *Roi Théodore à Venise, Le*
[*Héroique*].
>   Th. de l'Odéon (**1**); Th. de la Citoyenne Montansier (**79**); Th. de la Cité
>   (**1**); Th. du Feydeau (de Monsieur) (**36**); **Total: 117.**

_____. *Trasime et Timagène* [*Tragédie* in 5 acts, Prem. in 3-1787, Pub. in
1787].
>   Th. du Marais (**7**); **Total: 7.**

_____. *Trois mariages, Les* [*Opéra*].
>   Th. Français, Comique et Lyrique (**16**); **Total: 16.**

_____. *Vieux garçon, Le* [*Comédie* in 5 acts, Prem. on 16-12-1782, Pub. in
1783].
>   Th. Lyrique des Amis de la Patrie (**3**); **Total: 3.**

_____. *Villageoise enlevée, La* [*Vaudeville* in 3 acts, Prem. on 5-7-1790].
>   Th. Français, Comique et Lyrique (**11**); **Total: 11.**

_____., Deshayes, Prosper-D. (comp). *Zelia ou La Grille enchantée*
[Prem. on 4-4-1797].
>   Th. de la Rue Martin (**1**); Th. des Italiens (Opéra-Comique) (**7**); **Total: 8.**

_____., Deshayes, Prosper-D. (comp). *Zelia ou Le Mari à deux femmes*
[*Drame* in 3 acts, Prem. on 29-10-1791, Pub. in 1793].
>   Th. du Lycée des Arts (**45**); Th. Lyrique des Amis de la Patrie (**97**); **Total:
>   142.**

Total Performances, Du Buisson, Paul-U.: **745**

Ducaire., Jadin, Louis-E. (comp). *Loizerolles ou L'Héroïsme paternel*
[In 1 act, Prem. on 21-12-1795].
>   Th. de la Rue Martin (**2**); Th. Lyrique des Amis de la Patrie (**14**); **Total:
>   16.**

Du Mersan, T., Marion, Ps.-T., Mme. Olympe., Moreau., Chazet,
René-A.-P. de. *Cassandre aveugle ou Le Concert d'Arlequin*
[*Comédie* in 1 act, Prem. on 19-9-1799, Pub. in 1803].
>   Th. des Jeunes Artistes (**2**); **Total: 2.**

_____., Vieillard, Pierre-A. *Noir et blanc* [*Drame* in 1 act, Pub. in 1806].
> Th. du Palais (Cité)-Variétés (3); **Total: 3**.
> **Total Performances**, Du Mersan, T., Marion, Ps.-T., Mme. Olympe: **5**

Du Roullet, François-L. Gand Lebland., Gluck, Christoph (comp). *Alceste* [*Opéra* in 3 acts, Prem. on 16-4-1776, Pub. in 1776].
> Académie de la Musique (Opéra) (58); Th. Français (de la rue Richelieu) (de la République) (10); **Total: 68**.

_____., Gluck, Christoph (comp). *Iphigénie en Aulide* [*Tragédie-Lyrique* in 3 acts, Prem. on 12-4-1774, Pub. in 1774].
> Académie de la Musique (Opéra) (121); Th. de l'Odéon (4); Th. du Marais (2); Th. Français (de la rue Richelieu) (de la République) (6); **Total: 133**.
> **Total Performances**, Du Roullet, François-L. Gand Lebland: **201**

Du Vaure, Jacques. *Faux savant, Le, ou L'Amant précepteur* [*Comédie* in 5 acts, Prem. on 13-8-1749, Pub. in 1749].
> Th. de la Citoyenne Montansier (1); Th. de la Nation (Comédie Française) (7); Th. du Marais (3); Th. Français (de la rue Richelieu) (de la République) (12); Th. Patriotique et de Momus (5); **Total: 28**.

Dubois, Alexis. *Mort du chevalier d'Assas, Le, ou Le Bataille de Clostercamp* [*Pantomime* in 3 acts, Prem. on 3-10-1788, Pub. in 1791].
> Th. de l'Ambigu Comique (10); Th. du Marais (6); **Total: 16**.

Dubois, Jean-B., Benda, George (comp). *Ariane abandonnée dans l'île de Naxe* [*Mélodrame* in 3 acts, Prem. in 1775, Pub. in 1781].
> Th. de la Cité (1); **Total: 1**.

Dubois-Fontanelle, Joseph-G. *Ericie ou La Vestale* [*Drame* in 3 acts, Prem. in 6-1768, Pub. in 1768].
> Th. de la Nation (Comédie Française) (2); **Total: 2**.

Dubreuil, Alphonse-D., Desaugiers, Marc-A. (comp). *Amant travesti, L'* [*Opéra-Bouffe* in 2 acts, Prem. on 2-11-1790].
> Th. du Feydeau (de Monsieur) (7); Th. Lyrique du Foire St. Germain (4); **Total: 11**.

_____., Le Sueur, Jean-F. (comp). *Paulin et Virginie* [*Comédie* in 3 acts, Prem. on 15-1-1794, Pub. in 1794].
> Th. du Feydeau (de Monsieur) (49); **Total: 49**.

_____., Cambini, Giuseppe-M. (comp). *Rose et Carloman ou La Rose d'amour* [*Comédie* in 3 acts, Prem. on 24-4-1779, Pub. in 1779].
> Th. des Italiens (Opéra-Comique) (1); Th. du Marais (1); **Total: 2**.
> **Total Performances**, Dubreuil, Alphonse-D.: **62**

Dubut, Laurent. *Pierrot roi de Cocagne* [*Pantomime* in 2 acts, Prem. on 10-1-1764, Pub. in 1764].
> Th. des Grands Danseurs (Gaîté) (20); **Total: 20**.

Ducancel, Charles-P. *Intérieur des comités révolutionnaires, L', ou Les Aristides modernes* [*Comédie* in 3 acts, Prem. on 27-4-1795, Pub. in 1795].
> Maison Egalité (29); Th. de la Citoyenne Montansier (1); Th. de la Cité (58); Th. des Variétés Amusantes, Comiques et Lyriques (3); Th. du Palais (Cité)-Variétés (21); **Total: 112**.

Duchaume., Barral. *Hérolhe de Mithier, L'* [*Vaudeville*, Pub. in 1794].
> Th. du Vaudeville (16); **Total: 16**.

_____., Sewrin, Charles-A. de Bassompierre, dit. *Hiver, L', ou Les Deux moulins* [*Opéra* in 1 act, Prem. on 27-3-1793, Pub. in 1793].
Maison Egalité (**2**); Th. du Palais (Cité)-Variétés (**37**); **Total: 39.**
Total Performances, Duchaume: **55**

Ducis, Jean-F. *Abufar ou La Famille arabe* [*Tragédie* in 5 acts, Prem. on 12-4-1795, Pub. in 1795].
n/a (**1**); Th. Français (de la rue Richelieu) (de la République) (**33**); **Total: 34.**

_____. *Hamlet* [*Tragédie* in 5 acts, Prem. on 30-9-1769, Pub. in 1770].
Th. de la Nation (Comédie Française) (**2**); **Total: 2.**

_____. *Jean-sans-terre ou La Mort d'Arthur* [*Tragédie* in 3 acts, Prem. on 18-6-1791, Pub. in 1792].
Th. Français (de la rue Richelieu) (de la République) (**7**); **Total: 7.**

_____. *Macbeth* [*Tragédie* in 5 acts, Prem. on 1-6-1790, Pub. in 1790].
Th. de la Cité (**1**); Th. de la Nation (Comédie Française) (**5**); Th. du Feydeau (de Monsieur) (**1**); Th. Français (de la rue Richelieu) (de la République) (**22**); **Total: 29.**

_____. *Oedipe à Colone* [*Tragédie* in 3 acts, Prem. on 5-6-1797, Pub. in 1826].
Académie de la Musique (Opéra) (**8**); Th. Français (de la rue Richelieu) (de la République) (**6**); **Total: 14.**

_____. *Oedipe chez Admète* [*Tragédie* in 5 acts].
Th. Français (de la rue Richelieu) (de la République) (**3**); **Total: 3.**

_____. *Othello ou Le More de Venise* [*Tragédie* in 5 acts, Prem. on 26-11-1792].
Th. des Elèves Dramatiques (**1**); Th. des Variétés Amusantes, Comiques et Lyriques (**1**); Th. du Marais (**2**); Th. Français (de la rue Richelieu) (de la République) (**56**); **Total: 60.**

_____. *Roi Lear, Le* [*Tragédie* in 5 acts, Prem. on 12-5-1792].
Th. Français (de la rue Richelieu) (de la République) (**7**); **Total: 7.**

_____. *Romeo et Juliette* [*Tragédie* in 4 acts, Prem. on 27-6-1772, Pub. in 1772].
Th. de la Nation (Comédie Française) (**1**); Th. des Italiens (Opéra-Comique) (**3**); **Total: 4.**
Total Performances, Ducis, Jean-F.: **160**

Duclos, Pierre-G. *Connaisseur, Le, ou L'Auteur par amour* [*Comédie* in 4 acts, Prem. on 30-1-1784, Pub. in 1809].
Th. de la Citoyenne Montansier (**14**); **Total: 14.**

Ducray-Duminil, François-G. *Deux Martines, Les, ou Le Procureur dupé* [*Comédie* in 1 act, Prem. on 13-2-1786, Pub. in 1786].
Th. de la Rue Antoine (**1**); Th. de Molière (**2**); Th. des Victoires (**2**); Th. des Victoires Nationales (**1**); **Total: 6.**

_____., Demautort, Jacques-B. *Taverne, La* [*Vaudeville* in 1 act, Prem. on 28-5-1796].
Th. du Vaudeville (**9**); **Total: 9.**
Total Performances, Ducray-Duminil, François-G.: **15**

Dudoyer de Gastels, Gérard. *Vindicatif, Le* [*Drame* in 5 acts, Prem. on 2-7-1774, Pub. in 1774].
Th. de la Rue Martin (**2**); **Total: 2.**

Dufresnoy, Citoyenne. *Petit Armand, Le, ou Le Bienfait des perruques* [*Vaudeville* in 1 act, Prem. on 21-8-1799].
Th. des Troubadours (**19**); **Total: 19.**

Dumaniant, see Bourlin, Antoine-J., Pseud. Dumaniant.

Dupaty, Louis-E. *Arlequin sentinelle* [*Vaudeville*, Prem. on 30-6-1798, Pub. in 1797].
> Th. du Vaudeville (**16**); **Total: 16.**

_____. *Arlequin tout seul* [*Comédie* in 1 act, Prem. on 4-12-1798, Pub. in 1798].
> Th. de la Citoyenne Montansier (**1**); Th. du Vaudeville (**38**); **Total: 39.**

_____. *Chapitre second* [*Comédie*, Pub. in 1798].
> Th. des Italiens (Opéra-Comique) (**24**); **Total: 24.**
>> **Total Performances**, Dupaty, Louis-E.: **79**

Duperche, J.-J.-M. *Arlequin protégé par l'amour et les génies infernaux* [*Mélodrame* in 4 acts, Prem. on 9-8-1797].
> Th. de la Citoyenne Montansier (**3**); Th. des Variétés Amusantes (Lazzari) (**11**); Th. des Variétés Amusantes, Comiques et Lyriques (**22**); **Total: 36.**

Dupeuty, Charles., Villeneuve, Mme., de la Salle. *Ménage du savetier, Le, ou La Richesse du pauvre* [*Comédie* in 1 act].
> Th. des Grands Danseurs (Gaîté) (**2**); Th. des Ombres de J.-J. Rousseau (**5**); **Total: 7.**

Dupin, Richard. *Préjugé de la naissance, La* [*Comédie* in 2 acts, Prem. on 22-6-1789].
> Th. des Grands Danseurs (Gaîté) (**9**); **Total: 9.**

Duprat de Latouloubre., Méreaux, Nicolas-J. (comp). *Oedipe à Thèbes ou Jocaste et Oedipe* [*Tragédie-Lyrique* in 3 acts, Prem. on 30-12-1791, Pub. in 1791].
> Académie de la Musique (Opéra) (**6**); **Total: 6.**

Dupuis, Amable-J. *Artiste patriote, L', ou La Vente des biens* [*Comédie* in 5 acts, Prem. on 1-8-1791, Pub. in 1791].
> Th. Français, Comique et Lyrique (**12**); **Total: 12.**

Durival., Deshayes, Prosper-D. (comp). *Auteur à la mode, L', ou Le Mari complaisant* [*Comédie* in 2 acts, Prem. on 23-12-1786, Pub. in 1786].
> Th. du Vaudeville (**5**); **Total: 5.**

Durosoi, see Rosoi, Barnabé-F. de, dit Durosoi.

Duryrer. *Mutius Scaevola* [*Trait civique* in 5 acts, Prem. on 29-11-1792, Pub. in 1792].
> Th. de la Citoyenne Montansier (**7**); **Total: 7.**

Duval, Alexandre-V.P., Deshayes, Prosper-D. (comp). *Bella ou La Femme à deux maris* [*Opéra* in 3 acts, Prem. on 15-6-1795, Pub. in 1795].
> Th. Lyrique des Amis de la Patrie (**14**); **Total: 14.**

_____. *Montoni ou Le Château d'Udolphe* [*Drame* in 5 acts, Prem. on 28-8-1798, Pub. in 1798].
> Th. de la Cité (**1**); Th. du Palais (Cité)-Variétés (**23**); **Total: 24.**

_____., Della-Maria, Dominique (comp). *Oncle valet, L'* [*Comédie* in 1 act, Prem. on 8-12-1798, Pub. in 1802].
> Th. des Italiens (Opéra-Comique) (**33**); **Total: 33.**

_____., Lemière, Jean.-F.-A. de Corvey (comp). *Prise de Toulon, La* [*Tableau-Patriotique* in 1 act, Prem. on 21-1-1794, Pub. in 1794].
> Th. des Grands Danseurs (Gaîté) (**1**); Th. des Italiens (Opéra-Comique) (**40**); **Total: 41.**

_____. *Prisonnier, Le, ou La Ressemblance* [*Comédie* in 1 act, Prem. on 29-1-1798, Pub. in 1798].
> Th. de la Citoyenne Montansier (**2**); Th. de Molière (**4**); Th. des Italiens (Opéra-Comique) (**103**); **Total: 109.**

_____. *Projets de mariage, Les, ou Les Deux militaires* [*Comédie* in 1 act, Prem. on 5-8-1798, Pub. in 1798].
> Th. du Feydeau (de Monsieur) (**8**); Th. du Vaudeville (**5**); Th. Français (de la rue Richelieu) (de la République) (**22**); Th. Patriotique et de Momus (**27**); **Total: 62.**

_____. *Souper imprévu, Le, ou Le Chanoine de Milan* [*Comédie* in 1 act, Prem. on 10-9-1796, Pub. in 1799].
> Th. de l'Emulation (Gaîté) (**1**); Th. des Variétés Amusantes, Comiques et Lyriques (**3**); Th. du Marais (**3**); Th. du Palais (Cité)-Variétés (**3**); Th. Français (de la rue Richelieu) (de la République) (**54**); **Total: 64.**

_____., Tarchi, Angelo (comp). *Trente et quarante ou Le Portrait* [*Opéra-Comique* in 1 act, Prem. on 18-5-1799, Pub. in 1803].
> Th. des Italiens (Opéra-Comique) (**36**); **Total: 36.**

_____., Dominique, Pierre-A. (comp). *Vieux château, Le, ou La Rencontre* [*Comédie* in 1 act, Prem. on 15-3-1798, Pub. in 1797].
> Th. de l'Odéon (**1**); Th. du Feydeau (de Monsieur) (**26**); **Total: 27.**
> > **Total Performances**, Duval, Alexandre-V.P.: **410**

Duval, Georges-L.-J., Gouffé, Armand Alexandre Duval. *Clément Marot* [*Vaudeville* in 1 act, Prem. on 8-5-1799, Pub. in 1798].
> Th. de Molière (**10**); Th. des Troubadours (**21**); Th. du Feydeau (de Monsieur) (**1**); **Total: 32.**

_____., Gouffé, Armand Alexandre Duval. *Vadé à la grenouillère* [*Vaudeville* in 1 act, Prem. on 9-9 -1799, Pub. in 1799].
> Th. des Troubadours (**35**); **Total: 35.**

_____., Gouffé, Armand Alexandre Duval. *Val de vivre, Le, ou Le Berceau du vaudeville* [*Divertissement/parade* in 1 act, Prem. on 7-6-1799, Pub. in 1798].
> Th. des Troubadours (**44**); **Total: 44.**
> > **Total Performances**, Duval, Georges-L.-J.: **111**

Duverger, C. *Frondeur, Le, ou L'Ami des moeurs* [*Comédie* in 5 acts, Prem. on 17-12-1788, Pub. in 1789].
> Th. de la Citoyenne Montansier (**16**); Th. Français (de la rue Richelieu) (de la République) (**1**); **Total: 17.**

Espic, Chevalier de Lirou, Jean-F., Piccinni, Niccolò. *Diane et Endimion* [*Opéra* in 3 acts, Prem. on 7-9-1784, Pub. in 1784].
> Académie de la Musique (Opéra) (**6**); **Total: 6.**

Etienne, Charles-G. *Nouveau réveil d'Epiménide, Le* [*Comédie* in 1 act, Prem. on 18-1-1794, Pub. in 1806].
> Th. Français (de la rue Richelieu) (de la République) (**5**); **Total: 5.**

_____., Gresnick, Antoine (comp). *Rêve, Le* [*Opéra-Comique* in 1 act, Prem. on 27-1-1799, Pub. in 1798].
> Th. des Italiens (Opéra-Comique) (**14**); **Total: 14.**
> > **Total Performances**, Etienne, Charles-G.: **19**

Eve, Antoine-F., dit Maillot., Dalayrac, N.M., Méhul, E.N., Grétry, E.M. *Congrès des rois, Le* [*Comédie* in 3 acts, Pub. in 1794].
> Th. des Italiens (Opéra-Comique) (**2**); **Total: 2.**

_____. *Madame Angot ou La Poissarde parvenue* [*Opéra-Comique* in 2 acts, Pub. in 1796].
> Th. de l'Emulation (Gaîté) (**94**); Th. de la Citoyenne Montansier (**27**); Th. de la Rue Antoine (**1**); Th. des Délassements Comiques (**14**); Th. des Jeunes Artistes (**8**); Th. Lyrique des Amis de la Patrie (**11**); **Total: 155.**

_____., Leblanc de Guillet, Antonio Blanc, dit (comp). *Mariage de Nanon, Le, ou La Suite de Madame Angot* [*Opéra-Comique* in 1 act, Pub. in 1797].
> Th. de l'Emulation (Gaîté) (**105**); Th. de la Citoyenne Montansier (**1**); Th. Lyrique des Amis de la Patrie (**10**); **Total: 116.**

_____. *Vieux soldat et sa pupille, Le* [*Opéra-Comique*].
> Th. des Jeunes Artistes (**18**); **Total: 18.**
>
> **Total Performances**, Eve, Antoine-F., dit Maillot: **291**

Eyraud., Deshayes, Prosper-D. (comp). *Paysan à prétention, Le* [*Opéra-Bouffe* in 1 act, Prem. on 12-6-1786].
> Th. des Beaujolais (**12**); **Total: 12.**

Fabre d'Eglantine, Philippe-F.-N., Foignet, Charles-G. (comp). *Apothicaire, L'* [*Comédie* in 2 acts, Prem. on 7-7-1790].
> Th. de la Citoyenne Montansier (**59**); Th. de la Montagne (**4**); Th. de la Rue Martin (**1**); **Total: 64.**

_____. *Collatéral, Le, ou L'Amour et l'intérêt* [*Comédie* in 3 acts, Prem. on 26-5-1789, Pub. in 1791].
> Th. du Feydeau (de Monsieur) (**21**); Th. Français (de la rue Richelieu) (de la République) (**5**); **Total: 26.**

_____. *Convalescent de qualité, Le, ou L'Aristocrate* [*Comédie* in 2 acts, Prem. on 28-1-1791, Pub. in 1791].
> Académie de la Musique (Opéra) (**1**); Th. des Italiens (Opéra-Comique) (**58**); Th. du Feydeau (de Monsieur) (**2**); **Total: 61.**

_____. *Héritière, L', ou Les Champs et la cour* [*Comédie* in 1 act, Prem. on 9-11-1791].
> Th. Français (de la rue Richelieu) (de la République) (**2**); **Total: 2.**

_____. *Intrigue épistolaire, L'* [*Comédie* in 5 acts, Prem. on 15-6-1791, Pub. in 1792].
> Th. de l'Emulation (Gaîté) (**7**); Th. de la Cité (**2**); Th. des Grands Danseurs (Gaîté) (**7**); Th. du Marais (**4**); Th. Français (de la rue Richelieu) (de la République) (**126**); **Total: 146.**

_____., Mengozzi, Bernardo (comp). *Isabelle de Salisbury* [*Comédie-Heroique* in 3 acts, Prem. on 20-8-1791].
> Th. de la Citoyenne Montansier (**56**); **Total: 56.**

_____. *Philinte de Molière, Le, ou La Suite du misanthrope* [*Comédie* in 5 acts, Prem. on 22-2-1790, Pub. in 1791].
> Th. de l'Odéon (**1**); Th. de la Nation (Comédie Française) (**29**); Th. du Feydeau (de Monsieur) (**21**); Th. Français (de la rue Richelieu) (de la République) (**7**); **Total: 58.**

_____. *Précepteurs, Les* [*Comédie* in 5 acts, Pub. in 1799].
> Th. Français (de la rue Richelieu) (de la République) (**23**); **Total: 23.**

_____. *Présomptueux, Le, ou L'Heureux imaginaire* [*Comédie* in 5 acts, Prem. on 20-2-1790, Pub. in 1790].
> Th. de la Nation (Comédie Française) (**10**); **Total: 10.**

_____. *Sot orgueilleux, Le, ou L'Ecole des élections* [*Comédie* in 5 acts].
> Th. Français (de la rue Richelieu) (de la République) (**1**); **Total: 1.**
>
> **Total Performances**, Fabre d'Eglantine, Philippe-F.-N.: **447**

Faciolle, C.-A. *Extravagante de qualité, L'* [*Comédie* in 3 acts, Prem. on 9-12-1788, Pub. in 1789].
> Th. du Palais Royal (**26**); **Total: 26.**

Fagan, Barthélemy-C. *Etourderie, L'* [*Comédie* in 1 act, Prem. on 18-7-1737, Pub. in 1761].
> Th. de la Nation (Comédie Française) (**11**); Th. des Troubadours (**2**); Th. Français (de la rue Richelieu) (de la République) (**2**); **Total: 15**.

_____. *Fermière, La* [*Comédie* in 3 acts, Prem. on 8-1-1748, Pub. in 1759].
> Th. Français (de la rue Richelieu) (de la République) (**5**); **Total: 5**.

_____. *Heureux retour, L'* [*Comédie* in 1 act, Pub. in 1744].
> Th. de l'Emulation (Gaîté) (**1**); **Total: 1**.

_____. *Originaux, Les* [*Comédie* in 1 act, Prem. on 18-7-1737, Pub. in 1760].
> n/a (**3**); Th. de l'Ambigu Comique (**2**); Th. de la Cité (**1**); Th. de la Nation (Comédie Française) (**11**); Th. de la Rue Martin (**1**); Th. du Marais (**1**); Th. Français (de la rue Richelieu) (de la République) (**45**); Th. Patriotique et de Momus (**4**); **Total: 68**.

_____. *Pupille, La* [*Comédie* in 1 act, Prem. on 5-7-1734, Pub. in 1734].
> Th. de l'Ambigu Comique (**6**); Th. de l'Odéon (**4**); Th. de la Citoyenne Montansier (**22**); Th. de la Concorde (**1**); Th. de la Liberté (**3**); Th. de la Nation (Comédie Française) (**19**); Th. de la Rue Martin (**6**); Th. de Molière (**9**); Th. des Délassements Comiques (**4**); Th. des Variétés Amusantes (Lazzari) (**1**); Th. des Variétés Amusantes, Comiques et Lyriques (**6**); Th. du Feydeau (de Monsieur) (**7**); Th. du Lycée Dramatique (**3**); Th. du Marais (**11**); Th. du Palais (Cité)-Variétés (**1**); Th. Français (de la rue Richelieu) (de la République) (**24**); Th. Français, Comique et Lyrique (**5**); Th. Lyrique des Amis de la Patrie (**6**); Th. Patriotique et de Momus (**14**); **Total: 152**.

_____. *Rendez-vous, Le* [*Comédie* in 1 act, Prem. on 27-5-1733, Pub. in 1733].
> Th. de l'Odéon (**2**); Th. de la Nation (Comédie Française) (**4**); Th. Français (de la rue Richelieu) (de la République) (**15**); Th. Français, Comique et Lyrique (**48**); **Total: 69**.

> **Total Performances**, Fagan, Barthélemy-C.: **310**

Falaise de Verneuil., Jadin, Louis-E. (comp). *Avare puni, L'* [*Opéra* in 1 act, Prem. on 4-8-1792].
> Th. du Feydeau (de Monsieur) (**7**); **Total: 7**.

Fallet, Nicolas., Dalayrac, Nicolas (comp). *Deux tuteurs, Les* [*Comédie* in 2 acts, Prem. on 8-5-1784, Pub. in 1784].
> Th. des Grands Danseurs (Gaîté) (**5**); Th. des Italiens (Opéra-Comique) (**50**); **Total: 55**.

_____., Champein, Stanislas (comp). *Noces cauchoises, Les* [*Opéra* in 2 acts, Prem. on 11-8-1790].
> Th. de la Citoyenne Montansier (**35**); **Total: 35**.

> **Total Performances**, Fallet, Nicolas: **90**

Famin, Pierre-N. *Deux perdrix, Les, ou Le Premier repas de noces* [*Comédie* in 2 acts, Prem. on 2-6-1798].
> Th. de l'Ambigu Comique (**7**); **Total: 7**.

_____. *Mariage impromptu, Le* [*Pièce* in 1 act, Pub. in 1775].
> Th. du Feydeau (de Monsieur) (**1**); Th. du Vaudeville (**1**); **Total: 2**.

_____. *Obligeant maladroit, L'* [*Comédie* in 3 acts, Prem. on 21-11-1792, Pub. in 1793].
> Th. du Vaudeville (**6**); Th. Français (de la rue Richelieu) (de la République) (**5**); **Total: 11**.

> **Total Performances**, Famin, Pierre-N.: **20**

Farin de Hautemer. *Maison à deux portes, La* [*Opéra-Comique* in 1 act, Prem. on 21-10-1791, Pub. in 1755].
> Th. Français (de la rue Richelieu) (de la République) (**2**); **Total: 2**.

Fatouville, Nolant de. *Arlequin chevalier du soleil* [*Comédie* in 3 acts, Pub. in 1685].
>   Th. des Variétés Amusantes, Comiques et Lyriques (2); **Total: 2**.

_____. *Arlequin empereur dans la lune* [*Vaudeville* in 3 acts].
>   Th. de l'Emulation (Gaîté) (5); Th. Lyrique des Amis de la Patrie (23); **Total: 28**.

>   **Total Performances**, Fatouville, Nolant de: **30**

Faur, Louis-F. *Amélie et Montrose* [*Drame* in 4 acts, Prem. on 19-9-1783, Pub. in 1783].
>   Th. des Italiens (Opéra-Comique) (2); **Total: 2**.

_____. *Amour à l'épreuve, L'* [*Comédie* in 1 act, Prem. on 13-8-1784, Pub. in 1784].
>   Th. de la Nation (Comédie Française) (2); Th. des Italiens (Opéra-Comique) (4); **Total: 6**.

_____. *Caractère colérique, Le* [*Comédie* in 2 acts, Prem. on 25-5-1789].
>   Th. des Grands Danseurs (Gaîté) (34); **Total: 34**.

_____., Dezède, C. (comp). *Fête de la cinquantaine, La* [*Opéra* in 2 acts, Prem. on 9-1-1796, Pub. in 1796].
>   n/a (1); Th. de la Citoyenne Montansier (16); Th. de la Cité (2); Th. du Lycée des Arts (15); **Total: 34**.

_____., Dezède. *Intrigant sans le vouloir, L'* [*Opéra* in 2 acts, Prem. on 4-4-1796].
>   Th. du Lycée des Arts (36); **Total: 36**.

_____., Persuis, Louis-L. (comp). *Phanor et Angela* [*Opéra*, Prem. on 11-7-1798].
>   Th. du Feydeau (de Monsieur) (1); **Total: 1**.

_____. *Plus de peur que de mal ou L'Heureux accident* [*Opéra-Comique* in 2 acts, Prem. on 22-8-1797].
>   Th. du Feydeau (de Monsieur) (25); **Total: 25**.

_____. *Veuve anglaise, La* [*Comédie* in 1 act, Prem. on 29-11-1786, Pub. in 1786].
>   Th. des Italiens (Opéra-Comique) (1); **Total: 1**.

>   **Total Performances**, Faur, Louis-F.: **139**

Favart, Charles-N. *Diable boiteux, Le, ou La Chose impossible* [*Vaudeville* in 1 act, Prem. on 27-9-1782, Pub. in 1782].
>   Th. des Italiens (Opéra-Comique) (3); **Total: 3**.

_____., Chapelle, Pierre-D.-A. (comp). *Famille réunie, La* [*Comédie* in 2 acts, Prem. on 6-12-1790, Pub. in 1790].
>   Th. des Italiens (Opéra-Comique) (4); **Total: 4**.

_____. *Joseph ou La Fin tragique de Madame Angot* [Prem. on 30-10-1797].
>   Th. des Jeunes Artistes (3); **Total: 3**.

_____., Mullot, Valentin. *Sagesse humaine, La, ou Arlequin memnon* [*Comédie* in 2 acts, Prem. on 5-10-1797].
>   Th. des Jeunes Artistes (11); **Total: 11**.

>   **Total Performances**, Favart, Charles-N.: **21**

Favart, Charles-S., Grétry, André-E.-M. (comp). *Amitié à l'épreuve, L'* [*Comédie* in 2 acts, Prem. on 13-11-1770, Pub. in 1770].
>   Th. des Italiens (Opéra-Comique) (6); **Total: 6**.

_____. *Anglais à Bordeaux, Les* [*Comédie* in 1 act, Prem. on 14-3-1763, Pub. in 1763].
      Th. de la Nation (Comédie Française) (**6**); **Total: 6.**

_____., Pannard, Charles-F. (comp). *Astrologue de village, L'* [*Opéra-Comique* in 1 act, Prem. on 15-6-1793].
      Th. du Vaudeville (**1**); **Total: 1.**

_____., Sodi, Charles (comp). *Baiocco et Serpilla* [*Parodie* in 3 acts, Prem. on 6-3-1753, Pub. in 1760].
      Th. des Variétés Amusantes, Comiques et Lyriques (**5**); **Total: 5.**

_____., Monsigny, Pierre-A. (comp). *Belle Arsène, La* [*Comédie* in 3 acts, Prem. on 6-11-1773, Pub. in 1773].
      Th. des Grands Danseurs (Gaîté) (**1**); Th. des Italiens (Opéra-Comique) (**61**); Th. du Marais (**1**); **Total: 63.**

_____., Dicapua, Rinaldo (comp). *Bohémienne, La* [*Comédie* in 2 acts, Prem. on 28-7-1755, Pub. in 1755].
      Th. des Jeunes Artistes (**38**); **Total: 38.**

_____. *Chercheuse d'esprit, La* [*Opéra-Comique* in 1 act, Prem. on 20-2-1741, Pub. in 1741].
      Th. des Grands Danseurs (Gaîté) (**24**); Th. du Vaudeville (**34**); **Total: 58.**

_____., Guérin de Frémicourt., Harny de Guerville. *Ensorcelés, Les, ou Jeannot et Jeannette* [*Parodie* in 1 act, Prem. on 1-9-1757, Pub. in 1758].
      Th. de Molière (**8**); Th. des Jeunes Artistes (**6**); **Total: 14.**

_____., Duni, Egidio-R. (comp). *Fée Urgèle, La* [*Comédie* in 4 acts, Prem. on 26-10-1765, Pub. in 1765].
      Th. du Marais (**1**); **Total: 1.**

_____. *Fête du château, La* [*Divertissement/parade*, Prem. on 25-9-1766, Pub. in 1766].
      Th. des Italiens (Opéra-Comique) (**2**); **Total: 2.**

_____., Duni, Egidio-R. (comp). *Fille mal gardée, La, ou Le Pédant amoureux* [*Parodie* in 2 acts, Prem. on 4-3-1758, Pub. in 1758].
      Th. Lyrique des Amis de la Patrie (**11**); **Total: 11.**

_____., Tarchi, Angelo (comp). *Général suédois, Le* [*Opéra-Comique* in 2 acts, Prem. on 23-5-1799].
      Th. des Italiens (Opéra-Comique) (**3**); **Total: 3.**

_____., Blaise, A.B. (comp). *Isabelle et Gertrude ou Les Sylphes supposés* [*Comédie* in 1 act, Prem. on 14-8-1765].
      Th. du Vaudeville (**12**); **Total: 12.**

_____. *Nymphes de Diane, Les* [*Opéra-Comique* in 1 act, Prem. on 22-9-1755, Pub. in 1755].
      Th. du Vaudeville (**5**); **Total: 5.**

_____., Anseaume, Louis. *Procès des ariettes et des vaudeville, Le* [*Pièce* in 1 act, Prem. on 28-6-1760, Pub. in 1760].
      Th. du Marais (**1**); Th. du Vaudeville (**53**); **Total: 54.**

_____., Guérin de Frémicourt. *Rêveries renouvellées des grecs, Les* [*Parodie* in 3 acts, Prem. on 26-6-1779, Pub. in 1779].
      Th. des Italiens (Opéra-Comique) (**13**); **Total: 13.**

_____. *Rosière de Salenci, La* [*Comédie* in 3 acts, Prem. on 25-10-1769, Pub. in 1769].

Th. de l'Ambigu Comique (2); Th. des Italiens (Opéra-Comique) (10); Total: 12.

_____. *Servante justifiée, La* [*Opéra-Comique* in 1 act, Prem. on 19-3-1740, Pub. in 1760].

Th. des Italiens (Opéra-Comique) (16); Total: 16.

_____. *Soirée des boulevards, La* [*Comédie* in 1 act, Prem. on 13-11-1758, Pub. in 1759].

Th. de Molière (2); Total: 2.

_____., Gibert, Paul-C. (comp). *Soliman II ou Les Trois sultanes* [*Comédie* in 3 acts, Prem. on 9-4-1761, Pub. in 1762].

Th. des Italiens (Opéra-Comique) (22); Total: 22.

_____., Jadin, Louis-E. (comp). *Vengeance du bailli, La* [*Comédie* in 2 acts, Prem. on 30-4-1791].

Th. du Feydeau (de Monsieur) (7); Total: 7.

Total Performances, Favart, Charles-S.: 351

Favart, Marie-J.-B.D. *Amours de Bastien et Bastienne, Les* [Pub. in 1789].

Th. des Grands Danseurs (Gaîté) (38); Total: 38.

_____., Lourdet de Santerre, Jean., Voisenon. *Annette et Lubin* [*Comédie* in 1 act, Prem. on 15-2-1762, Pub. in 1762].

Académie de la Musique (Opéra) (4); Th. de l'Ambigu Comique (92); Th. des Délassements Comiques (7); Th. des Italiens (Opéra-Comique) (17); Th. des Jeunes Artistes (1); Th. du Marais (1); Total: 122.

_____., Chevalier. *Fête d'amour, La, ou Lucas et Colinette* [*Divertissement/parade* in 1 act, Prem. on 5-12-1754, Pub. in 1754].

Cirque National (2); Th. de l'Emulation (Gaîté) (2); Th. de l'Estrapade au Panthéon (1); Th. de la Citoyenne Montansier (2); Th. de la Rue Martin (4); Th. de Molière (8); Th. des Jeunes Artistes (11); Th. du Lycée des Arts (1); Th. du Marais (4); Th. du Vaudeville (6); Th. Lyrique des Amis de la Patrie (1); Th. National (de la rue Richelieu) (1); Th. Patriotique et de Momus (5); Total: 48.

Total Performances, Favart, Marie-J.-B.D.: 208

Favières, Edmond-G.-F. de., Berton, Henri-M. (comp). *Christophe et Jérôme ou La Ferme hospitalière* [*Comédie* in 1 act, Prem. on 26-10-1796].

Th. des Italiens (Opéra-Comique) (1); Total: 1.

_____., Jadin, Louis-E. (comp). *Coin du feu, Le* [*Comédie* in 1 act, Prem. on 10-6-1793].

Th. des Italiens (Opéra-Comique) (11); Total: 11.

_____., Grétry, André-E.-M. (comp). *Elisca ou L'Amour maternel* [*Drame lyrique* in 3 acts, Prem. on 1-1-1799].

Th. des Italiens (Opéra-Comique) (16); Total: 16.

_____., Champein, Stanislas (comp). *Espiègleries de garnison, Les* [*Comédie* in 3 acts, Prem. on 21-9-1791, Pub. in 1792].

Th. des Italiens (Opéra-Comique) (9); Total: 9.

_____., Persuis, Louis-L.-L'O. (comp). *Fanny Morna ou L'Ecossaise* [*Drame* in 3 acts, Prem. on 22-8-1799, Pub. in 1799].

Th. des Italiens (Opéra-Comique) (13); Total: 13.

_____., Solié, Jean-P. (comp). *Jean et Geneviève* [*Opéra-Comique* in 1 act, Prem. on 3-12-1792, Pub. in 1810].
Th. des Italiens (Opéra-Comique) (**51**); **Total: 51.**

_____., Grétry, André-E.-M. (comp). *Lisbeth* [*Drame* in 3 acts, Pub. in 1797].
Th. des Italiens (Opéra-Comique) (**34**); **Total: 34.**

_____. *Mauvaise étoile, La* [*Comédie* in 5 acts, Prem. on 31-5-1792].
Th. Français (de la rue Richelieu) (de la République) (**1**); **Total: 1.**

_____. *Mauvaise tête et bon coeur* [*Comédie* in 3 acts, Prem. on 2-7-1789].
Th. du Palais (Cité)-Variétés (**13**); Th. du Palais Royal (**45**); **Total: 58.**

_____., Kreutzer, Rodolpho (comp). *Paul et Virginie* [*Comédie* in 3 acts, Prem. on 15-1-1791, Pub. in 1792].
Th. des Italiens (Opéra-Comique) (**150**); Th. des Variétés Amusantes, Comiques et Lyriques (**1**); Th. du Marais (**2**); **Total: 153.**

_____., Marsollier des Vivetières, Benoît-J., Dalayrac, Nicolas (comp). *Primerose* [*Opéra* in 3 acts, Prem. on 7-3-1799].
Th. des Italiens (Opéra-Comique) (**7**); **Total: 7.**

_____. *Seigneur supposé, Le* [*Comédie* in 2 acts, Prem. on 12-1-1789, Pub. in 1789].
Th. du Palais Royal (**47**); **Total: 47.**

_____., Devienne, François (comp). *Volicour* [*Comédie* in 1 act, Prem. on 22-3-1797].
Th. des Italiens (Opéra-Comique) (**1**); **Total: 1.**
Total Performances, Favières, Edmond-G.-F. de: **402**

Fédérico, Gennaro., Pergolesi, Giovanni-B. (comp). *Serva padrona, La* [*Opéra-Comique* in 2 acts, Prem. on 5-9-1733].
Th. du Feydeau (de Monsieur) (**13**); **Total: 13.**

Fenouillot de Falbaire de Quingey, Charles-G., Grétry, André-E.-M. (comp). *Deux Avares, Les* [*Comédie* in 2 acts, Prem. on 27-10-1770, Pub. in 1770].
Th. des Italiens (Opéra-Comique) (**23**); **Total: 23.**

_____. *Honnête criminel, L', ou L'Amour filial* [*Drame* in 5 acts, Prem. on 2-2-1768, Pub. in 1767].
Th. de l'Ambigu Comique (**1**); Th. de l'Emulation (Gaîté) (**9**); Th. de la Nation (Comédie Française) (**14**); Th. de la Rue Martin (**8**); Th. de Molière (**5**); Th. des Victoires (**2**); Th. des Victoires Nationales (**2**); Th. du Feydeau (de Monsieur) (**7**); Th. du Marais (**7**); Th. Français (de la rue Richelieu) (de la République) (**37**); Th. Lyrique des Amis de la Patrie (**2**); **Total: 94.**
Total Performances, Fenouillot de Falbaire de Quingey, Charles-G.: **117**

Ferrand, Comte Antoine-F.-C. *Philoctète* [*Tragédie* in 3 acts, Pub. in 1786].
Th. des Grands Danseurs (Gaîté) (**1**); **Total: 1.**

Ferrières, A. de., Plantade, Charles-H. (comp). *Souliers mordorés, Les, ou La Cordonnière allemande* [*Opéra-comique* in 2 acts, Prem. on 18-5-1793].
Th. du Feydeau (de Monsieur) (**6**); **Total: 6.**

Fiévée, Joseph. *Homme en loterie, L'* [*Comédie* in 2 acts, Prem. on 28-10-1789].
Th. du Feydeau (de Monsieur) (**32**); **Total: 32.**

_____. *Maison à vendre, La, ou La Nuit à Grenade* [*Comédie* in 3 acts, Prem. on 6-2-1789].
Th. du Feydeau (de Monsieur) (**11**); **Total: 11.**

_____. *Nuit espagnole, La, ou Le Contre-temps* [Prem. on 31-8-1797].
Th. de l'Ambigu Comique (**2**); **Total: 2.**

_____., Persuis, Louis-L.-L'O. (comp). *Nuit espagnole, La* [*Opéra* in 2 acts, Prem. on 14-6-1791].
Th. du Feydeau (de Monsieur) (**9**); **Total: 9.**

_____., Berton, Henri-M. (comp). *Rigueurs du cloître, Les* [*Comédie* in 2 acts, Prem. on 23-8-1790, Pub. in 1790].
Th. de Molière (**5**); Th. des Italiens (Opéra-Comique) (**66**); **Total: 71.**
Total Performances, Fiévée, Joseph: **125**

Fleury, Jacques. *Miroir magique, Le* [*Opéra-Comique* in 1 act, Prem. on 25-7-1752, Pub. in 1752].
Th. du Vaudeville (**5**); **Total: 5.**

Flins des Oliviers, see Carbon de Flins des Oliviers, Claude-M.

Florian, Jean-P.-C. de. *Arlequin bon père* [*Comédie* in 1 act].
Th. de l'Emulation (Gaîté) (**1**); Th. de la Citoyenne Montansier (**28**); Th. de la Cité (**4**); Th. de la Montagne (**1**); Th. des Victoires Nationales (**3**); Th. du Palais (Cité)-Variétés (**3**); **Total: 40.**

_____. *Azélie* [*Comédie* in 3 acts, Prem. on 4-7-1790].
Th. du Feydeau (de Monsieur) (**16**); **Total: 16.**

_____. *Baiser, Le, ou La Bonne fée* [*Comédie* in 3 acts, Prem. on 26-11-1781, Pub. in 1782].
Th. du Lycée des Arts (**1**); **Total: 1.**

_____. *Bon ménage, Le, ou La Suite des deux billets* [*Comédie* in 1 act, Prem. on 17-1-1783, Pub. in 1783].
Th. de l'Ambigu Comique (**1**); Th. de la Citoyenne Montansier (**19**); Th. des Italiens (Opéra-Comique) (**13**); Th. des Jeunes Artistes (**1**); **Total: 34.**

_____. *Bon père, Le, ou La Suite du bon ménage* [*Comédie* in 1 act, Prem. on 2-2-1783, Pub. in 1784].
Th. de l'Emulation (Gaîté) (**2**); Th. de la Citoyenne Montansier (**9**); Th. des Italiens (Opéra-Comique) (**7**); Th. des Jeunes Artistes (**17**); Th. Français (de la rue Richelieu) (de la République) (**1**); Th. Lyrique des Amis de la Patrie (**72**); Th. Patriotique et de Momus (**2**); **Total: 110.**

_____. *Bonne mère, La* [*Comédie* in 1 act, Prem. on 2-2-1785, Pub. in 1785].
Th. de l'Ambigu Comique (**1**); Th. de la Citoyenne Montansier (**22**); Th. des Italiens (Opéra-Comique) (**65**); Th. du Marais (**2**); Th. du Vaudeville (**1**); Th. National (de la rue Richelieu) (**1**); **Total: 92.**

_____. *Deux billets, Les* [*Comédie* in 1 act, Prem. on 9-2-1779, Pub. in 1780].
Maison Egalité (**2**); Th. de l'Emulation (Gaîté) (**9**); Th. de la Citoyenne Montansier (**26**); Th. de la Montagne (**6**); Th. de la Nation (Comédie Française) (**1**); Th. des Grands Danseurs (Gaîté) (**7**); Th. des Italiens (Opéra-Comique) (**38**); Th. des Variétés Amusantes (Lazzari) (**1**); Th. des Variétés Amusantes, Comiques et Lyriques (**11**); Th. des Victoires Nationales (**3**); Th. du Vaudeville (**3**); Th. Français, Comique et Lyrique (**1**); Th. Patriotique et de Momus (**6**); **Total: 114.**

_____. *Jumeaux de Bergame, Les* [*Comédie* in 1 act, Prem. on 6-8-1782, Pub. in 1782].
n/a (**1**); Th. de la Citoyenne Montansier (**19**); Th. de la Montagne (**4**); Th. de la Nation (Comédie Française) (**1**); Th. des Grands Danseurs (Gaîté) (**3**); Th. des Italiens (Opéra-Comique) (**26**); Th. des Variétés Amusantes (Lazzari) (**1**); Th. des Variétés Amusantes, Comiques et Lyriques (**3**); Th. du Vaudeville (**7**); Th. Patriotique et de Momus (**5**); **Total: 70.**
Total Performances, Florian, Jean-P.-C. de: **477**

Fonpré de Fracansalle. *Almanzor et Nadine* [*Comédie* in 1 act, Prem. on 6-12-1787].
Th. des Grands Danseurs (Gaîté) (**7**); **Total: 7.**

_____. *Amours de Montmartre, Les* [*Comédie* in 1 act, Prem. on 3-4-1774, Pub. in 1782].
Th. de l'Emulation (Gaîté) (**4**); Th. des Variétés Amusantes, Comiques et Lyriques (**23**); Th. du Palais (Cité)-Variétés (**2**); Th. du Palais Royal (**3**); **Total: 32.**

_____. *Bal favorable, Le, ou Le Rendez-vous manqué* [*Comédie* in 1 act, Prem. on 11-11-1780, Pub. in 1780].
Th. des Grands Danseurs (Gaîté) (**1**); **Total: 1.**

_____. *Bataille d'Antioche, La, ou Gargamelle vaincu* [*Tragédie* in 1 act, Prem. on 2-12-1778, Pub. in 1782].
Th. de l'Emulation (Gaîté) (**2**); **Total: 2.**

_____. *Six prétendus de la folle volontaire, Les* [*Comédie* in 3 acts, Prem. on 26-9-1786].
Th. des Grands Danseurs (Gaîté) (**39**); **Total: 39.**

Total Performances, Fonpré de Fracansalle: **81**

Fontenelle, Bernard le Bouyer de. *Comète, La* [*Comédie* in 1 act, Pub. in 1767].
Th. du Vaudeville (**3**); **Total: 3.**

Forgeot, Nicolas-J., Méhul, Etienne-N. (comp). *Caverne, La* [*Opéra* in 3 acts, Prem. on 5-12-1795, Pub. in 1793].
Th. des Italiens (Opéra-Comique) (**22**); **Total: 22.**

_____., **Champein, Stanislas (comp).** *Dettes, Les* [*Comédie* in 2 acts, Prem. on 8-1-1787, Pub. in 1787].
Th. des Italiens (Opéra-Comique) (**96**); **Total: 96.**

_____. *Deux oncles, Les* [*Comédie* in 1 act, Prem. on 29-9-1780, Pub. in 1780].
Th. des Italiens (Opéra-Comique) (**1**); **Total: 1.**

_____. *Double divorce, Le, ou Bienfait de la loi* [*Comédie* in 1 act, Prem. on 26-9-1794, Pub. in 1794].
Maison Egalité (**10**); Th. du Feydeau (de Monsieur) (**2**); Th. Français (de la rue Richelieu) (de la République) (**1**); **Total: 13.**

_____. *Epreuves, Les* [*Comédie* in 1 act, Prem. on 29-1-1785, Pub. in 1785].
Th. de la Nation (Comédie Française) (**8**); Th. du Feydeau (de Monsieur) (**2**); Th. Français (de la rue Richelieu) (de la République) (**1**); **Total: 11.**

_____., **Dezède, Florine (comp).** *Lucette et Lucas* [*Comédie* in 1 act, Prem. on 8-11-1781, Pub. in 1781].
Th. des Italiens (Opéra-Comique) (**10**); **Total: 10.**

_____., **Lemoyne, Jean-B. (comp).** *Mensonge officieux, Le* [*Comédie* in 1 act, Prem. on 13-3-1795, Pub. in 1796].
Cirque National (**8**); Th. du Feydeau (de Monsieur) (**25**); Th. du Lycée au Palais Egalité (**1**); **Total: 34.**

_____., **Lemoyne, Jean-B. (comp).** *Pommiers et le moulin, Les* [*Comédie* in 1 act, Prem. on 22-1-1790, Pub. in 1790].
Académie de la Musique (Opéra) (**21**); Th. du Feydeau (de Monsieur) (**40**); Th. du Palais (Cité)-Variétés (**1**); **Total: 62.**

_____. *Ressemblance, La* [*Comédie* in 3 acts, Prem. on 18-1-1788, Pub. in 1796].
Th. de Molière (**1**); **Total: 1.**

_____., Grétry, André-E.-M. (comp). *Rival confident, Le* [*Comédie* in 2 acts, Prem. on 26-6-1788, Pub. in 1788].
  Th. des Italiens (Opéra-Comique) (**7**); **Total: 7.**

_____. *Rivaux amis, Les* [*Comédie* in 1 act, Prem. on 13-11-1782, Pub. in 1782].
  Th. des Délassements Comiques (**8**); Th. du Feydeau (de Monsieur) (**2**); **Total: 10.**

_____. *Rupture inutile, La* [*Comédie*, Prem. on 2-7-1797].
  Th. du Feydeau (de Monsieur) (**6**); **Total: 6.**
  Total Performances, Forgeot, Nicolas-J.: **273**

Framery, Nicolas-E., Sacchini, Antonio (comp). *Colonie, La* [*Comédie* in 2 acts, Prem. on 16-8-1775, Pub. in 1775].
  Maison Egalité (**6**); Th. de l'Ambigu Comique (**1**); Th. de Molière (**2**); Th. des Grands Danseurs (Gaîté) (**1**); Th. des Italiens (Opéra-Comique) (**31**); Th. du Marais (**1**); Th. du Vaudeville (**1**); Th. Lyrique des Amis de la Patrie (**4**); Th. Patriotique et de Momus (**14**); **Total: 61.**

_____., Paisiello, Giovanni (comp). *Infante de Zamora, L'* [*Opéra* in 4 acts, Prem. in 1779, Pub. in 1781].
  Th. du Feydeau (de Monsieur) (**13**); **Total: 13.**
  Total Performances, Framery, Nicolas-E.: **74**

François de Coupigny, A. *Arlequin jaloux* [*Vaudeville*, Prem. on 2-1-1797, Pub. in 1797].
  Th. du Vaudeville (**1**); **Total: 1.**

François de Neufchâteau, Nicolas-L. *Paméla ou La Vertu récompensée* [*Comédie* in 5 acts, Prem. on 1-8-1793, Pub. in 1793].
  Th. de la Nation (Comédie Française) (**10**); Th. des Variétés Amusantes, Comiques et Lyriques (**3**); Th. du Feydeau (de Monsieur) (**23**); Th. du Marais (**1**); Th. Patriotique et de Momus (**38**); **Total: 75.**

Friedel, Adrien C. *Menzikow ou Les Ennemis généreux* [*Drame* in 2 acts, Pub. in 1780].
  Th. de l'Emulation (Gaîté) (**3**); Th. des Grands Danseurs (Gaîté) (**1**); **Total: 4.**

Fuzelier, Louis., Rey, Jean-B. (comp). *Apollon et Coronis* [*Opéra* in 1 act, Prem. on 3-5-1781, Pub. in 1781].
  Académie de la Musique (Opéra) (**3**); **Total: 3.**

_____. *Arlequin devin par hasard ou Le Lendemain de noces* [*Opéra-Comique* in 1 act, Prem. on 24-7-1716, Pub. in 1717].
  Th. de la Citoyenne Montansier (**4**); Th. de la Montagne (**1**); Th. des Variétés Amusantes, Comiques et Lyriques (**2**); Th. du Feydeau (de Monsieur) (**1**); **Total: 8.**
  Total Performances, Fuzelier, Louis: **11**

Gabiot de Salins, Jean-L. *Auto-da-fé, L', ou Le Tribunal de l'Inquisition* [*Pièce* in 3 acts, Prem. on 2-11-1790, Pub. in 1790].
  Th. de l'Ambigu Comique (**66**); **Total: 66.**

_____. *Aveu délicat, L'* [*Fait Historique* in 1 act, Prem. on 3-9-1787, Pub. in 1787].
  Th. de l'Ambigu Comique (**68**); Th. des Jeunes Artistes (**59**); Th. des Jeunes Elèves (**5**); Th. du Marais (**1**); Th. Patriotique et de Momus (**2**); **Total: 135.**

_____. *Baron de Trenck, Le, ou Le Prisonnier prussien* [*Fait Historique* in 1 act, Prem. on 8-6-1788, Pub. in 1788].
  Th. de l'Ambigu Comique (**47**); **Total: 47.**

_____. *Confédération nationale, La* [*Fait Historique* in 1 act, Prem. on 20-7-1790].
  Th. de l'Ambigu Comique (**19**); **Total: 19**.

_____., Cambini, Giuseppe-M. (comp). *Cora ou La Prêtresse du soleil* [*Drame* in 3 acts, Prem. on 26-3-1789].
  Th. des Beaujolais (**35**); **Total: 35**.

_____. *Deux Babillards, Les* [*Comédie* in 1 act, Prem. on 14-6-1789, Pub. in 1789].
  Th. des Beaujolais (**14**); Th. des Délassements Comiques (**14**); **Total: 28**.

_____. *Deux cousins rivaux, Les* [*Comédie* in 2 acts, Prem. on 24-5-1790, Pub. in 1790].
  Th. des Beaujolais (**23**); **Total: 23**.

_____. *Deux neveux, Les* [*Comédie* in 2 acts, Prem. in 1788, Pub. in 1788].
  Th. des Beaujolais (**50**); Th. des Jeunes Artistes (**63**); **Total: 113**.

_____. *Divorce inutile, Le* [*Comédie* in 1 act, Prem. in 3-1788].
  Th. des Beaujolais (**34**); **Total: 34**.

_____. *Enfant du bonheur, L'* [*Pantomime* in 4 acts, Prem. on 15-6-1797, Pub. in 1797].
  Th. de l'Ambigu Comique (**1**); Th. de l'Emulation (Gaîté) (**85**); Th. Lyrique des Amis de la Patrie (**16**); **Total: 102**.

_____. *Esope aux boulevards* [*Episodique* in 1 act, Prem. on 14-3-1779, Pub. in 1784].
  Th. de l'Ambigu Comique (**5**); **Total: 5**.

_____. *Etrennes critiques, Les* [*Episodique* in 1 act, Prem. on 1-1-1789].
  Th. des Beaujolais (**4**); **Total: 4**.

_____. *Filet, Le, ou Les Bons et les méchants* [*Pantomime* in 1 act, Prem. on 27-10-1785].
  Th. de l'Ambigu Comique (**16**); **Total: 16**.

_____. *Goûter, Le, ou Un Bienfait n'est jamais perdu* [*Comédie* in 1 act, Prem. on 19-10-1784, Pub. in 1784].
  Th. du Lycée des Arts (**10**); **Total: 10**.

_____. *Mari fille, Le* [*Comédie* in 1 act, Prem. on 28-4-1789].
  Th. des Beaujolais (**25**); Th. des Jeunes Artistes (**19**); **Total: 44**.

_____. *Mort d'Hercule, La* [*Pantomime* in 3 acts, Prem. in 1784, Pub. in 1784].
  Th. de l'Ambigu Comique (**36**); **Total: 36**.

_____. *Orgueilleuse, L'* [*Comédie* in 1 act, Prem. on 5-7-1786, Pub. in 1787].
  Th. de l'Ambigu Comique (**7**); Th. du Lycée des Arts (**7**); **Total: 14**.

_____. *Paris sauvé ou La Conspiration manquée* [*Drame* in 3 acts, Prem. on 10-2-1790, Pub. in 1790].
  Th. de l'Ambigu Comique (**47**); **Total: 47**.

_____. *Soufflet, Le* [*Comédie* in 1 act, Prem. on 9-9-1789].
  Th. de l'Ambigu Comique (**18**); Th. de l'Emulation (Gaîté) (**7**); Th. Lyrique des Amis de la Patrie (**2**); **Total: 27**.

_____., Anfossi, Pasquale., Cambini, Giovanni-G. (comp). *Tuteur avare, Le* [*Opéra-Bouffe* in 3 acts, Prem. on 15-3-1787].
  Th. des Beaujolais (**62**); Th. du Lycée des Arts (**3**); Veillée de Thalie (**1**); **Total: 66**.

  Total Performances, Gabiot de Salins, Jean-L.: **871**

Gallet, Sébastien., Rochefort, Jean-B. (comp). *Bacchus et Ariane* [*Ballet*, Prem. on 11-12-1791].
> Académie de la Musique (Opéra) (**25**); Th. des Variétés Amusantes, Comiques et Lyriques (**6**); **Total: 31**.

_____. *Fête civique, La* [*Divertissement/parade* in 1 act, Pub. in 1793].
> Th. National (de la rue Richelieu) (**44**); **Total: 44**.

_____. *Journée de l'amour, La* [*Pantomime*, Prem. on 13-3-1794, Pub. in 1794].
> Maison Egalité (**4**); Th. National (de la rue Richelieu) (**12**); **Total: 16**.
> **Total Performances**, Gallet, Sébastien: **91**

Gamas. *Cange ou Le Commissionnaire de Lazare* [*Fait Historique* in 1 act, Prem. on 30-10-1794, Pub. in 1794].
> Th. Français (de la rue Richelieu) (de la République) (**2**); **Total: 2**.

_____. *Emigrés aux terres australes, Les, ou Le Dernier chapitre d'une grande révolution* [*Comédie* in 1 act, Prem. on 24-11-1792, Pub. in 1794].
> Th. Lyrique des Amis de la Patrie (**18**); **Total: 18**.

_____., Foignet, Charles-G. (comp). *Michel Cervantes* [*Opéra-Comique* in 3 acts, Prem. on 24-12-1793, Pub. in 1794].
> Th. du Lycée des Arts (**13**); Th. Lyrique des Amis de la Patrie (**59**); **Total: 72**.

_____., Foignet, Charles-G. (comp). *Plan d'Opéra, Le* [*Comédie* in 1 act, Prem. on 27-10-1794, Pub. in 1794].
> Maison Egalité (**14**); Th. de la Citoyenne Montansier (**1**); Th. de la Cité (**13**); Th. des Variétés Amusantes, Comiques et Lyriques (**7**); Th. du Palais (Cité)-Variétés (**18**); **Total: 53**.
> **Total Performances**, Gamas: **145**

Gardel, Maximilien. *Chercheuse d'esprit, La* [*Ballet* in 1 act, Prem. on 23-10-1771, Pub. in 1777].
> Académie de la Musique (Opéra) (**61**); Th. de l'Emulation (Gaîté) (**1**); Th. des Troubadours (**3**); **Total: 65**.

_____., Monsigny, Pierre-A. (comp). *Déserteur, Le* [*Ballet* in 3 acts, Prem. on 21-10-1786, Pub. in 1786].
> Académie de la Musique (Opéra) (**113**); Th. de l'Odéon (**3**); Th. de la Rue Martin (**1**); Th. de Molière (**13**); Th. des Délassements Comiques (**22**); Th. des Grands Danseurs (Gaîté) (**25**); Th. des Victoires Nationales (**4**); Th. du Marais (**4**); Th. Français (de la rue Richelieu) (de la République) (**7**); **Total: 192**.

_____. *Grâces, Les* [*Ballet* in 1 act, Prem. on 4-2-1779, Pub. in 1779].
> Th. de l'Emulation (Gaîté) (**16**); Th. des Grands Danseurs (Gaîté) (**7**); Th. du Lycée des Arts (**11**); Th. Patriotique et de Momus (**3**); **Total: 37**.

_____. *Jugement de Pâris, Le* [*Ballet* in 3 acts, Prem. on 23-1-1789, Pub. in 1800].
> Académie de la Musique (Opéra) (**2**); Th. de l'Ambigu Comique (**3**); Th. des Ombres Chinoises (**12**); Th. des Ombres de J.-J. Rousseau (**9**); Th. Français (de la rue Richelieu) (de la République) (**5**); **Total: 31**.

_____. *Jugement du berger Pâris, Le* [*Ballet* in 3 acts, Prem. on 6-3-1793].
> Académie de la Musique (Opéra) (**57**); **Total: 57**.

_____. *Mirza* [*Ballet* in 3 acts, Prem. on 8-11-1779].
> Académie de la Musique (Opéra) (**67**); Th. de la Citoyenne Montansier (**17**); Th. du Vaudeville (**1**); **Total: 85**.

_____. *Nid d'oiseau, Le, ou Colin et Colette* [*Ballet* in 1 act, Pub. in 1786].
    Th. de l'Ambigu Comique (**68**); **Total: 68**.

_____., Gossec, François-J. (comp). *Pied de boeuf, Le*
[*Divertissement/parade* in 1 act, Prem. on 17-6-1787].
    Académie de la Musique (Opéra) (**4**); **Total: 4**.

_____., Grétry, André-E.-M. (comp). *Premier navigateur, Le, ou Le*
Pouvoir de l'amour [*Ballet* in 3 acts, Prem. on 26-7-1785, Pub. in 1785].
    Académie de la Musique (Opéra) (**53**); **Total: 53**.

_____. *Rosière, La* [*Ballet* in 2 acts, Prem. on 29-7-1783, Pub. in 1783].
    Académie de la Musique (Opéra) (**35**); Th. du Lycée des Arts (**6**); Th. Pa-
    triotique et de Momus (**23**); **Total: 64**.
                                          Total Performances, Gardel, Maximilien: **656**

Gardel, Pierre-G., Muller, Ernest-L. (comp). *Psyché* [*Ballet* in 3 acts, Prem.
on 14-12-1790].
    Académie de la Musique (Opéra) (**243**); **Total: 243**.

_____. *Télémaque dans l'île de Calypso* [*Ballet* in 3 acts, Prem. on 23-2-
1790, Pub. in 1790].
    Académie de la Musique (Opéra) (**201**); Th. du Feydeau (de Monsieur) (**2**);
    Total: 203.

                                          Total Performances, Gardel, Pierre-G.: **446**

Garnier, Comte Germain. *Girandols, Les, ou La Tricherie revient à*
son maître [Prem. on 9-12-1780, Pub. in 1780].
    Th. de l'Emulation (Gaîté) (**2**); Th. des Grands Danseurs (Gaîté) (**8**); **To-**
    tal: 10.

Gassier, J.-M., Pseud. L. de Saint-Hughes. *Ami du peuple, L', ou La*
Mort de Marat [*Fait Historique* in 1 act, Pub. in 1794].
    Th. de l'Ambigu Comique (**1**); **Total: 1**.

_____. *Liberté des nègres, La* [*Pantomime* in 1 act, Pub. in 1794].
    Maison Egalité (**4**); Th. des Variétés Amusantes, Comiques et Lyriques
    (**2**); Th. National (de la rue Richelieu) (**2**); **Total: 8**.

_____. *Rival inattendu, Le* [N/A].
    Th. des Variétés Amusantes (Lazzari) (**23**); Th. des Variétés Amusantes,
    Comiques et Lyriques (**1**); **Total: 24**.
                                          Total Performances, Gassier, J.-M.: **33**

Gaullard de Saudray, Charles-E. *Capucins aux frontières, Les* [*Pantom-*
ime in 3 acts, Prem. on 16-10-1798, Pub. in 1793].
    Académie de la Musique (Opéra) (**2**); Th. de la Rue Martin (**7**); Th. des
    Variétés Amusantes (Lazzari) (**29**); Th. des Variétés Amusantes, Comiques
    et Lyriques (**6**); Th. du Lycée des Arts (**141**); Th. Lyrique des Amis de la
    Patrie (**8**); **Total: 193**.

Gautier., Bréval, Jean-B. (comp). *Inez et Léonore ou La Soeur jalouse*
[*Comédie* in 3 acts, Prem. on 14-11-1788, Pub. in 1788].
    Th. des Italiens (Opéra-Comique) (**17**); **Total: 17**.

Genlis, Stéphanie-F., Comtesse de. *Cloison, La* [*Comédie* in 1 act, Prem. on
4-4-1792, Pub. in 1781].
    Th. de la Citoyenne Montansier (**1**); **Total: 1**.

_____. *Curieuse, La* [*Comédie* in 5 acts, Prem. on 29-10-1779].
    Th. du Palais (Cité)-Variétés (**8**); **Total: 8**.
                                          Total Performances, Genlis, Stéphanie-F.: **9**

Gentillâtre, Nicolas. *Poule au pot, La* [*Opéra-Comique* in 2 acts, Pub. in
1778].
    Th. des Ombres de J.-J. Rousseau (**2**); **Total: 2**.

Gérès de Camarsac. *Ainsi va le monde* [*Comédie* in 5 acts, Pub. in 1782].
Th. du Vaudeville (2); Th. Patriotique et de Momus (3); **Total: 5.**

Gersin, N., Année, Antoine. *Ne pas croire ce qu'on voit* [*Vaudeville* in 1 act, Prem. on 18-4-1799, Pub. in 1799].
Th. du Vaudeville (25); **Total: 25.**

Gibert, François-B. *Amant locataire, L', ou Le Faux somnambule* [*Vaudeville* in 2 acts, Prem. on 11-2-1789].
Th. des Beaujolais (4); **Total: 4.**

Godard d'Aucourt de Saint-Just, Claude., Boïeldieu, François-A. (comp). *Famille Suisse, La* [*Opéra-Vaudeville* in 1 act, Prem. on 11-2-1797].
Th. du Feydeau (de Monsieur) (19); **Total: 19.**

_____., Boïeldieu, François-A. (comp). *Zoraime et Zulnar* [*Opéra* in 3 acts, Prem. on 10-5-1798, Pub. in 1798].
Th. des Italiens (Opéra-Comique) (37); **Total: 37.**

Total Performances, Godard d'Aucourt de Saint-Just, Claude: **56**

Godefroy-Menilglaise. *Ami généreux, L'* [*Tableau-Patriotique* in 3 acts, Pub. in 1776].
Th. de Molière (1); Th. des Délassements Comiques (14); **Total: 15.**

Goldoni, Carlo. *Bourru bienfaisant, Le* [*Comédie* in 3 acts, Prem. on 4-11-1771, Pub. in 1771].
Th. de l'Ambigu Comique (1); Th. de l'Emulation (Gaîté) (3); Th. de l'Odéon (1); Th. de la Citoyenne Montansier (6); Th. de la Montagne (1); Th. de la Nation (Comédie Française) (35); Th. de la Rue Martin (3); Th. de Molière (6); Th. du Feydeau (de Monsieur) (21); Th. du Marais (1); Th. du Palais (Cité)-Variétés (2); Th. Français (de la rue Richelieu) (de la République) (11); Th. Lyrique des Amis de la Patrie (1); Th. National (de la rue Richelieu) (15); **Total: 107.**

_____., Piccinni, Niccolò (comp). *Buona figliola, La* [*Opéra*].
Th. du Feydeau (de Monsieur) (6); Veillée de Thalie (3); **Total: 9.**

_____. *Nozze di Dorina, Delle* [*Opéra* in 2 acts].
Th. du Feydeau (de Monsieur) (50); **Total: 50.**

Total Performances, Goldoni, Carlo: **166**

Gosse, Etienne. *Auteur dans son ménage, L'* [*Comédie* in 1 act, Prem. on 28-3-1799, Pub. in 1798].
Th. de l'Ambigu Comique (1); Th. du Feydeau (de Monsieur) (24); **Total: 25.**

_____. *Epreuve par ressemblance, L'* [*Comédie* in 1 act, Prem. on 21-12-1798, Pub. in 1798].
Th. de la Citoyenne Montansier (7); **Total: 7.**

_____. *Femmes politiques, Les* [*Comédie* in 3 acts, Prem. on 15-9-1799, Pub. in 1799].
Th. des Victoires (22); Th. des Victoires Nationales (5); **Total: 27.**

_____. *Roman, Le* [*Tableau-Patriotique* in 1 act, Prem. on 2-12-1791].
Th. de l'Emulation (Gaîté) (23); Th. Lyrique des Amis de la Patrie (5); **Total: 28.**

Total Performances, Gosse, Etienne: **87**

Gossec, François-J. (comp). *Offrande à la Liberté, L'* [*Opéra*, Prem. on 3-7-1792, Pub. in 1792].
Académie de la Musique (Opéra) (143); Ampithéâtre National (21); Th. de Molière (1); Th. des Variétés Amusantes (Lazzari) (7); Th. du Lycée des Arts (1); Th. du Palais (Cité)-Variétés (1); **Total: 174.**

Gouffé, Armand Alexandre Duval. *Coco-ricco* [*Vaudeville*, Pub. in 1796].
    Th. de l'Emulation (Gaîté) (**20**); **Total: 20**.

_____. *Deux jocrisses, Les, ou Le Commerce à l'eau* [*Vaudeville* in 1 act,
Prem. on 3-1-1796, Pub. in 1796].
    Th. de la Citoyenne Montansier (**1**); Th. de la Cité (**47**); Th. des Variétés
    Amusantes, Comiques et Lyriques (**4**); Th. du Palais (Cité)-Variétés (**34**);
    Total: 86.

_____. *Nouvelle cacophonie, La, ou Faites donc aussi la paix* [*Vaude-
ville*, Pub. in 1797].
    Th. de la Citoyenne Montansier (**1**); Th. de la Cité (**18**); **Total: 19**.

_____. *Panorama, Le* [*Vaudeville* in 1 act, Prem. on 27-9-1799].
    Th. des Troubadours (**8**); **Total: 8**.

_____. *Revue de l'an V* [In 1 act, Pub. in 1800].
    Th. du Vaudeville (**1**); **Total: 1**.

_____. *Tivoli ou Le Jardin à la mode* [*Vaudeville* in 1 act, Pub. in 1797].
    Th. de la Citoyenne Montansier (**4**); Th. de la Cité (**39**); Th. des Variétés
    Amusantes, Comiques et Lyriques (**1**); **Total: 44**.
                    Total Performances, Gouffé, Armand Alexandre Duval: **170**

Gouges, Marie Gouze, dite Olympe de. *Bienfaisance récompensée, La,
ou La Vertu couronnée* [*Comédie mêlée d'ariettes* in 1 act, Pub. in 1788].
    Th. de la Citoyenne Montansier (**5**); **Total: 5**.

_____. *Couvent, Le, ou Les Voeux forcés* [*Drame* in 2 acts, Prem. in 10-1790,
Pub. in 1792].
    Th. Français, Comique et Lyrique (**42**); **Total: 42**.

_____. *Entrée de Dumouriez à Bruxelles, L', ou Les Vivandiers* [*Pièce*
in 5 acts, Prem. in 1-1793, Pub. in 1793].
    Th. Français (de la rue Richelieu) (de la République) (**3**); **Total: 3**.

_____. *Esclavage des noirs, L', ou L'Heureux naufrage* [*Drame* in 3 acts,
Prem. in 12-1789, Pub. in 1792].
    Th. de la Nation (Comédie Française) (**1**); **Total: 1**.

_____. *Mirabeau aux Champs Elysées* [*Comédie* in 1 act, Prem. on 15-4-
1791].
    n/a (**1**); **Total: 1**.
                    Total Performances, Gouges, Marie Gouze, dite Olympe de: **52**

Gougibus, J.-T. Gougy, dit., Leblanc de Guillet, Antonio Blanc, dit
    (comp). *Gonzalve et Zuleima ou La Destruction des moeurs* [*Pan-
tomime* in 3 acts, Prem. on 12-9-1797].
    Th. de la Cité (**13**); **Total: 13**.

Goulard, Jean-F.-T. *Florestan ou La Leçon* [*Comédie* in 2 acts, Prem. on 10-
10-1798, Pub. in 1798].
    Th. du Vaudeville (**18**); **Total: 18**.

Gourbillon, C.-Joseph., Paisiello, Giovanni (comp). *Bon maître, Le, ou
Les Esclaves par amour* [*Opéra* in 3 acts, Prem. in 1786].
    Th. du Feydeau (de Monsieur) (**28**); **Total: 28**.

Gourbillon, Joseph-A., Paisiello, Giovanni (comp). *Marquis de Tulipano, Le* [*Opéra-Bouffe* in 2 acts, Prem. in 1779, Pub. in 1803].
    Th. de la Rue Martin (**1**); Th. de Molière (**1**); Th. du Feydeau (de Mon-
    sieur) (**124**); Th. du Palais (Cité)-Variétés (**1**); Th. Lyrique des Amis de la
    Patrie (**3**); Veillée de Thalie (**5**); **Total: 135**.

Gourgault, J.B. pseud. Henri Dugazon *Modéré, Le* [*Comédie* in 1 act, Pub. in 1793].
> Th. Français (de la rue Richelieu) (de la République) (**36**); **Total: 36**.

Grenier., Champein, Stanislas (comp). *Mélomanie, La* [*Comédie* in 1 act, Prem. on 23-1-1781, Pub. in 1783].
> Académie de la Musique (Opéra) (**1**); Th. de l'Ambigu Comique (**2**); Th. de l'Odéon (**1**); Th. de la Citoyenne Montansier (**15**); Th. de la Cité (**1**); Th. de la Montagne (**1**); Th. de la Rue Martin (**5**); Th. de Molière (**5**); Th. des Italiens (Opéra-Comique) (**156**); Th. du Lycée des Arts (**25**); Th. du Marais (**1**); Th. Français (de la rue Richelieu) (de la République) (**1**); **Total: 214**.

_____. *Monsieur de Craquignac ou Le Pauvre ermite* [*Comédie* in 1 act, Pub. in 1799].
> Th. de l'Ambigu Comique (**3**); **Total: 3**.
> > **Total Performances**, Grenier: **217**

Gresset, Jean-B.-L. *Méchant, Le* [*Comédie* in 5 acts, Prem. in 4-1747, Pub. in 1747].
> Maison Egalité (**2**); Th. de l'Odéon (**1**); Th. de la Nation (Comédie Française) (**5**); Th. du Feydeau (de Monsieur) (**1**); Th. du Marais (**4**); Th. Français (de la rue Richelieu) (de la République) (**20**); Th. National (de la rue Richelieu) (**4**); **Total: 37**.

Grétry, André-J., Grétry, André-E.-M. (comp). *Barbier de village, Le, ou Le Revenant* [*Opéra-Comique*, Prem. on 6-5-1797, Pub. in 1797].
> Th. du Feydeau (de Monsieur) (**7**); **Total: 7**.

Grouvelle, Philippe-A. *Epreuve délicate, L'* [*Comédie* in 3 acts, Prem. on 20-6-1785, Pub. in 1785].
> Th. du Feydeau (de Monsieur) (**2**); Th. Français (de la rue Richelieu) (de la République) (**1**); **Total: 3**.

Gueroult, Jean-F. *Journée de Marathon, La, ou Le Triomphe de la liberté* [*Héroique* in 4 acts, Prem. on 26-8-1793].
> Th. National (de la rue Richelieu) (**12**); **Total: 12**.

Gueulette, Thomas-S. *Arlequin Pluton* [*Comédie* in 3 acts, Prem. in 1719, Pub. in 1879].
> Th. des Ombres de J.-J. Rousseau (**10**); **Total: 10**.

Guibert, Jacques-A.-H. *Anne de Boleyn* [*Tragédie* in 5 acts, Prem. on 6-10-1791, Pub. in 1825].
> Th. de Molière (**1**); **Total: 1**.

Guichard, Jean-F., Charpentier (comp). *Bûcheron, Le, ou Les Trois souhaits* [*Comédie* in 1 act, Prem. on 28-2-1763, Pub. in 1763].
> Th. de l'Emulation (Gaîté) (**3**); Th. des Italiens (Opéra-Comique) (**3**); Th. des Ombres Chinoises (**8**); Th. des Ombres de J.-J. Rousseau (**41**); **Total: 55**.

"Guilbert, citoyen." *Léonidas ou Le Départ des spartiates* [*Tableau-Patriotique* in 1 act].
> Th. Français (de la rue Richelieu) (de la République) (**1**); **Total: 1**.

Guilbert de Pixerécourt, René-C. *Château des Appenins, Le, ou Le Fantôme vivant* [*Drame* in 5 acts, Prem. on 9-12-1798, Pub. in 1798].
> Th. de l'Ambigu Comique (**4**); **Total: 4**.

_____. *Deux valets, Les* [*Comédie* in 3 acts, Prem. on 30-10-1789, Pub. in 1803].
> Th. de l'Ambigu Comique (**18**); **Total: 18**.

_____. *Forêt de Sicile, La* [*Opéra* in 2 acts, Prem. on 23-4-1798].
Th. de la Citoyenne Montansier (37); **Total: 37.**

_____., Persuis, Louis-L.-L'O. (comp). *Léonidas ou Les Spartiates*
[*Opéra* in 3 acts, Prem. on 15-8-1799].
Académie de la Musique (Opéra) (2); **Total: 2.**

_____. *Nuit espagnole, La, ou La Cloison* [*Comédie* in 2 acts, Prem. on 15-3-1798].
Th. de l'Ambigu Comique (4); **Total: 4.**

_____., Morange (comp). *Petits auvergnats, Les* [*Opéra*, Prem. on 24-11-1797].
Th. de l'Ambigu Comique (41); **Total: 41.**

_____., Mengozzi, Bernardo (comp). *Selico ou Les Nègres généreux*
[*Drame* in 4 acts, Prem. on 5-10-1793].
Th. National (de la rue Richelieu) (34); **Total: 34.**

_____. *Soirée des Champs Elysées, La* [*Comédie* in 1 act, Pub. in 1799].
Th. de la Citoyenne Montansier (29); **Total: 29.**

_____. *Victor ou L'Enfant de la forêt* [*Mélodrame* in 3 acts, Prem. on 10-6-1798, Pub. in 1798].
Th. de l'Ambigu Comique (47); Th. de l'Emulation (Gaîté) (29); Th. du
Marais (1); Th. Lyrique des Amis de la Patrie (6); **Total: 83.**

_____. *Zozo ou Le Mal avisé* [*Comédie*, Prem. on 16-10-1799].
Th. de la Citoyenne Montansier (8); **Total: 8.**

Total Performances, Guilbert de Pixerécourt, René-C.: **260**

Guillard, Nicolas-F., Sacchini, Antonio (comp). *Arvire et Evelina*
[*Drame* in 3 acts, Prem. on 29-4-1788, Pub. in 1788].
Académie de la Musique (Opéra) (32); Th. Français (de la rue Richelieu)
(de la République) (1); **Total: 33.**

_____., Sacchini, Antonio (comp). *Chimène ou Le Cid* [*Tragédie-Lyrique*
in 3 acts, Prem. on 18-11-1783, Pub. in 1783].
Académie de la Musique (Opéra) (13); **Total: 13.**

_____. *Elfrida* [Prem. on 17-12-1791].
Th. des Italiens (Opéra-Comique) (6); **Total: 6.**

_____. *Elisca ou L'Habitant de Madagascar* [Prem. on 28-8-1799].
Th. des Italiens (Opéra-Comique) (6); **Total: 6.**

_____., Salieri, Antonio (comp). *Horaces, Les* [*Tragédie-Lyrique* in 3 acts,
Prem. on 2-12-1786, Pub. in 1786].
Th. de la Citoyenne Montansier (6); **Total: 6.**

_____., Gluck, Christoph (comp). *Iphigénie en Tauride* [*Tragédie-Lyrique*
in 4 acts, Prem. on 18-5-1779, Pub. in 1779].
Académie de la Musique (Opéra) (133); Th. Français (de la rue Richelieu)
(de la République) (1); **Total: 134.**

_____., Andrieux, François-G.-J.-S., Lemoyne, Jean-B. (comp). *Louis
IX en Egypte* [*Opéra* in 3 acts, Prem. on 15-6-1790, Pub. in 1790].
Académie de la Musique (Opéra) (10); **Total: 10.**

_____., Lemoyne, Jean-B. (comp). *Miltiade à Marathon* [*Opéra-
Vaudeville* in 2 acts].
Académie de la Musique (Opéra) (67); Th. du Palais (Cité)-Variétés (1);
Total: 68.

_____., Sacchini, Antonio (comp). *Oedipe à Colone* [*Tragédie-Lyrique* in 3 acts, Prem. on 4-1-1786, Pub. in 1786].
Académie de la Musique (Opéra) (**194**); Th. de l'Odéon (**1**); Th. Lyrique des Amis de la Patrie (**1**); **Total: 196.**

_____., Kalkbrenner, Christian (comp). *Olimpie* [*Tragédie* in 3 acts, Prem. on 18-12-1798].
Académie de la Musique (Opéra) (**3**); **Total: 3.**
Total Performances, Guillard, Nicolas-F.: **475**

Guillemain, Charles-J. *Alexis et Rosette* [*Mélodrame* in 1 act, Prem. on 18-5-1786, Pub. in 1786].
Th. des Beaujolais (**18**); Th. des Jeunes Artistes (**37**); **Total: 55.**

_____., Chardiny, Louis-A. (comp). *Annette et Basile* [Prem. on 17-11-1785, Pub. in 1785].
n/a (**1**); Th. des Beaujolais (**25**); Th. des Délassements Comiques (**1**); Th. des Jeunes Artistes (**90**); **Total: 117.**

_____., Raymond, B. (comp). *Armoire, L'* [*Opéra-Bouffe* in 1 act, Prem. on 6-9-1789, Pub. in 1789].
Th. des Beaujolais (**21**); Th. des Jeunes Artistes (**43**); **Total: 64.**

_____. *Auberge isolée, L'* [*Comédie* in 1 act, Prem. on 6-8-1794, Pub. in 1794].
Th. du Vaudeville (**39**); **Total: 39.**

_____. *Boniface pointu et sa famille* [*Comédie* in 1 act, Prem. on 1-2-1782, Pub. in 1782].
Th. de la Citoyenne Montansier (**94**); Th. de la Cité (**1**); Th. de la Montagne (**17**); Th. de Molière (**26**); Th. des Grands Danseurs (Gaîté) (**5**); Th. des Jeunes Artistes (**2**); Th. du Marais (**3**); Th. du Palais Royal (**4**); Th. Lyrique des Amis de la Patrie (**11**); **Total: 163.**

_____. *Bonnes gens, Les, ou Boniface à Paris* [*Comédie* in 1 act, Prem. on 26-3-1783, Pub. in 1783].
Maison Egalité (**13**); Th. de l'Ambigu Comique (**1**); Th. de la Citoyenne Montansier (**30**); Th. de la Cité (**28**); Th. de la Montagne (**17**); Th. de Molière (**4**); Th. des Variétés Amusantes, Comiques et Lyriques (**2**); Th. du Palais (Cité)-Variétés (**3**); Th. du Palais Royal (**29**); Th. du Vaudeville (**9**); Th. National (de la rue Richelieu) (**1**); **Total: 137.**

_____. *Bouquets, Les* [*Vaudeville* in 1 act, Prem. on 6-9-1785, Pub. in 1785].
Th. de l'Ambigu Comique (**14**); **Total: 14.**

_____. *Café des halles, Le* [*Comédie* in 1 act, Prem. on 8-7-1780, Pub. in 1781].
Th. du Palais Royal (**22**); **Total: 22.**

_____. *Cent écus, Les* [*Drame* in 1 act, Prem. on 20-11-1783, Pub. in 1784].
Maison Egalité (**6**); Th. de l'Emulation (Gaîté) (**6**); Th. du Palais (Cité)-Variétés (**3**); Th. du Palais Royal (**14**); **Total: 29.**

_____. *Cheveux, Les* [*Comédie* in 1 act].
Th. des Jeunes Artistes (**29**); **Total: 29.**

_____. *Demande en mariage, La* [Prem. in 1789].
Th. des Ombres Chinoises (**5**); Th. des Ombres de J.-J. Rousseau (**8**); **Total: 13.**

_____. *Ecrivain public, L'* [N/A].
Th. des Ombres Chinoises (**2**); Th. des Ombres de J.-J. Rousseau (**9**); **Total: 11.**

_____. *Encore des bonnes gens* [*Comédie* in 1 act, Pub. in 1793].
Th. du Vaudeville (**64**); **Total: 64.**

_____. *Enrôlement supposé, L'* [*Comédie* in 1 act, Prem. on 25-6-1781, Pub. in 1781].

> Maison Egalité (**28**); Th. de l'Emulation (Gaîté) (**14**); Th. de la Citoyenne Montansier (**67**); Th. de la Cité (**30**); Th. des Délassements Comiques (**5**); Th. des Variétés Amusantes (Lazzari) (**22**); Th. des Variétés Amusantes, Comiques et Lyriques (**33**); Th. du Marais (**1**); Th. du Mareux (**2**); Th. du Palais (Cité)-Variétés (**45**); Th. du Palais Royal (**44**); Th. Patriotique et de Momus (**12**); **Total: 303**.

_____. *Entrepreneur de spectacle, L'* [Prem. on 20-6-1796].

> Th. du Vaudeville (**5**); Th. Patriotique et de Momus (**8**); **Total: 13**.

_____. *Esope seigneur de village* [*Vaudeville* in 1 act, Prem. on 14-8-1790].

> Th. Français, Comique et Lyrique (**22**); **Total: 22**.

_____. *Faux talisman, Le, ou Rira bien qui rira le dernier* [*Comédie* in 1 act, Prem. on 28-6-1782, Pub. in 1782].

> Th. de la Citoyenne Montansier (**12**); Th. de la Montagne (**11**); Th. des Jeunes Artistes (**9**); Th. du Palais Royal (**32**); **Total: 64**.

_____. *Femme battue et contente, La* [N/A].

> Th. des Ombres Chinoises (**1**); Th. des Ombres de J.-J. Rousseau (**13**); **Total: 14**.

_____. *Gagne-petit, Le* [*Pièce* in 1 act, Prem. in 1776, Pub. in 1776].

> Th. des Grands Danseurs (Gaîté) (**9**); Th. des Ombres Chinoises (**4**); Th. des Ombres de J.-J. Rousseau (**22**); **Total: 35**.

_____. *Gilles le niais* [N/A].

> Th. des Ombres de J.-J. Rousseau (**15**); **Total: 15**.

_____. *Grands et les petits, Les* [*Comédie* in 1 act, Prem. on 26-3-1789].

> Th. du Feydeau (de Monsieur) (**3**); **Total: 3**.

_____. *Matinée du ménage des bons citoyens, La* [*Comédie* in 1 act, Prem. on 10-11-1791].

> Th. Français, Comique et Lyrique (**4**); **Total: 4**.

_____. *Mensonge excusable, Le* [*Comédie* in 1 act, Prem. on 29-1-1783, Pub. in 1783].

> Th. de l'Emulation (Gaîté) (**4**); Th. de la Citoyenne Montansier (**1**); Th. de la Cité (**33**); Th. des Grands Danseurs (Gaîté) (**10**); Th. du Palais (Cité)-Variétés (**24**); Th. du Palais Royal (**62**); Th. Français (de la rue Richelieu) (de la République) (**6**); **Total: 140**.

_____. *Menuisier de Bagdad, Le* [*Comédie* in 1 act, Prem. on 22-12-1789, Pub. in 1790].

> Th. des Beaujolais (**52**); Th. des Jeunes Artistes (**36**); **Total: 88**.

_____. *Nègre aubergiste, Le* [*Fait Historique* in 1 act, Prem. on 3-9-1793, Pub. in 1794].

> Th. du Vaudeville (**67**); **Total: 67**.

_____. *Nouveau parvenu, Le* [*Comédie* in 1 act, Prem. on 14-9-1782, Pub. in 1782].

> Th. de la Cité (**7**); Th. du Palais Royal (**32**); **Total: 39**.

_____. *Patriotisme des français, Le* [*Vaudeville* in 1 act, Prem. on 19-9-1789].

> Th. des Beaujolais (**19**); **Total: 19**.

_____. *Politique à la halle, La* [*Opéra-Comique* in 1 act, Prem. on 18-8-1789].

> Th. des Beaujolais (**31**); **Total: 31**.

_____. *Prisonniers français à Liège, Les* [*Comédie* in 1 act, Pub. in 1792].

> Th. du Vaudeville (**16**); **Total: 16**.

_____. *Sans-culottides, Les* [*Comédie* in 1 act].

> Th. du Lycée des Arts (**10**); **Total: 10**.

_____. *Solitude, La* [*Comédie* in 1 act, Prem. on 23-6-1786, Pub. in 1787].
　　　Th. des Beaujolais (**26**); Th. des Délassements Comiques (**1**); Th. des
　　　Jeunes Artistes (**81**); Th. du Marais (**2**); **Total: 110.**

_____. *Veuve espagnole, La* [*Comédie* in 1 act, Prem. on 12-12-1789].
　　　Th. des Beaujolais (**30**); **Total: 30.**
　　　　　　　　　　　Total Performances, Guillemain, Charles-J.: **1780**

Guillet. *Prisonnier français, Le, ou Le Bienfait récompensé* [*Fait Historique* in 1 act, Prem. on 1-10-1798].
　　　Th. de la Citoyenne Montansier (**31**); Th. de Molière (**7**); **Total: 38.**

Guimond de la Touche, Claude. *Iphigénie en Tauride* [*Tragédie* in 5 acts,
Prem. on 4-6-1757, Pub. in 1758].
　　　Académie de la Musique (Opéra) (**24**); Maison Egalité (**1**); Th. de l'Odéon
　　　(**3**); Th. de la Citoyenne Montansier (**5**); Th. de la Nation (Comédie
　　　Française) (**7**); Th. de la Rue Martin (**4**); Th. du Feydeau (de Monsieur)
　　　(**7**); Th. du Lycée Dramatique (**4**); Th. du Marais (**9**); Th. Français (de la
　　　rue Richelieu) (de la République) (**18**); **Total: 82.**

Guy, Jean-H., Grétry, André-E.-M. (comp). *Anacréon chez Polycrate*
[*Opéra* in 3 acts, Prem. on 17-1-1797, Pub. in 1797].
　　　Académie de la Musique (Opéra) (**33**); Th. Français (de la rue Richelieu)
　　　(de la République) (**6**); **Total: 39.**

_____., Gaveaux, Pierre (comp). *Sophie et Moncars ou L'Intrigue portugaise* [*Opéra-Vaudeville* in 3 acts, Prem. on 30-9-1797, Pub. in 1797].
　　　Th. des Italiens (Opéra-Comique) (**5**); Th. du Feydeau (de Monsieur) (**45**);
　　　Th. Français (de la rue Richelieu) (de la République) (**1**); **Total: 51.**
　　　　　　　　　　　Total Performances, Guy, Jean-H.: **90**

Guyot de Merville, Michel. *Apparence trompeuse, L', ou Le Capricieux* [*Comédie* in 1 act, Prem. on 22-3-1790, Pub. in 1744].
　　　Th. des Beaujolais (**1**); **Total: 1.**

_____. *Consentement forcé, Le* [*Comédie* in 1 act, Prem. on 13-8-1738, Pub. in
1738].
　　　Th. de l'Ambigu Comique (**21**); Th. de l'Odéon (**1**); Th. de la Citoyenne
　　　Montansier (**13**); Th. de la Liberté (**1**); Th. de la Nation (Comédie
　　　Française) (**25**); Th. de la Rue Martin (**13**); Th. de Molière (**5**); Th. des
　　　Grands Danseurs (Gaîté) (**13**); Th. des Victoires (**4**); Th. du Feydeau (de
　　　Monsieur) (**14**); Th. du Lycée des Arts (**2**); Th. du Marais (**18**); Th.
　　　Français (de la rue Richelieu) (de la République) (**56**); Th. Lyrique des
　　　Amis de la Patrie (**4**); Th. National (de la rue Richelieu) (**12**); **Total: 207.**
　　　　　　　　Total Performances, Guyot de Merville, Michel: **208**

Hapdé, Jean-B.-A. *Arlequin Jacob et Gilles Esaü ou Le Droit
d'aînesse* [*Vaudeville*, Prem. on 3-12-1797, Pub. in 1798].
　　　Th. de l'Ambigu Comique (**1**); Th. des Jeunes Artistes (**42**); Th. du Marais
　　　(**1**); **Total: 44.**

_____. *Arlequin jokei ou L'Equitomanie* [*Vaudeville* in 1 act, Prem. on 15-8-
1798].
　　　Th. des Jeunes Artistes (**14**); Th. du Marais (**1**); **Total: 15.**

_____. *Arlequin rentier* [*Vaudeville*, Prem. on 23-5-1797].
　　　Th. des Jeunes Artistes (**39**); **Total: 39.**

_____. *Bon magister, Le* [*Vaudeville*].
　　　Th. de la Cité (**1**); Th. des Jeunes Artistes (**59**); **Total: 60.**

_____. *Buffet, Le, ou Les Deux cousins* [*Comédie* in 1 act, Prem. on 4-10-
1796].
　　　Th. des Jeunes Artistes (**70**); Th. du Marais (**1**); **Total: 71.**

_____. *Deux pères pour un, Les, ou Le Mariage aux Invalides* [*Comédie* in 1 act, Prem. on 24-7-1799, Pub. in 1799].
> Th. de la Cité (**13**); Th. de Molière (**1**); Th. des Grands Danseurs (Gaîté) (**1**); Th. du Palais (Cité)-Variétés (**15**); **Total: 30.**

_____. *Faux nicaise, Le* [N/A].
> Th. de l'Ambigu Comique (**7**); **Total: 7.**

_____. *Gilles éléphant* [*Vaudeville*, Prem. on 16-2-1799].
> Th. des Jeunes Artistes (**10**); Th. du Marais (**3**); **Total: 13.**

_____. *Homme entre deux femmes, L'* [*Comédie* in 2 acts].
> Th. de la Rue Martin (**1**); Th. des Jeunes Artistes (**42**); **Total: 43.**

_____. *Parc de mousseaux, Le* [*Vaudeville*, Prem. on 2-8-1798].
> Th. du Palais (Cité)-Variétés (**4**); **Total: 4.**

_____., Corsange de la Plant, Jean-F.-J. *Pauvre aveugle, Le* [*Opéra-Comique*, Prem. on 24-7-1797, Pub. in 1792].
> Th. de l'Ambigu Comique (**54**); Th. de Molière (**4**); Th. des Délassements Comiques (**18**); **Total: 76.**

_____., Corsange de la Plant, Jean-F.-J. *Pierre Luc ou Le Cultivateur du Mont-blanc* [In 3 acts, Prem. on 21-8-1799].
> Th. des Jeunes Artistes (**22**); Th. du Marais (**2**); **Total: 24.**

_____., Dabaytua, Joachim E. *Sérail, Le, ou La Fête du grand Mogol* [*Pantomime* in 3 acts, Prem. on 2-10-1799].
> Th. de la Cité (**11**); **Total: 11.**

> **Total Performances**, Hapdé, Jean-B.-A.: **437**

Harny de Guerville., Mme. Favart., Sodi, Charles (comp)., Favart, Charles-S. *Amours de Bastien et Bastienne, Les* [*Parodie* in 1 act, Prem. on 4-8-1753, Pub. in 1753].
> Th. des Italiens (Opéra-Comique) (**6**); Th. du Vaudeville (**7**); **Total: 13.**

_____. *Georget et Georgette* [*Opéra-Comique* in 1 act, Prem. on 28-7-1761, Pub. in 1761].
> Th. de l'Ambigu Comique (**9**); **Total: 9.**

_____. *Liberté conquise, La* [*Drame* in 5 acts, Prem. on 4-1-1791].
> Th. de la Nation (Comédie Française) (**32**); **Total: 32.**

> **Total Performances**, Harny de Guerville: **54**

Hauteroche, Noel de. *Bourgeoises de qualité, Les* [*Comédie* in 5 acts, Pub. in 1691].
> Th. Français (de la rue Richelieu) (de la République) (**4**); **Total: 4.**

_____. *Cocher, Le* [*Comédie* in 1 act, Pub. in 1685].
> Th. de l'Odéon (**2**); Th. de la Citoyenne Montansier (**10**); Th. de la Nation (Comédie Française) (**5**); Th. des Grands Danseurs (Gaîté) (**49**); Th. du Feydeau (de Monsieur) (**1**); Th. du Marais (**13**); Th. Français (de la rue Richelieu) (de la République) (**22**); Th. Lyrique des Amis de la Patrie (**1**); Th. National (de la rue Richelieu) (**1**); **Total: 104.**

_____. *Crispin médecin* [*Comédie* in 3 acts, Prem. in 1673, Pub. in 1680].
> Maison Egalité (**1**); Th. de l'Estrapade au Panthéon (**4**); Th. de l'Odéon (**10**); Th. de la Citoyenne Montansier (**4**); Th. de la Liberté (**1**); Th. de la Montagne (**4**); Th. de la Nation (Comédie Française) (**17**); Th. de la Rue Martin (**11**); Th. de Molière (**4**); Th. des Grands Danseurs (Gaîté) (**9**); Th. des Victoires (**7**); Th. du Feydeau (de Monsieur) (**16**); Th. du Lycée Dramatique (**6**); Th. du Marais (**11**); Th. Français (de la rue Richelieu) (de la République) (**35**); Th. National (de la rue Richelieu) (**3**); **Total: 143.**

_____. *Deuil, Le* [*Comédie* in 1 act, Pub. in 1673].
  Th. du Marais (4); Th. Français (de la rue Richelieu) (de la République) (3); **Total: 7.**

_____. *Esprit follet, L', ou La Dame invisible* [*Comédie* in 5 acts, Prem. in 1684, Pub. in 1684].
  Th. de la Cité (5); Th. de la Nation (Comédie Française) (3); **Total: 8.**
  Total Performances, Hauteroche, Noel de: **266**

Hèle, Thomas d'., Grétry, André-E.-M. (comp). *Evénements imprévus, Les* [*Comédie* in 3 acts, Prem. on 11-11-1779].
  Th. de la Citoyenne Montansier (33); Th. des Italiens (Opéra-Comique) (68); Th. National (de la rue Richelieu) (3); **Total: 104.**

_____. *Fausses apparences, Les, ou L'Amant jaloux* [*Comédie* in 3 acts, Prem. on 20-11-1778, Pub. in 1778].
  Th. de l'Ambigu Comique (1); Th. de la Citoyenne Montansier (18); Th. des Italiens (Opéra-Comique) (106); Th. National (de la rue Richelieu) (4); **Total: 129.**

_____. *Gilles ravisseur* [*Comédie* in 1 act, Prem. on 1-3-1781, Pub. in 1781].
  Th. de la Citoyenne Montansier (2); Th. du Palais Royal (2); **Total: 4.**

_____., Grétry, André-E.-M. (comp). *Jugement de Midas, Le* [*Comédie* in 3 acts, Prem. on 27-6-1778, Pub. in 1778].
  Th. des Italiens (Opéra-Comique) (51); **Total: 51.**
  Total Performances, Hèle, Thomas d': **288**

Hennequin, Louis., Anfossi, Pasquale (comp). *Antiquaire, L'* [*Opéra-Comique* in 3 acts, Prem. on 9-3-1789].
  Th. du Feydeau (de Monsieur) (2); **Total: 2.**

_____., Lebrun, Louis-S. (comp). *Bon fils, Le* [*Opéra-Comique* in 1 act, Prem. on 17-9-1795, Pub. in 1795].
  Th. Français, Comique et Lyrique (27); **Total: 27.**

_____., Lebrun, Louis-S. (comp). *Emilie et Melcour ou La Leçon villageoise* [*Comédie* in 1 act, Prem. on 3-7-1795, Pub. in 1795].
  Th. du Lycée des Arts (67); Th. Lyrique des Amis de la Patrie (27); **Total: 94.**

_____., Quaisin, Adrian (comp). *Estelle et Nemorin* [*Comédie* in 2 acts, Pub. in 1789].
  Th. de l'Ambigu Comique (22); Th. des Variétés Amusantes, Comiques et Lyriques (8); Th. National (de la rue Richelieu) (6); **Total: 36.**

_____. *Moment d'humeur, Un* [*Comédie* in 1 act, Prem. on 21-7-1796].
  Th. du Lycée des Arts (16); **Total: 16.**

_____., Gaveaux, Pierre (comp). *Partie carrée, La* [*Opéra-Bouffe* in 1 act, Prem. on 26-6-1793, Pub. in 1793].
  Th. du Feydeau (de Monsieur) (59); Th. Patriotique et de Momus (10); **Total: 69.**
  Total Performances, Hennequin, Louis: **244**

Henrion, Charles. *Amours de la halle, Les* [In 1 act, Pub. in 1802].
  Th. des Variétés Amusantes (Lazzari) (1); Th. Patriotique et de Momus (2); **Total: 3.**

_____. *Laitière, La* [*Comédie* in 1 act, Prem. on 22-9-1795, Pub. in 1806].
  Th. des Italiens (Opéra-Comique) (1); Th. Patriotique et de Momus (11); **Total: 12.**

_____. *Rosenthal ou Le Vol à tire d'aile* [*Vaudeville*, Prem. on 29-10-1799].
  Th. de Molière (3); **Total: 3.**
  Total Performances, Henrion, Charles: **18**

Henriquez, L.-M., Gouffé, Armand Alexandre Duval. *Chaudronnier de St.-Flour, Le* [*Comédie* in 1 act, Prem. on 20-5-1798, Pub. in 1799].
Th. de l'Emulation (Gaîté) (35); Th. du Marais (1); Th. du Mareux (1); Th. du Palais (Cité)-Variétés (1); Th. Lyrique des Amis de la Patrie (31); Total: 69.

Hérissant, Louis-T., Anson, Pierre-H. *Deux seigneurs, Les, ou L'Alchimiste* [*Comédie* in 2 acts, Pub. in 1783].
Petits Comédiens de Palais Royal (4); Total: 4.

Hippolite., Paisiello, Giovanni (comp). *Valet rival et confident, Le* [*Parodie* in 2 acts, Prem. on 27-10-1789].
Th. du Feydeau (de Monsieur) (21); Total: 21.

Hoffman, François-B. *Adélaïde ou La Victime* [*Drame* in 3 acts, Prem. on 25-7-1793].
Th. des Italiens (Opéra-Comique) (1); Total: 1.

_____., Méhul, Etienne-N. (comp). *Adrien empereur de Rome* [*Opéra* in 3 acts, Prem. on 4-6-1799, Pub. in 1798].
Académie de la Musique (Opéra) (4); Total: 4.

_____., Méhul, Etienne-N. (comp). *Ariodant* [*Opéra* in 3 acts, Prem. on 10-10-1799].
Th. des Italiens (Opéra-Comique) (12); Total: 12.

_____. *Azeline* [*Comédie* in 3 acts, Prem. on 5-12-1796].
Th. des Italiens (Opéra-Comique) (29); Total: 29.

_____., Kreutzer, Rodolpho (comp). *Brigand, Le* [*Drame* in 3 acts, Prem. on 25-7-1795, Pub. in 1795].
Th. des Italiens (Opéra-Comique) (11); Total: 11.

_____., Grétry, André-E.-M. (comp). *Callias ou Nature et patrie* [*Opéra* in 1 act, Prem. on 19-9-1794, Pub. in 1794].
Th. des Italiens (Opéra-Comique) (7); Total: 7.

_____., Méhul, Etienne-N. (comp). *Euphrosine et Coradin* [*Opéra* in 3 acts, Pub. in 1790].
Th. des Italiens (Opéra-Comique) (58); Total: 58.

_____., Méhul, Etienne-N. (comp). *Euphrosine ou Le Tyran corrigé* [*Comédie* in 3 acts, Prem. on 4-9-1790, Pub. in 1791].
Th. des Italiens (Opéra-Comique) (62); Total: 62.

_____., Solié, Jean-P. (comp). *Femme de 45 ans, La* [*Comédie* in 1 act, Prem. on 19-11-1798, Pub. in 1798].
Th. des Italiens (Opéra-Comique) (1); Total: 1.

_____. *Folle épreuve, La* [*Comédie* in 1 act, Prem. on 6-11-1787, Pub. in 1788].
Th. de l'Ambigu Comique (146); Total: 146.

_____., Méhul, Etienne-N. (comp). *Jeune sage et le vieux fou, Le* [*Comédie* in 1 act, Prem. on 28-3-1793, Pub. in 1802].
Th. des Italiens (Opéra-Comique) (33); Total: 33.

_____., Solié, Jean-P. (comp). *Jockey, Le* [*Comédie* in 1 act, Prem. on 6-1-1796, Pub. in 1796].
Th. des Italiens (Opéra-Comique) (80); Total: 80.

_____., Dalayrac, Nicolas (comp). *Léon ou Le Château de Montenero* [*Drame* in 3 acts, Prem. on 15-10-1798, Pub. in 1817].
Th. des Italiens (Opéra-Comique) (41); Total: 41.

_____., Chérubini, Luigi (comp). *Médée* [*Opéra* in 3 acts, Prem. on 13-3-1797].
>   Th. du Feydeau (de Monsieur) (**39**); **Total: 39.**

_____., Lemoyne, Jean-B. (comp). *Nephte, reine d'Egypte* [*Tragédie-Lyrique* in 3 acts, Prem. on 15-12-1789, Pub. in 1790].
>   Académie de la Musique (Opéra) (**36**); **Total: 36.**

_____. *Original, L'* [*Comédie* in 1 act, Prem. on 30-7-1796].
>   Th. du Feydeau (de Monsieur) (**11**); **Total: 11.**

_____., Lemoyne, Jean-B. (comp). *Phèdre* [*Tragédie-Lyrique* in 3 acts, Prem. on 26-10-1786, Pub. in 1786].
>   Académie de la Musique (Opéra) (**29**); Th. du Feydeau (de Monsieur) (**2**); Th. du Marais (**4**); Th. Français (de la rue Richelieu) (de la République) (**7**); **Total: 42.**

_____., Solié, Jean-P. (comp). *Secret, Le* [*Comédie* in 1 act, Prem. on 20-4-1796, Pub. in 1796].
>   Th. de la Rue Martin (**2**); Th. des Italiens (Opéra-Comique) (**117**); Th. du Feydeau (de Monsieur) (**1**); Th. du Mareux (**1**); Th. du Palais (Cité)-Variétés (**2**); **Total: 123.**

_____., Solié, Jean-P. (comp). *Soubrette, La, ou L'Etui de harpe* [*Comédie* in 1 act, Prem. on 3-12-1794].
>   Th. des Italiens (Opéra-Comique) (**33**); **Total: 33.**

_____., Méhul, Etienne-N. (comp). *Stratonice* [*Comédie* in 1 act, Prem. on 3-5-1792, Pub. in 1792].
>   Th. des Italiens (Opéra-Comique) (**98**); **Total: 98.**
>   **Total Performances**, Hoffman, François-B.: **867**

Hourcastrème, Pierre. *Nouvelle Eve, La* [*Comédie mêlée d'ariettes* in 3 acts, Prem. on 28-11-1793, Pub. in 1773].
>   Th. du Lycée des Arts (**6**); **Total: 6.**

Hus, Eugène., Gaveaux, Pierre (comp). *Lise et Colin ou La Surveillance inutile* [*Opéra* in 2 acts, Prem. on 4-8-1796].
>   Th. du Feydeau (de Monsieur) (**22**); **Total: 22.**

_____. *Muses, Les, ou Le Triomphe d'Apollon* [*Ballet*, Prem. on 13-11-1792].
>   Académie de la Musique (Opéra) (**4**); **Total: 4.**

_____. *Nid d'amours, Le, ou Les Amours vengés* [*Ballet*, Prem. on 3-9-1798].
>   Th. de Molière (**1**); Th. des Jeunes Artistes (**45**); **Total: 46.**
>   **Total Performances**, Hus, Eugène: **72**

Imbert, Barthélemy. *Deux noms, Les* [*Comédie* in 3 acts, Prem. on 3-10-1790].
>   Th. du Feydeau (de Monsieur) (**1**); **Total: 1.**

_____. *Fausse apparence, La, ou Le Jaloux malgré lui* [*Comédie* in 3 acts, Prem. on 24-4-1789, Pub. in 1789].
>   Th. de la Nation (Comédie Française) (**5**); **Total: 5.**

_____. *Griffonet* [*Opéra-Comique* in 1 act, Prem. on 1-3-1790].
>   Th. des Beaujolais (**6**); **Total: 6.**

_____. *Inauguration du Théâtre Français, L'* [*Vaudeville* in 2 acts, Pub. in 1782].
>   Petits Comédiens de Palais Royal (**15**); **Total: 15.**

_____. *Jaloux sans amour, Le* [*Comédie* in 5 acts, Prem. on 8-1-1781, Pub. in 1781].
    Th. de la Nation (Comédie Française) (**16**); Th. du Feydeau (de Monsieur) (**14**); Th. Français (de la rue Richelieu) (de la République) (**3**); **Total: 33.**

_____. *Marie de Brabant, reine de France* [*Tragédie* in 5 acts, Prem. on 9-9-1789, Pub. in 1790].
    Th. de la Nation (Comédie Française) (**10**); **Total: 10.**
        Total Performances, Imbert, Barthélemy: **70**

Jacquelin, Jacques-A. *Antiquomanie, L', ou Le Mariage sous la cheminée* [*Comédie* in 1 act, Prem. on 27-5-1799, Pub. in 1799].
    Th. des Jeunes Artistes (**5**); **Total: 5.**

_____. *Clef forée, La* [*Comédie* in 1 act, Prem. on 3-8-1799, Pub. in 1799].
    Th. des Jeunes Artistes (**3**); Th. des Troubadours (**11**); **Total: 14.**

_____. *Enfant de l'amour, L'* [*Tragi-Comédie* in 1 act, Prem. on 2-3-1799, Pub. in 1798].
    Th. des Jeunes Artistes (**3**); Th. du Marais (**2**); **Total: 5.**

_____., Philidor Rochelle. *Fureurs de l'amour, Les* [*Tragi-Comédie*, Prem. on 10-5-1798, Pub. in 1798].
    Th. des Jeunes Artistes (**40**); Th. du Marais (**1**); **Total: 41.**

_____. *Jean la Fontaine* [*Comédie* in 1 act, Prem. on 23-9-1798, Pub. in 1798].
    Th. des Jeunes Artistes (**17**); Th. du Marais (**1**); **Total: 18.**

_____. *Jean Racine avec ses enfants* [*Comédie* in 1 act, Prem. on 21-4-1799, Pub. in 1798].
    Th. des Jeunes Artistes (**26**); **Total: 26.**
        Total Performances, Jacquelin, Jacques-A.: **109**

Jardin. *Déjeuneur des volontaires, Le* [*Tableau-Patriotique*, Prem. on 4-3-1794, Pub. in 1794].
    Th. du Palais (Cité)-Variétés (**1**); **Total: 1.**

Joigny., Trial, Armand-E. (comp). *Cécile et Julien ou Le Siège de Lille* [*Fait Historique* in 3 acts, Prem. on 21-11-1792, Pub. in 1792].
    Th. des Italiens (Opéra-Comique) (**72**); **Total: 72.**

_____., Berton, Henri-M. (comp). *Dénouement inattendu, Le* [In 1 act, Prem. on 10-11-1791].
    Th. des Italiens (Opéra-Comique) (**1**); **Total: 1.**

_____., Quaisin, Adrian (comp). *Vendange, La, ou Silvain et Lucette* [*Opéra-Comique*, Prem. on 16-5-1798].
    Th. de Molière (**21**); **Total: 21.**
        Total Performances, Joigny: **94**

Jolly, François-A. *Capricieuse, La* [*Comédie* in 3 acts, Prem. on 11-5-1726, Pub. in 1726].
    Th. des Grands Danseurs (Gaîté) (**5**); **Total: 5.**

_____. *Henri IV à Meulan ou Les Dames françaises* [*Comédie* in 1 act, Prem. on 28-12-1789].
    Th. des Grands Danseurs (Gaîté) (**20**); **Total: 20.**
        Total Performances, Jolly, François-A.: **25**

Joly de Saint-Just. *Heureux procès, L'* [N/A].
    Th. du Feydeau (de Monsieur) (**2**); **Total: 2.**

Jouffroy, Comte A. *Soldat généreux, Le, ou La Suite du maréchal des logis* [*Comédie* in 1 act, Pub. in 1788].
> Th. de Molière (**4**); Th. des Variétés Amusantes (Lazzari) (**8**); Th. des Variétés Amusantes, Comiques et Lyriques (**7**); Th. Patriotique et de Momus (**11**); **Total: 30**.

Jouy, Victor-J. Etienne, dit de., Longchamps, Charles de. *Arbitre, L', ou Les Consultations de l'an VII* [*Comédie* in 1 act, Pub. in 1798].
> Th. du Vaudeville (**6**); **Total: 6**.

_____., **Dieulafoy, Michel., Longchamps, Charles de.** *Comment faire ou Les Epreuves de misanthropie et repentir* [*Comédie* in 1 act, Prem. on 16-3-1799, Pub. in 1798].
> Th. du Vaudeville (**57**); **Total: 57**.

_____., **Chérubini, Luigi (comp)., Longchamps, Charles de.** *Prisonnière, La* [*Opéra-Comique* in 1 act, Prem. on 12-9-1799, Pub. in 1803].
> Th. de la Citoyenne Montansier (**29**); **Total: 29**.
> **Total Performances**, Jouy, Victor-J. Etienne, dit de: **92**

Kotzebue, Auguste. *Enfant de l'amour, L'* [*Drame* in 3 acts].
> Th. du Palais (Cité)-Variétés (**1**); **Total: 1**.

_____. *Fils naturel, Le* [*Drame* in 5 acts, Prem. on 6-11-1798].
> Th. de l'Odéon (**1**); Th. de Molière (**3**); **Total: 4**.
> **Total Performances**, Kotzebue, Auguste: **5**

La Chapelle, Jean. *Carrosses d'Orléans, Les* [*Comédie* in 1 act, Prem. on 3-1-1793, Pub. in 1680].
> Th. des Grands Danseurs (Gaîté) (**2**); **Total: 2**.

La Chaussée, Pierre-C. N. de. *Ecole de la jeunesse, L', ou Le Retour sur soi-même* [*Comédie* in 5 acts, Prem. on 22-2-1749, Pub. in 1762].
> Th. de l'Emulation (Gaîté) (**1**); Th. des Grands Danseurs (Gaîté) (**1**); **Total: 2**.

_____. *Ecole des mères, L'* [*Comédie* in 5 acts, Prem. on 27-4-1744, Pub. in 1745].
> Th. de la Nation (Comédie Française) (**8**); Th. de Molière (**5**); Th. Français (de la rue Richelieu) (de la République) (**16**); **Total: 29**.

_____. *Eloge de la folie, L'* [*Comédie* in 3 acts, Prem. on 26-10-1791].
> Th. Français, Comique et Lyrique (**4**); **Total: 4**.

_____. *Gouvernante, La* [*Comédie* in 5 acts, Prem. on 18-1-1747, Pub. in 1747].
> Th. de la Nation (Comédie Française) (**19**); Th. de Molière (**1**); Th. du Marais (**3**); Th. du Palais Royal (**4**); Th. Français (de la rue Richelieu) (de la République) (**5**); **Total: 32**.

_____. *Maximien* [*Tragédie*, Prem. on 28-2-1738, Pub. in 1738].
> Th. de l'Odéon (**3**); **Total: 3**.

_____. *Mélanide* [*Comédie* in 5 acts, Prem. in 5-1741, Pub. in 1741].
> Th. de l'Estrapade au Panthéon (**1**); Th. de l'Odéon (**4**); Th. de la Citoyenne Montansier (**3**); Th. du Marais (**6**); **Total: 14**.

_____. *Préjugé à la mode, Le* [*Comédie* in 5 acts, Prem. on 3-2-1735, Pub. in 1735].
> Th. de la Nation (Comédie Française) (**5**); **Total: 5**.
> **Total Performances**, La Chaussée, Pierre-C. N. de: **89**

La Fosse, Antoine de. *Manlius Capitolinus* [*Tragédie* in 5 acts, Prem. in 1698, Pub. in 1806].
> Th. de la Nation (Comédie Française) (**8**); **Total: 8**.

La Harpe, Jean-F. de. *Comte de Warwick, Le* [*Tragédie* in 5 acts, Prem. on 7-11-1763, Pub. in 1764].
      Th. de la Nation (Comédie Française) (1); **Total: 1.**
_____. *Mélanie ou La Religieuse* [*Drame* in 3 acts, Prem. on 7-12-1791, Pub. in 1792].
      Th. de l'Ambigu Comique (2); Th. de l'Emulation (Gaîté) (1); Th. de la Rue Martin (27); Th. de Molière (14); Th. des Victoires (7); Th. des Victoires Nationales (3); Th. du Feydeau (de Monsieur) (1); Th. du Marais (8); Th. Français (de la rue Richelieu) (de la République) (19); **Total: 82.**
_____. *Menzicoff ou Les Exilés* [*Tragédie* in 5 acts, Prem. on 10-11-1775, Pub. in 1781].
      Th. de Molière (1); **Total: 1.**
_____. *Muses rivales, Les* [In 1 act, Prem. on 10-7-1791].
      Th. Français (de la rue Richelieu) (de la République) (4); **Total: 4.**
_____. *Philoctète* [*Tragédie* in 3 acts, Prem. on 16-6-1783, Pub. in 1781].
      Maison Egalité (4); n/a (2); Th. de l'Odéon (4); Th. de la Bienfaisance (2); Th. de la Nation (Comédie Française) (17); Th. de la Rue Martin (1); Th. des Victoires Nationales (1); Th. du Feydeau (de Monsieur) (7); Th. du Marais (7); Th. Français (de la rue Richelieu) (de la République) (11); Th. Lyrique des Amis de la Patrie (1); Th. National (de la rue Richelieu) (1); **Total: 58.**
_____. *Timoléon* [*Tragédie* in 5 acts, Prem. on 1-8-1764, Pub. in 1764].
      Th. Français (de la rue Richelieu) (de la République) (21); **Total: 21.**
_____. *Virginie* [*Tragédie* in 5 acts, Prem. on 11-7-1786, Pub. in 1793].
      Th. de la Nation (Comédie Française) (4); Th. des Jeunes Artistes (29); Th. du Feydeau (de Monsieur) (1); Th. du Marais (1); Th. Français (de la rue Richelieu) (de la République) (29); Th. Français, Comique et Lyrique (25); Th. Patriotique et de Momus (12); **Total: 101.**
                  Total Performances, La Harpe, Jean-F. de: **268**
La Lande. *Adélaïde et Sainville* [*Comédie* in 1 act, Prem. on 22-10-1790].
      Th. du Feydeau (de Monsieur) (2); **Total: 2.**
La Martelière, Jean-H.-F. *Robert, chef de brigands* [*Drame* in 5 acts, Prem. on 6-3-1792, Pub. in 1793].
      Th. de l'Emulation (Gaîté) (19); Th. de la Rue Martin (1); Th. de Molière (3); Th. des Grands Danseurs (Gaîté) (2); Th. des Victoires (3); Th. des Victoires Nationales (6); Th. du Feydeau (de Monsieur) (1); Th. du Marais (73); Th. Français (de la rue Richelieu) (de la République) (49); Th. Lyrique des Amis de la Patrie (3); **Total: 160.**
_____. *Tribunal Redoutable, Le, ou La Suite de "Robert, chef de brigands"* [*Drame* in 5 acts, Prem. on 10-11-1792, Pub. in 1792].
      Th. du Marais (12); **Total: 12.**
_____. *Trois amants, Les* [*Comédie* in 3 acts, Prem. on 14-1-1791].
      Th. du Feydeau (de Monsieur) (1); **Total: 1.**
_____. *Trois espiègles, Les, ou Les Arts et la folie* [*Comédie* in 3 acts, Prem. on 11-8-1798, Pub. in 1798].
      Th. Lyrique des Amis de la Patrie (12); **Total: 12.**
                  Total Performances, La Martelière, Jean-H.-F.: **185**
La Montagne, Pierre de. *Café de Rouen, Le* [*Comédie* in 1 act, Prem. on 4-11-1785, Pub. in 1786].
      Th. du Palais Royal (13); **Total: 13.**

La Motte, Antoine H. de. *Inès de Castro* [*Tragédie* in 5 acts, Prem. on 6-4-1723, Pub. in 1723].
> Th. de la Citoyenne Montansier (2); Th. de la Nation (Comédie Française) (3); **Total: 5.**

La Ribardière, de., Desbrosses (comp). *Deux cousins, Les, ou La Bonne amie* [*Comédie* in 1 act, Prem. on 21-5-1763, Pub. in 1763].
> Th. des Italiens (Opéra-Comique) (8); **Total: 8.**

La Rochefoucould, Alexis-Niçolas de, Mis. de Surgerès. *Comment l'esprit vient aux filles* [*Comédie* in 3 acts, Prem. in 1738, Pub. in 1738].
> Th. des Jeunes Artistes (10); **Total: 10.**

La Salle d'Offremont, Adrien-N. P. *Esclave à la mode, L'* [*Comédie* in 2 acts, Prem. on 24-6-1789].
> Th. du Feydeau (de Monsieur) (1); **Total: 1.**

_____., Lebrun, Louis-S. (comp). *Ils ne savent pas lire* [*Opéra* in 1 act, Prem. on 21-6-1791].
> Th. de la Citoyenne Montansier (2); **Total: 2.**

_____. *Officieux, L'* [*Comédie* in 3 acts, Prem. on 18-8-1780, Pub. in 1780].
> Th. des Italiens (Opéra-Comique) (1); **Total: 1.**

_____., Gossec, François-J. (comp). *Pêcheurs, Les* [*Comédie* in 1 act, Prem. on 23-4-1766, Pub. in 1766].
> Th. des Italiens (Opéra-Comique) (9); Th. du Marais (1); Veillée de Thalie (2); **Total: 12.**

_____., Beaumesnil, Henriette-A. (comp). *Plaire c'est commander* [*Opéra* in 2 acts, Prem. on 12-5-1792, Pub. in 1792].
> Th. de la Citoyenne Montansier (27); **Total: 27.**
> > **Total Performances**, La Salle d'Offremont, Adrien-N. P.: **43**

Labussière, Charles-H.-D. de. *Inventaire, L'* [*Comédie* in 1 act, Prem. on 17-8-1777, Pub. in 1777].
> Th. Français, Comique et Lyrique (1); **Total: 1.**

Lachabeaussière, Auguste-E.-X. P. de., Dalayrac, Nicolas (comp). *Azémia ou Les Sauvages* [*Comédie* in 3 acts, Prem. on 17-10-1786, Pub. in 1786].
> Th. des Italiens (Opéra-Comique) (145); **Total: 145.**

_____. *Corsaire, Le* [*Comédie* in 3 acts, Prem. on 7-3-1783, Pub. in 1783].
> Th. de Molière (3); Th. des Italiens (Opéra-Comique) (13); **Total: 16.**

_____. *Eclipse de lune, L', ou L'Astrologue qui tombe dans un puits* [*Comédie* in 1 act, Prem. on 13-7-1799].
> Th. de la Citoyenne Montansier (38); Th. du Mareux (1); **Total: 39.**

_____. *Intrigante, L'* [*Comédie* in 5 acts, Pub. in 1789].
> Th. des Grands Danseurs (Gaîté) (3); **Total: 3.**

_____. *Maris corrigés, Les* [*Comédie* in 3 acts, Prem. on 7-8-1781, Pub. in 1781].
> Th. des Italiens (Opéra-Comique) (3); **Total: 3.**

_____. *Sourd, Le* [*Comédie* in 1 act, Prem. on 25-4-1780, Pub. in 1780].
> Th. de l'Ambigu Comique (95); **Total: 95.**
> > **Total Performances**, Lachabeaussière, Auguste-E.-X. P. de: **301**

Ladoucette, Baron Jean de. *Helvétius à Voré* [*Fait Historique* in 1 act, Prem. on 7-7-1798, Pub. in 1797].
> Th. de Molière (14); **Total: 14.**

Laffichard, Thomas. *Banquier, Le* [*Comédie* in 3 acts, Pub. in 1753].
    Th. de la Citoyenne Montansier (21); **Total: 21.**

_____., **Valois d'Orville, Adrien-J. de.** *Epreuve amoureuse, L'* [*Opéra-Comique* in 1 act, Prem. on 23-7-1737].
    Th. des Grands Danseurs (Gaîté) (3); **Total: 3.**
                                    Total Performances, Laffichard, Thomas: **24**

Laffile, Charles. *Fête de l'hymen, La* [*Tableau-Patriotique*, Pub. in 1633].
    Th. de l'Ambigu Comique (4); **Total: 4.**

Laffillard, Eugène-H., Pseud. Decour., St. Honorine. *Amour au village, L'* [*Opéra* in 1 act, Pub. in 1804].
    Th. de l'Emulation (Gaîté) (4); Th. des Enfans Comiques (1); **Total: 5.**

Lafont, Joseph de., Gilliers, Jean-C. (comp). *Naufrage, Le, ou La Pompe funèbre de Crispin* [*Comédie* in 1 act, Prem. on 14-6-1710, Pub. in 1789].
    Th. de l'Ambigu Comique (18); Th. de la Nation (Comédie Française) (7); **Total: 25.**

_____. *Provençale, La* [*Ballet*, Prem. on 17-9-1722, Pub. in 1735].
    Th. du Palais (Cité)-Variétés (16); **Total: 16.**

_____. *Trois frères rivaux, Les* [*Comédie* in 1 act, Prem. on 4-8-1713, Pub. in 1713].
    Petits Comédiens de Palais Royal (31); Th. de l'Estrapade au Panthéon (3); Th. de l'Odéon (2); Th. de la Citoyenne Montansier (3); Th. de la Nation (Comédie Française) (3); Th. de la Rue Martin (7); Th. de Molière (7); Th. des Variétés Amusantes, Comiques et Lyriques (1); Th. du Lycée Dramatique (1); Th. du Marais (2); Th. du Palais Royal (3); Th. Français (de la rue Richelieu) (de la République) (4); Th. Lyrique des Amis de la Patrie (8); Th. Patriotique et de Momus (1); **Total: 76.**
                                    Total Performances, Lafont, Joseph de: **117**

Lafontaine, Jean de., Chevillet de Champmeslé, Charles. *Coupe enchantée, La* [*Comédie* in 1 act, Pub. in 1710].
    Th. de la Cité (6); Th. de la Nation (Comédie Française) (2); Th. Français (de la rue Richelieu) (de la République) (25); **Total: 33.**

_____., **Chevillet de Champmeslé, Charles.** *Florentin, Le* [*Comédie* in 1 act, Prem. on 20-7-1683, Pub. in 1685].
    Th. de l'Odéon (2); Th. de la Cité (1); Th. de la Nation (Comédie Française) (6); Th. du Marais (1); Th. du Palais (Cité)-Variétés (3); **Total: 13.**
                                    Total Performances, Lafontaine, Jean de: **46**

Lagrange, Nicolas., Procope-Couteau, M. Cottelli dit. *Gageure, La* [*Comédie* in 3 acts, Prem. on 9-2-1741, Pub. in 1752].
    Th. des Grands Danseurs (Gaîté) (3); **Total: 3.**

Laignelot, Joseph-F. *Rienzy* [*Tragédie* in 5 acts, Prem. on 2-3-1791, Pub. in 1791].
    Th. de la Nation (Comédie Française) (1); **Total: 1.**

Lajonchère, Venard de. *Amphitrion* [*Ballet* in 3 acts, Prem. on 18-2-1792, Pub. in 1772].
    Th. des Grands Danseurs (Gaîté) (15); **Total: 15.**

Lambert, L.-T. *Arlequin tailleur* [*Comédie* in 1 act, Prem. on 29-7-1793, Pub. in 1793].
    Th. du Vaudeville (43); **Total: 43.**

_____. *Plaque retournée, La* [*Vaudeville* in 1 act, Prem. on 8-1-1794, Pub. in 1794].
>Th. du Vaudeville (**19**); **Total: 19.**
>>**Total Performances**, Lambert, L.-T.: **62**

Lamontagne, Pierre de. *Enthousiaste, L'* [*Comédie* in 2 acts, Prem. on 19-4-1784, Pub. in 1785].
>Th. du Palais (Cité)-Variétés (**4**); **Total: 4.**

Landrin. *Bouquet du sentiment, Le* [*Comédie* in 1 act, Prem. on 28-1-1789, Pub. in 1789].
>Th. du Feydeau (de Monsieur) (**1**); **Total: 1.**

_____. *Bureau de mariages, Le* [Prem. on 14-8-1799].
>Th. des Troubadours (**3**); **Total: 3.**

_____. *Colère d'Achille, La* [N/A].
>Th. des Ombres Chinoises (**4**); Th. des Ombres de J.-J. Rousseau (**12**); **Total: 16.**

_____., Levacher de Charnois, Jean-C. *Esope à la foire* [*Comédie* in 1 act, Prem. on 30-7-1782, Pub. in 1782].
>Th. du Palais Royal (**33**); Th. Lyrique des Amis de la Patrie (**7**); **Total: 40.**

_____. *Fabuliste, Le* [*Comédie* in 2 acts, Prem. on 12-3-1789].
>Th. du Feydeau (de Monsieur) (**9**); **Total: 9.**

_____. *Sabotier, Le, ou Les Huit sols* [*Comédie* in 1 act, Prem. on 13-9-1781, Pub. in 1781].
>Th. des Grands Danseurs (Gaîté) (**15**); Th. des Ombres Chinoises (**2**); **Total: 17.**

_____. *Trois Horaces, Les* [N/A].
>Th. des Ombres Chinoises (**4**); Th. des Ombres de J.-J. Rousseau (**10**); **Total: 14.**
>>**Total Performances**, Landrin: **100**

Langeron, see Andrault de Langeron.

Lanoue, Jean-B. Sauvé, dit. *Coquette corrigée, La* [*Comédie* in 5 acts, Prem. on 5-8-1756, Pub. in 1757].
>Th. de l'Emulation (Gaîté) (**2**); Th. de l'Odéon (**5**); Th. de la Citoyenne Montansier (**4**); Th. de la Nation (Comédie Française) (**22**); Th. de la Rue Martin (**2**); Th. de Molière (**3**); Th. du Feydeau (de Monsieur) (**17**); Th. du Lycée Dramatique (**1**); Th. du Marais (**12**); Th. du Mareux (**1**); Th. Français (de la rue Richelieu) (de la République) (**14**); Th. National (de la rue Richelieu) (**4**); **Total: 87.**

Lantier, Etienne-F. *Impatient, L'* [*Comédie* in 1 act, Prem. on 3-9-1778, Pub. in 1779].
>Th. de l'Odéon (**2**); Th. de la Nation (Comédie Française) (**13**); Th. du Marais (**2**); Th. National (de la rue Richelieu) (**4**); **Total: 21.**

Laperière. *Edouard et Emilie ou Le Triomphe de l'amour et de l'amitié* [*Pantomime* in 4 acts, Prem. on 30-5-1793].
>Th. du Palais (Cité)-Variétés (**7**); **Total: 7.**

Lapierre de Châteauneuf. *Bienfaisant, Le* [*Comédie* in 1 act, Prem. on 10-10-1791, Pub. in 1787].
>Th. Lyrique des Amis de la Patrie (**2**); **Total: 2.**

Larnac, François. *Thémistocle* [*Tragédie* in 3 acts, Prem. on 9-3-1798].
>Th. de l'Odéon (**4**); **Total: 4.**

Laroche., Guillemain, Charles-J. *Bienfait récompensé, Le, ou La Suite des bonnes gens* [*Comédie* in 1 act, Prem. on 15-12-1783, Pub. in 1784].
    Th. de la Citoyenne Montansier (1); Th. de la Rue Martin (1); Th. de Molière (3); Th. des Italiens (Opéra-Comique) (1); Th. du Lycée des Arts (11); Th. du Palais Royal (2); **Total: 19**.

_____. *Deux voisins, Les* [*Comédie* in 2 acts, Prem. on 25-1-1791].
    Th. des Italiens (Opéra-Comique) (1); **Total: 1**.

_____. *Dumont ou Le Modèle des amis* [*Comédie* in 2 acts, Prem. on 8-6-1787, Pub. in 1787].
    Th. du Palais Royal (7); **Total: 7**.

_____. *Tuteur trompé, Le* [*Comédie* in 3 acts, Pub. in 1779].
    Th. de Molière (4); **Total: 4**.
                                   Total Performances, Laroche: **31**

Lasante, Gilles de. *Héritiers, Les* [In 3 acts, Prem. on 9-3-1742, Pub. in 1742].
    Th. Français (de la rue Richelieu) (de la République) (28); **Total: 28**.

Lauchery, Etienne. *Mariée de village, La* [*Ballet*, Pub. in 1784].
    Th. du Lycée des Arts (5); **Total: 5**.

Laugier, Marie., Champein, Stanislas (comp). *Epreuves du républicain, Les, ou L'Amour de la patrie* [*Comédie* in 3 acts, Prem. on 4-8-1794].
    Th. de la Rue Martin (1); Th. des Italiens (Opéra-Comique) (8); **Total: 9**.

Laujon, Pierre., Martini, Jean.-P.-E. (comp). *Amoureux de quinze ans, L', ou La Double fête* [*Comédie* in 3 acts, Prem. on 18-4-1771, Pub. in 1771].
    Th. des Italiens (Opéra-Comique) (30); **Total: 30**.

_____. *Couvent, Le, ou Les Fruits du caractère* [*Comédie* in 1 act, Prem. on 16-4-1790, Pub. in 1822].
    Th. de la Nation (Comédie Française) (26); Th. du Feydeau (de Monsieur) (2); **Total: 28**.

_____. *Matin, Le, ou La Toilette de Vénus* [*Divertissement/parade* in 5 acts, Prem. on 25-2-1750].
    Th. des Jeunes Artistes (43); **Total: 43**.
                                   Total Performances, Laujon, Pierre: **101**

Laus de Boissy, Louis de. *Portrait, Le* [*Divertissement/parade*, Prem. on 13-1-1799].
    Th. de l'Odéon (5); **Total: 5**.

_____. *Tête sans cervelle, La* [*Comédie* in 1 act, Prem. on 15-12-1793, Pub. in 1794].
    Th. Lyrique des Amis de la Patrie (7); **Total: 7**.

_____. *Trois rivaux, Les* [*Opéra-Bouffe* in 2 acts, Pub. in 1778].
    Th. de Molière (1); Th. des Grands Danseurs (Gaîté) (1); **Total: 2**.
                                   Total Performances, Laus de Boissy, Louis de: **14**

Lavallée, Joseph. *Constitution à Constantinople, La* [*Tableau-Patriotique* in 1 act, Prem. on 15-8-1793, Pub. in 1793].
    Th. National (de la rue Richelieu) (31); **Total: 31**.

_____. *Départ des volontaires villageois pour les frontières, Le* [*Comédie* in 1 act, Pub. in 1793].
    Th. de la Citoyenne Montansier (22); Th. de la Montagne (2); Th. de la Rue Martin (1); Th. du Lycée des Arts (3); Th. National (de la rue Richelieu) (3); **Total: 31**.

_____., Foignet, Charles-G. (comp). *Femme qui sait se taire, La* [*Opéra* in 1 act, Prem. on 28-10-1793].
>Th. National (de la rue Richelieu) (**3**); **Total: 3.**

_____. *Manlius Torquatus* [*Tragédie*, Prem. on 4-2-1794].
>Th. National (de la rue Richelieu) (**11**); **Total: 11.**

_____. *Nègre comme il y a peu de blancs, Le* [*Comédie* in 1 act, Prem. on 4-8-1789].
>Th. de l'Ambigu Comique (**44**); **Total: 44.**

_____., Foignet, Charles-G. (comp). *Roi et le pèlerin, Le* [*Opéra* in 2 acts, Prem. on 2-6-1792].
>Th. de la Citoyenne Montansier (**17**); **Total: 17.**
>**Total Performances**, Lavallée, Joseph: **137**

Laya, Jean-L. *Ami des loix, L'* [*Comédie* in 5 acts, Prem. on 2-1-1793, Pub. in 1793].
>Th. de la Nation (Comédie Française) (**6**); Th. du Feydeau (de Monsieur) (**12**); **Total: 18.**

_____. *Dangers de l'opinion, Les* [*Drame* in 5 acts, Prem. on 19-1-1790, Pub. in 1790].
>Th. de la Nation (Comédie Française) (**18**); **Total: 18.**

_____. *Falkland* [*Drame* in 5 acts, Prem. on 25-5-1798].
>Th. du Feydeau (de Monsieur) (**5**); **Total: 5.**

_____. *Jean Calas* [*Drame* in 5 acts, Prem. on 18-12-1790, Pub. in 1791].
>Th. de la Nation (Comédie Française) (**7**); Th. de Molière (**2**); Th. des Italiens (Opéra-Comique) (**3**); Th. du Marais (**7**); **Total: 19.**
>**Total Performances**, Laya, Jean-L.: **60**

Lazzari, Ange. *Amour puni par Vénus, L'* [*Pantomime* in 2 acts, Pub. in 1792].
>Th. des Jeunes Artistes (**5**); Th. des Variétés Amusantes (Lazzari) (**55**); Th. des Variétés Amusantes, Comiques et Lyriques (**32**); Th. du Marais (**2**); **Total: 94.**

_____. *Ariston ou Le Pouvoir de la magie* [*Pantomime* in 2 acts, Prem. on 11-7-1792, Pub. in 1792].
>Maison Egalité (**1**); Th. de la Citoyenne Montansier (**3**); Th. des Variétés Amusantes, Comiques et Lyriques (**165**); **Total: 169.**

_____. *Arlequin boulanger* [*Pantomime* in 2 acts, Pub. in 1795].
>Th. des Variétés Amusantes, Comiques et Lyriques (**1**); **Total: 1.**

_____. *Arlequin gardien des femmes* [*Comédie*].
>Th. des Variétés Amusantes (Lazzari) (**27**); Th. des Variétés Amusantes, Comiques et Lyriques (**54**); Th. Français, Comique et Lyrique (**1**); **Total: 82.**

_____. *Arlequin honnête homme et fripon* [*Vaudeville* in 3 acts, Pub. in 1793].
>Th. de la Citoyenne Montansier (**1**); Th. des Variétés Amusantes, Comiques et Lyriques (**4**); **Total: 5.**

_____. *Arlequin médecin* [*Pantomime* in 3 acts, Pub. in 1793].
>Th. des Grands Danseurs (Gaîté) (**6**); Th. des Variétés Amusantes (Lazzari) (**15**); Th. des Variétés Amusantes, Comiques et Lyriques (**8**); **Total: 29.**

_____. *Arlequin mort et vivant* [*Pantomime* in 3 acts, Pub. in 1793].
>Th. des Variétés Amusantes (Lazzari) (**8**); Th. des Variétés Amusantes, Comiques et Lyriques (**17**); **Total: 25.**

_____. *Boîte enchantée, La* [*Pantomime* in 3 acts].
Th. des Variétés Amusantes (Lazzari) (**12**); Th. des Variétés Amusantes,
Comiques et Lyriques (**17**); **Total: 29.**

_____. *Bûcherons de Potsdam, Les* [*Pantomime* in 1 act, Pub. in 1792].
Th. des Variétés Amusantes, Comiques et Lyriques (**4**); **Total: 4.**

_____. *Cinquantaine infernale, La, ou La Baleine avalée par Arlequin*
[*Pantomime* in 5 acts, Prem. on 9-1-1796].
Th. des Variétés Amusantes (Lazzari) (**49**); Th. des Variétés Amusantes,
Comiques et Lyriques (**123**); Th. du Lycée des Arts (**49**); **Total: 221.**

_____. *Commerce du Jardin Egalité, Le* [*Pantomime* in 2 acts, Pub. in 1795].
Th. des Variétés Amusantes, Comiques et Lyriques (**14**); **Total: 14.**

_____. *Deux Arlequins jumeaux, Les* [*Pantomime* in 3 acts, Pub. in 1793].
Th. de la Citoyenne Montansier (**1**); Th. des Grands Danseurs (Gaîté) (**8**);
Th. des Variétés Amusantes (Lazzari) (**26**); Th. du Vaudeville (**1**); **Total:
36.**

_____. *Deux Arlequins rivaux, Les* [*Pantomime* in 3 acts, Pub. in 1793].
Th. des Variétés Amusantes, Comiques et Lyriques (**11**); **Total: 11.**

_____. *Diable à quatre, Le* [*Pantomime* in 1 act, Pub. in 1795].
Th. des Variétés Amusantes (Lazzari) (**28**); Th. des Variétés Amusantes,
Comiques et Lyriques (**19**); **Total: 47.**

_____. *Fête de Bacchus, La* [*Pantomime* in 3 acts, Pub. in 1795].
Th. des Variétés Amusantes, Comiques et Lyriques (**8**); **Total: 8.**

_____. *Tartane de Venise, La* [*Comédie* in 2 acts, Pub. in 1791].
Th. des Variétés Amusantes (Lazzari) (**48**); Th. des Variétés Amusantes,
Comiques et Lyriques (**42**); **Total: 90.**

Total Performances, Lazzari, Ange: **865**

Le Blanc de Guillet, Antoine Blanc, dit. *Albert I ou Adeline* [*Comédie* in
3 acts, Prem. on 4-2-1775, Pub. in 1775].
Th. des Italiens (Opéra-Comique) (**21**); **Total: 21.**

Le Boeuf, Jean-J. *Apothéose de Beaurepaire, L', ou La Patrie reconnaissante* [*Opéra* in 1 act, Prem. on 2-1-1793, Pub. in 1793].
Académie de la Musique (Opéra) (**3**); **Total: 3.**

_____., Sacchini, Antonio (comp). *Renaud* [*Tragédie-Lyrique* in 3 acts,
Prem. on 28-2-1783, Pub. in 1783].
Académie de la Musique (Opéra) (**78**); **Total: 78.**

Total Performances, Le Boeuf, Jean-J.: **81**

Le Fèvre, Pierre-F.-A. *Zuma* [*Tragédie*, Prem. on 10-10-1776, Pub. in 1777].
Th. de la Nation (Comédie Française) (**5**); **Total: 5.**

Le Mière de Corvey, Jean. *Deux Crispins, Les, ou Encore des jumeaux*
[*Opéra-Comique* in 1 act, Prem. on 15-6-1798, Pub. in 1798].
Th. de Molière (**13**); **Total: 13.**

Le Mierre d'Argy, Auguste-J. *Calas ou Le Fanatisme* [*Drame* in 4 acts,
Prem. on 17-12-1790].
Th. du Palais Royal (**15**); **Total: 15.**

Lemierre, Antoine-M. *Barnevelt, grand pensionnaire de Hollande*
[*Tragédie* in 5 acts, Prem. in 1784, Pub. in 1784].
Th. de la Nation (Comédie Française) (**7**); **Total: 7.**

_____. *Guillaume Tell* [*Tragédie* in 5 acts, Prem. on 17-11-1766, Pub. in 1767].
Th. de la Nation (Comédie Française) (**14**); Th. des Victoires Nationales
(**2**); Th. du Feydeau (de Monsieur) (**4**); Th. du Palais (Cité)-Variétés (**3**);
Th. Français (de la rue Richelieu) (de la République) (**15**); Th. National (de
la rue Richelieu) (**12**); **Total: 50.**

_____. *Hypermnestre* [*Tragédie* in 5 acts, Prem. on 31-8-1758, Pub. in 1759].
Th. de l'Emulation (Gaîté) (**2**); Th. de l'Odéon (**2**); Th. de la Nation (Comédie Française) (**7**); Th. de la Rue Martin (**4**); Th. des Délassements Comiques (**8**); Th. du Feydeau (de Monsieur) (**3**); Th. du Marais (**1**); **Total: 27.**

_____. *Veuve du Malabar, La, ou L'Empire des coutumes* [*Tragédie* in 5 acts, Prem. on 30-7-1770, Pub. in 1780].
Th. de l'Emulation (Gaîté) (**1**); Th. de l'Odéon (**5**); Th. de la Nation (Comédie Française) (**16**); Th. de la Rue Martin (**5**); Th. de Molière (**4**); Th. des Délassements Comiques (**13**); Th. du Feydeau (de Monsieur) (**8**); Th. du Marais (**6**); Th. Français (de la rue Richelieu) (de la République) (**1**); **Total: 59.**

Total Performances, Lemierre, Antoine-M.: **143**

Le Prévost d'Iray, Vicomte Chrétien., Gresnick, Antoine (comp). *Alphonse et Léonore ou L'Heureux procès* [*Comédie* in 1 act, Prem. on 29-5-1789, Pub. in 1798].
Th. de l'Ambigu Comique (**16**); Th. du Feydeau (de Monsieur) (**11**); **Total: 27.**

_____. *Clubomanie, La* [*Comédie* in 3 acts, Pub. in 1795].
Th. de la Rue Martin (**1**); **Total: 1.**

_____., Philipon, Louis. *Maître Adam ou Le Menuisier de Nevers* [*Vaudeville* in 1 act, Prem. on 17-7-1795, Pub. in 1795].
Th. du Vaudeville (**78**); **Total: 78.**

_____., Philipon, Louis. *Troubadours, Les* [*Comédie* in 1 act, Prem. on 18-3-1797, Pub. in 1797].
Th. du Vaudeville (**51**); **Total: 51.**

Total Performances, Le Prévost d'Iray, Vicomte Chrétien: **157**

Le Prieur de Blainvilliers, Anne-C.-H.-B. *Port de Morlaix, Le* [*Pantomime* in 1 act].
Th. des Variétés Amusantes, Comiques et Lyriques (**1**); **Total: 1.**

Le Roy., Aldey (comp). *Geneviève de Brabant* [*Mélodrame* in 2 acts, Prem. on 23-11-1791, Pub. in 1793].
Th. Lyrique des Amis de la Patrie (**68**); **Total: 68.**

Lebailly, Antoine-F. *Suprises, Les, ou Les Rencontres imprévues* [*Comédie* in 1 act, Prem. on 4-7-1786].
Th. des Grands Danseurs (Gaîté) (**12**); **Total: 12.**

Lebas., Champein, Stanislas (comp). *Florette et Colin* [*Opéra-Bouffe* in 3 acts, Prem. on 7-7-1787].
Th. des Beaujolais (**46**); **Total: 46.**

_____. *Jeunes amants, Les* [*Comédie* in 1 act, Prem. on 4-5-1786].
Th. des Beaujolais (**15**); **Total: 15.**

Total Performances, Lebas: **61**

Lebrun. *Hippocrate amoureux* [Prem. on 8-11-1797].
Th. du Vaudeville (**5**); **Total: 5.**

Lebrun Tossa, Jean-A., Lesueur, Jean-F. (comp). *Arabelle et Vascos ou Les Jacobins de Goa* [*Drame* in 3 acts, Prem. on 7-9-1794, Pub in 1794-5].
Th. des Italiens (Opéra-Comique) (**17**); **Total: 17.**

_____., Gresnick, Antoine (comp). *Faux mendiants, Les* [*Opéra-Comique* in 2 acts, Prem. on 23-5-1784].
> Académie de la Musique (Opéra) (**1**); Th. de la Citoyenne Montansier (**34**); Th. de la Cité (**5**); Th. du Lycée des Arts (**8**); **Total: 48**.

_____. *Folie de Georges, La, ou L'Ouverture du parlement d'Angleterre* [*Comédie* in 3 acts, Pub. in 1794].
> Th. du Palais (Cité)-Variétés (**14**); **Total: 14**.

_____. *Honnête aventurier, L'* [*Comédie* in 1 act, Prem. 28-5-1788].
> Th. de la Citoyenne Montansier (**20**); Th. Lyrique des Amis de la Patrie (**39**); **Total: 59**.

_____., Foignet, Charles-G. (comp). *Mont Alphea, Le, ou Le Français jatabite* [*Opéra* in 3 acts, Prem. on 6-12-1792, Pub. in 1793].
> Th. de la Citoyenne Montansier (**93**); Th. de la Montagne (**3**); **Total: 96**.

_____. *Noirs et les blancs, Les, ou Les Conspirateurs généreux* [*Tableau-Patriotique*, Prem. on 24-1-1791].
> Th. Français, Comique et Lyrique (**13**); **Total: 13**.

_____., Gresnick, Antoine (comp). *Savoir faire, Le* [*Opéra* in 2 acts, Prem. on 4-4-1795, Pub. in 1795].
> Th. de la Citoyenne Montansier (**11**); Th. du Lycée des Arts (**10**); Th. Lyrique des Amis de la Patrie (**76**); **Total: 97**.
> **Total Performances**, Lebrun Tossa, Jean-A.: **344**

Lefèbre de Saint-Ildephont. *Gasconnades, Les* [*Comédie* in 2 acts, Prem. on 26-2-1792].
> Th. des Variétés Amusantes, Comiques et Lyriques (**2**); **Total: 2**.

Lefèbvre, Philippe. *Honnête homme, L'* [*Comédie* in 5 acts].
> Th. du Vaudeville (**2**); Th. Patriotique et de Momus (**18**); **Total: 20**.

Lefranc de Pompignan, Jean-G. *Didon* [*Tragédie* in 5 acts, Prem. on 21-6-1734, Pub. in 1734].
> Th. de la Citoyenne Montansier (**3**); Th. de la Nation (Comédie Française) (**7**); **Total: 10**.

Léger, François-P.-A. *Alain et Rosette* [*Comédie* in 1 act, Prem. on 14-12-1792, Pub. in 1795].
> Th. de la Cité (**4**); Th. des Troubadours (**10**); Th. du Palais (Cité)-Variétés (**2**); **Total: 16**.

_____. *Angélique et Melcour ou Le Procès* [*Comédie* in 1 act, Prem. on 29-12-1795].
> Th. de l'Odéon (**2**); Th. de Molière (**2**); Th. des Troubadours (**14**); Th. du Vaudeville (**15**); **Total: 33**.

_____., Jadin, Louis-E. (comp). *Apothéose du jeune Barra, L'* [*Tableau-Patriotique* in 1 act, Prem. on 5-6-1794, Pub. in 1794].
> Th. du Feydeau (de Monsieur) (**27**); **Total: 27**.

_____. *Belle et bonne ou Les Deux soeurs* [*Comédie* in 1 act, Prem. on 25-11-1797, Pub. in 1798].
> Th. de Molière (**3**); Th. des Troubadours (**16**); Th. du Vaudeville (**38**); **Total: 57**.

_____. *Billet de logement, Le* [*Comédie* in 1 act, Prem. on 4-5-1799, Pub. in 1805].
> Th. des Troubadours (**25**); **Total: 25**.

_____. *Christophe Dubois* [*Fait Historique* in 1 act, Prem. on 12-10-1794, Pub. in 1795].
Th. des Variétés Amusantes, Comiques et Lyriques (1); Th. du Vaudeville (**68**); **Total: 69.**

_____. *Danger des conseils, Le, ou La Folle inconstance* [*Comédie* in 1 act, Prem. on 26-6-1790].
Th. Français, Comique et Lyrique (**25**); **Total: 25.**

_____., Philipon, Louis. *Dedit mal gardé, Le* [*Vaudeville* in 1 act, Prem. on 22-6-1794, Pub. in 1794].
Th. du Vaudeville (**21**); **Total: 21.**

_____., Leblanc de Guillet, Antonio Blanc, dit (comp). *Folle gageure, La* [*Comédie* in 1 act, Prem. on 30-6-1790, Pub. in 1790].
Th. Français, Comique et Lyrique (**61**); **Total: 61.**

_____., Radet, Jean-B., Desfontaines, François-G. Fouques, dit. *Gageure inutile, La, ou Plus de peur que de mal* [*Comédie* in 1 act, Prem. on 7-1-1793].
Th. de Molière (**6**); Th. des Troubadours (**15**); Th. des Variétés Amusantes, Comiques et Lyriques (**2**); Th. du Marais (**1**); Th. du Vaudeville (**135**); **Total: 159.**

_____. *Georges et Gros-Jean ou L'Enfant trouvé* [*Fait Historique* in 1 act, Pub. in 1793].
Th. de Molière (**3**); Th. des Troubadours (**10**); Th. du Vaudeville (**86**); **Total: 99.**

_____. *Gilles Lovelace* [*Parodie* in 5 acts, Prem. on 25-4-1792].
Th. du Vaudeville (**9**); **Total: 9.**

_____. *Heureuse ivresse, L', ou Le Mari de retour* [*Opéra*, Prem. on 30-6-1791].
Th. Français, Comique et Lyrique (**9**); **Total: 9.**

_____. *Homme sans façon, L', ou Le Vieux cousin* [*Comédie* in 3 acts, Prem. on 10-2-1798, Pub. in 1798].
Th. de l'Odéon (**8**); **Total: 8.**

_____. *Joconde* [*Comédie* in 2 acts, Prem. on 31-10-1792].
Th. des Troubadours (**2**); Th. du Palais (Cité)-Variétés (**12**); **Total: 14.**

_____. *Nicaise, peintre* [*Comédie* in 1 act, Prem. on 26-2-1793, Pub. in 1793].
Th. du Vaudeville (**95**); **Total: 95.**

_____. *Orphelin et le curé, L'* [*Fait Historique* in 1 act, Prem. on 29-7-1790].
Th. Français, Comique et Lyrique (**45**); **Total: 45.**

_____. *Papesse Jeanne, La* [*Opéra-Bouffe* in 1 act, Prem. on 26-1-1793].
Th. de la Rue Martin (**36**); Th. du Feydeau (de Monsieur) (**29**); Th. du Vaudeville (**7**); **Total: 72.**

_____., Leblanc de Guillet, Antonio Blanc, dit (comp). *Rosine et Zelis* [*Vaudeville* in 1 act, Prem. on 4-9-1790].
Th. Français, Comique et Lyrique (**5**); **Total: 5.**

_____., Barré, Pierre-Y. *Sourd guéri, Le, ou Les Tu et les vous* [*Comédie* in 1 act, Prem. on 31-1-1794, Pub. in 1793].
Th. du Vaudeville (**36**); **Total: 36.**

Total Performances, Léger, François-P.-A.: **885**

Legouvé, Gabriel-M.-J.-B. *Epicharis et Néron ou La Conspiration pour la liberté* [*Tragédie* in 5 acts, Prem. on 3-2-1794, Pub. in 1794].
n/a (2); Th. des Délassements Comiques (9); Th. du Lycée des Arts (1); Th. du Marais (6); Th. Français (de la rue Richelieu) (de la République) (58); Th. Lyrique des Amis de la Patrie (2); **Total: 78.**

_____. *Etéocle et Polinice* [In 5 acts, Prem. on 19-10-1799].
Th. Français (de la rue Richelieu) (de la République) (7); **Total: 7.**

_____. *Laurence et Orzano* [*Tragédie* in 5 acts].
Th. de la Nation (Comédie Française) (6); **Total: 6.**

_____. *Mort d'Abel, La* [*Tragédie* in 3 acts, Prem. on 6-3-1792, Pub. in 1793].
n/a (3); Th. de l'Odéon (8); Th. de la Citoyenne Montansier (5); Th. de la Nation (Comédie Française) (45); Th. des Jeunes Elèves (1); Th. des Victoires (4); Th. du Feydeau (de Monsieur) (12); Th. du Marais (7); Th. Lyrique des Amis de la Patrie (2); **Total: 87.**

_____. *Quintus Fabius ou La Discipline romaine* [*Tragédie* in 3 acts, Pub. in 1795].
Th. Français (de la rue Richelieu) (de la République) (20); **Total: 20.**
Total Performances, Legouvé, Gabriel-M.-J.-B.: **198**

Legrand, Marc-A., Biancolleli, Pierre-F. dit Dominique. *Agnès de Chaillot* [*Comédie* in 1 act, Pub. in 1723].
Th. des Grands Danseurs (Gaîté) (6); **Total: 6.**

_____., Fuzelier, Louis. *Amazones modernes, Les, ou Le Triomphe des dames* [*Comédie* in 3 acts, Prem. on 29-10-1727, Pub. in 1727].
Th. de l'Emulation (Gaîté) (13); **Total: 13.**

_____. *Amour diable, L'* [*Comédie* in 1 act, Prem. on 30-3-1708, Pub. in 1708].
Th. de la Rue Martin (1); **Total: 1.**

_____. *Aveugle clairvoyant, L'* [*Comédie* in 1 act, Prem. on 18-9-1716, Pub. in 1716].
Académie de la Musique (Opéra) (2); Th. de l'Ambigu Comique (2); Th. de l'Odéon (3); Th. de la Nation (Comédie Française) (13); Th. de la Rue Martin (4); Th. de Molière (15); Th. du Feydeau (de Monsieur) (7); Th. du Lycée des Arts (1); Th. du Marais (2); Th. du Vaudeville (4); Th. Français (de la rue Richelieu) (de la République) (24); Th. Lyrique des Amis de la Patrie (3); **Total: 80.**

_____. *Cartouche ou Les Voleurs* [*Comédie* in 3 acts, Prem. on 14-10-1721, Pub. in 1721].
Th. de l'Emulation (Gaîté) (26); **Total: 26.**

_____. *Famille extravagante, La* [*Comédie* in 1 act, Prem. on 7-6-1709, Pub. in 1709].
Th. de la Nation (Comédie Française) (8); Th. du Marais (4); Th. Français (de la rue Richelieu) (de la République) (7); **Total: 19.**

_____. *Femme fille et veuve, La* [*Comédie* in 1 act, Prem. on 26-5-1707, Pub. in 1707].
Th. des Grands Danseurs (Gaîté) (9); **Total: 9.**

_____. *Fleuve d'oubli, Le* [*Comédie* in 1 act, Prem. on 12-9-1721, Pub. in 1723].
Th. de l'Estrapade au Panthéon (1); Th. du Vaudeville (5); Th. Patriotique et de Momus (14); **Total: 20.**

_____. *Galant coureur, Le, ou L'Ouvrage d'un moment* [*Comédie* in 1 act, Prem. on 11-8-1722, Pub. in 1722].
Th. de la Nation (Comédie Française) (2); Th. de Molière (1); Th. des Grands Danseurs (Gaîté) (19); Th. du Marais (9); Th. Français (de la rue Richelieu) (de la République) (2); **Total: 33.**

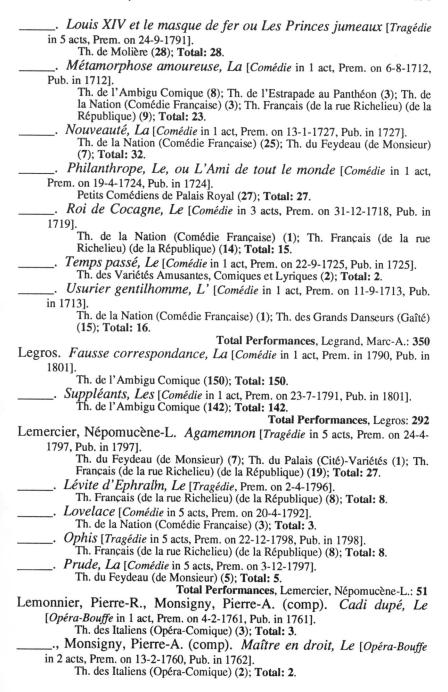

_____. *Louis XIV et le masque de fer ou Les Princes jumeaux* [*Tragédie* in 5 acts, Prem. on 24-9-1791].
Th. de Molière (**28**); **Total: 28.**

_____. *Métamorphose amoureuse, La* [*Comédie* in 1 act, Prem. on 6-8-1712, Pub. in 1712].
Th. de l'Ambigu Comique (**8**); Th. de l'Estrapade au Panthéon (**3**); Th. de la Nation (Comédie Française) (**3**); Th. Français (de la rue Richelieu) (de la République) (**9**); **Total: 23.**

_____. *Nouveauté, La* [*Comédie* in 1 act, Prem. on 13-1-1727, Pub. in 1727].
Th. de la Nation (Comédie Française) (**25**); Th. du Feydeau (de Monsieur) (**7**); **Total: 32.**

_____. *Philanthrope, Le, ou L'Ami de tout le monde* [*Comédie* in 1 act, Prem. on 19-4-1724, Pub. in 1724].
Petits Comédiens de Palais Royal (**27**); **Total: 27.**

_____. *Roi de Cocagne, Le* [*Comédie* in 3 acts, Prem. on 31-12-1718, Pub. in 1719].
Th. de la Nation (Comédie Française) (**1**); Th. Français (de la rue Richelieu) (de la République) (**14**); **Total: 15.**

_____. *Temps passé, Le* [*Comédie* in 1 act, Prem. on 22-9-1725, Pub. in 1725].
Th. des Variétés Amusantes, Comiques et Lyriques (**2**); **Total: 2.**

_____. *Usurier gentilhomme, L'* [*Comédie* in 1 act, Prem. on 11-9-1713, Pub. in 1713].
Th. de la Nation (Comédie Française) (**1**); Th. des Grands Danseurs (Gaîté) (**15**); **Total: 16.**

Total Performances, Legrand, Marc-A.: **350**

Legros. *Fausse correspondance, La* [*Comédie* in 1 act, Prem. in 1790, Pub. in 1801].
Th. de l'Ambigu Comique (**150**); **Total: 150.**

_____. *Suppléants, Les* [*Comédie* in 1 act, Prem. on 23-7-1791, Pub. in 1801].
Th. de l'Ambigu Comique (**142**); **Total: 142.**

Total Performances, Legros: **292**

Lemercier, Népomucène-L. *Agamemnon* [*Tragédie* in 5 acts, Prem. on 24-4-1797, Pub. in 1797].
Th. du Feydeau (de Monsieur) (**7**); Th. du Palais (Cité)-Variétés (**1**); Th. Français (de la rue Richelieu) (de la République) (**19**); **Total: 27.**

_____. *Lévite d'Ephraïm, Le* [*Tragédie*, Prem. on 2-4-1796].
Th. Français (de la rue Richelieu) (de la République) (**8**); **Total: 8.**

_____. *Lovelace* [*Comédie* in 5 acts, Prem. on 20-4-1792].
Th. de la Nation (Comédie Française) (**3**); **Total: 3.**

_____. *Ophis* [*Tragédie* in 5 acts, Prem. on 22-12-1798, Pub. in 1798].
Th. Français (de la rue Richelieu) (de la République) (**8**); **Total: 8.**

_____. *Prude, La* [*Comédie* in 5 acts, Prem. on 3-12-1797].
Th. du Feydeau (de Monsieur) (**5**); **Total: 5.**

Total Performances, Lemercier, Népomucène-L.: **51**

Lemonnier, Pierre-R., Monsigny, Pierre-A. (comp). *Cadi dupé, Le* [*Opéra-Bouffe* in 1 act, Prem. on 4-2-1761, Pub. in 1761].
Th. des Italiens (Opéra-Comique) (**3**); **Total: 3.**

_____., Monsigny, Pierre-A. (comp). *Maître en droit, Le* [*Opéra-Bouffe* in 2 acts, Prem. on 13-2-1760, Pub. in 1762].
Th. des Italiens (Opéra-Comique) (**2**); **Total: 2.**

_____. *Mariage clandestin, Le* [*Comédie* in 3 acts, Prem. on 12-8-1775, Pub. in 1775].
> Th. de la Citoyenne Montansier (**14**); **Total: 14**.
> **Total Performances**, Lemonnier, Pierre-R.: **19**

Lemontey., Plantade, Charles-H. (comp). *Palma ou Le Voyage en Grèce* [*Opéra* in 2 acts, Prem. on 22-8-1798].
> Th. de Molière (**2**); Th. du Feydeau (de Monsieur) (**48**); **Total: 50**.

Lenoble, Eustache. *Deux Arlequins, Les* [*Vaudeville* in 3 acts].
> Th. de la Citoyenne Montansier (**2**); Th. des Grands Danseurs (Gaîté) (**29**); **Total: 31**.

Lépidor, M.-J. Mathieu, dit., Paisiello, Giovanni (comp). *Orgon dans la lune ou Crédule trompé* [*Opéra* in 3 acts].
> Th. du Feydeau (de Monsieur) (**6**); **Total: 6**.

Lepitre, Jacques-F., Deshayes, Prosper-D. (comp). *Arlequin imprimeur ou Pourquoi écoutait-il?* [*Comédie* in 1 act, Prem. on 16-6-1794, Pub. in 1794].
> Maison Egalité (**1**); Th. de la Cité (**4**); Th. du Palais (Cité)-Variétés (**26**); **Total: 31**.

_____., Cambini, Giuseppe-M. (comp). *Bon père, Le* [*Opéra-Bouffe* in 1 act, Prem. on 8-10-1788, Pub. in 1788].
> Th. de la Citoyenne Montansier (**2**); Th. de la Cité (**1**); Th. de Molière (**1**); Th. des Beaujolais (**72**); Th. des Jeunes Artistes (**19**); Th. des Victoires Nationales (**1**); Th. du Lycée des Arts (**1**); **Total: 97**.

_____. *Renouvellement du bail, Le* [*Opéra* in 1 act, Prem. on 29-3-1794, Pub. in 1794].
> Th. du Palais (Cité)-Variétés (**13**); **Total: 13**.
> **Total Performances**, Lepitre, Jacques-F.: **141**

Leprêtre. *Pierre de Provence* [*Pantomime* in 4 acts, Pub. in 1781].
> Th. de l'Ambigu Comique (**2**); **Total: 2**.

Lesage, Alain-R. *Crispin rival de son maître* [*Comédie* in 1 act, Prem. on 12-3-1707, Pub. in 1707].
> Th. de l'Estrapade au Panthéon (**3**); Th. de l'Odéon (**10**); Th. de la Citoyenne Montansier (**3**); Th. de la Cité (**2**); Th. de la Montagne (**1**); Th. de la Nation (Comédie Française) (**9**); Th. de la Rue Martin (**3**); Th. de Molière (**1**); Th. des Grands Danseurs (Gaîté) (**40**); Th. des Victoires Nationales (**2**); Th. du Marais (**9**); Th. du Palais (Cité)-Variétés (**2**); Th. du Palais Royal (**7**); Th. Français (de la rue Richelieu) (de la République) (**48**); Th. Patriotique et de Momus (**2**); **Total: 142**.

_____. *Point d'honneur, Le* [*Comédie* in 5 acts, Pub. in 1702].
> Th. du Palais Royal (**3**); **Total: 3**.

_____., Fuzelier, Louis., Coupartantoine M. *Retour d'Arlequin à la foire, Le* [*Divertissement/parade*].
> Th. des Jeunes Artistes (**32**); **Total: 32**.

_____. *Turcaret* [*Comédie* in 5 acts, Prem. on 14-2-1709, Pub. in 1709].
> Th. de l'Estrapade au Panthéon (**2**); Th. de la Citoyenne Montansier (**6**); Th. de la Nation (Comédie Française) (**13**); Th. de la Rue Martin (**1**); Th. du Feydeau (de Monsieur) (**4**); Th. Français (de la rue Richelieu) (de la République) (**18**); **Total: 44**.
> **Total Performances**, Lesage, Alain-R.: **221**

Lescène-Desmaisons, Jacques. *Retour aux isles des amis, Le, ou Le Capitaine Cook* [*Opéra* in 2 acts, Prem. on 30-11-1790].
> Th. du Feydeau (de Monsieur) (**4**); **Total: 4**.

Lesueur, Abraham-N. *Déguisements villageois, Les, ou Le Retour de la noce* [*Opéra-Comique* in 2 acts].
Th. de l'Ambigu Comique (**5**); Th. Français, Comique et Lyrique (**20**); Total: **25**.

Lesur, Charles-L., Berton, Henri-M. (comp). *Amour bizarre, L', ou Les Projets dérangés* [*Opéra-Comique*, Prem. on 30-8-1799].
Th. des Italiens (Opéra-Comique) (**2**); Total: **2**.

———. *Apothéose de Beaurepaire, L'* [*Héroique* in 1 act, Prem. on 21-11-1792].
Th. de la Nation (Comédie Française) (**12**); Total: **12**.

———. *Veuve du républicain, La, ou Le Calomniateur* [*Comédie* in 3 acts, Prem. on 23-11-1793].
Th. des Italiens (Opéra-Comique) (**24**); Total: **24**.
Total Performances, Lesur, Charles-L.: **38**

Letourneur, dit Valville. *Deux tableaux parlants, Les, ou Le Dîner interrompu* [*Comédie*, Pub. in 1799].
Th. des Grands Danseurs (Gaîté) (**13**); Total: **13**.

Levigni, F., Paisiello, Giovanni (comp). *Frascatana, La* [*Opéra* in 3 acts, Pub. in 1774].
Th. du Feydeau (de Monsieur) (**35**); Total: **35**.

Lévrier de Champ-Rion, Guillaume-D.-T., Gaveaux, Pierre (comp). *Diable couleur de rose, Le, ou Le Bonhomme misère* [*Opéra-Bouffe* in 1 act, Prem. on 23-10-1798, Pub. in 1799].
Th. de Molière (**24**); Total: **24**.

———. *Geneviève de Brabant* [*Mélodrame* in 2 acts, Prem. on 23-11-1791, Pub. in 1793].
Th. de Molière (**3**); Total: **3**.

———. *Joseph Barra* [*Fait Historique*, Prem. on 5-6-1794].
Th. des Italiens (Opéra-Comique) (**9**); Total: **9**.

———. *Suite de Geneviève de Brabant, La* [*Mélodrame* in 1 act, Pub. in 1791].
Th. Lyrique des Amis de la Patrie (**16**); Total: **16**.

———. *Trois cousins, Les* [*Comédie* in 2 acts, Prem. on 18-6-1792, Pub. in 1792].
Th. Français (de la rue Richelieu) (de la République) (**28**); Total: **28**.
Total Performances, Lévrier de Champ-Rion, Guillaume-D.-T.: **80**

Lheureux, C.-F. *Incroyables, Les, ou Le Danger des plaisirs* [*Comédie* in 2 acts, Pub. in 1799].
Th. de la Citoyenne Montansier (**3**); Total: **3**.

Linière, Comte de., Lebailly, Antoine-F., Langle, Honoré-F.-M. (comp). *Corisandre ou Les Fous par enchantement* [*Comédie-Opéra* in 3 acts, Prem. on 8-3-1791, Pub. in 1791].
Académie de la Musique (Opéra) (**37**); Total: **37**.

Lisle de Ladrevetière, Louis-F. de. *Arlequin sauvage* [*Comédie* in 3 acts, Prem. on 17-6-1721, Pub. in 1722].
Th. de la Citoyenne Montansier (**2**); Th. des Variétés Amusantes, Comiques et Lyriques (**2**); Total: **4**.

_____. *Faucon, Le, ou Les Oies de Bocace* [*Comédie* in 3 acts, Prem. on 6-2-1725, Pub. in 1725].
Th. des Grands Danseurs (Gaîté) (**23**); **Total: 23.**
Total Performances, Lisle de Ladrevetière, Louis-F. de: **27**

Livigni, F., Anfossi, Pasquale., Cambini, Giovanni-G. (comp). *Viaggiatori felici, I* [*Dramma Giocoso* in 2 acts, Prem. on 30-6-1790].
Th. du Feydeau (de Monsieur) (**33**); **Total: 33.**

Loaisel de Tréogate, Joseph-M. *Amour arrange tout, L'* [*Comédie* in 1 act, Prem. on 22-7-1788, Pub. in 1788].
Th. des Beaujolais (**37**); **Total: 37.**

_____. *Bizarrerie de la fortune, La, ou Le Jeune philosophe* [*Comédie* in 5 acts, Prem. on 16-4-1793, Pub. in 1793].
Th. de la Rue Martin (**8**); Th. du Feydeau (de Monsieur) (**4**); Th. du Marais (**15**); Th. Français (de la rue Richelieu) (de la République) (**11**); **Total: 38.**

_____. *Château du diable, Le* [*Comédie* in 4 acts, Prem. on 5-12-1792, Pub. in 1793].
Elysée (**2**); Th. de l'Emulation (Gaîté) (**7**); Th. de la Rue Martin (**66**); Th. du Lycée des Arts (**1**); **Total: 76.**

_____. *Combat des Thermopyles, Le* [*Fait Historique* in 3 acts, Prem. on 23-7-1794, Pub. in 1794].
Th. de la Cité (**2**); Th. du Palais (Cité)-Variétés (**4**); **Total: 6.**

_____. *Fontaine merveilleuse, La, ou Les époux musulmans* [*Pantomime* in 5 acts, Prem. on 11-9-1799, Pub. in 1799].
Th. de l'Ambigu Comique (**26**); **Total: 26.**

_____. *Forêt périlleuse, La, ou Les Brigands de la Calabre* [*Drame* in 3 acts, Prem. on 17-5-1797, Pub. in 1797].
Th. de l'Ambigu Comique (**1**); Th. de la Cité (**29**); Th. de Molière (**1**); Th. des Grands Danseurs (Gaîté) (**4**); Th. du Palais (Cité)-Variétés (**18**); **Total: 53.**

_____. *Lucile et Dercourt* [*Comédie* in 2 acts, Prem. on 2-5-1790].
Th. des Beaujolais (**20**); **Total: 20.**

_____. *Roland de Montglave* [*Drame* in 4 acts, Prem. on 28-1-1799, Pub. in 1790].
Th. de l'Ambigu Comique (**11**); Th. des Grands Danseurs (Gaîté) (**3**); **Total: 14.**

_____. *Vol par amour, Le* [*Comédie* in 2 acts, Pub. in 1796].
Th. de l'Ambigu Comique (**31**); **Total: 31.**
Total Performances, Loaisel de Tréogate, Joseph-M.: **301**

Loeillard d'Arvigny, Charles-J., Berton, Henri-M. (comp). *Brouilleries, Les* [*Comédie* in 3 acts, Prem. on 1-3-1790].
Th. de la Citoyenne Montansier (**10**); Th. des Italiens (Opéra-Comique) (**2**); **Total: 12.**

_____., Legouvé, Gabriel M.-J.-B., Méhul, Etienne-N. (comp). *Doria* [*Opéra* in 3 acts, Prem. on 12-3-1795].
Th. des Italiens (Opéra-Comique) (**1**); **Total: 1.**

_____., Berton, Henri-M. (comp). *Eugène, ou La Piété filiale* [*Opéra* in 3 acts, Prem. on 11-3-1793].
Th. du Feydeau (de Monsieur) (**3**); **Total: 3.**

_____., Parenti, Paolo-F. (comp). *Homme et le malheur, L'* [*Drame* in 1 act, Prem. on 22-10-1793].
Th. des Italiens (Opéra-Comique) (**5**); **Total: 5.**

_____. *Lettre, La* [*Vaudeville* in 1 act, Pub. in 1794].
  Th. du Palais (Cité)-Variétés (**1**); Th. du Vaudeville (**21**); **Total: 22.**

_____., Jadin, Louis-E. (comp). *Mariage de la veille, Le* [*Comédie* in 1 act, Prem. on 2-1-1796].
  Th. des Italiens (Opéra-Comique) (**23**); **Total: 23.**

_____., Dejaure., Jadin, Louis-E. (comp). *Négociant de Boston, Le* [*Comédie* in 1 act, Prem. on 23-3-1796].
  Th. des Italiens (Opéra-Comique) (**2**); **Total: 2.**

_____., Jadin, Louis-E. (comp). *Supercherie par amour, La, ou Le Fils supposé* [*Comédie* in 3 acts, Prem. on 7-5-1795, Pub. in 1788].
  Académie de la Musique (Opéra) (**1**); Th. des Italiens (Opéra-Comique) (**29**); **Total: 30.**
  Total Performances, Loeillard d'Arvigny, Charles-J.: **98**

Lombard de Langres, Vincent. *Journaliste, Le, ou L'Ami des moeurs* [*Comédie* in 1 act, Pub. in 1797].
  Th. des Variétés Amusantes, Comiques et Lyriques (**3**); Th. Français (de la rue Richelieu) (de la République) (**1**); **Total: 4.**

_____. *Meunier de Sans-Souci, Le* [*Vaudeville*, Prem. on 11-7-1798, Pub. in 1798].
  Th. de la Citoyenne Montansier (**25**); **Total: 25.**

_____. *Prêtres et les rois, Les, ou Les Français dans l'Inde* [*Tableau-Patriotique*, Pub. in 1793].
  Th. National (de la rue Richelieu) (**19**); **Total: 19.**

_____. *Têtes à la Titus, Les* [*Vaudeville* in 1 act, Prem. on 21-7-1798].
  Th. de la Citoyenne Montansier (**47**); Th. des Délassements Comiques (**3**); **Total: 50.**
  Total Performances, Lombard de Langres, Vincent: **98**

Longchamps, C. de., Pergolesi, Giovanni-B. (comp). *Pari, Le* [Prem. on 15-12-1797].
  n/a (**3**); **Total: 3.**

Longepierre, Hilaire-B.-R., Baron de. *Médée* [*Tragédie* in 5 acts, Pub. in 1694].
  Académie de la Musique (Opéra) (**1**); Th. de la Nation (Comédie Française) (**20**); Th. Français (de la rue Richelieu) (de la République) (**7**); **Total: 28.**

Longueil, Charles-H. de. *Orphelin anglais, L'* [*Drame* in 3 acts, Prem. on 26-1-1769, Pub. in 1769].
  Th. de l'Estrapade au Panthéon (**2**); Th. de la Nation (Comédie Française) (**4**); Th. de Molière (**4**); Th. Français (de la rue Richelieu) (de la République) (**3**); **Total: 13.**

Loraux, Claude-F. Fillette, dit., Chérubini, Luigi (comp). *Lodoiska* [*Comédie* in 3 acts, Prem. on 18-7-1791, Pub. in 1805].
  Th. du Feydeau (de Monsieur) (**112**); Th. Patriotique et de Momus (**7**); **Total: 119.**

Lorville, L.-T. *Double feinte, La, ou Le Prêt rendu* [*Comédie* in 2 acts, Prem. on 24-2-1789].
  Th. des Italiens (Opéra-Comique) (**1**); **Total: 1.**

Lourdet de Santerre, Jean., Grétry, André-E.-M. (comp). *Double épreuve, La, ou Colinette à la cour* [*Comédie* in 3 acts, Prem. on 1-1-1782].
> Académie de la Musique (Opéra) (**8**); Th. de l'Ambigu Comique (**19**); Total: **27**.

_____., Grétry, André-E.-M. (comp). *Embarras des richesses, L'* [*Comédie* in 3 acts, Prem. on 26-11-1782, Pub. in 1782].
> Th. des Grands Danseurs (Gaîté) (**4**); Total: **4**.

_____., Rigel, Henri-J. (comp). *Savetier et le financier, Le* [*Comédie* in 2 acts, Prem. on 23-10-1778, Pub. in 1778].
> Th. des Italiens (Opéra-Comique) (**1**); Total: **1**.
> **Total Performances**, Lourdet de Santerre, Jean: **32**

Luce de Lancival, Jean-C.-J. *Mutius Scaevola* [*Tragédie* in 3 acts, Prem. on 23-7-1793, Pub. in 1794].
> Th. de la Citoyenne Montansier (**1**); Th. Français (de la rue Richelieu) (de la République) (**8**); Total: **9**.

Luce, M. *Fernandez* [*Tragédie*, Prem. on 15-8-1797].
> Th. de la Nation (Comédie Française) (**5**); Total: **5**.

Lutaine., Leblanc de Guillet, Antonio Blanc, dit (comp). *Lord et le jockey, Le* [*Comédie* in 3 acts, Prem. on 8-10-1788].
> Th. des Beaujolais (**3**); Total: **3**.

_____., Leblanc de Guillet, Antonio Blanc, dit (comp). *Noce béarnaise, La, ou Le Secret* [*Opéra-Comique* in 3 acts, Prem. on 14-11-1787].
> Th. des Beaujolais (**28**); Th. du Lycée des Arts (**7**); Total: **35**.
> **Total Performances**, Lutaine: **38**

Mague de Saint-Aubin, Jacques. *Cabinet de figures, Le, ou Le Sculpteur en bois* [*Comédie* in 1 act, Prem. on 25-7-1782, Pub. in 1784].
> Th. de l'Ambigu Comique (**10**); Total: **10**.

_____. *Etape, L'* [*Tableau-Patriotique* in 2 acts, Prem. on 9-7-1794].
> Th. de l'Ambigu Comique (**28**); Th. Patriotique et de Momus (**7**); Total: **35**.

_____. *Matinée comique, La, ou Les Acteurs à l'épreuve* [*Pièce* in 1 act, Prem. in 1787].
> Th. des Variétés Amusantes, Comiques et Lyriques (**10**); Total: **10**.

_____. *Nuit champêtre, La, ou Les Mariages de dépit* [*Comédie mêlée d'ariettes* in 2 acts, Prem. on 4-12-1787, Pub. in 1787].
> Th. de la Citoyenne Montansier (**1**); Th. des Variétés Amusantes, Comiques et Lyriques (**6**); Th. du Vaudeville (**3**); Th. Patriotique et de Momus (**29**); Total: **39**.

_____. *Parisien dépaysé, Le, ou Chaque oiseau trouve son nid beau* [*Proverbe/allégorique* in 1 act, Prem. on 17-10-1787, Pub. in 1786].
> Th. de l'Ambigu Comique (**1**); Th. de la Citoyenne Montansier (**1**); Th. des Variétés Amusantes, Comiques et Lyriques (**10**); Total: **12**.

_____. *Pour et contre* [*Comédie* in 1 act, Pub. in 1786].
> Th. du Vaudeville (**4**); Total: **4**.
> **Total Performances**, Mague de Saint-Aubin, Jacques: **110**

Maillé de Lamalle. *Fille généreuse, La, ou Le Tapissier de Saint-Germain en Laye* [*Comédie* in 2 acts, Prem. on 18-12-1787].
> Th. des Grands Danseurs (Gaîté) (**26**); Total: **26**.

_____. *Lanterne magique, La, ou Les Pourquoi* [*Comédie* in 1 act, Prem. in 1772, Pub. in 1772].
  Th. de l'Ambigu Comique (**49**); **Total: 49.**
          Total Performances, Maillé de Lamalle: **75**

Maillé de Marencour. *Homme noir, L', ou Spleen* [*Comédie* in 2 acts, Prem. on 2-6-1783, Pub. in 1786].
  Th. de l'Ambigu Comique (**9**); **Total: 9.**

_____., Chardiny, Louis-A. (comp). *Pouvoir de la nature, Le, ou La Suite de la ruse d'amour* [*Comédie* in 2 acts, Prem. on 4-3-1786, Pub. in 1787].
  Petits Comédiens de Palais Royal (**19**); Th. des Jeunes Artistes (**66**); **Total: 85.**

_____., Chardiny, Louis-A. (comp). *Ruse d'amour, La, ou L'Epreuve* [*Comédie* in 1 act, Prem. on 25-8-1785, Pub. in 1786].
  Th. des Beaujolais (**13**); Th. des Grands Danseurs (Gaîté) (**6**); Th. des Jeunes Artistes (**44**); Th. du Marais (**2**); **Total: 65.**

_____. *Sexagénaire, Le, ou L'Homme comme il y en a peu* [*Comédie* in 2 acts, Prem. on 28-7-1783, Pub. in 1783].
  Th. de l'Ambigu Comique (**15**); **Total: 15.**
       Total Performances, Maillé de Marencour: **174**

Maillot, see Eve, Antoine-F., dit Maillot.

Mantauffeld, Baron Ernest de., Dezède, Nicolas (comp). *Auguste et Théodore ou Les Deux pages* [*Comédie* in 2 acts, Prem. on 6-3-1789, Pub. in 1789].
  Th. de la Nation (Comédie Française) (**53**); Th. du Feydeau (de Monsieur) (**12**); Th. Français (de la rue Richelieu) (de la République) (**1**); **Total: 66.**

Marchand, François., Champein, Stanislas (comp) *Ruses de Frontin, Les* [In 3 acts, Prem. in 1787].
  Th. du Feydeau (de Monsieur) (**14**); Th. du Marais (**6**); **Total: 20.**

Marcouville, Pierre-A. Lefèvre de. *Heureux déguisement, L', ou La Gouvernante supposée* [*Comédie* in 2 acts, Prem. on 7-8-1758, Pub. in 1758].
  Th. du Palais Royal (**13**); **Total: 13.**

_____. *Trois jumeaux vénitiens, Les* [*Comédie* in 4 acts, Prem. on 7-12-1773, Pub. in 1777].
  Th. de la Citoyenne Montansier (**1**); Th. de Molière (**4**); **Total: 5.**
    Total Performances, Marcouville, Pierre-A. Lefèvre de: **18**

Maréchal, Pierre-Sylvain., Grétry, André-E.-M. (comp). *Denys le tyran, maître d'école à Corinthe* [*Opéra* in 1 act, Prem. on 21-8-1794].
  Académie de la Musique (Opéra) (**8**); **Total: 8.**

_____. *Jugement dernier des rois, Le* [*Prophétie* in 1 act, Prem. on 17-10-1793].
  Th. du Marais (**1**); Th. Français (de la rue Richelieu) (de la République) (**21**); **Total: 22.**

_____. *Missionnaires républicains, Les* [*Tableau-Patriotique* in 1 act, Prem. on 4-4-1794].
  Th. des Italiens (Opéra-Comique) (**1**); **Total: 1.**

_____., Grétry, André-E.-M. (comp). *Rosière républicaine, La, ou La Fête de la vertu* [*Opéra* in 1 act, Prem. on 2-9-1794].
 Académie de la Musique (Opéra) (**7**); **Total: 7.**
       Total Performances, Maréchal, Pierre-Sylvain: **38**
Marivaux, Pierre-C. de C. de. *Dénouement imprévu, Le* [*Comédie* in 1 act, Prem. on 2-12-1724, Pub. in 1727].
 Th. de la Nation (Comédie Française) (**3**); **Total: 3.**

_____. *Ecole des mères, L'* [*Comédie* in 1 act, Prem. in 1732, Pub. in 1732].
 Th. du Vaudeville (**10**); **Total: 10.**

_____. *Epreuve, L'* [*Comédie* in 1 act, Prem. on 19-11-1740, Pub. in 1740].
 Th. de l'Emulation (Gaîté) (**2**); Th. de la Citoyenne Montansier (**7**); Th. de la Cité (**7**); Th. de la Nation (Comédie Française) (**6**); Th. de Molière (**1**); Th. des Variétés Amusantes (Lazzari) (**4**); **Total: 27.**

_____. *Fausses confidences, Les* [*Comédie* in 3 acts, Prem. on 16-3-1737, Pub. in 1738].
 Académie de la Musique (Opéra) (**1**); Maison Egalité (**2**); Th. de l'Emulation (Gaîté) (**8**); Th. de la Montagne (**1**); Th. de la Nation (Comédie Française) (**7**); Th. du Feydeau (de Monsieur) (**17**); Th. du Marais (**1**); Th. Français (de la rue Richelieu) (de la République) (**14**); Th. Lyrique des Amis de la Patrie (**1**); Th. National (de la rue Richelieu) (**3**); **Total: 55.**

_____. *Ile des esclaves, L'* [Prem. on 7-9-1791].
 Th. des Grands Danseurs (Gaîté) (**5**); **Total: 5.**

_____. *Jeu de l'amour et du hasard, Le* [*Comédie* in 3 acts, Prem. on 23-1-1730, Pub. in 1730].
 Maison Egalité (**1**); Th. de l'Ambigu Comique (**3**); Th. de l'Emulation (Gaîté) (**7**); Th. de l'Estrapade au Panthéon (**3**); Th. de l'Odéon (**10**); Th. de la Citoyenne Montansier (**5**); Th. de la Cité (**3**); Th. de la Concorde (**1**); Th. de la Liberté (**3**); Th. de la Rue Martin (**14**); Th. de Molière (**10**); Th. des Délassements Comiques (**1**); Th. des Grands Danseurs (Gaîté) (**44**); Th. des Variétés Amusantes, Comiques et Lyriques (**7**); Th. des Victoires Nationales (**1**); Th. du Feydeau (de Monsieur) (**9**); Th. du Marais (**10**); Th. du Mareux (**1**); Th. du Palais Royal (**9**); Th. Français (de la rue Richelieu) (de la République) (**20**); Th. Lyrique des Amis de la Patrie (**5**); Th. Lyrique du Foire St. Germain (**2**); **Total: 169.**

_____. *Legs, Le* [*Comédie* in 1 act, Prem. on 11-6-1736, Pub. in 1736].
 Th. de l'Odéon (**3**); Th. de la Citoyenne Montansier (**1**); Th. de la Nation (Comédie Française) (**20**); Th. de Molière (**8**); Th. du Feydeau (de Monsieur) (**13**); Th. du Marais (**13**); Th. du Palais (Cité)-Variétés (**1**); Th. Français (de la rue Richelieu) (de la République) (**25**); Th. Lyrique des Amis de la Patrie (**2**); Th. National (de la rue Richelieu) (**1**); **Total: 87.**

_____. *Mère confidente, La* [*Comédie* in 3 acts, Prem. on 9-5-1735, Pub. in 1735].
 Th. du Lycée des Arts (**3**); Th. Français (de la rue Richelieu) (de la République) (**14**); Th. National (de la rue Richelieu) (**3**); **Total: 20.**

_____. *Nouvelle épreuve, La* [*Comédie* in 1 act, Prem. on 8-2-1791].
 Th. de l'Odéon (**11**); Th. de la Citoyenne Montansier (**10**); Th. de la Liberté (**3**); Th. de la Montagne (**3**); Th. de la Rue Martin (**11**); Th. de Molière (**11**); Th. des Variétés Amusantes, Comiques et Lyriques (**7**); Th. du Lycée des Arts (**10**); Th. du Marais (**4**); Th. du Palais (Cité)-Variétés (**2**); Th. Français (de la rue Richelieu) (de la République) (**31**); Th. Lyrique des Amis de la Patrie (**10**); Th. National (de la rue Richelieu) (**3**); Th. Patriotique et de Momus (**2**); **Total: 118.**

_____. *Préjugé vaincu, Le, ou La Vertu récompensée* [*Comédie* in 1 act, Prem. on 6-8-1746, Pub. in 1747].
Th. de l'Emulation (Gaîté) (**1**); Th. de la Nation (Comédie Française) (**8**); Th. de Molière (**5**); Th. des Variétés Amusantes, Comiques et Lyriques (**1**); **Total: 15.**

_____. *Serments indiscrets, Les* [N/A].
Th. Français (de la rue Richelieu) (de la République) (**5**); **Total: 5.**

_____. *Surprise de l'amour, La* [*Comédie* in 3 acts, Prem. on 3-5-1722, Pub. in 1733].
Maison Egalité (**3**); Th. de la Liberté (**1**); Th. de la Nation (Comédie Française) (**14**); Th. de Molière (**2**); Th. du Feydeau (de Monsieur) (**8**); Th. du Marais (**4**); Th. Français (de la rue Richelieu) (de la République) (**13**); **Total: 45.**

Total Performances, Marivaux, Pierre-C. de C. de: **559**

Marmontel, Jean F., Grétry, André-E.-M. (comp). *Ami de la maison, L'* [*Comédie* in 3 acts, Prem. on 26-10-1771, Pub. in 1771].
Th. de la Citoyenne Montansier (**6**); Th. des Italiens (Opéra-Comique) (**27**); **Total: 33.**

_____., Zingarelli, Nicolas-A. (comp). *Antigone* [*Opéra* in 3 acts, Prem. on 30-4-1790, Pub. in 1790].
Académie de la Musique (Opéra) (**2**); **Total: 2.**

_____., Piccinni, Niccolò (comp). *Atys* [*Tragédie-Lyrique* in 3 acts, Prem. on 22-2-1780, Pub. in 1780].
Académie de la Musique (Opéra) (**13**); **Total: 13.**

_____., Chérubini, Luigi (comp). *Démophoon* [*Opéra* in 3 acts, Prem. on 2-12-1789, Pub. in 1788].
Académie de la Musique (Opéra) (**14**); **Total: 14.**

_____., Piccinni, Niccolò (comp). *Didon* [*Tragédie* in 3 acts, Prem. on 16-10-1783, Pub. in 1793].
Académie de la Musique (Opéra) (**88**); Th. de la Nation (Comédie Française) (**3**); **Total: 91.**

_____., Piccinni, Niccolò (comp). *Dormeur éveillé, Le* [*Opéra-Comique* in 4 acts, Prem. on 14-11-1783, Pub. in 1783].
Th. de la Citoyenne Montansier (**8**); **Total: 8.**

_____., Grétry, André-E.-M. (comp). *Fausse magie, La* [*Opéra-Comique* in 2 acts, Prem. on 1-2-1775, Pub. in 1775].
Maison Egalité (**1**); Th. des Italiens (Opéra-Comique) (**55**); Th. du Marais (**1**); **Total: 57.**

_____., Grétry, André-E.-M. (comp). *Huron, Le* [*Comédie* in 2 acts, Prem. on 20-8-1768, Pub. in 1768].
Th. des Italiens (Opéra-Comique) (**3**); **Total: 3.**

_____., Grétry, André-E.-M. (comp). *Lucile* [*Comédie* in 1 act, Prem. on 5-1-1769, Pub. in 1769].
Th. des Italiens (Opéra-Comique) (**11**); **Total: 11.**

_____., Piccinni, Niccolò (comp). *Roland* [*Opéra* in 3 acts, Prem. on 17-1-1777].
Académie de la Musique (Opéra) (**12**); **Total: 12.**

_____., Grétry, André-E.-M. (comp). *Silvain* [*Comédie* in 1 act, Prem. on 19-2-1770, Pub. in 1770].
Th. de la Citoyenne Montansier (**20**); Th. des Italiens (Opéra-Comique) (**41**); Th. du Marais (**3**); Th. de Molière (**1**); **Total: 65.**

_____., Grétry, André-E.-M. (comp). *Zémire et Azor* [*Comédie* in 4 acts, Prem. on 9-11-1771, Pub. in 1771].
>Th. des Italiens (Opéra-Comique) (**66**); Th. du Marais (**1**); **Total: 67.**
>**Total Performances,** Marmontel, Jean F.: **376**

Marsollier des Vivetières, Benoît-J., Dalayrac, Nicolas (comp). *Adèle et Dorsan* [*Drame* in 3 acts, Prem. on 27-4-1795, Pub. in 1796].
>Th. des Italiens (Opéra-Comique) (**46**); **Total: 46.**

_____., Dalayrac, Nicolas (comp). *Adolphe et Clara ou Les Deux prisonniers* [*Comédie* in 1 act, Prem. on 10-2-1799].
>Th. de l'Ambigu Comique (**5**); Th. des Italiens (Opéra-Comique) (**62**); **Total: 67.**

_____., Dalayrac, Nicolas (comp). *Alexis ou L'Erreur d'un bon père* [In 1 act, Prem. on 24-1-1798, Pub. in 1802].
>Th. de Molière (**1**); Th. du Feydeau (de Monsieur) (**45**); **Total: 46.**

_____., Dalayrac, Nicolas (comp). *Arnill ou Le Prisonnier américain* [*Comédie* in 1 act, Pub. in 1797].
>Th. des Italiens (Opéra-Comique) (**7**); **Total: 7.**

_____., Dalayrac, Nicolas (comp). *Asgill ou Le Prisonnier de guerre* [*Opéra* in 1 act, Prem. on 2-5-1793].
>Th. des Italiens (Opéra-Comique) (**8**); **Total: 8.**

_____., Dalayrac, Nicolas (comp). *Camille ou Le Souterrain* [*Comédie* in 3 acts, Prem. on 19-3-1791, Pub. in 1791].
>Th. de Molière (**1**); Th. des Italiens (Opéra-Comique) (**131**); Th. du Marais (**2**); **Total: 134.**

_____. *Céphise ou L'Erreur de l'esprit* [*Comédie* in 1 act, Prem. on 23-1-1783, Pub. in 1784].
>Th. de l'Ambigu Comique (**2**); Th. des Grands Danseurs (Gaîté) (**1**); Th. des Italiens (Opéra-Comique) (**11**); Th. du Feydeau (de Monsieur) (**5**); Th. du Marais (**4**); Th. du Mareux (**1**); Th. Français (de la rue Richelieu) (de la République) (**3**); **Total: 27.**

_____. *Chevalier de La Barre, Le* [*Comédie* in 1 act, Prem. on 6-7-1791, Pub. in 1791].
>Th. des Italiens (Opéra-Comique) (**6**); **Total: 6.**

_____. *Confiance trahie, La* [*Comédie* in 1 act, Prem. on 28-2-1784, Pub. in 1784].
>Th. du Feydeau (de Monsieur) (**9**); **Total: 9.**

_____., Dalayrac, Nicolas (comp). *Détenus, Les, ou Cange* [*Fait Historique* in 1 act, Prem. on 18-11-1794, Pub. in 1794].
>Th. des Italiens (Opéra-Comique) (**25**); **Total: 25.**

_____., Dalayrac, Nicolas (comp). *Deux petits savoyards, Les* [*Comédie* in 1 act, Prem. on 14-1-1789, Pub. in 1789].
>Th. de l'Ambigu Comique (**2**); Th. des Italiens (Opéra-Comique) (**213**); Th. Français, Comique et Lyrique (**3**); **Total: 218.**

_____. *Edmond et Caroline* [*Comédie* in 1 act, Prem. on 10-10-1793].
>Th. du Feydeau (de Monsieur) (**1**); **Total: 1.**

_____. *Emma ou Le Soupçon* [*Opéra* in 3 acts, Prem. on 15-10-1799].
>Th. du Feydeau (de Monsieur) (**7**); **Total: 7.**

_____., Darcis, François-J. (comp). *Fausse peur, La, ou Les Vendanges de Taverni* [*Opéra* in 1 act, Prem. on 18-6-1774, Pub. in 1774].
>Cirque National (**1**); Th. de l'Emulation (Gaîté) (**6**); Th. Lyrique des Amis de la Patrie (**25**); **Total: 32.**

_____. *Gulnare ou L'Esclave persane* [*Comédie* in 1 act, Prem. on 9-1-1798, Pub. in 1802].
> Th. des Italiens (Opéra-Comique) (**48**); **Total: 48.**

_____. *Laure ou L'Actrice chez-elle* [Prem. on 25-9-1799].
> Th. des Italiens (Opéra-Comique) (**9**); **Total: 9.**

_____., Dalayrac, Nicolas (comp). *Leçon, La, ou La Tasse de glaces* [*Comédie* in 1 act, Prem. on 24-5-1797, Pub. in 1797].
> Th. du Feydeau (de Monsieur) (**10**); **Total: 10.**

_____., Dalayrac, Nicolas (comp). *Maison isolée, La, ou Le Vieillard des Vosges* [*Comédie* in 2 acts, Prem. on 11-5-1797, Pub. in 1802].
> Th. des Italiens (Opéra-Comique) (**41**); **Total: 41.**

_____., Dalayrac, Nicolas (comp). *Marianne ou L'Amour maternel* [*Comédie* in 1 act, Prem. on 7-7-1796, Pub. in 1797].
> Th. des Italiens (Opéra-Comique) (**52**); **Total: 52.**

_____., Dalayrac, Nicolas (comp). *Nina ou La Folle par amour* [*Comédie* in 1 act, Prem. on 15-5-1786, Pub. in 1786].
> Th. des Italiens (Opéra-Comique) (**107**); Th. du Marais (**5**); **Total: 112.**

_____. *Pauvre femme, La* [*Comédie* in 1 act, Prem. on 8-4-1795, Pub. in 1795].
> Académie de la Musique (Opéra) (**10**); Th. de la Rue Martin (**1**); Th. des Italiens (Opéra-Comique) (**40**); Th. des Variétés Amusantes, Comiques et Lyriques (**1**); Th. du Feydeau (de Monsieur) (**1**); Th. du Marais (**2**); **Total: 55.**

_____., Gaveaux, Pierre (comp). *Traité nul, Le* [*Comédie* in 1 act, Prem. on 23-6-1797, Pub. in 1797].
> Th. du Feydeau (de Monsieur) (**53**); **Total: 53.**
> > **Total Performances**, Marsollier des Vivetières, Benoît-J.: **1013**

Martainville, Alphonse. *Assemblées primaires, Les, ou Les Elections* [*Vaudeville* in 1 act, Prem. on 19-3-1797].
> Th. des Jeunes Artistes (**7**); **Total: 7.**

_____. *Dentiste, Le* [*Comédie* in 1 act, Prem. on 23-1-1797, Pub. in 1797].
> n/a (**18**); Th. de Molière (**5**); **Total: 23.**

_____. *Général et le charbonnier, Le, ou Le Retour d'Italie* [Prem. on 21-1-1798].
> Th. de l'Emulation (Gaîté) (**6**); **Total: 6.**

_____. *Noé ou Le Monde repeuplé* [*Vaudeville* in 1 act, Prem. on 14-5-1798, Pub. in 1797].
> Th. des Jeunes Artistes (**44**); Th. du Marais (**1**); **Total: 45.**

_____. *René ou Le Berger philosophe* [*Pantomime*, Prem. on 21-11-1798].
> Th. de l'Emulation (Gaîté) (**3**); Th. Lyrique des Amis de la Patrie (**6**); **Total: 9.**
> > **Total Performances**, Martainville, Alphonse: **90**

Martin, Marie-J.-D., dit Barouillet., Méreaux, Nicolas-J. (comp). *Fabius* [*Opéra* in 3 acts, Prem. on 9-8-1793, Pub. in 1792].
> Académie de la Musique (Opéra) (**18**); **Total: 18.**

Martineau, Louis-S. *Bouquet de famille, Le, ou Le 25 août* [*Vaudeville* in 2 acts, Pub. in 1816].
> Th. des Jeunes Artistes (**80**); **Total: 80.**

Massip, Jean-B. *Fêtes nouvelles, Les* [*Ballet* in 3 acts, Prem. on 22-7-1734, Pub. in 1734].
> Th. de la Rue Martin (**1**); **Total: 1.**

Masson de Pezay, Alexandre-F.-J., Grétry, André-E.-M. (comp).
Rosière de Salency, La [*Opéra-Comique* in 4 acts, Prem. on 23-10-1773, Pub. in 1773].
    Th. des Italiens (Opéra-Comique) (**15**); **Total: 15.**

Mathelin. *Marat dans le souterrain des Cordeliers ou La Journée du 10 août* [*Fait Historique* in 2 acts, Prem. on 7-12-1793].
    Th. des Italiens (Opéra-Comique) (**21**); **Total: 21.**

Maupinot. *Nuit de Cadix, La, ou La Mère rivale de sa fille* [*Comédie* in 1 act].
    Th. des Grands Danseurs (Gaîté) (**2**); **Total: 2.**

Maurin, see Pompigny, Maurin de.

Mayeur de St.-Paul., Champein, Stanislas (comp). *Déguisements amoureux, Les* [*Opéra-Bouffe* in 2 acts, Prem. on 9-8-1789, Pub. in 1783].
    Th. des Beaujolais (**72**); Th. Lyrique des Amis de la Patrie (**16**); **Total: 88.**

Mayeur de St.-Paul, François-M. *Charette républicaine, La, ou La Paix en Vendée* [*Pantomime* in 1 act, Pub. in 1795].
    Th. du Feydeau (de Monsieur) (**1**); Th. du Palais (Cité)-Variétés (**2**); **Total: 3.**

_____. *Dorval ou Le Bon procureur* [*Comédie* in 2 acts, Prem. on 26-3-1790].
    Th. des Grands Danseurs (Gaîté) (**2**); **Total: 2.**

_____. *Etrennes villageois, Les, ou La Vertu récompensée* [*Comédie* in 1 act, Prem. on 1-1-1789].
    Th. de l'Ambigu Comique (**21**); **Total: 21.**

_____. *Fou par amour, Le, ou La Fatale épreuve* [*Comédie* in 2 acts, Prem. on 26-2-1787, Pub. in 1788].
    Th. des Grands Danseurs (Gaîté) (**68**); **Total: 68.**

_____. *Gargouille ou Le Raccommodeur de faïence* [*Comédie* in 1 act, Prem. on 26-9-1787].
    Th. des Grands Danseurs (Gaîté) (**6**); **Total: 6.**

_____. *Héroïsme d'Alexandre, L'* [*Pantomime*, Prem. on 9-1-1791].
    Th. des Grands Danseurs (Gaîté) (**13**); **Total: 13.**

_____. *Jeune homme du jour, Le, ou La Journée d'un jeune homme* [*Comédie* in 2 acts, Prem. in 1787, Pub. in 1787].
    Th. des Grands Danseurs (Gaîté) (**3**); **Total: 3.**

_____. *Mine est trompeuse, La* [*Pièce* in 1 act, Prem. on 20-6-1785].
    Th. des Grands Danseurs (Gaîté) (**50**); **Total: 50.**

_____. *Oiseau de Lubin, L', ou Il n'y a pas de souris qui ne trouve son trou* [*Comédie* in 1 act, Prem. on 5-8-1780].
    Th. des Grands Danseurs (Gaîté) (**34**); **Total: 34.**

_____. *Pierre de Provence ou La Belle Maguelonne* [*Pantomime* in 3 acts].
    Th. de l'Ambigu Comique (**5**); **Total: 5.**

_____. *Scieur de pierres, Le, ou Guillerot alcalde* [*Comédie* in 3 acts, Prem. in 1785, Pub. in 1785].
    Th. des Grands Danseurs (Gaîté) (**21**); **Total: 21.**

_____. *Tout le monde s'en mêle ou La Manie du commerce* [*Vaudeville*, Prem. on 21-7-1796].
    Th. du Vaudeville (**29**); **Total: 29.**

_____. *Turelure ou Le Cahos perpétuel* [*Divertissement/parade* in 1 act, Prem. on 4-7-1787].
>   Th. des Grands Danseurs (Gaîté) (**5**); **Total: 5.**
>   **Total Performances**, Mayeur de St.-Paul, François-M.: **260**

Mercier, Louis-S. *Brouette du vinaigrier, La* [*Drame* in 3 acts, Prem. in 1774, Pub. in 1775].
>   Th. de la Rue Martin (**4**); Th. des Italiens (Opéra-Comique) (**5**); Th. du Marais (**10**); Th. Français (de la rue Richelieu) (de la République) (**4**); **Total: 23.**

_____. *Déserteur, Le* [*Drame* in 5 acts, Prem. on 23-1-1771, Pub. in 1770].
>   Th. de Molière (**3**); Th. des Grands Danseurs (Gaîté) (**3**); Th. des Italiens (Opéra-Comique) (**59**); Th. des Variétés Amusantes, Comiques et Lyriques (**1**); Th. des Victoires (**2**); Th. du Marais (**4**); **Total: 72.**

_____. *Habitant de la Guadeloupe, L'* [*Comédie* in 4 acts, Prem. on 15-4-1786, Pub. in 1782].
>   Th. de l'Emulation (Gaîté) (**11**); Th. de l'Odéon (**8**); Th. de la Citoyenne Montansier (**5**); Th. de la Liberté (**2**); Th. de la Rue Martin (**9**); Th. de Molière (**8**); Th. du Marais (**16**); Th. Français (de la rue Richelieu) (de la République) (**5**); Th. Lyrique des Amis de la Patrie (**1**); **Total: 65.**

_____. *Indigent, L'* [*Drame* in 4 acts, Prem. on 22-11-1782, Pub. in 1772].
>   Th. de la Rue Martin (**6**); Th. des Délassements Comiques (**2**); Th. des Italiens (Opéra-Comique) (**7**); Th. du Marais (**5**); Th. Patriotique et de Momus (**3**); **Total: 23.**

_____. *Jean Hennuyer ou L'Evêque de Lisieux* [*Drame* in 3 acts, Pub. in 1773].
>   Th. du Marais (**8**); **Total: 8.**

_____. *Jenneval ou Le Barnevelt français* [*Drame* in 5 acts, Prem. on 13-2-1781, Pub. in 1769].
>   Th. du Marais (**2**); **Total: 2.**

_____. *Libérateur, Le* [*Comédie* in 2 acts, Prem. on 7-4-1791].
>   Th. de la Citoyenne Montansier (**7**); Th. Lyrique des Amis de la Patrie (**33**); **Total: 40.**

_____. *Maison de Molière, La* [*Drame* in 4 acts, Prem. on 20-10-1787, Pub. in 1788].
>   Th. de la Nation (Comédie Française) (**17**); Th. du Feydeau (de Monsieur) (**2**); **Total: 19.**

_____. *Nouveau doyen de Killerine, Le* [*Comédie* in 3 acts, Prem. on 17-10-1788, Pub. in 1790].
>   Th. de l'Ambigu Comique (**31**); Th. du Palais Royal (**1**); **Total: 32.**
>   **Total Performances**, Mercier, Louis-S.: **284**

Merey. *A Bon chat bon rat ou Le Bailli dupé* [*Proverbe/allégorique* in 1 act, Prem. in 1776, Pub. in 1776].
>   Th. des Grands Danseurs (Gaîté) (**17**); **Total: 17.**

Metastasio, Pietro., Mengozzi, Bernardo (comp). *Isola disabitata, L'* [*Opéra*, Pub. in 1789].
>   Th. du Feydeau (de Monsieur) (**3**); **Total: 3.**

Milcent, Jean-B.-G.-M. de. *Deux frères, Les* [*Comédie* in 2 acts, Prem. on 11-1-1785, Pub. in 1785].
>   Th. des Italiens (Opéra-Comique) (**3**); **Total: 3.**

Mittié, Jean-C. *Conspirateur confondu, Le, ou La Patrie sauvée* [*Comédie* in 3 acts, Prem. on 10-7-1791, Pub. in 1790].
>   Th. Lyrique du Foire St. Germain (**1**); **Total: 1.**

_____., Rochefort, Jean-B. (comp). *Descente en Angleterre, La*
[*Prophétie* in 2 acts, Prem. on 24-12-1797, Pub. in 1798].
> Th. de la Cité (5); Th. du Palais (Cité)-Variétés (2); **Total: 7.**

_____. *Matinée bien employée, La* [*Comédie* in 1 act].
> Th. de la Citoyenne Montansier (21); **Total: 21.**

_____. *Paix, La, ou Les Amants réunis* [*Comédie*, Prem. on 29-10-1797, Pub. in 1797].
> Th. de l'Ambigu Comique (1); Th. de l'Emulation (Gaîté) (1); Th. de la Citoyenne Montansier (3); Th. des Délassements Comiques (29); Th. des Jeunes Artistes (13); Th. des Variétés Amusantes, Comiques et Lyriques (6); Th. du Vaudeville (1); Th. Français (de la rue Richelieu) (de la République) (7); **Total: 61.**
> **Total Performances,** Mittié, Jean-C.: **90**

Moithey., Bellement, André-P. *Amour et valeur ou La Gamelle*
[*Comédie* in 2 acts, Pub. in 1793].
> Th. de l'Ambigu Comique (22); **Total: 22.**

Molière, Jean-B. Poquelin de. *Amphitryon* [*Comédie* in 3 acts, Prem. on 13-1-1688, Pub. in 1668].
> Th. de l'Emulation (Gaîté) (2); Th. de l'Odéon (3); Th. de la Nation (Comédie Française) (21); Th. de Molière (2); Th. du Feydeau (de Monsieur) (6); Th. du Marais (2); Th. Français (de la rue Richelieu) (de la République) (11); **Total: 47.**

_____. *Avare, L'* [*Comédie* in 5 acts, Prem. on 9-9-1668, Pub. in 1669].
> Maison Egalité (2); Th. de l'Odéon (10); Th. de la Citoyenne Montansier (4); Th. de la Cité (2); Th. de la Nation (Comédie Française) (20); Th. des Italiens (Opéra-Comique) (1); Th. du Feydeau (de Monsieur) (6); Th. du Lycée Dramatique (3); Th. du Marais (7); Th. Français (de la rue Richelieu) (de la République) (40); **Total: 95.**

_____. *Bourgeois gentilhomme, Le* [*Comédie* in 5 acts, Prem. on 14-10-1670, Pub. in 1670].
> Th. de la Cité (1); Th. de la Nation (Comédie Française) (8); Th. Français (de la rue Richelieu) (de la République) (16); **Total: 25.**

_____. *Comtesse d'Escarbagnas, La* [*Comédie* in 1 act, Prem. in 12-1671].
> Th. de la Nation (Comédie Française) (21); Th. Français (de la rue Richelieu) (de la République) (3); **Total: 24.**

_____. *Dépit amoureux, Le* [*Comédie* in 5 acts, Prem. in 1656].
> Académie de la Musique (Opéra) (2); Maison Egalité (1); Th. de l'Ambigu Comique (17); Th. de l'Emulation (Gaîté) (17); Th. de l'Estrapade au Panthéon (1); Th. de l'Odéon (2); Th. de la Citoyenne Montansier (26); Th. de la Cité (3); Th. de la Concorde (1); Th. de la Liberté (1); Th. de la Montagne (3); Th. de la Nation (Comédie Française) (11); Th. de la Rue Antoine (3); Th. de la Rue Martin (5); Th. de Molière (4); Th. des Beaujolais (6); Th. des Délassements Comiques (4); Th. des Grands Danseurs (Gaîté) (11); Th. des Jeunes Artistes (11); Th. des Variétés Amusantes (Lazzari) (15); Th. des Variétés Amusantes, Comiques et Lyriques (42); Th. des Victoires (2); Th. des Victoires Nationales (6); Th. du Feydeau (de Monsieur) (7); Th. du Lycée des Arts (11); Th. du Lycée Dramatique (1); Th. du Marais (1); Th. du Palais (Cité)-Variétés (7); Th. du Vaudeville (1); Th. Français (de la rue Richelieu) (de la République) (40); Th. Français, Comique et Lyrique (11); Th. Lyrique des Amis de la Patrie (7); Th. National (de la rue Richelieu) (10); Th. Patriotique et de Momus (17); **Total: 307.**

_____. *Ecole des femmes, L'* [*Comédie* in 5 acts, Prem. on 26-12-1662].
Th. de l'Odéon (**8**); Th. de la Citoyenne Montansier (**1**); Th. de la Nation (Comédie Française) (**34**); Th. de la Rue Martin (**1**); Th. de Molière (**1**); Th. du Feydeau (de Monsieur) (**7**); Th. du Lycée Dramatique (**1**); Th. du Marais (**1**); Th. Français (de la rue Richelieu) (de la République) (**17**); Th. Lyrique des Amis de la Patrie (**4**); **Total: 75.**

_____. *Ecole des maris, L'* [*Comédie* in 3 acts, Prem. on 24-6-1661, Pub. in 1680].
Maison Egalité (**1**); n/a (**3**); Th. de l'Ambigu Comique (**72**); Th. de l'Estrapade au Panthéon (**2**); Th. de l'Odéon (**11**); Th. de la Citoyenne Montansier (**34**); Th. de la Cité (**6**); Th. de la Montagne (**2**); Th. de la Nation (Comédie Française) (**45**); Th. de la Rue Martin (**6**); Th. de Molière (**10**); Th. des Beaujolais (**1**); Th. des Délassements Comiques (**7**); Th. des Variétés Amusantes, Comiques et Lyriques (**10**); Th. du Feydeau (de Monsieur) (**9**); Th. du Lycée des Arts (**5**); Th. du Lycée Dramatique (**1**); Th. du Marais (**9**); Th. du Mareux (**3**); Th. du Palais (Cité)-Variétés (**9**); Th. du Vaudeville (**1**); Th. Français (de la rue Richelieu) (de la République) (**43**); Th. Lyrique des Amis de la Patrie (**5**); Th. National (de la rue Richelieu) (**12**); Th. Patriotique et de Momus (**9**); **Total: 316.**

_____. *Etourdi, L', ou Les Contretemps* [*Comédie* in 5 acts, Prem. in 1656].
Th. de la Nation (Comédie Française) (**1**); Th. de Molière (**1**); Th. du Feydeau (de Monsieur) (**1**); Th. du Marais (**4**); Th. Français (de la rue Richelieu) (de la République) (**9**); Th. Français, Comique et Lyrique (**1**); **Total: 17.**

_____. *Femmes savantes, Les* [*Comédie* in 5 acts, Prem. on 11-3-1672, Pub. in 1672].
Th. de la Nation (Comédie Française) (**16**); Th. de Molière (**1**); Th. du Feydeau (de Monsieur) (**4**); Th. Français (de la rue Richelieu) (de la République) (**27**); **Total: 48.**

_____. *Fourberies de Scapin, Les* [*Comédie* in 3 acts, Prem. on 24-5-1671, Pub. in 1671].
Académie de la Musique (Opéra) (**2**); Th. de l'Odéon (**2**); Th. de la Citoyenne Montansier (**10**); Th. de la Montagne (**4**); Th. de la Nation (Comédie Française) (**6**); Th. de la Rue Martin (**13**); Th. des Grands Danseurs (Gaîté) (**78**); Th. des Victoires Nationales (**1**); Th. du Marais (**5**); Th. Français (de la rue Richelieu) (de la République) (**27**); **Total: 148.**

_____. *George Dandin ou Le Mari confondu* [*Comédie* in 3 acts, Prem. on 18-7-1668, Pub. in 1668].
Th. de l'Ambigu Comique (**34**); Th. de la Citoyenne Montansier (**4**); Th. de la Nation (Comédie Française) (**19**); Th. Français (de la rue Richelieu) (de la République) (**6**); **Total: 63.**

_____. *Malade imaginaire, Le* [*Comédie* in 3 acts, Prem. on 10-2-1673, Pub. in 1674].
Th. de la Nation (Comédie Française) (**6**); Th. de la Rue Martin (**2**); Th. de Molière (**2**); Th. Français (de la rue Richelieu) (de la République) (**10**); **Total: 20.**

_____. *Mariage forcé, Le* [*Comédie* in 1 act, Prem. on 29-1-1664, Pub. in 1664].
Th. Français (de la rue Richelieu) (de la République) (**4**); Th. Lyrique des Amis de la Patrie (**10**); **Total: 14.**

_____. *Médecin malgré lui, Le* [*Comédie* in 3 acts, Prem. on 6-8-1666, Pub. in 1667].

Maison Egalité (1); Th. de l'Emulation (Gaîté) (1); Th. de l'Estrapade au Panthéon (2); Th. de l'Odéon (8); Th. de la Citoyenne Montansier (3); Th. de la Cité (4); Th. de la Liberté (3); Th. de la Montagne (5); Th. de la Nation (Comédie Française) (22); Th. de la Rue Martin (10); Th. de Molière (2); Th. des Grands Danseurs (Gaîté) (104); Th. des Variétés Amusantes, Comiques et Lyriques (5); Th. du Feydeau (de Monsieur) (36); Th. du Lycée des Arts (1); Th. du Lycée Dramatique (4); Th. du Marais (1); Th. du Vaudeville (4); Th. Français (de la rue Richelieu) (de la République) (56); Th. Lyrique des Amis de la Patrie (3); Th. National (de la rue Richelieu) (2); Th. Patriotique et de Momus (7); **Total: 284.**

_____. *Misanthrope, Le* [*Comédie* in 5 acts, Prem. on 4-6-1666, Pub. in 1667].

Maison Egalité (3); Th. de la Citoyenne Montansier (1); Th. de la Liberté (1); Th. de la Nation (Comédie Française) (14); Th. de la Rue Martin (1); Th. de Molière (2); Th. du Feydeau (de Monsieur) (7); Th. du Marais (7); Th. Français (de la rue Richelieu) (de la République) (22); Th. Lyrique des Amis de la Patrie (3); Th. National (de la rue Richelieu) (2); **Total: 63.**

_____., Mengozzi, Bernardo (comp). *Monsieur de Pourceaugnac* [*Comédie* in 2 acts, Prem. in 9-1669].

Th. de la Citoyenne Montansier (32); Th. de la Nation (Comédie Française) (14); Th. de la Rue Martin (3); Th. des Délassements Comiques (3); Th. du Feydeau (de Monsieur) (9); Th. Français (de la rue Richelieu) (de la République) (7); Th. National (de la rue Richelieu) (6); **Total: 74.**

_____. *Précieuses ridicules, Les* [*Comédie* in 1 act, Prem. on 18-11-1659, Pub. in 1660].

Th. de la Citoyenne Montansier (12); Th. de la Liberté (1); Th. de la Rue Martin (2); Th. des Grands Danseurs (Gaîté) (43); Th. des Jeunes Elèves (1); Th. des Variétés Amusantes, Comiques et Lyriques (3); Th. du Lycée Dramatique (5); Th. du Marais (6); Th. Français (de la rue Richelieu) (de la République) (21); **Total: 94.**

_____. *Sganarelle ou Le Cocu imaginaire* [*Comédie* in 1 act, Prem. on 28-5-1660, Pub. in 1660].

Th. de la Citoyenne Montansier (2); **Total: 2.**

_____. *Tartuffe* [*Comédie* in 5 acts, Prem. in 1667, Pub. in 1677].

Maison Egalité (2); Th. de l'Estrapade au Panthéon (2); Th. de l'Odéon (11); Th. de la Citoyenne Montansier (7); Th. de la Liberté (1); Th. de la Nation (Comédie Française) (21); Th. de la Rue Martin (11); Th. de Molière (3); Th. du Feydeau (de Monsieur) (18); Th. du Lycée des Arts (1); Th. du Lycée Dramatique (3); Th. du Marais (7); Th. du Palais (Cité)-Variétés (1); Th. du Vaudeville (2); Th. Français (de la rue Richelieu) (de la République) (34); Th. Français, Comique et Lyrique (7); Th. Lyrique des Amis de la Patrie (5); Th. Lyrique du Foire St. Germain (1); Th. National (de la rue Richelieu) (7); Th. Patriotique et de Momus (4); **Total: 148.**

Total Performances, Molière, Jean-B. Poquelin de: **1864**

Moline, Pierre-L., Carpentier (comp). *Alchimistes, Les, ou La Folie et la sagesse* [*Opéra-Comique* in 1 act, Prem. on 3-9-1791, Pub. in 1806].

Th. Lyrique des Amis de la Patrie (24); **Total: 24.**

_____. *Amour anglois, L'* [*Comédie* in 3 acts, Prem. on 9-7-1788, Pub. in 1788].

Th. du Palais Royal (21); **Total: 21.**

_____., Edelman, Johann-F. (comp). *Ariane dans l'île de Naxos* [*Opéra* in 1 act, Prem. on 24-9-1782, Pub. in 1782].

Académie de la Musique (Opéra) (11); **Total: 11.**

_____., Paisiello, Giovanni (comp). *Duel comique, Le* [*Opéra-Bouffe* in 2 acts, Pub. in 1776].
   Th. de l'Ambigu Comique (**22**); Th. des Grands Danseurs (Gaîté) (**4**); **Total: 26.**

_____., Mozart, Wolfgang-A. (comp). *Enlèvement au sérail, L'* [*Opéra* in 3 acts, Pub in 1782].
   Th. Français, Comique et Lyrique (**3**); Th. Lyrique des Amis de la Patrie (**5**); **Total: 8.**

_____., Gluck, Christoph (comp). *Orphée et Euridice* [*Drame* in 3 acts, Prem. on 2-8-1774, Pub. in 1774].
   Académie de la Musique (Opéra) (**79**); **Total: 79.**

_____., Paisiello, Giovanni (comp). *Roi Théodore à Venise, Le* [*Opéra-Comique* in 2 acts, Prem. on 11-9-1787, Pub. in 1787].
   Th. de l'Ambigu Comique (**25**); **Total: 25.**
   Total Performances, Moline, Pierre-L.: **194**

Moller, Heinrich-F., Dalainval, Cavanas, dit. *Comte de Waltron, Le, ou La Subordination* [*Pièce* in 3 acts, Prem. on 16-9-1789, Pub. in 1789].
   Th. de la Citoyenne Montansier (**6**); Th. du Feydeau (de Monsieur) (**12**); **Total: 18.**

Moncrif, François-A.-P. de. *Fausse magie, La* [*Comédie* in 3 acts, Prem. on 4-5-1719].
   Th. de la Citoyenne Montansier (**13**); Th. de la Rue Martin (**1**); Th. des Italiens (Opéra-Comique) (**19**); Th. du Marais (**2**); **Total: 35.**

Monnet, Jean. *Amants sans amour, Les* [*Comédie* in 1 act, Prem. in 1789, Pub. in 1793].
   Th. de la Citoyenne Montansier (**56**); Th. de la Cité (**1**); Th. des Variétés Amusantes (Lazzari) (**1**); Th. du Palais (Cité)-Variétés (**10**); **Total: 68.**

_____. *Inconséquente, L', ou Le Fat dupé* [*Comédie* in 1 act, Prem. on 20-8-1787, Pub. in 1787].
   Th. des Jeunes Artistes (**25**); Th. du Palais Royal (**17**); **Total: 42.**

_____., Scio, Etienne (comp). *Lisia* [*Opéra* in 1 act, Prem. on 8-7-1793, Pub. in 1794].
   Th. du Feydeau (de Monsieur) (**37**); **Total: 37.**

_____., Scio, Etienne (comp). *Lisidore et Monrose* [*Opéra* in 3 acts, Prem. on 26-4-1792].
   Th. du Feydeau (de Monsieur) (**13**); **Total: 13.**

_____., Foignet, Charles-G. (comp). *Orage, L'* [*Opéra* in 1 act, Prem. on 31-5-1798, Pub. in 1798].
   Th. de la Citoyenne Montansier (**32**); **Total: 32.**

_____. *Rêve de Kamailliaka, Le* [*Opéra* in 2 acts, Prem. on 16-7-1791].
   Th. de Molière (**12**); **Total: 12.**

_____., Scio, Etienne (comp). *Tambourin de province, Le, ou L'Heureuse incertitude* [*Opéra* in 1 act, Prem. on 13-9-1793, Pub. in 1793].
   Th. de la Cité (**1**); Th. du Palais (Cité)-Variétés (**22**); **Total: 23.**

_____., Gaveaux, Pierre (comp). *Tout par hasard* [In 1 act, Prem. on 22-10-1796].
   Th. du Feydeau (de Monsieur) (**1**); **Total: 1.**
   Total Performances, Monnet, Jean: **228**

Monnet, Marie-M. *Intrigue secrète, L', ou La Veuve* [*Comédie* in 1 act].
   Th. du Palais (Cité)-Variétés (**33**); **Total: 33.**

_____. *Montagnards, Les* [*Comédie* in 3 acts, Pub. in 1793].
   Th. de la Citoyenne Montansier (1); Th. Français (de la rue Richelieu) (de la République) (1); Th. National (de la rue Richelieu) (22); **Total: 24.**
                    Total Performances, Monnet, Marie-M.: **57**
"Monsieur de B." *Heureuse découverte, L'* [*Opéra-Comique* in 1 act, Pub. in 1756].
   Th. des Grands Danseurs (Gaîté) (14); **Total: 14.**
_____. *Tuteur dupé, Le* [*Comédie* in 1 act, Pub. in 1789].
   Th. des Grands Danseurs (Gaîté) (12); **Total: 12.**
                    Total Performances, Monsieur de B.: **26**
Montanclos, Mme. Marie M. de. *Bonne maîtresse, La* [*Comédie*, Pub. in 1803].
   Th. du Marais (5); **Total: 5.**
_____. *Fauteuil, Le* [*Comédie*, Prem. on 11-10-1798, Pub. in 1798].
   Th. de Molière (6); **Total: 6.**
_____. *Robert le Bossu ou Les Trois soeurs* [N/A].
   Th. de la Citoyenne Montansier (55); **Total: 55.**
                    Total Performances, Montanclos, Mme. Marie M. de: **66**
Montfleury, Antoine Jacob, dit. *Femme juge et partie, La* [*Comédie* in 5 acts, Prem. in 3-1669, Pub. in 1670].
   Th. de la Citoyenne Montansier (6); Th. de la Rue Martin (5); Th. du Lycée des Arts (1); Th. du Palais (Cité)-Variétés (3); Th. Français (de la rue Richelieu) (de la République) (6); **Total: 21.**
_____. *Fille capitaine, La* [*Comédie* in 5 acts, Pub. in 1672].
   Th. de la Nation (Comédie Française) (4); Th. Français (de la rue Richelieu) (de la République) (4); **Total: 8.**
                    Total Performances, Montfleury, Antoine Jacob, dit: **29**
Montorcier. *Oies du frère Philippe, Les* [*Pièce* in 1 act, Prem. in 1771, Pub. in 1771].
   Th. de l'Ambigu Comique (66); **Total: 66.**
Monvel, see Boutet de Monvel.
Morel de Chédeville, Etienne., Grétry, André-E.-M. (comp). *Aspasie*
   [*Opéra* in 3 acts, Prem. on 17-3-1789, Pub. in 1789].
   Académie de la Musique (Opéra) (15); **Total: 15.**
_____., Grétry, André-E.-M. (comp). *Caravane du Caire, La* [*Opéra-Ballet* in 3 acts, Prem. on 30-10-1783, Pub. in 1783].
   Académie de la Musique (Opéra) (42); Th. Français (de la rue Richelieu) (de la République) (1); **Total: 43.**
_____., Grétry, André-E.-M. (comp). *Panurge dans l'isle des Lanternes* [*Comédie*-Lyrique in 3 acts, Prem. on 25-1-1785, Pub. in 1785].
   Académie de la Musique (Opéra) (77); **Total: 77.**
                    Total Performances, Morel de Chédeville, Etienne: **135**
Mouslier de Moissy, Alexandre. *Diamants, Les* [*Comédie* in 1 act, Prem. on 21-11-1791].
   Th. des Enfans Comiques (1); **Total: 1.**
_____. *Fausses inconstances, Les* [*Comédie* in 1 act, Prem. on 22-9-1750, Pub. in 1751].
   Th. des Enfans Comiques (1); **Total: 1.**
_____. *Heureux malheur, L'* [*Comédie* in 1 act, Prem. on 23-11-1791].
   Th. des Enfans Comiques (1); **Total: 1.**

_____. *Jolie servante, La* [In 1 act].
Th. des Enfans Comiques (2); **Total: 2.**
_____. *Vicieux malade, Le* [N/A].
Th. des Enfans Comiques (1); **Total: 1.**
Total Performances, Mouslier de Moissy, Alexandre: **6**
Noël., Trial, Armand-E. (comp). *Deux petits aveugles, Les* [*Comédie*,
Prem. on 28-7-1792].
Th. des Italiens (Opéra-Comique) (9); **Total: 9.**
Nogaret, François-F., P.S. Aristenete., Corebus. *Bataille de Fleurus,*
La [*Fait Historique*].
Maison Egalité (5); **Total: 5.**
Nougaret, Pierre-J.-B. *Arlequin amoureux ou L'Ecole du monde*
[*Comédie*, Pub. in 1762].
Th. des Grands Danseurs (Gaîté) (2); **Total: 2.**
_____. *Il n'y a plus d'enfants* [*Comédie*, Prem. on 8-4-1772, Pub. in 1772].
Th. des Jeunes Artistes (4); **Total: 4.**
Total Performances, Nougaret, Pierre-J.-B.: **6**
Noverre, Jean-G., Rodolphe, Jean-J. (comp). *Caprices de Galathée,*
Les [Prem. on 6-10-1776].
Th. de l'Ambigu Comique (1); Th. Français (de la rue Richelieu) (de la
République) (1); Th. Lyrique des Amis de la Patrie (1); **Total: 3.**
_____. *Triomphe de Neptune, Le* [*Ballet*, Prem. on 11-2-1763, Pub. in 1763].
Th. des Grands Danseurs (Gaîté) (1); **Total: 1.**
Total Performances, Noverre, Jean-G.: **4**
Orel de Chedeville. *Panurge* [Prem. in 1785].
Académie de la Musique (Opéra) (2); **Total: 2.**
Pagès, François-X. *Amélie et Mainfroi* [*Tragédie* in 5 acts, Pub. in 1794].
Th. Patriotique et de Momus (1); **Total: 1.**
Paillardelle, A. *Conseil imprudent, Le* [*Comédie* in 2 acts, Prem. on 30-4-
1789].
Th. du Feydeau (de Monsieur) (55); **Total: 55.**
Pain, Joseph-M. *Appartement à louer, L'* [*Comédie* in 1 act, Prem. on 1-3-
1799, Pub. in 1798].
Th. de la Citoyenne Montansier (21); **Total: 21.**
_____., Riou de Kesauln, François-M.-J. *Chouans, Les, ou*
Républicaine de Malestroit [*Fait Historique* in 1 act, Prem. on 29-7-1795,
Pub. in 1794].
Th. de l'Ambigu Comique (38); **Total: 38.**
_____. *Connaisseur, Le* [*Comédie* in 1 act, Prem. on 2-11-1799].
Th. des Troubadours (4); **Total: 4.**
Total Performances, Pain, Joseph-M.: **63**
Palaprat, Joseph. *Grondeur, Le* [*Comédie* in 3 acts, Prem. in 1691, Pub. in
1771].
Th. de la Nation (Comédie Française) (11); **Total: 11.**
Palissot de Montenoy, Charles. *Courtisanes, Les, ou L'Ecole des*
moeurs [*Comédie* in 3 acts, Prem. in 1782, Pub. in 1775].
Th. Français (de la rue Richelieu) (de la République) (3); **Total: 3.**
Palomba, Giuseppe., Guglielmi, Pietro.-A. (comp). *Due gemelle, Le*
[*Opéra* in 3 acts, Prem. on 12-6-1786, Pub. in 1790].
Th. du Feydeau (de Monsieur) (3); **Total: 3.**

_____., Paisiello, Giovanni (comp). *Molinarella, La, ou L'Amor con-trasto* [*Opéra*, Prem. in 1788].
>   Th. du Feydeau (de Monsieur) (**25**); **Total: 25.**
> **Total Performances,** Palomba, Giuseppe: **28**

Pannard, Charles-F. *Amant supposé, L', ou Le Miroir* [*Opéra-Comique* in 1 act, Prem. on 2-9-1739].
>   Th. de l'Emulation (Gaîté) (**13**); **Total: 13.**

_____. *Armoire, L', ou La Pièce à deux acteurs* [*Opéra-Comique* in 1 act, Prem. on 6-2-1738, Pub. in 1738].
>   Th. de l'Emulation (Gaîté) (**1**); Th. des Jeunes Artistes (**4**); Th. des Ombres de J.-J. Rousseau (**9**); **Total: 14.**

_____. *Compliment, Le* [*Vaudeville*, Prem. on 7-9-1731].
>   Th. des Beaujolais (**1**); Th. des Grands Danseurs (Gaîté) (**1**); **Total: 2.**

_____. *Fée bienfaisante, La* [*Prologue* in 1 act, Prem. on 11-8-1736].
>   Th. des Variétés Amusantes (Lazzari) (**12**); Th. des Variétés Amusantes, Comiques et Lyriques (**4**); **Total: 16.**

_____. *Gageure, La* [*Opéra-Comique* in 1 act, Prem. on 19-3-1740, Pub. in 1745].
>   Académie de la Musique (Opéra) (**1**); Th. de la Citoyenne Montansier (**1**); **Total: 2.**

> **Total Performances,** Pannard, Charles-F.: **47**

Paoli, Chevalier. *Fête flamande, La, ou Le Prix des arts* [*Comédie* in 1 act, Pub. in 1791].
>   Th. des Jeunes Artistes (**15**); **Total: 15.**

Parisau, Pierre-G., La Houssaye (comp). *Amours de Coucy, Les, ou Le Tournoy* [*Pantomime* in 3 acts, Prem. on 22-8-1790].
>   Th. du Feydeau (de Monsieur) (**2**); **Total: 2.**

_____., Dupré (comp). *Deux amis, Les, ou L'Héroïsme de l'amitié* [*Pantomime* in 3 acts, Prem. on 12-12-1781].
>   Th. des Grands Danseurs (Gaîté) (**1**); **Total: 1.**

_____. *Deux font la paire, Les, ou Les Bottes de foin* [*Comédie* in 1 act, Prem. on 30-4-1783, Pub. in 1783].
>   Th. des Grands Danseurs (Gaîté) (**74**); **Total: 74.**

_____. *Dinde du Mans, La* [*Comédie* in 1 act, Prem. on 1-3-1783, Pub. in 1773].
>   Th. des Grands Danseurs (Gaîté) (**8**); **Total: 8.**

_____. *Honnête étourdi, L'* [*Comédie* in 1 act, Prem. in 1773].
>   Th. du Palais Royal (**12**); **Total: 12.**

_____. *Jean la Fontaine* [*Comédie* in 2 acts, Prem. on 21-3-1790].
>   Th. des Jeunes Artistes (**2**); Th. du Feydeau (de Monsieur) (**25**); **Total: 27.**

_____., Trial, Armand-E. (comp). *Julien et Colette ou La Milice* [*Opéra* in 1 act, Prem. on 3-3-1788].
>   Cirque National (**10**); **Total: 10.**

_____. *Prix académique, Le* [*Comédie* in 1 act, Pub. in 1783].
>   Th. de la Citoyenne Montansier (**1**); **Total: 1.**

_____. *Réconciliation des ennemis généreux, La* [*Tableau-Patriotique* in 1 act, Prem. on 25-7-1782].
>   Th. des Grands Danseurs (Gaîté) (**7**); **Total: 7.**

_____. *Repentir de Figaro, Le* [*Comédie* in 1 act, Prem. on 28-6-1784, Pub. in 1785].
>   Th. de l'Ambigu Comique (**13**); **Total: 13.**

_____. *Richard* [*Parodie* in 1 act, Prem. on 2-9-1781, Pub. in 1781].
>   Th. des Italiens (Opéra-Comique) (**2**); **Total: 2.**

_____. *Rosalie* [*Comédie* in 1 act, Prem. on 13-2-1790].
Th. du Feydeau (de Monsieur) (**2**); **Total: 2.**

_____. *Soirée d'été, La* [*Opéra-Comique* in 1 act, Prem. on 5-2-1782, Pub. in 1782].
Th. du Palais (Cité)-Variétés (**1**); **Total: 1.**

_____., Dupré (comp). *Sophie de Brabant* [*Pantomime* in 3 acts, Prem. on 15-6-1781, Pub. in 1781].
Th. des Grands Danseurs (Gaîté) (**33**); **Total: 33.**

_____. *Veuve de Cancale, La* [*Parodie* in 3 acts, Prem. on 3-10-1780, Pub. in 1780].
Th. des Italiens (Opéra-Comique) (**4**); **Total: 4.**

Total Performances, Parisau, Pierre-G.: **197**

Pascali. *Timide, Le* [*Comédie* in 1 act, Prem. on 11-8-1788, Pub. in 1788].
Th. de la Citoyenne Montansier (**16**); Th. du Palais Royal (**44**); **Total: 60.**

Patrat, Joseph., Trial, Armand-E. (comp). *Adélaïde et Mirval ou La Vengeance paternelle* [*Opéra* in 3 acts, Prem. on 6-6-1791].
Th. des Italiens (Opéra-Comique) (**15**); **Total: 15.**

_____. *Amants protées, Les, ou Qui compte sans son hôte compte deux fois* [*Comédie* in 1 act, Prem. on 3-10-1798, Pub. in 1823].
Th. de la Citoyenne Montansier (**99**); **Total: 99.**

_____. *Complot inutile, Le* [*Comédie* in 3 acts, Prem. on 28-11-1799, Pub. in 1822].
Th. de l'Odéon (**10**); Th. du Feydeau (de Monsieur) (**18**); **Total: 28.**

_____., Mengozzi, Bernardo (comp). *Débat des muses, Le* [*Opéra* in 1 act, Prem. on 31-12-1791].
Th. de la Citoyenne Montansier (**24**); **Total: 24.**

_____. *Déguisements amoureux, Les* [*Opéra-Bouffe* in 2 acts, Prem. on 18-11-1783, Pub. in 1783].
Th. de l'Ambigu Comique (**8**); Th. de l'Emulation (Gaîté) (**5**); Th. de la Citoyenne Montansier (**10**); Th. de la Cité (**1**); Th. des Grands Danseurs (Gaîté) (**7**); Th. des Italiens (Opéra-Comique) (**14**); Th. du Lycée des Arts (**5**); Th. du Marais (**4**); Th. Français (de la rue Richelieu) (de la République) (**32**); **Total: 86.**

_____., Weiss, Matthias., Jauffret, Louis-F. *Deux frères, Les* [*Comédie* in 4 acts, Prem. on 29-7-1799, Pub. in 1822].
Th. de la Citoyenne Montansier (**1**); Th. du Palais Royal (**4**); Th. Français (de la rue Richelieu) (de la République) (**15**); **Total: 20.**

_____. *Deux grenadiers, Les, ou Les Quiproquos* [*Comédie* in 3 acts, Pub. in 1799].
Maison Egalité (**1**); Th. de la Citoyenne Montansier (**65**); Th. de la Cité (**25**); Th. des Variétés Amusantes, Comiques et Lyriques (**1**); Th. du Marais (**1**); Th. du Palais (Cité)-Variétés (**47**); **Total: 140.**

_____. *Deux morts, Les, ou La Ruse de carnaval* [*Opéra-Comique* in 1 act, Prem. on 27-2-1781, Pub. in 1781].
Th. de l'Emulation (Gaîté) (**30**); Th. de la Citoyenne Montansier (**7**); **Total: 37.**

_____. *Espiègle, L'* [*Vaudeville* in 2 acts, Prem. on 18-11-1797, Pub. in 1797].
Th. de l'Emulation (Gaîté) (**7**); Th. de l'Odéon (**13**); Th. du Marais (**1**); Th. du Mareux (**2**); Th. Lyrique des Amis de la Patrie (**33**); **Total: 56.**

_____. *Fausse nièce, La* [*Comédie* in 3 acts, Prem. on 6-9-1790].
Th. du Palais Royal (**9**); **Total: 9.**

_____. *Fou raisonnable, Le, ou L'Anglais* [*Comédie* in 1 act, Prem. on 9-7-1781, Pub. in 1781].
> Th. de la Citoyenne Montansier (4); Th. de la Rue Martin (10); Th. de Molière (13); Th. des Jeunes Artistes (2); Th. du Lycée des Arts (1); Th. du Marais (3); Th. du Palais Royal (28); **Total: 61.**

_____. *François et Rouffignac* [*Comédie*, Prem. on 23-5-1799, Pub. in 1798].
> Th. de la Citoyenne Montansier (17); **Total: 17.**

_____. *Heureuse erreur, L'* [*Comédie* in 1 act, Prem. on 22-7-1783, Pub. in 1783].
> Th. de la Citoyenne Montansier (7); Th. des Italiens (Opéra-Comique) (7); Th. du Feydeau (de Monsieur) (7); Th. du Marais (6); **Total: 27.**

_____. *Heureuse supercherie, L'* [*Comédie* in 3 acts, Prem. on 26-10-1782].
> Th. de la Citoyenne Montansier (5); **Total: 5.**

_____. *Heureux quiproquo, L', ou Le Présent* [*Comédie*, Pub. in 1786].
> Maison Égalité (27); Th. de l'Ambigu Comique (1); Th. de la Citoyenne Montansier (21); Th. de la Cité (25); Th. des Italiens (Opéra-Comique) (1); Th. des Variétés Amusantes, Comiques et Lyriques (10); Th. du Lycée des Arts (1); Th. du Palais (Cité)-Variétés (66); **Total: 152.**

_____. *Menteuse par point d'honneur, La* [*Comédie* in 2 acts, Prem. on 28-10-1791].
> Th. du Feydeau (de Monsieur) (5); **Total: 5.**

_____., Grétry, André-E.-M. (comp). *Méprises par ressemblance, Les* [*Comédie* in 3 acts, Prem. on 7-11-1786, Pub. in 1786].
> Th. de la Cité (10); Th. des Italiens (Opéra-Comique) (34); Th. des Variétés Amusantes, Comiques et Lyriques (2); Th. du Palais (Cité)-Variétés (15); **Total: 61.**

_____. *Mirza ou Le Préjugé de l'amitié* [*Comédie* in 3 acts, Pub. in 1797].
> Académie de la Musique (Opéra) (13); Th. de la Citoyenne Montansier (1); **Total: 14.**

_____., Bruni, Antonio-B. (comp). *Officier de fortune, L', ou Les Deux militaires* [*Opéra* in 2 acts, Prem. on 24-9-1792].
> Th. du Feydeau (de Monsieur) (66); **Total: 66.**

_____. *Orpheline, L'* [*Vaudeville* in 1 act, Prem. on 4-4-1796].
> Th. du Feydeau (de Monsieur) (10); **Total: 10.**

_____. *Petite ruse, La* [*Opéra*-Vaudeville].
> Th. de l'Odéon (9); Th. de la Citoyenne Montansier (22); Th. de la Cité (1); **Total: 32.**

_____. *Résolution inutile, La, ou Les Déguisements amoureux* [*Comédie* in 1 act, Prem. on 18-11-1783, Pub. in 1783].
> Th. de la Citoyenne Montansier (4); Th. Lyrique des Amis de la Patrie (1); **Total: 5.**

_____. *Sourd et l'aveugle, Le* [*Comédie* in 1 act, Prem. on 21-11-1790, Pub. in 1791].
> Th. des Beaujolais (18); Th. Lyrique des Amis de la Patrie (33); **Total: 51.**

_____. *Toberne ou Le Pécheur suédois* [*Opéra-Comique* in 2 acts, Prem. on 2-12-1795, Pub. in 1798].
> Th. du Feydeau (de Monsieur) (61); **Total: 61.**

_____. *Valet mal servi, Le* [*Comédie* in 1 act, Prem. on 27-6-1793].
> Th. du Palais (Cité)-Variétés (6); **Total: 6.**

_____. *Vengeance, La* [*Comédie* in 1 act, Prem. on 31-10-1798, Pub. in 1799].
> Th. de l'Odéon (3); **Total: 3.**

> **Total Performances**, Patrat, Joseph: **1090**

Pein, Thomas., Midet. *Naufrage au port, Le* [*Comédie* in 1 act, Prem. on 30-8-1794, Pub. in 1795].
> Th. de l'Emulation (Gaîté) (**4**); Th. du Vaudeville (**47**); **Total: 51.**

Pellegrin, Abbé S.-J. *Vrais amis, Les, ou Le Père intéressé* [*Comédie* in 5 acts, Prem. on 26-11-1720, Pub. in 1720].
> Th. de l'Emulation (Gaîté) (**1**); **Total: 1.**

Pelletier de Volmeranges, Benoît. *Devoir et la nature, Le* [*Drame* in 5 acts, Prem. on 2-9-1797, Pub. in 1798].
> Th. de l'Odéon (**12**); Th. des Variétés Amusantes, Comiques et Lyriques (**1**); **Total: 13.**

_____. *Mariage du capucin, Le* [*Comédie* in 3 acts, Prem. on 30-5-1798, Pub. in 1798].
> Th. de l'Emulation (Gaîté) (**8**); Th. Lyrique des Amis de la Patrie (**47**); **Total: 55.**

> **Total Performances**, Pelletier de Volmeranges, Benoît: **68**

Pépin de Degrouette., Gebauer, Michel.-J. (comp). *Aimée ou La Fausse apparence* [*Opéra-Bouffe* in 1 act, Prem. on 20-5-1790].
> Th. de la Citoyenne Montansier (**1**); **Total: 1.**

Person de Bérainville, L.-C. *Belphégor ou Le Diable à Florence* [*Comédie* in 1 act, Prem. on 10-3-1785].
> Th. des Grands Danseurs (Gaîté) (**2**); **Total: 2.**

_____. *Bouquet et la veuve, Le* [*Comédie* in 1 act, Prem. on 3-11-1791].
> Th. de Molière (**4**); **Total: 4.**

_____. *Epreuve du sentiment, L', ou Les Deux frères* [*Comédie* in 1 act, Prem. on 7-3-1789, Pub. in 1789].
> Th. de l'Emulation (Gaîté) (**1**); **Total: 1.**

> **Total Performances**, Person de Bérainville, L.-C.: **7**

Petit, Abbé. *David et Bethsabée* [*Tragédie* in 5 acts, Pub. in 1754].
> Th. de l'Ambigu Comique (**22**); **Total: 22.**

Petitain, Louis-G. *Français à Cythère, Les* [*Héroique* in 1 act, Prem. on 17-3-1798, Pub. in 1798].
> Th. du Vaudeville (**29**); **Total: 29.**

Petitot, Claude-B. *Geta* [*Tragédie* in 5 acts, Prem. on 25-5-1797, Pub. in 1797].
> Th. de la Nation (Comédie Française) (**5**); **Total: 5.**

_____. *Myrrha* [*Tragédie* in 5 acts, Prem. on 2-1-1796].
> Th. du Feydeau (de Monsieur) (**5**); **Total: 5.**

> **Total Performances**, Petitot, Claude-B.: **10**

Philipon, Louis de la Madeleine., Jadin, Louis-E. (comp). *Agricole Viala ou Le Jeune héros de la Durance* [*Fait Historique* in 1 act, Prem. on 1-7-1794].
> Th. des Italiens (Opéra-Comique) (**11**); Th. du Feydeau (de Monsieur) (**5**); Th. Lyrique des Amis de la Patrie (**20**); **Total: 36.**

_____., Plantade, Charles-H. (comp). *Aux plus braves les plus belles* [*Comédie* in 1 act, Prem. on 6-10-1794, Pub. in 1795].
> Th. Lyrique des Amis de la Patrie (**22**); **Total: 22.**

> **Total Performances**, Philipon, Louis de la Madeleine: **58**

Picard, Louis-B. *Amis de collège, Les, ou L'Homme oisif et l'artisan* [*Comédie* in 3 acts, Prem. on 14-12-1795, Pub. in 1796].
> Th. de la Rue Antoine (**1**); Th. du Feydeau (de Monsieur) (**4**); Th. Français (de la rue Richelieu) (de la République) (**34**); **Total: 39.**

_____., Duval, Alexandre-V.-P., Lemière, Jean.-F.-A. de Corvey (comp). *Andros et Almona ou Le Français à Bassora* [*Comédie mêlée d'ariettes* in 3 acts, Prem. on 5-2-1794, Pub. in 1794].
Th. des Italiens (Opéra-Comique) (**17**); **Total: 17.**

_____. *Arlequin friand* [*Comédie* in 1 act, Prem. on 24-5-1793, Pub. in 1793].
Th. du Vaudeville (**14**); **Total: 14.**

_____., Fiévée, Joseph. *Badinage dangereux, Le* [*Comédie* in 1 act, Prem. on 27-11-1789].
Th. du Feydeau (de Monsieur) (**19**); **Total: 19.**

_____. *Collatéral, Le, ou La Diligence à Gorguy* [*Comédie* in 5 acts, Prem. on 6-11-1799].
Th. du Feydeau (de Monsieur) (**2**); **Total: 2.**

_____., Devienne, François (comp). *Comédiens ambulants, Les* [*Vaudeville* in 2 acts, Prem. on 28-12-1798].
Th. du Feydeau (de Monsieur) (**45**); **Total: 45.**

_____. *Conjectures, Les* [*Comédie* in 3 acts, Prem. on 20-10-1795].
Th. du Feydeau (de Monsieur) (**7**); **Total: 7.**

_____. *Conteur, Le, ou Les Deux postes* [*Comédie* in 3 acts, Prem. on 4-2-1793, Pub. in 1793].
Th. de l'Odéon (**7**); Th. de la Cité (**3**); Th. de la Nation (Comédie Française) (**35**); Th. des Variétés Amusantes, Comiques et Lyriques (**1**); Th. du Feydeau (de Monsieur) (**20**); Th. du Marais (**1**); Th. du Palais (Cité)-Variétés (**2**); Th. Français (de la rue Richelieu) (de la République) (**32**); **Total: 101.**

_____. *Cousin de tout le monde, Le* [*Comédie* in 1 act, Prem. on 22-7-1793, Pub. in 1793].
Maison Egalité (**8**); Th. de la Cité (**7**); Th. des Variétés Amusantes, Comiques et Lyriques (**2**); Th. du Palais (Cité)-Variétés (**44**); **Total: 61.**

_____., Jadin, Louis-E. (comp). *Ecolier en vacances, L'* [*Opéra* in 1 act, Prem. on 13-10-1794, Pub. in 1794].
Académie de la Musique (Opéra) (**1**); Th. des Italiens (Opéra-Comique) (**26**); **Total: 27.**

_____. *Encore des Ménechmes* [*Comédie* in 3 acts, Prem. on 9-6-1791].
Th. du Feydeau (de Monsieur) (**9**); **Total: 9.**

_____., Mazares, Edouard-J.-E. *Enfant trouvé, L'* [*Comédie* in 3 acts, Pub. in 1794].
Maison Egalité (**2**); **Total: 2.**

_____. *Entrée dans le monde, L'* [*Comédie* in 5 acts, Prem. on 15-6-1799].
Th. de la Cité (**2**); Th. du Feydeau (de Monsieur) (**1**); Th. du Marais (**3**); Th. du Palais (Cité)-Variétés (**18**); **Total: 24.**

_____. *Masque, Le* [*Comédie* in 2 acts, Prem. on 10-6-1790].
Th. du Feydeau (de Monsieur) (**10**); **Total: 10.**

_____. *Médiocre et rampant ou Le Moyen de parvenir* [*Comédie* in 5 acts, Pub. in 1797].
Th. de l'Odéon (**21**); Th. de la Cité (**4**); Th. du Marais (**2**); Th. du Palais (Cité)-Variétés (**4**); Th. Lyrique des Amis de la Patrie (**2**); **Total: 33.**

_____. *Moitié du chemin, La* [*Comédie* in 3 acts, Prem. on 21-10-1793, Pub. in 1794].
Th. Français (de la rue Richelieu) (de la République) (**11**); **Total: 11.**

_____. *Perruque blonde, La* [*Comédie* in 1 act, Pub. in 1794].
Académie de la Musique (Opéra) (2); Th. de l'Emulation (Gaîté) (1); Th. de la Rue Martin (1); Th. du Feydeau (de Monsieur) (1); Th. Français (de la rue Richelieu) (de la République) (11); **Total: 16.**

_____., Dalayrac, Nicolas (comp). *Prise de Toulon, La* [*Tableau-Patriotique* in 1 act, Prem. on 21-1-1794, Pub. in 1794].
Th. de la Montagne (2); Th. du Feydeau (de Monsieur) (18); Th. du Lycée des Arts (1); **Total: 21.**

_____., Devienne, François (comp). *Rose et Aurèle* [*Opéra* in 1 act, Prem. on 8-8-1794].
Th. du Feydeau (de Monsieur) (18); **Total: 18.**

_____., Moreau., Lemiere, Jean.-F.-A. de Corvey (comp). *Suspects, Les* [*Comédie* in 1 act, Prem. on 19-5-1795, Pub. in 1797].
Maison Egalité (58); Th. de la Citoyenne Montansier (1); Th. de la Cité (3); Th. des Variétés Amusantes, Comiques et Lyriques (3); Th. du Lycée des Arts (18); Th. du Vaudeville (1); Th. Lyrique des Amis de la Patrie (66); **Total: 150.**

_____. *Trois voisins, Les* [*Comédie* in 1 act, Prem. on 9-7-1799].
Th. du Palais (Cité)-Variétés (11); **Total: 11.**

_____., Devienne, François (comp). *Visitandines, Les* [*Comédie* in 2 acts, Prem. on 7-8-1792, Pub. in 1792].
n/a (9); Th. de l'Odéon (1); Th. de la Rue Martin (1); Th. de Molière (5); Th. des Délassements Comiques (29); Th. du Feydeau (de Monsieur) (233); Th. du Marais (4); Th. du Palais (Cité)-Variétés (1); Th. Lyrique des Amis de la Patrie (3); **Total: 286.**

_____. *Voisins, Les* [*Comédie* in 1 act, Pub. in 1799].
Th. de la Cité (7); Th. du Marais (5); **Total: 12.**

_____. *Voyage interrompu, Le* [*Comédie* in 3 acts, Prem. on 17-11-1798, Pub. in 1802].
Académie de la Musique (Opéra) (1); Th. de l'Odéon (28); Th. de la Cité (2); Th. des Italiens (Opéra-Comique) (1); Th. du Marais (3); Th. du Palais (Cité)-Variétés (8); Th. Lyrique des Amis de la Patrie (1); **Total: 44.**

_____., Duval, Alexandre-V.-P. *Vraie bravoure, La* [*Comédie* in 1 act, Prem. on 3-12-1793, Pub. in 1793].
Th. Français (de la rue Richelieu) (de la République) (25); **Total: 25.**
Total Performances, Picard, Louis-B.: **1004**

Piccinni, Joseph-M., Piccinni, Niccolò (comp). *Faux lord, Le* [*Opéra-Comique* in 2 acts, Prem. on 5-12-1783, Pub. in 1783].
Th. de la Citoyenne Montansier (7); **Total: 7.**

Picot-Belloc, Jean. *Père comme il y en a peu, Le, ou Le Mariage assorti* [*Comédie* in 3 acts, Pub. in 1797].
Th. de l'Emulation (Gaîté) (3); Th. Lyrique des Amis de la Patrie (1); **Total: 4.**

Picot-Clainville. *Dangers de la calomnie, Les* [N/A].
Th. du Lycée des Arts (2); **Total: 2.**

Pieyre, Alexandre. *Ecole des pères, L'* [*Comédie* in 5 acts, Prem. on 1-6-1787, Pub. in 1788].
Th. de l'Odéon (3); Th. de la Nation (Comédie Française) (17); Th. du Feydeau (de Monsieur) (3); Th. du Marais (2); Th. Français (de la rue Richelieu) (de la République) (15); **Total: 40.**

Pigault-Lebrun, Charles-A.P. de L'Epinoy, dit. *Amour et la raison, L'*
[*Comédie* in 1 act, Prem. on 30-10-1790, Pub. in 1791].
> Maison Egalité (**3**); n/a (**2**); Th. de l'Ambigu Comique (**1**); Th. de la Cité
> (**1**); Th. de Molière (**6**); Th. du Feydeau (de Monsieur) (**10**); Th. du Marais
> (**4**); Th. du Palais (Cité)-Variétés (**31**); Th. du Palais Royal (**19**); Th.
> Français (de la rue Richelieu) (de la République) (**12**); **Total: 89.**

_____. *Charles et Caroline ou Les Abus de l'Ancien Régime* [*Comédie* in
5 acts, Prem. on 28-6-1790, Pub. in 1790].
> Th. de Molière (**3**); Th. des Victoires (**2**); Th. des Victoires Nationales (**5**);
> Th. du Feydeau (de Monsieur) (**1**); Th. du Marais (**1**); Th. du Palais
> (Cité)-Variétés (**2**); Th. du Palais Royal (**20**); Th. Français (de la rue
> Richelieu) (de la République) (**48**); **Total: 82.**

_____. *Claudine de Florian* [*Comédie* in 3 acts, Prem. on 15-7-1797, Pub. in
1804].
> Th. de la Citoyenne Montansier (**15**); **Total: 15.**

_____. *Contretemps sur contretemps* [*Comédie* in 3 acts, Prem. on 23-10-
1792].
> Maison Egalité (**5**); Th. de l'Ambigu Comique (**4**); Th. de la Cité (**9**); Th.
> du Palais (Cité)-Variétés (**25**); **Total: 43.**

_____. *Cordonnier de Damas, Le, ou La Lanterne magique* [*Pièce* in 3
acts, Prem. on 13-1-1798].
> Th. de la Cité (**17**); **Total: 17.**

_____. *Dragons en cantonnement, Les* [*Comédie* in 1 act, Prem. on 13-2-
1794, Pub. in 1794].
> Maison Egalité (**16**); Th. de la Citoyenne Montansier (**1**); Th. de la Cité
> (**12**); Th. des Variétés Amusantes, Comiques et Lyriques (**10**); Th. du
> Palais (Cité)-Variétés (**77**); **Total: 116.**

_____. *Dragons et les bénédictines, Les* [*Comédie* in 1 act, Prem. on 6-2-
1794, Pub. in 1794].
> Maison Egalité (**15**); Th. de la Citoyenne Montansier (**1**); Th. de la Cité
> (**14**); Th. des Variétés Amusantes, Comiques et Lyriques (**11**); Th. du
> Palais (Cité)-Variétés (**102**); **Total: 143.**

_____. *Empiriques, Les* [*Comédie* in 3 acts, Prem. on 21-12-1794, Pub. in 1795].
> Maison Egalité (**1**); Th. du Palais (Cité)-Variétés (**2**); **Total: 3.**

_____. *Esprit follet, L', ou Le Cabaret des Pyrénées* [*Comédie* in 1 act,
Pub. in 1796].
> Th. de la Citoyenne Montansier (**2**); Th. de la Cité (**28**); **Total: 30.**

_____. *Jaloux corrigé, Le* [*Comédie* in 1 act, Prem. on 28-6-1788, Pub. in 1788].
> Th. du Palais Royal (**7**); **Total: 7.**

_____. *Joueuse, La* [*Drame* in 3 acts, Prem. on 17-6-1789, Pub. in 1789].
> Th. du Palais (Cité)-Variétés (**2**); Th. du Palais Royal (**30**); Th. Français
> (de la rue Richelieu) (de la République) (**3**); **Total: 35.**

_____. *Journée du 9 thermidor, La, ou La Chute du tyran* [*Drame* in 2
acts, Prem. on 4-9-1794, Pub. in 1794].
> Th. du Palais (Cité)-Variétés (**6**); **Total: 6.**

_____., **Bruni, Antonio-B. (comp).** *Major Palmer, Le* [*Drame* in 3 acts,
Prem. on 26-1-1797, Pub. in 1797].
> Th. de l'Odéon (**1**); Th. du Feydeau (de Monsieur) (**38**); **Total: 39.**

_____. *Marchand provençal, Le* [*Comédie* in 2 acts, Prem. on 4-1-1790, Pub. in
1789].
> Th. du Palais Royal (**34**); Th. Français (de la rue Richelieu) (de la
> République) (**16**); **Total: 50.**

_____. *Mère rivale, La* [*Comédie* in 1 act, Prem. on 1-10-1791, Pub. in 1791].
Maison Egalité (1); Th. de la Cité (2); Th. des Variétés Amusantes, Comiques et Lyriques (6); Th. du Palais (Cité)-Variétés (28); Th. Français (de la rue Richelieu) (de la République) (6); **Total: 43.**

_____. *Orphelin, L'* [*Comédie* in 3 acts, Prem. on 20-5-1794, Pub. in 1794].
Maison Egalité (2); Th. de la Cité (4); Th. du Palais (Cité)-Variétés (38); **Total: 44.**

_____. *Orpheline, L'* [*Comédie* in 3 acts, Prem. on 4-8-1789, Pub. in 1791].
Th. du Palais (Cité)-Variétés (20); Th. du Palais Royal (33); Th. Français (de la rue Richelieu) (de la République) (3); **Total: 56.**

_____. *Pessimiste, Le, ou L'Homme mécontent de tout* [*Comédie* in 1 act, Prem. on 21-3-1789, Pub. in 1789].
Maison Egalité (2); Th. de l'Emulation (Gaîté) (27); Th. des Variétés Amusantes, Comiques et Lyriques (7); Th. du Palais (Cité)-Variétés (16); Th. du Palais Royal (38); Th. Français (de la rue Richelieu) (de la République) (4); Th. Lyrique des Amis de la Patrie (2); **Total: 96.**

_____., Gaveaux, Pierre (comp). *Petit matelot, Le, ou Le Mariage impromptu* [*Comédie* in 1 act, Prem. on 18-12-1795, Pub. in 1796].
n/a (1); Th. de l'Ambigu Comique (1); Th. de l'Emulation (Gaîté) (1); Th. de la Rue Martin (1); Th. de Molière (6); Th. du Feydeau (de Monsieur) (73); Th. du Mareux (1); **Total: 84.**

_____. *Rivaux d'eux-mêmes, Les* [*Comédie* in 1 act, Prem. on 9-8-1798].
Th. de Molière (1); Th. du Palais (Cité)-Variétés (44); **Total: 45.**

_____., Bruni, Antonio-B. (comp). *Sabotiers, Les* [*Comédie* in 1 act, Prem. on 23-6-1796, Pub. in 1796].
Maison Egalité (1); Th. de l'Emulation (Gaîté) (27); Th. de la Citoyenne Montansier (5); Th. de Molière (10); Th. des Grands Danseurs (Gaîté) (2); Th. des Ombres Chinoises (2); Th. des Variétés Amusantes, Comiques et Lyriques (8); Th. du Feydeau (de Monsieur) (8); Th. du Marais (1); Th. du Palais (Cité)-Variétés (11); **Total: 75.**

Total Performances, Pigault-Lebrun, Charles-A.P. de L'Epinoy, dit: **1118**

Piis, Chevalier P.-A.-A. de., Barré, Pierre-Y. *Deux Panthéons, Les, ou L'Inauguration du Théâtre du Vaudeville* [*Comédie* in 3 acts, Prem. on 12-1-1792].
Th. du Vaudeville (15); **Total: 15.**

_____., Propriac, Catherine-J.-F.-G. de (comp). *Fausse paysanne, La, ou L'Heureuse inconséquence* [*Comédie* in 3 acts, Prem. on 26-3-1789, Pub. in 1789].
Th. des Italiens (Opéra-Comique) (15); **Total: 15.**

_____. *Limosins, Les* [*Opéra-Comique* in 1 act, Prem. on 28-3-1792].
Th. du Vaudeville (10); **Total: 10.**

_____., Barré, Pierre-Y. *Nourrice républicaine, La* [*Comédie* in 1 act, Prem. on 25-3-1794, Pub. in 1794].
Th. du Vaudeville (37); **Total: 37.**

_____. *Plaisirs de l'hospitalité, Les* [*Opéra-Comique* in 1 act, Prem. on 13-11-1794, Pub. in 1794].
Th. du Vaudeville (95); **Total: 95.**

_____. *Saint déniché, Le, ou La Saint-Nicolas d'été* [*Comédie* in 2 acts, Prem. on 28-12-1792, Pub. in 1793].
Th. du Vaudeville (2); **Total: 2.**

_____., Propriac, Catherine-J.-F.-G. de (comp). *Savoyards, Les, ou La Continence de Bayard* [*Comédie* in 1 act, Prem. on 30-5-1789, Pub. in 1789].
> Th. des Italiens (Opéra-Comique) (**8**); **Total: 8.**

_____. *Seigneur d'à présent, Le* [*Comédie* in 1 act, Prem. on 25-8-1790].
> Th. Français, Comique et Lyrique (**18**); **Total: 18.**

_____. *Solitaires de Normandie, Les* [*Opéra-Comique* in 1 act, Prem. on 15-1-1788, Pub. in 1788].
> Th. des Italiens (Opéra-Comique) (**20**); Th. du Vaudeville (**25**); **Total: 45.**

_____., Barré, Pierre-Y. *Suite des solitaires de Normandie, La* [*Opéra-Comique* in 1 act, Prem. on 4-5-1790].
> Th. des Italiens (Opéra-Comique) (**4**); **Total: 4.**

_____., Propriac, Catherine-J.-F.-G. de (comp). *Trois déesses rivales, Les, ou Le Double jugement de Pâris* [*Divertissement/parade* in 1 act, Prem. on 28-7-1788, Pub. in 1788].
> Th. des Italiens (Opéra-Comique) (**5**); **Total: 5.**

_____., Desfontaines, François-G. Fouques, dit., Barré, Pierre-Y., Radet, Jean-B. *Vallée de Montmorency, La, ou Jean-Jacques Rousseau à l'hermitage* [*Opéra-Comique* in 3 acts, Prem. on 11-6-1798, Pub. in 1798].
> Th. du Vaudeville (**32**); **Total: 32.**
>   **Total Performances**, Piis, Chevalier P.-A.-A. de: **286**

Pilhes, André-F. de., Austin. *Curieux puni, Le* [*Comédie* in 1 act, Prem. on 24-1-1793].
> Th. du Lycée au Palais Egalité (**1**); **Total: 1.**

Pilhes, Joseph. *Bienfait anonyme, Le* [*Comédie* in 4 acts, Prem. on 6-10-1783, Pub. in 1785].
> Th. de la Nation (Comédie Française) (**19**); Th. de la Rue Martin (**1**); Th. du Feydeau (de Monsieur) (**5**); Th. du Marais (**1**); Th. Français (de la rue Richelieu) (de la République) (**4**); Th. National (de la rue Richelieu) (**7**); **Total: 37.**

Pillet, F., Ladurner, Ignaz.-A. (comp). *Wenzel ou Le Magistrat du peuple* [*Comédie*, Prem. on 10-4-1794, Pub. in 1794].
> Th. National (de la rue Richelieu) (**8**); **Total: 8.**

Piron, Alexis. *Ecole des pères, L'* [*Comédie* in 5 acts, Pub. in 1728].
> Th. National (de la rue Richelieu) (**10**); **Total: 10.**

_____. *Fernand Cortez* [*Tragédie* in 5 acts, Prem. on 8-1-1744, Pub. in 1757].
> Th. Français, Comique et Lyrique (**13**); **Total: 13.**

_____. *Fils ingrats, Les* [*Comédie* in 5 acts, Prem. on 10-10-1728, Pub. in 1729].
> Th. de la Nation (Comédie Française) (**3**); **Total: 3.**

_____. *Gustave Wasa* [*Tragédie* in 5 acts, Prem. on 3-2-1733, Pub. in 1733].
> Th. de la Nation (Comédie Française) (**5**); **Total: 5.**

_____. *Métromanie, La, ou Le Poète* [*Comédie* in 5 acts, Prem. on 10-1-1738, Pub. in 1738].
> Th. de l'Estrapade au Panthéon (**2**); Th. de l'Odéon (**6**); Th. de la Citoyenne Montansier (**2**); Th. de la Liberté (**1**); Th. de la Nation (Comédie Française) (**19**); Th. de la Rue Martin (**5**); Th. de Molière (**3**); Th. du Feydeau (de Monsieur) (**5**); Th. du Lycée des Arts (**1**); Th. du Marais (**9**); Th. Français (de la rue Richelieu) (de la République) (**40**); Th. Français, Comique et Lyrique (**6**); Th. Lyrique des Amis de la Patrie (**2**); Th. National (de la rue Richelieu) (**7**); **Total: 108.**

_____. *Roze, La, ou Les Festes de l'hymen* [*Opéra-Comique* in 1 act, Prem. on 8-3-1752, Pub. in 1754].
> Th. de l'Emulation (Gaîté) (**4**); Th. des Grands Danseurs (Gaîté) (**4**); **Total: 8.**
> > **Total Performances**, Piron, Alexis: **147**

Pitrot, Antoine. *Brouetteur italien, Le* [*Ballet*, Prem. in 6-1762, Pub. in 1762].
> Th. des Grands Danseurs (Gaîté) (**2**); **Total: 2.**

Pixerécourt, see Guilbert de Pixerécourt, René-.C.

Placide, Alexandre-P. Bussart, dit. *Amours de Nicodème et du bûcheron, Les* [*Pantomime* in 1 act, Prem. on 25-1-1781].
> Th. des Grands Danseurs (Gaîté) (**14**); **Total: 14.**

_____. *Arlequin dogue d'Angleterre* [*Pantomime* in 2 acts, Prem. in 1772].
> Th. des Grands Danseurs (Gaîté) (**56**); Th. des Variétés Amusantes, Comiques et Lyriques (**1**); **Total: 57.**

_____. *Arlequin péruvien, L'* [*Pantomime* in 5 acts, Prem. in 1772].
> Th. des Grands Danseurs (Gaîté) (**1**); **Total: 1.**

_____. *Colombine invisible* [*Pantomime*, Pub. in 1770].
> Th. des Grands Danseurs (Gaîté) (**44**); **Total: 44.**

_____. *Enrôlement du bûcheron, L', ou Le Recruteur* [*Pantomime* in 2 acts, Prem. on 13-9-1781].
> Th. des Grands Danseurs (Gaîté) (**80**); **Total: 80.**

_____. *Fragments, Les, ou Le Malade jaloux* [*Pantomime* in 1 act, Prem. on 17-9-1779].
> Th. des Grands Danseurs (Gaîté) (**55**); Th. des Variétés Amusantes (Lazzari) (**1**); Th. des Variétés Amusantes, Comiques et Lyriques (**6**); Tivoli (**2**); **Total: 64.**
> > **Total Performances**, Placide, Alexandre-P. Bussart, dit: **260**

Plancher de Valcour, dit Aristide. *A Bon vin point d'enseigne* [*Proverbe/allégorique* in 1 act, Prem. on 2-4-1781, Pub. in 1781].
> Th. des Variétés Amusantes, Comiques et Lyriques (**5**); **Total: 5.**

_____. *Brave Thénard, Le, ou Le Soldat de la liberté* [*Tableau-Patriotique*, Prem. on 28-5-1792].
> Th. de Molière (**8**); **Total: 8.**

_____. *Campagnard révolutionnaire, Le* [*Comédie* in 2 acts].
> Th. de la Montagne (**8**); **Total: 8.**

_____. *Charles et Victoire ou Les Amants de Plailly* [*Comédie*, Prem. on 18-10-1793].
> Th. du Palais (Cité)-Variétés (**15**); **Total: 15.**

_____., Destival de Brabant. *Débarquement de la Sainte Famille à Alger, Le* [*Tableau-Patriotique*, Prem. on 9-5-1792].
> Th. de Molière (**16**); **Total: 16.**

_____. *Discipline républicaine, La* [*Fait Historique*, Prem. on 20-4-1794].
> Th. des Italiens (Opéra-Comique) (**15**); **Total: 15.**

_____. *Homme à la minute, L', ou Le Petit cousin* [*Opéra-Comique*].
> Th. des Grands Danseurs (Gaîté) (**10**); **Total: 10.**

_____. *Mariage du curé, Le* [*Opéra* in 2 acts, Prem. on 25-12-1791].
> Th. des Variétés Amusantes, Comiques et Lyriques (**17**); **Total: 17.**

_____., Foignet, Charles-G. (comp). *Petits montagnards, Les* [*Opéra-Bouffe* in 3 acts, Prem. on 17-1-1794, Pub. in 1794].
 Maison Egalité (4); Th. de la Cité (1); Th. du Palais (Cité)-Variétés (29); **Total: 34.**

_____. *Piques, Les* [*Opéra* in 2 acts, Prem. on 7-3-1792].
 Th. des Variétés Amusantes, Comiques et Lyriques (11); **Total: 11.**

_____. *Pourquoi pas ou Le Roturier parvenu* [*Comédie* in 1 act, Prem. on 7-11-1781, Pub. in 1780].
 Th. de l'Emulation (Gaîté) (1); Th. des Grands Danseurs (Gaîté) (14); **Total: 15.**

_____. *Premier coup de canon aux frontières, Le* [In 2 acts, Prem. on 26-1-1792].
 Th. des Variétés Amusantes, Comiques et Lyriques (19); **Total: 19.**

_____. *Talismans, Les* [*Comédie* in 1 act, Prem. on 30-8-1778].
 Th. Lyrique des Amis de la Patrie (7); **Total: 7.**

_____. *Vous et le toi, Le* [*Vaudeville* in 1 act, Prem. on 29-11-1793, Pub. in 1794].
 Th. de la Cité (1); Th. du Palais (Cité)-Variétés (37); **Total: 38.**
 Total Performances, Plancher de Valcour, dit Aristide: **218**

Planterre, Barthélemy., Loise (comp). *Agnès de Châtillon ou Le Siège de Saint-Jean d'Acre* [*Opéra* in 3 acts, Prem. on 12-5-1792, Pub. in 1792].
 Th. Lyrique des Amis de la Patrie (38); **Total: 38.**

_____., Jadin, Louis-E. (comp). *Bons voisins, Les* [*Opéra-Comique*, Prem. on 1-11-1797].
 Th. du Feydeau (de Monsieur) (1); **Total: 1.**

_____., Gaveaux, Pierre (comp). *Deux hermites, Les* [*Opéra* in 1 act, Prem. on 20-4-1793].
 Th. de l'Emulation (Gaîté) (1); Th. de l'Odéon (1); Th. des Italiens (Opéra-Comique) (1); Th. du Feydeau (de Monsieur) (91); **Total: 94.**

_____., Gaveaux, Pierre (comp). *Famille indigente, La* [*Fait Historique* in 1 act, Prem. on 24-3-1794, Pub. in 1794].
 n/a (1); Th. de l'Odéon (3); Th. des Grands Danseurs (Gaîté) (1); Th. du Feydeau (de Monsieur) (100); **Total: 105.**

_____., Desvignes (comp). *Fête de l'égalité, La* [*Mélodrame* in 1 act, Prem. on 14-11-1793, Pub. in 1794].
 Th. du Palais (Cité)-Variétés (18); Th. du Vaudeville (3); **Total: 21.**

_____. *Jour de l'an, Le, ou Les Etrennes* [*Comédie* in 1 act, Pub. in 1779].
 Th. du Palais Royal (6); **Total: 6.**

_____. *Midas au Parnasse* [*Opéra* in 1 act, Prem. on 7-1-1793, Pub. in 1793].
 Th. de la Cité (1); Th. du Palais (Cité)-Variétés (18); **Total: 19.**
 Total Performances, Planterre, Barthélemy: **284**

Plaute, Marcus-A. *Captifs, Les* [*Comédie* in 5 acts, Prem. on 16-1-1789, Pub. in 1666].
 Th. de l'Ambigu Comique (40); **Total: 40.**

Pleinchesne, Roger-T.-R. de. *Fameux siège, Le, ou La Pucelle d'Orléans* [*Pantomime* in 3 acts, Prem. on 27-12-1729].
 Th. des Grands Danseurs (Gaîté) (62); **Total: 62.**

_____. *Joseph vendu par ses frères* [*Pantomime* in 3 acts, Prem. on 3-11-1791, Pub. in 1779].
 Th. des Grands Danseurs (Gaîté) (12); **Total: 12.**

_____. *Malentendu, Le* [*Comédie* in 3 acts, Prem. on 27-1-1769].
    Th. de l'Ambigu Comique (**3**); **Total: 3.**

_____. *Mariage par exemple, Le, ou Les époux à l'épreuve* [*Comédie*,
Pub. in 1789].
    Th. de l'Ambigu Comique (**1**); **Total: 1.**

_____. *Pouvoir de l'amour, Le* [*Pantomime* in 1 act, Pub. in 1770].
    Th. des Grands Danseurs (Gaîté) (**1**); **Total: 1.**
        Total Performances, Pleinchesne, Roger-T.-R. de: **79**

Poinsinet, Antoine-A.-H. *Cercle, Le, ou La Soirée à la mode* [*Comédie* in
1 act, Prem. on 7-9-1764, Pub. in 1764].
    n/a (**1**); Th. de la Nation (Comédie Française) (**22**); Th. du Feydeau (de
    Monsieur) (**18**); Th. du Marais (**8**); Th. Français (de la rue Richelieu) (de la
    République) (**9**); Th. Patriotique et de Momus (**1**); **Total: 59.**

_____., Philidor, François-A. Danican (comp). *Sorcier, Le* [*Opéra-
Comique* in 2 acts, Prem. on 2-1-1764, Pub. in 1768].
    Th. de l'Ambigu Comique (**17**); Th. de Molière (**4**); Th. des Italiens
    (Opéra-Comique) (**11**); **Total: 32.**

_____., Philidor, André-D. (comp). *Tom Jones* [*Comédie* in 3 acts, Prem. on
27-2-1765, Pub. in 1765].
    Th. de Molière (**2**); Th. des Italiens (Opéra-Comique) (**3**); **Total: 5.**
        Total Performances, Poinsinet, Antoine-A.-H.: **96**

Poinsinet de Sivry, Louis. *Briséis ou La Colère d'Achille* [*Tragédie* in 5
acts, Prem. on 25-6-1759, Pub. in 1763].
    Th. de l'Odéon (**14**); Th. de la Nation (Comédie Française) (**1**); Th. des
    Ombres de J.-J. Rousseau (**2**); Th. du Marais (**1**); Th. Français (de la rue
    Richelieu) (de la République) (**4**); Th. Lyrique des Amis de la Patrie (**2**);
    Total: 24.

Poisson, Philippe. *Impromptu de campagne, L'* [*Comédie* in 1 act, Prem. in
1733].
    n/a (**1**); Th. de l'Ambigu Comique (**38**); Th. de l'Emulation (Gaîté) (**2**); Th.
    de l'Estrapade au Panthéon (**1**); Th. de la Liberté (**1**); Th. de la Nation
    (Comédie Française) (**6**); Th. de la Rue Antoine (**1**); Th. de la Rue Martin
    (**4**); Th. de Molière (**7**); Th. des Grands Danseurs (Gaîté) (**1**); Th. des
    Variétés Amusantes, Comiques et Lyriques (**7**); Th. des Victoires (**3**); Th.
    du Lycée Dramatique (**5**); Th. du Marais (**13**); Th. Français (de la rue
    Richelieu) (de la République) (**19**); Th. Lyrique des Amis de la Patrie (**1**);
    Total: 110.

_____. *Procureur arbitre, Le* [*Comédie* in 1 act, Prem. on 25-2-1728, Pub. in
1728].
    n/a (**1**); Th. de l'Estrapade au Panthéon (**2**); Th. de la Citoyenne Montan-
    sier (**11**); Th. de la Nation (Comédie Française) (**5**); Th. de la Rue Martin
    (**8**); Th. de Molière (**13**); Th. des Délassements Comiques (**6**); Th. du Fey-
    deau (de Monsieur) (**1**); Th. du Lycée des Arts (**3**); Th. du Marais (**5**); Th.
    Français (de la rue Richelieu) (de la République) (**7**); Th. Lyrique des
    Amis de la Patrie (**10**); Th. Lyrique du Foire St. Germain (**1**); **Total: 73.**

_____. *Ruses d'amour, Les* [*Comédie* in 3 acts, Prem. on 30-4-1736, Pub. in
1736].
    Th. de la Rue Martin (**1**); Th. des Jeunes Artistes (**92**); Th. du Marais (**3**);
    Total: 96.
        Total Performances, Poisson, Philippe: **279**

Poisson, Raymond. *Fou raisonnable, Le* [*Comédie* in 1 act, Pub. in 1664].
　　Th. de l'Emulation (Gaîté) (**2**); Th. de la Citoyenne Montansier (**46**); Th.
　　de la Cité (**2**); Th. de la Rue Martin (**1**); Th. du Lycée des Arts (**7**); Th.
　　Français (de la rue Richelieu) (de la République) (**4**); Th. Lyrique des
　　Amis de la Patrie (**10**); **Total: 72.**

Pompigny, Maurin de. *Artisan philosophe, L', ou L'Ecole des pères*
　[*Comédie* in 1 act, Prem. on 17-12-1787, Pub. in 1788].
　　Th. de l'Ambigu Comique (**160**); **Total: 160.**

_____. *Barogo ou La Suite du Ramoneur prince* [*Comédie* in 2 acts, Prem.
　on 24-7-1785, Pub. in 1786].
　　Th. de la Citoyenne Montansier (**92**); Th. de la Montagne (**1**); Th. des Om-
　　bres Chinoises (**4**); Th. du Palais Royal (**11**); Th. Lyrique des Amis de la
　　Patrie (**9**); **Total: 117.**

_____. *Bon valet, Le, ou Il était temps* [*Comédie* in 1 act, Prem. on 3-11-1790,
　Pub. in 1784].
　　Th. de l'Emulation (Gaîté) (**9**); Th. de la Citoyenne Montansier (**29**); Th.
　　des Grands Danseurs (Gaîté) (**31**); Th. du Palais Royal (**5**); **Total: 74.**

_____. *Bonne soeur, La, ou Elle en avait besoin* [*Comédie* in 2 acts, Prem.
　on 17-12-1789, Pub. in 1790].
　　Th. de l'Ambigu Comique (**27**); Th. des Variétés Amusantes (Lazzari) (**9**);
　　Th. des Variétés Amusantes, Comiques et Lyriques (**2**); **Total: 38.**

_____. *Comminges ou Les Amants malheureux* [*Pantomime*, Pub. in 1790].
　　Th. des Délassements Comiques (**3**); Th. du Feydeau (de Monsieur) (**3**);
　　Th. du Marais (**1**); **Total: 7.**

_____. *Epoux républicain, L'* [*Drame* in 2 acts, Prem. on 14-2-1794, Pub. in
　1794].
　　Th. du Palais (Cité)-Variétés (**21**); **Total: 21.**

_____., Foignet, Charles-G. (comp). *Franc marin, Le, ou La Gageure
　indiscrète* [*Comédie* in 2 acts, Prem. on 3-12-1795, Pub. in 1796].
　　Th. de la Rue Martin (**1**); Th. du Lycée des Arts (**39**); **Total: 40.**

_____., Foignet, Charles-G. (comp). *Gascon tel qu'il est, Le* [*Opéra*,
　Prem. on 10-7-1797].
　　Th. de la Citoyenne Montansier (**8**); **Total: 8.**

_____. *Héritage, L', ou L'Epreuve raisonnable* [*Comédie* in 1 act, Prem. on
　8-7-1789, Pub. in 1788].
　　Th. de l'Ambigu Comique (**195**); **Total: 195.**

_____. *Mari à deux femmes, Le* [*Pantomime* in 1 act, Pub. in 1784].
　　Th. du Palais Royal (**4**); **Total: 4.**

_____. *Mariée de village, La* [*Comédie* in 1 act, Pub. in 1790].
　　Th. de l'Ambigu Comique (**76**); **Total: 76.**

_____. *Mieux fait douceur que violence ou Le Père comme il y en a
　peu* [*Comédie* in 2 acts, Prem. on 24-2-1785, Pub. in 1786].
　　Th. du Palais (Cité)-Variétés (**8**); Th. du Palais Royal (**1**); **Total: 9.**

_____. *Officieux maladroit, L'* [*Tableau-Patriotique*, Pub. in 1795].
　　Th. Français (de la rue Richelieu) (de la République) (**2**); **Total: 2.**

_____. *Parents supposés, Les* [*Comédie*, Prem. on 8-8-1799].
　　Th. de la Citoyenne Montansier (**1**); **Total: 1.**

_____. *Pontignac ou A femme adroite homme rusé* [*Comédie* in 2 acts,
　Prem. on 26-12-1796, Pub. in 1797].
　　Th. de l'Emulation (Gaîté) (**8**); **Total: 8.**

_____., Gouges, Marie Gouze, dite Olympe de. *Prélat d'autrefois, Le, ou St. Elme et Sophie* [*Comédie* in 3 acts, Prem. on 18-3-1794, Pub. in 1795].
>Maison Egalité (1); Th. de la Cité (1); Th. du Palais (Cité)-Variétés (18); **Total: 20.**

_____. *Ramoneur prince et le prince Ramoneur, Le* [*Comédie* in 1 act, Prem. on 11-12-1784, Pub. in 1785].
>Th. de la Citoyenne Montansier (28); Th. de la Cité (1); Th. du Palais Royal (8); **Total: 37.**

_____. *Ruse inutile, La* [*Comédie* in 1 act, Prem. on 28-10-1783, Pub. in 1784].
>Th. du Mareux (1); **Total: 1.**
>**Total Performances**, Pompigny, Maurin de: **818**

Pont de Veyle, A. de Feriol, Comte de. *Fat puni, Le* [*Comédie* in 1 act, Prem. on 7-4-1738, Pub. in 1738].
>Th. du Lycée des Arts (1); Th. du Marais (1); **Total: 2.**

_____. *Somnambule, Le* [*Comédie* in 1 act, Prem. on 19-1-1739, Pub. in 1739].
>n/a (1); Th. de l'Estrapade au Panthéon (1); Th. de l'Odéon (4); Th. de la Citoyenne Montansier (10); Th. de la Cité (12); Th. de la Nation (Comédie Française) (19); Th. de la Rue Martin (2); Th. de Molière (7); Th. des Victoires (7); Th. du Feydeau (de Monsieur) (7); Th. du Lycée Dramatique (6); Th. du Marais (1); Th. du Vaudeville (6); Th. Français (de la rue Richelieu) (de la République) (26); Th. Lyrique des Amis de la Patrie (8); Th. National (de la rue Richelieu) (1); Th. Patriotique et de Momus (4); **Total: 122.**
>**Total Performances**, Pont-De-Veyle, A. de Feriol, Comte de: **124**

Pontaud. *Double prévention, La* [*Comédie* in 3 acts, Prem. on 28-5-1789].
>Th. du Palais Royal (22); **Total: 22.**

_____. *Faux billets doux, Les, ou Les Trahisons réciproques* [*Comédie* in 1 act, Pub. in 1787].
>Th. de l'Ambigu Comique (3); **Total: 3.**
>**Total Performances**, Pontaud: **25**

Ponte, Lorenzo., Martin y Soler, Vincente (comp). *Una Cosa rara, o Sia bellezza ed onesta* [*Opéra*, Prem. on 17-5-1781].
>Th. du Feydeau (de Monsieur) (21); **Total: 21.**

Ponteuil, Triboulet, J.B., dit. *Ecole des frères, L', ou L'Incertitude paternelle* [*Comédie* in 2 acts, Prem. on 26-8-1790].
>Th. du Palais Royal (8); **Total: 8.**

_____. *Hôtel prussien, L'* [*Comédie* in 5 acts, Prem. on 14-9-1791].
>Th. du Feydeau (de Monsieur) (2); **Total: 2.**

_____., Bruni, Antonio-B. (comp). *Mort imaginaire, Le* [*Opéra-Comique* in 2 acts, Prem. on 27-4-1790, Pub. in 1751].
>Th. de la Citoyenne Montansier (32); Th. du Marais (9); **Total: 41.**
>**Total Performances**, Ponteuil, Triboulet, J.B., dit: **51**

Poultier d'Elmotte, François-M., Bruni, Antonio-B. (comp). *Galathée* [*Mélodrame*, Prem. on 1-2-1795, Pub. in 1795].
>Th. Français (de la rue Richelieu) (de la République) (2); **Total: 2.**

Prévost de St.-Lucien, Roch-H. *Arlequin aux enfers ou L'Enlèvement de Colombine* [*Comédie* in 1 act, Pub. in 1760].
>Th. des Grands Danseurs (Gaîté) (4); **Total: 4.**

Prévost, Abbé A.F. *Tout pour l'amour ou Le Monde bien perdu* [*Tragédie* in 5 acts, Pub. in 1735].
>Th. des Italiens (Opéra-Comique) (2); **Total: 2.**

Prévost, Augustin. *Cadet Roussel* [*Comédie* in 1 act, Prem. in 1784, Pub. in 1801].
>   Th. de l'Estrapade au Panthéon (1); Th. de la Citoyenne Montansier (1); Th. de la Cité (39); Th. du Vaudeville (1); Th. Patriotique et de Momus (17); **Total: 59.**

_____. *Ribotte le savetier* [*Comédie* in 2 acts, Pub. in 1802].
>   Th. de l'Estrapade au Panthéon (1); Th. des Grands Danseurs (Gaîté) (5); **Total: 6.**

_____. *Victor ou L'Enfant de la forêt* [*Mélodrame* in 3 acts, Prem. on 10-6-1798, Pub. in 1798].
>   Th. des Jeunes Artistes (1); Th. du Marais (1); **Total: 2.**
>   **Total Performances**, Prévost, Augustin: **67**

Prévost-Montfort, P., Arquier, Joseph (comp). *Bon ermite, Le* [In 1 act, Prem. on 2-5-1793, Pub. in 1794].
>   Th. du Palais (Cité)-Variétés (48); **Total: 48.**

_____. *Esprit des prêtres, L', ou La Persécution des Français en Espagne* [*Drame* in 3 acts].
>   Th. du Palais (Cité)-Variétés (7); **Total: 7.**

_____. *Soeurs du pot, Les, ou Double rendez-vous* [*Comédie* in 1 act, Prem. on 30-9-1792, Pub. in 1792].
>   Th. de l'Ambigu Comique (68); **Total: 68.**
>   **Total Performances**, Prévost-Montfort, P.: **123**

Prevot d'Ivrai, Tardu (comp). *Aurore de Gusman, L'* [*Opéra* in 1 act, Prem. on 24-10-1799].
>   Th. du Feydeau (de Monsieur) (6); **Total: 6.**

Pujoulx, Jean-B. *Anti-célibataire, L', ou Les Mariages* [*Comédie* in 3 acts, Prem. on 5-6-1790].
>   Th. des Grands Danseurs (Gaîté) (3); **Total: 3.**

_____., Bruni, Antonio-B. (comp). *Cadichon ou Les Bohémiennes* [*Comédie* in 1 act, Prem. on 12-3-1792, Pub. in 1795].
>   Th. du Feydeau (de Monsieur) (60); **Total: 60.**

_____. *Dangers de l'absence, Les, ou Le Souper de famille* [*Comédie* in 2 acts, Prem. on 11-11-1788, Pub. in 1789].
>   Th. des Italiens (Opéra-Comique) (41); Th. du Vaudeville (3); **Total: 44.**

_____. *Dangers de l'ivresse ou Philippe, Les* [*Comédie* in 1 act, Prem. on 24-5-1794].
>   Th. Français (de la rue Richelieu) (de la République) (5); **Total: 5.**

_____., Gaveaux, Pierre (comp). *Deux jockeys, Les* [In 2 acts, Prem. on 17-1-1799].
>   Th. du Feydeau (de Monsieur) (2); **Total: 2.**

_____., Devienne, François (comp). *Ecole des parvenus, L', ou La Suite des deux petits Savoyards* [*Comédie* in 1 act, Prem. on 11-10-1789].
>   Th. des Italiens (Opéra-Comique) (4); **Total: 4.**

_____., Devienne, François (comp). *Encore des Savoyards ou L'Ecole des parvenus* [*Opéra-Comique* in 1 act, Prem. on 8-2-1792].
>   Th. des Italiens (Opéra-Comique) (27); **Total: 27.**

_____. *Mirabeau à son lit de mort* [*Fait Historique* in 1 act, Prem. on 24-5-1791].
>   Th. du Feydeau (de Monsieur) (10); **Total: 10.**

_____. *Modernes enrichis, Les* [*Comédie* in 3 acts, Prem. on 16-12-1797, Pub. in 1798].
>> Th. du Vaudeville (3); Th. Français (de la rue Richelieu) (de la République) (24); **Total: 27.**

_____. *Montagnards, Les, ou L'Ecole de la bienfaisance* [*Comédie* in 1 act, Prem. on 2-9-1794, Pub. in 1794].
>> Th. des Italiens (Opéra-Comique) (1); Th. du Feydeau (de Monsieur) (16); **Total: 17.**

_____., Gaveaux, Pierre (comp). *Noms supposés, Les* [*Comédie* in 2 acts, Prem. on 6-12-1798].
>> Th. du Feydeau (de Monsieur) (10); **Total: 10.**

_____., Bruni, Antonio-B. (comp). *Rencontre en voyage, La* [*Opéra* in 1 act, Prem. on 28-4-1798, Pub. in 1797].
>> Th. du Feydeau (de Monsieur) (41); **Total: 41.**

_____., Berton, Henri-M. (comp). *Rendez-vous supposé, Le, ou Le Souper de famille* [*Comédie* in 2 acts, Prem. on 5-8-1798, Pub. in 1798].
>> Th. des Italiens (Opéra-Comique) (8); **Total: 8.**

_____. *Veuve Calas à Paris, La* [*Comédie* in 1 act, Prem. on 31-7-1791, Pub. in 1791].
>> Th. des Italiens (Opéra-Comique) (6); Th. du Marais (4); **Total: 10.**
>> **Total Performances**, Pujoulx, Jean-B.: **268**

Puységur, Amand-M.-J. de Chastenet, Marquis de., Fay, Etienne (comp). *Intérieur d'un ménage républicain, L'* [*Opéra-Comique* in 1 act, Prem. on 4-1-1794, Pub. in 1794].
>> Th. des Italiens (Opéra-Comique) (46); **Total: 46.**

_____. *Juge bienfaisant, Le* [*Comédie* in 3 acts, Prem. on 15-10-1799].
>> Th. du Feydeau (de Monsieur) (1); Th. du Marais (5); **Total: 6.**

_____. *Paul et Philippe ou La Suite de l'intérieur d'un ménage républicain* [*Vaudeville*, Pub. in 1795].
>> Th. des Variétés Amusantes, Comiques et Lyriques (1); Th. du Vaudeville (3); **Total: 4.**
>> **Total Performances**, Puységur, Amand-M.-J. de Chastenet, Marquis de: **56**

Quétant, Antoine-F. *Ecolier devenu maître, L', ou Le Pédant joue* [*Comédie* in 3 acts, Prem. on 6-11-1767, Pub. in 1768].
>> Th. de l'Emulation (Gaîté) (1); Th. des Grands Danseurs (Gaîté) (1); **Total: 2.**

_____., Vachon, Pierre (comp). *Femmes et le secret, Les* [*Comédie* in 1 act, Prem. on 9-11-1767, Pub. in 1768].
>> Th. de la Citoyenne Montansier (21); Th. de la Montagne (8); Th. des Italiens (Opéra-Comique) (2); **Total: 31.**

_____., Philidor, François-A. Danican (comp). *Maréchal Ferrant, Le* [*Opéra-Comique* in 1 act, Prem. on 22-8-1761, Pub. in 1761].
>> Th. des Enfans Comiques (1); Th. des Italiens (Opéra-Comique) (20); Th. du Vaudeville (1); **Total: 22.**

_____. *Quiproquo de l'hôtellerie, Le* [*Comédie* in 2 acts, Prem. on 8-5-1779, Pub. in 1779].
>> Th. des Grands Danseurs (Gaîté) (60); **Total: 60.**

_____. *Savetier et le financier, Le, ou Contentement passe richesse* [*Parodie*, Pub. in 1779].
>> Th. du Vaudeville (46); **Total: 46.**
>> **Total Performances**, Quétant, Antoine-F.: **161**

Quinault, Philippe., Gluck, Christoph (comp). *Armide* [*Drame-Heroique* in 5 acts, Prem. on 23-9-1777].
    Académie de la Musique (Opéra) (**67**); **Total: 67**.

_____. *Coups de l'amour et de la fortune, Les* [*Comédie* in 3 acts, Pub. in 1655].
    Th. de la Nation (Comédie Française) (**3**); **Total: 3**.

_____. *Pausanias* [*Tragédie* in 5 acts, Pub. in 1669].
    Th. du Feydeau (de Monsieur) (**10**); **Total: 10**.
        Total Performances, Quinault, Philippe: **80**

Quiney, J.S. *Colin-Maillard* [*Parodie* in 2 acts, Prem. in 9-1787, Pub. in 1787].
    Th. du Lycée des Arts (**1**); **Total: 1**.

Racine, Jean. *Andromaque* [*Tragédie* in 5 acts, Prem. in 11-1667, Pub. in 1668].
    n/a (**1**); Th. de l'Odéon (**4**); Th. de la Citoyenne Montansier (**1**); Th. de la Nation (Comédie Française) (**11**); Th. de la Rue Martin (**5**); Th. du Feydeau (de Monsieur) (**4**); Th. du Lycée Dramatique (**3**); Th. du Marais (**2**); Th. Français (de la rue Richelieu) (de la République) (**7**); **Total: 38**.

_____. *Athalie* [*Tragédie* in 5 acts, Prem. on 3-3-1716, Pub. in 1691].
    Th. de la Nation (Comédie Française) (**16**); Th. des Italiens (Opéra-Comique) (**5**); **Total: 21**.

_____. *Bajazet* [*Tragédie* in 5 acts, Pub. in 1672].
    Th. de l'Odéon (**2**); Th. de la Citoyenne Montansier (**2**); Th. de la Nation (Comédie Française) (**12**); Th. Français (de la rue Richelieu) (de la République) (**2**); **Total: 18**.

_____. *Bérénice* [*Tragédie* in 5 acts, Pub. in 1671].
    Th. de la Nation (Comédie Française) (**6**); **Total: 6**.

_____. *Britannicus* [*Tragédie* in 5 acts, Prem. on 15-12-1669, Pub. in 1670].
    n/a (**2**); Th. de l'Odéon (**3**); Th. de la Citoyenne Montansier (**6**); Th. de la Nation (Comédie Française) (**12**); Th. du Feydeau (de Monsieur) (**2**); Th. Français (de la rue Richelieu) (de la République) (**12**); **Total: 37**.

_____. *Iphigénie en Aulide* [*Tragédie* in 5 acts, Prem. on 18-8-1674, Pub. in 1675].
    Th. de l'Odéon (**1**); Th. de la Citoyenne Montansier (**10**); Th. de la Nation (Comédie Française) (**15**); Th. du Feydeau (de Monsieur) (**1**); Th. du Marais (**3**); Th. du Palais (Cité)-Variétés (**1**); Th. Français (de la rue Richelieu) (de la République) (**5**); Th. Lyrique des Amis de la Patrie (**1**); **Total: 37**.

_____. *Mithridate* [*Tragédie*, Pub. in 1673].
    Th. de la Nation (Comédie Française) (**2**); Th. du Lycée Dramatique (**2**); **Total: 4**.

_____. *Phèdre et Hippolyte* [*Tragédie* in 5 acts, Prem. on 1-1-1677, Pub. in 1677].
    Th. de l'Emulation (Gaîté) (**1**); Th. de l'Odéon (**8**); Th. de la Citoyenne Montansier (**14**); Th. de la Liberté (**3**); Th. de la Nation (Comédie Française) (**20**); Th. du Feydeau (de Monsieur) (**4**); Th. du Lycée Dramatique (**2**); Th. du Marais (**3**); Th. Français (de la rue Richelieu) (de la République) (**9**); **Total: 64**.

_____. *Plaideurs, Les* [*Comédie* in 3 acts, Prem. in 11-1668, Pub. in 1669].
    Th. de l'Odéon (**1**); Th. de la Nation (Comédie Française) (**19**); Th. du Feydeau (de Monsieur) (**3**); Th. du Marais (**7**); Th. Français (de la rue Richelieu) (de la République) (**37**); Th. Patriotique et de Momus (**6**); **Total: 73**.
        Total Performances, Racine, Jean: **298**

Radcliffe, Ann. *Mystères d'Udolphe, Les* [Prem. on 4-7-1798].
>Th. de l'Emulation (Gaîté) (**25**); **Total: 25.**

Radet, Jean-B., Desfontaines, François-G. Fouques, dit. *Au retour*
[*Tableau-Patriotique* in 1 act, Prem. on 4-11-1793, Pub. in 1793].
>Th. de l'Ambigu Comique (**54**); Th. de la Montagne (**11**); Th. du Lycée des Arts (**20**); Th. du Vaudeville (**39**); Th. Français, Comique et Lyrique (**2**); **Total: 126.**

_____. *Beaufils ou Le Petit bonhomme vit encore* [*Parodie* in 1 act, Prem. on 7-1-1799].
>Th. du Vaudeville (**4**); **Total: 4.**

_____. *Bonne aubaine, La* [*Comédie* in 1 act, Prem. on 28-1-1793, Pub. in 1793].
>Th. du Palais (Cité)-Variétés (**1**); Th. du Vaudeville (**129**); **Total: 130.**

_____., Champein, Stanislas (comp). *Canonnier convalescent, Le* [*Fait Historique* in 1 act, Prem. on 29-6-1794, Pub. in 1794].
>Th. du Vaudeville (**24**); **Total: 24.**

_____., Madame Kennens. *Dîner au Pré Saint-Gervais, Le* [*Comédie* in 1 act, Prem. on 19-11-1796, Pub. in 1797].
>Th. du Marais (**1**); Th. du Vaudeville (**88**); **Total: 89.**

_____., Desfontaines, François-G. Fouques, dit. *Encore un curé* [*Fait Historique* in 1 act, Prem. on 20-11-1793, Pub. in 1793].
>Th. de la Montagne (**12**); Th. du Vaudeville (**12**); **Total: 24.**

_____. *Faucon, Le* [*Comédie* in 1 act, Prem. on 23-9-1793].
>Th. du Marais (**1**); Th. du Vaudeville (**117**); **Total: 118.**

_____., Desfontaines, François-G. Fouques, dit. *Fête de l'égalité, La*
[*Comédie* in 1 act, Prem. on 25-2-1794, Pub. in 1795].
>Th. du Vaudeville (**41**); **Total: 41.**

_____. *Honorine* [*Comédie* in 3 acts, Prem. on 25-2-1794, Pub. in 1797].
>Th. du Vaudeville (**70**); **Total: 70.**

_____. *Matrone d'Ephèse, La* [*Comédie* in 1 act, Prem. on 13-10-1792, Pub. in 1793].
>Th. du Vaudeville (**134**); **Total: 134.**

_____. *Noble roturier, Le* [*Comédie* in 1 act, Prem. on 14-3-1794, Pub. in 1794].
>Th. du Vaudeville (**81**); **Total: 81.**

_____. *Pauline ou La Fille naturelle* [*Comédie* in 3 acts, Prem. on 11-4-1796, Pub. in 1797].
>Th. du Vaudeville (**30**); Th. Français (de la rue Richelieu) (de la République) (**4**); **Total: 34.**

_____. *Prix, Le, ou L'Embarras du choix* [*Vaudeville* in 1 act, Prem. on 27-2-1792].
>Th. du Vaudeville (**113**); **Total: 113.**

_____., Barré., Dalayrac, Nicolas (comp). *Renaud d'Ast* [*Comédie mêlée d'ariettes* in 2 acts, Prem. on 19-7-1787, Pub. in 1787].
>Académie de la Musique (Opéra) (**1**); Maison Egalité (**2**); Th. des Italiens (Opéra-Comique) (**124**); Th. du Lycée des Arts (**6**); Th. du Palais (Cité)-Variétés (**1**); **Total: 134.**

_____. *Rencontre sur rencontre* [N/A].
>Th. du Lycée des Arts (**1**); **Total: 1.**

_____., Dalayrac, Nicolas (comp). *Soirée orageuse, La* [*Comédie* in 1 act, Prem. on 29-5-1790, Pub. in 1790].
   Th. des Italiens (Opéra-Comique) (**132**); Th. du Feydeau (de Monsieur) (**1**); **Total: 133.**

_____. *Testament, Le* [*Comédie* in 1 act, Prem. on 5-10-1797, Pub. in 1797].
   Th. du Vaudeville (**15**); **Total: 15.**
   Total Performances, Radet, Jean-B.: **1271**

Raffard-Brienne, J.S. *Coureur de successions, Le* [*Comédie* in 5 acts].
   Th. de Molière (**6**); **Total: 6.**

_____. *Volontaires en route, Les, ou L'Enlèvement des cloches* [*Vaudeville* in 1 act, Prem. on 22-1-1794, Pub. in 1794].
   Th. du Vaudeville (**25**); **Total: 25.**
   Total Performances, Raffard-Brienne, J.S.: **31**

Raisin. *Niais de Sologne, Le* [*Comédie* in 1 act, Pub. in 1686].
   Th. de la Citoyenne Montansier (**57**); **Total: 57.**

Rauquil-Lieutaud. *Duel, Le, ou La Force du préjugé* [*Comédie* in 3 acts, Pub. in 1786].
   Th. des Italiens (Opéra-Comique) (**1**); **Total: 1.**

_____., Chapelle, Pierre-D.-A. (comp). *Heureux dépit, L', ou Les Enfantillages de l'amour* [*Opéra-Comique* in 1 act, Prem. on 16-11-1785, Pub. in 1788].
   Th. des Beaujolais (**5**); **Total: 5.**
   Total Performances, Rauquil-Lieutaud: **6**

Ravrio, Antoine-A. *Arlequin journaliste* [*Comédie* in 1 act, Prem. on 1-8-1797].
   Th. de la Cité (**8**); Th. du Vaudeville (**15**); **Total: 23.**

_____. *Sorcière, La* [*Vaudeville* in 1 act, Prem. on 27-3-1797, Pub. in 1799].
   Th. de la Cité (**10**); Th. du Vaudeville (**13**); **Total: 23.**
   Total Performances, Ravrio, Antoine-A.: **46**

Raymond, B.-Louis., Raymond, B. (comp). *Amateur de musique, L'* [*Comédie* in 1 act, Prem. on 3-7-1785, Pub. in 1785].
   Th. des Beaujolais (**17**); **Total: 17.**

Regnard, Jean-F. Renard, dit., Rivière-Dufresney, Charles. *Attendez-moi sous l'orme* [*Comédie* in 1 act, Pub. in 1694].
   Th. du Vaudeville (**4**); Th. Patriotique et de Momus (**16**); **Total: 20.**

_____., Campra, André (comp). *Carnaval de Venise, Le* [*Opéra* in 3 acts, Prem. in 1699, Pub. in 1699].
   Th. des Ombres de J.-J. Rousseau (**3**); Th. Lyrique des Amis de la Patrie (**16**); Tivoli (**1**); **Total: 20.**

_____. *Démocrite* [*Comédie* in 5 acts, Prem. on 12-1-1700, Pub. in 1700].
   n/a (**9**); Th. de la Nation (Comédie Française) (**1**); Th. des Variétés Amusantes, Comiques et Lyriques (**3**); Th. du Vaudeville (**4**); Th. Français (de la rue Richelieu) (de la République) (**9**); Th. Français, Comique et Lyrique (**1**); Th. Lyrique des Amis de la Patrie (**2**); Th. Patriotique et de Momus (**4**); **Total: 33.**

_____. *Descente de Mezzetin aux enfers, La* [*Parodie*, Pub. in 1700].
   Maison Ruggieri (**5**); **Total: 5.**

_____. *Distrait, Le* [*Comédie* in 5 acts, Pub. in 1697].
Th. de l'Odéon (**2**); Th. de la Citoyenne Montansier (**3**); Th. de la Nation (Comédie Française) (**11**); Th. de Molière (**3**); Th. des Victoires Nationales (**1**); Th. du Feydeau (de Monsieur) (**7**); Th. du Marais (**2**); Th. Français (de la rue Richelieu) (de la République) (**20**); Th. Lyrique des Amis de la Patrie (**1**); Th. Patriotique et de Momus (**11**); **Total: 61.**

_____. *Folies amoureuses, Les* [*Comédie* in 3 acts, Prem. on 15-1-1704, Pub. in 1704].
Maison Egalité (**1**); n/a (**2**); Th. de l'Emulation (Gaîté) (**1**); Th. de l'Estrapade au Panthéon (**4**); Th. de l'Odéon (**8**); Th. de la Citoyenne Montansier (**20**); Th. de la Cité (**14**); Th. de la Montagne (**2**); Th. de la Nation (Comédie Française) (**38**); Th. de la Rue Martin (**19**); Th. de Molière (**6**); Th. des Beaujolais (**1**); Th. des Délassements Comiques (**8**); Th. des Grands Danseurs (Gaîté) (**55**); Th. des Variétés Amusantes (Lazzari) (**4**); Th. des Variétés Amusantes, Comiques et Lyriques (**12**); Th. des Victoires (**1**); Th. des Victoires Nationales (**3**); Th. du Feydeau (de Monsieur) (**6**); Th. du Lycée des Arts (**4**); Th. du Lycée Dramatique (**5**); Th. du Marais (**9**); Th. du Palais (Cité)-Variétés (**9**); Th. Français (de la rue Richelieu) (de la République) (**23**); Th. Français, Comique et Lyrique (**4**); Th. Lyrique des Amis de la Patrie (**7**); Th. Lyrique du Foire St. Germain (**1**); Th. National (de la rue Richelieu) (**4**); Th. Patriotique et de Momus (**9**); **Total: 280.**

_____. *Joueur, Le* [*Comédie* in 5 acts, Prem. in 1696, Pub. in 1700].
Th. de l'Estrapade au Panthéon (**1**); Th. de l'Odéon (**1**); Th. de la Citoyenne Montansier (**7**); Th. de la Nation (Comédie Française) (**14**); Th. de Molière (**3**); Th. des Variétés Amusantes, Comiques et Lyriques (**4**); Th. des Victoires Nationales (**1**); Th. du Feydeau (de Monsieur) (**1**); Th. du Lycée Dramatique (**7**); Th. du Vaudeville (**2**); Th. Français (de la rue Richelieu) (de la République) (**9**); Th. Patriotique et de Momus (**11**); **Total: 61.**

_____. *Légataire universel, Le* [*Comédie* in 5 acts, Prem. on 9-1-1708, Pub. in 1714].
Th. de l'Estrapade au Panthéon (**5**); Th. de la Nation (Comédie Française) (**33**); Th. de la Rue Martin (**6**); Th. de Molière (**3**); Th. des Variétés Amusantes, Comiques et Lyriques (**3**); Th. du Feydeau (de Monsieur) (**2**); Th. du Marais (**3**); Th. du Vaudeville (**2**); Th. Français (de la rue Richelieu) (de la République) (**12**); Th. Patriotique et de Momus (**3**); **Total: 72.**

_____. *Ménechmes, Les, ou Les Jumeaux* [*Comédie* in 5 acts, Prem. on 5-12-1705, Pub. in 1706].
Th. de l'Estrapade au Panthéon (**2**); Th. de la Citoyenne Montansier (**4**); Th. de la Nation (Comédie Française) (**7**); Th. de Molière (**3**); Th. des Variétés Amusantes, Comiques et Lyriques (**5**); Th. du Marais (**3**); **Total: 24.**

_____. *Retour imprévu, Le* [*Comédie* in 1 act, Prem. on 11-2-1700, Pub. in 1700].
Th. de l'Estrapade au Panthéon (**3**); Th. de la Nation (Comédie Française) (**3**); Th. des Victoires (**2**); Th. du Lycée Dramatique (**4**); Th. du Marais (**5**); Th. Français (de la rue Richelieu) (de la République) (**18**); **Total: 35.**

_____. *Sérénade, La* [*Comédie* in 1 act, Pub. in 1695].
Th. de la Nation (Comédie Française) (**4**); Th. Français (de la rue Richelieu) (de la République) (**9**); **Total: 13.**
Total Performances, Regnard, Jean-F. Renard, dit: **624**

Renou, Antoine. *Ballon aérostatique, Le, ou Les Imbroglios d'Arlequin* [*Prologue* in 2 acts, Prem. in 1783, Pub. in 1780].
> Th. Lyrique des Amis de la Patrie (**8**); **Total: 8**.

Renout, Jean-J.-C. *Deux Arlequins, Les* [*Farce* in 1 act, Prem. in 1786, Pub. in 1786].
> Th. des Grands Danseurs (Gaîté) (**5**); **Total: 5**.

_____. *Savant jardinier, Le, ou Lison eut peur* [*Pantomime* in 1 act, Prem. on 4-3-1780].
> Th. des Grands Danseurs (Gaîté) (**16**); **Total: 16**.
> **Total Performances**, Renout, Jean-J.-C.: **21**

Restier. *Arlequin protégé par Vulcain* [*Pantomime* in 5 acts, Prem. in 1765].
> Th. des Grands Danseurs (Gaîté) (**30**); **Total: 30**.

Reveroni Saint-Cyr, Baron Jacques-A. de. *Club des sans-soucis, Le, ou Les Deux pupilles* [*Vaudeville* in 1 act, Pub. in 1794].
> Th. du Feydeau (de Monsieur) (**38**); **Total: 38**.

_____., Cherubini, Luigi (comp). *Elisa ou Le Voyage aux glaciers du mont St.-Bernard* [*Opéra* in 2 acts, Pub. in 1795].
> Th. du Feydeau (de Monsieur) (**56**); **Total: 56**.

_____., Foignet, Charles-G. (comp). *Hélena ou Les Miquelets* [*Opéra-Comique* in 2 acts, Prem. on 27-9-1794, Pub. in 1795].
> Th. Lyrique des Amis de la Patrie (**20**); **Total: 20**.

_____. *Hospice de village, L'* [*Opéra* in 1 act, Pub. in 1795].
> Maison Egalité (**14**); Th. de la Rue Martin (**1**); Th. du Palais (Cité)-Variétés (**4**); **Total: 19**.
> **Total Performances**, Reveroni Saint-Cyr, Baron Jacques-A. de: **133**

Rézicourt., Lemoyne, Jean-B. (comp). *Vrais sans-culottes, Les, ou L'Hospitalité républicaine* [*Tableau-Patriotique* in 1 act, Prem. on 12-5-1794, Pub. in 1794].
> Th. du Feydeau (de Monsieur) (**48**); **Total: 48**.

Ribié, César. *Avantageux puni, L'* [*Comédie* in 1 act, Prem. on 30-11-1786].
> Th. des Grands Danseurs (Gaîté) (**30**); **Total: 30**.

_____. *Bombardement de la ville des Arméniens* [*Pantomime* in 3 acts, Prem. on 19-9-1786].
> Th. des Grands Danseurs (Gaîté) (**3**); **Total: 3**.

_____. *Bon seigneur, Le, ou La Vertu récompensée* [*Drame* in 1 act, Prem. on 2-9-1782, Pub. in 1782].
> Th. des Grands Danseurs (Gaîté) (**45**); **Total: 45**.

_____. *Courtisane vertueuse, La* [*Comédie* in 1 act, Prem. on 3-10-1782].
> Th. des Grands Danseurs (Gaîté) (**8**); **Total: 8**.

_____. *Enfants du soleil, Les, ou Les Vestales du nouveau monde* [*Pantomime* in 3 acts, Prem. on 30-10-1788].
> Th. de l'Emulation (Gaîté) (**26**); Th. des Grands Danseurs (Gaîté) (**87**); **Total: 113**.

_____. *Geneviève de Brabant* [*Mélodrame* in 3 acts].
> Th. de Molière (**3**); **Total: 3**.

_____. *Habitant de St.-Domingue, L'* [*Comédie* in 3 acts, Prem. on 23-12-1790].
> Th. des Grands Danseurs (Gaîté) (**16**); **Total: 16**.

_____. *Héros américain, Le* [*Pantomime* in 3 acts, Prem. on 17-6-1786].
> Th. de l'Emulation (Gaîté) (**11**); Th. des Grands Danseurs (Gaîté) (**50**); **Total: 61**.

_____. *Héros anglais, Le* [*Pantomime* in 3 acts, Prem. on 28-7-1788].
Th. des Grands Danseurs (Gaîté) **(20)**; **Total: 20.**

_____. *Oncle et le neveu, amateurs de comédie, L'* [*Comédie* in 2 acts, Prem. on 21-1-1786].
Th. des Grands Danseurs (Gaîté) **(38)**; **Total: 38.**

_____. *Paysan seigneur, Le* [*Comédie* in 1 act, Prem. on 16-10-1786].
Th. des Grands Danseurs (Gaîté) **(3)**; **Total: 3.**

_____. *Prise de Mytilène, La* [N/A].
Th. de l'Emulation (Gaîté) **(3)**; **Total: 3.**

_____. *Richard Coeur de Lion* [*Pantomime* in 3 acts, Pub. in 1788].
Th. des Grands Danseurs (Gaîté) **(14)**; **Total: 14.**

_____. *Tel père tel fils* [N/A].
Th. de l'Emulation (Gaîté) **(22)**; **Total: 22.**

_____., Destival de Brabant. *Vieillard amoureux, Le, ou Les Quipro-quos* [*Comédie* in 1 act, Prem. in 1789].
Th. des Grands Danseurs (Gaîté) **(13)**; Th. des Ombres Chinoises **(2)**; **Total: 15.**

Total Performances, Ribié, César: **394**

Riccoboni, Antoine-F., Goldoni, Carlo., Riccoboni, Marie-J.-L. de Mézières, Mme. *Caquets, Les* [*Comédie* in 3 acts, Prem. on 4-2-1761, Pub. in 1761].
Th. de la Citoyenne Montansier **(26)**; Th. de la Rue Martin **(1)**; Th. du Vaudeville **(5)**; Th. National (de la rue Richelieu) **(1)**; Th. Patriotique et de Momus **(12)**; **Total: 45.**

_____. *Zéphire et Flore* [*Pastoral* in 3 acts, Prem. on 23-8-1727].
Th. des Jeunes Artistes **(100)**; **Total: 100.**

Total Performances, Riccoboni, Antoine-F.: **145**

Riccoboni, Marie-J.-L. de Mézières, Mme. *Fausse délicatesse, La, ou The False Delicacy* [*Comédie* in 5 acts, Prem. on 30-3-1798].
Th. du Feydeau (de Monsieur) **(1)**; **Total: 1.**

Richaud-Martelly, Honoré-A. *Deux Figaro, Les* [*Comédie* in 5 acts, Prem. on 25-11-1791, Pub. in 1790].
Th. du Palais (Cité)-Variétés **(21)**; Th. du Palais Royal **(29)**; Th. Français (de la rue Richelieu) (de la République) **(7)**; **Total: 57.**

Richerolles d'Avallon. *Astyanax* [*Tragédie* in 5 acts, Prem. on 7-2-1789, Pub. in 1818].
Th. de la Nation (Comédie Française) **(1)**; **Total: 1.**

Rigaud, Antoine-F. *Inconnu, L', ou Misanthropie et repentir* [*Drame* in 5 acts, Prem. on 29-8-1799].
Th. de l'Odéon **(37)**; Th. de la Cité **(3)**; Th. de Molière **(3)**; Th. des Italiens (Opéra-Comique) **(2)**; Th. des Jeunes Artistes **(22)**; Th. du Marais **(7)**; Th. du Palais (Cité)-Variétés **(12)**; Th. Lyrique des Amis de la Patrie **(7)**; **Total: 93.**

Rivière-Dufresny, Charles. *Dédit, Le* [*Comédie* in 1 act, Prem. on 12-5-1719, Pub. in 1719].
Th. des Jeunes Artistes **(26)**; Th. du Marais **(1)**; Th. Français (de la rue Richelieu) (de la République) **(35)**; **Total: 62.**

_____. *Double veuvage, Le* [*Comédie* in 3 acts, Prem. in 1692, Pub. in 1701].
Th. de la Nation (Comédie Française) **(10)**; **Total: 10.**

_____. *Esprit de contradiction, L'* [*Comédie* in 1 act, Prem. on 27-8-1700, Pub. in 1700].
> Th. de l'Odéon (**12**); Th. de la Montagne (**2**); Th. de la Nation (Comédie Française) (**40**); Th. de la Rue Martin (**12**); Th. de Molière (**3**); Th. des Variétés Amusantes, Comiques et Lyriques (**2**); Th. des Victoires (**2**); Th. des Victoires Nationales (**4**); Th. du Feydeau (de Monsieur) (**5**); Th. du Lycée des Arts (**4**); Th. du Marais (**9**); Th. du Palais (Cité)-Variétés (**2**); Th. Français (de la rue Richelieu) (de la République) (**16**); Th. Lyrique des Amis de la Patrie (**11**); Th. Lyrique du Foire St. Germain (**2**); **Total: 126.**

_____. *Mariage fait et rompu, Le* [*Comédie* in 3 acts, Prem. on 14-2-1721, Pub. in 1721].
> Th. de la Nation (Comédie Française) (**2**); **Total: 2.**
> **Total Performances,** Rivière-Dufresny, Charles: **200**

Robert. *Fausses présomptions, Les, ou Le Jeune gouverneur* [*Comédie* in 5 acts, Prem. on 12-8-1789].
> Th. de la Nation (Comédie Française) (**1**); **Total: 1.**

Robillard de Magnanville. *Deux orphelins, Les* [*Comédie* in 2 acts, Prem. in 11-1775, Pub. in 1775].
> Th. des Grands Danseurs (Gaîté) (**2**); **Total: 2.**

Robineau de Beaunoir, see Beaunoir, Alexandre-L.-B. Robineau dit.

Rochelle, J.H. Flacon, dit, Pseud. Philidor. *Bélisaire* [*Opéra* in 3 acts, Prem. on 3-10-1796, Pub. in 1796].
> Th. des Italiens (Opéra-Comique) (**10**); **Total: 10.**

Rochon de Chabannes, Marc. *Amants généreux, Les* [*Comédie* in 5 acts, Prem. on 13-10-1774, Pub. in 1774].
> Th. de la Nation (Comédie Française) (**3**); Th. de la Rue Martin (**8**); Th. du Feydeau (de Monsieur) (**8**); **Total: 19.**

_____. *Coupe enchantée, La* [*Opéra-Comique* in 1 act, Prem. on 19-7-1753, Pub. in 1753].
> Th. des Grands Danseurs (Gaîté) (**15**); **Total: 15.**

_____. *Heureusement* [*Comédie* in 1 act, Prem. on 29-11-1762, Pub. in 1762].
> Th. de la Nation (Comédie Française) (**13**); Th. de Molière (**4**); Th. des Délassements Comiques (**1**); Th. des Victoires (**4**); Th. du Feydeau (de Monsieur) (**2**); Th. du Marais (**1**); Th. du Vaudeville (**3**); Th. Français (de la rue Richelieu) (de la République) (**2**); Th. Patriotique et de Momus (**13**); **Total: 43.**

_____. *Ile des femmes, L'* [*Opéra* in 3 acts, Pub. in 1789].
> Th. du Vaudeville (**75**); **Total: 75.**

_____. *Jaloux, Le* [*Comédie* in 5 acts, Prem. on 11-3-1784, Pub. in 1785].
> Th. de la Nation (Comédie Française) (**10**); Th. de Molière (**1**); **Total: 11.**

_____. *Manie des arts, La* [*Comédie* in 1 act, Prem. on 1-6-1763, Pub. in 1763].
> Th. de la Nation (Comédie Française) (**9**); **Total: 9.**

_____., Lemoyne, Jean-B. (comp). *Prétendus, Les* [*Comédie* in 2 acts, Prem. on 2-6-1789, Pub. in 1789].
> Académie de la Musique (Opéra) (**106**); Th. des Grands Danseurs (Gaîté) (**12**); Th. du Marais (**1**); Th. Lyrique des Amis de la Patrie (**1**); **Total: 120.**
> **Total Performances,** Rochon de Chabannes, Marc: **292**

Roger. *Epreuve délicate, L'* [*Comédie* in 1 act, Pub. in 1798].
> Th. du Feydeau (de Monsieur) (**4**); **Total: 4.**

_____., Devienne, François (comp). *Valet de deux maîtres, Le* [*Comédie* in 1 act, Prem. on 3-11-1799].
>> Th. du Feydeau (de Monsieur) (4); **Total: 4.**
>>> **Total Performances**, Roger: **8**

Rolland, J.J. *Amour filial, L'* [*Comédie* in 1 act, Prem. on 16-1-1768, Pub. in 1768].
>> Th. du Feydeau (de Monsieur) (3); **Total: 3.**

_____., Clairville, Nicolas, dit. *Arlequin perruquier* [*Opéra* in 1 act, Pub. in 1795].
>> Th. du Palais (Cité)-Variétés (1); **Total: 1.**
>>> **Total Performances**, Rolland, J.J.: **4**

Romagnesi, Jean-A. *Arlequin horloger* [*Pantomime* in 3 acts].
>> Th. des Grands Danseurs (Gaîté) (1); **Total: 1.**

Ronsin, Charles-P. *Arétaphile ou La Révolution de Cyrène* [*Tragédie* in 5 acts, Prem. on 23-6-1792, Pub. in 1793].
>> Th. Français (de la rue Richelieu) (de la République) (5); Th. Lyrique des Amis de la Patrie (5); **Total: 10.**

_____. *Bal et le souper des poètes, Le* [*Comédie* in 1 act, Prem. on 25-2-1789].
>> Th. du Feydeau (de Monsieur) (14); **Total: 14.**

_____. *Dîner des patriotes, Le* [*Comédie* in 1 act, Prem. on 12-7-1790, Pub. in 1790].
>> Th. du Palais Royal (6); Th. Français (de la rue Richelieu) (de la République) (2); **Total: 8.**

_____. *Ligue des fanatiques et des tyrans, La* [*Tragédie* in 3 acts, Prem. on 18-6-1791].
>> Th. de Molière (44); **Total: 44.**

_____. *Louis XII, père du peuple* [*Tragédie* in 3 acts, Prem. on 12-2-1790, Pub. in 1790].
>> Th. de la Nation (Comédie Française) (1); Th. des Variétés Amusantes, Comiques et Lyriques (9); **Total: 10.**
>>> **Total Performances**, Ronsin, Charles-P.: **86**

Rosière, H. *Triomphe de la raison, Le, ou Les Fêtes républicaines* [*Comédie* in 1 act, Pub. in 1792].
>> Th. des Variétés Amusantes, Comiques et Lyriques (4); **Total: 4.**

Rosimond, Jean-B. Dumesnil, dit. *Nouveau festin de Pierre, Le* [*Tragi-Comédie* in 5 acts, Pub. in 1670].
>> Th. des Variétés Amusantes (Lazzari) (17); **Total: 17.**

_____. *Savetier avocat, Le* [*Comédie* in 1 act, Prem. on 12-10-1763, Pub. in 1763].
>> Th. des Grands Danseurs (Gaîté) (40); **Total: 40.**
>>> **Total Performances**, Rosimond, Jean-B. Dumesnil, dit: **57**

Rosny, Antoine-J.-N., Fay, Etienne (comp). *Rendez-vous espagnols, Les* [*Comédie* in 3 acts, Prem. on 10-6-1796].
>> Th. des Italiens (Opéra-Comique) (3); **Total: 3.**

Rosoi, Barnabé-F. de, dit Durosoi. *Fourberies de marine, Les, ou Le Tuteur juge et partie* [*Opéra-Comique* in 3 acts, Prem. on 11-9-1789].
>> Th. du Feydeau (de Monsieur) (1); **Total: 1.**

_____., Martini, Jean P.E. (comp). *Henri IV ou La Bataille d'Ivry*
[*Drame* in 3 acts, Pub. in 1774].
> Th. de l'Estrapade au Panthéon (1); Th. des Italiens (Opéra-Comique) (6);
> **Total: 7.**
> > **Total Performances**, Rosoi, Barnabé-F. de, dit Durosoi: **8**

Rotrou, Jean. *Venceslas* [*Tragédie* in 5 acts, Prem. in 1647, Pub. in 1774].
> Th. de la Nation (Comédie Française) (2); Th. Français (de la rue
> Richelieu) (de la République) (1); **Total: 3.**

Rouget de Lisle, Claude J., Champein, Stanislas (comp). *Bayard dans
bresse* [*Opéra* in 2 acts, Prem. on 21-2-1791, Pub. in 1791].
> Th. des Italiens (Opéra-Comique) (2); **Total: 2.**

Rouhier-Deschamps, J., Renault (comp). *Amours villageois, Les*
[*Opéra-Comique* in 2 acts, Prem. in 1770].
> Th. des Variétés Amusantes, Comiques et Lyriques (2); **Total: 2.**

_____., Gouffé, Armand Alexandre Duval. *Dîner d'un héros, Le* [*Fait
Historique* in 1 act, Prem. on 24-1-1798, Pub. in 1798].
> Th. de la Cité (8); Th. du Palais (Cité)-Variétés (2); **Total: 10.**

_____., Deshayes, Prosper-D. (comp). *Fin du jour, La* [*Opéra* in 1 act,
Prem. on 1-8-1793].
> Th. du Palais (Cité)-Variétés (6); **Total: 6.**

_____. *Marianne et Dumont* [*Comédie* in 3 acts, Prem. on 18-10-1788, Pub. in
1789].
> Th. de la Cité (15); Th. du Palais (Cité)-Variétés (16); Th. du Palais Royal
> (27); **Total: 58.**

_____., Gouffé, Armand Alexandre Duval. *Médard, fils de Gros-Jean*
[*Parodie* in 2 acts, Prem. on 23-6-1796].
> Th. de la Cité (9); **Total: 9.**

_____., Gouffé, Armand Alexandre Duval. *Nicodème à Paris ou La
Décade et le dimanche* [*Vaudeville* in 1 act, Prem. on 24-1-1796].
> Th. des Variétés Amusantes, Comiques et Lyriques (1); Th. du Palais
> (Cité)-Variétés (14); **Total: 15.**

_____., Léger, François-P.-A., Beaupré., Deshayes, Prosper-D. (comp).
Petit Orphée, Le [*Opéra-Comique* in 4 acts, Prem. on 13-6-1792].
> Th. de la Cité (6); Th. du Palais (Cité)-Variétés (43); **Total: 49.**

_____. *Saint-Aubin ou Le Bienfait et la reconnaissance* [*Comédie* in 3
acts, Prem. on 10-3-1790].
> Th. du Palais Royal (9); **Total: 9.**
> > **Total Performances**, Rouhier-Deschamps, J.: **158**

Rousseau, Jean-Baptiste. *Café, Le* [*Comédie* in 1 act, Prem. in 8-1695, Pub. in
1694].
> Th. des Variétés Amusantes, Comiques et Lyriques (4); **Total: 4.**

_____. *Capricieux, Le, ou Les Apparences trompeuses* [*Comédie* in 5 acts,
Prem. on 17-12-1700, Pub. in 1701].
> Th. de l'Odéon (1); Th. de la Citoyenne Montansier (11); **Total: 12.**

_____. *Ceinture magique, La* [*Comédie* in 1 act, Prem. on 3-2-1702, Pub. in
1694].
> Th. de la Rue Antoine (1); Th. Patriotique et de Momus (4); **Total: 5.**

_____. *Dupe de soi-même, La, ou Le Défiant confondu* [*Comédie* in 1 act, Pub. in 1751].
>> Th. du Marais (**3**); Th. Français (de la rue Richelieu) (de la République) (**1**); Th. Lyrique des Amis de la Patrie (**1**); **Total: 5.**
>> **Total Performances**, Rousseau, Jean-Baptiste: **26**

Rousseau, Jean-Jacques. *Devin du village, Le* [*Intermède* in 1 act, Prem. on 18-10-1752, Pub. in 1753].
>> Académie de la Musique (Opéra) (**33**); n/a (**2**); Th. de l'Ambigu Comique (**52**); Th. de l'Emulation (Gaîté) (**1**); Th. de l'Estrapade au Panthéon (**4**); Th. de la Citoyenne Montansier (**41**); Th. de la Liberté (**2**); Th. de la Montagne (**4**); Th. de la Rue Martin (**1**); Th. de Molière (**9**); Th. des Beaujolais (**7**); Th. des Délassements Comiques (**1**); Th. des Grands Danseurs (Gaîté) (**1**); Th. des Jeunes Artistes (**8**); Th. des Variétés Amusantes (Lazzari) (**1**); Th. du Lycée des Arts (**16**); Th. du Lycée Dramatique (**8**); Th. du Marais (**14**); Th. Français (de la rue Richelieu) (de la République) (**5**); Th. Français, Comique et Lyrique (**4**); Th. Lyrique des Amis de la Patrie (**41**); Th. Lyrique du Foire St. Germain (**6**); Th. Patriotique et de Momus (**3**); **Total: 264.**

_____. *Pygmalion* [*Opéra* in 1 act, Prem. in 1770, Pub. in 1775].
>> Th. de l'Ambigu Comique (**15**); Th. de l'Estrapade au Panthéon (**1**); Th. de la Bienfaisance (**1**); Th. de la Montagne (**2**); Th. de la Nation (Comédie Française) (**10**); Th. de la Rue Martin (**3**); Th. de Molière (**1**); Th. des Délassements Comiques (**1**); Th. des Grands Danseurs (Gaîté) (**2**); Th. des Jeunes Artistes (**50**); Th. des Variétés Amusantes (Lazzari) (**3**); Th. des Variétés Amusantes, Comiques et Lyriques (**5**); Th. du Feydeau (de Monsieur) (**2**); Th. du Lycée Dramatique (**2**); Th. du Marais (**12**); Th. du Palais (Cité)-Variétés (**1**); Th. du Vaudeville (**1**); Th. Français (de la rue Richelieu) (de la République) (**15**); Th. Patriotique et de Momus (**8**); Veillée de Thalie (**1**); **Total: 136.**
>> **Total Performances**, Rousseau, Jean-Jacques: **400**

Roussel, Pierre.-J.-A. *Encore un tuteur dupé* [*Opéra*, Prem. on 22-2-1798, Pub. in 1798].
>> Th. de la Citoyenne Montansier (**7**); **Total: 7.**

Sade, Donatien Alphonse François, Marquis de. *Comte Oxtiern, Le* [*Comédie* in 3 acts, Prem. on 22-10-1791].
>> Th. de Molière (**1**); **Total: 1.**

Saint-Aignan, E., Cherubini, Luigi (comp). *Hôtellerie portugaise, L'* [*Opéra-Comique* in 1 act, Prem. on 25-7-1798].
>> Th. du Feydeau (de Monsieur) (**4**); **Total: 4.**

Saint-Brice. *Thalie aux boulevards ou La Singulière entreprise* [*Comédie* in 1 act, Pub. in 1798].
>> Th. de l'Ambigu Comique (**15**); **Total: 15.**

Saint-Foix, Germain-F.-P. de. *Colonie, La* [*Comédie* in 3 acts, Prem. on 25-10-1749, Pub. in 1750].
>> n/a (**2**); Th. de l'Ambigu Comique (**1**); Th. de la Citoyenne Montansier (**2**); Th. de Molière (**6**); Th. des Grands Danseurs (Gaîté) (**1**); Th. du Feydeau (de Monsieur) (**24**); Th. du Marais (**3**); Th. du Palais (Cité)-Variétés (**2**); Th. Patriotique et de Momus (**4**); Veillée de Thalie (**2**); **Total: 47.**

_____. *Derviche, Le* [*Comédie* in 1 act, Prem. on 15-9-1755].
>> Th. de l'Ambigu Comique (**11**); Th. des Grands Danseurs (Gaîté) (**22**); Th. du Lycée Dramatique (**1**); **Total: 34.**

_____., Giraud, François-J. (comp). *Hommes, Les* [*Comédie-Ballet* in 1 act, Prem. on 27-6-1753, Pub. in 1753].
   Th. du Feydeau (de Monsieur) (1); **Total: 1.**

_____. *Métamorphoses, Les* [*Comédie* in 4 acts, Prem. in 1748].
   Th. de la Citoyenne Montansier (1); **Total: 1.**

_____. *Oracle, L'* [*Comédie* in 1 act, Prem. on 22-3-1740, Pub. in 1740].
   Th. de l'Ambigu Comique (1); Th. de l'Odéon (10); Th. de la Citoyenne Montansier (1); Th. de la Nation (Comédie Française) (24); Th. Lyrique des Amis de la Patrie (1); Th. Patriotique et de Momus (5); **Total: 42.**
   Total Performances, Saint-Foix, Germain-F.-P. de: **125**

Saint-Marcel, A.-Philippe Tardieu. *Caton d'Utique* [*Trait civique*, Prem. on 16-4-1796].
   Th. Français (de la rue Richelieu) (de la République) (5); **Total: 5.**

Saint-Just, see Godard d'Aucourt de Saint-Just, Claude.

Salieri, Antonio. *Scuola de gelosi, La* [*Opéra*, Prem. on 20-5-1791].
   Th. du Feydeau (de Monsieur) (2); **Total: 2.**

Salm-Reifferscheid-Dyck, Constance-M., Martini, Jean.-P.-E. (comp). *Sapho* [*Tragédie-Lyrique* in 3 acts, Prem. on 14-12-1794].
   Th. Lyrique des Amis de la Patrie (69); **Total: 69.**

Salverte, Aglaé d'Arcambal, Dame C. de F. *Pauline* [*Comédie* in 2 acts, Prem. on 1-7-1791, Pub. in 1791].
   Th. de la Nation (Comédie Française) (3); Th. du Vaudeville (19); **Total: 22.**

Sarti. *Gelosie villane, Delle* [*Opéra*, Prem. on 14-4-1790].
   Th. du Feydeau (de Monsieur) (29); **Total: 29.**

Saugiers, Marc-A., Plantade, Charles-H. (comp). *Romagnesi* [*Opéra*, Prem. on 3-9-1799].
   Th. du Feydeau (de Monsieur) (6); **Total: 6.**

Saulnier, Guillaume.-N.-F., Jadin, Louis-E. (comp). *Heureux stratagème, L', ou Le Vol supposé* [*Opéra-Bouffe* in 2 acts, Prem. on 13-9-1791].
   Académie de la Musique (Opéra) (3); **Total: 3.**

_____. *Portrait, Le* [*Comédie* in 2 acts, Pub. in 1793].
   Th. du Feydeau (de Monsieur) (13); **Total: 13.**

_____., Champein, Stanislas (comp). *Portrait, Le, ou La Divinité du sauvage* [*Drame-Lyrique* in 2 acts, Prem. on 14-6-1793].
   Académie de la Musique (Opéra) (8); **Total: 8.**

_____., Dutilh., Jadin, Louis-E. (comp). *Siège de Thionville, Le* [*Drame-Lyrique* in 2 acts, Prem. on 14-6-1793].
   Académie de la Musique (Opéra) (27); **Total: 27.**
   Total Performances, Saulnier, Guillaume.-N.-F.: **51**

Saurin, Bernard-J. *Anglomanie, L'* [*Vaudeville* in 2 acts, Prem. on 9-2-1799].
   Th. du Marais (3); Th. du Vaudeville (1); **Total: 4.**

_____. *Beverley* [*Tragédie* in 5 acts, Prem. on 7-5-1768, Pub. in 1768].
n/a (1); Th. de l'Emulation (Gaîté) (1); Th. de l'Estrapade au Panthéon (2); Th. de l'Odéon (1); Th. de la Citoyenne Montansier (2); Th. de la Liberté (2); Th. de la Nation (Comédie Française) (6); Th. de la Rue Martin (7); Th. de Molière (3); Th. des Grands Danseurs (Gaîté) (8); Th. des Variétés Amusantes, Comiques et Lyriques (1); Th. du Feydeau (de Monsieur) (5); Th. du Marais (2); Th. du Palais Royal (4); Th. du Vaudeville (1); Th. Français (de la rue Richelieu) (de la République) (2); Th. Lyrique du Foire St. Germain (1); Th. Patriotique et de Momus (16); **Total: 65.**

_____. *Mariage de Julie, Le* [*Comédie* in 1 act, Prem. in 10-1772, Pub. in 1772].
Th. du Palais Royal (1); **Total: 1.**

_____. *Spartacus* [*Tragédie* in 5 acts, Prem. on 20-2-1760, Pub. in 1760].
Maison Egalité (2); Th. de la Nation (Comédie Française) (7); Th. du Feydeau (de Monsieur) (4); **Total: 13.**

Total Performances, Saurin, Bernard-J.: **83**

Savin-Desplasses., Cimarosa, Domenico (comp). *Cousin et la cousine, Le* [*Opéra-Comique* in 3 acts, Pub. in 1787].
Th. du Feydeau (de Monsieur) (1); **Total: 1.**

Scarron, Paul. *Jodelet ou Le Maître valet* [*Comédie* in 5 acts, Pub. in 1645].
Th. de la Nation (Comédie Française) (3); Th. Français (de la rue Richelieu) (de la République) (2); **Total: 5.**

Schroeder, F.-L. *Enseigne, L', ou Le Jeune militaire* [*Comédie* in 3 acts, Prem. on 8-4-1799].
Th. de la Cité (7); **Total: 7.**

Sedaine de Sarcy, Jean-F. *Convention matrimoniale, La* [*Comédie* in 2 acts, Prem. on 29-5-1790].
Th. du Palais Royal (9); **Total: 9.**

_____. *Défauts supposés, Les* [*Comédie* in 1 act, Prem. on 28-1-1788, Pub. in 1788].
Th. du Palais (Cité)-Variétés (7); Th. du Palais Royal (45); Th. Français (de la rue Richelieu) (de la République) (2); **Total: 54.**

_____. *Fausses bonnes fortunes, Les* [*Comédie* in 2 acts, Prem. on 17-10-1791].
Th. Français (de la rue Richelieu) (de la République) (3); **Total: 3.**

_____., Bruni, Antonio-B. (comp). *Ile enchantée, L'* [*Opéra-Comique* in 3 acts, Prem. on 3-8-1789].
Th. du Feydeau (de Monsieur) (34); **Total: 34.**

_____. *Jean qui pleure et Jean qui rit* [*Comédie* in 1 act, Prem. on 18-10-1781, Pub. in 1781].
Th. de l'Ambigu Comique (13); **Total: 13.**

_____. *Malentendu, Le, ou Il ne faut jurer de rien* [*Comédie* in 1 act, Prem. on 5-12-1782, Pub. in 1782].
Th. de l'Ambigu Comique (94); Th. des Jeunes Artistes (1); **Total: 95.**

_____. *Manteau écalarte, Le, ou Le Rêve supposé* [*Comédie* in 1 act, Prem. on 5-4-1784, Pub. in 1784].
Th. de l'Ambigu Comique (93); **Total: 93.**

_____. *Marchand d'esprit et le marchand de mémoire, Le* [*Comédie* in 1 act, Prem. on 24-11-1786, Pub. in 1788].
Th. des Variétés Amusantes (Lazzari) (1); **Total: 1.**

_____. *Sérail à l'encan, Le* [*Comédie* in 1 act, Prem. in 1781, Pub. in 1783].
Th. de l'Ambigu Comique (16); **Total: 16.**

_____. *Tout comme il vous plaira ou La Gageure favorable* [*Comédie* in 1 act, Prem. on 5-5-1786, Pub. in 1786].
   Th. de l'Ambigu Comique (**32**); **Total: 32.**

_____. *Trois Léandres, Les, ou Les Noms changés* [*Comédie* in 1 act, Prem. on 22-4-1785, Pub. in 1786].
   Th. de l'Ambigu Comique (**39**); **Total: 39.**
                        Total Performances, Sedaine de Sarcy, Jean-F.: **389**
Sedaine, Michel-J., Grétry, André-E.-M. (comp). *Albert ou Le Service récompensé* [*Comédie* in 3 acts, Prem. in 1786, Pub. in 1775].
   Th. des Italiens (Opéra-Comique) (**6**); **Total: 6.**

_____., Grétry, André-E.-M. (comp). *Amphitrion* [*Opéra-Vaudeville* in 3 acts, Prem. on 15-3-1786, Pub. in 1786].
   Th. de Molière (**3**); **Total: 3.**

_____., Grétry, André-E.-M. (comp). *Aucassin et Nicolette ou Les Moeurs du bon temps* [*Comédie* in 4 acts, Prem. on 30-12-1779, Pub. in 1780].
   Th. des Italiens (Opéra-Comique) (**38**); **Total: 38.**

_____., Grétry, André-E.-M. (comp). *Basile ou A trompeur trompeur et demi* [*Comédie* in 1 act, Prem. on 17-10-1792, Pub. in 1792].
   Th. des Italiens (Opéra-Comique) (**2**); **Total: 2.**

_____., Grétry, André-E.-M. (comp). *Comte d'Albert, Le* [*Drame* in 2 acts, Prem. on 13-11-1786, Pub. in 1787].
   Th. des Italiens (Opéra-Comique) (**53**); **Total: 53.**

_____., Monsigny, Pierre-A. (comp). *Déserteur, Le* [*Drame* in 3 acts, Prem. on 6-3-1769, Pub. in 1769].
   Th. de l'Emulation (Gaîté) (**7**); Th. de la Rue Antoine (**1**); Th. de la Rue Martin (**6**); Th. des Italiens (Opéra-Comique) (**11**); Th. du Marais (**1**); Th. Patriotique et de Momus (**10**); **Total: 36.**

_____. *Diable à quatre, Le, ou La Double métamorphose* [*Comédie* in 3 acts, Pub. in 1756].
   Th. des Italiens (Opéra-Comique) (**15**); Th. des Variétés Amusantes, Comiques et Lyriques (**4**); **Total: 19.**

_____., Monsigny, Pierre-A. (comp). *Felix ou L'Enfant trouvé* [*Comédie* in 3 acts, Prem. on 10-11-1777, Pub. in 1777].
   Th. de l'Ambigu Comique (**6**); Th. des Italiens (Opéra-Comique) (**74**); **Total: 80.**

_____., Philidor, François-A. Danican (comp). *Femmes vengées, Les* [*Opéra-Comique* in 1 act, Prem. on 20-3-1775, Pub. in 1775].
   Th. des Italiens (Opéra-Comique) (**34**); **Total: 34.**

_____. *Gageure imprévue, La* [*Comédie* in 1 act, Prem. on 27-5-1768, Pub. in 1768].
   Maison Egalité (**1**); Th. de l'Estrapade au Panthéon (**1**); Th. de l'Odéon (**4**); Th. de la Citoyenne Montansier (**3**); Th. de la Nation (Comédie Française) (**16**); Th. de la Rue Martin (**10**); Th. de Molière (**12**); Th. des Variétés Amusantes (Lazzari) (**4**); Th. des Variétés Amusantes, Comiques et Lyriques (**4**); Th. du Feydeau (de Monsieur) (**11**); Th. du Lycée des Arts (**8**); Th. du Marais (**12**); Th. du Palais (Cité)-Variétés (**4**); Th. Français (de la rue Richelieu) (de la République) (**19**); Th. National (de la rue Richelieu) (**7**); **Total: 116.**

_____., Grétry, André-E.-M. (comp). *Guillaume Tell* [*Opéra* in 3 acts, Prem. on 9-4-1791, Pub. in 1794].
> Th. de l'Ambigu Comique (**36**); Th. de la Rue Martin (**2**); Th. des Italiens (Opéra-Comique) (**85**); Th. des Victoires (**1**); Th. du Marais (**4**); Th. du Vaudeville (**1**); **Total: 129.**

_____., Philidor, François-A. Danican (comp). *Jardinier et son seigneur, Le* [*Opéra-Comique* in 1 act, Prem. on 18-2-1761, Pub. in 1761].
> Th. des Italiens (Opéra-Comique) (**2**); **Total: 2.**

_____., Grétry, André-E.-M. (comp). *Magnifique, Le* [*Comédie* in 3 acts, Prem. on 4-3-1773, Pub. in 1773].
> Th. des Italiens (Opéra-Comique) (**25**); **Total: 25.**

_____. *Mort marié, Le* [*Comédie* in 2 acts, Prem. in 1771, Pub. in 1771].
> Th. de Molière (**4**); Th. des Italiens (Opéra-Comique) (**3**); **Total: 7.**

_____., Monsigny, Pierre-A. (comp). *On ne s'avise jamais de tout* [*Opéra-Comique* in 1 act, Prem. on 14-9-1761].
> Th. de Molière (**1**); Th. des Italiens (Opéra-Comique) (**2**); **Total: 3.**

_____., Porta, Bernado (comp). *Pagamin de moneque* [*Opéra-Comique* in 1 act, Prem. on 29-3-1792].
> Th. Lyrique des Amis de la Patrie (**2**); **Total: 2.**

_____. *Philosophe sans le savoir, Le* [*Comédie* in 5 acts, Prem. on 2-11-1765, Pub. in 1766].
> Th. de la Nation (Comédie Française) (**11**); Th. du Feydeau (de Monsieur) (**13**); Th. Français (de la rue Richelieu) (de la République) (**11**); **Total: 35.**

_____., Grétry, André-E.-M. (comp). *Raoul Barbe-bleue* [*Comédie* in 3 acts, Prem. on 2-3-1789, Pub. in 1791].
> Th. des Italiens (Opéra-Comique) (**108**); **Total: 108.**

_____. *Raymond V, comte de Toulouse ou L'épreuve inutile* [*Comédie* in 5 acts, Prem. on 22-9-1789].
> Th. de la Nation (Comédie Française) (**2**); **Total: 2.**

_____., Grétry, André-E.-M. (comp). *Richard Coeur-de-Lion* [*Comédie* in 3 acts, Prem. on 21-10-1784, Pub. in 1786].
> Th. des Italiens (Opéra-Comique) (**29**); **Total: 29.**

_____., Monsigny, Pierre-A. (comp). *Roi et le fermier, Le* [*Comédie* in 3 acts, Prem. on 22-11-1762, Pub. in 1762].
> Th. des Italiens (Opéra-Comique) (**2**); **Total: 2.**

_____., Monsigny, Pierre-A. (comp). *Rose et Colas* [*Comédie* in 1 act, Prem. on 8-3-1764, Pub. in 1764].
> n/a (**1**); Th. de Molière (**10**); Th. des Délassements Comiques (**11**); Th. des Italiens (Opéra-Comique) (**54**); Th. du Marais (**5**); Th. du Mareux (**1**); **Total: 82.**

_____., Duni, Egidio-R. (comp)., Cazotte, Jacques. *Sabots, Les* [In 1 act, Prem. on 26-10-1768, Pub. in 1768].
> Th. des Italiens (Opéra-Comique) (**38**); Th. du Marais (**1**); **Total: 39.**
> > **Total Performances**, Sedaine, Michel-J.: **852**

Séguier, Baron Maurice. *Maréchal-ferrant de la ville d'Anvers, Le* [*Anecdotique* in 1 act, Prem. on 12-5-1799, Pub. in 1799].
> Th. du Vaudeville (**28**); **Total: 28.**

Ségur, Alexander-J.-P., Vte. de. *Amant arbitre, L'* [*Comédie* in 1 act, Pub. in 1799].
> Th. de la Cité (**2**); Th. du Marais (**3**); Th. du Palais (Cité)-Variétés (**7**); **Total: 12.**

_____. *Bon fermier, Le* [*Comédie* in 1 act, Pub. in 1795].
Th. des Variétés Amusantes, Comiques et Lyriques (1); Th. du Feydeau (de Monsieur) (5); **Total: 6.**

_____. *C'est le même* [*Vaudeville* in 1 act, Prem. on 30-5-1798, Pub. in 1798].
Th. du Vaudeville (17); **Total: 17.**

_____., Tarchi, Angelo (comp). *Cabriolet jaune, Le, ou Le Phénix d'Angoulême* [*Opéra-Bouffe*, Prem. on 7-11-1798, Pub. in 1799].
Th. des Italiens (Opéra-Comique) (8); **Total: 8.**

_____., Philipon, Louis. *Chaulieu à Fontenay* [*Comédie* in 1 act, Prem. on 31-8-1799, Pub. in 1799].
Th. du Vaudeville (47); **Total: 47.**

_____. *Deux veuves, Les* [*Comédie* in 2 acts, Prem. on 12-12-1796, Pub. in 1797].
Th. de l'Odéon (5); Th. du Marais (1); Th. du Vaudeville (67); **Total: 73.**

_____. *Dorval ou Le Fou par amour* [*Comédie* in 1 act, Prem. on 29-1-1791].
Th. de la Nation (Comédie Française) (5); **Total: 5.**

_____. *Elize dans les bois* [*Comédie* in 1 act, Pub. in 1797].
Maison Egalité (8); Th. de la Cité (10); Th. du Palais (Cité)-Variétés (4); **Total: 22.**

_____., Desprez, Jean-B.-D. *Nice* [*Parodie* in 1 act, Prem. on 6-6-1792, Pub. in 1793].
Th. du Vaudeville (123); **Total: 123.**

_____., Dupaty, Louis-E., Della Maria, Dominique (comp). *Opéra-comique, L'* [*Opéra-Comique* in 1 act, Prem. on 9-7-1798].
Th. des Italiens (Opéra-Comique) (55); **Total: 55.**

_____. *Retour du mari, Le* [*Comédie* in 1 act, Prem. on 25-1-1792, Pub. in 1792].
Th. de la Montagne (2); Th. de la Nation (Comédie Française) (10); Th. du Feydeau (de Monsieur) (10); Th. Français (de la rue Richelieu) (de la République) (2); Th. National (de la rue Richelieu) (15); **Total: 39.**

_____. *Roméo et Juliette* [*Opéra* in 3 acts, Prem. on 10-9-1794].
Th. de Molière (4); Th. du Feydeau (de Monsieur) (153); **Total: 157.**

_____. *Rosaline et Floricourt* [*Comédie* in 2 acts, Prem. on 17-11-1787, Pub. in 1790].
Th. de la Nation (Comédie Française) (1); **Total: 1.**

_____. *Saint-Elmont et Verseuil ou Le Danger d'un soupçon* [*Drame* in 5 acts, Prem. on 12-2-1797, Pub. in 1797].
Th. de la Nation (Comédie Française) (1); Th. Français (de la rue Richelieu) (de la République) (6); **Total: 7.**

_____., Ladurner, Ignaz.-A. (comp). *Vieux fous, Les, ou Plus de peur que de mal* [*Opéra-Comique* in 1 act, Prem. on 16-1-1796, Pub. in 1796].
Th. du Feydeau (de Monsieur) (11); **Total: 11.**
                                        Total Performances, Ségur, Alexander-J.-P.: **583**

Ségur, Louis-Philippe, Cte. de., Devienne, François (comp). *Mariage clandestin, Le* [*Opéra* in 1 act, Prem. on 11-11-1790, Pub. in 1779].
Th. de la Citoyenne Montansier (35); Th. National (de la rue Richelieu) (1); **Total: 36.**

_____. *Revenants, Les* [*Comédie* in 1 act, Prem. on 16-4-1798, Pub. in 1798].
Th. du Vaudeville (24); **Total: 24.**
                                Total Performances, Ségur, Louis-Philippe, Cte. de: **60**

Serrières., Coupartantoine-M. *Vengeance pour vengeance ou Le Cadi de Smyrne* [Prem. on 15-7-1797].
>Th. de la Citoyenne Montansier (3); Th. des Variétés Amusantes (Lazzari) (18); Th. des Variétés Amusantes, Comiques et Lyriques (17); **Total: 38.**

Servandoni, Jean-N., Geminiani, Francesco-S. (comp). *Forêt enchantée, La* [*Divertissement/parade* in 5 acts, Prem. on 31-3-1754, Pub. in 1754].
>Th. des Grands Danseurs (Gaîté) (29); **Total: 29.**

Sewrin, Charles-A. de Bassompierre, dit. *Blonde et la brune, La, ou Les Deux n'en font qu'une* [*Comédie* in 1 act, Prem. on 10-7-1798, Pub. in 1795].
>Th. de l'Ambigu Comique (1); Th. des Jeunes Artistes (50); Th. des Variétés Amusantes, Comiques et Lyriques (3); Th. du Marais (1); **Total: 55.**

_____. *Chasse aux loups, La* [*Opéra-Comique* in 1 act, Prem. on 26-4-1797, Pub. in 1796].
>Th. de la Cité (15); **Total: 15.**

_____., Jadin, Louis-E. (comp). *Coucou* [*Opéra-Comique*, Prem. on 10-5-1798].
>Th. de la Citoyenne Montansier (2); **Total: 2.**

_____. *Deux orphelines, Les* [*Opéra*, Prem. on 26-5-1798, Pub. in 1797].
>Th. de Molière (12); **Total: 12.**

_____., Solié, Jean-P. (comp). *Ecole du village, L'* [*Opéra-Comique* in 1 act, Prem. on 10-5-1794, Pub. in 1794].
>Th. des Italiens (Opéra-Comique) (1); **Total: 1.**

_____. *Ecu de six francs, L', ou L'Héritage* [*Comédie* in 1 act].
>Th. des Ombres Chinoises (6); Th. des Ombres de J.-J. Rousseau (15); **Total: 21.**

_____., Chazet, René-A.-P. de. *Folie et la raison, La* [*Comédie* in 1 act, Pub. in 1804].
>Th. de l'Ambigu Comique (1); **Total: 1.**

_____., Gresnick, Antoine (comp). *Grotte des Cévennes, La* [*Opéra-Comique* in 1 act, Prem. on 6-1-1798, Pub. in 1797].
>Th. de la Citoyenne Montansier (12); **Total: 12.**

_____., Lefranc-Ponteuil, Nicolas. *Hermitage, L'* [*Opéra-Comique* in 2 acts, Prem. on 15-2-1793, Pub. in 1793].
>Th. Lyrique des Amis de la Patrie (42); Th. National (de la rue Richelieu) (1); **Total: 43.**

_____. *Julia ou Les Souterrains du château de Mazzini* [*Mélodrame* in 3 acts, Prem. on 2-12-1798, Pub. in 1798].
>Th. des Jeunes Artistes (32); Th. du Marais (1); **Total: 33.**

_____. *Loups et les brebis, Les, ou La Nuit d'été* [*Divertissement/parade* in 1 act, Prem. on 16-3-1793].
>Th. Lyrique des Amis de la Patrie (50); **Total: 50.**

_____., Solié, Jean-P. (comp). *Moisson, La* [*Opéra-Comique* in 2 acts, Prem. on 5-9-1793, Pub. in 1793].
>Th. des Italiens (Opéra-Comique) (11); **Total: 11.**

_____., Solié, Jean-P. (comp). *Plaisir et la gloire, Le* [*Tableau-Patriotique*, Prem. on 19-1-1794, Pub. in 1794].
>Th. des Italiens (Opéra-Comique) (19); **Total: 19.**

_____., Chapelle, Pierre-D.-A. (comp). *Ruse villageoise, La* [*Opéra-Comique* in 1 act, Prem. on 2-7-1793, Pub. in 1794].
>Th. Lyrique des Amis de la Patrie (62); **Total: 62.**

_____. *Sorcière, La* [*Comédie* in 1 act, Prem. on 14-9-1799].
>Th. du Vaudeville (10); **Total: 10.**

_____. *Villageois qui cherche son veau, Le* [*Opéra-Comique* in 1 act, Prem. on 27-9-1797].
>Th. de la Cité (6); **Total: 6.**
>>**Total Performances,** Sewrin, Charles-A. de Bassompierre, dit: **353**

Simon, Edouard-T. *A propos de la nature, L', ou Le Dédit confirmé* [*Comédie* in 1 act, Prem. on 17-10-1791].
>Th. de la Citoyenne Montansier (11); **Total: 11.**

Simonnet de Maisonneuve, L.-J.-B. *Faux insouciant, Le* [*Comédie* in 5 acts, Pub. in 1824].
>Th. de la Nation (Comédie Française) (4); **Total: 4.**

_____. *Roxelane et Mustapha* [*Tragédie* in 5 acts, Prem. on 6-6-1785, Pub. in 1785].
>Th. de la Nation (Comédie Française) (7); **Total: 7.**
>>**Total Performances,** Simonnet de Maisonneuve, L.-J.-B.: **11**

Simonot, J.-F. *Gilles tout seul* [*Vaudeville*, Prem. on 19-2-1799, Pub. in 1798].
>Th. des Victoires Nationales (10); Th. du Palais (Cité)-Variétés (8); **Total: 18.**

Souriguière de Saint-Marc, J.-M. *Artémidore ou Le Roi citoyen* [*Tragédie* in 3 acts, Prem. on 29-9-1791].
>Th. du Marais (5); **Total: 5.**

_____. *Cécile ou La Reconnaissance* [*Comédie* in 1 act, Prem. on 15-1-1797, Pub. in 1797].
>Th. de l'Odéon (1); Th. de la Nation (Comédie Française) (2); Th. Français (de la rue Richelieu) (de la République) (15); **Total: 18.**

_____., Gaveaux, Pierre (comp). *Céliane* [*Opéra* in 1 act, Prem. on 31-12-1796].
>Th. du Feydeau (de Monsieur) (1); **Total: 1.**

_____. *Tout par l'opium ou Juliette et Purgono* [*Parodie*].
>Th. de la Citoyenne Montansier (13); **Total: 13.**
>>**Total Performances,** Souriguière de Saint-Marc, J.-M.: **37**

Sylvestre. *Deux fermiers, Les* [*Comédie* in 1 act, Prem. on 14-1-1788, Pub. in 1788].
>Maison Egalité (21); Th. de la Citoyenne Montansier (22); Th. de la Cité (12); Th. des Variétés Amusantes, Comiques et Lyriques (3); Th. du Palais (Cité)-Variétés (37); Th. du Palais Royal (56); **Total: 151.**

_____. *Lot mal employé, Le* [*Comédie* in 2 acts, Prem. on 25-4-1790].
>Th. du Feydeau (de Monsieur) (2); **Total: 2.**
>>**Total Performances,** Sylvestre: **153**

Taconet, Toussaint-G. *Baiser donné et le baiser rendu, Le* [*Opéra-Comique* in 2 acts, Prem. on 19-5-1770, Pub. in 1771].
>Th. du Lycée des Arts (11); Th. Lyrique des Amis de la Patrie (45); **Total: 56.**

_____. *Compliment sans compliment* [*Prologue*, Prem. on 27-6-1761, Pub. in 1761].
>Th. de Molière (1); **Total: 1.**

_____. *Homme aux deux femmes, L'* [*Comédie* in 1 act, Prem. in 1767].
 Th. des Grands Danseurs (Gaîté) (**2**); **Total: 2.**
_____. *Labyrinthe d'amour, Le* [*Opéra-Comique* in 1 act, Prem. in 6-1756,
 Pub. in 1757].
 Th. des Jeunes Artistes (**22**); **Total: 22.**
_____. *Mort du boeuf gras, La* [*Tragi-Comédie* in 1 act, Prem. on 26-2-1767,
 Pub. in 1767].
 Th. des Grands Danseurs (Gaîté) (**2**); **Total: 2.**
_____. *Nostradamus* [*Parodie* in 1 act, Pub. in 1756].
 Th. des Grands Danseurs (Gaîté) (**51**); **Total: 51.**
_____. *Savetier gentilhomme, Le* [*Comédie* in 3 acts, Prem. in 1766].
 Th. des Grands Danseurs (Gaîté) (**1**); **Total: 1.**
 Total Performances, Taconet, Toussaint-G.: **135**

Tarchi, Angelo (comp). *Don Chisciotte della Mancia* [*Vaudeville*, Prem. on
 2-8-1790].
 Th. du Feydeau (de Monsieur) (**3**); **Total: 3.**

Testard. *Bible à ma tante, La* [*Comédie* in 1 act, Prem. on 7-3-1798, Pub. in
 1798].
 Th. de l'Emulation (Gaîté) (**24**); Th. de la Citoyenne Montansier (**3**); Th.
 Lyrique des Amis de la Patrie (**16**); **Total: 43.**

Theaulon de Lambert, Marie-E.-G.-M. Ps. Léon. *Ramoneur, Le* [*Vaude-
 ville* in 2 acts].
 Th. de la Citoyenne Montansier (**3**); Th. des Ombres Chinoises (**8**); Th. des
 Ombres de J.-J. Rousseau (**28**); **Total: 39.**

Thésigny, F. Domillier de. *Arlequin journaliste* [*Comédie* in 1 act, Prem. on
 30-1-1793].
 n/a (**14**); Th. de la Citoyenne Montansier (**15**); **Total: 29.**

Thiemet. *Comédien de société, Le* [*Comédie* in 1 act, Prem. on 14-3-1789, Pub.
 in 1793].
 Th. de l'Ambigu Comique (**93**); Th. du Lycée Dramatique (**1**); Th. du
 Palais (Cité)-Variétés (**8**); **Total: 102.**
_____. *Deux voyageurs, Les* [*Comédie* in 3 acts, Prem. on 10-3-1792].
 Th. de l'Ambigu Comique (**1**); **Total: 1.**
_____. *Embarras comique, L'* [*Proverbe/allégorique* in 1 act, Pub. in 1787].
 Echiquier (**1**); Th. de l'Ambigu Comique (**50**); Th. du Lycée Dramatique
 (**1**); Th. du Palais (Cité)-Variétés (**15**); **Total: 67.**
_____. *Moines gourmands, Les* [*Comédie*].
 Th. de l'Ambigu Comique (**2**); Th. du Lycée Dramatique (**2**); Th. du Palais
 (Cité)-Variétés (**2**); **Total: 6.**
_____. *Nuit blanche, La* [N/A].
 Th. du Lycée Dramatique (**4**); **Total: 4.**
 Total Performances, Thiemet: **180**

Thouvenin. *Bonheur inattendu, Le* [*Opéra-Comique* in 2 acts, Prem. on 18-7-
 1793].
 Th. de la Citoyenne Montansier (**6**); **Total: 6.**

Tissot, Charles-L. *Cri de la nature, Le, ou Le Fils repentant* [*Comédie* in
 2 acts, Prem. on 31-10-1793].
 Th. du Palais (Cité)-Variétés (**2**); **Total: 2.**
_____., Kreutzer, Rodolpho (comp). *On respire* [*Comédie* in 1 act, Prem. on
 9-3-1795, Pub. in 1795].
 Th. des Italiens (Opéra-Comique) (**6**); **Total: 6.**

_____. *Salpêtriers républicains, Les* [*Comédie* in 1 act, Prem. on 26-6-1794, Pub. in 1794].
　Th. du Palais (Cité)-Variétés (**10**); **Total: 10.**

_____. *Tout pour la liberté* [*Comédie* in 1 act, Prem. on 20-10-1792, Pub. in 1794].
　Th. du Palais (Cité)-Variétés (**15**); **Total: 15.**
　　　Total Performances, Tissot, Charles-L.: **33**

Tolmer, Louis, dit Vallier. *Arlequin esclave à Bagdad ou Le Calife généreux* [*Comédie* in 1 act, Prem. on 20-10-1797, Pub. in 1798].
　Th. de l'Emulation (Gaîté) (**3**); Th. Lyrique des Amis de la Patrie (**15**); **Total: 18.**

Tonioli, G., Paisiello, Giovanni (comp). *Locandiera, La* [*Opéra*, Prem. on 29-1-1791].
　Th. du Feydeau (de Monsieur) (**2**); **Total: 2.**

Tritto, Giacomo. *Vicende amorose, Le* [*Opéra-Comique* in 2 acts, Prem. in 4-1787].
　Th. du Feydeau (de Monsieur) (**12**); **Total: 12.**

Trouvé, C.-J. *Comédie sans comédie, La* [*Comédie* in 5 acts, Pub. in 1657].
　Th. Lyrique des Amis de la Patrie (**11**); **Total: 11.**

Vacherot. *Amours de Nanterre, Les* [*Tragi-Comédie* in 1 act, Prem. on 18-12-1788].
　Th. des Grands Danseurs (Gaîté) (**3**); **Total: 3.**

Vadé, Jean-J. *Il était temps* [*Parodie* in 1 act, Prem. on 28-6-1754, Pub. in 1754].
　Th. de l'Emulation (Gaîté) (**22**); Th. des Grands Danseurs (Gaîté) (**7**); Th. Lyrique des Amis de la Patrie (**4**); **Total: 33.**

_____. *Jérôme et Fanchonette* [*Pastoral* in 1 act, Prem. on 18-2-1755, Pub. in 1755].
　Th. du Vaudeville (**4**); Th. Patriotique et de Momus (**3**); **Total: 7.**

_____., Léger, François-P.-A., Bambini, Arnauldo (comp). *Nicaise* [*Opéra-Comique* in 1 act, Prem. on 18-1-1792, Pub. in 1756].
　Th. de l'Ambigu Comique (**12**); Th. de la Citoyenne Montansier (**23**); Th. de la Cité (**23**); Th. des Variétés Amusantes, Comiques et Lyriques (**6**); Th. du Palais (Cité)-Variétés (**9**); Th. du Vaudeville (**72**); **Total: 145.**

_____. *Poirier, Le* [*Opéra-Comique* in 1 act, Prem. on 7-8-1752, Pub. in 1752].
　Th. de l'Ambigu Comique (**18**); **Total: 18.**

_____. *Racoleurs, Les* [*Opéra-Comique* in 1 act, Prem. on 11-3-1756, Pub. in 1756].
　Th. de l'Ambigu Comique (**11**); Th. de la Citoyenne Montansier (**6**); Th. de Molière (**2**); Th. des Délassements Comiques (**3**); Th. Français, Comique et Lyrique (**1**); **Total: 23.**

_____., Dauvergne (comp). *Troqueurs, Les* [*Opéra-Comique* in 1 act, Prem. on 30-7-1753].
　Th. de la Cité (**1**); **Total: 1.**

_____., Anseaume, Louis., Duni, Egidio-R. (comp). *Veuve indécise, La* [*Opéra-Comique* in 1 act, Prem. on 24-9-1759, Pub. in 1759].
　Th. de l'Ambigu Comique (**15**); **Total: 15.**
　　　Total Performances, Vadé, Jean-J.: **242**

Val, Citoyen. *Expériences physique, Les* [*Tableau-Patriotique*, Pub. in 1793].
Maison Egalité (6); Th. de la Citoyenne Montansier (5); Th. des Variétés Amusantes, Comiques et Lyriques (1); Th. du Lycée des Arts (5); Th. du Palais (Cité)-Variétés (2); **Total: 19.**

Valadier., Méhul, Etienne-N. (comp). *Cora* [*Opéra* in 4 acts, Prem. on 15-2-1791].
Académie de la Musique (Opéra) (5); **Total: 5.**

Valcour, see Plancher de Valcour, dit Aristide.

Valentin. *Prétendu sans le savoir, Le* [*Comédie* in 1 act, Prem. in 1775].
Th. des Grands Danseurs (Gaîté) (95); Th. des Jeunes Artistes (8); **Total: 103.**

Valienne., Bizet. *Caserne ou Le Départ de la première réquisition* [*Tableau-Patriotique* in 1 act, Pub. in 1793].
Th. du Palais (Cité)-Variétés (11); **Total: 11.**

Valigny, P. de. *Valet rusé, Le, ou Arlequin muet* [*Comédie* in 1 act, Prem. on 4-3-1785, Pub. in 1785].
Th. de la Citoyenne Montansier (1); Th. de Molière (5); **Total: 6.**

Vaqué, Pierre. *Citoyens français, Les, ou Le Triomphe de la Révolution* [*Drame* in 5 acts, Prem. on 3-7-1791, Pub. in 1791].
Th. du Lycée Dramatique (3); **Total: 3.**

Vaulabelle, Eléonore de. *Tireuse de cartes, La* [*Mélodrame* in 3 acts, Prem. on 18-5-1797].
Th. des Délassements Comiques (6); **Total: 6.**

Velier., Navoigille, Julien (comp). *Orage, L', ou Quel guignon* [*Pantomime* in 1 act, Prem. on 16-5-1793].
Th. du Palais (Cité)-Variétés (20); **Total: 20.**

Verdan, Anne-P. de. *Narcisse* [*Mélodrame*, Prem. on 2-1-1789, Pub. in 1786].
Th. de l'Ambigu Comique (30); Th. des Délassements Comiques (3); **Total: 33.**

Verment-Mariton. *Folle prétention, La* [*Comédie* in 1 act, Prem. on 6-3-1798, Pub. in 1798].
Th. de l'Ambigu Comique (13); **Total: 13.**

Vial, Jean-B. *Clémentine ou La Belle mère* [*Comédie* in 1 act, Prem. on 18-9-1799, Pub. in 1799].
Th. de Molière (1); Th. des Jeunes Artistes (3); Th. des Troubadours (8); Th. du Feydeau (de Monsieur) (20); **Total: 32.**

_____. *Elève de la nature, L'* [*Comédie* in 1 act, Prem. on 8-3-1795].
Th. des Italiens (Opéra-Comique) (10); **Total: 10.**
Total Performances, Vial, Jean-B.: **42**

Vigée, Louis-J.-B.-E. *Aveux difficiles, Les* [*Comédie* in 1 act, Prem. on 24-2-1783, Pub. in 1783].
Th. du Feydeau (de Monsieur) (2); **Total: 2.**

_____. *Entrevue, L'* [*Comédie* in 1 act, Prem. on 6-12-1788, Pub. in 1788].
Th. de la Nation (Comédie Française) (17); Th. du Feydeau (de Monsieur) (17); Th. Français (de la rue Richelieu) (de la République) (3); **Total: 37.**

_____. *Matinée d'une jolie femme, La* [*Comédie* in 1 act, Prem. on 29-12-1792, Pub. in 1793].
Th. de l'Ambigu Comique (30); Th. de la Nation (Comédie Française) (10); **Total: 40.**

_____., Fay, Etienne (comp). *Projet extravagant, Le* [*Opéra* in 2 acts, Prem. on 11-7-1792].
    Th. Lyrique des Amis de la Patrie (3); **Total: 3.**

_____. *Vivacité à l'épreuve, La* [*Comédie* in 3 acts, Prem. on 5-7-1793].
    Th. de la Nation (Comédie Française) (3); **Total: 3.**
        Total Performances, Vigée, Louis-J.-B.-E.: **85**

Villemain d'Abancourt, François-J. *Arrivée de Voltaire à Romilly, L'* [*Fait Historique* in 1 act, Prem. on 10-7-1791].
    Th. de Molière (2); **Total: 2.**

_____. *Bienfaisance de Voltaire, La* [*Pièce* in 1 act, Prem. on 30-5-1791, Pub. in 1791].
    Th. de la Nation (Comédie Française) (4); **Total: 4.**

_____. *Chevalier de Faublas, Le* [*Comédie* in 1 act, Prem. on 3-2-1789, Pub. in 1789].
    Th. du Feydeau (de Monsieur) (16); **Total: 16.**

_____. *Journée de Henri IV, La* [*Comédie* in 3 acts, Prem. on 12-10-1791, Pub. in 1792].
    Th. de Molière (36); **Total: 36.**
        Total Performances, Villemain d'Abancourt, François-J.: **58**

Villeterque, Alexandre. *Mari jaloux et rival de lui-même, Le* [*Comédie*, Prem. on 14-6-1793, Pub. in 1792].
    Th. du Marais (11); **Total: 11.**

Villiers, Pierre-A.-B. *Apothicaire (dévalisé), L'* [*Comédie* in 1 act].
    Th. de la Citoyenne Montansier (4); **Total: 4.**

_____., Capelle, Pierre-A. *Bébée et jargon* [*Opéra*, Prem. on 27-3-1797, Pub. in 1797].
    Th. de la Citoyenne Montansier (17); **Total: 17.**

_____., Ferrière, Alexandre de. *Bustes, Les, ou Arlequin sculpteur* [*Comédie* in 1 act, Pub. in 1795].
    Maison Egalité (9); Th. du Palais (Cité)-Variétés (6); **Total: 15.**

_____. *Cange ou Le Commissionaire bienfaisant* [*Fait Historique* in 1 act, Prem. on 31-10-1794, Pub. in 1794].
    Th. du Palais (Cité)-Variétés (11); **Total: 11.**
        Total Performances, Villiers, Pierre-A.-B.: **47**

Voisenon, Abbé-C.-H. de Fusée de. *Coquette fixée, La* [*Comédie* in 3 acts, Prem. on 10-3-1746, Pub. in 1746].
    Th. des Italiens (Opéra-Comique) (2); **Total: 2.**

_____. *Mariages assortis, Les* [*Comédie* in 3 acts, Prem. on 10-2-1744, Pub. in 1744].
    Th. de l'Ambigu Comique (32); **Total: 32.**
        Total Performances, Voisenon, Abbé-C.-H. de Fusée de: **34**

Voligni, B.-V.-M. *Henri et Boulen* [*Parodie*, Prem. on 6-10-1791, Pub. in 1791].
    Th. de Molière (3); **Total: 3.**

Voltaire, F.-M. Arouet, dit Arouet de. *Adélaïde du Guesclin* [*Tragédie* in 5 acts, Prem. on 18-1-1734, Pub. in 1765].
Académie de la Musique (Opéra) (2); Th. de l'Odéon (5); Th. de la Citoyenne Montansier (1); Th. de la Liberté (2); Th. de la Nation (Comédie Française) (9); Th. de Molière (2); Th. des Délassements Comiques (6); Th. du Lycée Dramatique (5); Th. du Marais (2); Th. Français (de la rue Richelieu) (de la République) (2); Th. Lyrique des Amis de la Patrie (1); **Total: 37.**

_____. *Alzire ou Les Américains* [*Tragédie* in 5 acts, Prem. on 27-1-1736, Pub. in 1736].
n/a (6); Th. de l'Odéon (4); Th. de la Citoyenne Montansier (1); Th. de la Nation (Comédie Française) (20); Th. de la Rue Martin (3); Th. du Feydeau (de Monsieur) (6); Th. du Marais (2); Th. Français (de la rue Richelieu) (de la République) (10); **Total: 52.**

_____. *Brutus* [*Tragédie* in 5 acts, Prem. on 11-12-1730, Pub. in 1731].
Maison Egalité (1); Th. de l'Estrapade au Panthéon (1); Th. de l'Odéon (1); Th. de la Citoyenne Montansier (3); Th. de la Nation (Comédie Française) (22); Th. de Molière (1); Th. des Beaujolais (3); Th. des Délassements Comiques (3); Th. des Grands Danseurs (Gaîté) (8); Th. des Variétés Amusantes, Comiques et Lyriques (1); Th. des Victoires Nationales (2); Th. du Feydeau (de Monsieur) (4); Th. du Lycée Dramatique (6); Th. du Marais (11); Th. Français (de la rue Richelieu) (de la République) (37); Th. Français, Comique et Lyrique (2); Th. National (de la rue Richelieu) (1); **Total: 107.**

_____. *Café, Le, ou L'Ecossaise* [*Comédie* in 5 acts, Prem. on 26-7-1760, Pub. in 1760].
Th. de la Nation (Comédie Française) (4); Th. de la Rue Martin (2); Th. Français (de la rue Richelieu) (de la République) (1); **Total: 7.**

_____. *Catilina ou Rome sauvée* [*Tragédie*, Prem. on 24-2-1752, Pub. in 1752].
Th. de la Nation (Comédie Française) (2); **Total: 2.**

_____. *Droit du seigneur, Le, ou L'Ecueil du sage* [*Comédie* in 5 acts, Prem. on 18-1-1762, Pub. in 1763].
Th. des Italiens (Opéra-Comique) (1); **Total: 1.**

_____. *Enfant prodigue, L'* [*Comédie* in 5 acts, Prem. on 10-10-1736, Pub. in 1738].
Th. de l'Estrapade au Panthéon (1); Th. de la Nation (Comédie Française) (20); Th. de la Rue Martin (13); Th. de Molière (5); Th. des Victoires Nationales (4); Th. du Marais (2); Th. Français (de la rue Richelieu) (de la République) (14); **Total: 59.**

_____. *Envieux, L'* [*Comédie* in 3 acts, Pub. in 1834].
Th. de l'Odéon (1); **Total: 1.**

_____. *Femme qui a raison, La* [*Comédie* in 3 acts, Prem. in 1758, Pub. in 1759].
Th. de l'Ambigu Comique (44); **Total: 44.**

_____. *Mahomet* [*Tragédie* in 5 acts, Prem. on 9-8-1742, Pub. in 1742].
Maison Egalité (3); Th. de l'Ambigu Comique (3); Th. de l'Emulation (Gaîté) (8); Th. de l'Odéon (4); Th. de la Citoyenne Montansier (3); Th. de la Cité (1); Th. de la Nation (Comédie Française) (23); Th. des Beaujolais (1); Th. des Délassements Comiques (9); Th. du Feydeau (de Monsieur) (6); Th. du Lycée Dramatique (7); Th. du Marais (9); Th. du Palais (Cité)-Variétés (1); Th. Français (de la rue Richelieu) (de la République) (17); **Total: 95.**

_____. *Mérope* [*Tragédie* in 5 acts, Prem. on 20-2-1743, Pub. in 1744].
Th. de l'Odéon (1); Th. de la Citoyenne Montansier (20); Th. de la Liberté (3); Th. de la Nation (Comédie Française) (20); Th. des Grands Danseurs (Gaîté) (1); Th. du Lycée Dramatique (7); Th. du Marais (5); Th. Français (de la rue Richelieu) (de la République) (1); **Total: 58.**

_____. *Mort de César, La* [*Tragédie* in 3 acts, Prem. on 11-8-1735, Pub. in 1735].
Maison Egalité (1); n/a (4); Th. de l'Ambigu Comique (1); Th. de l'Estrapade au Panthéon (1); Th. de la Citoyenne Montansier (1); Th. de la Nation (Comédie Française) (5); Th. des Délassements Comiques (3); Th. du Feydeau (de Monsieur) (7); Th. du Marais (7); Th. Français (de la rue Richelieu) (de la République) (25); Th. National (de la rue Richelieu) (1); **Total: 56.**

_____. *Nanine* [*Comédie* in 3 acts, Prem. on 16-6-1749, Pub. in 1749].
n/a (2); Th. de l'Emulation (Gaîté) (6); Th. de l'Estrapade au Panthéon (4); Th. de l'Odéon (9); Th. de la Bienfaisance (1); Th. de la Citoyenne Montansier (33); Th. de la Cité (3); Th. de la Liberté (3); Th. de la Nation (Comédie Française) (13); Th. de la Rue Martin (8); Th. de Molière (10); Th. des Délassements Comiques (1); Th. des Variétés Amusantes (Lazzari) (4); Th. des Variétés Amusantes, Comiques et Lyriques (10); Th. des Victoires Nationales (1); Th. du Feydeau (de Monsieur) (9); Th. du Lycée des Arts (2); Th. du Lycée Dramatique (3); Th. du Marais (8); Th. du Palais (Cité)-Variétés (3); Th. du Vaudeville (2); Th. Français (de la rue Richelieu) (de la République) (23); Th. Lyrique des Amis de la Patrie (4); Th. National (de la rue Richelieu) (10); Th. Patriotique et de Momus (20); **Total: 192.**

_____. *Oedipe* [*Tragédie* in 5 acts, Prem. on 18-11-1718, Pub. in 1719].
Académie de la Musique (Opéra) (5); Th. de la Nation (Comédie Française) (7); Th. de Molière (2); Th. du Lycée Dramatique (2); **Total: 16.**

_____. *Oreste* [*Tragédie*, Pub. in 1750].
Th. de la Nation (Comédie Française) (3); **Total: 3.**

_____. *Orphelin de la Chine, L'* [*Tragédie* in 5 acts, Prem. on 20-8-1755, Pub. in 1755].
Th. de la Citoyenne Montansier (8); Th. de la Nation (Comédie Française) (11); **Total: 19.**

_____. *Sémiramis* [*Tragédie* in 5 acts, Prem. on 29-8-1748, Pub. in 1749].
Th. de l'Odéon (2); Th. de la Citoyenne Montansier (17); Th. de la Liberté (1); Th. de la Nation (Comédie Française) (15); Th. du Marais (6); Th. Français (de la rue Richelieu) (de la République) (10); **Total: 51.**

_____. *Tancrède* [*Tragédie* in 5 acts, Prem. on 3-9-1760, Pub. in 1760].
Th. de l'Odéon (2); Th. de la Citoyenne Montansier (11); Th. de la Nation (Comédie Française) (22); Th. des Délassements Comiques (4); Th. des Victoires Nationales (2); Th. du Marais (5); Th. Français (de la rue Richelieu) (de la République) (9); **Total: 55.**

_____. *Zaïre* [*Tragédie* in 5 acts, Prem. on 13-8-1732, Pub. in 1733].
n/a (2); Th. de la Citoyenne Montansier (2); Th. de la Nation (Comédie Française) (25); Th. des Délassements Comiques (3); Th. du Lycée Dramatique (3); Th. du Marais (1); Th. Français (de la rue Richelieu) (de la République) (5); **Total: 41.**

Total Performances, Voltaire, F.-M. Arouet, dit Arouet de: **896**

Watelet, Claude-H. *Statuaires d'Athènes, Les* [*Comédie* in 3 acts, Prem. on 28-8-1799].
Th. Français (de la rue Richelieu) (de la République) (1); **Total: 1.**

Ymond, B. Louis. *Muette, La* [*Comédie* in 1 act, Prem. on 16-10-1790].
    Th. de la Citoyenne Montansier (**17**); **Total: 17.**
Zini, Francesco-S., Guglielmi, Pietro.-A. (comp). *Bella Pescatrice, La*
    [*Comedia per Musica* in 2 acts, Prem. in 10-1789, Pub. in 1790].
        Th. du Feydeau (de Monsieur) (**4**); **Total: 4.**
_____., Cimarosa, Domenico (comp). *Fanatico burlato, Il* [*Comedia per*
Musica in 2 acts, Prem. on 28-11-1789].
        Th. du Feydeau (de Monsieur) (**4**); **Total: 4.**
_____., Guglielmi, Pietro.-A. (comp). *Pastorella nobile, La* [*Opéra* in 2
acts, Prem. in 4-1788, Pub. in 1789].
        Th. du Feydeau (de Monsieur) (**21**); **Total: 21.**
                        Total Performances, Zini, Francesco-S.: **29**

12

Repertory of Anonymous or Unattributed Plays

Sorted by title with number of performances by theatre.

A Bas les diables, à bas les bêtes [N/A].
    Th. de Molière (**12**); Th. des Troubadours (**12**); **Total: 24.**
A Quelque chose malheur et bon [N/A].
    Th. des Variétés Amusantes, Comiques et Lyriques (**3**); **Total: 3.**
A Qui la faute? [*Opéra*, Prem. on 29-1-1799].
    Th. du Mareux (**1**); **Total: 1.**
A Tout péché miséricorde [*Parodie* in 1 act].
    Th. du Vaudeville (**3**); **Total: 3.**
Abbé chez la mère Duchesne, L' [*Tableau-Patriotique* in 1 act, Prem. on 31-3-1791].
    Th. des Grands Danseurs (Gaîté) (**26**); **Total: 26.**
Abbé vert, L' [*Fait Historique* in 1 act, Prem. on 4-5-1793].
    Th. du Vaudeville (**16**); **Total: 16.**
Abonnements, Les [N/A].
    Th. du Marais (**5**); **Total: 5.**
Absents ont tort, Les [N/A].
    Th. des Jeunes Artistes (**1**); **Total: 1.**
Abus de la presse, L' [N/A].
    Th. de l'Ambigu Comique (**18**); **Total: 18.**
Abus de pouvoir de l'Ancien Régime [*Fait Historique*, Pub. in 1794].
    Th. de l'Ambigu Comique (**13**); **Total: 13.**
Accord poissard, L' [N/A].
    Th. des Ombres Chinoises (**3**); **Total: 3.**
Accordées de village, Les [*Opéra-Comique* in 3 acts, Prem. on 4-5-1791].
    Th. de la Citoyenne Montansier (**11**); Th. des Grands Danseurs (Gaîté) (**20**); **Total: 31.**
Accords de Julie, Les, ou Le Savant dupé [*Comédie* in 1 act, Prem. on 6-1-1791].
    Th. des Beaujolais (**5**); Th. des Grands Danseurs (Gaîté) (**4**); **Total: 9.**

Acteur chez lui, L' [*Prologue* in 1 act, Prem. on 8-1-1781].
Th. des Variétés Amusantes, Comiques et Lyriques (12); **Total: 12.**

Acteur débutant, L' [*Comédie* in 2 acts, Prem. on 24-10-1791].
Cirque National (8); **Total: 8.**

Adélaïde de Lussan [*Comédie* in 3 acts, Pub. in 1790].
Th. de l'Ambigu Comique (39); **Total: 39.**

Adèle de Crécy [*Drame* in 4 acts, Prem. on 3-5-1793].
Th. de la Nation (Comédie Française) (6); **Total: 6.**

Adèle de Sacy ou Le Siège du Mont-Cenis [*Pantomime* in 3 acts, Prem. on
24-8-1793, Pub. in 1795].
Th. de la Rue Martin (4); Th. des Italiens (Opéra-Comique) (1); Th. du
Lycée des Arts (95); **Total: 100.**

Adèle et Edwin [*Comédie* in 1 act, Prem. on 19-8-1791].
Th. Lyrique des Amis de la Patrie (19); **Total: 19.**

Adèle et Julien [Prem. on 22-5-1798].
Th. du Palais (Cité)-Variétés (11); **Total: 11.**

Adèle ou La Chaumière [*Opéra*, Prem. on 1-2-1798].
Th. de la Citoyenne Montansier (1); Th. des Jeunes Artistes (19); Th. des
Variétés Amusantes, Comiques et Lyriques (7); Th. du Marais (2); **Total:
29.**

Adeline et Tracy ou La Suite des naufrages [*Pantomime*, Prem. on 23-8-
1797].
Th. de l'Ambigu Comique (39); **Total: 39.**

Adolphe ou La Vengeance [*Pantomime*].
Th. du Palais (Cité)-Variétés (1); **Total: 1.**

Africains, Les [N/A].
Th. Patriotique et de Momus (2); **Total: 2.**

Agard [N/A].
Th. du Vaudeville (1); **Total: 1.**

Ah! ah! C'est inconcevable [*Parodie*].
Th. de l'Emulation (Gaîté) (12); **Total: 12.**

Ahuris de Chaillot, Les [N/A].
Th. de l'Ambigu Comique (10); **Total: 10.**

Ailes de l'amour, Les [N/A].
Th. de Molière (1); Th. des Jeunes Artistes (11); **Total: 12.**

Aimable viellard, L' [N/A].
Th. de l'Emulation (Gaîté) (1); **Total: 1.**

Aînée, L', ou La Cadette [N/A].
Th. du Vaudeville (13); **Total: 13.**

Airos, L' [N/A].
Th. du Palais (Cité)-Variétés (1); **Total: 1.**

Albert ou L'Origine de la République Lucques [*Comédie* in 3 acts, Prem. on
6-12-1792].
Th. du Vaudeville (2); **Total: 2.**

Alexis et Basile [N/A].
Th. des Jeunes Artistes (1); **Total: 1.**

Alexis et Fanchette [*Opéra* in 2 acts, Prem. on 11-11-1790].
Th. des Délassements Comiques (2); **Total: 2.**

Alix de Valdemar [N/A].
Th. de la Citoyenne Montansier (21); Th. de la Cité (1); **Total: 22.**

Allemande à trois, L' [N/A].
Th. des Grands Danseurs (Gaîté) (3); **Total: 3.**
Amant astrologue et médecin, L' [*Comédie* in 1 act, Pub. in 1795].
Th. des Variétés Amusantes, Comiques et Lyriques (3); **Total: 3.**
Amant au tombeau, L' [*Pantomime*, Pub. in 1788].
Th. des Grands Danseurs (Gaîté) (78); **Total: 78.**
Amant bienvenu, L', ou Les Deux soeurs rivales [*Comédie* in 2 acts, Prem. on 9-11-1774].
Th. des Grands Danseurs (Gaîté) (36); **Total: 36.**
Amant femme-de-chambre, L' [Prem. on 16-3-1799].
Th. du Palais (Cité)-Variétés (6); **Total: 6.**
Amant flatté, L' [*Comédie*].
Th. des Italiens (Opéra-Comique) (2); **Total: 2.**
Amant hermite, L' [N/A].
Th. de la Citoyenne Montansier (1); Th. de la Rue Antoine (1); Th. des Variétés Amusantes, Comiques et Lyriques (60); **Total: 62.**
Amant inquiet, L', ou Le Rival supposé [*Comédie*, Prem. on 8-11-1791].
Th. du Marais (1); **Total: 1.**
Amant invisible, L' [N/A].
Th. des Grands Danseurs (Gaîté) (23); **Total: 23.**
Amant maître d'école, L' [In 1 act].
Th. des Grands Danseurs (Gaîté) (2); **Total: 2.**
Amant protégé par Vulcain, L' [N/A].
Th. des Grands Danseurs (Gaîté) (1); **Total: 1.**
Amant sculpteur, L' [*Vaudeville* in 1 act, Prem. on 15-9-1790].
Th. Français, Comique et Lyrique (30); **Total: 30.**
Amant volage, L' [N/A].
Th. des Variétés Amusantes, Comiques et Lyriques (2); **Total: 2.**
Amants à l'épreuve, Les [*Comédie* in 1 act, Prem. on 3-8-1793].
Th. Lyrique des Amis de la Patrie (18); **Total: 18.**
Amants anglais, Les [*Drame* in 3 acts, Prem. on 27-10-1791].
Th. de la Citoyenne Montansier (23); Th. National (de la rue Richelieu) (1); **Total: 24.**
Amants invisibles, Les [*Pantomime*].
Th. des Grands Danseurs (Gaîté) (42); **Total: 42.**
Amants par vengeance, Les [*Comédie* in 1 act, Prem. on 26-11-1791].
Th. de l'Ambigu Comique (6); Th. des Jeunes Artistes (3); **Total: 9.**
Amants rivaux, Les [N/A].
n/a (2); **Total: 2.**
Amants siciliens, Les, ou Les Apparences trompeuses [*Comédie*, Prem. on 19-1-1799].
Th. de Molière (1); **Total: 1.**
Amants surpris, Les [N/A].
Th. des Grands Danseurs (Gaîté) (2); **Total: 2.**
Amants voleurs, Les [Prem. on 28-9-1799].
Th. des Grands Danseurs (Gaîté) (2); Th. des Ombres Chinoises (1); **Total: 3.**
Amélie [In 3 acts].
Th. de l'Ambigu Comique (6); **Total: 6.**
Amélie et Melcour [N/A].
Th. du Lycée des Arts (1); **Total: 1.**

Amélie ou Le Couvent [*Comédie* in 2 acts, Prem. on 3-3-1791].
Th. du Feydeau (de Monsieur) (**30**); **Total: 30**.

Amis, Les [*Comédie* in 3 acts, Prem. on 13-8-1791, Pub. in 1779].
Th. de Molière (**11**); **Total: 11**.

Amour dragon, L' [*Opéra* in 2 acts, Prem. on 25-6-1792].
Th. de la Citoyenne Montansier (**2**); **Total: 2**.

Amour et courage [*Pantomime*].
Th. du Palais (Cité)-Variétés (**2**); **Total: 2**.

Amour et humanité [N/A].
Th. des Jeunes Artistes (**50**); **Total: 50**.

Amour et jeunesse ou Le Sous-lieutenant [*Vaudeville* in 2 acts].
Th. des Variétés Amusantes (Lazzari) (**2**); Th. du Palais (Cité)-Variétés (**3**); **Total: 5**.

Amour et la paix, L' [Prem. on 12-5-1797].
Th. de l'Ambigu Comique (**2**); **Total: 2**.

Amour et la vieillesse, L' [Prem. on 25-5-1797].
Th. des Variétés Amusantes, Comiques et Lyriques (**3**); **Total: 3**.

Amour et les lettres, L' [Prem. on 30-6-1797].
Th. de l'Emulation (Gaîté) (**28**); **Total: 28**.

Amour maternel, L' [*Ballet*].
Th. de l'Ambigu Comique (**6**); **Total: 6**.

Amour par ressemblance, L' [*Opéra* in 2 acts, Prem. on 27-4-1792].
Th. de la Citoyenne Montansier (**4**); **Total: 4**.

Amour rend capable de tout, L' [N/A].
Th. des Variétés Amusantes, Comiques et Lyriques (**6**); **Total: 6**.

Amours d'Alain, Les [N/A].
Th. des Grands Danseurs (Gaîté) (**1**); **Total: 1**.

Amours de blanquette et de restaurant, Les [*Tragédie-Parade* in 1 act, Prem. on 5-8-1785, Pub. in 1772].
Th. des Grands Danseurs (Gaîté) (**9**); **Total: 9**.

Amours de chasseur [*Comédie*].
Th. des Grands Danseurs (Gaîté) (**1**); **Total: 1**.

Amours de Colin et Colinette, Les [*Comédie* in 1 act, Pub. in 1783].
Th. des Grands Danseurs (Gaîté) (**1**); **Total: 1**.

Amours de Colin et d'Agathe, Les [*Comédie*].
Th. des Grands Danseurs (Gaîté) (**2**); **Total: 2**.

Amours de Colombine et Arlequin, Les [N/A].
Th. des Grands Danseurs (Gaîté) (**6**); **Total: 6**.

Amours de Colombine et Delorme, Les [*Comédie*].
Th. des Grands Danseurs (Gaîté) (**4**); **Total: 4**.

Amours de Cora, Les [*Comédie*].
Th. des Grands Danseurs (Gaîté) (**3**); **Total: 3**.

Amours de Gargotin et Blanquette, Les [N/A].
Th. des Grands Danseurs (Gaîté) (**2**); **Total: 2**.

Amours de Gilles au camp de Châlons, Les [*Vaudeville* in 1 act].
Th. de l'Estrapade au Panthéon (**3**); **Total: 3**.

Amours de Jeannette, Les [N/A].
Th. des Grands Danseurs (Gaîté) (**1**); **Total: 1**.

Amours de M. Barbarus et de Mme. Neviège [N/A].
Th. des Grands Danseurs (Gaîté) (**1**); **Total: 1**.

Amours de M. Cuirvieux et de Mme. Beurrefort, Les [*Tragi-Comédie* in 1 act, Pub. in 1787].
> Th. des Grands Danseurs (Gaîté) (**49**); **Total: 49.**

Amours de M. Thurin, Les [*Comédie*].
> Th. des Grands Danseurs (Gaîté) (**1**); **Total: 1.**

Amours de Madame Angot, Les [N/A].
> Th. des Jeunes Artistes (**7**); **Total: 7.**

Amours de Mme. Martin, Les, ou L'Enrôlement de Pierrot [*Comédie* in 1 act, Prem. on 23-7-1782].
> Th. des Grands Danseurs (Gaîté) (**15**); **Total: 15.**

Amours de Mme. Mirotin et de M. Gargotin [*Comédie*].
> Th. des Grands Danseurs (Gaîté) (**14**); **Total: 14.**

Amours de Mme Revêche, Les [*Comédie*].
> Th. des Grands Danseurs (Gaîté) (**1**); **Total: 1.**

Amours de Nicaise et de Silvandre [N/A].
> Th. des Grands Danseurs (Gaîté) (**14**); **Total: 14.**

Amours de Nice et de Valère, Les [*Comédie*].
> Th. des Grands Danseurs (Gaîté) (**5**); **Total: 5.**

Amours de Nicodème, Les, ou Le Désespoir favorable [*Pantomime* in 2 acts, Pub. in 1783].
> Th. de l'Emulation (Gaîté) (**2**); Th. des Grands Danseurs (Gaîté) (**16**); **Total: 18.**

Amours de Pierrot et de Thérèse, Les [*Comédie*].
> Th. des Grands Danseurs (Gaîté) (**1**); **Total: 1.**

Amours de Plailly, Les [*Fait Historique* in 1 act, Prem. on 28-9-1793].
> Th. du Lycée des Arts (**32**); **Total: 32.**

Amours de Prométhée et de Pandore, Les [*Pantomime*].
> Th. des Grands Danseurs (Gaîté) (**34**); **Total: 34.**

Amours de Thérèse et de François, Les [*Comédie*].
> Th. des Grands Danseurs (Gaîté) (**1**); **Total: 1.**

Amours du meunier et du charbonnier, Les [*Pantomime* in 1 act, Prem. on 19-11-1786].
> Th. des Grands Danseurs (Gaîté) (**5**); **Total: 5.**

Amours du précepteur et de la gouvernante, Les [*Comédie*, Pub. in 1790].
> Th. des Grands Danseurs (Gaîté) (**8**); **Total: 8.**

Amours du quai de la Ferraille, Les [*Comédie* in 1 act, Prem. on 31-7-1787].
> Th. de l'Ambigu Comique (**95**); Th. du Vaudeville (**1**); **Total: 96.**

Amours du savetier, Les [*Comédie*].
> Th. des Grands Danseurs (Gaîté) (**1**); **Total: 1.**

An 1788, 1789 et 1792, L' [*Vaudeville*, Pub. in 1792].
> Th. de Molière (**1**); **Total: 1.**

Anacréon, L' [*Parodie*, Prem. on 13-3-1797].
> Th. de l'Emulation (Gaîté) (**19**); Th. Lyrique des Amis de la Patrie (**2**); **Total: 21.**

Ancien et le nouveau régime, L' [*Comédie* in 2 acts, Prem. on 5-5-1791].
> Petits Comédiens de Palais Royal (**10**); **Total: 10.**

Ane et le procureur, L' [N/A].
> Th. de l'Emulation (Gaîté) (**45**); **Total: 45.**

Angélique et Vilmard [*Comédie* in 3 acts].
> Th. de la Citoyenne Montansier (**2**); Th. de la Montagne (**1**); **Total: 3.**

Anglais travestis, Les [*Comédie* in 1 act, Pub. in 1792].
> Th. des Variétés Amusantes, Comiques et Lyriques (1); Th. Français, Comique et Lyrique (5); **Total: 6.**

Anglaise, L' [N/A].
> Th. des Grands Danseurs (Gaîté) (1); **Total: 1.**

Annette et Rosette [N/A].
> Th. des Jeunes Artistes (1); **Total: 1.**

Anniversaire du 10 août, L' [*Tableau-Patriotique* in 1 act, Pub. in 1794].
> Th. National (de la rue Richelieu) (1); **Total: 1.**

Annonciades, Les [*Comédie* in 1 act, Prem. in 1793].
> Th. Français, Comique et Lyrique (1); **Total: 1.**

Anti-dramaturge, L' [*Comédie* in 3 acts, Prem. on 6-6-1790, Pub. in 1790].
> Th. des Beaujolais (24); **Total: 24.**

Antigone [N/A].
> Th. des Délassements Comiques (6); **Total: 6.**

Antipathie, L' [*Opéra*, Prem. on 11-12-1798].
> Th. de la Citoyenne Montansier (1); **Total: 1.**

Antiquaire, L' [*Comédie* in 1 act, Pub. in 1789].
> Th. des Beaujolais (10); **Total: 10.**

Antiques d'Italie, Les [N/A].
> Th. de la Citoyenne Montansier (18); Th. de la Cité (1); **Total: 19.**

Apheline, L' [N/A].
> Th. du Palais (Cité)-Variétés (1); **Total: 1.**

Apollon ou Le Triomphe des arts utiles [*Proverbe/allégorique*, Prem. on 18-5-1794].
> Th. du Lycée des Arts (44); **Total: 44.**

Apothéose de Favart, L', ou Favart aux Champs-Elysées [N/A].
> Th. du Vaudeville (17); **Total: 17.**

Apothéose de Mirabeau, Voltaire et Rousseau [*Tableau-Patriotique*].
> Th. de Molière (1); **Total: 1.**

Araminthe [Prem. on 8-10-1799].
> Th. des Jeunes Artistes (3); **Total: 3.**

Arbre de Diane, L' [*Vaudeville* in 3 acts, Prem. on 6-5-1790].
> Th. de la Citoyenne Montansier (15); **Total: 15.**

Arbre de la liberté, L' [*Opéra* in 1 act, Prem. on 3-1-1793].
> Th. de la Citoyenne Montansier (1); **Total: 1.**

Arbre enchanté, L' [N/A].
> Th. des Variétés Amusantes (Lazzari) (39); **Total: 39.**

Archevêque de Lisbonne, L' [N/A].
> Th. de l'Emulation (Gaîté) (1); **Total: 1.**

Argent vient en chantant, L' [N/A].
> Th. des Ombres de J.-J. Rousseau (2); **Total: 2.**

Ariane [Prem. on 4-11-1797].
> Th. des Italiens (Opéra-Comique) (1); **Total: 1.**

Aristocratie démasquée, L' [*Comédie*].
> Th. des Grands Danseurs (Gaîté) (11); **Total: 11.**

Arlequin [*Pantomime*].
> Th. des Jeunes Artistes (13); Th. des Variétés Amusantes (Lazzari) (3); Th. des Variétés Amusantes, Comiques et Lyriques (2); **Total: 18.**

Arlequin aîné et cadet [N/A].
> Th. des Grands Danseurs (Gaîté) (3); **Total: 3.**

Arlequin amant rebuté [*Pantomime*].
Th. des Grands Danseurs (Gaîté) (**1**); **Total: 1**.
Arlequin apprenti magicien [*Pantomime* in 5 acts, Pub. in 1767].
Th. des Grands Danseurs (Gaîté) (**2**); **Total: 2**.
Arlequin au désespoir [*Pantomime*].
Th. des Grands Danseurs (Gaîté) (**1**); **Total: 1**.
Arlequin auteur et Gilles musicien [N/A].
Th. des Grands Danseurs (Gaîté) (**25**); **Total: 25**.
Arlequin automate [N/A].
Th. des Variétés Amusantes, Comiques et Lyriques (**1**); **Total: 1**.
Arlequin bon fils [Prem. on 13-6-1796].
Th. du Vaudeville (**5**); **Total: 5**.
Arlequin brouetteur [Prem. on 28-2-1799].
Th. des Grands Danseurs (Gaîté) (**4**); **Total: 4**.
Arlequin charcutier [*Pantomime* in 2 acts, Prem. on -3-1778].
Th. des Grands Danseurs (Gaîté) (**1**); **Total: 1**.
Arlequin dégraisseur [N/A].
Th. du Vaudeville (**1**); **Total: 1**.
Arlequin dentiste [Prem. on 3-4-1797].
Th. du Vaudeville (**12**); **Total: 12**.
Arlequin doge de Venise [Prem. on 23-1-1799].
Th. du Vaudeville (**1**); **Total: 1**.
Arlequin et Angélique invisibles [*Pantomime*].
Th. des Grands Danseurs (Gaîté) (**9**); **Total: 9**.
Arlequin et Colombine invisibles [*Pantomime* in 2 acts, Prem. on 13-3-1785].
Th. des Grands Danseurs (Gaîté) (**24**); **Total: 24**.
Arlequin et Isabelle invisibles [*Pantomime*].
Th. des Grands Danseurs (Gaîté) (**3**); **Total: 3**.
Arlequin et Scapin rivaux [*Pantomime* in 3 acts, Pub. in 1770].
Th. des Variétés Amusantes (Lazzari) (**35**); Th. des Variétés Amusantes, Comiques et Lyriques (**8**); **Total: 43**.
Arlequin frippier [N/A].
Th. de la Cité (**8**); **Total: 8**.
Arlequin garçon traiteur [Prem. on 21-4-1796].
Th. du Vaudeville (**3**); **Total: 3**.
Arlequin incendiaire [N/A].
Th. des Variétés Amusantes, Comiques et Lyriques (**1**); **Total: 1**.
Arlequin incombustible ou L'Onguent pour la brûlure [*Parodie* in 1 act].
Th. du Vaudeville (**24**); **Total: 24**.
Arlequin infidèle [*Pantomime* in 2 acts].
Th. des Grands Danseurs (Gaîté) (**1**); **Total: 1**.
Arlequin jardinier [*Pantomime*].
Tivoli (**2**); **Total: 2**.
Arlequin machiniste [*Comédie* in 1 act, Prem. on 31-3-1793].
Th. des Grands Danseurs (Gaîté) (**1**); Th. du Vaudeville (**30**); **Total: 31**.
Arlequin et Madame Pataffia [N/A].
Th. des Variétés Amusantes, Comiques et Lyriques (**1**); **Total: 1**.
Arlequin magicien [*Comédie* in 3 acts, Pub. in 1739].
Th. des Grands Danseurs (Gaîté) (**6**); **Total: 6**.
Arlequin Mahomet ou Le Cabriolet volant [*Drame*, Prem. on 5-6-1798].
Th. de l'Emulation (Gaîté) (**1**); Th. Lyrique des Amis de la Patrie (**5**); **Total: 6**.

Arlequin maître d'école [N/A].
   Th. des Variétés Amusantes (Lazzari) (**42**); Th. des Variétés Amusantes, Comiques et Lyriques (**24**); **Total: 66**.

Arlequin maître d'esprit [N/A].
   Th. des Variétés Amusantes (Lazzari) (**27**); **Total: 27**.

Arlequin maître et valet [*Pantomime* in 3 acts].
   Th. de la Citoyenne Montansier (**1**); **Total: 1**.

Arlequin mannequin [*Vaudeville* in 1 act, Pub. in 1793].
   Th. des Variétés Amusantes (Lazzari) (**7**); Th. des Variétés Amusantes, Comiques et Lyriques (**8**); **Total: 15**.

Arlequin marchand d'esprit [*Opéra*].
   Th. de l'Emulation (Gaîté) (**4**); Th. des Jeunes Artistes (**1**); Th. des Variétés Amusantes (Lazzari) (**1**); Th. des Variétés Amusantes, Comiques et Lyriques (**23**); **Total: 29**.

Arlequin marchand d'oeufs [*Pantomime* in 1 act].
   Th. des Grands Danseurs (Gaîté) (**3**); **Total: 3**.

Arlequin médecin du malade jaloux [*Pantomime* in 3 acts, Prem. on 3-1-1782].
   Th. des Grands Danseurs (Gaîté) (**13**); **Total: 13**.

Arlequin médecin par amour [N/A].
   Th. de la Nation (Comédie Française) (**1**); Th. des Grands Danseurs (Gaîté) (**9**); Th. des Variétés Amusantes, Comiques et Lyriques (**3**); **Total: 13**.

Arlequin messager des paysans de qualité [*Pantomime*].
   Th. des Grands Danseurs (Gaîté) (**10**); **Total: 10**.

Arlequin meunier [*Comédie* in 1 act].
   Th. de la Citoyenne Montansier (**1**); **Total: 1**.

Arlequin nécromancien [*Pantomime* in 2 acts].
   Th. des Grands Danseurs (Gaîté) (**30**); **Total: 30**.

Arlequin par amour [*Pantomime*].
   Th. des Grands Danseurs (Gaîté) (**1**); **Total: 1**.

Arlequin pâtissier ou Le Cochon de lait [*Pantomime* in 2 acts, Prem. on 13-2-1781].
   Th. des Grands Danseurs (Gaîté) (**35**); Th. des Variétés Amusantes, Comiques et Lyriques (**4**); **Total: 39**.

Arlequin postillon [*Pantomime*].
   Th. des Grands Danseurs (Gaîté) (**3**); **Total: 3**.

Arlequin protégé par la fortune [Prem. on 16-5-1797].
   Th. de l'Émulation (Gaîté) (**3**); **Total: 3**.

Arlequin protégé par la magie [N/A].
   Th. de la Citoyenne Montansier (**1**); **Total: 1**.

Arlequin protégé par le diable boiteur [*Pantomime* in 3 acts, Prem. on 2-6-1781].
   Th. des Grands Danseurs (Gaîté) (**1**); **Total: 1**.

Arlequin protégé par Nostradamus [*Pantomime*].
   Th. des Grands Danseurs (Gaîté) (**24**); Th. des Variétés Amusantes, Comiques et Lyriques (**7**); **Total: 31**.

Arlequin qui rit et Gilles qui pleure [*Vaudeville* in 1 act].
   Th. du Vaudeville (**4**); **Total: 4**.

Arlequin receveur de loterie [Prem. on 7-4-1798].
   Th. de la Citoyenne Montansier (**3**); **Total: 3**.

Arlequin restaurateur ou La Gageure [N/A].
   Th. du Vaudeville (**8**); **Total: 8**.

Arlequin rival de son oncle [*Pantomime*].
  Th. des Grands Danseurs (Gaîté) (**1**); **Total: 1.**
Arlequin rival du capitaine hollandois [*Pantomime*].
  Th. des Grands Danseurs (Gaîté) (**1**); **Total: 1.**
Arlequin squelette par amour [*Pantomime* in 1 act, Pub. in 1775].
  Th. des Grands Danseurs (Gaîté) (**2**); Th. des Variétés Amusantes (Laz-
  zari) (**5**); Th. des Variétés Amusantes, Comiques et Lyriques (**21**); **Total:
  28.**
Arlequin triomphant [*Pantomime*].
  Th. des Grands Danseurs (Gaîté) (**5**); **Total: 5.**
Arlequin vainqueur de son rival [*Pantomime*].
  Th. des Grands Danseurs (Gaîté) (**1**); **Total: 1.**
Arlequin voleur sans le savoir [*Farce* in 1 act, Prem. on 25-10-1780].
  Th. des Grands Danseurs (Gaîté) (**3**); **Total: 3.**
Arrivée d'Arlequin, L' [N/A].
  Th. des Grands Danseurs (Gaîté) (**7**); **Total: 7.**
Arrivée de Beaumarchais aux Champs Elysées, L' [N/A].
  Th. du Vaudeville (**1**); **Total: 1.**
Arrivée de Henri IV à Paris, L' [*Comédie* in 2 acts, Prem. on 20-3-1790].
  Th. des Grands Danseurs (Gaîté) (**47**); **Total: 47.**
Arrivée de Jean Bart à Marseille reçu par le père Duchesne, L'
  [*Comédie* in 1 act].
  Th. de l'Emulation (Gaîté) (**5**); **Total: 5.**
Arrivée de la jeune Thalie, L' [*Intermède* in 1 act].
  Th. des Délassements Comiques (**2**); **Total: 2.**
Arrivée de mon oncle Colas, L' [Pub. in 1792].
  Th. des Grands Danseurs (Gaîté) (**3**); **Total: 3.**
Arrivée du maître, L' [N/A].
  Th. de la Citoyenne Montansier (**14**); Th. de la Cité (**1**); **Total: 15.**
Arrivée et le couronnement de Mirabeau aux Champs-Elysées, L'
  [*Tableau-Patriotique* in 3 acts].
  Th. de la Liberté (**2**); **Total: 2.**
Artiste, L' [*Comédie* in 1 act, Prem. on 27-7-1797].
  Th. de l'Emulation (Gaîté) (**1**); **Total: 1.**
Arts et les femmes, Les [*Comédie* in 1 act, Pub. in 1795].
  Th. des Variétés Amusantes (Lazzari) (**2**); **Total: 2.**
Au Feu d'artifice [N/A].
  Th. des Variétés Amusantes, Comiques et Lyriques (**1**); **Total: 1.**
Auberge à Bruxelles, L', ou Le Jour de l'an [*Vaudeville* in 2 acts].
  Th. de l'Estrapade au Panthéon (**13**); **Total: 13.**
Auberge supposé, L' [N/A].
  Académie de la Musique (Opéra) (**1**); Th. de l'Odéon (**1**); **Total: 2.**
Aubomanie, L' [Pub. in 1795].
  Th. de la Rue Martin (**1**); **Total: 1.**
Auguste et Marianne [N/A].
  Th. de Molière (**2**); **Total: 2.**
Autel de la patrie, L' [*Opéra-Comique* in 1 act, Prem. on 15-7-1792].
  Th. Lyrique des Amis de la Patrie (**3**); **Total: 3.**
Auteur aux expédients, L' [*Comédie* in 1 act, Prem. on 23-11-1789].
  Th. de l'Ambigu Comique (**10**); **Total: 10.**

Auteur mécontent, L' [*Comédie* in 1 act].
Th. de l'Estrapade au Panthéon (**7**); **Total: 7.**

Avènement du Mustapha au trône, L' [*Vaudeville* in 3 acts, Pub. in 1792].
Th. Français (de la rue Richelieu) (de la République) (**2**); **Total: 2.**

Aventures de don Quichotte, Les [N/A].
Ampithéâtre National (**21**); **Total: 21.**

Aventures de la nuit espagnole, Les [*Comédie* in 3 acts].
Th. des Grands Danseurs (Gaîté) (**3**); **Total: 3.**

Aventures des halles, Les [N/A].
Th. des Ombres Chinoises (**3**); **Total: 3.**

Aventures du matin dans les ombres, Les [N/A].
Th. des Ombres Chinoises (**5**); Th. des Ombres de J.-J. Rousseau (**20**); **Total: 25.**

Aventurier gascon, L' [*Comédie* in 1 act, Prem. on 4-2-1792].
Th. Français, Comique et Lyrique (**2**); **Total: 2.**

Aveu supposé, L' [Prem. on 12-8-1797].
Th. du Vaudeville (**9**); **Total: 9.**

Avocat Patelin, L' [*Opéra-Comique*, Prem. on 13-1-1794, Pub. in 1794].
Th. de la Montagne (**6**); Th. du Marais (**1**); **Total: 7.**

Aymar et Azalais ou Le Château de Sendar [*Drame*].
Th. du Palais (Cité)-Variétés (**5**); **Total: 5.**

Azémire ou Les Réfugiés péruviens [*Pantomime*, Prem. on 17-10-1798].
Th. de l'Emulation (Gaîté) (**27**); Th. Lyrique des Amis de la Patrie (**7**); **Total: 34.**

Babet et Paulin ou Le Paysan supposé [*Opéra* in 2 acts].
Th. de l'Estrapade au Panthéon (**1**); **Total: 1.**

Bah! c'est singulier [Prem. on 6-12-1797].
Th. des Jeunes Artistes (**17**); **Total: 17.**

Bal, Le, ou L'Amour et la fortune [*Pantomime* in 1 act, Prem. on 10-5-1788].
Th. des Grands Danseurs (Gaîté) (**13**); **Total: 13.**

Ballet américain, Le [N/A].
Th. des Italiens (Opéra-Comique) (**1**); **Total: 1.**

Ballet de la guinguette, Le [N/A].
Th. de l'Emulation (Gaîté) (**1**); **Total: 1.**

Ballet de Paris [*Ballet*].
Académie de la Musique (Opéra) (**6**); **Total: 6.**

Ballet des fleurs, Le [*Ballet*].
Th. de l'Emulation (Gaîté) (**3**); Th. des Grands Danseurs (Gaîté) (**2**); **Total: 5.**

Ballet des foux, Le [*Ballet*].
Th. du Palais (Cité)-Variétés (**2**); **Total: 2.**

Ballet des nègres, Le [*Ballet*].
Th. de la Cité (**1**); Th. National (de la rue Richelieu) (**2**); **Total: 3.**

Barbe-bleue [*Comédie* in 2 acts, Prem. on 28-9-1795].
Th. des Italiens (Opéra-Comique) (**3**); Th. des Ombres Chinoises (**8**); **Total: 11.**

Barbe-bleue dans les marionnettes [N/A].
Th. des Ombres de J.-J. Rousseau (**12**); **Total: 12.**

Barbier babillard, Le [*Comédie* in 3 acts, Pub. in 1776].
Th. des Grands Danseurs (Gaîté) (**2**); **Total: 2.**

Baron de Roquetin, Le [*Comédie* in 2 acts, Pub. in 1788].
Th. des Beaujolais (**4**); **Total: 4.**

Barrogo [N/A].
Th. de la Citoyenne Montansier (**2**); **Total: 2**.

Basque, Le [N/A].
Th. des Grands Danseurs (Gaîté) (**7**); **Total: 7**.

Bassville à Rome [*Comédie* in 1 act, Prem. on 4-3-1793].
Th. de l'Ambigu Comique (**6**); **Total: 6**.

Bastien et Colette [*Opéra* in 1 act, Prem. on 16-6-1791].
Th. de la Citoyenne Montansier (**1**); **Total: 1**.

Bastille, La, ou Le Régime intérieur [*Drame* in 3 acts, Prem. on 6-6-1791].
Th. Français, Comique et Lyrique (**34**); **Total: 34**.

Bathilde et Eloy [Pub. in 1795].
Th. des Italiens (Opéra-Comique) (**17**); **Total: 17**.

Batilde et Ferdinand [*Vaudeville* in 3 acts, Prem. on 10-2-1793].
Th. de l'Estrapade au Panthéon (**7**); **Total: 7**.

Belle bouquetière, La [*Comédie*].
Th. des Grands Danseurs (Gaîté) (**18**); **Total: 18**.

Belle capricieuse, La [In 3 acts, Pub. in 1749].
Th. des Grands Danseurs (Gaîté) (**27**); **Total: 27**.

Belle créole, La [N/A].
Th. de la Rue Martin (**1**); Th. du Lycée des Arts (**3**); **Total: 4**.

Belle fille, La [*Comédie* in 3 acts, Prem. on 24-10-1789].
Th. du Palais Royal (**1**); **Total: 1**.

Belle-mère, La [Prem. on 1-11-1798].
Th. des Jeunes Artistes (**25**); **Total: 25**.

Bienfait récompensé, Le [*Pantomime* in 4 acts, Prem. on 7-6-1784].
Th. de la Citoyenne Montansier (**5**); Th. des Grands Danseurs (Gaîté) (**1**);
Th. des Variétés Amusantes (Lazzari) (**6**); **Total: 12**.

Bienfaiteur rival, Le [*Comédie*].
Th. des Victoires (**2**); **Total: 2**.

Bièvre ou L'Abus de l'esprit [N/A].
Th. des Jeunes Artistes (**2**); Th. des Troubadours (**4**); Th. du Feydeau (de
Monsieur) (**1**); **Total: 7**.

Billet au porteur, Le [Prem. on 3-6-1797].
Th. des Jeunes Artistes (**3**); **Total: 3**.

Billet de loterie, Le [*Comédie*].
Th. des Ombres Chinoises (**1**); Th. des Ombres de J.-J. Rousseau (**3**); **Total: 4**.

Blaise ensorcelé ou L'Amant magicien [N/A].
Th. des Jeunes Artistes (**2**); **Total: 2**.

Boëtes, Les, ou Le Réveille-matin [*Vaudeville*, Pub. in 1796].
Th. de la Cité (**5**); **Total: 5**.

Boeuf à la mode, Le [Prem. on 10-6-1797].
Th. des Délassements Comiques (**23**); **Total: 23**.

Bohémiens, Les [*Comédie*].
Th. des Variétés Amusantes, Comiques et Lyriques (**9**); **Total: 9**.

Boiteuse, La [*Comédie* in 1 act, Prem. on 22-1-1793].
Th. de la Citoyenne Montansier (**3**); **Total: 3**.

Bon curé, Le, ou Conciliateur villageois [*Vaudeville* in 2 acts, Prem. on 4-2-
1792].
Th. des Variétés Amusantes, Comiques et Lyriques (**3**); **Total: 3**.

Bon époux, Le, ou Petite école des maris [*Comédie* in 3 acts, Prem. on 6-7-1789].
  Th. des Beaujolais (**7**); **Total: 7**.
Bon marin, Le [N/A].
  Th. de l'Emulation (Gaîté) (**2**); **Total: 2**.
Bon nègre, Le [N/A].
  Th. des Variétés Amusantes, Comiques et Lyriques (**5**); **Total: 5**.
Bon paysan, Le [N/A].
  Th. des Grands Danseurs (Gaîté) (**6**); **Total: 6**.
Bon turc, Le, ou Arlequin à Bagdad [Prem. on 21-10-1797].
  Th. de l'Emulation (Gaîté) (**18**); Th. Lyrique des Amis de la Patrie (**2**); **Total: 20**.
Bonheur, fruit du travail, Le [*Vaudeville*, Prem. on 13-7-1798].
  Th. de l'Emulation (Gaîté) (**1**); Th. des Délassements Comiques (**1**); **Total: 2**.
Bonne petite fille, La [N/A].
  Th. de l'Emulation (Gaîté) (**3**); Th. des Grands Danseurs (Gaîté) (**16**); **Total: 19**.
Bons apôtres, Les, ou Les Dangers de la superstition [N/A].
  Th. de l'Ambigu Comique (**33**); **Total: 33**.
Bons patriotes, Les [Pub. in 1793].
  Th. de l'Ambigu Comique (**3**); **Total: 3**.
Bords de la Loire, Les [N/A].
  Th. Patriotique et de Momus (**15**); **Total: 15**.
Bossus, Les [N/A].
  Th. du Vaudeville (**4**); Th. Patriotique et de Momus (**4**); **Total: 8**.
Bostonien, Le [N/A].
  Th. de l'Emulation (Gaîté) (**13**); Th. du Mareux (**1**); Th. Lyrique des Amis de la Patrie (**9**); **Total: 23**.
Boularc, Le [N/A].
  Th. Lyrique des Amis de la Patrie (**1**); **Total: 1**.
Bouquet, Le, ou La Matinée champêtre [*Ballet* in 2 acts, Prem. on 25-4-1792, Pub. in 1768].
  Th. des Variétés Amusantes, Comiques et Lyriques (**3**); **Total: 3**.
Bouquet de Lucinde, Le [*Opéra* in 1 act].
  Th. de l'Estrapade au Panthéon (**10**); **Total: 10**.
Bourgeois, Le [N/A].
  Th. des Variétés Amusantes (Lazzari) (**1**); **Total: 1**.
Boutique du perruquier, La [N/A].
  Th. de l'Emulation (Gaîté) (**2**); **Total: 2**.
Brave Rousselot, Le, ou Le Combat de Moscou [*Fait Historique* in 2 acts, Prem. on 12-7-1792].
  Th. des Grands Danseurs (Gaîté) (**20**); **Total: 20**.
Brigands de Pologne, Les [N/A].
  n/a (**2**); **Total: 2**.
Brindavoine [*Pièce* in 1 act, Pub. in 1788].
  Th. de l'Ambigu Comique (**53**); **Total: 53**.
Brunet et Caroline ou Le Chansonnier impromptu [Prem. on 5-7-1799].
  Th. de la Citoyenne Montansier (**17**); **Total: 17**.
Bûcherons, Les [N/A].
  Th. de la Liberté (**2**); **Total: 2**.

Buonaparte en Italie [N/A].
　　Th. de l'Emulation (Gaîté) (**2**); **Total: 2.**
Ca vaut mieux qu'un divorce [*Comédie* in 1 act].
　　Th. de la Cité (**3**); **Total: 3.**
C'est l'un ou l'autre [*Fait Historique*, Prem. on 24-12-1798].
　　Th. du Vaudeville (**13**); **Total: 13.**
C'est toujours lui [N/A].
　　Th. de l'Emulation (Gaîté) (**4**); **Total: 4.**
Ca vaut mieux qu'un divorce [N/A].
　　Th. de la Cité (**1**); **Total: 1.**
Cadet la gingeole ou Les Deux frères de lait [*Comédie*, Prem. on 1-6-1799].
　　Th. de la Cité (**1**); Th. du Palais (Cité)-Variétés (**2**); **Total: 3.**
Cadet professeur [N/A].
　　Th. de la Citoyenne Montansier (**1**); **Total: 1.**
Cadet Roussel aux enfers [N/A].
　　Echiquier (**2**); **Total: 2.**
Café, Le [*Prologue* in 1 act].
　　Th. de la Citoyenne Montansier (**9**); **Total: 9.**
Café à l'encan, Le [In 2 acts].
　　Th. du Lycée Dramatique (**1**); **Total: 1.**
Café de la Révolution, Le [*Comédie* in 2 acts, Prem. on 23-3-1790].
　　Th. de l'Ambigu Comique (**16**); **Total: 16.**
Café des patriotes, Le [*Comédie* in 1 act, Prem. on 12-10-1793].
　　Th. du Lycée des Arts (**29**); **Total: 29.**
Cahin Cola ou Parodie de mort d'Abel [*Parodie*].
　　Th. de Molière (**3**); **Total: 3.**
Calendrier des vieillards, Le [*Comédie* in 1 act, Prem. on 20-8-1793].
　　Th. du Vaudeville (**3**); **Total: 3.**
Cambyse ou L'Embrassement de Mytilène [N/A].
　　Th. de l'Emulation (Gaîté) (**45**); **Total: 45.**
Candeille [N/A].
　　Académie de la Musique (Opéra) (**5**); **Total: 5.**
Cange [*Fait Historique* in 1 act, Pub. in 1794].
　　Th. de l'Ambigu Comique (**15**); Th. des Grands Danseurs (Gaîté) (**17**); Th. des Variétés Amusantes, Comiques et Lyriques (**3**); **Total: 35.**
Carmagnole à Chambéry, La [*Tableau-Patriotique* in 3 acts, Pub. in 1792].
　　Th. de la Citoyenne Montansier (**6**); **Total: 6.**
Capana et le bon religieux [*Pantomime* in 3 acts, Prem. on 27-11-1790].
　　Th. des Grands Danseurs (Gaîté) (**18**); **Total: 18.**
Capucins, Les, ou Faisons la paix [*Comédie* in 2 acts, Prem. on 15-3-1791].
　　Th. du Feydeau (de Monsieur) (**1**); **Total: 1.**
Carnaval du sérail, Le [*Parodie*].
　　Th. des Jeunes Artistes (**1**); **Total: 1.**
Caroline [Prem. on 2-12-1789].
　　Th. de l'Ambigu Comique (**1**); Th. des Italiens (Opéra-Comique) (**1**); **Total: 2.**
Caron-Beaumarchais aux Champs Elysées [N/A].
　　Th. de Molière (**1**); Th. des Jeunes Artistes (**3**); Th. du Marais (**2**); **Total: 6.**
Cartel républicain, Le [*Tableau-Patriotique*, Pub. in 1795].
　　Th. de l'Ambigu Comique (**5**); **Total: 5.**

Cassandre bouquiniste [N/A].
Th. des Jeunes Artistes (**37**); **Total: 37.**

Cassandre égoïste [*Vaudeville*].
Th. du Vaudeville (**4**); **Total: 4.**

Cassandre sculpteur [*Vaudeville*].
Th. des Grands Danseurs (Gaîté) (**1**); Th. des Jeunes Artistes (**6**); **Total: 7.**

Cassandre traiteur et restaurateur [Prem. on 4-9-1798].
Th. des Jeunes Artistes (**16**); Th. du Marais (**1**); **Total: 17.**

Castel du lac, Le, ou Les Amants piémontais [*Pantomime* in 3 acts, Prem. on 30-3-1799].
Th. de l'Ambigu Comique (**1**); Th. de la Cité (**15**); **Total: 16.**

Causes et les effets, Les, ou Le Réveil du peuple [*Comédie* in 5 acts, Prem. on 17-8-1793].
Th. des Italiens (Opéra-Comique) (**7**); Th. du Lycée des Arts (**1**); **Total: 8.**

Caverne enchantée, La [*Pantomime* in 5 acts, Prem. on 7-9-1782].
Th. des Grands Danseurs (Gaîté) (**67**); **Total: 67.**

Cécile ou La Suite de Zélia [*Opéra* in 3 acts, Prem. on 25-2-1792].
Th. Lyrique des Amis de la Patrie (**10**); **Total: 10.**

Céladon moderne, Le [Prem. on 27-6-1797].
Th. des Variétés Amusantes, Comiques et Lyriques (**9**); **Total: 9.**

Céleste ou L'Auberge de la forêt des Ardennes [N/A].
Th. des Variétés Amusantes, Comiques et Lyriques (**9**); **Total: 9.**

Censeur, Le [N/A].
Th. du Feydeau (de Monsieur) (**1**); **Total: 1.**

Cérémonie Turque, La [N/A].
Th. de la Cité (**1**); **Total: 1.**

Cervantès [N/A].
Th. du Lycée des Arts (**1**); **Total: 1.**

Chanson des Marseillais, La [*Tableau-Patriotique* in 3 acts, Pub. in 1792].
Th. de l'Ambigu Comique (**3**); Th. de la Citoyenne Montansier (**2**); **Total: 5.**

Chant des victoires, Le [*Chanson*].
Académie de la Musique (Opéra) (**2**); Th. du Feydeau (de Monsieur) (**2**); **Total: 4.**

Chant triomphal, Le [N/A].
Th. Français (de la rue Richelieu) (de la République) (**1**); **Total: 1.**

Chapeau merveilleux, Le [Prem. on 24-7-1798].
Th. de l'Emulation (Gaîté) (**17**); Th. Lyrique des Amis de la Patrie (**3**); **Total: 20.**

Charbonnier gentilhomme, Le [N/A].
Th. des Grands Danseurs (Gaîté) (**5**); **Total: 5.**

Charlatan, Le [*Opéra-Bouffe* in 2 acts].
Th. de l'Emulation (Gaîté) (**5**); **Total: 5.**

Charlatans, Les [*Opéra* in 1 act, Prem. on 15-9-1794].
Th. des Jeunes Artistes (**4**); Th. du Palais (Cité)-Variétés (**3**); **Total: 7.**

Charles IV [*Fait Historique*].
Th. Français (de la rue Richelieu) (de la République) (**1**); **Total: 1.**

Charlot ou La Nuit des fiançailles [*Vaudeville* in 1 act, Prem. on 14-2-1792].
Th. des Variétés Amusantes, Comiques et Lyriques (**1**); **Total: 1.**

Chasseur anglais, Le [*Pantomime* in 4 acts, Prem. on 14-11-1791].
Th. des Grands Danseurs (Gaîté) (**28**); **Total: 28.**

Chasseurs généreux, Les [Pub. in 1793].
Th. de l'Ambigu Comique (**13**); **Total: 13.**

Chat perdu ou Les Fausses conjectures [N/A].
Th. du Vaudeville (**15**); **Total: 15.**

Château assiégé, Le [*Pantomime* in 3 acts, Prem. on 18-9-1789, Pub. in 1789].
Th. de l'Emulation (Gaîté) (**4**); Th. des Grands Danseurs (Gaîté) (**11**); **Total: 15.**

Château de Montenero, Le [N/A].
Th. des Italiens (Opéra-Comique) (**6**); **Total: 6.**

Chaumière, La [*Comédie*, Prem. on 22-7-1797].
Th. de l'Ambigu Comique (**4**); Th. des Jeunes Artistes (**3**); **Total: 7.**

Chaumière des Alpes, La [*Vaudeville* in 1 act].
Th. Lyrique des Amis de la Patrie (**13**); **Total: 13.**

Chéri et Emilie [*Comédie*].
Th. de la Citoyenne Montansier (**9**); Th. de la Cité (**1**); **Total: 10.**

D. de B., Lemière de Corvey (comp). *Chevaliers errants, Les* [*Opéra* in 1 act, Prem. on 20-3-1792].
Th. de la Citoyenne Montansier (**1**); **Total: 1.**

Choeur de Marathon, Le [*Opéra*].
Th. de la Citoyenne Montansier (**2**); Th. National (de la rue Richelieu) (**7**); **Total: 9.**

Choeur patriotique, Le [*Tableau-Patriotique*, Pub. in 1794].
Th. de l'Ambigu Comique (**8**); **Total: 8.**

Chouchou ou Les Amants lutins [N/A].
Th. de l'Emulation (Gaîté) (**14**); Th. Lyrique des Amis de la Patrie (**1**); **Total: 15.**

Christophe Morin ou Que je suis fâché d'être riche [Prem. on 10-10-1799].
Th. des Troubadours (**15**); **Total: 15.**

Chute de Nicodème en Brabant, La, ou La Révolution fanatique [*Fait Historique*, Prem. on 17-3-1791].
Th. de la Liberté (**5**); **Total: 5.**

Citoyen Lamblée, Le [N/A].
Th. du Lycée des Arts (**1**); **Total: 1.**

Clara [N/A].
Th. des Italiens (Opéra-Comique) (**1**); **Total: 1.**

Clarice et Belthon [*Comédie* in 3 acts, Prem. on 23-3-1793].
Th. des Italiens (Opéra-Comique) (**11**); **Total: 11.**

Clarté dans l'ombre, La [N/A].
Th. des Délassements Comiques (**2**); **Total: 2.**

Clavecin, Le [*Opéra*-Vaudeville].
Th. de l'Ambigu Comique (**8**); **Total: 8.**

Clef, La, ou Le Tuteur italien [N/A].
Th. de l'Emulation (Gaîté) (**25**); **Total: 25.**

Clémence et Formose [*Ballet*, Prem. on 9-9-1799].
Th. des Grands Danseurs (Gaîté) (**26**); **Total: 26.**

Clémentine ou Les Deux portraits [Prem. on 18-9-1799].
Th. des Troubadours (**9**); **Total: 9.**

Cloche de minuit, Le [Prem. on 5-11-1798].
Th. de l'Emulation (Gaîté) (**11**); **Total: 11.**

Club, Le [*Comédie* in 1 act, Prem. on 12-5-1790].
Th. de l'Ambigu Comique (**1**); **Total: 1.**

Club des émigrants, Le [*Vaudeville* in 3 acts, Prem. on 8-12-1791].
    Th. des Variétés Amusantes, Comiques et Lyriques (17); **Total: 17.**

Coclambin Gilles [Prem. on 16-8-1799].
    Th. des Grands Danseurs (Gaîté) (1); **Total: 1.**

Coeur de Jeannette, La [N/A].
    Th. du Vaudeville (1); **Total: 1.**

Colas trente fois Colas [Prem. on 19-9-1797].
    Th. des Variétés Amusantes, Comiques et Lyriques (11); **Total: 11.**

Colinette à la cour ou La Double épreuve [*Opéra*, Pub. in 1782].
    Th. de l'Ambigu Comique (5); Th. du Vaudeville (7); Th. Patriotique et de Momus (20); **Total: 32.**

Colinette ou Les Vendangeurs [N/A].
    Th. de l'Emulation (Gaîté) (1); **Total: 1.**

Collation, La [N/A].
    Th. des Ombres Chinoises (1); **Total: 1.**

Collier dans les marionnettes, Le [N/A].
    Th. des Ombres Chinoises (6); Th. des Ombres de J.-J. Rousseau (1); **Total: 7.**

Colombine Arlequin ou Arlequin sorcier [Prem. on 4-5-1799].
    Th. du Vaudeville (2); **Total: 2.**

Colombine Gilles [N/A].
    Th. des Grands Danseurs (Gaîté) (14); **Total: 14.**

Colombine revenante [*Vaudeville*, Prem. on 2-10-1799].
    Th. des Jeunes Elèves (1); **Total: 1.**

Colporteur, Le [Prem. on 17-10-1798].
    Th. du Palais (Cité)-Variétés (2); **Total: 2.**

Combat de Moscou, Le [N/A].
    Th. des Grands Danseurs (Gaîté) (6); **Total: 6.**

Comédie de campagne, La [Prem. on 6-7-1798].
    Th. de la Citoyenne Montansier (25); **Total: 25.**

Comédien par amour, Le [*Comédie*].
    Th. des Variétés Amusantes (Lazzari) (9); Th. des Variétés Amusantes, Comiques et Lyriques (1); Th. Patriotique et de Momus (20); **Total: 30.**

Comédiens, Les, ou Les Moines diables [*Comédie*, Pub. in 1793].
    Th. du Vaudeville (6); **Total: 6.**

Comité des diables, Le [N/A].
    Th. de l'Ambigu Comique (4); Th. de la Cité (1); **Total: 5.**

Comité infernal, Le [N/A].
    Th. de l'Ambigu Comique (14); **Total: 14.**

Commissionnaire et le secret, Le [N/A].
    Th. des Italiens (Opéra-Comique) (2); **Total: 2.**

Communauté de Copenhague, La [*Opéra* in 3 acts, Prem. on 13-12-1790].
    Th. de la Citoyenne Montansier (30); **Total: 30.**

Compagnons du diable, Les [*Comédie* in 1 act, Pub. in 1795].
    Th. des Variétés Amusantes, Comiques et Lyriques (1); **Total: 1.**

Compère Luc ou Les dangers de l'ivrognerie [*Opéra* in 2 acts].
    Th. du Feydeau (de Monsieur) (2); **Total: 2.**

Concert aux éléphants, Le [*Vaudeville* in 1 act].
    Th. du Vaudeville (21); **Total: 21.**

Concurrents, Les [*Comédie*, Prem. on 29-12-1793].
    Th. Lyrique des Amis de la Patrie (1); **Total: 1.**

Confidence forcée, La [*Comédie*].
  Th. des Jeunes Artistes (5); **Total: 5.**
Confidences trompeuses, Les [Prem. on 7-8-1798].
  Th. de Molière (3); **Total: 3.**
Congé du volontaire, Le [*Opéra-Comique* in 1 act, Prem. on 21-1-1794].
  Th. de la Montagne (5); **Total: 5.**
Connaisseurs, Les [*Comédie* in 3 acts].
  Th. de la Montagne (1); **Total: 1.**
Conquête de la Chine, La [N/A].
  Th. des Ombres Chinoises (2); Th. des Ombres de J.-J. Rousseau (12); **Total: 14.**
Adet. *Conseil impérial, Le* [Prem. on 10-01-1794].
  Th. de la Cité (1); **Total: 1.**
Constance et Linval [*Comédie* in 2 acts, Prem. on 25-4-1789].
  Th. du Palais Royal (2); **Total: 2.**
Constance ou La Journée bien employée [*Opéra*, Prem. on 9-10-1798].
  Th. Lyrique des Amis de la Patrie (13); **Total: 13.**
Constitution villageoise, La [*Comédie* in 2 acts, Prem. on 25-4-1791].
  Th. des Délassements Comiques (20); **Total: 20.**
Contrat de mariage, Le [Prem. on 5-7-1797].
  Th. du Vaudeville (2); **Total: 2.**
Contrat forcé, Le [N/A].
  Th. de l'Ambigu Comique (1); **Total: 1.**
Contrat viager, Le [*Comédie* in 1 act, Prem. on 28-5-1791].
  Th. de l'Ambigu Comique (33); **Total: 33.**
"D, citoyen." *Contretemps, Les* [Pub. in 1793].
  Th. de l'Ambigu Comique (33); **Total: 33.**
Contre-révolutionnaires juges, Les [*Comédie* in 3 acts, Prem. on 17-1-1796].
  Th. Français (de la rue Richelieu) (de la République) (4); **Total: 4.**
Convalescence du roi et le retour du Te deum au Champ-de-Mars, La
  [*Fait Historique*].
  Th. des Délassements Comiques (6); **Total: 6.**
Coquette inutile, La [N/A].
  Th. du Vaudeville (1); **Total: 1.**
Coquettes dupées, Les [*Comédie* in 1 act].
  Th. Français, Comique et Lyrique (18); **Total: 18.**
Coquettes, Les [N/A].
  Th. des Délassements Comiques (3); **Total: 3.**
Coraly ou La Petite orpheline indienne [Prem. on 11-7-1796].
  Th. du Vaudeville (1); **Total: 1.**
Corde lâche, La [N/A].
  Th. des Grands Danseurs (Gaîté) (12); **Total: 12.**
Cordonnier allemand, Le [*Vaudeville* in 1 act, Prem. on 18-8-1798].
  Th. du Vaudeville (31); **Total: 31.**
Cordonnier de Colmar, Le [N/A].
  Th. du Vaudeville (1); **Total: 1.**
Cornets de dragées, Les [*Fait Historique*, Pub. in 1787].
  Th. de l'Ambigu Comique (7); **Total: 7.**
Corps de garde patriotique, Le [*Vaudeville*].
  Th. Lyrique des Amis de la Patrie (34); **Total: 34.**

Corrupteur, Le [*Comédie* in 5 acts, Prem. on 14-10-1790].
　　　Th. du Palais Royal (3); **Total: 3.**

Corsaire comme il n'y en a point, Le [*Comédie* in 3 acts, Pub. in 1788].
　　　Th. de l'Ambigu Comique (43); **Total: 43.**

Corsaire provençal, Le, ou Le capitaine Sabart [Prem. on 13-5-1799].
　　　Th. de la Citoyenne Montansier (16); **Total: 16.**

Cossier ou Le Médecin de Cadix [*Comédie* in 3 acts].
　　　Th. de l'Estrapade au Panthéon (3); **Total: 3.**

Couplets, Les [*Comédie* in 2 acts, Prem. on 26-2-1789].
　　　Th. du Palais Royal (5); **Total: 5.**

Cousin de Dannière, Le [N/A].
　　　Th. des Jeunes Artistes (10); **Total: 10.**

Coutelier de Bagdad, Le, ou Les Trois bossus [*Opéra* in 1 act, Pub. in 1792].
　　　Th. du Palais (Cité)-Variétés (2); **Total: 2.**

Couvent de bénédictines, Le [*Comédie* in 1 act, Prem. on 21-2-1791].
　　　Th. du Palais Royal (1); **Total: 1.**

Cravatte et le ruban, La [N/A].
　　　Th. du Vaudeville (13); **Total: 13.**

Crève-coeur ou Le Brigand par amour [Prem. on 7-7-1798].
　　　Th. Lyrique des Amis de la Patrie (2); **Total: 2.**

Cri de vengeance, Le [Prem. on 30-5-1799].
　　　Th. de l'Ambigu Comique (5); Th. du Vaudeville (1); **Total: 6.**

Crime de Rastadt, Le [N/A].
　　　Th. du Palais (Cité)-Variétés (2); **Total: 2.**

Crime et la vertu, Le [N/A].
　　　Th. de l'Ambigu Comique (5); **Total: 5.**

Crispin à Madrid [*Comédie* in 1 act, Pub. in 1792].
　　　Th. de l'Ambigu Comique (6); **Total: 6.**

Croisée, La [*Comédie* in 2 acts, Prem. on 26-4-1788].
　　　Th. des Beaujolais (40); Th. du Lycée des Arts (1); **Total: 41.**

Croyables, Les [Prem. on 14-2-1797].
　　　Th. de la Rue Martin (8); **Total: 8.**

Curé amoureux, Le, ou Le Mariage des prêtres [*Comédie*].
　　　Th. Français, Comique et Lyrique (6); **Total: 6.**

Curiosité punie, La [N/A].
　　　Th. de l'Ambigu Comique (9); **Total: 9.**

Dalmakzi [Prem. on 20-8-1798].
　　　Th. des Délassements Comiques (7); **Total: 7.**

Dangers de l'ambition, Les [*Drame*, Prem. on 23-9-1799].
　　　Th. des Victoires (3); **Total: 3.**

Danières à Paris [N/A].
　　　Th. de la Cité (1); **Total: 1.**

Danse anglaise, La [*Ballet*].
　　　Th. des Grands Danseurs (Gaîté) (5); **Total: 5.**

Danse de l'échelle, La [N/A].
　　　Th. des Grands Danseurs (Gaîté) (2); **Total: 2.**

Darina et ses trois fils [Prem. on 27-5-1798].
　　　Th. de l'Emulation (Gaîté) (30); **Total: 30.**

De par et pour le peuple [*Tableau-Patriotique*].
　　　Académie de la Musique (Opéra) (1); **Total: 1.**

Débarquement hollandais, Le [*Pantomime* in 3 acts, Prem. on 20-3-1781].
    Th. des Grands Danseurs (Gaîté) (**29**); **Total: 29.**

Débats, Les [*Prologue*].
    Th. de la Cité (**2**); **Total: 2.**

Début, Le [N/A].
    Th. des Variétés Amusantes, Comiques et Lyriques (**1**); Th. du Marais (**1**);
    Total: 2.

Débutante, La [N/A].
    Th. des Jeunes Artistes (**96**); **Total: 96.**

Débutants, Les [N/A].
    Th. du Vaudeville (**5**); **Total: 5.**

Débuts, Les [N/A].
    Th. de l'Ambigu Comique (**2**); **Total: 2.**

Décence, La, ou Les Filles mères [*Parodie*, Prem. on 10-4-1797].
    Th. du Vaudeville (**40**); **Total: 40.**

Dédit du gendre embarrassant, Le [*Comédie*].
    Th. des Grands Danseurs (Gaîté) (**17**); **Total: 17.**

Défenseur officieux, Le [*Comédie* in 3 acts, Pub. in 1795].
    Th. du Palais (Cité)-Variétés (**1**); **Total: 1.**

Défi des sauteurs, Le, ou Le Défi hasardeux [*Opéra-Comique* in 2 acts, Prem.
  on 8-8-1796].
    Th. des Grands Danseurs (Gaîté) (**1**); **Total: 1.**

Défi, Le [*Opéra*, Prem. on 27-5-1797].
    Th. de l'Odéon (**1**); Th. de la Citoyenne Montansier (**25**); Th. de la Rue
    Martin (**2**); Th. du Lycée des Arts (**4**); **Total: 32.**

Délicatesse mal entendue, La [N/A].
    Th. des Variétés Amusantes, Comiques et Lyriques (**11**); **Total: 11.**

Démosthènes [*Tableau-Patriotique* in 1 act].
    Th. des Italiens (Opéra-Comique) (**2**); **Total: 2.**

Denise et Alexis [*Comédie* in 1 act, Prem. on 14-5-1791].
    Th. du Lycée Dramatique (**5**); **Total: 5.**

Denise et Assima [N/A].
    Th. des Jeunes Artistes (**5**); **Total: 5.**

Départ des patriotes, Le, ou La Loterie des filles [*Tableau-Patriotique*,
  Prem. on 8-8-1793].
    Th. des Grands Danseurs (Gaîté) (**78**); **Total: 78.**

Départ des patriotes pour les frontières, Le [*Comédie* in 1 act, Prem. on 20-
  8-1791].
    Th. du Lycée Dramatique (**2**); **Total: 2.**

Départ des volontaires [N/A].
    Th. du Lycée des Arts (**5**); **Total: 5.**

Départ du général français de l'isle de Malte, Le [Prem. on 9-7-1798].
    Th. du Palais (Cité)-Variétés (**2**); **Total: 2.**

Dépit, Le [N/A].
    Th. de la Citoyenne Montansier (**2**); **Total: 2.**

Déserteur par amour, Le [*Pantomime* in 2 acts].
    Th. de la République des Arts (**1**); Th. des Grands Danseurs (Gaîté) (**2**);
    Total: 3.

Désespoir de Colombine et Arlequin, Le [*Pantomime*].
    Th. des Grands Danseurs (Gaîté) (**2**); **Total: 2.**

Despotisme monacal, Le [*Fait Historique*, Prem. on 1-11-1792].
　　Th. des Italiens (Opéra-Comique) (**4**); **Total: 4.**

Deux Amphitryons et les deux sosies, Les [N/A].
　　Th. des Grands Danseurs (Gaîté) (**2**); **Total: 2.**

Deux anneaux, Les [N/A].
　　Th. des Variétés Amusantes, Comiques et Lyriques (**4**); **Total: 4.**

Deux Arlequins frères rivaux, Les [*Pantomime* in 2 acts, Pub. in 1769].
　　Th. des Grands Danseurs (Gaîté) (**51**); **Total: 51.**

Deux célibataires, Les [Prem. on 31-7-1797].
　　Th. des Jeunes Artistes (**14**); **Total: 14.**

Deux cent francs, Les [N/A].
　　Th. de la Citoyenne Montansier (**2**); Th. de la Cité (**11**); Th. du Palais
　　(Cité)-Variétés (**1**); **Total: 14.**

Deux chambres du diable, Les [*Comédie*].
　　Th. de Molière (**2**); **Total: 2.**

Deux clercs, Les, ou L'Avoué supposé [N/A].
　　Th. des Jeunes Artistes (**5**); **Total: 5.**

Deux coffrets, Les [*Pantomime*].
　　Th. de l'Ambigu Comique (**9**); Th. de la Cité (**7**); Th. du Palais (Cité)-
　　Variétés (**48**); **Total: 64.**

Deux cousines, Les [*Comédie* in 3 acts].
　　Th. des Variétés Amusantes (Lazzari) (**1**); Th. Patriotique et de Momus
　　(**22**); **Total: 23.**

Deux curés, Les, ou Le Lever du rideau [*Vaudeville* in 1 act].
　　Th. des Variétés Amusantes, Comiques et Lyriques (**8**); **Total: 8.**

Deux dévotes, Les [Prem. on 28-4-1799].
　　Th. des Jeunes Artistes (**25**); **Total: 25.**

Deux docteurs dans les marionnettes, Les [N/A].
　　Th. des Ombres Chinoises (**3**); Th. des Ombres de J.-J. Rousseau (**1**); **To-
　　tal: 4.**

Deux français à Naples, Les [*Comédie* in 3 acts].
　　Cirque National (**10**); **Total: 10.**

Deux frères, Les [*Opéra* in 3 acts, Prem. on 10-1-1792, Pub. in 1792].
　　Th. Français (de la rue Richelieu) (de la République) (**2**); **Total: 2.**

Deux frères à Paris [*Comédie* in 2 acts, Prem. on 16-6-1789].
　　Th. des Grands Danseurs (Gaîté) (**1**); **Total: 1.**

Deux fripons, Les [*Comédie* in 3 acts].
　　Th. des Variétés Amusantes, Comiques et Lyriques (**2**); Th. du Palais
　　(Cité)-Variétés (**1**); **Total: 3.**

Deux généraux, Les [N/A].
　　Th. de l'Ambigu Comique (**17**); **Total: 17.**

Deux Henriettes, Les [Prem. on 31-8-1797].
　　Th. du Vaudeville (**8**); **Total: 8.**

Deux hérolhes de St.-Amand, Les [*Tableau-Patriotique* in 1 act, Pub. in 1792].
　　Th. de la Citoyenne Montansier (**11**); **Total: 11.**

Deux journalistes, Les, ou Erreur n'est pas comptée [*Comédie* in 2 acts,
　　Prem. on 26-1-1799, Pub. in 1797].
　　Th. de Molière (**2**); Th. des Troubadours (**11**); Th. du Vaudeville (**11**); **To-
　　tal: 24.**

Deux jumelles, Les [*Pantomime* in 1 act, Prem. on 6-5-1786].
　　Th. des Beaujolais (**3**); **Total: 3.**

Deux Léonards, Les, ou Le Quiproquo [*Comédie* in 1 act, Prem. on 30-8-1784].
    Th. des Grands Danseurs (Gaîté) (**25**); **Total: 25.**
Deux martyrs, Les [N/A].
    Th. des Victoires Nationales (**1**); **Total: 1.**
Deux morts vivants, Les [*Opéra* in 1 act].
    Th. du Lycée des Arts (**3**); **Total: 3.**
Deux muets, Les [*Comédie* in 1 act, Prem. on 16-9-1790].
    Th. des Grands Danseurs (Gaîté) (**2**); **Total: 2.**
Deux Nicodèmes, Les [*Opéra* in 2 acts, Prem. on 21-11-1791].
    Th. du Feydeau (de Monsieur) (**8**); **Total: 8.**
Deux noces, Les [*Opéra* in 2 acts, Prem. on 15-4-1793].
    Th. du Palais (Cité)-Variétés (**3**); **Total: 3.**
Deux petits frères, Les [*Comédie* in 4 acts, Prem. on 10-5-1792, Pub. in 1785].
    Th. de l'Ambigu Comique (**63**); **Total: 63.**
Deux petits guerriers, Les [N/A].
    Th. de l'Ambigu Comique (**1**); **Total: 1.**
Deux procureurs, Les [N/A].
    Th. des Grands Danseurs (Gaîté) (**8**); **Total: 8.**
Deux rivaux de la laitière, Les [*Pantomime* in 1 act, Prem. on 11-5-1791, Pub. in 1785].
    Th. des Grands Danseurs (Gaîté) (**19**); **Total: 19.**
Deux rivaux, Les [*Pantomime* in 1 act, Prem. on 12-9-1782].
    Th. des Grands Danseurs (Gaîté) (**4**); **Total: 4.**
Deux soeurs, Les [*Comédie* in 3 acts, Prem. on 17-4-1755].
    Th. du Feydeau (de Monsieur) (**10**); **Total: 10.**
Deux Sophies, Les [*Drame* in 5 acts].
    Th. de la Montagne (**1**); Th. National (de la rue Richelieu) (**3**); **Total: 4.**
Deux sourds, Les [*Comédie*, Prem. on 20-1-1798].
    Th. de la Cité (**2**); Th. du Vaudeville (**9**); **Total: 11.**
Deux sous-lieutenants, Les [Prem. on 19-5-1792].
    Th. des Italiens (Opéra-Comique) (**2**); **Total: 2.**
Deux suisses, Les [N/A].
    Th. de la Rue Antoine (**1**); **Total: 1.**
Deux vieilles, Les [*Vaudeville* in 1 act, Prem. on 7-1-1794].
    Th. Lyrique des Amis de la Patrie (**3**); **Total: 3.**
Deux voleurs, Les [*Opéra-Comique*].
    Th. des Ombres Chinoises (**5**); Th. des Ombres de J.-J. Rousseau (**15**); **Total: 20.**
Deux voyageurs, Les, ou A beau mentir qui vient de loin [*Comédie* in 1 act, Prem. on 30-9-1799].
    Th. de la Cité (**9**); **Total: 9.**
Dévotes, Les, ou La Triple vengeance [*Comédie* in 3 acts, Prem. on 23-12-1793].
    Th. du Palais (Cité)-Variétés (**1**); **Total: 1.**
Dévouement conjugal, Le, ou Le Prisonnier d'Olmutz [N/A].
    Th. de l'Ambigu Comique (**6**); **Total: 6.**
Diable, Le, ou Arlequin incendiaire [N/A].
    Th. des Variétés Amusantes, Comiques et Lyriques (**1**); **Total: 1.**
Diable et le pâtissier, Le [Prem. on 3-10-1797].
    Th. de l'Emulation (Gaîté) (**5**); **Total: 5.**

Didon [*Tragédie*].
> Th. de l'Odéon (**2**); Th. Français (de la rue Richelieu) (de la République) (**6**); **Total: 8**.

Dieu veille sur tout ou L'Accouchée [Prem. on 30-7-1797].
> Th. de l'Emulation (Gaîté) (**2**); **Total: 2**.

Diletante, Il [*Intermède*, Prem. on 13-11-1790].
> Th. du Feydeau (de Monsieur) (**2**); **Total: 2**.

Dîner de carton, Le [N/A].
> Th. de l'Emulation (Gaîté) (**9**); **Total: 9**.

Dîner des bossus, Le [Prem. on 23-7-1799].
> Th. des Grands Danseurs (Gaîté) (**4**); **Total: 4**.

Dîner des ci-devants, Le [*Comédie*].
> Th. du Palais (Cité)-Variétés (**5**); **Total: 5**.

Dîner des peuples, Le [*Tableau-Patriotique*, Prem. on 4-5-1794, Pub. in 1794].
> Th. du Vaudeville (**9**); **Total: 9**.

Dîner du roi de Prusse à Paris, Le [*Fait Historique* in 2 acts].
> Th. de Molière (**9**); **Total: 9**.

Dîner interrompu, Le [*Comédie*].
> Th. de la Rue Martin (**1**); **Total: 1**.

Directeur villageois, Le [In 1 act].
> Cirque National (**13**); **Total: 13**.

Dispute pour rien, La [N/A].
> Th. des Ombres de J.-J. Rousseau (**2**); **Total: 2**.

Divertissement, Un [*Pantomime*, Prem. on 7-6-1797].
> Th. des Jeunes Artistes (**1**); **Total: 1**.

Divorce pour rien, Le [Prem. on 17-4-1799].
> Th. de la Citoyenne Montansier (**1**); **Total: 1**.

Dix Louis, Les [N/A].
> Th. des Variétés Amusantes, Comiques et Lyriques (**5**); **Total: 5**.

Dom Pedre et Emilie [N/A].
> Th. des Délassements Comiques (**4**); **Total: 4**.

Don, Le [N/A].
> Th. de l'Ambigu Comique (**1**); **Total: 1**.

Dons de l'amitié, Les [Prem. on 31-8-1799].
> Th. de l'Ambigu Comique (**16**); **Total: 16**.

Double récompense, La, ou Le Stratagème inutile [*Comédie* in 1 act, Prem. on 10-1-1789].
> Th. de la Citoyenne Montansier (**1**); Th. des Beaujolais (**16**); **Total: 17**.

Double retraite, La [Prem. on 12-7-1799].
> Th. du Vaudeville (**4**); **Total: 4**.

Double salamandre, La [Prem. on 18-6-1796].
> Tivoli (**1**); **Total: 1**.

Double surprise, La, ou Les Etrennes mutuelles [Prem. on 10-4-1797].
> Th. des Jeunes Artistes (**48**); **Total: 48**.

Douze francs, Les [Pub. in 1793].
> Th. de l'Ambigu Comique (**2**); **Total: 2**.

Douze thermidor, Le [*Tableau-Patriotique*].
> Th. de l'Ambigu Comique (**16**); **Total: 16**.

Dragons, Les [N/A].
> Th. des Variétés Amusantes (Lazzari) (**7**); Th. du Palais (Cité)-Variétés (**1**); **Total: 8**.

Drôles de gens, Les, ou La Place publique [N/A].
Th. des Jeunes Artistes (**12**); **Total: 12.**

Duel d'Arlequin, Le [*Comédie* in 1 act, Prem. on 9-2-1793].
Th. des Grands Danseurs (Gaîté) (**23**); Th. du Vaudeville (**12**); **Total: 35.**

Duel protégé par Vulcain, Le [*Vaudeville*].
Th. des Grands Danseurs (Gaîté) (**3**); **Total: 3.**

Duelliste plastronné, Le [*Comédie* in 2 acts, Prem. on 16-2-1790, Pub. in 1790].
Th. des Grands Danseurs (Gaîté) (**2**); **Total: 2.**

Duellistes, Les [Prem. on 21-6-1791].
Th. des Grands Danseurs (Gaîté) (**3**); **Total: 3.**

Duels, Les [*Comédie* in 1 act, Prem. on 4-1-1792].
Th. de Molière (**1**); **Total: 1.**

Dupes, Les, ou Le Mariage bien assorti [Prem. on 2-6-1797].
Th. de l'Ambigu Comique (**2**); **Total: 2.**

Dupes des girandolles, Les [*Comédie* in 2 acts, Pub. in 1788].
Th. des Grands Danseurs (Gaîté) (**29**); **Total: 29.**

Duval ou Les Remords [*Drame* in 3 acts, Prem. on 24-3-1798].
Th. de l'Odéon (**3**); **Total: 3.**

Eaux de l'Aix-la-Chapelle, Les [*Fait Historique*, Pub. in 1792].
Th. de Molière (**5**); **Total: 5.**

Echange, L', ou La Dupe de soi-même [*Comédie* in 1 act, Prem. on 23-8-1791, Pub. in 1785].
Th. Français (de la rue Richelieu) (de la République) (**2**); Th. Français, Comique et Lyrique (**5**); **Total: 7.**

Echange des portraits, L' [*Comédie* in 1 act].
Th. des Variétés Amusantes, Comiques et Lyriques (**3**); **Total: 3.**

Echappé de Lyon, L' [Prem. on 18-11-1793].
Th. du Lycée des Arts (**23**); **Total: 23.**

Eclipse, L' [N/A].
Th. du Mareux (**1**); **Total: 1.**

Ecole de bienfaisance, L' [*Comédie*, Pub. in 1792].
Th. des Grands Danseurs (Gaîté) (**3**); **Total: 3.**

Ecole de cartouche, L' [N/A].
Th. des Variétés Amusantes, Comiques et Lyriques (**2**); **Total: 2.**

Ecole des enfants, L' [N/A].
Th. des Jeunes Artistes (**44**); **Total: 44.**

Ecole des jeunes gens, L' [*Comédie* in 2 acts, Prem. on 7-12-1791, Pub. in 1771].
Th. Lyrique des Amis de la Patrie (**12**); **Total: 12.**

Ecole des prêtres, L' [*Comédie* in 3 acts, Prem. on 4-11-1791].
Th. du Palais Royal (**4**); **Total: 4.**

Ecole du républicain, L' [Prem. on 23-1-1794].
Th. du Lycée des Arts (**10**); **Total: 10.**

Ecole du sentiment, L', ou Les Crimes réparés [*Drame* in 5 acts, Prem. on 14-1-1793].
Th. de l'Estrapade au Panthéon (**8**); **Total: 8.**

Ecoles en vacances, Les [N/A].
Th. des Variétés Amusantes, Comiques et Lyriques (**1**); **Total: 1.**

Ecoliers de Sainte Barbe, Les, ou La Soutane [N/A].
Th. des Jeunes Artistes (**48**); **Total: 48.**

Ecrivain, L' [N/A].
Th. des Ombres Chinoises (**1**); **Total: 1.**

Edmond et Fonrose ou Les crimes de l'amour [*Drame* in 3 acts, Prem. on 15-6-1792].
Th. de Molière (3); **Total: 3.**

Education de l'ancien et du nouveau régime, L' [*Comédie* in 3 acts].
Th. National (de la rue Richelieu) (1); **Total: 1.**

Effets au porteur, Les [Prem. on 17-7-1797].
Th. du Vaudeville (20); **Total: 20.**

Effets de la calomnie, Les [N/A].
Th. de l'Ambigu Comique (3); **Total: 3.**

Effets de la pièce "Misanthropie et repentir", Les [*Anecdotique* in 2 acts, Prem. on 9-3-1799].
Th. Lyrique des Amis de la Patrie (2); **Total: 2.**

Effets de repentir, Les [N/A].
Th. du Marais (3); **Total: 3.**

Effort surnaturel, L' [N/A].
Th. du Vaudeville (13); **Total: 13.**

Eléanore et Ferdinand [*Pantomime*].
Th. du Lycée des Arts (2); **Total: 2.**

Elise et Melval ou Les Parvenus à leur place [Prem. on 6-8-1799].
Th. de Molière (3); Th. des Victoires (5); Th. des Victoires Nationales (11); **Total: 19.**

Embarquement de Brest, L' [Prem. on 10-2-1798].
Th. des Jeunes Artistes (10); **Total: 10.**

Embarras du ménage, L' [N/A].
Th. des Ombres Chinoises (11); Th. des Ombres de J.-J. Rousseau (46); **Total: 57.**

Embarras imprévu, L' [*Comédie* in 2 acts, Prem. on 24-3-1791].
Th. de la Citoyenne Montansier (3); **Total: 3.**

Emigrante, L', ou Le Père Jacobin [*Comédie* in 3 acts].
Th. Français (de la rue Richelieu) (de la République) (11); **Total: 11.**

Emigration de Paris à Sèvres, L' [N/A].
Th. de l'Emulation (Gaîté) (5); **Total: 5.**

Emigrés à Spa, Les [N/A].
Th. du Vaudeville (1); **Total: 1.**

Emigrés chassés de Spa, Les [Pub. in 1793].
Th. du Vaudeville (3); **Total: 3.**

Emprunt contre l'Angleterre, L' [*Comédie*].
Th. de l'Ambigu Comique (1); **Total: 1.**

Emprunt forcé, L' [N/A].
Th. de l'Ambigu Comique (1); Th. de l'Emulation (Gaîté) (6); Th. des Jeunes Artistes (6); Th. des Variétés Amusantes (Lazzari) (27); Th. du Palais (Cité)-Variétés (7); Th. Patriotique et de Momus (9); **Total: 56.**

Enchantements de Circé, Les [N/A].
Unknown (1); **Total: 1.**

Enchantements de la forêt, Les [N/A].
Th. des Grands Danseurs (Gaîté) (3); **Total: 3.**

Encore des moines [*Vaudeville* in 1 act, Pub. in 1792].
Th. de l'Estrapade au Panthéon (17); **Total: 17.**

Encore des nones [N/A].
Th. de la Cité (3); **Total: 3.**

Encore le retour d'un mari [N/A].
> Th. des Variétés Amusantes (Lazzari) (**6**); Th. des Variétés Amusantes, Comiques et Lyriques (**5**); **Total: 11.**

Encore Madame Angot ou Le Mariage à la courte paille [N/A].
> Th. des Délassements Comiques (**28**); **Total: 28.**

Encore un ballon ou Le Mariage en l'air [Prem. on 3-5-1798].
> Th. des Jeunes Artistes (**7**); **Total: 7.**

Encore un concert [Pub. in 1795].
> Th. des Grands Danseurs (Gaîté) (**4**); **Total: 4.**

Encore un crime [N/A].
> Th. des Délassements Comiques (**3**); **Total: 3.**

Encore un diable [*Opéra*, Prem. on 13-6-1799].
> Th. des Victoires Nationales (**4**); **Total: 4.**

Encore un Figaro ou Le Rendez-vous manqué [N/A].
> Th. des Grands Danseurs (Gaîté) (**3**); **Total: 3.**

Enée à Carthage [N/A].
> Th. des Ombres Chinoises (**4**); Th. des Ombres de J.-J. Rousseau (**11**); **Total: 15.**

Enfance et la jeunesse, L' [N/A].
> Th. des Grands Danseurs (Gaîté) (**1**); Th. des Jeunes Artistes (**14**); **Total: 15.**

Enfant bien corrigé, L' [*Comédie* in 1 act, Prem. on 17-10-1790].
> Th. des Beaujolais (**2**); **Total: 2.**

Enfant de la joie, L' [*Parodie*, Prem. on 10-2-1798].
> Th. des Délassements Comiques (**4**); **Total: 4.**

Enfant perdu et retrouvé, L' [*Comédie* in 3 acts, Pub. in 1772].
> Th. des Grands Danseurs (Gaîté) (**7**); **Total: 7.**

Enfant républicain, L' [*Opéra* in 1 act, Prem. on 1-6-1794].
> Th. du Palais (Cité)-Variétés (**1**); **Total: 1.**

Enfants dans les bois, Les, ou La Tourterelle [*Opéra*, Prem. on 2-8-1797].
> Th. du Feydeau (de Monsieur) (**1**); **Total: 1.**

Enfants de la lune, Les [Prem. on 20-9-1796].
> Th. de la Rue Martin (**1**); **Total: 1.**

Engagement supposé, L' [N/A].
> Th. de l'Emulation (Gaîté) (**10**); Th. des Variétés Amusantes (Lazzari) (**2**); Th. des Variétés Amusantes, Comiques et Lyriques (**1**); Th. Patriotique et de Momus (**1**); **Total: 14.**

Enlèvement d'Europe, L' [*Pantomime* in 3 acts, Pub. in 1773].
> Th. de l'Emulation (Gaîté) (**9**); Th. des Grands Danseurs (Gaîté) (**53**); **Total: 62.**

Enlèvement des Sabines, L' [*Vaudeville* in 2 acts, Prem. on 31-10-1792].
> Th. du Feydeau (de Monsieur) (**7**); **Total: 7.**

Enlèvement du ballon, L' [N/A].
> Th. des Grands Danseurs (Gaîté) (**1**); **Total: 1.**

Enlèvement du bûcheron, L' [*Pantomime* in 2 acts, Prem. on 13-9-1781].
> Th. des Grands Danseurs (Gaîté) (**15**); **Total: 15.**

Enlèvement du globe, L' [*Pantomime* in 1 act, Prem. on 6-11-1787].
> Th. des Grands Danseurs (Gaîté) (**11**); **Total: 11.**

Enlèvement involontaire, L' [*Comédie* in 3 acts, Prem. on 9-2-1792].
> Th. Lyrique des Amis de la Patrie (**5**); **Total: 5.**

Enlèvement précipité, L' [*Pantomime*].
> Th. des Grands Danseurs (Gaîté) (**12**); **Total: 12.**

Enrôlement de Cadet Roussel, L' [*Comédie* in 1 act, Pub. in 1793].
   Th. du Palais (Cité)-Variétés (**3**); **Total: 3**.
Enrôlement par désespoir, L' [N/A].
   Th. des Grands Danseurs (Gaîté) (**2**); **Total: 2**.
Epée, L', ou Le Général et ses soldats [N/A].
   Th. des Jeunes Artistes (**4**); **Total: 4**.
Epiménide français, L' [*Comédie* in 1 act, Prem. on 26-1-1790].
   Th. du Feydeau (de Monsieur) (**21**); **Total: 21**.
Eponine et Sabinus [*Opéra* in 3 acts, Prem. on 25-1-1796].
   Th. du Lycée des Arts (**37**); **Total: 37**.
Epouse fidèle condamnée à mort par son mari cruel, L' [N/A].
   Unknown (**2**); **Total: 2**.
Epoux de seize ans, L', ou Le Berceau [*Opéra*, Prem. on 18-7-1798].
   Th. de Molière (**1**); **Total: 1**.
Epoux divorcés, Les [*Comédie* in 3 acts, Prem. on 24-8-1799].
   Th. de la Cité (**3**); Th. du Palais (Cité)-Variétés (**4**); **Total: 7**.
Epoux portugais, Les, ou Les Victimes de l'inquisition [*Drame* in 4 acts,
   Prem. on 18-7-1798, Pub. in 1793].
      Th. de l'Emulation (Gaîté) (**17**); Th. du Feydeau (de Monsieur) (**3**); Th. du
      Marais (**17**); Th. Lyrique des Amis de la Patrie (**4**); **Total: 41**.
Epreuve de la nature, L' [N/A].
   Th. des Jeunes Artistes (**1**); **Total: 1**.
Epreuve paternelle, L' [N/A].
   Th. des Variétés Amusantes, Comiques et Lyriques (**7**); Th. du Vaudeville
   (**1**); Th. Patriotique et de Momus (**27**); **Total: 35**.
Equilibrés, Les [N/A].
   Th. des Grands Danseurs (Gaîté) (**13**); **Total: 13**.
Equivoque en équivoque, D' [N/A].
   Th. des Variétés Amusantes, Comiques et Lyriques (**16**); **Total: 16**.
Esclave persanne, L' [N/A].
   Th. des Italiens (Opéra-Comique) (**2**); **Total: 2**.
Espagnol rival du héros américain, L' [*Fait Historique*].
   Th. des Grands Danseurs (Gaîté) (**3**); **Total: 3**.
Esprits, Les, ou Le Mariage par sortilège [Prem. on 10-10-1799].
   Th. des Victoires (**14**); **Total: 14**.
Etats généraux, Les [*Mélodrame* in 2 acts].
   Th. des Enfans Comiques (**1**); **Total: 1**.
Etourdi, L', ou La Première faction [Prem. on 20-3-1798].
   Th. des Variétés Amusantes, Comiques et Lyriques (**1**); Th. Français (de la
   rue Richelieu) (de la République) (**4**); **Total: 5**.
Etourdi corrigé, L' [N/A].
   Th. Patriotique et de Momus (**1**); **Total: 1**.
Etrennes des bonnes gens, Les [N/A].
   Th. de l'Ambigu Comique (**14**); **Total: 14**.
Etrennes du moment, Les [In 1 act, Prem. on 1-1-1790].
   Th. des Beaujolais (**2**); **Total: 2**.
Etrennes patriotiques, Les [*Tableau-Patriotique* in 1 act, Prem. on 1-1-1792].
   Th. Français, Comique et Lyrique (**8**); **Total: 8**.
Eugénie et les deux chambres [*Drame* in 5 acts].
   Th. de Molière (**2**); **Total: 2**.
Eugénie et Linval ou Le Mauvais fils [*Opéra-Comique*, Prem. on 20-9-1798].
   Th. de la Citoyenne Montansier (**4**); **Total: 4**.

Europe et Junon [N/A].
Th. de l'Emulation (Gaîté) (**17**); **Total: 17.**

Eustache chez lui [*Comédie*].
Th. de la Montagne (**1**); **Total: 1.**

Evêque et le curé, L' [N/A].
Th. de l'Ambigu Comique (**20**); **Total: 20.**

Exercises sur la corde [N/A].
Th. des Jeunes Elèves (**1**); **Total: 1.**

Exigence, L' [*Comédie* in 1 act, Prem. on 8-5-1792].
Th. Français (de la rue Richelieu) (de la République) (**1**); **Total: 1.**

Expulsion des Tarquins, L' [*Fait Historique*].
Th. Français (de la rue Richelieu) (de la République) (**4**); **Total: 4.**

Extravagance de la vieillesse, L' [*Opéra* in 2 acts, Prem. on 21-5-1796].
Th. du Lycée des Arts (**8**); **Total: 8.**

Famille de tous les Pointus, La [N/A].
Th. de l'Emulation (Gaîté) (**1**); Th. des Grands Danseurs (Gaîté) (**5**); **Total: 6.**

Fanchette et Julien [*Opéra-Comique* in 1 act, Prem. on 30-7-1792].
Th. du Vaudeville (**3**); **Total: 3.**

Fanchette ou L'Amour d'une femme [*Vaudeville* in 3 acts].
Th. des Italiens (Opéra-Comique) (**1**); **Total: 1.**

Farce russe, La [N/A].
Th. des Ombres Chinoises (**1**); Th. des Ombres de J.-J. Rousseau (**11**); **Total: 12.**

Fat corrigé, Le [*Drame*, Prem. on 27-2-1798].
Th. des Délassements Comiques (**1**); **Total: 1.**

Fatime et Zenor [*Comédie* in 1 act, Prem. on 1-2-1792].
Th. Français (de la rue Richelieu) (de la République) (**1**); **Total: 1.**

Fausse amie, La [N/A].
Th. de l'Emulation (Gaîté) (**10**); **Total: 10.**

Fausse auberge, La [*Comédie* in 2 acts, Prem. on 16-6-1789].
Th. des Italiens (Opéra-Comique) (**4**); **Total: 4.**

Fausse dénonciation, La [N/A].
Th. des Variétés Amusantes, Comiques et Lyriques (**3**); **Total: 3.**

Faux artistes, Les [N/A].
Th. de l'Emulation (Gaîté) (**1**); **Total: 1.**

Faux brave protégé par Vulcain, Le [*Pantomime*].
Th. des Grands Danseurs (Gaîté) (**1**); **Total: 1.**

Faux d'amis ou Le Mariage fait et rompu de Dufresny, Le [N/A].
Th. des Victoires (**4**); **Total: 4.**

Faux dépit, Le [N/A].
Th. de la Rue Martin (**1**); **Total: 1.**

Faux juifs, Les [N/A].
Th. de l'Emulation (Gaîté) (**1**); **Total: 1.**

Faux Roxas, Les, ou L'Aventurier [*Comédie* in 3 acts].
Th. Français, Comique et Lyrique (**16**); **Total: 16.**

Fée vindicative, La [N/A].
Th. des Variétés Amusantes, Comiques et Lyriques (**5**); **Total: 5.**

Felix ou Le Triomphe de l'innocence [N/A].
Th. du Marais (**2**); **Total: 2.**

Fellamar ou La Suite de Tom-Jones [*Comédie* in 5 acts].
Th. de la Citoyenne Montansier (**6**); Th. de la Rue Martin (**7**); **Total: 13.**

Femme artiste, La [N/A].
    Th. du Vaudeville (7); **Total: 7.**

Femme auteur, La [Prem. on 3-11-1798].
    Th. du Vaudeville (1); **Total: 1.**

Femme bijoutier, La [N/A].
    Th. Patriotique et de Momus (34); **Total: 34.**

Femme fidèle, La [N/A].
    Th. des Grands Danseurs (Gaîté) (1); **Total: 1.**

Femme fille, veuve et mariée, La [N/A].
    Th. des Variétés Amusantes (Lazzari) (3); **Total: 3.**

Femme invincible, La [*Pantomime*].
    Th. des Grands Danseurs (Gaîté) (1); **Total: 1.**

Femme invisible, La [N/A].
    Th. des Grands Danseurs (Gaîté) (1); **Total: 1.**

Femme soldat, La, ou L'effet du patriotisme [*Comédie* in 2 acts, Prem. on 4-3-1790].
    Th. des Grands Danseurs (Gaîté) (4); **Total: 4.**

Femme vertueuse, La, ou Le Pantalon débauché [*Comédie* in 3 acts, Pub. in 1716].
    Th. des Grands Danseurs (Gaîté) (6); **Total: 6.**

Femmes et les arts, Les [N/A].
    Th. du Marais (1); **Total: 1.**

Ferdinand XV ou Les Barons allemands [*Vaudeville*, Prem. on 8-7-1799].
    Th. de la Cité (7); Th. de Molière (1); Th. du Palais (Cité)-Variétés (11); **Total: 19.**

Fermier bienfaisant, Le [N/A].
    Th. de l'Ambigu Comique (25); Th. des Grands Danseurs (Gaîté) (11); Th. du Feydeau (de Monsieur) (2); **Total: 38.**

Fermier bijoutier, Le [N/A].
    Th. Patriotique et de Momus (1); **Total: 1.**

Fermier hospitalier ou Le Bon laboureur, Le [N/A].
    Th. de l'Emulation (Gaîté) (12); **Total: 12.**

Fermier républicain, Le [*Vaudeville* in 2 acts, Pub. in 1794].
    Th. National (de la rue Richelieu) (6); **Total: 6.**

Fermière jalouse, La [N/A].
    Th. des Victoires (1); Th. Lyrique des Amis de la Patrie (1); **Total: 2.**

Festin de Pierre à la foire, Le [*Comédie* in 5 acts].
    Th. de l'Emulation (Gaîté) (4); Th. de la Rue Martin (3); Th. des Grands Danseurs (Gaîté) (37); Th. des Variétés Amusantes (Lazzari) (9); Th. du Feydeau (de Monsieur) (1); Th. Français (de la rue Richelieu) (de la République) (4); **Total: 58.**

Festin des sans-culottes, Le [*Vaudeville* in 2 acts, Prem. on 6-1-1793].
    Th. de l'Estrapade au Panthéon (5); **Total: 5.**

Fête américaine, La [*Ballet*, Prem. on 18-8-1794, Pub. in 1794].
    Th. de la Citoyenne Montansier (1); Th. des Italiens (Opéra-Comique) (12); Th. des Variétés Amusantes (Lazzari) (10); **Total: 23.**

Fête au château, La [Prem. on 7-9-1797].
    Th. des Jeunes Artistes (3); **Total: 3.**

Fête champêtre, La [*Ballet*].
    Th. des Grands Danseurs (Gaîté) (18); **Total: 18.**

Fête civique, La [*Vaudeville*, Pub. in 1794].
    Th. de l'Ambigu Comique (**57**); Th. des Grands Danseurs (Gaîté) (**1**); **Total: 58.**

Fête d'arquebuse, La [*Vaudeville* in 2 acts, Prem. on 6-1-1790].
    Th. des Beaujolais (**11**); **Total: 11.**

Fête de la fraternité, La [*Drame* in 3 acts, Pub. in 1793].
    Th. du Palais (Cité)-Variétés (**5**); **Total: 5.**

Fête de la paix, La [Prem. on 7-11-1797].
    Th. de la Cité (**7**); **Total: 7.**

Fête de la rose, La [*Comédie*, Prem. on 14-6-1797].
    Th. de l'Ambigu Comique (**2**); **Total: 2.**

Fête de la soixantaine, La [Prem. on 31-12-1796].
    Th. des Jeunes Artistes (**1**); **Total: 1.**

Fête de Sophie ou Deux amis soupçonnés [*Ballet* in 3 acts, Prem. on 23-1-1788].
    Th. des Beaujolais (**10**); **Total: 10.**

Fête de village interrompue, La [N/A].
    Th. du Vaudeville (**1**); **Total: 1.**

Fête des bonnes gens, La [Prem. on 18-4-1796].
    Th. Patriotique et de Momus (**6**); **Total: 6.**

Fête des nègres, La [*Vaudeville*].
    Th. National (de la rue Richelieu) (**11**); **Total: 11.**

Fête des vieillards, La [N/A].
    Th. des Jeunes Artistes (**1**); **Total: 1.**

Fête du grenadier, La, ou La Fête de la liberté [*Pantomime* in 1 act, Prem. on 3-9-1789].
    Th. de l'Ambigu Comique (**49**); **Total: 49.**

Fête du prix, La [N/A].
    Th. des Grands Danseurs (Gaîté) (**1**); **Total: 1.**

Fête du savetier, La [N/A].
    Th. des Grands Danseurs (Gaîté) (**1**); **Total: 1.**

Fête du voisin, La [N/A].
    Th. des Délassements Comiques (**2**); **Total: 2.**

Fête en petit, La [*Tableau-Patriotique* in 2 acts].
    Th. de la Citoyenne Montansier (**1**); **Total: 1.**

Fête et ballet chinois [Prem. on 7-12-1797].
    Th. des Ombres Chinoises (**11**); Th. des Ombres de J.-J. Rousseau (**51**); **Total: 62.**

Fête genevoise, La, ou Les Moeurs du bon temps [Prem. on 29-9-1797].
    Th. des Jeunes Artistes (**41**); **Total: 41.**

Feuille des bénéfices, La [Prem. on 1-7-1791].
    Th. de Molière (**1**); **Total: 1.**

Feux pyrrhiques et hydrauliques [N/A].
    Th. des Ombres Chinoises (**20**); Th. des Ombres de J.-J. Rousseau (**33**); **Total: 53.**

Fiancé de Falaire, Le [*Comédie* in 1 act, Pub. in 1795].
    Th. des Variétés Amusantes, Comiques et Lyriques (**3**); **Total: 3.**

Figaro grand vizir [N/A].
    Th. des Grands Danseurs (Gaîté) (**2**); **Total: 2.**

Fil de laiton, Le [N/A].
    Th. des Grands Danseurs (Gaîté) (**1**); **Total: 1.**

Fille à la mode, La [N/A].
    Th. des Grands Danseurs (Gaîté) (**15**); **Total: 15.**

Fille en loterie, La [*Comédie* in 2 acts, Prem. on 26-9-1799].
    Th. du Vaudeville (**8**); **Total: 8.**

Fille généreuse de St.-Germain, La [Prem. in 1787].
    Th. des Grands Danseurs (Gaîté) (**43**); **Total: 43.**

Fille indécise, La [*Vaudeville* in 2 acts, Prem. on 23-1-1793].
    Th. de l'Estrapade au Panthéon (**7**); **Total: 7.**

Fille peintre, La [N/A].
    Th. de l'Ambigu Comique (**9**); **Total: 9.**

Fille rusée, La [*Comédie* in 1 act].
    Cirque National (**1**); **Total: 1.**

Fille vindicative [N/A].
    Th. des Variétés Amusantes, Comiques et Lyriques (**2**); **Total: 2.**

Filles mères, Les [N/A].
    Th. du Vaudeville (**1**); **Total: 1.**

Filoli et Mioco [Prem. on 29-4-1797].
    Th. de la Cité (**6**); **Total: 6.**

Fils adoptif, Le [N/A].
    Th. des Grands Danseurs (Gaîté) (**3**); Th. du Vaudeville (**1**); **Total: 4.**

Fin contre fin [N/A].
    Th. de l'Ambigu Comique (**23**); **Total: 23.**

Fin contre fin ou Les Deux clefs [*Comédie* in 1 act, Prem. on 27-5-1782, Pub. in
1782].
    Th. de l'Ambigu Comique (**9**); Th. des Grands Danseurs (Gaîté) (**7**); **To-
tal: 16.**

Fin du monde, La, ou La Comète [*Divertissement/parade*, Prem. on 25-1-1798].
    Th. de l'Ambigu Comique (**8**); Th. de la Citoyenne Montansier (**2**); Th. des
Délassements Comiques (**22**); Th. du Vaudeville (**31**); Tivoli (**5**); **Total:
68.**

Fin du monde, La, ou Le Faux prophète [*Vaudeville*].
    Th. du Vaudeville (**1**); **Total: 1.**

Financier amoureux, Le [*Opéra* in 2 acts, Prem. on 5-11-1791].
    Cirque National (**6**); **Total: 6.**

Flageolet enchanté, Le [*Comédie*, Prem. on 22-3-1792].
    Th. de la Citoyenne Montansier (**23**); Th. de Molière (**2**); **Total: 25.**

Floride, La [N/A].
    Th. du Palais (Cité)-Variétés (**1**); **Total: 1.**

Foire des fées, La [Prem. on 3-9-1796].
    Th. du Vaudeville (**8**); **Total: 8.**

Folie de Jérôme Pointu, La [N/A].
    Th. du Lycée des Arts (**4**); **Total: 4.**

Fontaine de Jouvence [N/A].
    Th. des Ombres Chinoises (**2**); **Total: 2.**

Forces d'Hercule, Les [N/A].
    Th. des Grands Danseurs (Gaîté) (**11**); **Total: 11.**

Forêt de Bondy, La [*Pantomime*, Prem. on 30-1-1797].
    Th. des Variétés Amusantes (Lazzari) (**3**); **Total: 3.**

Forêt des Ardennes, La [N/A].
    Th. des Variétés Amusantes, Comiques et Lyriques (**2**); **Total: 2.**

Forges de Vulcain, Les [*Pantomime* in 1 act, Pub. in 1773].
    Th. des Grands Danseurs (Gaîté) (**47**); **Total: 47.**

Forges du père Duchesne, Les [Prem. on 22-2-1794].
Th. du Lycée des Arts (8); **Total: 8.**

Forte gageure, La [N/A].
Th. de l'Emulation (Gaîté) (1); **Total: 1.**

Fossoyeurs, Les [*Parodie*].
Th. de la Citoyenne Montansier (2); **Total: 2.**

Fou malgré lui, Le [*Opéra*, Prem. on 24-11-1798].
Th. de Molière (2); **Total: 2.**

Fou par terreur, Le [Prem. on 26-8-1797].
Th. des Jeunes Artistes (6); **Total: 6.**

Fourberies d'Arlequin, Les [*Pantomime*].
Th. des Variétés Amusantes (Lazzari) (1); Th. des Variétés Amusantes, Comiques et Lyriques (1); **Total: 2.**

Fourberies de Frontin, Les [*Opéra*].
Th. Lyrique du Foire St. Germain (9); **Total: 9.**

Fous de Médine, Les [*Comédie* in 3 acts, Prem. on 1-5-1790].
Th. des Italiens (Opéra-Comique) (1); **Total: 1.**

Français à Madrid, Le [*Pièce* in 2 acts, Prem. on 10-8-1789].
Th. de l'Ambigu Comique (1); Th. du Palais Royal (6); **Total: 7.**

Français à Tunis, Les [N/A].
Th. des Variétés Amusantes (Lazzari) (11); Th. des Variétés Amusantes, Comiques et Lyriques (21); **Total: 32.**

Français à Worms, Le [*Tableau-Patriotique*, Prem. on 21-12-1792].
Th. de l'Ambigu Comique (21); **Total: 21.**

Français dans l'Inde, Les [*Tragédie* in 3 acts].
Th. National (de la rue Richelieu) (3); **Total: 3.**

Français dans l'isle de la liberté, Les [*Comédie* in 1 act, Pub. in 1789].
Th. du Marais (1); **Total: 1.**

Français en Espagne, Les [*Vaudeville*].
Th. de l'Ambigu Comique (12); **Total: 12.**

Françaises, Les [In 1 act].
Th. des Beaujolais (1); **Total: 1.**

Franche et Monmutin [Prem. on 5-11-1798].
Th. du Vaudeville (11); **Total: 11.**

Frère barbare, Le [*Comédie*].
Th. des Grands Danseurs (Gaîté) (1); **Total: 1.**

Frère Jean ou Le Pont de coupe-gorge [Prem. on 14-7-1797].
Th. de l'Ambigu Comique (22); Th. des Grands Danseurs (Gaîté) (20); **Total: 42.**

Frère retrouvé, Le [N/A].
Th. des Grands Danseurs (Gaîté) (13); Th. des Ombres Chinoises (1); **Total: 14.**

Frère supposé, Le [N/A].
Th. du Palais (Cité)-Variétés (1); **Total: 1.**

Fricassée, La [*Divertissement/parade*, Pub. in 1772].
Th. des Grands Danseurs (Gaîté) (2); **Total: 2.**

Frippier marchand de modes, Le [*Pantomime* in 1 act, Pub. in 1782].
Th. de l'Ambigu Comique (22); **Total: 22.**

Frippon démasqué, Le [N/A].
Th. de la Citoyenne Montansier (1); **Total: 1.**

Farce russe, La [N/A].
  Th. des Ombres Chinoises (4); Th. des Ombres de J.-J. Rousseau (1); **Total: 5.**

Gages d'amour, Les [*Opéra*, Prem. on 20-1-1792].
  Th. de Molière (16); **Total: 16.**

Gageure, La [N/A].
  Th. de la Citoyenne Montansier (1); Th. de la Rue Antoine (1); Th. de la Rue Martin (1); Th. des Variétés Amusantes, Comiques et Lyriques (2); Th. du Vaudeville (8); Th. Français (de la rue Richelieu) (de la République) (1); Th. Patriotique et de Momus (1); **Total: 15.**

Gageure du pèlerin, La [*Opéra* in 2 acts].
  Th. de la Citoyenne Montansier (12); **Total: 12.**

Gageure imprudente, La [N/A].
  Th. des Grands Danseurs (Gaîté) (3); **Total: 3.**

Gageure indiscrète, La [N/A].
  Th. du Lycée des Arts (1); **Total: 1.**

Gageure villageoise, La, ou Le Baiser [*Comédie* in 1 act].
  Th. de Molière (4); **Total: 4.**

Gargamelle, La [N/A].
  Th. de l'Emulation (Gaîté) (1); **Total: 1.**

Gascon tel qu'il est, Le [*Opéra-Vaudeville*, Prem. on 10-7-1797].
  Th. de la Citoyenne Montansier (2); **Total: 2.**

Gasconnade [*Opéra* in 1 act, Prem. on 10-10-1796].
  Th. du Feydeau (de Monsieur) (1); **Total: 1.**

Gâteau des tyrans, Le [*Pantomime*, Prem. on 9-3-1794, Pub. in 1794].
  Th. de l'Ambigu Comique (35); **Total: 35.**

Gazetier, Le [*Comédie* in 1 act, Prem. on 9-12-1791].
  Th. de la Citoyenne Montansier (1); **Total: 1.**

Gazette de campagne, La [*Opéra-Comique* in 1 act].
  Th. de la Montagne (11); **Total: 11.**

Général Custine à Spire, Le [*Fait Historique* in 2 acts, Pub. in 1791].
  Th. de l'Ambigu Comique (24); **Total: 24.**

Généraux, Les [N/A].
  Th. de l'Ambigu Comique (4); **Total: 4.**

Généreuse patriote, La [*Tableau-Patriotique*].
  Th. des Grands Danseurs (Gaîté) (1); **Total: 1.**

Généreuse supercherie, La [*Comédie* in 3 acts, Prem. on 7-10-1793].
  Th. Lyrique des Amis de la Patrie (1); **Total: 1.**

Geneviève de Brabant [*Mélodrame* in 2 acts, Prem. on 23-11-1791, Pub. in 1793].
  Th. de l'Emulation (Gaîté) (30); Th. de l'Odéon (16); Th. de Molière (2); Th. des Grands Danseurs (Gaîté) (46); Th. du Lycée des Arts (31); Th. du Marais (5); Th. du Palais (Cité)-Variétés (2); Th. du Vaudeville (8); **Total: 140.**

Gengis Kan [N/A].
  Th. des Ombres de J.-J. Rousseau (2); **Total: 2.**

Gilles afficheur [Prem. on 23-9-1798].
  Th. des Jeunes Artistes (26); Th. du Marais (1); Th. du Palais (Cité)-Variétés (1); **Total: 28.**

Gilles dupé [*Comédie* in 1 act, Prem. on 12-2-1792, Pub. in 1792].
  Th. du Vaudeville (24); **Total: 24.**

Gilles garnement ou Le Ballon-biron [Prem. on 26-8-1797].
  Th. du Vaudeville (19); **Total: 19.**

Gilles Georges et Arlequin Pitt [*Parodie* in 3 acts, Pub. in 1794].
>   Th. du Vaudeville (**25**); **Total: 25.**

Gilles le niais [N/A].
>   Th. des Ombres Chinoises (**1**); Th. des Ombres de J.-J. Rousseau (**1**); **Total: 2.**

Gilles musicien [N/A].
>   Th. des Grands Danseurs (Gaîté) (**3**); **Total: 3.**

Gilles toujours Gilles, rival d'Arlequin ou La Cassette [*Vaudeville* in 2 acts].
>   Th. de l'Estrapade au Panthéon (**11**); Th. de Molière (**1**); Th. des Variétés Amusantes, Comiques et Lyriques (**1**); **Total: 13.**

Gliska [N/A].
>   Th. des Italiens (Opéra-Comique) (**5**); **Total: 5.**

Goanna et Jennuy [N/A].
>   Th. de l'Ambigu Comique (**20**); **Total: 20.**

Goburge dans l'isle des falots [N/A].
>   Th. des Jeunes Artistes (**34**); **Total: 34.**

Goute, La, ou L'Aimable vieillard [Prem. on 17-3-1798].
>   Th. de l'Emulation (Gaîté) (**2**); **Total: 2.**

Goute des halles [*Vaudeville* in 1 act, Pub. in 1793].
>   Th. des Variétés Amusantes, Comiques et Lyriques (**5**); **Total: 5.**

Grand festin de Pierre, Le [*Pantomime* in 3 acts, Pub. in 1787].
>   Th. des Grands Danseurs (Gaîté) (**8**); **Total: 8.**

Grand genre, Le [Prem. on 13-1-1799].
>   Th. de l'Ambigu Comique (**3**); **Total: 3.**

Grande famille, La [N/A].
>   Th. des Délassements Comiques (**1**); **Total: 1.**

Grande revue de l'armée noire et blanche d'Outre-Rhin, La [*Mélodrame* in 1 act, Prem. on 25-7-1791].
>   Th. de Molière (**25**); **Total: 25.**

Grande rosace, La [*Proverbe/allégorique*].
>   Tivoli (**5**); **Total: 5.**

Grandes ombres impalpables, Les [*Comédie* in 3 acts].
>   Th. de Jean-Jacques Rousseau (**1**); **Total: 1.**

Gras et les maigres, Les [N/A].
>   Th. des Ombres de J.-J. Rousseau (**4**); **Total: 4.**

Grégoire et ses filles ou L'Intendant puni [*Opéra* in 1 act, Prem. on 5-11-1789].
>   Th. des Beaujolais (**6**); **Total: 6.**

Guadeloupe reconquise, La [N/A].
>   Th. du Lycée des Arts (**30**); **Total: 30.**

Guibert et Raffile [N/A].
>   Th. de la Cité (**1**); **Total: 1.**

Guillaume tout coeur [*Opéra* in 2 acts, Prem. on 23-1-1792].
>   Th. Français, Comique et Lyrique (**4**); **Total: 4.**

Guillot gorju [N/A].
>   Th. de l'Ambigu Comique (**1**); **Total: 1.**

Guinguette, La [*Ballet*].
>   Th. de l'Emulation (Gaîté) (**1**); Th. Lyrique des Amis de la Patrie (**15**); **Total: 16.**

Habitants du Vaucluse, Les [*Opéra*, Prem. on 1-6-1799].
 Th. de la Citoyenne Montansier (**16**); **Total: 16.**
Hâbleur de la Vendée, Le [*Comédie* in 3 acts, Pub. in 1794].
 Maison Egalité (**1**); Th. du Palais (Cité)-Variétés (**5**); **Total: 6.**
Hagard, fils de son père [*Parodie* in 2 acts, Prem. on 21-6-1796].
 Th. du Vaudeville (**17**); **Total: 17.**
Hélène et Paulin [*Vaudeville* in 1 act, Prem. on 2-10-1790].
 Th. Français, Comique et Lyrique (**10**); **Total: 10.**
Héloïse américaine, L' [N/A].
 Th. de la Rue Martin (**13**); Th. du Lycée des Arts (**2**); **Total: 15.**
Henri et Sophie [N/A].
 Th. de l'Emulation (Gaîté) (**17**); **Total: 17.**
Henriot et Boulotte [*Parodie*, Pub. in 1791].
 Th. de Molière (**9**); **Total: 9.**
Héritage et l'honnête huissier, L' [*Tableau-Patriotique*, Prem. on 24-2-1790].
 Th. des Grands Danseurs (Gaîté) (**15**); **Total: 15.**
Héritage inattendu, L' [*Comédie* in 2 acts, Prem. on 6-12-1790].
 Th. de la Citoyenne Montansier (**1**); **Total: 1.**
Héritiers, Les, ou Le Naufrage [*Comédie*, Prem. on 28-11-1796].
 Th. Français (de la rue Richelieu) (de la République) (**14**); **Total: 14.**
Héritiers de Jean-bête, Les [N/A].
 Th. des Délassements Comiques (**7**); **Total: 7.**
Herman et Flora [N/A].
 Th. Lyrique des Amis de la Patrie (**1**); **Total: 1.**
Hermitage, L', ou Les Brigands de Pologne [*Pantomime*].
 n/a (**3**); **Total: 3.**
Hermite amoureux, L' [N/A].
 Th. des Grands Danseurs (Gaîté) (**1**); **Total: 1.**
Herneval et Saint-Méry [*Comédie* in 3 acts, Prem. on 4-3-1793].
 Th. Français (de la rue Richelieu) (de la République) (**1**); **Total: 1.**
Hérolhe, L' [N/A].
 Th. de l'Ambigu Comique (**1**); **Total: 1.**
Hérolhe corse, L' [*Fait Historique* in 4 acts, Prem. on 2-6-1792].
 Th. de l'Ambigu Comique (**2**); **Total: 2.**
Hérolhe française, L' [*Fait Historique*, Prem. on 11-8-1799].
 Th. des Grands Danseurs (Gaîté) (**8**); **Total: 8.**
Hérolsme mutuel, L' [*Fait Historique*].
 Th. Français, Comique et Lyrique (**5**); **Total: 5.**
Heureuse espérance, L' [N/A].
 Th. de la Cité (**2**); **Total: 2.**
Heureuse extravagance, L' [N/A].
 Th. du Palais (Cité)-Variétés (**3**); **Total: 3.**
Heureuse journée, L' [N/A].
 Th. Lyrique des Amis de la Patrie (**1**); **Total: 1.**
Heureuse nouvelle, L' [*Comédie*, Prem. on 7-11-1797].
 Th. du Feydeau (de Monsieur) (**1**); **Total: 1.**
Heureuse rencontre, L' [N/A].
 Th. de l'Ambigu Comique (**17**); **Total: 17.**
Heureux ménage, L' [*Vaudeville*].
 Th. des Jeunes Artistes (**2**); **Total: 2.**

Heureux naturels, Les [*Comédie* in 1 act, Prem. on 29-4-1790].
Th. des Grands Danseurs (Gaîté) (12); **Total: 12.**

Heureux stratagème, L', ou Le Bachelier de Salamanque [*Comédie* in 3 acts, Prem. on 25-5-1799].
Th. des Jeunes Artistes (5); Th. du Marais (3); **Total: 8.**

Heureux voyage, L' [*Comédie* in 1 act, Prem. on 7-11-1789].
Th. de l'Ambigu Comique (15); **Total: 15.**

Hola trico [N/A].
Th. des Jeunes Artistes (2); **Total: 2.**

Hollandais dupé, L' [N/A].
Th. des Grands Danseurs (Gaîté) (1); **Total: 1.**

Hollandaise, La [N/A].
Th. des Variétés Amusantes (Lazzari) (1); Th. des Variétés Amusantes, Comiques et Lyriques (10); **Total: 11.**

Hommage mérité, L' [N/A].
Th. du Lycée Dramatique (1); **Total: 1.**

Hommage rendu à la liberté, L' [*Tableau-Patriotique*].
Th. de l'Estrapade au Panthéon (3); **Total: 3.**

Homme aux huit sols, L' [N/A].
Th. de l'Emulation (Gaîté) (7); **Total: 7.**

Homme de rien et l'homme de bien, L' [N/A].
Th. de l'Ambigu Comique (5); **Total: 5.**

Homme marin, L', ou Le Poisson d'avril [*Comédie* in 1 act].
Th. du Palais (Cité)-Variétés (4); **Total: 4.**

Homme mécontent, L' [N/A].
Th. de l'Emulation (Gaîté) (3); Th. Lyrique des Amis de la Patrie (1); **Total: 4.**

Homme vertueux, L', ou Le Vrai républicain [*Comédie* in 1 act, Prem. on 15-6-1794, Pub. in 1788].
Th. des Italiens (Opéra-Comique) (10); Th. des Variétés Amusantes, Comiques et Lyriques (5); Th. du Palais (Cité)-Variétés (4); **Total: 19.**

Hommes à projets, Les [*Comédie* in 3 acts, Prem. on 17-2-1791, Pub. in 1784].
Th. Français, Comique et Lyrique (1); **Total: 1.**

Honneur et richesse [Prem. on 25-4-1799].
Th. des Jeunes Artistes (4); **Total: 4.**

Honneurs funèbres, Les, ou Le Tombeau des sans-culottes [*Tableau-Patriotique* in 1 act, Prem. on 2-2-1794, Pub. in 1794].
Th. du Palais (Cité)-Variétés (2); **Total: 2.**

Honorine et Julien [N/A].
Th. de l'Ambigu Comique (3); **Total: 3.**

Honorine muet malgré lui [*Vaudeville*].
Th. des Variétés Amusantes, Comiques et Lyriques (1); **Total: 1.**

Hospice, L' [N/A].
Th. des Jeunes Artistes (1); Th. des Variétés Amusantes, Comiques et Lyriques (1); **Total: 2.**

Hospitalité trahie, L' [N/A].
Th. de l'Ambigu Comique (4); **Total: 4.**

Hôtellerie, L' [*Vaudeville* in 1 act].
Th. des Grands Danseurs (Gaîté) (8); **Total: 8.**

Hôtellerie de Fontainebleau, L' [*Opéra* in 3 acts, Prem. on 18-5-1793].
Th. de la Citoyenne Montansier (4); **Total: 4.**

Houlans, Les, ou Les Effets de la liberté [*Tableau-Patriotique*, Prem. on 30-3-1794].
>Th. de l'Ambigu Comique (**37**); **Total: 37**.

Houlvary des sauteurs, L' [*Divertissement/parade*].
>Th. des Grands Danseurs (Gaîté) (**1**); **Total: 1**.

Hulla de Samarcande ou Le Divorce tartare [*Comédie* in 5 acts, Pub. in 1793].
>Th. Français (de la rue Richelieu) (de la République) (**3**); **Total: 3**.

Hussards du Ier régiment, Les [*Fait Historique* in 2 acts, Prem. on 2-6-1792].
>Th. de Molière (**7**); **Total: 7**.

Hymen volé par l'amour, L' [N/A].
>Th. des Jeunes Artistes (**87**); **Total: 87**.

Hymne à Jean-Jacques Rousseau [*Fait Historique*].
>Académie de la Musique (Opéra) (**1**); **Total: 1**.

Hymne à l'indépendance, L' [*Tableau-Patriotique*, Pub. in 1794].
>Th. du Palais (Cité)-Variétés (**1**); **Total: 1**.

Hymne à la liberté, L' [*Tableau-Patriotique*, Prem. on 10-12-1793, Pub. in 1794].
>Th. de la Citoyenne Montansier (**1**); Th. de la Rue Martin (**1**); Th. des Grands Danseurs (Gaîté) (**31**); Th. du Marais (**5**); **Total: 38**.

Hymne à la paix [*Opéra*].
>Th. des Italiens (Opéra-Comique) (**2**); Th. du Feydeau (de Monsieur) (**8**); **Total: 10**.

Hymne à la victoire, L' [*Chanson*].
>Académie de la Musique (Opéra) (**3**); Th. du Lycée des Arts (**4**); **Total: 7**.

Hypocrite en révolution, L' [*Comédie* in 1 act, Prem. on 20-7-1794, Pub. in 1794].
>Th. du Palais (Cité)-Variétés (**7**); **Total: 7**.

Il a voulu, il n'a pas pu [Prem. on 29-7-1799].
>Th. des Grands Danseurs (Gaîté) (**12**); **Total: 12**.

Il est bon de s'entendre [*Vaudeville* in 1 act, Prem. on 21-9-1790].
>Th. Français, Comique et Lyrique (**9**); **Total: 9**.

Il est temps ou La Découverte [Prem. on 10-3-1794].
>Th. des Grands Danseurs (Gaîté) (**4**); **Total: 4**.

Il était tant [N/A].
>Th. de l'Emulation (Gaîté) (**2**); **Total: 2**.

Il ne boira plus [*Comédie* in 1 act, Prem. on 17-2-1795].
>Th. des Grands Danseurs (Gaîté) (**11**); **Total: 11**.

Il ne faut pas dire fontaine, je ne boirai pas de ton eau [*Comédie* in 1 act, Prem. on 19-3-1791].
>n/a (**2**); **Total: 2**.

Ile d'Ormus heureuse, L', ou La Suite de Tarare [In 3 acts, Prem. on 30-10-1790].
>Th. des Beaujolais (**8**); **Total: 8**.

Ils n'y pensaient pas [*Comédie* in 3 acts, Prem. on 13-7-1792].
>Th. Lyrique des Amis de la Patrie (**2**); **Total: 2**.

Ils ont le diable au corps faute de s'entendre dans les marionnettes [N/A].
>Th. des Ombres Chinoises (**10**); Th. des Ombres de J.-J. Rousseau (**3**); **Total: 13**.

Ils sont libres enfin [N/A].
>Th. du Lycée des Arts (**4**); **Total: 4**.

Imbroglio, L', ou Les Métamorphoses d'Arlequin [Prem. on 23-8-1798].
 Th. Lyrique des Amis de la Patrie (**2**); **Total: 2**.
Inconséquente et Basile, L' [N/A].
 Th. des Jeunes Artistes (**63**); **Total: 63**.
Inconstance sans inconstance [*Opéra*, Prem. on 22-10-1798].
 Th. de la Citoyenne Montansier (**2**); **Total: 2**.
Indicateur, L' [N/A].
 Th. du Vaudeville (**6**); **Total: 6**.
Indifférence vaincue, L', ou Aglaure [*Ballet*, Prem. on 11-3-1788].
 Th. des Grands Danseurs (Gaîté) (**3**); **Total: 3**.
Inès ou La Victime cloîtrée [N/A].
 Th. de l'Ambigu Comique (**19**); **Total: 19**.
Infidélités imaginaires, Les [N/A].
 Th. Lyrique des Amis de la Patrie (**1**); **Total: 1**.
Innocence protégée du ciel, L' [N/A].
 Th. des Variétés Amusantes, Comiques et Lyriques (**9**); **Total: 9**.
Innocente supercherie, L' [N/A].
 Th. de la Cité (**2**); **Total: 2**.
Inquisition, L' [N/A].
 Th. de l'Emulation (Gaîté) (**2**); **Total: 2**.
Insulaires, Les [N/A].
 Th. du Vaudeville (**3**); **Total: 3**.
Insurrection des ombres, L' [*Pantomime* in 1 act, Prem. on 17-1-1791].
 Th. de l'Ambigu Comique (**37**); **Total: 37**.
Intendant, L' [N/A].
 Th. du Vaudeville (**19**); **Total: 19**.
Intendant comédien malgré lui, L', ou La Fête de campagne [*Comédie* in 1 act, Pub. in 1789].
 Th. de la Citoyenne Montansier (**12**); **Total: 12**.
Intendant comédien, L' [N/A].
 Th. de l'Emulation (Gaîté) (**5**); Th. de la Citoyenne Montansier (**21**); Th. des Victoires Nationales (**3**); Th. du Marais (**2**); Th. du Vaudeville (**16**); Th. Lyrique des Amis de la Patrie (**10**); **Total: 57**.
Intendant supposé, L' [*Comédie* in 2 acts, Prem. on 22-10-1788].
 Th. des Beaujolais (**38**); **Total: 38**.
Intéressés, Les [N/A].
 Th. des Jeunes Artistes (**2**); **Total: 2**.
Intérieur de la maison, L' [*Comédie* in 3 acts, Pub. in 1792].
 Th. du Marais (**3**); **Total: 3**.
Intérieur des comités de spectacle, L' [N/A].
 Th. des Jeunes Artistes (**3**); **Total: 3**.
Intrigue portugaise, L' [N/A].
 Th. du Feydeau (de Monsieur) (**1**); **Total: 1**.
Intrigues nocturnes, Les [*Comédie*].
 Th. du Marais (**1**); **Total: 1**.
Irlandais unis, Les [*Drame*, Prem. on 23-1-1799].
 Th. du Palais (Cité)-Variétés (**7**); **Total: 7**.
Isabelle somnambule [*Comédie*, Prem. on 26-11-1798].
 Th. du Vaudeville (**5**); **Total: 5**.
Italien, L' [N/A].
 Th. de l'Emulation (Gaîté) (**6**); **Total: 6**.

J.-J.Rousseau dans l'isle St.-Pierre [*Drame* in 5 acts, Prem. on 15-12-1791].
   Th. de la Nation (Comédie Française) (1); **Total: 1.**

Jacobins du 9 thermidor, Les [*Opéra* in 1 act, Pub. in 1795].
   Maison Egalité (2); Th. du Palais (Cité)-Variétés (1); **Total: 3.**

Jacques le fataliste et son maître [Prem. on 31-7-1798].
   Th. du Vaudeville (1); **Total: 1.**

Jako et Zulica [*Pantomime*, Prem. on 12-8-1798].
   Th. du Marais (1); **Total: 1.**

Jalousie de campagne, La [*Comédie* in 1 act, Prem. on 23-6-1792].
   Th. de la Citoyenne Montansier (1); **Total: 1.**

Jalousie villageoise, La [N/A].
   Th. de la Rue Martin (1); Th. du Lycée des Arts (2); **Total: 3.**

Jaloux guéris, Les [N/A].
   Th. du Lycée des Arts (4); **Total: 4.**

Janot bohémienne [N/A].
   Th. de la Citoyenne Montansier (39); **Total: 39.**

Jardin de la révolution, Le [N/A].
   Th. du Lycée des Arts (3); **Total: 3.**

Jardiniers galants, Les [Prem. on 11-6-1791].
   Th. des Grands Danseurs (Gaîté) (32); **Total: 32.**

Jean Monet [N/A].
   Th. du Vaudeville (16); **Total: 16.**

Jean Racine [N/A].
   Th. de la Cité (1); Th. de Molière (1); Th. des Jeunes Artistes (3); **Total: 5.**

Jean-Jacques Rousseau [N/A].
   Th. du Marais (1); **Total: 1.**

Jean-Jacques Rousseau à l'hermitage [N/A].
   Th. du Vaudeville (2); **Total: 2.**

Jean-Jacques Rousseau au paraclet [*Comédie* in 3 acts].
   Th. National (de la rue Richelieu) (26); Th. Patriotique et de Momus (11);
   Total: 37.

Jean-Jacques Rousseau dans son ménage [N/A].
   Th. du Feydeau (de Monsieur) (1); **Total: 1.**

Jeannette et Bastien [*Vaudeville* in 1 act, Prem. on 18-9-1791].
   Th. du Lycée des Arts (1); Th. Lyrique des Amis de la Patrie (31); **Total:
   32.**

Jérôme spirituel ou Les Scudéry [*Vaudeville* in 1 act, Prem. on 9-11-1799].
   Th. des Troubadours (1); **Total: 1.**

Jeune parisienne, La [N/A].
   Th. Patriotique et de Momus (2); **Total: 2.**

Jeune savoyarde, La [N/A].
   Th. de l'Ambigu Comique (5); **Total: 5.**

Jeux d'amour et du hasard [N/A].
   Th. du Lycée des Arts (1); **Total: 1.**

Jeux d'amour, Les [*Ballet*].
   Th. de l'Emulation (Gaîté) (6); **Total: 6.**

Jocrisse [N/A].
   Th. des Variétés Amusantes, Comiques et Lyriques (1); **Total: 1.**

Jocrisse à Longchamp [*Vaudeville*, Prem. on 17-4-1798].
   Th. de la Citoyenne Montansier (2); **Total: 2.**

Jocrisse à Tivoli [N/A].
   Th. des Délassements Comiques (1); **Total: 1.**

Jocrisse ou La Poule aux oeufs d'or [*Opéra-Comique* in 1 act, Pub. in 1792].
Th. du Vaudeville (**35**); **Total: 35.**

Jocrisse presque seul [Prem. on 9-3-1799].
Th. de la Citoyenne Montansier (**2**); **Total: 2.**

Joli conciliateur, Le [*Comédie* in 1 act].
Th. du Palais (Cité)-Variétés (**2**); **Total: 2.**

Jolie gouvernante, La [*Comédie* in 2 acts, Prem. on 11-11-1791].
Cirque National (**7**); **Total: 7.**

Jolie savoyarde, La [N/A].
Th. de l'Ambigu Comique (**6**); **Total: 6.**

Joseph la valse [N/A].
Th. de la Citoyenne Montansier (**1**); **Total: 1.**

Jour des noces, Le [*Vaudeville*, Prem. on 31-8-1798].
Th. de l'Emulation (Gaîté) (**21**); Th. Lyrique des Amis de la Patrie (**1**); **Total: 22.**

Journaliste, Le [N/A].
Th. de la Citoyenne Montansier (**5**); **Total: 5.**

Journée d'un rentier, La [N/A].
Th. des Jeunes Artistes (**4**); **Total: 4.**

Journée de Ferney, Une [*Comédie* in 3 acts].
Th. du Vaudeville (**37**); **Total: 37.**

Journée de Varennes, La [*Fait Historique* in 2 acts, Prem. on 20-7-1791].
Th. de l'Ambigu Comique (**18**); **Total: 18.**

Journée dérangée, La [*Tableau-Patriotique* in 1 act, Pub. in 1790].
Th. du Feydeau (de Monsieur) (**22**); **Total: 22.**

Journée du jeune Néron, Une [*Comédie* in 1 act].
Th. de l'Odéon (**7**); **Total: 7.**

Juge de paix, Le [*Fait Historique* in 1 act, Pub. in 1792].
Maison Egalité (**1**); Th. de la Rue Martin (**1**); Th. de Molière (**1**); Th. du Palais (Cité)-Variétés (**6**); Th. Français, Comique et Lyrique (**1**); **Total: 10.**

Jugement de Visapour, Le [N/A].
Th. des Ombres Chinoises (**1**); Th. des Ombres de J.-J. Rousseau (**7**); **Total: 8.**

Jugements précipités, Les, ou Les Suites de misanthropie et repentir [N/A].
Th. de la Citoyenne Montansier (**5**); **Total: 5.**

Julie chez les sauvages [N/A].
Th. des Variétés Amusantes, Comiques et Lyriques (**10**); **Total: 10.**

Jumeau et la jumelle, Le [*Comédie*, Prem. on 16-4-1798].
Th. de la Citoyenne Montansier (**3**); **Total: 3.**

Jupiter, Europe et Junon [N/A].
Th. de l'Emulation (Gaîté) (**3**); **Total: 3.**

Kanko [*Pantomime*, Prem. on 3-10-1798].
Th. Lyrique des Amis de la Patrie (**32**); **Total: 32.**

Laitière prussienne, La [N/A].
Th. de l'Ambigu Comique (**39**); **Total: 39.**

Laure et Angélique [N/A].
Th. du Feydeau (de Monsieur) (**1**); **Total: 1.**

Laure et Félino [Pub. in 1795].
Th. de l'Ambigu Comique (**47**); **Total: 47.**

Laure et Zulme [*Opéra* in 3 acts].
Th. Lyrique des Amis de la Patrie (**54**); **Total: 54.**

Léandre devin, escamoteur [Prem. on 14-10-1799].
 Th. de l'Ambigu Comique (4); **Total: 4**.

Leçon aux fermiers, La [N/A].
 Th. de la Citoyenne Montansier (9); **Total: 9**.

Leçon utile, La, ou Le Mariage du charbonnier [Prem. on 12-4-1798].
 Th. des Jeunes Artistes (9); **Total: 9**.

Lendemain de la S. Barthélemy, Le, ou L'évêque de Lizieux [N/A].
 Th. des Victoires Nationales (4); **Total: 4**.

Lever de l'amour, Le [*Prologue* in 1 act, Pub. in 1786].
 Th. de l'Ambigu Comique (30); **Total: 30**.

Liberté au port de la montagne, La [N/A].
 Th. de la Montagne (4); **Total: 4**.

Liberté barreau, La, ou Les Hérolhes républicaines [*Tableau-Patriotique*,
 Pub. in 1794].
 Th. du Lycée des Arts (19); **Total: 19**.

Liberté de la presse, La [*Opéra* in 1 act, Pub. in 1794].
 Th. des Variétés Amusantes, Comiques et Lyriques (6); **Total: 6**.

Liberté des costumes, La, ou Il n'a pas perdu sa journée [Prem. on 14-8-
 1798].
 Th. de l'Emulation (Gaîté) (3); Th. des Grands Danseurs (Gaîté) (33); Th.
 du Marais (2); Th. Français, Comique et Lyrique (1); Th. Lyrique des
 Amis de la Patrie (30); **Total: 69**.

Liberté des femmes, La [*Comédie* in 3 acts, Prem. on 23-6-1793].
 Th. Français (de la rue Richelieu) (de la République) (1); **Total: 1**.

Lise et Justin [*Opéra* in 2 acts].
 Th. de l'Estrapade au Panthéon (22); **Total: 22**.

Lise et Lucas [N/A].
 Th. des Variétés Amusantes, Comiques et Lyriques (6); **Total: 6**.

Livia ou L'Italienne à Londres [*Opéra* in 3 acts, Prem. on 13-4-1790, Pub. in
 1787].
 Th. de la Citoyenne Montansier (37); Th. du Feydeau (de Monsieur) (30);
 Total: 67.

Lol'ska ou Les Enfants du château [In 4 acts, Prem. on 18-1-1799].
 Th. des Délassements Comiques (5); **Total: 5**.

Loisserolles [N/A].
 Th. du Lycée des Arts (14); **Total: 14**.

Lombardeur, Le, ou La Maison de prêt [N/A].
 Th. de l'Emulation (Gaîté) (4); Th. des Grands Danseurs (Gaîté) (8); Th.
 Lyrique des Amis de la Patrie (4); **Total: 16**.

Loriadoe [*Ballet*].
 Th. Lyrique des Amis de la Patrie (1); **Total: 1**.

Lubies, Les [N/A].
 Th. des Variétés Amusantes, Comiques et Lyriques (4); **Total: 4**.

Lucette et Gercourt [*Opéra* in 1 act].
 Th. Lyrique des Amis de la Patrie (2); **Total: 2**.

Lucinde et Raimond [*Opéra* in 3 acts, Pub. in 1794].
 Maison Egalité (2); Th. National (de la rue Richelieu) (3); **Total: 5**.

Madame Angot dans les marionnettes [N/A].
 Th. des Ombres de J.-J. Rousseau (1); **Total: 1**.

Madame des Travers [*Comédie*].
 Th. des Grands Danseurs (Gaîté) (49); **Total: 49**.

Madame Hautaine ou L'Amant voleur [*Pantomime* in 3 acts, Prem. on -2-1778, Pub. in 1778].
>Th. des Grands Danseurs (Gaîté) (**20**); **Total: 20**.

Madame Pincebec [N/A].
>Th. de l'Ambigu Comique (**6**); **Total: 6**.

Madrigal, Le, ou Les Poètes rivaux [*Comédie* in 2 acts, Prem. on 1-5-1789].
>Th. de l'Ambigu Comique (**17**); **Total: 17**.

Magicien, Le [N/A].
>Th. des Grands Danseurs (Gaîté) (**1**); Th. des Ombres Chinoises (**13**); Th. des Ombres de J.-J. Rousseau (**44**); **Total: 58**.

Magicien Glaucus, Le [N/A].
>Th. des Grands Danseurs (Gaîté) (**1**); **Total: 1**.

Main de fer, La [N/A].
>Th. des Délassements Comiques (**1**); **Total: 1**.

Maire, Le, ou Le Triomphe de l'innocence [*Drame* in 3 acts, Prem. on 21-8-1791].
>Th. du Lycée Dramatique (**9**); **Total: 9**.

Maison du diable, La [N/A].
>Th. de l'Emulation (Gaîté) (**6**); **Total: 6**.

Maison du Marais, La, ou Trois ans d'absence [*Comédie* in 3 acts, Prem. on 8-11-1799].
>Th. des Italiens (Opéra-Comique) (**1**); **Total: 1**.

Maître d'école, Le [N/A].
>Th. des Ombres Chinoises (**2**); Th. des Variétés Amusantes (Lazzari) (**13**); **Total: 15**.

Maître d'école dans les ombres, Le [N/A].
>Th. des Ombres de J.-J. Rousseau (**12**); **Total: 12**.

Maître d'esprit, Le [N/A].
>Th. des Variétés Amusantes (Lazzari) (**1**); **Total: 1**.

Maître de danse supposé, Le [*Opéra* in 3 acts].
>Th. de la Citoyenne Montansier (**6**); **Total: 6**.

Maîtresse de pension, La [Prem. on 20-3-1795].
>Th. du Vaudeville (**11**); **Total: 11**.

Major prussien, Le [N/A].
>Th. du Vaudeville (**1**); **Total: 1**.

Mal veut, mal lui tourne [Prem. on 7-11-1799].
>Th. des Jeunes Artistes (**2**); **Total: 2**.

Malade, Le [N/A].
>Th. des Ombres de J.-J. Rousseau (**6**); **Total: 6**.

Malencontreux, Le [*Comédie* in 3 acts, Prem. on 21-5-1790].
>Th. du Feydeau (de Monsieur) (**14**); **Total: 14**.

Malices de l'amour, Les [*Pièce* in 1 act, Prem. on 22-7-1780].
>Th. des Grands Danseurs (Gaîté) (**1**); **Total: 1**.

Mandats, Les [Prem. on 19-6-1796].
>Th. Patriotique et de Momus (**2**); **Total: 2**.

Manie corrigée, La [N/A].
>Th. des Ombres de J.-J. Rousseau (**1**); **Total: 1**.

Manie des bals, La, ou Les Abus de la mode [N/A].
>Th. de l'Ambigu Comique (**6**); **Total: 6**.

Manie des perruques, La [N/A].
>Th. de l'Ambigu Comique (**8**); **Total: 8**.

Mannequin, Le [*Comédie* in 1 act, Prem. on 5-7-1793].
    Th. de Molière (**1**); Th. Lyrique des Amis de la Patrie (**37**); **Total: 38.**

Maraudeurs de l'Ancien Régime, Les [*Comédie* in 2 acts].
    Th. de l'Ambigu Comique (**6**); **Total: 6.**

Marcel ou Le Jeune français [N/A].
    Th. des Jeunes Artistes (**4**); Th. du Marais (**1**); **Total: 5.**

Marcel [*Opéra* in 1 act, Pub. in 1795].
    Th. des Variétés Amusantes, Comiques et Lyriques (**8**); **Total: 8.**

Marchands de la mode, Les [N/A].
    Th. de l'Emulation (Gaîté) (**12**); **Total: 12.**

Mardi gras, Le [*Divertissement/parade*].
    Th. des Ombres de J.-J. Rousseau (**1**); **Total: 1.**

Maréchal, Le [N/A].
    Th. de la Citoyenne Montansier (**2**); Th. Lyrique des Amis de la Patrie (**3**);
    Veillée de Thalie (**1**); **Total: 6.**

Maréchal de France, Le [N/A].
    Th. du Marais (**1**); **Total: 1.**

Margot la résolue ou L'Adjucation manquée [Prem. on 3-11-1796].
    Th. de l'Ambigu Comique (**2**); **Total: 2.**

Marguerite [N/A].
    Th. des Grands Danseurs (Gaîté) (**3**); **Total: 3.**

Mari bohémien, Le [N/A].
    Th. Patriotique et de Momus (**1**); **Total: 1.**

Mari borgne, Le [N/A].
    Th. de l'Ambigu Comique (**2**); **Total: 2.**

Mari comme il y en a tant, Le, ou L'Ecole des épouses [*Comédie* in 3 acts,
    Pub. in 1764].
    Th. de Molière (**16**); **Total: 16.**

Mari confesseur, Le, ou Le Carme [Prem. on 23-2-1798].
    Th. des Délassements Comiques (**23**); **Total: 23.**

Mari corrigé, Le [*Comédie*, Prem. on 21-2-1791].
    Th. Français, Comique et Lyrique (**24**); **Total: 24.**

Mari de quinze ans, Le [*Comédie* in 1 act, Prem. on 21-8-1788, Pub. in 1788].
    Th. des Grands Danseurs (Gaîté) (**1**); Th. des Jeunes Artistes (**15**); **Total:
    16.**

Mari jaloux, Le [*Opéra* in 2 acts, Prem. on 4-6-1791].
    Th. des Grands Danseurs (Gaîté) (**1**); Th. du Feydeau (de Monsieur) (**1**);
    Th. Lyrique du Foire St. Germain (**9**); **Total: 11.**

Mari revenant, Le [Prem. on 19-9-1796].
    Th. du Vaudeville (**4**); **Total: 4.**

Mari supposé, Le [Prem. on 10-9-1799].
    Th. du Vaudeville (**10**); Th. Patriotique et de Momus (**1**); **Total: 11.**

Mari volage, Le [N/A].
    Th. du Vaudeville (**11**); Th. Patriotique et de Momus (**13**); **Total: 24.**

Mariage à la paix, Le [N/A].
    Th. de l'Odéon (**4**); **Total: 4.**

Mariage aux frais de la nation, Le [*Pantomime*, Prem. on 31-10-1793].
    Th. du Lycée des Arts (**36**); **Total: 36.**

Mariage civique, Le [*Vaudeville* in 1 act, Prem. on 6-8-1794].
    Th. Lyrique des Amis de la Patrie (**24**); **Total: 24.**

Mariage d'Arlequin, Le [*Pantomime* in 3 acts, Pub. in 1749].
    Th. des Grands Danseurs (Gaîté) (**2**); **Total: 2.**

Mariage de convenance, Le [*Comédie* in 1 act, Prem. on 29-5-1790].
Th. de la Citoyenne Montansier (**11**); **Total: 11.**

Mariage de Danières ou La Suite du sourd [*Comédie* in 2 acts, Prem. on 14-12-1791].
Th. de Molière (**1**); **Total: 1.**

Mariage de Dufresny, Le [N/A].
Th. des Jeunes Artistes (**1**); **Total: 1.**

Mariage de Garriga, Le, ou Les Deux maréchaux ferrants [*Ballet*, Prem. on 4-10-1794].
Th. des Italiens (Opéra-Comique) (**2**); **Total: 2.**

Mariage de Jean Jacques Rousseau, Le [*Intermède* in 1 act, Prem. on 26-10-1794].
Maison Egalité (**1**); **Total: 1.**

Mariage de Jocrisse, Le [N/A].
Th. de la Cité (**11**); Th. des Jeunes Artistes (**8**); **Total: 19.**

Mariage de Rosette, Le [*Comédie* in 2 acts, Prem. on 15-3-1792].
Th. de Molière (**9**); **Total: 9.**

Mariage du savetier, Le [N/A].
Th. des Grands Danseurs (Gaîté) (**2**); **Total: 2.**

Mariage de Valmier, Le [*Comédie* in 1 act, Pub. in 1791].
Th. de l'Ambigu Comique (**13**); **Total: 13.**

Mariage des trois cousines, Le [N/A].
Th. des Grands Danseurs (Gaîté) (**2**); **Total: 2.**

Mariage du chaudronnier de Saint-Flour, Le [Prem. on 11-9-1798].
Th. Lyrique des Amis de la Patrie (**11**); **Total: 11.**

Mariage du politique, Le [N/A].
Th. des Grands Danseurs (Gaîté) (**12**); **Total: 12.**

Mariage enfantin, Le, ou Mari de quinze ans [*Comédie* in 1 act, Prem. on 21-8-1788].
Th. des Beaujolais (**15**); **Total: 15.**

Mariage fait au tour, Le [*Vaudeville* in 1 act, Prem. on 8-3-1793].
Th. de la Citoyenne Montansier (**16**); **Total: 16.**

Mariage militaire, Le [N/A].
Th. de l'Ambigu Comique (**6**); **Total: 6.**

Mariage par procuration, Le [*Comédie* in 3 acts, Prem. on 27-10-1791].
Cirque National (**2**); **Total: 2.**

Mariage par stratagème, Le [*Comédie* in 1 act, Pub. in 1782].
Th. de l'Ambigu Comique (**33**); **Total: 33.**

Mariage patriotique, Le [*Comédie* in 2 acts, Prem. on 19-12-1793].
Th. du Palais (Cité)-Variétés (**22**); **Total: 22.**

Mariage renoué, Le, ou Les Méprises [*Comédie* in 1 act].
Th. du Vaudeville (**4**); **Total: 4.**

Mariage rompu par le bon valet, Le [*Pantomime* in 1 act, Prem. on 2-4-1791].
Th. des Grands Danseurs (Gaîté) (**1**); **Total: 1.**

Mariages persans, Les [*Opéra* in 3 acts, Prem. on 5-1-1792].
Th. de la Citoyenne Montansier (**2**); **Total: 2.**

Marie Christine ou La Promenade militaire [*Opéra*, Prem. on 12-11-1793].
Th. du Lycée des Arts (**5**); **Total: 5.**

Marie de Courbevois [*Fait Historique* in 1 act].
Th. Français, Comique et Lyrique (**1**); **Total: 1.**

Marin, Le [N/A].
Th. du Vaudeville (2); Th. Patriotique et de Momus (4); **Total: 6**.

Marquis de Bièvre, Le [N/A].
Th. des Troubadours (57); **Total: 57**.

Mascarades, Les, ou Le Carnaval de l'amour [*Comédie*, Prem. on 10-10-1799].
Th. de la Cité (11); **Total: 11**.

Matinée de Frédéric II, La [N/A].
Th. de la Citoyenne Montansier (2); Th. de la Rue Martin (8); **Total: 10**.

Matinée de Molière, La [*Comédie* in 1 act, Prem. on 20-4-1789].
Th. du Feydeau (de Monsieur) (2); **Total: 2**.

Matinée des petits pères, La [*Opéra* in 1 act, Prem. on 2-5-1794, Pub. in 1794].
Th. du Palais (Cité)-Variétés (3); **Total: 3**.

Matinée des rues de Paris, La [N/A].
Th. des Ombres Chinoises (3); Th. des Ombres de J.-J. Rousseau (9); **Total: 12**.

Matinée du jardin public, La [*Comédie* in 1 act, Prem. on 27-1-1787].
Th. des Beaujolais (43); **Total: 43**.

Matinée du sultan dans les ombres, La [N/A].
Th. des Ombres Chinoises (10); Th. des Ombres de J.-J. Rousseau (15); **Total: 25**.

Matinée poissarde, La [N/A].
Th. du Vaudeville (5); Th. Patriotique et de Momus (12); **Total: 17**.

Matinée républicaine, La [*Vaudeville* in 1 act].
Th. Lyrique des Amis de la Patrie (33); **Total: 33**.

Mauvais sujet corrigé, Le [*Comédie* in 2 acts, Prem. on 2-3-1789].
Th. de l'Ambigu Comique (6); **Total: 6**.

Méconnu, Le [N/A].
Th. du Lycée des Arts (1); **Total: 1**.

Mécontent, Le [N/A].
Th. de l'Emulation (Gaîté) (4); **Total: 4**.

Médecin d'amour, Le [*Comédie* in 3 acts, Prem. on 13-7-1786].
Th. des Grands Danseurs (Gaîté) (5); **Total: 5**.

Médecine de Grégoire, La [Prem. on 27-11-1798].
Th. de la Citoyenne Montansier (1); **Total: 1**.

Médée ou L'Hospitalité des fous [N/A].
Th. de l'Ambigu Comique (1); **Total: 1**.

Médisance, La [N/A].
Th. des Variétés Amusantes, Comiques et Lyriques (2); **Total: 2**.

Mélinde et Ferval [*Opéra* in 2 acts, Prem. on 20-2-1796].
Th. du Feydeau (de Monsieur) (4); **Total: 4**.

Mélite [*Comédie* in 2 acts, Prem. on 19-3-1792].
Th. des Italiens (Opéra-Comique) (3); **Total: 3**.

Ménage d'Arlequin, Le [N/A].
Th. de la Citoyenne Montansier (9); **Total: 9**.

Ménage de Justine, Le [N/A].
Th. des Jeunes Artistes (1); **Total: 1**.

Ménage du charbonnier, Le [N/A].
Th. des Jeunes Artistes (19); Th. du Marais (1); **Total: 20**.

Mensonge innocent, Le [*Comédie* in 1 act, Prem. on 15-3-1790].
Th. de l'Ambigu Comique (11); **Total: 11**.

Mensonge par discrétion, Le [*Comédie*, Prem. on 13-10-1798].
Th. Lyrique des Amis de la Patrie (3); **Total: 3.**

Menteur maladroit, Le [*Opéra-Comique*, Prem. on 29-12-1798].
Th. de Molière (4); **Total: 4.**

Mentruo [N/A].
Th. Français (de la rue Richelieu) (de la République) (1); **Total: 1.**

Méprise en voyage, La [N/A].
Th. du Vaudeville (8); **Total: 8.**

Méprises, Les [N/A].
Th. de l'Ambigu Comique (9); **Total: 9.**

Mercredi des cendres, Le [N/A].
Th. des Ombres de J.-J. Rousseau (1); **Total: 1.**

Mère désabusée, La [N/A].
Th. des Délassements Comiques (3); **Total: 3.**

Mère laitue, La [N/A].
Th. des Jeunes Artistes (42); **Total: 42.**

Mère Simone, La [N/A].
Th. des Grands Danseurs (Gaîté) (1); **Total: 1.**

Merseuil ou Le Libertin corrigé [*Drame* in 3 acts, Prem. on 26-6-1791].
Th. Lyrique du Foire St. Germain (2); **Total: 2.**

Messager boiteux, Le [N/A].
Th. des Variétés Amusantes (Lazzari) (23); **Total: 23.**

Métamorphoses d'Arlequin, Les [N/A].
Th. des Variétés Amusantes, Comiques et Lyriques (4); **Total: 4.**

Michel Montaigne [*Comédie*, Prem. on 12-11-1798].
Th. Français (de la rue Richelieu) (de la République) (6); **Total: 6.**

Millier de sucre, Le [*Comédie*].
Th. de la Citoyenne Montansier (7); **Total: 7.**

Ministres français à Rastadt, Les [*Mélodrame*].
Th. des Grands Danseurs (Gaîté) (3); **Total: 3.**

Minuit ou 1796 et l'an 5 [N/A].
Th. de l'Ambigu Comique (8); Th. du Feydeau (de Monsieur) (14); Th. du Marais (1); **Total: 23.**

Miroir de la vérité, Le [*Opéra*].
Th. des Délassements Comiques (13); **Total: 13.**

Mirtil et Licoris [*Opéra*, Prem. on 9-4-1791].
Th. de l'Ambigu Comique (14); **Total: 14.**

Mésange, La, ou L'Oiseau plumé [N/A].
Th. des Délassements Comiques (1); **Total: 1.**

Misanthrope corrigé, Le [N/A].
Th. des Grands Danseurs (Gaîté) (1); **Total: 1.**

Modèles des époux, Les [*Comédie* in 3 acts, Prem. on 14-4-1790].
Th. de l'Ambigu Comique (20); **Total: 20.**

Modernes, Les [N/A].
Th. du Vaudeville (1); **Total: 1.**

Moeurs de l'Ancien Régime, Les [*Drame* in 5 acts, Prem. on 23-5-1794].
Th. Français (de la rue Richelieu) (de la République) (9); **Total: 9.**

Moine généreux, Le [*Opéra* in 4 acts].
Th. Français (de la rue Richelieu) (de la République) (1); **Total: 1.**

Mois de mai, Le, ou La Partie d'ânes [*Opéra-Comique*, Prem. on 15-5-1792].
Th. du Vaudeville (1); **Total: 1.**

Molière à Lyon [*Comédie* in 1 act].
>   Th. du Vaudeville (**22**); **Total: 22.**

Momie [N/A].
>   Th. du Vaudeville (**5**); **Total: 5.**

Momus aux Variétés [*Prologue* in 1 act].
>   Th. du Palais (Cité)-Variétés (**2**); **Total: 2.**

Momus chez les enfants [*Prologue*, Prem. on 6-9-1799].
>   Th. du Mareux (**1**); **Total: 1.**

Monde repeuplé, Le [N/A].
>   Th. des Jeunes Artistes (**4**); **Total: 4.**

Monsieur de la canardière [*Comédie* in 3 acts, Prem. on 3-7-1792].
>   Th. de la Citoyenne Montansier (**3**); **Total: 3.**

Morale au sucre, La [Prem. on 11-8-1799].
>   Th. de l'Ambigu Comique (**2**); **Total: 2.**

Mort de Calas, La [Prem. on 13-11-1796].
>   Th. de la Rue Martin (**4**); **Total: 4.**

Mort de Dampierre, La [*Comédie* in 2 acts, Prem. on 5-6-1793].
>   Th. du Palais (Cité)-Variétés (**9**); **Total: 9.**

Mort de Don Quichotte, La [N/A].
>   Th. du Palais (Cité)-Variétés (**1**); **Total: 1.**

Mort de Gouvion, La [N/A].
>   Th. de Molière (**1**); **Total: 1.**

Mort de Lucrèce dans les marionnettes, La [N/A].
>   Th. des Ombres Chinoises (**7**); Th. des Ombres de J.-J. Rousseau (**2**); **Total: 9.**

Mort de Marat, La [Prem. on 5-2-1794].
>   n/a (**3**); **Total: 3.**

Mort de Simoneau, maire d'Etampes, La [*Tableau-Patriotique*, Prem. on 1-5-1792].
>   Th. du Marais (**6**); **Total: 6.**

Mort du brave Gouvion, La [*Fait Historique* in 2 acts, Pub. in 1792].
>   Th. de l'Ambigu Comique (**14**); **Total: 14.**

Mort du capitaine Lapérouse, La, ou La Cruauté anglaise [Prem. on 10-2-1798].
>   Th. des Variétés Amusantes, Comiques et Lyriques (**6**); **Total: 6.**

Mort du général Hoche, La [Prem. on 5-11-1797].
>   Académie de la Musique (Opéra) (**4**); Th. des Délassements Comiques (**10**); Th. du Feydeau (de Monsieur) (**4**); **Total: 18.**

Mort du général Marceau, La [N/A].
>   Th. de l'Ambigu Comique (**18**); Th. de l'Emulation (Gaîté) (**3**); **Total: 21.**

Mort du mardi gras, La [*Tragédie* in 1 act, Prem. on 6-3-1791].
>   Th. de la Liberté (**3**); **Total: 3.**

Mort par spéculation, La [*Vaudeville*, Prem. on 20-1-1799].
>   Th. de Molière (**5**); **Total: 5.**

Muet malgré lui, Le [N/A].
>   Th. du Vaudeville (**9**); **Total: 9.**

Mutius Scévola [*Tragédie* in 5 acts, Pub. in 1793].
>   Th. de Molière (**1**); **Total: 1.**

[53 Personnes.] *Mystère de la vie et histoire de Mgr. Saint Martin, Le* [N/A].
>   Th. des Délassements Comiques (**1**); **Total: 1.**

Narcisse ou Echo et Narcisse [*Pantomime*, Prem. on 11-2-1793].
    Th. de l'Ambigu Comique (**18**); **Total: 18.**
Nature vengée par la liberté, La [*Pantomime*, Prem. on 7-2-1794].
    Th. du Lycée des Arts (**18**); **Total: 18.**
Naufrage d'Allonzo, Le, ou L'Isle ténébreuse [*Tragédie* in 3 acts, Prem. on
    24-3-1792].
    Th. des Variétés Amusantes, Comiques et Lyriques (**3**); **Total: 3.**
Nautilde et Dagobert [*Opéra* in 3 acts, Prem. on 1-10-1791].
    Th. Lyrique des Amis de la Patrie (**24**); **Total: 24.**
Nécromancien, Le [*Pantomime*].
    Th. des Grands Danseurs (Gaîté) (**61**); **Total: 61.**
Neptune protecteur d'Arlequin [*Pantomime* in 3 acts, Pub. in 1759].
    Th. des Grands Danseurs (Gaîté) (**1**); **Total: 1.**
Ni trop ni trop peu [N/A].
    Th. de l'Ambigu Comique (**4**); **Total: 4.**
Nicaise vaudeville [N/A].
    Th. de la Citoyenne Montansier (**1**); **Total: 1.**
Nicette et Robin [N/A].
    Th. des Jeunes Artistes (**2**); **Total: 2.**
Nicette ou La Folle gageure [*Comédie* in 1 act, Prem. on 30-10-1786].
    Th. de l'Emulation (Gaîté) (**3**); Th. des Grands Danseurs (Gaîté) (**1**); **To-
    tal: 4.**
Nicodème de retour du soleil [*Comédie* in 1 act, Prem. on 1-9-1791].
    Th. de Molière (**11**); **Total: 11.**
Nièce généreuse, La [N/A].
    Th. des Grands Danseurs (Gaîté) (**1**); **Total: 1.**
Niza [*Pantomime*].
    Th. du Lycée des Arts (**6**); **Total: 6.**
Noce, La [*Comédie* in 2 acts, Pub. in 1794].
    Th. du Palais (Cité)-Variétés (**11**); **Total: 11.**
Noce enchantée, La [N/A].
    Th. des Grands Danseurs (Gaîté) (**1**); **Total: 1.**
Noce hollandaise, La [*Pantomime* in 3 acts, Prem. on 20-9-1782].
    Th. des Grands Danseurs (Gaîté) (**44**); **Total: 44.**
Noce interrompue, La, ou Le Serpent magicien [*Pantomime* in 3 acts, Prem.
    on 19-10-1780].
    Th. des Grands Danseurs (Gaîté) (**23**); Th. du Vaudeville (**1**); **Total: 24.**
Noce provençale, La [*Ballet* in 1 act, Prem. on 11-3-1793].
    Th. du Palais (Cité)-Variétés (**19**); **Total: 19.**
Noce turque, La [N/A].
    Th. des Grands Danseurs (Gaîté) (**3**); **Total: 3.**
Noce villageoise dans les marionnettes, La [N/A].
    Th. des Ombres Chinoises (**4**); Th. des Ombres de J.-J. Rousseau (**3**); **To-
    tal: 7.**
Noces de Lucette, Les [Prem. on 8-11-1798].
    Th. de la Citoyenne Montansier (**19**); **Total: 19.**
None de Lindenberg, La, ou La Nuit merveilleuse [Prem. on 23-6-1798].
    Th. des Jeunes Artistes (**54**); **Total: 54.**
Nono et Ninie [N/A].
    Th. des Grands Danseurs (Gaîté) (**34**); **Total: 34.**

Nous sommes libres aussi [*Tableau-Patriotique* in 1 act].
　　　Th. des Variétés Amusantes, Comiques et Lyriques (2); **Total: 2.**
Nous verrons [N/A].
　　　Th. de Molière (8); Th. des Troubadours (1); **Total: 9.**
Nouveau divertissement, Le [N/A].
　　　Th. des Jeunes Artistes (1); **Total: 1.**
Nouveau fermier bijoutier, Le [N/A].
　　　Th. Patriotique et de Momus (23); **Total: 23.**
Nouveaux enrichis, Les [N/A].
　　　Th. de la Rue Martin (6); **Total: 6.**
Nouveaux malheurs du Petit Poucet, Les [Prem. on 8-9-1799].
　　　Th. des Jeunes Elèves (8); **Total: 8.**
Nouvelle allemande à trois, La [N/A].
　　　Th. des Grands Danseurs (Gaîté) (1); **Total: 1.**
Nouvelle Arsène, La [N/A].
　　　Th. de l'Emulation (Gaîté) (4); **Total: 4.**
Nouvelle au camp de l'assassinat des ministres français à Rastadt [*Pièce*
　　　in 1 act, Prem. on 14-6-1799].
　　　　　Académie de la Musique (Opéra) (2); **Total: 2.**
Nouvelle épreuve, La [N/A].
　　　Th. de l'Odéon (1); Th. de la Rue Martin (1); Th. du Vaudeville (1); Th.
　　　Patriotique et de Momus (2); **Total: 5.**
Nouvelle journée, La [Prem. on 28-7-1797].
　　　Th. des Jeunes Artistes (2); **Total: 2.**
Nouvelles du jour, Les [N/A].
　　　Th. du Marais (1); **Total: 1.**
Nouvellistes de Pantin, Les, ou Le Retour inattendu [*Vaudeville*, Prem. on
　　　30-10-1799].
　　　　　Th. des Victoires (5); **Total: 5.**
Nuit de Bergame, La [N/A].
　　　Th. des Jeunes Artistes (16); **Total: 16.**
Nuit de Madrid, La [N/A].
　　　Th. des Grands Danseurs (Gaîté) (9); **Total: 9.**
Nuit du charbonnier, La [N/A].
　　　Th. des Jeunes Artistes (1); **Total: 1.**
Numéraire, Le, ou Le Négociant de la rue Vivienne [*Comédie* in 1 act,
　　　Prem. on 3-7-1791].
　　　　　Th. du Lycée Dramatique (1); **Total: 1.**
Observateur en défaut, L' [N/A].
　　　Th. du Vaudeville (1); **Total: 1.**
Offrande à l'amour, L' [Prem. on 17-3-1791].
　　　Petits Comédiens de Palais Royal (28); **Total: 28.**
Offrande villageoise, L' [N/A].
　　　Th. des Grands Danseurs (Gaîté) (13); **Total: 13.**
Oiseau plumé, L', ou L'Education villageoise [Prem. on 8-5-1798].
　　　Th. de l'Emulation (Gaîté) (4); **Total: 4.**
Oiseau, L' [*Pantomime* in 1 act, Prem. on 4-6-1786].
　　　Th. des Grands Danseurs (Gaîté) (1); **Total: 1.**
Olivia [*Opéra* in 1 act, Prem. on 4-1-1796].
　　　Th. du Feydeau (de Monsieur) (2); **Total: 2.**

On la tire aujourd'hui [N/A].
> Th. des Délassements Comiques (6); **Total: 6.**

Oncle, L' [N/A].
> Th. Patriotique et de Momus (1); **Total: 1.**

Oncle et le neveux rivaux, L' [*Comédie*].
> Th. des Grands Danseurs (Gaîté) (7); **Total: 7.**

Oncle rival de son neveu, L' [*Comédie*].
> Th. des Grands Danseurs (Gaîté) (7); **Total: 7.**

Oncle supposé, L', ou Alexis et Henriette [*Comédie* in 2 acts, Prem. on 15-12-1793].
> Th. Lyrique des Amis de la Patrie (2); **Total: 2.**

Onsy [Prem. on 12-6-1796].
> Th. de la Citoyenne Montansier (1); **Total: 1.**

Or faux, L' [N/A].
> Th. des Ombres Chinoises (4); Th. des Ombres de J.-J. Rousseau (13); **Total: 17.**

Oracles du bois de Boulogne, Les [Prem. on 19-3-1791].
> n/a (2); **Total: 2.**

Orage favorable, L' [N/A].
> Th. de l'Ambigu Comique (1); Th. des Grands Danseurs (Gaîté) (5); **Total: 6.**

Orphée aux enfers [N/A].
> Th. des Ombres Chinoises (8); Th. des Ombres de J.-J. Rousseau (1); **Total: 9.**

Orphée moderne, L' [N/A].
> Th. de l'Emulation (Gaîté) (38); **Total: 38.**

Ouverture du jeune Henri, L' [Prem. on 1-5-1797].
> Th. de la Cité (1); Th. des Italiens (Opéra-Comique) (2); **Total: 3.**

Palemon et Lavinia [*Pantomime*, Prem. on 25-4-1791].
> Petits Comédiens de Palais Royal (18); **Total: 18.**

Pardon mérité, Le [*Comédie* in 1 act, Prem. on 1-1-1793].
> Th. Lyrique des Amis de la Patrie (6); **Total: 6.**

Pari de 24 heures, Le, ou La Nouvelle prise de Toulon [*Opéra* in 1 act, Pub. in 1794].
> Th. du Palais (Cité)-Variétés (15); **Total: 15.**

Paris [*Ballet*, Prem. on 27-4-1798].
> Académie de la Musique (Opéra) (20); **Total: 20.**

Paris en miniature [*Bleuette*, Prem. on 26-9-1799].
> Th. de la Cité (9); **Total: 9.**

Parrain et la marraine de village, Le [*Comédie* in 1 act, Prem. on 3-8-1789].
> Th. des Beaujolais (13); **Total: 13.**

Pas des trois sabotiers, Le [*Ballet*].
> Th. des Grands Danseurs (Gaîté) (4); Th. des Variétés Amusantes, Comiques et Lyriques (1); **Total: 5.**

Pasquin maître et valet [*Opéra-Comique*].
> Th. de Molière (1); **Total: 1.**

Passé, le présent et le futur, Le [*Vaudeville*, Prem. on 25-4-1791].
> Th. des Délassements Comiques (1); **Total: 1.**

Patriote à l'épreuve, Le [N/A].
> Th. de l'Ambigu Comique (1); **Total: 1.**

Patriote du 10 août [*Comédie* in 2 acts].
> Th. Français (de la rue Richelieu) (de la République) (4); **Total: 4.**

Patriotes, Les [*Ballet*].
    Th. des Grands Danseurs (Gaîté) (3); **Total: 3.**
Patriotisme du village, Le [*Pantomime* in 3 acts].
    Th. des Grands Danseurs (Gaîté) (5); **Total: 5.**
Patriotisme récompensé, Le, ou L'Arrivée à Paris des sauveurs de la patrie [*Héroique*, Prem. on 2-7-1791].
    Th. Lyrique du Foire St. Germain (3); **Total: 3.**
Pauline et Justine [N/A].
    Th. de l'Ambigu Comique (3); **Total: 3.**
Pauline et Linrose [*Comédie* in 2 acts, Prem. on 26-11-1791].
    Th. de Molière (6); **Total: 6.**
Pauvre hermite, Le [Prem. on 1-9-1799].
    Th. de l'Ambigu Comique (4); **Total: 4.**
Paysan et son seigneur, Le [*Comédie* in 1 act, Pub. in 1781].
    Th. du Palais Royal (1); **Total: 1.**
Paysan magistrat, Le [In 5 acts].
    Th. Français (de la rue Richelieu) (de la République) (2); **Total: 2.**
Pédant d'amour, Le [N/A].
    Th. des Grands Danseurs (Gaîté) (1); **Total: 1.**
Pédant scrupuleux, Le [In 1 act].
    Th. des Grands Danseurs (Gaîté) (11); **Total: 11.**
Peintre dans son ménage, Le [Prem. on 21-10-1799].
    Th. des Jeunes Artistes (5); **Total: 5.**
Pèlerinage de Sainte Cunégonde, Le [N/A].
    Th. des Délassements Comiques (5); **Total: 5.**
Pépinière de Virginie, La, ou Un brin de laurier de l'armée d'Italie [N/A].
    Th. de l'Ambigu Comique (1); **Total: 1.**
Pépite, La [N/A].
    Th. de la Citoyenne Montansier (1); **Total: 1.**
Père adolescent, Le [N/A].
    Th. du Marais (4); **Total: 4.**
Père Angot, Le [Prem. on 23-9-1797].
    Th. de l'Emulation (Gaîté) (2); **Total: 2.**
Père Duchesne de 88, Le [N/A].
    Th. de l'Emulation (Gaîté) (16); Th. du Vaudeville (4); **Total: 20.**
Père Gérard de retour à sa ferme, Le [*Comédie* in 1 act, Prem. on 31-10-1791].
    Th. de Molière (48); **Total: 48.**
Père rival et le fils dans les marionnettes, Le [N/A].
    Th. des Ombres Chinoises (1); Th. des Ombres de J.-J. Rousseau (2); **Total: 3.**
Périandre [*Tragédie*, Prem. on 17-12-1798].
    Th. de l'Odéon (4); **Total: 4.**
Persico ou Le Souper dérangé [Prem. on 25-1-1797].
    Th. du Vaudeville (39); **Total: 39.**
Bawr, Alexandrine-S. de. *Petit commissionnaire, Le* [*Comédie*].
    Th. du Feydeau (de Monsieur) (18); Th. du Lycée des Arts (24); Th. Lyrique des Amis de la Patrie (3); **Total: 45.**
Petit cousin, Le [*Comédie* in 1 act, Prem. on 7-6-1799].
    Th. des Grands Danseurs (Gaîté) (9); **Total: 9.**

Petit Jacquot, Le [*Comédie* in 2 acts, Pub. in 1773].
Th. des Grands Danseurs (Gaîté) (1); **Total: 1.**

Petit ramoneur, Le [N/A].
Th. de la Citoyenne Montansier (1); **Total: 1.**

Petit savoyard, Le, ou Le Prix de la sagesse [*Vaudeville* in 1 act].
Th. de la Montagne (8); **Total: 8.**

Petit Télémaque, Le [N/A].
Th. de la Cité (1); **Total: 1.**

Petit voltigeur, Le [N/A].
Th. des Grands Danseurs (Gaîté) (2); **Total: 2.**

Petite chaconne d'Arlequin, La [*Pantomime*].
Th. des Grands Danseurs (Gaîté) (17); **Total: 17.**

Petite école des mères, La [*Comédie* in 1 act, Pub. in 1783].
Th. Français (de la rue Richelieu) (de la République) (2); **Total: 2.**

Petite épreuve, La [N/A].
Th. de l'Emulation (Gaîté) (1); Th. de la Cité (6); Th. du Marais (1); Th. du Palais (Cité)-Variétés (4); **Total: 12.**

Petite fête civique, La [*Vaudeville* in 1 act].
Th. de la Montagne (6); **Total: 6.**

Petite fille du grand Mogol à Marseille, La [Prem. on 24-11-1798].
Th. de l'Emulation (Gaîté) (15); **Total: 15.**

Petite maison de Proserpine, La, ou Pluton comédien sans le savoir [Prem. on 21-1-1799].
Th. de l'Ambigu Comique (1); **Total: 1.**

Petite Marie, La, ou La Bouquetière [Prem. on 27-6-1797].
Th. de l'Ambigu Comique (14); **Total: 14.**

Petite Mariette, La [N/A].
Th. du Feydeau (de Monsieur) (1); **Total: 1.**

Petite orpheline, La [*Fait Historique* in 1 act].
Th. de la Citoyenne Montansier (6); **Total: 6.**

Petite ruse de guerre, La, ou L'Aimable allemande [Prem. on 20-7-1798].
Th. de l'Ambigu Comique (4); Th. de la Citoyenne Montansier (1); **Total: 5.**

Petite veilleuse, La [N/A].
Th. de l'Ambigu Comique (2); **Total: 2.**

Petits écoliers, Les [*Comédie*].
Th. du Palais (Cité)-Variétés (1); **Total: 1.**

Peureux, Le [N/A].
Th. des Jeunes Artistes (9); **Total: 9.**

Phanor et Zulima [*Pantomime*, Prem. on 17-6-1797].
Th. de l'Ambigu Comique (10); **Total: 10.**

Philocrate [*Tragédie*].
Th. du Feydeau (de Monsieur) (1); **Total: 1.**

Philosophe amoureux, Le, ou Le Mort du faucon [*Comédie*].
Th. des Grands Danseurs (Gaîté) (2); **Total: 2.**

Philosophes soldats, Les [*Comédie* in 3 acts, Prem. on 4-4-1793, Pub. in 1792].
Th. du Marais (7); **Total: 7.**

Pic Repic et Capot ou L'Imbroglio des petites affiches [Prem. on 26-5-1792].
Th. de Molière (12); **Total: 12.**

Pièce nouvelle, La [N/A].
 Th. de l'Ambigu Comique (1); **Total: 1.**

Pied de nez, Le, ou La Nouvelle de la paix [Prem. on 13-11-1797].
 Th. des Variétés Amusantes, Comiques et Lyriques (1); **Total: 1.**

Pierre Dandin [*Opéra*, Prem. on 11-2-1792].
 Th. Français, Comique et Lyrique (3); **Total: 3.**

Pierre l'Engourdi [N/A].
 Th. des Grands Danseurs (Gaîté) (4); **Total: 4.**

Pierre ou Le Coupable innocent [*Drame* in 5 acts, Prem. on 26-9-1797].
 Th. de la Cité (4); **Total: 4.**

Pierre, soldat français [*Comédie* in 2 acts, Prem. on 26-6-1792].
 Th. de Molière (3); **Total: 3.**

Piété filiale, La [N/A].
 Th. du Feydeau (de Monsieur) (1); Th. du Marais (2); **Total: 3.**

Pigmalion [*Ballet*].
 Th. de l'Ambigu Comique (12); Th. Lyrique des Amis de la Patrie (2); **Total: 14.**

Pille, La [N/A].
 Th. Français (de la rue Richelieu) (de la République) (1); **Total: 1.**

Pinçon de Lubin, Le [N/A].
 Th. des Grands Danseurs (Gaîté) (20); **Total: 20.**

Pirates, Les [*Pantomime* in 3 acts, Prem. on 5-3-1794, Pub. in 1794].
 Th. de la Cité (1); Th. du Palais (Cité)-Variétés (19); **Total: 20.**

Pison [N/A].
 Th. du Feydeau (de Monsieur) (3); **Total: 3.**

Pitt roi de la petite Bretagne [N/A].
 Th. de l'Ambigu Comique (2); **Total: 2.**

Plaisirs du printemps, Les [*Ballet*, Pub. in 1795].
 Petits Comédiens de Palais Royal (34); Th. des Jeunes Artistes (1); Th. des Variétés Amusantes, Comiques et Lyriques (27); **Total: 62.**

Plan de comédie, Le [*Comédie* in 3 acts, Pub. in 1634].
 Th. Français, Comique et Lyrique (1); **Total: 1.**

Plume de l'ange Gabriel, La [*Tableau-Patriotique*].
 Th. de la Montagne (5); **Total: 5.**

Poinsinet [*Comédie* in 1 act, Prem. on 13-4-1793].
 Th. du Vaudeville (17); **Total: 17.**

Pointus, Les [N/A].
 Th. de l'Emulation (Gaîté) (1); **Total: 1.**

Policarpe et Pancrace, Le [N/A].
 Th. de la Citoyenne Montansier (16); Th. de la Rue Martin (3); **Total: 19.**

Pomme de Rambour, La [Prem. on 21-7-1793, Pub. in 1793].
 Th. de l'Ambigu Comique (64); **Total: 64.**

Pompe funèbre du général Hoche, La [N/A].
 Académie de la Musique (Opéra) (1); Th. du Feydeau (de Monsieur) (1); **Total: 2.**

Pont cassé, Le [N/A].
 Th. des Ombres Chinoises (19); Th. des Ombres de J.-J. Rousseau (44); **Total: 63.**

Pont de coupe-gorge, Le [N/A].
 Th. de l'Ambigu Comique (4); **Total: 4.**

Pont de Lodi, Le [Prem. on 16-12-1797].
 Th. du Feydeau (de Monsieur) (4); **Total: 4.**

Port de mer, Le [*Pantomime* in 3 acts, Prem. on 2-8-1788].
  Th. des Grands Danseurs (Gaîté) (3); **Total: 3.**
Porteur d'eau, Le, ou Le Porte-feuille perdu [N/A].
  Th. Lyrique des Amis de la Patrie (10); **Total: 10.**
Portrait de Gilles, Le [N/A].
  Th. du Vaudeville (4); **Total: 4.**
Portraits de famille, Les, ou La Sainte-Christine [*Pantomime*].
  Th. de l'Emulation (Gaîté) (33); Th. des Grands Danseurs (Gaîté) (9); **Total: 42.**
Portraits du jour, Les, ou Le Nouveau cercle [Prem. on 26-5-1797].
  Th. de l'Ambigu Comique (5); **Total: 5.**
Pot pourri, Le [*Vaudeville* in 1 act, Pub. in 1792].
  Th. du Vaudeville (45); **Total: 45.**
Potier de terre, Le [In 3 acts, Prem. on 11-2-1791].
  Th. du Palais Royal (1); **Total: 1.**
Poule plumée, La [N/A].
  Th. des Ombres Chinoises (18); Th. des Ombres de J.-J. Rousseau (33); **Total: 51.**
Pouvoir du nécromancien, Le [N/A].
  Th. des Grands Danseurs (Gaîté) (1); **Total: 1.**
Précepteur amoureux, Le [N/A].
  Th. des Grands Danseurs (Gaîté) (1); **Total: 1.**
Précieux du jour, Les [Prem. on 16-4-1797].
  Th. de la Cité (1); **Total: 1.**
Préjugé du point d'honneur, Le [*Comédie* in 3 acts, Prem. on 3-1-1791].
  Th. de l'Ambigu Comique (20); **Total: 20.**
Premier mai, Le, ou Les Bons paysans [*Opéra* in 1 act].
  Th. du Lycée Dramatique (9); **Total: 9.**
Première réquisition, La, ou Le Serment des français [*Tableau-Patriotique* in 1 act, Pub. in 1793].
  Th. de l'Ambigu Comique (1); Th. de la Citoyenne Montansier (1); Th. Français (de la rue Richelieu) (de la République) (7); Th. National (de la rue Richelieu) (8); **Total: 17.**
Prenez-garde à vous [*Comédie* in 1 act, Pub. in 1795].
  Th. des Variétés Amusantes, Comiques et Lyriques (17); **Total: 17.**
Près, Les [N/A].
  Th. du Vaudeville (1); **Total: 1.**
Prétention ridicule, La [*Comédie* in 3 acts, Prem. on 8-7-1790].
  Th. Français, Comique et Lyrique (19); **Total: 19.**
Prêtres russes, Les [*Drame*].
  Th. des Délassements Comiques (1); **Total: 1.**
Prêtresse au temple de l'indifférence, La [N/A].
  Th. des Grands Danseurs (Gaîté) (1); **Total: 1.**
Prévenu d'émigration, Le, ou Les Trois clefs [*Fait Historique*, Prem. on 20-7-1797].
  Th. de la Citoyenne Montansier (1); Th. des Variétés Amusantes, Comiques et Lyriques (16); **Total: 17.**
Prévoyance en défaut, La [*Vaudeville*, Prem. on 3-1-1799].
  Th. de Molière (4); **Total: 4.**
Prince devenu ramoneur, Le [*Comédie* in 1 act].
  Th. de la Citoyenne Montansier (9); **Total: 9.**

Princesse blanquette, La [N/A].
Th. des Grands Danseurs (Gaîté) (1); **Total: 1.**

Prise de la Bastille, La [In 3 acts, Prem. on 25-8-1791].
Th. Français (de la rue Richelieu) (de la République) (5); **Total: 5.**

Prise de la ville de Mayence par les français, La [*Drame* in 2 acts, Pub. in 1792].
Th. de l'Estrapade au Panthéon (4); **Total: 4.**

Prise de la ville de Mons, La [*Fait Historique* in 2 acts].
Th. des Grands Danseurs (Gaîté) (21); **Total: 21.**

Prise de la ville des arméniens par Cambise, La [*Pantomime* in 5 acts, Prem. on 17-4-1788].
Th. des Grands Danseurs (Gaîté) (16); **Total: 16.**

Prise de Mantoue, La [Prem. on 27-2-1797].
Th. de l'Ambigu Comique (8); Th. de l'Emulation (Gaîté) (8); **Total: 16.**

Prise de Mauritanie, La [N/A].
Th. de l'Ambigu Comique (1); **Total: 1.**

Prise de possession, La [N/A].
Th. de la Cité (2); **Total: 2.**

Prise de Toulon, La [*Tableau-Patriotique* in 1 act].
Th. des Variétés Amusantes, Comiques et Lyriques (1); **Total: 1.**

Prisonnier américain, Le [N/A].
Th. des Italiens (Opéra-Comique) (4); **Total: 4.**

Prisonniers français patriotes, Les [*Tableau-Patriotique*, Prem. on 26-8-1794].
Th. de l'Ambigu Comique (50); **Total: 50.**

Prisonniers pour dettes, Les [Prem. on 16-8-1796].
Th. du Vaudeville (11); **Total: 11.**

Prix, Le [N/A].
Th. du Vaudeville (7); **Total: 7.**

Prix de l'hospitalité ou Le Chevalier [*Opéra* in 2 acts].
Th. du Palais (Cité)-Variétés (1); **Total: 1.**

Prix de la fidélité, Le [*Comédie* in 1 act, Prem. on 11-2-1794].
Th. de l'Ambigu Comique (7); **Total: 7.**

Procès du cerisier, Le [N/A].
Th. des Grands Danseurs (Gaîté) (5); **Total: 5.**

Procureur d'autrefois, Le [N/A].
Th. du Marais (1); **Total: 1.**

Procureur trompeur trompé, Le [*Pièce* in 2 acts, Prem. on 1-12-1784].
Th. des Grands Danseurs (Gaîté) (2); **Total: 2.**

Prodigue, Le, ou Les Femmes discrètes [*Comédie* in 3 acts, Prem. on 9-12-1789, Pub. in 1789].
Th. de l'Ambigu Comique (82); **Total: 82.**

Prodigue et l'hypocrite, Le [N/A].
Th. de l'Emulation (Gaîté) (1); **Total: 1.**

Projet de fortune, Le [*Vaudeville* in 1 act].
Th. de la Cité (2); Th. du Palais (Cité)-Variétés (38); **Total: 40.**

Prologue d'inauguration, Le [*Prologue*, Pub. in 1790].
Th. du Palais Royal (2); **Total: 2.**

Prologue d'ouverture, Le [Prem. on 19-1-1799].
Th. de l'Odéon (4); Th. Lyrique des Amis de la Patrie (1); Veillée de Thalie (1); **Total: 6.**

Prompt avertisseur, Le [N/A].
 Th. des Jeunes Artistes (**1**); **Total: 1**.
Propriétaire et le fermier, Le [N/A].
 Th. du Vaudeville (**59**); **Total: 59**.
Puce perdue, La [N/A].
 Th. du Vaudeville (**5**); **Total: 5**.
Pucelle d'Orléans, La, ou Les Anglais vaincus [*Pantomime*, Prem. on 24-2-1798].
 Th. de l'Emulation (Gaîté) (**16**); **Total: 16**.
Punition, La [*Opéra-Vaudeville* in 1 act].
 Th. du Feydeau (de Monsieur) (**6**); **Total: 6**.
Pupitre, Le [*Comédie* in 2 acts].
 Th. des Délassements Comiques (**5**); **Total: 5**.
Pygmalion [N/A].
 Th. du Lycée des Arts (**6**); **Total: 6**.
Pyramides d'Hercule, Les [N/A].
 Th. des Variétés Amusantes, Comiques et Lyriques (**2**); **Total: 2**.
Quaker, Le [N/A].
 Th. de l'Ambigu Comique (**8**); **Total: 8**.
Quakers irlandais, Les [*Pantomime* in 1 act, Prem. on 27-2-1789].
 Th. des Grands Danseurs (Gaîté) (**4**); **Total: 4**.
Quatre héros français, Les [*Pantomime* in 3 acts].
 Ampithéâtre National (**3**); **Total: 3**.
Quatre soeurs, Les [*Comédie* in 3 acts, Prem. on 23-5-1793].
 Th. de la Nation (Comédie Française) (**1**); **Total: 1**.
Quatre rendez-vous du ménage à la mode, Les [*Comédie* in 3 acts].
 Th. des Grands Danseurs (Gaîté) (**56**); **Total: 56**.
Queue, La [N/A].
 Th. de l'Ambigu Comique (**3**); **Total: 3**.
Qui a bu boira [N/A].
 Th. de la Citoyenne Montansier (**19**); **Total: 19**.
Quiproquo, Le [*Comédie*].
 Th. de l'Emulation (Gaîté) (**1**); **Total: 1**.
Rabelais [Prem. on 1-2-1799].
 Th. du Palais (Cité)-Variétés (**1**); Th. du Vaudeville (**30**); **Total: 31**.
Raisin d'amour, Le [N/A].
 Th. des Grands Danseurs (Gaîté) (**8**); **Total: 8**.
Ranuccio [N/A].
 Th. des Jeunes Artistes (**14**); **Total: 14**.
Raoul de Coucy [*Pantomime*, Prem. on 8-12-1791].
 Cirque National (**1**); **Total: 1**.
Ravissement d'Europe par Jupiter, Le [*Pantomime* in 1 act, Prem. on 1-6-1786].
 Th. des Grands Danseurs (Gaîté) (**5**); **Total: 5**.
Raymond et Felix [N/A].
 Th. des Variétés Amusantes (Lazzari) (**23**); Th. des Variétés Amusantes, Comiques et Lyriques (**3**); **Total: 26**.
Réception des gendarmes, La [*Tableau-Patriotique*, Pub. in 1794].
 Th. de l'Ambigu Comique (**3**); **Total: 3**.
Réconciliation, La [N/A].
 Th. des Jeunes Artistes (**10**); **Total: 10**.

Réconciliation générale, La [*Tableau-Patriotique* in 1 act, Prem. on 17-2-1791].
    Th. des Grands Danseurs (Gaîté) (**10**); **Total: 10.**
Réconciliation inutile, La [N/A].
    Th. du Lycée des Arts (**1**); **Total: 1.**
Réconciliés, Les [*Pantomime*, Prem. on 1-3-1784].
    Th. des Grands Danseurs (Gaîté) (**2**); **Total: 2.**
Reconnaissance des deux frères, La [N/A].
    Th. des Variétés Amusantes, Comiques et Lyriques (**1**); **Total: 1.**
Reddition de Mantoue, La [N/A].
    Th. de la Rue Martin (**1**); **Total: 1.**
Redoute, La [N/A].
    Th. du Marais (**1**); **Total: 1.**
Religieuse malgré elle, La [Prem. on 28-3-1790].
    Th. du Palais Royal (**5**); **Total: 5.**
Remède à l'ennui, Le, ou Faire des heureux, c'est l'être [*Comédie*, Pub. in
    1792].
    Th. de l'Ambigu Comique (**9**); **Total: 9.**
Remède au divorce, Le [Prem. on 12-1-1796].
    Th. des Jeunes Artistes (**27**); **Total: 27.**
Rencontre sur rencontre [Prem. on 1-8-1799].
    Th. de la Citoyenne Montansier (**7**); **Total: 7.**
Rendez-vous, Le, ou Roséide [*Opéra-Comique* in 1 act, Pub. in 1785].
    Th. du Vaudeville (**1**); **Total: 1.**
Rentier du marais, Le [N/A].
    Th. de l'Emulation (Gaîté) (**18**); **Total: 18.**
Repos interrompu, Le [N/A].
    Th. de l'Emulation (Gaîté) (**6**); **Total: 6.**
Réquisition, La, ou Le Départ d'un volontaire [*Tableau-Patriotique* in 1 act,
    Prem. on 7-10-1793].
    Th. de la Citoyenne Montansier (**2**); **Total: 2.**
Restauration, Le, ou La Gageure [Prem. on 1-6-1799].
    Th. du Vaudeville (**1**); **Total: 1.**
Reste à un [N/A].
    Th. des Ombres Chinoises (**6**); Th. des Ombres de J.-J. Rousseau (**17**); **Total: 23.**
Restitution forcée, La [N/A].
    Th. du Vaudeville (**1**); Th. Patriotique et de Momus (**3**); **Total: 4.**
Résurrection de Cadet Roussel, La [*Vaudeville*, Prem. on 1-12-1798].
    Th. des Délassements Comiques (**1**); Th. du Palais (Cité)-Variétés (**4**); **Total: 5.**
Retour à l'espérance, Le, ou L'Arrivée du général Bonaparte [*Comédie*,
    Prem. on 19-10-1799].
    Th. de Molière (**7**); **Total: 7.**
Retour de l'inconstant, Le, ou Le Mariage rompu [*Comédie* in 2 acts, Pub.
    in 1789].
    Th. des Beaujolais (**6**); **Total: 6.**
Retour de la flotte nationale, Le [Prem. on 30-9-1793].
    Th. du Lycée des Arts (**19**); **Total: 19.**
Retour de la gaité, Le [*Prologue*].
    Th. des Grands Danseurs (Gaîté) (**8**); **Total: 8.**

Retour de la noce, Le [Pub. in 1794].
    Th. de l'Ambigu Comique (1); **Total: 1.**
Retour de la pantomime, Le [N/A].
    Th. des Grands Danseurs (Gaîté) (5); **Total: 5.**
Retour de Rastadt, Le, ou Le Cri de la France [N/A].
    Th. des Jeunes Artistes (2); **Total: 2.**
Retour des bûcherons, Le [*Ballet*].
    Th. de la Liberté (1); **Total: 1.**
Retour des sabotiers, Le [*Ballet* in 1 act].
    Th. des Grands Danseurs (Gaîté) (18); Th. des Variétés Amusantes,
    Comiques et Lyriques (1); **Total: 19.**
Retour du ballon mousseux, Le [Prem. on 19-10-1797].
    Th. du Vaudeville (8); **Total: 8.**
Retour du guerrier, Le [N/A].
    Th. des Délassements Comiques (5); **Total: 5.**
Retour du héros, Le [Prem. on 17-12-1797].
    Th. des Délassements Comiques (2); **Total: 2.**
Retour du héros d'Egypte, Le [Prem. on 26-10-1799].
    Th. des Grands Danseurs (Gaîté) (11); **Total: 11.**
Retour du maître, Le [N/A].
    Th. de la Citoyenne Montansier (1); **Total: 1.**
Retour inattendu, Le [*Comédie* in 1 act, Prem. on 4-3-1790].
    Th. du Palais Royal (1); Th. Lyrique des Amis de la Patrie (1); **Total: 2.**
Retraite d'Arlequin, La [Prem. on 1-1-1796].
    Th. des Variétés Amusantes (Lazzari) (2); **Total: 2.**
Rêve supposé, Le [N/A].
    Th. de l'Ambigu Comique (1); **Total: 1.**
Revenant, Le [In 1 act, Prem. on 30-5-1790].
    Th. des Grands Danseurs (Gaîté) (3); **Total: 3.**
Rêveries grecques, Les [N/A].
    Th. de la Citoyenne Montansier (3); Th. de Molière (3); **Total: 6.**
Révolte des nègres, La [*Pantomime*].
    Th. du Lycée au Palais Egalité (1); Th. du Lycée des Arts (19); **Total: 20.**
Revue de l'an VI, La [N/A].
    Th. des Troubadours (8); **Total: 8.**
Revue de l'an VII, La [N/A].
    Th. des Jeunes Elèves (5); **Total: 5.**
Richard et Isabelle [N/A].
    Th. de la Citoyenne Montansier (19); Th. du Marais (1); **Total: 20.**
Riche du jour, Le [N/A].
    Th. du Vaudeville (6); **Total: 6.**
Ridicules, Les [N/A].
    Th. des Variétés Amusantes, Comiques et Lyriques (1); **Total: 1.**
Rien n'est difficile en amour [*Pantomime* in 5 acts, Prem. on 7-9-1782].
    Th. des Grands Danseurs (Gaîté) (2); **Total: 2.**
Rien ou peu de chose [*Parodie*, Prem. on 1-7-1799].
    Th. des Grands Danseurs (Gaîté) (7); **Total: 7.**
Rival par occasion, Le [*Comédie* in 1 act, Prem. on 26-9-1791].
    Th. Lyrique des Amis de la Patrie (3); **Total: 3.**
Rivale maîtresse, La [Prem. on 7-2-1798].
    Th. du Vaudeville (3); **Total: 3.**

Rivaux, Les, ou La Peau de l'ours [*Opéra-Comique* in 1 act, Prem. on 6-9-1791].
Th. du Lycée Dramatique (3); Th. du Marais (2); **Total: 5.**

Rivaux d'eux-mêmes, Les [Prem. on 4-10-1799].
Th. de la Cité (5); Th. Français (de la rue Richelieu) (de la République) (5); **Total: 10.**

Rivaux généreux, Les [N/A].
Th. des Variétés Amusantes, Comiques et Lyriques (1); **Total: 1.**

Rivaux joués, Les [*Vaudeville* in 1 act, Prem. on 18-12-1791].
Th. des Variétés Amusantes, Comiques et Lyriques (11); **Total: 11.**

Robert et Célestine [*Pantomime*].
n/a (7); **Total: 7.**

Rocher de Pierre le Grand, Le [N/A].
Th. des Ombres de J.-J. Rousseau (10); **Total: 10.**

Roger ou Le Sage [N/A].
Th. des Italiens (Opéra-Comique) (9); **Total: 9.**

Roi de Pique, Le [*Comédie* in 1 act].
Th. des Jeunes Artistes (4); **Total: 4.**

Roi tampon, Le [N/A].
Th. des Ombres de J.-J. Rousseau (12); **Total: 12.**

Romagnesi [*Opéra-Vaudeville*, Prem. on 3-9-1799].
Th. du Feydeau (de Monsieur) (9); **Total: 9.**

Roméo et Juliette [*Opéra* in 3 acts, Prem. on 10-9-1794].
Th. de l'Odéon (1); Th. du Marais (1); **Total: 2.**

Ronde, La [N/A].
Th. des Délassements Comiques (1); Th. Lyrique des Amis de la Patrie (1); **Total: 2.**

Rose [*Vaudeville* in 1 act, Pub. in 1792].
Th. du Palais (Cité)-Variétés (1); **Total: 1.**

Rose d'Agathe prise par Colin, La [N/A].
Th. des Grands Danseurs (Gaîté) (8); **Total: 8.**

Rose et Delmont [N/A].
Th. du Vaudeville (3); **Total: 3.**

Rose et Félix [N/A].
Th. des Jeunes Artistes (5); **Total: 5.**

Rose sans épines, La [In 1 act, Prem. on 5-3-1791].
Petits Comédiens de Palais Royal (35); **Total: 35.**

Roselle ou Le Moment d'erreur [Prem. on 16-9-1797].
Th. des Délassements Comiques (1); **Total: 1.**

Rosière de Cholet, La [N/A].
Th. de la Citoyenne Montansier (5); Th. Patriotique et de Momus (2); **Total: 7.**

Rosière, La, ou Le Triomphe de la vertu [N/A].
Académie de la Musique (Opéra) (13); Th. du Vaudeville (1); **Total: 14.**

Rossignol, Le [*Opéra-Comique* in 1 act, Prem. in 1798].
Th. du Palais (Cité)-Variétés (2); **Total: 2.**

Rozelli ou Le Crime et la vertu [Prem. on 7-7-1799].
Th. de l'Ambigu Comique (16); **Total: 16.**

Rue Martin, La, ou Le Retour [N/A].
Th. de Molière (2); Th. du Marais (2); **Total: 4.**

Ruse innocente, La [*Comédie* in 1 act, Pub. in 1792].
Th. du Palais (Cité)-Variétés (1); **Total: 1.**

Russes en Pologne, Les, ou Poleska et Nourinski [*Pantomime* in 3 acts, Prem. on 6-12-1795].
>Th. des Variétés Amusantes, Comiques et Lyriques (1); Th. du Palais (Cité)-Variétés (13); **Total: 14.**

Sabinus ou Le Triomphe de l'amour et de la vertu [*Tragédie* in 5 acts, Pub. in 1785].
>Th. du Lycée des Arts (2); **Total: 2.**

Sabotiers du bois de Vincennes, Les [N/A].
>Th. des Ombres de J.-J. Rousseau (15); **Total: 15.**

Sac, Le [*Comédie* in 1 act, Prem. on 27-4-1793].
>Th. du Vaudeville (11); **Total: 11.**

Sacrifice d'Isaac, Le [*Vaudeville*, Prem. on 20-1-1798].
>Th. des Jeunes Artistes (10); **Total: 10.**

Sage femme, La [*Parodie*, Prem. on 21-5-1792].
>Th. de la Citoyenne Montansier (3); **Total: 3.**

Saint-Charles ou L'Homme raisonnable [Prem. on 10-7-1799].
>Th. des Victoires Nationales (7); **Total: 7.**

Sainte omelette, La [*Farce*].
>Th. de la Montagne (14); **Total: 14.**

Salamandre, La [N/A].
>Tivoli (2); **Total: 2.**

Salon, Le [N/A].
>Th. du Vaudeville (1); **Total: 1.**

Sancho Pança ou Le Paysan parvenu [*Comédie*, Pub. in 1754].
>Th. de Molière (1); Th. du Marais (6); **Total: 7.**

Sans-culottes, Les, ou Le Dîner interrompu [*Opéra* in 1 act, Pub. in 1794].
>Th. du Palais (Cité)-Variétés (3); **Total: 3.**

Sauteurs, Les [*Divertissement/parade*].
>Th. des Grands Danseurs (Gaîté) (57); **Total: 57.**

Savetier, Le [N/A].
>Th. des Ombres de J.-J. Rousseau (7); **Total: 7.**

Savetier apprenti coiffeur de femmes, Le [*Comédie* in 1 act, Prem. on 2-6-1789].
>Th. des Grands Danseurs (Gaîté) (2); **Total: 2.**

Savetier apprenti comédien, Le [N/A].
>Th. des Variétés Amusantes (Lazzari) (4); **Total: 4.**

Savetier du Jura, Le [Prem. on 11-8-1797].
>Th. de l'Emulation (Gaîté) (29); Th. Lyrique des Amis de la Patrie (1); **Total: 30.**

Savetier galant, Le [N/A].
>Th. des Grands Danseurs (Gaîté) (9); **Total: 9.**

Savetier parvenu, Le [N/A].
>Th. des Grands Danseurs (Gaîté) (1); **Total: 1.**

Savetier tragique, Le [N/A].
>Th. de l'Emulation (Gaîté) (2); **Total: 2.**

Savoir rendu, Le [N/A].
>Th. Lyrique des Amis de la Patrie (1); **Total: 1.**

Scaramouche capitaine [N/A].
>Th. des Grands Danseurs (Gaîté) (1); **Total: 1.**

Scarron [N/A].
>Th. du Vaudeville (54); **Total: 54.**

Scelle, Le [N/A].
>   Th. du Vaudeville (**48**); **Total: 48**.

Scène civique, Une [N/A].
>   Th. National (de la rue Richelieu) (**2**); **Total: 2**.

Scieur de bois et la ravaudeuse, Le [N/A].
>   Th. des Jeunes Artistes (**2**); **Total: 2**.

Sept mariages, Les [N/A].
>   Th. des Grands Danseurs (Gaîté) (**6**); **Total: 6**.

Sept péchés capitaux, Les [N/A].
>   Th. des Variétés Amusantes, Comiques et Lyriques (**1**); **Total: 1**.

Sept travestissements d'Arlequin, Les [N/A].
>   Th. du Palais (Cité)-Variétés (**1**); **Total: 1**.

Sérail, Le [*Ballet*].
>   Th. de l'Emulation (Gaîté) (**4**); **Total: 4**.

Séraphine et Mendoce [*Comédie*, Prem. on 19-9-1799].
>   Th. de la Cité (**5**); Th. du Palais (Cité)-Variétés (**2**); **Total: 7**.

Serment des prêtres, Le, ou Le 9 janvier 1791 [In 2 acts, Prem. on 28-3-1791].
>   Petits Comédiens de Palais Royal (**26**); **Total: 26**.

Serment du vicaire, Le [*Fait Historique* in 3 acts, Prem. on 13-11-1791].
>   Th. des Variétés Amusantes, Comiques et Lyriques (**9**); **Total: 9**.

Serment républicain, Le [N/A].
>   Académie de la Musique (Opéra) (**3**); **Total: 3**.

Serpent magicien, Le, ou Le Débarquement [*Pantomime* in 3 acts, Prem. on 19-10-1780].
>   Th. des Grands Danseurs (Gaîté) (**17**); **Total: 17**.

Serva patrona, La [*Vaudeville*].
>   Veillée de Thalie (**1**); **Total: 1**.

Servante de Molière, La, ou La Revue de quelques auteurs [Prem. on 9-10-1799].
>   Th. des Grands Danseurs (Gaîté) (**4**); **Total: 4**.

Sigisbert [*Drame*, Prem. on 6-12-1798].
>   Th. de Molière (**6**); **Total: 6**.

Soeur aînée, La [N/A].
>   Th. des Jeunes Artistes (**5**); **Total: 5**.

Soirée d'une vieille femme, La [*Comédie* in 2 acts, Prem. on 25-3-1793, Pub. in 1793].
>   Th. de la Nation (Comédie Française) (**1**); **Total: 1**.

Soirée des dupes, La [N/A].
>   Th. du Vaudeville (**1**); Th. Patriotique et de Momus (**4**); **Total: 5**.

Soirée rustique, La [*Comédie*].
>   Th. des Délassements Comiques (**1**); **Total: 1**.

Soirée villageoise, La [*Pantomime* in 1 act, Prem. on 30-12-1781].
>   Th. des Grands Danseurs (Gaîté) (**10**); **Total: 10**.

Soixante francs, Les [N/A].
>   Th. des Ombres Chinoises (**1**); **Total: 1**.

Soldat de Louis XII, Le [*Fait Historique* in 3 acts, Prem. on 17-8-1791].
>   Th. de l'Ambigu Comique (**13**); **Total: 13**.

Soldat et l'homme de lettres, Le [N/A].
>   Th. de l'Emulation (Gaîté) (**8**); Th. des Grands Danseurs (Gaîté) (**6**); Th. Lyrique des Amis de la Patrie (**3**); **Total: 17**.

Soldat supposé, Le [*Opéra-Comique* in 1 act].
Th. des Délassements Comiques (**13**); Th. des Variétés Amusantes (Lazzari) (**1**); **Total: 14**.

Soldats du pape, Les [N/A].
Th. de l'Emulation (Gaîté) (**10**); **Total: 10**.

Soliman ou Le Mariage de Roxelane [N/A].
Th. du Marais (**1**); **Total: 1**.

Solitaire par amour, Le [N/A].
Th. des Jeunes Artistes (**11**); **Total: 11**.

Solitaires anglais, Les, ou Le Triomphe des femmes [*Fait Historique*, Prem. on 4-10-1791].
Th. de Molière (**5**); **Total: 5**.

Songe agréable, Le, ou Le Réveil du charbonnier [*Comédie* in 3 acts, Prem. on 22-7-1790].
Th. des Grands Danseurs (Gaîté) (**33**); **Total: 33**.

Sopha [*Opéra*, Prem. on 26-8-1791].
Th. de Molière (**11**); **Total: 11**.

Sophocle et Aristophane ou La Réconciliation des arts [*Héroique*, Prem. on 19-4-1797].
Th. du Vaudeville (**3**); **Total: 3**.

Sot intrigant, Le, ou La Manie d'être quelque chose [N/A].
Th. Français (de la rue Richelieu) (de la République) (**1**); **Total: 1**.

Sottinet ou Le Voyage inutile [Prem. on 24-7-1798].
Th. Lyrique des Amis de la Patrie (**2**); **Total: 2**.

Souper, Le [*Comédie* in 3 acts, Pub. in 1754].
Th. des Grands Danseurs (Gaîté) (**1**); **Total: 1**.

Souper du chanoine, Le [N/A].
Th. de l'Ambigu Comique (**1**); **Total: 1**.

Souper de Henri IV chez le charbonnier, Le [*Pantomime*].
Th. des Grands Danseurs (Gaîté) (**8**); **Total: 8**.

Souper de l'Opéra-comique, Le [*Vaudeville* in 1 act, Prem. on 6-8-1799].
Th. des Troubadours (**9**); **Total: 9**.

Souper de la courtisane vertueuse, Le [N/A].
Th. des Grands Danseurs (Gaîté) (**9**); **Total: 9**.

Souper de Molière par Voltaire, Le [N/A].
Th. du Vaudeville (**16**); **Total: 16**.

Souper des vieillards dupés, Le [N/A].
Th. des Grands Danseurs (Gaîté) (**1**); **Total: 1**.

Souper du Champ de Mars, Le [*Comédie*, Prem. on 17-7-1790].
Th. Français, Comique et Lyrique (**8**); **Total: 8**.

Souper magique, Le, ou Les Deux siècles [*Comédie* in 1 act, Prem. on 11-2-1790].
Th. de la Nation (Comédie Française) (**4**); **Total: 4**.

Spéculateur du jour, Le [Prem. on 3-5-1799].
Th. des Jeunes Artistes (**15**); **Total: 15**.

Spleen, Le [N/A].
Th. de l'Ambigu Comique (**2**); **Total: 2**.

St. Clément et Valois [*Comédie* in 3 acts, Prem. on 23-5-1791].
Petits Comédiens de Palais Royal (**2**); **Total: 2**.

Statues, Les [N/A].
Th. des Variétés Amusantes (Lazzari) (**8**); **Total: 8**.

Stratagème inutile, Le [In 1 act, Prem. on 4-7-1792].
Th. du Vaudeville (11); **Total: 11.**

Stratagème par amour, Le [N/A].
Th. de l'Ambigu Comique (2); **Total: 2.**

Stratagème superflu, Le [*Comédie* in 3 acts, Prem. on 10-1-1792].
Th. Français, Comique et Lyrique (8); **Total: 8.**

Sucre et le café, Le [*Drame* in 1 act, Prem. on 13-2-1792].
Th. des Variétés Amusantes, Comiques et Lyriques (9); **Total: 9.**

Suicide du 28 décembre 1791, Le [*Fait Historique* in 2 acts, Prem. on 1-2-1792].
Th. de Molière (12); **Total: 12.**

Suite, La [N/A].
Th. de l'Emulation (Gaîté) (35); Th. des Variétés Amusantes, Comiques et Lyriques (9); Th. du Palais (Cité)-Variétés (1); **Total: 45.**

Surprise de l'amour français, La [*Comédie* in 3 acts, Prem. on 30-3-1791, Pub. in 1727].
Th. de la Citoyenne Montansier (1); **Total: 1.**

Surprise réciproque, La [*Comédie* in 1 act, Prem. on 29-11-1786].
Th. des Beaujolais (6); **Total: 6.**

Surprises du paravent, Les [N/A].
Th. des Grands Danseurs (Gaîté) (4); **Total: 4.**

Suzanne [N/A].
Th. du Vaudeville (13); **Total: 13.**

Symphonie de Haydn [*Chanson*].
Th. du Feydeau (de Monsieur) (7); **Total: 7.**

Table, La [N/A].
Th. des Jeunes Artistes (4); **Total: 4.**

Table d'ébène dans les marionnettes, La [N/A].
Th. des Ombres Chinoises (3); Th. des Ombres de J.-J. Rousseau (5); **Total: 8.**

Tableau de famille, Le [*Comédie* in 3 acts, Prem. on 6-1-1793].
Th. Lyrique des Amis de la Patrie (21); **Total: 21.**

Tableau du mariage dans les marionnettes, Le [N/A].
Th. des Ombres Chinoises (5); Th. des Ombres de J.-J. Rousseau (3); **Total: 8.**

Talmire ou L'Amitié vaincue par l'amour [Prem. on 14-10-1799].
Th. des Jeunes Artistes (6); **Total: 6.**

Tambourins, Les [*Ballet*].
Th. des Jeunes Artistes (8); **Total: 8.**

Tampon dans les ombres, Le [N/A].
Th. des Ombres Chinoises (6); **Total: 6.**

Tartuffe révolutionnaire [N/A].
Th. Français (de la rue Richelieu) (de la République) (10); **Total: 10.**

Tasse de glace, La [N/A].
Th. du Feydeau (de Monsieur) (6); **Total: 6.**

Taugaine [Prem. on 7-8-1797].
Th. de l'Ambigu Comique (3); **Total: 3.**

Temple de Diane, Le [N/A].
Tivoli (2); **Total: 2.**

Temps passé n'est plus, Le [N/A].
Th. du Vaudeville (10); **Total: 10.**

Testament, Le [*Comédie* in 3 acts, Prem. on 5-10-1797, Pub. in 1836].
Th. du Vaudeville (**27**); **Total: 27.**

Testament du mort vivant, Le [*Pièce* in 2 acts, Prem. on 26-8-1787].
Th. des Grands Danseurs (Gaîté) (**27**); **Total: 27.**

Tête des femmes, La [N/A].
Th. des Variétés Amusantes, Comiques et Lyriques (**7**); Th. Patriotique et de Momus (**8**); **Total: 15.**

Thé, Le, ou Les Parvenus [*Vaudeville* in 2 acts].
Th. du Mareux (**3**); Th. du Palais (Cité)-Variétés (**1**); **Total: 4.**

Théâtre de l'amour, Le [*Comédie* in 1 act, Pub. in 1795].
Th. des Variétés Amusantes, Comiques et Lyriques (**1**); **Total: 1.**

Thémire protégé par l'amour [*Ballet*, Prem. on 20-8-1797].
Th. des Délassements Comiques (**17**); **Total: 17.**

Théodore Gambois [N/A].
Th. de l'Estrapade au Panthéon (**1**); **Total: 1.**

Théodose le jeune [*Comédie* in 5 acts, Prem. on 7-11-1791].
Th. du Marais (**1**); **Total: 1.**

Thérèse [*Comédie* in 1 act].
Cirque National (**1**); **Total: 1.**

Thiase [Prem. on 8-5-1797].
Th. de l'Odéon (**4**); **Total: 4.**

Thomas le crédule [*Comédie*, Prem. on 17-2-1798].
Th. de l'Ambigu Comique (**7**); **Total: 7.**

Titus et Caracalla [Prem. on 27-7-1798].
Th. de l'Ambigu Comique (**12**); **Total: 12.**

Tombeau de Nostradamus, Le [*Pantomime*].
Th. des Grands Danseurs (Gaîté) (**36**); **Total: 36.**

Toulon reconquis ou La Fête du port [*Fait Historique* in 1 act, Prem. on 23-1-1794].
Th. Lyrique des Amis de la Patrie (**3**); **Total: 3.**

Tour du page, Le, ou Volicour [Prem. on 22-3-1797].
Th. des Italiens (Opéra-Comique) (**2**); **Total: 2.**

Tour de Roquelaure, Un [N/A].
Th. des Jeunes Artistes (**30**); Th. du Marais (**1**); Th. du Palais (Cité)-Variétés (**1**); Th. Lyrique des Amis de la Patrie (**1**); **Total: 33.**

Tourneuse, La [N/A].
Th. des Grands Danseurs (Gaîté) (**4**); **Total: 4.**

Toute neuve, La [N/A].
Th. des Grands Danseurs (Gaîté) (**1**); **Total: 1.**

Tracasseries inutiles, Les [*Opéra* in 2 acts].
Th. des Délassements Comiques (**4**); **Total: 4.**

Tragédie impromptu, La [*Tragédie* in 1 act, Prem. on 16-8-1791].
Th. Lyrique des Amis de la Patrie (**4**); **Total: 4.**

Travail et plaisir [N/A].
Th. des Jeunes Artistes (**35**); **Total: 35.**

Trente et un ou La Joueuse corrigée [*Comédie* in 3 acts, Prem. on 17-9-1791].
Th. des Grands Danseurs (Gaîté) (**7**); Th. Lyrique des Amis de la Patrie (**9**); **Total: 16.**

Trésor d'Arlequin, Le [N/A].
Th. du Vaudeville (**3**); **Total: 3.**

Trésor et les trois derviches, Le [N/A].
Th. des Jeunes Artistes (**11**); **Total: 11.**

Triomphe de l'amour conjugal, Le [*Pantomime* in 3 acts, Prem. on 2-6-1789].
Th. des Grands Danseurs (Gaîté) (**90**); **Total: 90.**

Triomphe de l'amour et de la nature, Le [*Comédie*].
Th. de l'Ambigu Comique (**2**); **Total: 2.**

Triomphe de l'amour, Le [*Opéra* in 3 acts].
Th. des Enfans Comiques (**2**); **Total: 2.**

Triomphe de l'humanité, Le [N/A].
Th. de la Cité (**1**); **Total: 1.**

Triomphe de l'innocence, Le [*Vaudeville* in 1 act, Prem. on 7-8-1793].
Th. Lyrique des Amis de la Patrie (**3**); **Total: 3.**

Triomphe de Merlin, Le [*Comédie* in 1 act, Pub. in 1783].
Th. des Grands Danseurs (Gaîté) (**23**); **Total: 23.**

Triste ruse, La, ou Les Trois n'en font qu'un [Prem. on 8-1-1799].
Th. Lyrique des Amis de la Patrie (**3**); **Total: 3.**

Trois ans de l'histoire de France [*Fait Historique*].
Th. de Molière (**12**); **Total: 12.**

Trois aveugles, Les [N/A].
Th. de la Cité (**4**); **Total: 4.**

Trois bâtards, Les [*Vaudeville*].
Th. de Molière (**1**); **Total: 1.**

Trois coquettes dupées, Les [*Comédie* in 1 act, Prem. on 29-9-1790].
Th. Français, Comique et Lyrique (**15**); **Total: 15.**

Trois Figaro, Les [*Comédie* in 3 acts, Prem. on 9-3-1791].
Th. de la Liberté (**2**); **Total: 2.**

Trois fils, Les, ou L'Héroïsme filial [*Drame*, Prem. on 26-2-1797].
Th. du Feydeau (de Monsieur) (**3**); **Total: 3.**

Trois généraux, Les [N/A].
Th. de l'Ambigu Comique (**1**); **Total: 1.**

Trois intrigants, Les [Prem. on 19-6-1790].
Th. des Grands Danseurs (Gaîté) (**2**); **Total: 2.**

Trois Jocrisses, Les [N/A].
Th. du Vaudeville (**4**); **Total: 4.**

Trois nones qui ne s'entendent pas [N/A].
Th. des Grands Danseurs (Gaîté) (**1**); **Total: 1.**

Trois nouvelles, Les [Prem. on 16-11-1797].
Th. des Jeunes Artistes (**11**); **Total: 11.**

Trompettes du jugement dernier, Les [N/A].
Th. du Marais (**5**); **Total: 5.**

Trône de l'amour dans les marionnettes, Le [N/A].
Th. des Ombres de J.-J. Rousseau (**4**); **Total: 4.**

Troubadours, Les, ou L'Imprudence désastreuse [*Drame* in 3 acts].
Th. des Troubadours (**1**); Th. du Marais (**7**); Th. du Vaudeville (**3**); **Total: 11.**

Tulipano [N/A].
Th. du Feydeau (de Monsieur) (**2**); **Total: 2.**

Tuteur malade, Le [N/A].
Th. des Délassements Comiques (**15**); Th. du Marais (**1**); **Total: 16.**

Tuteur original, Le [Prem. on 19-1-1799].
Th. de Molière (**8**); **Total: 8.**

Ulysse moderne, L' [N/A].
Th. des Jeunes Artistes (**6**); **Total: 6.**

Un bienfait n'est jamais perdu [N/A].
    Th. des Grands Danseurs (Gaîté) (**6**); **Total: 6.**
Un officier à Metz [*Vaudeville* in 1 act, Prem. on 9-10-1793].
    Th. des Italiens (Opéra-Comique) (**32**); **Total: 32.**
Un ou l'autre, L' [N/A].
    Th. du Vaudeville (**8**); **Total: 8.**
Une folie du vaudeville ou Les Mariages par adjudication [*Vaudeville*, Prem. on 4-11-1799].
    Th. du Vaudeville (**1**); **Total: 1.**
Union fraternelle, L' [*Fait Historique* in 1 act, Prem. on 14-2-1789].
    Th. de l'Ambigu Comique (**2**); **Total: 2.**
Valet à tout le monde, Le [*Comédie* in 3 acts].
    Th. de l'Estrapade au Panthéon (**8**); **Total: 8.**
Valet maître et le maître valet, Le [*Vaudeville*].
    Th. des Grands Danseurs (Gaîté) (**12**); **Total: 12.**
Valet rival de son maître, Le [*Pièce* in 1 act, Pub. in 1785].
    Th. des Grands Danseurs (Gaîté) (**8**); **Total: 8.**
Valets singes de leurs maîtres, Les [*Comédie* in 2 acts, Pub. in 1786].
    Th. du Palais Royal (**3**); **Total: 3.**
Valise perdue, La [N/A].
    Th. des Grands Danseurs (Gaîté) (**2**); **Total: 2.**
Veillée villageoise, La [N/A].
    Th. du Vaudeville (**10**); **Total: 10.**
Vendanges de Taverny, Les [N/A].
    Th. Lyrique des Amis de la Patrie (**8**); **Total: 8.**
Vengeances, Les [*Opéra* in 2 acts, Prem. on 10-10-1791].
    Th. du Feydeau (de Monsieur) (**1**); **Total: 1.**
Vénitiens, Les [N/A].
    Th. Français (de la rue Richelieu) (de la République) (**6**); **Total: 6.**
Véritable ami du peuple, Le [*Tableau-Patriotique* in 1 act].
    Th. des Grands Danseurs (Gaîté) (**22**); **Total: 22.**
Véritables honnêtes gens, Les [*Comédie*, Prem. on 20-10-1797].
    Th. Français (de la rue Richelieu) (de la République) (**7**); **Total: 7.**
Vertu récompense, La [N/A].
    Th. de l'Emulation (Gaîté) (**2**); **Total: 2.**
Vertus et les talents, Les [Prem. on 24-11-1798].
    Th. des Jeunes Artistes (**31**); **Total: 31.**
Veuve américaine, La [*Opéra-Comique* in 3 acts, Prem. on 20-9-1796].
    Th. du Lycée des Arts (**2**); Th. Lyrique des Amis de la Patrie (**5**); **Total: 7.**
Vice et la vertu, Le [N/A].
    Th. de l'Emulation (Gaîté) (**9**); **Total: 9.**
Victimes de l'orgueil, Les [N/A].
    Th. de l'Emulation (Gaîté) (**25**); **Total: 25.**
Vieillard amoureux dans les marionnettes, Le [N/A].
    Th. des Ombres de J.-J. Rousseau (**3**); **Total: 3.**
Vieillesse de Jean-Jacques Rousseau, La [N/A].
    Th. des Italiens (Opéra-Comique) (**1**); **Total: 1.**
Vieux coffre, Le [N/A].
    Th. des Jeunes Artistes (**28**); **Total: 28.**
Vieux cousin, Le [N/A].
    Th. de l'Odéon (**6**); Th. Lyrique des Amis de la Patrie (**1**); **Total: 7.**

Vieux élégants, Les [Prem. on 30-9-1794].
Th. du Vaudeville (12); **Total: 12.**

Vieux incroyables, Les [N/A].
Th. du Vaudeville (26); **Total: 26.**

Vieux militaire, Le [*Comédie* in 3 acts, Prem. on 12-1-1790].
Th. du Feydeau (de Monsieur) (1); **Total: 1.**

Vieux soldat, Le [N/A].
Th. des Jeunes Artistes (12); **Total: 12.**

Villageois à l'épreuve, Le [*Vaudeville* in 2 acts].
Th. des Beaujolais (1); **Total: 1.**

Villageois à la ville, Les [*Opéra-Comique*, Prem. on 22-11-1791].
Th. de l'Ambigu Comique (24); **Total: 24.**

Villageois philosophe, Le [N/A].
Th. des Jeunes Artistes (18); **Total: 18.**

Villageoise rusée, La [N/A].
Th. de l'Ambigu Comique (16); **Total: 16.**

Vingt-six métamorphoses de la fée bienfaisante, Les [*Féerie* in 3 acts, Prem. on 4-7-1780].
Th. des Grands Danseurs (Gaîté) (45); **Total: 45.**

Vingtièmes, Les [N/A].
Th. des Ombres de J.-J. Rousseau (1); **Total: 1.**

Vision des sots, La [Prem. on 31-1-1798].
Th. des Jeunes Artistes (6); **Total: 6.**

Visite de Racan, La, ou La Femme [Prem. on 1-8-1799].
Th. des Troubadours (9); **Total: 9.**

Volage, Le [*Comédie* in 1 act, Prem. on 22-9-1790].
Th. du Palais Royal (2); **Total: 2.**

Voleur converti par la dame secourable, Le [*Pièce* in 1 act, Prem. on 18-10-1788].
Th. des Grands Danseurs (Gaîté) (40); **Total: 40.**

Volontaires de Sambre et Meuse, Les [N/A].
Th. du Vaudeville (15); **Total: 15.**

Voltaire [N/A].
Th. du Vaudeville (1); **Total: 1.**

Voltige, La [N/A].
Th. des Grands Danseurs (Gaîté) (2); **Total: 2.**

Voltigeurs, Les, ou Grand voltigeur, Le [*Divertissement/parade*].
Th. des Grands Danseurs (Gaîté) (6); **Total: 6.**

Voyage aérien de Madame Angot dans le ballon, Le [*Opéra*].
Th. du Palais (Cité)-Variétés (23); **Total: 23.**

Voyage de St. Cloud par mer et le retour par terre, Le [Prem. on 13-12-1798].
Th. de la Citoyenne Montansier (3); **Total: 3.**

Voyage du Parisien, Le [N/A].
Th. des Ombres Chinoises (1); **Total: 1.**

Voyages de Jean-Jacques Rousseau, Les [N/A].
Th. des Délassements Comiques (7); **Total: 7.**

Vrais sujet corrigé, Le [*Comédie* in 2 acts, Prem. on 2-3-1789].
Th. de l'Ambigu Comique (1); **Total: 1.**

Vulcain [*Pantomime*].
Th. des Grands Danseurs (Gaîté) (2); **Total: 2.**

Washington ou Le Règne des lois [*Opéra* in 3 acts, Prem. on 5-5-1796].
 Th. Lyrique des Amis de la Patrie (**5**); **Total: 5**.
Young ou La Vie [*Comédie*, Prem. on 8-10-1799].
 Th. du Vaudeville (**8**); **Total: 8**.
Zabbi et Dorville [*Pantomime* in 4 acts, Prem. on 23-5-1796].
 Th. de la Cité (**41**); **Total: 41**.
Zabeau et Courville [N/A].
 Th. du Lycée au Palais Egalité (**1**); **Total: 1**.
Zélis et l'hymen [*Opéra-Comique* in 3 acts, Prem. on 31-12-1791].
 Th. de l'Ambigu Comique (**50**); **Total: 50**.
Zing-zing [*Divertissement/parade* in 1 act].
 Th. de l'Emulation (Gaîté) (**15**); Th. des Grands Danseurs (Gaîté) (**4**); **Total: 19**.
Zirphee [N/A].

13

Index of Titles and Authors

*First author is shown in **bold**. Consult Chapter 11 for complete listing.*

Demoustier, Charles-A., Devienne, François (comp).

Agnès et Olivier, **Boutet de Monvel, Jacques-M.,** Dalayrac, Nicolas (comp).

Agricole Viala ou Le Jeune héros de la Durance, **Philipon, Louis de la Madeleine.,** Jadin, Louis-E. (comp).

Aimée ou La Fausse apparence, **Pépin de Degrouette.,** Gebauer, Michel.-J. (comp).

Aîné et le cadet, L', **Collot d'Herbois, J.-M.**

Ainsi va le monde, **Gérès de Camarsac.**

Akancas, Les, **Cuvelier de Trie, Jean G.-A.**

Alain et Rosette, **Léger, François-P.-A.**

Alain et Suzette ou Le Fils adoptif, **Brazier, Nicolas.**

Alarmiste, L', **Després, Jean-B.-D.**

*Albert I ou Adeline,***Le Blanc de Guillet, Antoine Blanc, dit.**

Albert ou Le Service récompensé, **Sedaine, Michel-J.,** Grétry, André-E.-M. (comp).

Alceste, **Du Roullet, François-L. Gand Lebland.,** Gluck, Christoph (comp).

Alceste à la campagne ou Le Misanthrope corrigé, **Demoustier, Charles-A.,** Devienne, François (comp).

Alchimistes, Les, ou La Folie et la sagesse, **Moline, Pierre-L.,** Carpentier (comp).

Alcine, **Danchet, Antoine.**

Alexis et Justine, **Boutet de Monvel, Jacques-M.,** Dalayrac, Nicolas (comp).

Alexis et Rosette, **Guillemain, Charles-J.**

Alexis ou L'Erreur d'un bon père, **Marsollier des Vivetières, Benoît-J.,** Dalayrac, Nicolas (comp).

Alisbelle ou Les Crimes de la féodalité, **Desforges, Pierre-J.-B. Choudard de.,** Jadin, Louis-E. (comp).

Alix de Beaucaire, **Boutillier, Maximilien-J.,** Deshayes, Prosper-D. (comp).

Almanzor et Nadine, **Fonpré de Fracansalle.**

Alonse et Cora, **Bourlin, Antoine-J.,** Pseud. Dumaniant.

Alphonse et Léonore ou L'Heureux procès, **Le Prévost d'Iray, Vicomte Chrétien.,** Gresnick, Antoine (comp).

Alzire ou Les Américains, **Voltaire, F.-M. Arouet, dit Arouet de.**

Amant arbitre, L', **Ségur, Alexander-J.-P., Vte. de.**

Amant auteur et valet, L', **Cérou, Chevalier de.**

Amant bourru, L', **Boutet de Monvel, Jacques-M.,** Dalayrac, Nicolas (comp).

Amant femme-de-chambre, L', **Bourlin, Antoine-J., Pseud. Dumaniant.**

Amant locataire, L', ou Le Faux somnambule, **Gibert, François-B.**

Amant loup-garou, L', ou M. Rodomont, **Collot D'Herbois, J.-M.**

Amant statue, L', **Desfontaines, François-G. Fouques, dit.,** Dalayrac, Nicolas (comp).

Amant supposé, L', ou Le Miroir, **Pannard, Charles-F.**

Amant travesti, L', **Dubreuil, Alphonse-D.,** Desaugiers, Marc-A. (comp).

Amants déguisés, Les, **Collé, Charles.**

Amants généreux, Les, **Rochon de Chabannes, Marc.**

Amants malheureux, Les, ou Le Comte de Comminges, **Arnaud, François-T.-M. de B. d'.**

Amants Protées, Les, ou Qui compte sans son hôte compte deux fois, **Patrat, Joseph.,** Trial, Armand-E. (comp).

Amants réunis, Les, **Beauchamps, Pierre-F.-G. de.**

*Amants ridicules, Les, ou Les Deux jaloux,***Desaudrais, Chalres Emmanuel Gaulard de.**

Amants sans amour, Les, **Monnet, Jean.**

Amateur de musique, L', **Raymond, B.-Louis.,** Raymond, B. (comp).

Amazones, Les, **Du Boccage, Anne-M.-L.**

Amazones modernes, Les, ou Le Triomphe des dames, **Legrand, Marc-A.,** Biancolelli, Pierre-F., dit Dominique.

Ambigu-comique, L', ou L'Audience de

Amphitrion, **Sedaine, Michel-J.**, Grétry, André-E.-M. (comp).

Amphitryon, **Molière, Jean-B. Poquelin de.**

Anacréon à Suresnes, **Chaussier, Hector.**, Bizet.

Anacréon chez Polycrate, **Guy, Jean-H.**, Grétry, André-E.-M. (comp).

Andromaque, **Racine, Jean.**

Andros et Almona ou Le Français à Bassora, **Picard, Louis-B.**

Angélique et Melcour ou Le Procès, **Léger, François-P.-A.**

Anglais à Bordeaux, Les, **Favart, Charles-S.**, Grétry, André-E.-M. (comp).

Anglomanie, L', **Saurin, Bernard-J.**

Anne de Boleyn, **Guibert, Jacques-A.-H.**

Annette et Basile, **Guillemain, Charles-J.**

Annette et Jacques ou Les Semestriers alsaciens, **Beaupré-Larigaudière.**

Annette et Lubin, **Favart, Marie-J.-B.D.**

Anniversaire, L', ou La Fête de la souveraineté, **Cuvelier de Trie, Jean G.-A.**

Anti-célibataire, L', ou Les Mariages, **Pujoulx, Jean-B.**

Antigone, **Marmontel, Jean F.**, Grétry, André-E.-M. (comp).

Antiquaire, L', **Hennequin, Louis.**, Anfossi, Pasquale (comp).

Antiquomanie, L', ou Le Mariage sous la cheminée, **Jacquelin, Jacques-A.**

Apelle et Campaspe, **Demoustier, Charles-A.**, Devienne, François (comp).

Apollon et Coronis, **Fuzelier, Louis.**, Rey, Jean-B. (comp).

Apothéose de Beaurepaire, L', **Lesur, Charles-L.**, Berton, Henri-M. (comp).

Apothéose de Beaurepaire, L', ou La Patrie reconnaissante, **Le Boeuf, Jean-J.**

Apothéose du jeune Barra, L', **Léger, François-P.-A.**

Apothicaire, L', **Fabre D'Eglantine, Philippe-F.-N.**, Foignet, Charles-G. (comp).

Apothicaire (dévalisé), L', **Villiers, Pierre-A.-B.**

Apparence trompeuse, L', ou Le Capricieux, **Guyot de Merville, Michel.**

Appartement à louer, L', **Pain, Joseph-M.**

Arabelle et Vascos ou Les Jacobins de Goa, **Lebrun Tossa, Jean-A.**, Lesueur, Jean-F. (comp).

Arbitre, L', ou Les Consultations de l'an VII, **Jouy, Victor-J. Etienne, dit de.**, Longchamps, Charles de.

Arétaphile ou La Révolution de Cyrène, **Ronsin, Charles-P.**

Ariane, **Corneille, Thomas.**

Ariane abandonnée dans l'île de Naxe, **Dubois, Jean-B.**, Benda, George (comp).

Ariane dans l'île de Naxos, **Moline, Pierre-L.**, Carpentier (comp).

Ariodant, **Hoffman, François-B.**

Ariston ou Le Pouvoir de la magie, **Lazzari, Ange.**

Aristote amoureux ou Le Philosophe bridé, **Barré, Pierre-Y.**, Radet, Jean-B., Desfontaines, François-G. Fouques, dit.

Arlequin afficheur, **Barré, Pierre-Y.**, Radet, Jean-B., Desfontaines, François-G. Fouques, dit.

Arlequin amoureux ou L'Ecole du monde, **Nougaret, Pierre-J.-B.**

Arlequin au tombeau ou Le Tombeau magique, **Caffaut.**

Arlequin aux enfers ou L'Enlèvement de Colombine, **Prévost de St.-Lucien, Roch-H.**

Arlequin bon père, **Florian, Jean-P.-C. de.**

Arlequin boulanger, **Lazzari, Ange.**

Arlequin chevalier du soleil, **Fatouville, Nolant de.**

Arlequin corsaire, **Dorvigny, Louis-A.**

Arlequin cruello, **Barré, Pierre-Y.**, Radet, Jean-B., Desfontaines, François-G. Fouques, dit.

Arlequin décorateur, **Année, Antoine.**

Arlequin devin par hasard ou Le Lendemain de noces, **Fuzelier, Louis.**, Rey, Jean-B. (comp).

Arlequin dogue d'Angleterre, **Placide, Alexandre-P.-Bussart, dit.**

Arlequin empereur dans la lune, **Fatou-**

André-E.-M. (comp).

Au retour, **Radet, Jean-B.,** Desfontaines, François-G. Fouques, dit.

Auberge allemande, L', ou *Le Traître démasqué,* **Chazel, Père.**

Auberge isolée, L', **Guillemain, Charles-J.**

Aucassin et Nicolette ou Les Moeurs du bon temps, **Sedaine, Michel-J.,** Grétry, André-E.-M. (comp).

Auguste et Théodore ou Les Deux pages, **Mantauffeld, Baron Ernest de.,** Dezède, Nicolas (comp).

Augustin et Babet ou Le Fils naturel, **Corsange de la Plante, Jean-F.-J.**

Aujourd'hui ou Les Fous supposés, **Bonnefoy de Bouyon, Abbé.,** Mengozzi, Bernardo (comp).

Aurore de Gusman, L', **Prevot d'Irai, Tardu (comp).**

Auteur à la mode, L', ou *Le Mari complaisant,* **Durival.,** Deshayes, Prosper-D. (comp).

Auteur dans son ménage, L', **Gosse, Etienne.**

Auto-da-fé, L', ou *Le Tribunal de l'Inquisition,* **Gabiot de Salins, Jean-L.**

Autre Tartuffe, L', ou *La Mère coupable,* **Beaumarchais, Pierre-A.C. de.**

Aux plus braves les plus belles, **Philipon, Louis de la Madeleine.,** Jadin, Louis-E. (comp).

Avantageux puni, L', **Ribié, César.**

Avare, L', **Molière, Jean-B. Poquelin de.**

Avare puni, L', **Falaise de Verneuil.,** Jadin, Louis-E. (comp).

Aveu délicat, L', **Gabiot de Salins, Jean-L.**

Aveugle clairvoyant, L', **Legrand, Marc-A.,** Biancolleli, Pierre-F., dit Dominique.

Aveugle et le muet, L', ou *Les Nez cassés,* **Desfougerais, P.F.** Aubin, dit.

Aveux difficiles, Les, **Vigée, Louis-J.-B.-E.**

Avocat Patelin, L', **Brueys, David-A. de.,** Palaprat, Joseph.

Azélie, **Florian, Jean-P.-C. de.**

Azeline, **Hoffman, François-B.**

Azémia ou Les Sauvages, **Lachabeaussière, Auguste-E.-X. P. de.,** Dalayrac, Nicolas (comp).

Babillard, Le, **Boissy, Louis de.**

Bacchus et Ariane, **Gallet, Sébastien.,** Rochefort, Jean-B. (comp).

Badinage dangereux, Le, **Picard, Louis-B.**

Bagnaudière, La, ou *Le Fou malgré lui,* **Darhilly.**

Baiocco et Serpilla, **Favart, Charles-S.,** Grétry, André-E.-M. (comp).

Baiser donné et le baiser rendu, Le, **Taconet, Toussaint-G.**

Baiser, Le, ou *La Bonne fée,* **Florian, Jean-P.-C. de.**

Bajazet, **Racine, Jean.**

Bal et le souper des poètes, Le, **Ronsin, Charles-P.**

Bal favorable, Le, ou *Le Rendez-vous manqué,* **Fonpré de Fracansalle.**

Ballon aérostatique, Le, ou *Les Imbroglios d'Arlequin,* **Renou, Antoine.**

Banquier, Le, **Laffichard, Thomas.**

Barbe Bleue, **Daine.**

Barbier de Séville, Le, ou *La Précaution inutile,* **Beaumarchais, Pierre-A.C. de.**

Barbier de village, Le, ou *L'Officieux désobligeant,* **Beaunoir, Alexandre-L.-B. Robineau dit.**

Barbier de village, Le, ou *Le Revenant,* **Grétry, André-J.,** Grétry, André-E.-M. (comp).

Barnevelt, grand pensionnaire de Hollande, **Lemierre, Antoine-M.**

Barogo ou La Suite du Ramoneur prince, **Pompigny, Maurin de.**

Baron d'Albikrac, Le, **Corneille, Thomas.**

Baron de Trenck, Le, ou *Le Prisonnier Prussien,* **Gabiot de Salins, Jean-L.**

Baronne de Chantal, fondatrice de l'ordre de la visitation, La, **Cubières-Palmezeaux, Michel de.**

Bascule, La, **Arnould, Jean-F. Mussot, dit.**

Basile ou A trompeur trompeur et demi, **Sedaine, Michel-J.,** Grétry, André-E.-M. (comp).

Bataille d'Antioche, La, ou *Gargamelle vaincu,* **Fonpré de Fracansalle.**

Bon père, Le, ou La Suite du bon ménage, **Florian, Jean-P.-C. de.**

Bon seigneur, Le, ou La Vertu récompensée, **Ribié, César.**

Bon valet, Le, ou Il était temps, **Pompigny, Maurin de.**

Bonheur inattendu, Le, **Thouvenin.**

Boniface pointu et sa famille, **Guillemain, Charles-J.**

Bonne aubaine, La, **Radet, Jean-B.**, Desfontaines, François-G. Fouques, dit.

Bonne maîtresse, La, **Montanclos, Mme. Marie M. de.**

Bonne mère, La, **Florian, Jean-P.-C. de.**

Bonne soeur, La, ou Elle en avait besoin, **Pompigny, Maurin de.**

Bonnes gens, Les, ou Boniface à Paris, **Guillemain, Charles-J.**

Bons amis, Les, ou Il était temps, **Dorvigny, Louis-A.**

Bons enfants, Les, ou La Cabane dans les bois, **Blanchard, Pierre.**

Bons et des méchants, Des, ou Philémon et Baucis, **Audinot, Nicolas-M.**

Bons voisins, Les, **Planterre, Barthélemy.**, Loise (comp).

Bouquet de famille, Le, ou Le 25 août, **Martineau, Louis-S.**

Bouquet de Thalie, Le, **Collé, Charles.**

Bouquet du sentiment, Le, **Landrin.**

Bouquet et la veuve, Le, **Person de Bérainville, L.-C.**

Bouquets, Les, **Guillemain, Charles-J.**

Bourgeois gentilhomme, Le, **Molière, Jean-B. Poquelin de.**

Bourgeoises de qualité, Les, **Dancourt, Florent C.**

Bourgeoises de qualité, Les, **Hauteroche, Noel de.**

Bourru bienfaisant, Le, **Goldoni, Carlo.**

Braconnier anglais, Le, **Arnould, Jean-F. Mussot, dit.**

Brave poltron, Le, ou Trois contre un, **Beaunoir**, Alexandre-L.-B. Robineau dit.

Brave Thénard, Le, ou Le Soldat de la liberté, **Plancher de Valcour, dit Aristide.**

Brigand, Le, **Hoffman, François-B.**

Brigands de la Vendée, Les, **Boullault,** Mathurin-J.

Briséis ou La Colère d'Achille, **Poinsinet de Sivry, Louis.**

Britannicus, **Racine, Jean.**

Brouette du vinaigrier, La, **Mercier, Louis-S.**

Brouetteur italien, Le, **Pitrot, Antoine.**

Brouilleries, Les,**Loeillard d'Arvigny, Charles J.**, Berton, Henri-M. (comp).

Bruits de paix, Les, ou L'Heureuse espérance, **Aude, Joseph.**

Brutus, **Voltaire, F.-M. Arouet, dit Arouet de.**

Bûcheron, Le, ou Les Trois souhaits, **Guichard, Jean-F.**, Charpentier (comp).

Bûcherons de Potsdam, Les, **Lazzari, Ange**

Buffet, Le, ou Les Deux cousins, **Hapdé, Jean-B.-A.**

Buona figliola, La, **Goldoni, Carlo.**

Burbero di buon cuore, Il, **Da Ponte, Lorenzo.**, Martini, Vincente (comp).

Bureau de mariages, Le, **Landrin.**

Bustes, Les, ou Arlequin sculpteur, **Villiers, Pierre-A.-B.**

C'est le diable ou La Bohémienne, **Cuvelier de Trie, Jean G.-A.**

C'est le même, **Ségur, Alexander-J.-P., Vte. de.**

Ca ira ou Le Retour des fédérés, **Dorvigny, Louis-A.**

Ça n'en est pas ou Tout ce qui reluit n'est pas or, **Dorvigny, Louis-A.**

Cabinet de figures, Le, ou Le Sculpteur en bois, **Mague de Saint-Aubin, Jacques.**

Cabriolet jaune, Le, ou Le Phénix d'Angoulême, **Ségur, Alexander-J.-P., Vte. de.**

Cacophonie, La, **Beaunoir, Alexandre-L.-B. Robineau dit.**

Cadet Roussel, **Prévost, Augustin.**

Cadet Roussel barbier à la fontaine des innocents, **Aude, Joseph.**

Cadet Roussel misanthrope et Manon repentante, **Aude, Joseph.**

Cadet Roussel ou Le Café des aveugles, **Aude, Joseph.**

Cadi dupé, Le, **Lemonnier, Pierre-R.**, Monsigny, Pierre-A. (comp).

Cadichon ou Les Bohémiennes,

Cent Louis, Les, Briois, Belle-Roche, dit de.

Céphise ou L'Erreur de l'esprit, Marsollier des Vivetières, Benoît-J., Dalayrac, Nicolas (comp).

Cercle, Le, ou La Soirée à la mode, Poinsinet, Antoine-A.-H.

Cérémonie, La, Bernard, Pierre-Joseph.

Chacun son métier, Dorvigny, Louis-A.

Champagnac et Suzette ou Fait comme lui, Chazet, René-A.-P. de.

Chapitre second, Dupaty, Louis-E.

Charette républicaine, La, ou La Paix en Vendée, Mayeur de St.-Paul, François-M.

Charles et Caroline ou Les Abus de l'Ancien Régime, Pigault-Lebrun, Charles-A.P. de L'Epinoy, dit.

Charles et Victoire ou Les Amants de Plailly, Plancher de Valcour, dit Aristide.

Charles IX ou L'Ecole des rois, Chénier, Marie-J.

Charles Rivière Dufresny ou Le Mariage impromptu, Deschamps, Jacques-M.

Chasse aux loups, La, Sewrin, Charles-A. de Bassompierre, dit.

Chasse, La, Desfontaines, François-G. Fouques, dit., Dalayrac, Nicolas (comp).

Chasseurs, Les, Desportes, Philippe.

Chaste Suzanne, La, Barré, Pierre-Y., Radet, Jean-B., Desfontaines, François-G. Fouques, dit.

Château des Appenins, Le, ou Le Fantôme vivant, Guilbert de Pixerécourt, René-.C.

Château du diable, Le, Loaisel de Tréogate, Joseph-M.

Châteaux en Espagne, Les, Collin d'Harleville, Jean-F.

Chaudronnier de St.-Flour, Le, Henriquez, L.-M., Gouffé, Armand Alexandre Duval.

Chaulieu à Fontenay, Ségur, Alexander-J.-P., Vte. de.

Chêne patriotique, Le, ou La Matinée du 14 juillet 1790, Boutet de Monvel, Jacques-M., Dalayrac, Nicolas (comp).

Chercheuse d'esprit, La, Favart, Charles-S., Grétry, André-E.-M. (comp).

Chercheuse d'esprit, La, Gardel, Maximilien.

Chercheuses d'esprit, Les, Destival de Braban.

Chevalier à la mode, Le, Dancourt, Florent C.

Chevalier de Faublas, Le, Villemain d'Abancourt, François-J.

Chevalier de La Barre, Le, Marsollier des Vivetières, Benoît-J., Dalayrac, Nicolas (comp).

Cheveux, Les, Guillemain, Charles-J.

Chimène ou Le Cid, Guillard, Nicolas-F., Sacchini, Antonio (comp).

Chouans de Vitré, Les, Desfontaines, François-G. Fouques, dit., Dalayrac, Nicolas (comp).

Chouans, Les, ou Républicaine de Malestroit, Pain, Joseph-M.

Christophe Dubois, Léger, François-P.-A.

Christophe et Jérôme ou La Ferme hospitalière, Favières, Edmond-G.-F. de., Berton, Henri-M. (comp).

Christophe le Rond, Dorvigny, Louis-A.

Cid, Le, Corneille, Pierre.

Cinna ou La Clémence d'Auguste, Corneille, Pierre.

Cinquantaine, La, Desfontaines, François-G. Fouques, dit., Dalayrac, Nicolas (comp).

Cinquantaine infernale, La, ou La Baleine avalée par Arlequin, Lazzari, Ange

Citoyens français, Les, ou Le Triomphe de la Révolution, Vaqué, Pierre.

Claudine de Florian, Pigault-Lebrun, Charles-A.P. de L'Epinoy, dit.

Claudine ou Le Petit commissionnaire, Deschamps, Jacques-M.

Claudinet ou Le Dernier venu en graine, Bosquier-Gavaudan, Jean-S.-F., Langle, Honoré-F.-M. (comp).

Clef forée, La, Jacquelin, Jacques-A.

Clément Marot, Duval, Georges-L.-J., Gouffé, Armand Alexandre Duval.

Clémentine et Desormes, Boutet de Monvel, Jacques-M., Dalayrac, Nicolas (comp).

Nicolas (comp).

Congrès des rois, Le, Eve, Antoine-F. , dit Maillot.

Conjectures, Les, Picard, Louis-B.

Connaisseur, Le, Pain, Joseph-M.

Connaisseur, Le, ou L'Auteur par amour, Duclos, Pierre-G.

Conseil de Lucifer, Le, Cuvelier de Trie, Jean G.-A.

Conseil imprudent, Le, Paillardelle, A.

Consentement forcé, Le, Guyot de Merville, Michel.

Conspirateur confondu, Le, ou La Patrie sauvée, Mittié, Jean-C.

Constance, Demoustier, Charles-A., Devienne, François (comp).

Constance et Colignan, Desriaux, Philippe., Blasius, Mathieu-F. (comp).

Constance et Gernand, Desriaux, Philippe., Blasius, Mathieu-F. (comp).

Constitution à Constantinople, La, Lavallée, Joseph.

Contentement passe richesse, Beaunoir, Alexandre-L.-B. Robineau, dit.

Conteur, Le, ou Les Deux postes, Picard, Louis-B.

Contretemps sur contretemps, Pigault-Lebrun, Charles-A.P. de L'Epinoy, dit.

Convalescent de qualité, Le, ou L'Aristocrate, Fabre d'Eglantine, Philippe-F.-N., Foignet, Charles-G. (comp).

Convention matrimoniale, La, Sedaine de Sarcy, Jean-F.

Convitato di pietra, Il, Bertati, Giovanni.

Coquette corrigée, La, Lanoue, Jean-B. Sauvé, dit.

Coquette et la fausse prude, La, Baron, Michel Boyron, dit.

Coquette fixée, La, Voisenon, Abbé-C.-H. de Fusée de.

Coquette généreuse, La, Belat-Bonneille, J.-B.

Coquette surannée, La, Bonnefoy de Bouyon, Abbé., Mengozzi, Bernardo (comp).

Cora, Valadier., Méhul, Etienne-N. (comp).

Cora ou La Prêtresse du soleil, Gabiot de Salins, Jean-L.

Coraline ou L'Ecole du théâtre, Béraud, Louis-F.-G.

Cordonnier de Damas, Le, ou La Lanterne magique, Pigault-Lebrun, Charles-A.P. de L'Epinoy, dit.

Corisandre ou Les Fous par enchantement, Linière, Comte de., Lebailly, Antoine-F., Langle, Honoré-F.-M. (comp).

Corne de vérité, La, ou L'Honnête homme dupe de sa bonne foi, Beaunoir, Alexandre-L.-B. Robineau, dit.

Corsaire, Le, Lachabeaussière, Auguste-E.-X. P. de., Dalayrac, Nicolas (comp).

Coucou, Sewrin, Charles-A. de Bassompierre, dit.

Coupe enchantée, La, Lafontaine, Jean de., Chevillet de Champmeslé, Charles.

Coupe enchantée, La, Rochon de Chabannes, Marc.

Coups de l'amour et de la fortune, Les, Quinault, Philippe., Gluck, Christoph (comp).

Coureur de successions, Le, Raffard-Brienne, J.S.

Courtisan devenu citoyen, Le, Billardon de Sauvigny, Louis-E.

Courtisane vertueuse, La, Ribié, César.

Courtisanes, Les, ou L'Ecole des moeurs, Palissot de Montenoy, Charles.

Cousin de tout le monde, Le, Picard, Louis-B.

Cousin et la cousine, Le, Savin-Desplasses., Cimarosa, Domenico (comp).

Cousin Jacques hors du salon, Beffroy de Reigny, Louis-A.

Couvent, Le, ou Les Fruits du caractère, Laujon, Pierre., Martini, Jean.-P.-E. (comp).

Couvent, Le, ou Les Voeux forcés, Gouges, Marie Gouze, dite Olympe de.

Cri de la nature, Le, ou Le Fils repentant, Tissot, Charles-L.

Crispin médecin, Hauteroche, Noel de.

Crispin rival de son maître, Lesage, Alain-R.

Rivière-Dufresney, Charles.

Descente en Angleterre, La, **Mittié, Jean-C.**

Déserteur, Le, **Gardel, Maximilien.**

Déserteur, Le, **Mercier, Louis-S.**

Déserteur, Le, **Sedaine, Michel-J.,** Grétry, André-E.-M. (comp).

*Déserteur de la montagne du Hamm, Le,***Dejaure, Jean-E. Bédéno.,** Kreutzer, Rodolpho (comp).

Désespoir de Jocrisse, Le, **Dorvigny, Louis-A.**

Despotisme et la liberté, Le, **Chaussier, Hector.,** Bizet.

Destin et les parques, Le, **Desfontaines, François-G. Fouques, dit.,** Dalayrac, Nicolas (comp).

Détenus, Les, ou Cange, **Marsollier des Vivetières, Benoît-J.,** Dalayrac, Nicolas (comp).

Dettes, Les, **Forgeot Nicolas-J.,** Méhul, Etienne-N. (comp).

Deuil, Le, **Hauteroche, Noel de.**

Deuil prématuré, Le, **Boutet de Monvel, Jacques-M.,** Dalayrac, Nicolas (comp).

Deux amis, Les, ou L'Héroïsme de l'amitié, **Parisau, Pierre-G.,** La Houssaye (comp).

Deux amis, Les, ou Le Négociant de Lyon, **Beaumarchais, Pierre-A.C. de.**

Deux Arlequins, Les, **Lenoble, Eustache.**

Deux Arlequins, Les, **Renout, Jean-J.-C.**

Deux Arlequins jumeaux, Les, **Lazzari, Ange**

Deux Arlequins rivaux, Les, **Lazzari, Ange**

Deux avares, Les, **Fenouillot de Falbaire de Quingey, Charles-G.,** Grétry, André-E.-M. (comp).

Deux Babillards, Les, **Gabiot de Salins, Jean-L.**

Deux billets, Les, **Florian, Jean-P.-C. de.**

Deux charbonniers ou Les Contrastes, **Beffroy de Reigny, Louis-A.**

Deux chasseurs et la laitière, Les, **Anseaume, Louis.,** Duni, Egidio-R. (comp).

Deux contrats, Les, ou Le Mariage inattendu, **Cizos-Duplessis, François.**

Deux cousins, Les, ou La Bonne amie, **La Ribardière, de.,** Desbrosses (comp).

Deux cousins, Les, ou Les Français à Séville, **Bourlin, Antoine-J., Pseud. Dumaniant.**

Deux cousins rivaux, Les, **Gabiot de Salins, Jean-L.**

Deux Crispins, Les, ou Encore des jumeaux, **Le Mière de Corvey, Jean.**

Deux fermiers, Les, **Sylvestre.**

Deux Figaro, Les, **Richaud-Martelly, Honoré-A.**

Deux font la paire, Les, ou Les Bottes de foin, **Parisau, Pierre-G.,** La Houssaye (comp).

Deux frères, Les, **Milcent, Jean-B.-G.-M. de.**

Deux frères, Les, **Patrat, Joseph.,** Trial, Armand-E. (comp).

Deux frères, Les, **Du Buisson, Paul-U.,** Anfossi, Pasquale (comp).

Deux grenadiers, Les, ou Les Quiproquos, **Patrat, Joseph.,** Trial, Armand-E. (comp).

Deux hermites, Les, **Planterre, Barthélemy.,** Loise (comp).

Deux jockeys, Les, **Pujoulx, Jean-B.**

Deux Jocrisses, Les, ou Le Commerce à l'eau, **Gouffé, Armand Alexandre Duval.**

Deux Julies, Les, ou Le Père crédule, **Bret, Antoine.**

Deux lettres, Les, **Delrieu, Etienne-J.-B.**

Deux Martines, Les, ou Le Procureur dupé, **Ducray-Duminil, François-G.**

Deux morts, Les, ou La Ruse de carnaval, **Patrat, Joseph.,** Trial, Armand-E. (comp).

Deux neveux, Les, **Gabiot de Salins, Jean-L.**

Deux noms, Les, **Imbert, Barthélemy.**

Deux oncles, Les, **Forgeot Nicolas-J.,** Méhul, Etienne-N. (comp).

Deux orphelines, Les, **Sewrin, Charles-A. de Bassompierre, dit.**

Deux orphelins, Les, **Robillard de Magnanville.**

Deux Panthéons, Les, ou L'Inauguration

Doria, **Loeillard d'Arvigny, Charles J.**, Berton, Henri-M. (comp).

Dormeur éveillé, Le, **Marmontel, Jean F.**, Grétry, André-E.-M. (comp).

Dorothée, **Audinot, Nicolas-M.**

Dorval ou Le Bon procureur, **Mayeur de St.-Paul, François-M.**

Dorval ou Le Fou par amour, **Ségur, Alexander-J.-P., Vte. de.**

Dot, La, **Desfontaines, François-G. Fouques, dit.**, Dalayrac, Nicolas (comp).

Dot de Suzette, La, **Dejaure, Jean-E. Bédéno.**, Kreutzer, Rodolpho (comp).

Double divorce, Le, ou Bienfait de la loi, **Forgeot Nicolas-J.**, Méhul, Etienne-N. (comp).

Double épreuve, La, ou Colinette à la cour, **Lourdet de Santerre, Jean.**, Grétry, André-E.-M. (comp).

Double feinte, La, ou Le Prêt rendu, **Lorville, L.-T.**

Double intrigue, La, ou L'Aventure embarrassante, **Bourlin, Antoine-J., Pseud. Dumaniant.**

Double prévention, La, **Pontaud.**

Double réconciliation, La, **De Lille, B. Dupont.**

Double veuvage, Le, **Rivière-Dufresny, Charles.**

Dragon de Thionville, Le, **Bourlin, Antoine-J.**, Pseud. Dumaniant.

Dragons en cantonnement, Les, **Pigault-Lebrun, Charles-A.P. de L'Epinoy, dit.**

Dragons et les bénédictines, Les, **Pigault-Lebrun, Charles-A.P. de L'Epinoy, dit.**

Droit du seigneur, Le, **Desfontaines, François-G. Fouques, dit.**, Dalayrac, Nicolas (comp).

Droit du seigneur, Le, ou L'Ecueil du sage, **Voltaire, F.-M. Arouet, dit Arouet de.**

Duc de Monmouth, Le, **Bodard de Tézay, Nicolas-M.-F.**

Due gemelle, Le, **Palomba, Giuseppe.**, Guglielmi, Pietro.-A. (comp).

Duel, Le, ou La Force du préjugé, **Rauquil-Lieutaud.**

Duel comique, Le, **Moline, Pierre-L.**, Carpentier (comp).

Duel supposé, Le, **Andrault de Langeron.**

Dumont ou Le Modèle des amis, **Laroche.**, Guillemain, Charles-J.

Dupe de soi-même, La, ou Le Défiant confondu, **Rousseau, Jean-Baptiste.**

Dupuis et Desronais, **Collé, Charles.**

Eclipse de lune, L', ou L'Astrologue qui tombe dans un puits, **Lachabeaussière, Auguste-E.-X. P. de.**, Dalayrac, Nicolas (comp).

Ecole amoureuse, L', **Bret, Antoine.**

Ecole de l'adolescence, L', **Bertin d'Antilly, Auguste-L.**, Philidor, François-A. Danican., Berton, Henri-M. (comp).

Ecole de la jeunesse, L', ou Le Retour sur soi-même, **La Chaussée, Pierre-C. N. de.**

Ecole des bourgeois, L', **Alainval, Abbé-L.-J.-C.-S. d'.**

Ecole des femmes, L', **Molière, Jean-B. Poquelin de.**

Ecole des frères, L', ou L'Incertitude paternelle, **Ponteuil, Triboulet, J.B., dit.**

Ecole des maris, L', **Molière, Jean-B. Poquelin de.**

Ecole des mères, L', **Desfontaines, François-G. Fouques, dit.**, Dalayrac, Nicolas (comp).

Ecole des mères, L', **La Chaussée, Pierre-C. N. de.**

Ecole des mères, L', **Marivaux, Pierre-C. de C. de.**

Ecole des parvenus, L', ou La Suite des deux petits savoyards, **Pujoulx, Jean-B.**

Ecole des pères, L', **Pieyre, Alexandre.**

Ecole des pères, L', **Piron, Alexis.**

Ecole du village, L', **Sewrin, Charles-A. de Bassompierre, dit.**

Ecole tragique, L', ou Cadet Roussel maître de déclamation, **Aude, Joseph.**

Ecolier devenu maître, L', ou Le Pédant joue, **Quétant, Antoine-F.**

Ecolier en vacances, L', **Picard, Louis-B.**

Ecoliers, Les, **Charlemagne, Armand.**

Ecosseuse, L', **Anseaume, Louis.**, Duni, Egidio-R. (comp).

Enlèvement au sérail, L', **Moline, Pierre-L.**, Carpentier (comp).

Enlèvement de Proserpine, L', ou Arlequin bouffon des enfers, **Destival de Braban.**

Enlèvement, L', ou La Caverne dans les Pyrénées, **Cuvelier de Trie, Jean G.-A.**

Enragé, L', ou Madame Thomas, **Carmontelle, Louis-C.**

Enrôlement du bûcheron, L', ou Le Recruteur, **Placide, Alexandre-P.-Bussart, dit.**

Enrôlement supposé, L', **Guillemain, Charles-J.**

Enseigne, L', ou Le Jeune militaire, **Schroeder, F.-L.**

Ensorcelés, Les, ou Jeannot et Jeannette, **Favart, Charles-S.**, Grétry, André-E.-M. (comp).

Entêté, L', ou On ne connaît jamais son enfant, **Crêton de Villeneuve.**

Enthousiaste, L', **Lamontagne, Pierre de.**

Entrée dans le monde, L', **Picard, Louis-B.**

Entrée de Dumouriez à Bruxelles, L', ou Les Vivandiers, **Gouges, Marie Gouze, dite Olympe de.**

Entrepreneur de spectacle, L', **Guillemain, Charles-J.**

Entrevue, L', **Vigée, Louis-J.-B.-E.**

Envieux, L', **Voltaire, F.-M. Arouet, dit Arouet de.**

Epicharis et Néron ou La Conspiration pour la liberté, **Legouvé, Gabriel-M.-J.-B.**

Epouse imprudente, L', **Desforges, Pierre-J.-B. Choudard de.**, Jadin, Louis-E. (comp).

Epoux à la mode, Les, **Beaunoir, Alexandre-L.-B. Robineau dit.**

Epoux généreux, L', ou Le Pouvoir des procédés, **Dejaure, Jean-E. Bédéno.**, Kreutzer, Rodolpho (comp).

Epoux mécontents, Les, ou Le Divorce, **Du Buisson, Paul-U.**, Anfossi, Pasquale (comp).

Epoux par supercherie, L', **Boissy, Louis de.**

Epoux républicain, L', **Pompigny, Maurin de.**

Epoux réunis, Les, **Dejaure, Jean-E. Bédéno.**, Kreutzer, Rodolpho (comp).

Epreuve, L', **Marivaux, Pierre-C. de C. de.**

Epreuve amoureuse, L', **Laffichard, Thomas.**

Epreuve délicate, L', **Grouvelle, Philippe-A.**

Epreuve délicate, L', **Roger.**

Epreuve du sentiment, L', ou Les Deux frères, **Person de Bérainville, L.-C.**

Epreuve par ressemblance, L', **Gosse, Etienne.**

Epreuve réciproque, L', **Alain, Robert.**, Legrand, Marc-A.

Epreuve singulière, L', ou La Jambe de bois, **Cubières-Palmezeaux, Michel de.**

Epreuve villageoise, L', **Desforges, Pierre-J.-B. Choudard de.**, Jadin, Louis-E. (comp).

Epreuves, Les, **Forgeot Nicolas-J.**, Méhul, Etienne-N. (comp).

Epreuves de l'amour, Les, **Anseaume, Louis.**, Duni, Egidio-R. (comp).

Epreuves du républicain, Les, ou L'Amour de la patrie, **Laugier, Marie.**, Champein, Stanislas (comp).

Ericie ou La Vestale, **Dubois-Fontanelle, Joseph-G.**

Esclavage des noirs, L', ou L'Heureux naufrage, **Gouges, Marie Gouze, dite Olympe de.**

Esclave à la mode, L', **La Salle d'Offremont, Adrien-N. P.**

Esope à la cour, **Boursault, Edmonde.**

Esope à la foire, **Landrin.**

Esope aux boulevards, **Gabiot de Salins, Jean-L.**

Esope seigneur de village, **Guillemain, Charles-J.**

Espagnols dans la Floride, Les, **Cuvelier de Trie, Jean G.-A.**

Espiègle, L', **Patrat, Joseph.**, Trial, Armand-E. (comp).

Espiègleries de garnison, Les, **Favières, Edmond-G.-F. de.**, Berton, Henri-M. (comp).

Esprit de contradiction, L', **Rivière-Dufresny, Charles.**

Esprit des prêtres, L', ou La Persécution des français en Espagne, **Prévost-**

Fausse délicatesse, La, ou The False Delicacy, Riccoboni, Marie-J.-L. de Mézières, Mme.

Fausse inconstance, La, Beauchamps, Pierre-F.-G. de.

Fausse magie, La, Marmontel, Jean F., Grétry, André-E.-M. (comp).

Fausse magie, La, Moncrif, François-A.-P. de.

Fausse mère, La, ou Une faute de l'amour, Destival de Braban.

Fausse nièce, La, Patrat, Joseph., Trial, Armand-E. (comp).

Fausse paysanne, La, ou L'Heureuse inconséquence, Piis, Chevalier-P.-A.-A. de., Barré, Pierre-Y.

Fausse peur, La, ou Les Vendanges de Taverni, Marsollier des Vivetières, Benoît-J., Dalayrac, Nicolas (comp).

Fausse veuve, La, Destouches, Philippe-N.

Fausses apparences, Les, ou L'Amant jaloux, Hèle, Thomas d'., Grétry, André-E.-M. (comp).

Fausses bonnes fortunes, Les, Sedaine de Sarcy, Jean-F.

Fausses confidences, Les, Marivaux, Pierre-C. de C. de.

Fausses consultations, Les, Dorvigny, Louis-A.

Fausses inconstances, Les, Mouslier de Moissy, Alexandre.

Fausses infidélités, Les, Barthe, Nicolas-T.

Fausses présomptions, Les, ou Le Jeune gouverneur, Robert.

Fauteuil, Le, Montanclos, Mme. Marie M. de.

Faux billets doux, Les, ou Les Trahisons réciproques, Pontaud.

Faux député, Le, Dorvo, Hyacinthe.

Faux insouciant, Le, Simonnet de Maisonneuve, L.-J.-B.

Faux lord, Le, Piccinni, Joseph-M., Piccinni, Niccolò (comp).

Faux mendiants, Les, Lebrun Tossa, Jean-A., Lesueur, Jean-F. (comp).

Faux monnayeurs, Les, ou La Vengeance, Cuvelier de Trie, Jean G.-A.

Faux Nicaise, Le, Hapdé, Jean-B.-A.

Faux savant, Le, ou L'Amant précepteur, Du Vaure, Jacques.

Faux serment, Le, Bombarde.

Faux talisman, Le, ou Rira bien qui rira le dernier, Guillemain, Charles-J.

Favart aux Champs-Elysées ou L'Apothéose, Barré, Pierre-Y., Radet, Jean-B., Desfontaines, François-G. Fouques, dit.

Fée bienfaisante, La, Pannard, Charles-F.

Fée Urgèle, La, Favart, Charles-S., Grétry, André-E.-M. (comp).

Feinte jardinière, La, Bulle., Anfossi, Pasquale (comp).

Feinte par amour, La, Dorat, Claude-J.

Félix ou L'Enfant trouvé, Sedaine, Michel-J., Grétry, André-E.-M. (comp).

Femme battue et contente, La, Guillemain, Charles-J.

Femme de 45 ans, La, Hoffman, François-B.

Femme fille et veuve, La, Legrand, Marc-A., Biancolelli, Pierre-F. dit Dominique.

Femme jalouse, La, Desforges, Pierre-J.-B. Choudard de., Jadin, Louis-E. (comp).

Femme juge et partie, La, Montfleury, Antoine Jacob, dit.

Femme qui a raison, La, Voltaire, F.-M. Arouet, dit Arouet de.

Femme qui sait se taire, La, Lavallée, Joseph.

Femmes curieuses, Les, ou Les Francs-maçons, Castaing, J.

Femmes et le secret, Les, Quétant, Antoine-F.

Femmes politiques, Les, Gosse, Etienne.

Femmes savantes, Les, Molière, Jean-B. Poquelin de.

Femmes vengées, Les, Sedaine, Michel-J., Grétry, André-E.-M. (comp).

Femmes, Les, Demoustier, Charles-A., Devienne, François (comp).

Fénelon ou Les Religieuses de Cambrai, Chénier, Marie-J.

Féodor et Lisinka ou Novogorod sauvée, Desforges, Pierre-J.-B. Choudard de., Jadin, Louis-E. (comp).

de.
Folle prétention, La, Verment-Mariton.
Fonds perdus, Les, Dancourt, Florent C.
Fontaine merveilleuse, La, ou Les époux musulmans, Loaisel de Tréogate, Joseph-M.
Forêt de Sicile, La, Guilbert de Pixerécourt, René-C.
Forêt enchantée, La, Servandoni, Jean-N., Geminiani, Francesco-S. (comp).
Forêt noire, La, ou Le Fils naturel, Arnould, Jean-F. Mussot, dit.
Forêt périlleuse, La, ou Les Brigands de la Calabre, Loaisel de Tréogate, Joseph-M.
Forgeron, Le, Delautel, G.
Fou par amour, Le, ou La Fatale épreuve, Mayeur de St.-Paul, François-M.
Fou raisonnable, Le, ou L'Anglais, Patrat, Joseph., Trial, Armand-E. (comp).
Fou raisonnable, Le, Poisson, Raymond.
Fourberies de marine, Les, ou Le Tuteur juge et partie, Rosoi, Barnabé-F. de, dit Durosoi.
Fourberies de Scapin, Les, Molière, Jean-B. Poquelin de.
Fourberies de Sganarelle, Les, Arnould, Jean-F. Mussot, dit.
Fourbisseur patriote, Le, Dorvigny, Louis-A.
Fragments, Les, ou Le Malade jaloux, Placide, Alexandre-P.-Bussart, dit.
Franc breton, Le, ou Le Négociant de Nantes, Dejaure, Jean-E. Bédéno., Kreutzer, Rodolpho (comp).
Franc marin, Le, ou La Gageure indiscrète, Pompigny, Maurin de.
Français à Cythère, Les, Petitain, Louis-G.
Français à Londres, Le, Boissy, Louis de.
Français en Huronie, Le, Bourlin, Antoine-J., Pseud. Dumaniant.
France régénérée, La, Chaussard, Pierre-J., Scio, Etienne (comp).
François et Rouffignac, Patrat, Joseph.,

Trial, Armand-E. (comp).
Frascatana, La, Levigni, F., Paisiello, Giovanni (comp).
Frédégilde ou Le Démon familier, Cuvelier de Trie, Jean G.-A.
Frères amis, Les, Beaunoir, Alexandre-L.-B. Robineau, dit.
Frondeur, Le, ou L'Ami des moeurs, Duverger, C.
Fureurs de l'amour, Les, Jacquelin, Jacques-A.
Gabrielle de Vergy, Belloy, Pierre-L.B. de.
Gageure, La, Lagrange, Nicolas., Procope-Couteau, M. Cottelli, dit.
Gageure, La, Pannard, Charles-F.
Gageure imprévue, La, Sedaine, Michel-J., Grétry, André-E.-M. (comp).
Gageure inutile, La, ou Plus de peur que de mal, Léger, François-P.-A.
Gagne-petit, Le, Guillemain, Charles-J.
Galant coureur, Le, ou L'Ouvrage d'un moment, Legrand, Marc-A., Biancolelli, Pierre-F., dit Dominique.
Galant jardinier, Le, Dancourt, Florent C.
Galant savetier, Le, Cordier de Saint-Firmin, Edmond.
Galathée, Poultier d'Elmotte, François-M., Bruni, Antonio-B. (comp).
Gargouille ou Le Raccommodeur de faïence, Mayeur de St.-Paul, François-M.
Gascon tel qu'il est, Le, Pompigny, Maurin de.
Gasconnades, Les, Lefèbre de Saint-Ildephont.
Gaston et Bayard, Belloy, Pierre-L.B. de.
Gâteau des rois, Le, Destival de Braban.
Gelosie villane, Delle, Sarti.
Geloso in cimento, Il, Bertati, Giovanni.
Général et le charbonnier, Le, ou Le Retour d'Italie, Martainville, Alphonse.
Général suédois, Le, Favart, Charles-S., Grétry, André-E.-M. (comp).

Foignet, Charles-G. (comp).

Héritiers, Les, **Lasante, Gilles de.**

Hermitage, L', **Sewrin, Charles-A. de Bassompierre, dit.**

Hérolhe américaine, L', **Arnould, Jean-F. Mussot, dit.**

Hérolhe de Mithier, L', **Duchaume.,** Barral.

Hérolhe suisse, L', ou Amour et courage, **Cuvelier de Trie, Jean G.-A.**

Hérolsme d'Alexandre, L', **Mayeur de St.-Paul, François-M.**

Héros américain, Le, **Ribié, César.**

Héros anglais, Le, **Ribié, César.**

Heureuse décade, L', **Barré, Pierre-Y.,** Radet, Jean-B., Desfontaines, François-G. Fouques, dit.

Heureuse découverte, L', **"Monsieur de B."**

Heureuse erreur, L', **Patrat, Joseph.,** Trial, Armand-E. (comp).

Heureuse indiscrétion, L', **Boutet de Monvel, Jacques-M.,** Dalayrac, Nicolas (comp).

Heureuse ivresse, L', ou Le Mari de retour, **Léger, François-P.-A.**

Heureuse nouvelle, L', **Dard d'Aucourt de Saint-Just, Claude.,** Marmontel, Jean-F. et Longchamps., Boïeldieu, François-A. (comp).

Heureuse supercherie, L', **Patrat, Joseph.,** Trial, Armand-E. (comp).

Heureuse vengeance, L', **Chevalier de Mont-Rémy.**

Heureusement, **Rochon de Chabannes, Marc.**

Heureux déguisement, L', ou La Gouvernante supposée, **Marcouville, Pierre-A. Lefèvre de.**

Heureux dépit, L', ou Les Enfantillages de l'amour, **Rauquil-Lieutaud.**

Heureux malheur, L', **Mouslier de Moissy, Alexandre.**

Heureux naufrage, L', **Barbier, Nicolas.**

Heureux procès, L', **Joly de Saint-Just.**

Heureux quiproquo, L', ou Le Présent, **Patrat, Joseph.,** Trial, Armand-E. (comp).

Heureux retour, L', **Fagan, Barthélemy-C.**

Heureux stratagème, L', ou Le Vol

supposé, **Saulnier, Guillaume.-N.-F.,** Jadin, Louis-E. (comp).

Hippocrate amoureux, **Lebrun.**

Hirza ou Les Illinois, **Billardon de Sauvigny, Louis-E.**

Histoire universelle, L', **Beffroy de Reigny, Louis-A.**

Hiver, L', ou Les Deux moulins, **Duchaume.,** Barral.

Hochets, Les, **Cammaille-Saint-Aubin, M.-C.**

Hommage du petit Vaudeville au grand Racine, L', **Barré, Pierre-Y.,** Radet, Jean-B., Desfontaines, François-G. Fouques, dit.

Homme à bonnes fortunes, L', **Baron, Michel Boyron, dit.**

Homme à la minute, L', ou Le Petit cousin, **Plancher de Valcour, dit Aristide.**

Homme à sentiments, L', ou Le Tartuffe des moeurs, **Chéron de la Bruyère, Louis-C.**

Homme au masque de fer, L', ou Le Souterrain, **Arnould, Jean-F. Mussot, dit.**

Homme aux deux femmes, L', **Taconet, Toussaint-G.**

Homme de lettres et l'homme d'affaires, L', **Charlemagne, Armand.**

Homme en loterie, L', **Fiévée, Joseph.**

Homme entre deux femmes, L', **Hapdé, Jean-B.-A.**

Homme et la femme comme il n'y en a point, L', ou Le Double travestissement, **Beaunoir, Alexandre-L.-B. Robineau, dit.**

Homme et le malheur, L', **Loeillard d'Arvigny, Charles J.,** Berton, Henri-M. (comp).

Homme noir, L', ou Spleen, **Maillé de Marencour.**

Homme sans façon, L', ou Le Vieux cousin, **Léger, François-P.-A.**

Homme singulier, L', **Destouches, Philippe-N.**

Hommes du jour, Les, **Allaire, Henri-A.**

Hommes, Les, **Saint-Foix, Germain-F.-P. de.**

Honnête aventurier, L', **Lebrun Tossa, Jean-A.,** Lesueur, Jean-F. (comp).

Honnête criminel, L', ou L'Amour filial,

Charles-G. (comp).

Intrigue secrète, L', ou La Veuve, Monnet, **Marie-M.**

Inventaire, L', **Labussière, Charles-H.-D. de.**

Iphigénie en Aulide, **Du Roullet, François-L. Gand Lebland.**, Gluck, Christoph (comp).

Iphigénie en Aulide, **Racine, Jean.**

Iphigénie en Tauride, **Guillard, Nicolas-F.**, Sacchini, Antonio (comp).

Iphigénie en Tauride, **Guimond de la Touche, Claude.**

Isabelle de Salisbury, **Fabre d'Eglantine, Philippe-F.-N.**, Foignet, Charles-G. (comp).

Isabelle et Gertrude ou Les Sylphes supposés, **Favart, Charles-S.**, Grétry, André-E.-M. (comp).

Isaure et Gernance ou Les Réfugiés, **Bourlin, Antoine-J., Pseud. Dumaniant.**

Isle des femmes, L', **Du Berry.**

Isle des foux, L', **Anseaume, Louis.**, Duni, Egidio-R. (comp).

Isola disabitata, L', **Metastasio, Pietro.**, Mengozzi, Bernardo (comp).

J.-J. Rousseau à ses derniers moments, **Bouilly, Jean-N.**

Jacobins aux enfers, Les, **Chaussier, Hector.**, Bizet.

Jacquot ou L'Ecole des mères, **Després, Jean-B.-D.**

Jaloux, Le, **Rochon de Chabannes, Marc.**

Jaloux corrigé, Le, **Pigault-Lebrun, Charles-A.P. de L'Epinoy, dit.**

Jaloux désabusé, Le, **Campistron, Jean-G. de.**

Jaloux malgré lui, Le, **Delrieu, Etienne-J.-B.**

Jaloux sans amour, Le, **Imbert, Barthélemy.**

Janot chez le dégraisseur ou A quelque chose malheur est bon, **Dorvigny, Louis-A.**

Janot ou Les Battus paient l'amende, **Dorvigny, Louis-A.**

Jardinier et son seigneur, Le, **Sedaine, Michel-J.**, Grétry, André-E.-M. (comp).

Je cherche mon père, **Dorvo, Hya-**

cinthe.

Jean Baptiste, **Beffroy de Reigny, Louis-A.**

Jean bête à la foire ou Les Deux niais, **Beaumarchais, Pierre-A.C. de.**

Jean Calas, **Chénier, Marie-J.**

Jean Calas, **Laya, Jean-L.**

Jean et Geneviève, **Favières, Edmond-G.-F. de.**, Berton, Henri-M. (comp).

Jean Gilles ou Le Frère de Jocrisse, **Dorvigny, Louis-A.**

Jean Hennuyer ou L'Evêque de Lisieux, **Mercier, Louis-S.**

Jean la Fontaine, **Jacquelin, Jacques-A.**

Jean la Fontaine, **Parisau, Pierre-G.**, La Houssaye (comp).

Jean qui pleure et Jean qui rit, **Sedaine de Sarcy, Jean-F.**

Jean Racine avec ses enfants, **Jacquelin, Jacques-A.**

Jean-sans-terre ou La Mort d'Arthur, **Ducis, Jean-F.**

Jeanne d'Arc à Orléans, **Desforges, Pierre-J.-B. Choudard de.**, Jadin, Louis-E. (comp).

Jeannette ou Les Battus ne payent pas l'amende, **Beaunoir, Alexandre-L.-B. Robineau, dit.**

Jenneval ou Le Barnevelt français, **Mercier, Louis-S.**

Jérôme et Fanchonette, **Vadé, Jean-J.**

Jérôme pointu, **Beaunoir, Alexandre-L.-B. Robineau, dit.**

Jeu de l'amour et du hasard, Le, **Marivaux, Pierre-C. de C. de.**

Jeune homme à l'épreuve, Le, **Destouches, Philippe-N.**

Jeune homme du jour, Le, ou La Journée d'un jeune homme, **Mayeur de St.-Paul, François-M.**

Jeune homme, Le, **Bastide, Jean-F. de.**

Jeune hôtesse, La, **Carbon de Flins des Oliviers, Claude-M.**

Jeune indienne, La, **Chamfort, Sébastien-R.-N.**

Jeune sage et le vieux fou, Le, **Hoffman, François-B.**

Jeunes amants, Les, **Lebas.**, Champein, Stanislas (comp).

Jockey, Le, **Hoffman, François-B.**

Joconde, **Léger, François-P.-A.**

Légataire universel, Le, **Regnard, Jean-F. Renard,** dit., Rivière-Dufresney, Charles.

Legs, Le, **Marivaux, Pierre-C. de C. de.**

Lendemain de la bataille de Fleurus, Le, **Bertin D'Antilly, Auguste-L.,** Philidor, François-A. Danican et Berton, Henri-M. (comp).

Léon ou Le Château de Montenero, **Hoffman, François-B.**

Léonidas ou Le Départ des spartiates, **"Guilbert, Citoyen".**

Léonidas ou Les Spartiates, **Guilbert de Pixerécourt, René-.C.**

Léonore ou L'Amour conjugal, **Bouilly, Jean-N.**

Lettre de cachet, La, **Adolphe, D.**

Lettre, La, **Loeillard d'Arvigny, Charles J.,** Berton, Henri-M. (comp).

Lévite d'Ephraïm, Le, **Lemercier, Népomucène-L.**

Libérateur, Le, **Mercier, Louis-S.**

Liberté conquise, La, **Harny de Guerville.,** Mme Favart., Sodi, Charles (comp)., Favart, Charles-S.

Liberté des nègres, La, **Gassier, J.-M.,** Pseud. L. de Saint-Hughes.

Ligue des fanatiques et des tyrans, La, **Ronsin, Charles-P.**

Limosins, Les, **Piis, Chevalier-P.-A.-A. de.,** Barré, Pierre-Y.

Lion parlant, Le, **Charrin, Pierre-J.,** Lapotre, le P. Arthur.

Lisbeth, **Favières, Edmond-G.-F. de.,** Berton, Henri-M. (comp).

Lise et Colin ou La Surveillance inutile, **Gaveaux, Pierre (comp).**

Lisia, **Monnet, Jean.**

Lisidore et Monrose, **Monnet, Jean.**

Locandiera, La, **Tonioli, G.,** Paisiello, Giovanni (comp).

Lodoiska, **Loraux, Claude-F. Fillette,** dit., Chérubini, Luigi (comp).

Lodoiska ou Les Tartares, **Dejaure, Jean-E. Bédéno.,** Kreutzer, Rodolpho (comp).

Loi d'accord avec la nature, La, **Deschamps, Jacques-M.**

Loi de Jatab, Le, ou Le Turc à Paris, **Bourlin, Antoine-J.,** Pseud. Dumaniant.

Loizerolles ou L'Héroïsme paternel, **Ducaire.,** Jadin, Louis-E. (comp).

Lord et le jockey, Le, **Lutaine.,** Leblanc de Guillet, Antonio Blanc, dit (comp).

Lot mal employé, Le, **Sylvestre.**

Loterie, La, **Dancourt, Florent C.**

Louis IX en Egypte, **Guillard, Nicolas-F.,** Sacchini, Antonio (comp).

Louis XII, père du peuple, **Ronsin, Charles-P.**

Louis XIV et le masque de fer ou Les Princes jumeaux, **Legrand, Marc-A.,** Biancolelli, Pierre-F., dit Dominique.

Louise et Volsan, **Dejaure, Jean-E. Bédéno.,** Kreutzer, Rodolpho (comp).

Louise ou La Réconciliation, **Candeille, Amélie-Julie.**

Louise ou Le Théâtre, **Cammaille-Saint-Aubin, M.-C.**

Loups et les brebis, Les, ou La Nuit d'été, **Sewrin, Charles-A. de Bassompierre, dit.**

Lovelace, **Lemercier, Népomucène-L.**

Lovelace français, Le, **Boutet de Monvel, Jacques-M.,** Dalayrac, Nicolas (comp).

Lucette et Lucas, **Forgeot Nicolas-J.,** Méhul, Etienne-N. (comp).

Lucile, **Marmontel, Jean F.,** Grétry, André-E.-M. (comp).

Lucile et Dercourt, **Loaisel de Tréogate, Joseph-M.**

Lucrèce, **Arnault, Antoine-V.**

Macbeth, **Ducis, Jean-F.**

Madame Angot ou La Poissarde parvenue, **Eve, Antoine-F. , dit Maillot.**

Madame Miroton, **Beaunoir, Alexandre-L.-B. Robineau dit.**

Madame Tintamarre, **Beaunoir, Alexandre-L.-B. Robineau dit.**

Madelon Friquet et Monsieur Vacarmini, **Beaunoir, Alexandre-L.-B. Robineau dit.**

Magdelon, **Beffroy de Reigny, Louis-A.**

Magnifique, Le, **Sedaine, Michel-J.,** Grétry, André-E.-M. (comp).

Mahomet, **Voltaire, F.-M. Arouet, dit Arouet de.**

Maire de village, Le, **Boissy, Louis de.**

Maison à deux portes, La, **Farin de Hautemer.**

Bassompierre, dit.

Moitié du chemin, La, **Picard, Louis-B.**

Molinarella, La, ou L'Amor contrasto, **Palomba, Giuseppe.,** Guglielmi, Pietro.-A. (comp).

Moment d'humeur, Un, **Hennequin, Louis.,** Anfossi, Pasquale (comp).

Moment dangereux, Le, **Dorvigny, Louis-A.**

Monet, directeur de l'Opéra comique, **Barré, Pierre-Y.,** Radet, Jean-B., Desfontaines, François-G. Fouques, dit.

Monnaie ne fait rien en amour, **Beaunoir, Alexandre-L.-B. Robineau, dit.**

Monsieur de Bièvre ou L'Abus de l'esprit, **Chazet, René-A.-P. de.**

Monsieur de Crac à Paris, **Charlemagne, Armand.**

Monsieur de Crac dans son petit castel ou Les Gascons, **Collin D'Harleville, Jean-F.**

Monsieur de Craquignac ou Le Pauvre ermite, **Grenier.,** Champein, Stanislas (comp).

Monsieur de Pourceaugnac, **Molière, Jean-B. Poquelin de.**

Mont Alphea, Le, ou Le Français jatabite, **Lebrun Tossa, Jean-A.,** Lesueur, Jean-F. (comp).

Montagnards, Les, **Dehesse, Jean-F. Deshayes, dit.**

Montagnards, Les, **Monnet, Marie M.**

Montagnards, Les, ou L'Ecole de la bienfaisance, **Pujoulx, Jean-B.**

Montano et Stéphanie, **Dejaure, Jean-E. Bédéno.,** Kreutzer, Rodolpho (comp).

Montoni ou Le Château d'Udolphe, **Duval, Alexandre-V.P.,** Deshayes, Prosper-D. (comp).

Montre, La, ou Les Effets du repentir, **De Lille, B. Dupont.**

Mort d'Abel, La, **Legouvé, Gabriel-M.-J.-B.**

Mort d'Hercule, La, **Gabiot de Salins, Jean-L.**

Mort de Beaurepaire, La, ou Les Héros français, **Bourlin, Antoine-J., Pseud. Dumaniant.**

Mort de Cadet Roussel, La, **Boullault,**
Mathurin-J.

Mort de César, La, **Voltaire, F.-M. Arouet, dit Arouet de.**

Mort de Madame Angot, La, **Cordier de Saint-Firmin, Edmond.**

Mort de Molière, La, **Cubières-Palmezeaux, Michel de.**

Mort de Socrate, La, **Billardon de Sauvigny, Louis-E.**

Mort du boeuf gras, La, **Taconet, Toussaint-G.**

Mort du capitaine Cook à son troisième voyage au nouveau monde, **Arnould, Jean-F. Mussot, dit.**

Mort du chevalier d'Assas, Le, ou Le Bataille de Clostercamp, **Dubois, Alexis.**

Mort du Maréchal de Turenne, La, **Cuvelier de Trie, Jean G.-A.**

Mort imaginaire, Le, **Ponteuil, Triboulet, J.B., dit.**

Mort marié, Le, **Sedaine, Michel-J.,** Grétry, André-E.-M. (comp).

Mort vivant, Le, **Beaunoir, Alexandre-L.-B. Robineau, dit.**

Mort vivant, Le, **Boursault, Edmonde.**

Moulin de sans souci, Le, **Dieulafoy, Michel.**

Muet, Le, **Brueys, David-A. de.,** Palaprat, Joseph.

Muette, La, **Ymond, B. Louis.**

Mur mitoyen, Le, ou Le Divorce manqué, **Barré, Pierre-Y.,** Radet, Jean-B., Desfontaines, François-G. Fouques, dit.

Muses, Les, **Danchet, Antoine.**

Muses rivales, Les, **La Harpe, Jean-F. de.**

Muses, Les, ou Le Triomphe d'Apollon, **Hus, Eugène.**

Musicomanie, La, **Audinot, Nicolas-M.**

Mutius Scaevola, **Duryrer.**

Mutius Scaevola, **Luce de Lancival, Jean-C.-J.**

Myrrha, **Petitot, Claude-B.**

Mystères d'Udolphe, Les, **Radcliffe, Ann.**

Nadir ou Thamas Kouli-kan, **Du Buisson, Paul-U.,** Anfossi, Pasquale (comp).

Naissance de la pantomime, La, **Cuvelier de Trie, Jean G.-A.**

Antoine-J., Pseud. Dumaniant.

Nuit blanche, La, **Thiemet.**

Nuit champêtre, La, ou Les Mariages de dépit, **Mague de Saint-Aubin, Jacques.**

Nuit de Cadix, La, ou La Mère rivale de sa fille, **Maupinot.**

Nuit de Henri IV, La, ou Le Charbonnier est maître chez lui, **Destival de Braban.**

Nuit espagnole, La, **Fiévée, Joseph.**

Nuit espagnole, La, ou Le Frère jaloux et barbare, **Beaunoir, Alexandre-L.-B. Robineau, dit.**

Nuit espagnole, La, ou La Cloison, **Guilbert de Pixerécourt, René-.C.**

Nuit espagnole, La, ou Le Contre-temps, **Fiévée, Joseph.**

Nymphes de Diane, Les, **Favart, Charles-S.,** Grétry, André-E.-M. (comp).

Obligeant maladroit, L', **Famin, Pierre-N.**

Obstacle imprévu, L', ou L'Obstacle sans obstacle, **Destouches, Philippe-N.**

Oedipe, **Voltaire, F.-M. Arouet, dit Arouet de.**

Oedipe à Colone, **Ducis, Jean-F.**

Oedipe à Colone, **Guillard, Nicolas-F.,** Sacchini, Antonio (comp).

Oedipe à Thèbes ou Jocaste et Oedipe, **Duprat de Latouloubre.,** Méreaux, Nicolas-J. (comp).

Oedipe chez Admète, **Ducis, Jean-F.**

Officier de fortune, L', ou Les Deux militaires, **Patrat, Joseph.,** Trial, Armand-E. (comp).

Officieux, L', **La Salle d'Offremont, Adrien-N. P.**

Officieux maladroit, L', **Pompigny, Maurin de.**

Offrande à la liberté, L', **Gossec, François-J. (comp).**

Oies du frère Philippe, Les, **Montorcier.**

Oiseau de Lubin, L', ou Il n'y a pas de souris qui ne trouve son trou, **Mayeur de St.-Paul, François-M.**

Oiseau perdu et retrouvé, L', **Barré, Pierre-Y.,** Radet, Jean-B., Desfontaines, François-G. Fouques, dit.

Oiseaux d'Idalie, Les, **Chaussier, Hector.,** Bizet.

Olimpie, **Guillard, Nicolas-F.,** Sacchini, Antonio (comp).

Ombre de Jean-Jacques Rousseau, L', **Desriaux, Philippe.,** Blasius, Mathieu-F. (comp).

Ombre de Mirabeau, L', **Dejaure, Jean-E. Bédéno.,** Kreutzer, Rodolpho (comp).

Omelette miraculeuse, L', **Dorvigny, Louis-A.**

On fait ce qu'on peut et non pas ce qu'on veut, **Dorvigny, Louis-A.**

On ne s'avise jamais de tout, **Sedaine, Michel-J.,** Grétry, André-E.-M. (comp).

On respire, **Tissot, Charles-L.**

Oncle et le neveu, L', **Beaugeard, Jean-S.-F.**

Oncle et le neveu, amateurs de comédie, L', **Ribié, César.**

Oncle valet, L', **Duval, Alexandre-V.P.,** Deshayes, Prosper-D. (comp).

Opera-comique, L', **Ségur, Alexander-J.-P., Vte. de.**

Ophis, **Lemercier, Népomucène-L.**

Optimiste, L', ou L'Homme content de tout, **Collin d'Harleville, Jean-F.**

Oracle, L', **Saint-Foix, Germain-F.-P. de.**

Orage, L', **Monnet, Jean.**

Orage, L', ou Quel guignon, **Velier.,** Navoigille, Julien (comp).

Oreste, **Voltaire, F.-M. Arouet, dit Arouet de.**

Orgon dans la lune ou Crédule trompé, **Lépidor, M.-J. Mathieu, dit.,** Paisiello, Giovanni (comp).

Orgueilleuse, L', **Gabiot de Salins, Jean-L.**

Original, L', **Hoffman, François-B.**

Originaux, Les, **Fagan, Barthélemy-C.**

Orphée aux enfers, **Dorvigny, Louis-A.**

Orphée et Euridice, **Moline, Pierre-L.,** Carpentier (comp).

Orphelin, L', **Pigault-Lebrun, Charles-A.P. de L'Epinoy, dit.**

Orphelin anglais, L', **Longueil, Charles-H. de.**

Orphelin de la Chine, L', **Voltaire, F.-M. Arouet, dit Arouet de.**

Adrien-N. P.

Peintre amoureux de son modèle, Le, **Anseaume, Louis.**, Duni, Egidio-R. (comp).

Père aveugle, Le, **Charlemagne, Armand.**

Père comme il y en a peu, Le, ou Le Mariage assorti, **Picot-Belloc, Jean.**

Père de famille, Le, **Diderot, Denis.**

Père Duchesne, Le, ou La Mauvaise habitude, **Dorvigny, Louis-A.**

Père supposé, Le, ou Les époux dès le berceau, **Delrieu, Etienne-J.-B.**

Perruque blonde, La, **Picard, Louis-B.**

Perruque de laine ou L'Entêté, **Desforges, Pierre-J.-B. Choudard de.**, Jadin, Louis-E. (comp).

Pessimiste, Le, ou L'Homme mécontent de tout, **Pigault-Lebrun, Charles-A.P. de L'Epinoy, dit.**

Petit Armand, Le, ou Le Bienfait des perruques, **Dufresnoy, Citoyenne.**

Petit matelot, Le, ou Le Mariage impromptu, **Pigault-Lebrun, Charles-A.P. de L'Epinoy, dit.**

Petit Orphée, Le, **Rouhier-Deschamps, J.**, Renault (comp).

Petit poucet, Le, ou L'Orphelin de la forêt, **Cuvelier de Trie, Jean G.-A.**

Petit sacristain, Le, ou Le Départ des novices, **Demautort, Jacques-B.**

Petite métromanie, La, ou La Pièce nouvelle, **Chazet, René-A.-P. de.**

Petite Nanette, La, **Beffroy de Reigny, Louis-A.**

Petite ruse, La, **Patrat, Joseph.**, Trial, Armand-E. (comp).

Petits auvergnats, Les, **Guilbert de Pixerécourt, René-.C.**

Petits montagnards, Les, **Plancher de Valcour, dit Aristide.**

Peuples et les rois, Les, ou Le Tribunal de la raison, **Cizos-Duplessis, François.**

Phanor et Angela, **Faur, Louis-F.**

Phèdre et Hippolyte, **Racine, Jean.**

Phèdre, **Hoffman, François-B.**

Phénix, Le, ou L'Isle des vieilles, **Cuvelier de Trie, Jean G.-A.**

Philanthrope, Le, ou L'Ami de tout le monde, **Legrand, Marc-A.**, Biancolelli, Pierre-F., dit Dominique.

Philinte de Molière, Le, ou La Suite du misanthrope, **Fabre d'Eglantine, Philippe-F.-N.**, Foignet, Charles-G. (comp).

Philippe et Georgette, **Boutet de Monvel, Jacques-M.**, Dalayrac, Nicolas (comp).

Philoctète, **Ferrand, Comte Antoine-F.-C.**

Philoctète, **La Harpe, Jean-F. de.**

Philosophe imaginaire, Le, **Du Buisson, Paul-U.**, Anfossi, Pasquale (comp).

Philosophe marié, Le, ou Le Mari honteux de l'être, **Destouches, Philippe-N.**

Philosophe sans le savoir, Le, **Sedaine, Michel-J.**, Grétry, André-E.-M. (comp).

Philosophe soi-disant, Le, **Bernouilly, L.P. de.**

Philosophe soi-disant, Le, **Destival de Braban.**

Pied de Boeuf, Le, **Gardel, Maximilien.**

Pierre Bagnolet et Claude Bagnolet, son fils, **Deville, Jean-B.-L.**

Pierre de Provence, **Arnould, Jean-F. Mussot, dit.**

Pierre de Provence ou La Belle Maguelonne, **Mayeur de St.-Paul, François-M.**

Pierre de Provence, **Leprêtre.**

Pierre le cruel, **Belloy, Pierre-L.B. de.**

Pierre le grand, **Bouilly, Jean-N.**

Pierre Luc ou Le Cultivateur du Montblanc, **Hapdé, Jean-B.-A.**

Pierrot roi de Cocagne, **Dubut, Laurent.**

Piété filiale, La, ou La Jambe de bois, **Courtial.**

Piques, Les, **Plancher de Valcour, dit Aristide.**

Piron avec ses amis ou Les Moeurs du temps passé, **Deschamps, Jacques-M.**

Place Maubert, La, **Dorvigny, Louis-A.**

Plaideurs, Les, **Racine, Jean.**

Plaire c'est commander, **La Salle d'Offremont, Adrien-N. P.**

Plaisir et la gloire, Le, **Sewrin, Charles-A. de Bassompierre, dit.**

Plaisirs de l'hospitalité, Les, **Piis, Chevalier P.-A.-A. de.**, Barré, Pierre-Y.

Alexandre-V.P., Deshayes, Prosper-D. (comp).

Prise de Toulon, La, **Picard, Louis-B.**

Prisonnier, Le, ou La Ressemblance, **Duval, Alexandre-V.P.,** Deshayes, Prosper-D. (comp).

Prisonnier français, Le, ou Le Bienfait récompensé, **Guillet.**

Prisonnière, La, **Jouy, Victor-J. Etienne, dit de.,** Longchamps, Charles de.

Prisonniers français à Liège, Les, **Guillemain, Charles-J.**

Prisonniers français en Angleterre, Les, **Dognon, Jean-F.,** Foignet, Charles-G. (comp)., Rebory.

Prix, Le, ou L'Embarras du choix, **Radet, Jean-B.,** Desfontaines, François-G. Fouques, dit.

Prix académique, Le, **Parisau, Pierre-G.,** La Houssaye (comp).

Prix de la vertu, Le, ou Le Désespéré, **Dorvigny, Louis-A.**

Procès de Socrate, Le, ou Le Régime des anciens temps, **Collot d'Herbois, J.-M.**

Procès des ariettes et des vaudeville, Le, **Favart, Charles-S.,** Grétry, André-E.-M. (comp).

Procureur arbitre, Le, **Poisson, Philippe.**

Prodigue par bienfaisance et le chevalier d'industrie, Le, **Bourlin, Antoine-J.,** Pseud. Dumaniant.

Projet extravagant, Le, **Vigée, Louis-J.-B.-E.**

Projet manqué, Le, ou Arlequin taquin, **Barré, Pierre-Y.,** Radet, Jean-B., Desfontaines, François-G. Fouques, dit.

Projets de mariage, Les, ou Les Deux militaires, **Duval, Alexandre-V.P.,** Deshayes, Prosper-D. (comp).

Promesses de mariage, Les, **Desforges, Pierre-J.-B. Choudard de.,** Jadin, Louis-E. (comp).

Provençale, La, **Lafont, Joseph de.,** Gilliers, Jean-C. (comp).

Proverbes, Les, **Dorvigny, Louis-A.**

Prude, La, **Lemercier, Népomucène-L.**

Psyché, **Gardel, Pierre-G.,** Muller, Ernest-L. (comp).

Pulchérie, **Corneille, Pierre.**

Punition, La, **Desfaucherets, J.L.B.,** Lebrun, Louis-S. (comp).

Pupille, La, **Fagan, Barthélemy-C.**

Pygmalion, **Rousseau, Jean-Jacques.**

Quart d'heure de Rabelais, Le, **Dieulafoy, Michel.**

Quatre coins, Les, **Barré, Pierre-Y.,** Radet, Jean-B., Desfontaines, François-G. Fouques, dit.

Quatre fils Aymon, Les, **Arnould, Jean-F. Mussot, dit.**

Qui court deux lièvres n'en attrape aucun, **Dorvigny, Louis-A.**

Qui paye les violons ne danse pas toujours, **Beaunoir, Alexandre-L.-B. Robineau, dit.**

Quintius Cincinnatus, **Arnault, Antoine-V.**

Quintus Fabius ou La Discipline romaine, **Legouvé, Gabriel-M.-J.-B.**

Quiproco nocturnes, **Cuvelier de Trie, Jean G.-A.**

Quiproquo de l'hôtellerie, Le, **Quétant, Antoine-F.**

Racoleurs, Les, **Vadé, Jean-J.**

Ramoneur, Le, **Theaulon de Lambert, Marie-E.-G.-M. Ps. Léon.**

Ramoneur prince et le prince Ramoneur, Le, **Pompigny, Maurin de.**

Raoul Barbe-bleue, **Sedaine, Michel-J.,** Grétry, André-E.-M. (comp).

Raoul, sire de Créqui, **Boutet de Monvel, Jacques-M.,** Dalayrac, Nicolas (comp).

Raymond V, comte de Toulouse ou L'Epreuve inutile, **Sedaine, Michel-J.,** Grétry, André-E.-M. (comp).

Réclamations contre l'emprunt forcé, Les, **Dorvigny, Louis-A.**

Réconciliation des ennemis généreux, La, **Parisau, Pierre-G.,** La Houssaye (comp).

Relâche au petit théâtre de Cadet Roussel ou Le Déluge universel, **Aude, Joseph.**

Renaud, **Le Boeuf, Jean-J.**

Renaud d'Ast, **Radet, Jean-B.,** Desfontaines, François-G. Fouques, dit.

Rencontre en voyage, La, **Pujoulx, Jean-B.**

Rencontre sur rencontre, **Radet, Jean-**

inique.

Roi et le fermier, Le, Sedaine, Michel-J., Grétry, André-E.-M. (comp).

Roi et le pèlerin, Le, Lavallée, Joseph.

Roi Lear, Le, Ducis, Jean-F.

Roi Théodore à Venise, Le, Du Buisson, Paul-U., Anfossi, Pasquale (comp).

Roi Théodore à Venise, Le, Moline, Pierre-L., Carpentier (comp).

Roland, Marmontel, Jean F., Grétry, André-E.-M. (comp).

Roland de Montglave, Loaisel de Tréogate, Joseph-M.

Romagnesi, Saugiers, Marc-A., Plantade, Charles-H. (comp).

Roman, Le, Gosse, Etienne.

Roméo et Juliette, Ducis, Jean-F.

Roméo et Juliette, Ségur, Alexander-J.-P., Vte. de.

Rosalie, Parisau, Pierre-G., La Houssaye (comp).

Rosaline et Floricourt, Ségur, Alexander-J.-P., Vte. de.

Rose et Aurèle, Picard, Louis-B.

Rose et Carloman ou La Rose d'amour, Dubreuil, Alphonse-D., Desaugiers, Marc-A. (comp).

Rose et Colas, Sedaine, Michel-J., Grétry, André-E.-M. (comp).

Rose et le bouton, La, ou Le Temple de l'hymen, Beaunoir, Alexandre-L.-B. Robineau dit.

Rose et Picard ou La Suite de l'optimiste, Collin d'Harleville, Jean-F.

Rose ou La Suite de Fanfan et Colas, Beaunoir, Alexandre-L.-B. Robineau, dit.

Rosenthal ou Le Vol à tire d'aile, Henrion, Charles.

Rosière, La, Gardel, Maximilien.

Rosière de Salenci, La, Favart, Charles-S., Grétry, André-E.-M. (comp).

Rosière de Salency, La, Masson de Pezay, Alexandre-F.-J., Grétry, André-E.-M. (comp).

Rosière républicaine, La, ou La Fête de la vertu, Maréchal, Pierre-Sylvain., Grétry, André-E.-M. (comp).

Rosine et Zelis, Léger, François-P.-A.

Roxelane et Mustapha, Simonnet de Maisonneuve, L.-J.-B.

Royalistes de la Vendée, Les, ou Les époux républicains, Cuvelier de Trie, Jean G.-A.

Roze, ou Les Festes de l'hymen, La, Piron, Alexis.

Rupture inutile, La, Forgeot, Nicolas-J., Méhul, Etienne-N. (comp).

Ruse d'amour, La, ou L'épreuve, Maillé de Marencour.

Ruse d'aveugle, La, Avisse, J.-B.

Ruse inutile, La, Pompigny, Maurin de.

Ruse villageoise, La, Sewrin, Charles-A. de Bassompierre, dit.

Ruses d'amour, Les, Poisson, Philippe.

Ruses de Frontin, Les, Marchand.

Ruses déjouées, Les, Bourlin, Antoine-J., Pseud. Dumaniant.

Ruses du mari, Les, Delrieu, Etienne-J.-B.

Sabinus, Chabanon, Michel-P.-G. de., Gossec, François-J. (comp).

Sabotier, Le, ou Les Huit sols, Landrin.

Sabotiers, Les, Beaupré-Larigaudière.

Sabotiers, Les, Pigault-Lebrun, Charles-A.P. de L'Epinoy, dit.

Sabots, Les, Sedaine, Michel-J., Grétry, André-E.-M. (comp).

Sage étourdi, Le, Boissy, Louis de.

Sagesse humaine, La, ou Arlequin memnon, Favart, Charles-N.

Saint déniché, Le, ou La Saint-Nicolas d'été, Piis, Chevalier P.-A.-A. de., Barré, Pierre-Y.

Saint-Aubin ou Le Bienfait et la reconnaissance, Rouhier-Deschamps, J., Renault (comp).

Saint-Elmont et Verseuil ou Le Danger d'un soupçon, Ségur, Alexander-J.-P., Vte. de.

Salpêtriers républicains, Les, Tissot, Charles-L.

Sans-culottides, Les, Guillemain, Charles-J.

Santeuil et Dominique, Barré, Pierre-Y., Radet, Jean-B., Desfontaines, François-G. Fouques, dit.

Santeuil, ou Le Chanoine au cabaret, Brazier, Nicolas., Villeneuve, Ferdinand Vallon de., Charles de Livry.

Sapho, Salm-Reifferscheid-Dyck, Constance-M., Martini, Jean.-P.-E.

Soldat prussien, Le, ou Le Bon fils, **Bourlin, Antoine-J.**, Pseud. Dumaniant.

Soliman II ou Les Trois sultanes, **Favart, Charles-S.**, Grétry, André-E.-M. (comp).

Solitaires de Normandie, Les, **Piis, Chevalier P.-A.-A. de.**, Barré, Pierre-Y.

Solitude, La, **Guillemain, Charles-J.**

Somnambule, Le, **Pont-de-Veyle, A. de Feriol, Comte de.**

Sophie de Brabant, **Parisau, Pierre-G.**, La Houssaye (comp).

Sophie et Derville, **Colleville, Anne-H. de Saint-Léger, Dame de.**

Sophie et Moncars ou L'Intrigue portugaise, **Guy, Jean-H.**, Grétry, André-E.-M. (comp).

Sophronime ou La Reconnaisance, **Demoustier, Charles-A.**, Devienne, François (comp).

Sorcier, Le, **Poinsinet, Antoine-A.-H.**

Sorcière, La, **Ravrio, Antoine-A.**

Sorcière, La, **Sewrin, Charles-A. de Bassompierre, dit.**

Sot orgueilleux, Le, ou L'Ecole des élections, **Fabre d'Eglantine, Philippe-F.-N.**, Foignet, Charles-G. (comp).

Soubrette, La, ou L'Etui de harpe, **Hoffman, François-B.**

Soubrette rusée, La, **Cailleau, André-C.**

Soufflet, Le, **Gabiot de Salins, Jean-L.**

Souliers Mordorés, Les, ou La Cordonnière allemande, **Ferrières, A. de.**, Plantade, Charles-H. (comp).

Souper de Henri IV, Le, ou Le Laboureur devenu gentilhomme, **Boutillier, Maximilien-J.**, Deshayes, Prosper-D. (comp).

Souper de Molière, Le, ou La Soirée d'Auteuil, **Cadet de Gassicourt, Charles-L.**

Souper des dupes, Le, **Beaunoir, Alexandre-L.-B. Robineau, dit.**

Souper des Jacobins, Le, **Charlemagne, Armand.**

Souper imprévu, Le, ou Le Chanoine de Milan, **Duval, Alexandre-V.P.**, Deshayes, Prosper-D. (comp).

Sourd, Le, **Lachabeaussière, Auguste-E.-X. P. de.**, Dalayrac, Nicolas (comp).

Sourd, Le, ou L'Auberge pleine, **Desforges, Pierre-J.-B. Choudard de.**, Jadin, Louis-E. (comp).

Sourd et l'aveugle, Le, **Patrat, Joseph.**, Trial, Armand-E. (comp).

Sourd guéri, Le, ou Les Tu et les vous, **Léger, François-P.-A.**

Spartacus, **Saurin, Bernard-J.**

Spinette et Marini ou La Leçon conjugale, **Bodard de Tézay, Nicolas-M.-F.**

Statuaires d'Athènes, Les, **Watelet, Claude-H.**

Stratonice, **Hoffman, François-B.**

Suborneur, Le, **Billard-Dumonceau, Edme.**

Succession, La, **Deschamps, Jacques-M.**

Suisses de Châteauvieux, Les, **Dorvigny, Louis-A.**

Suite de Geneviève de Brabant, La, **Lévrier de Champ-Rion, Guillaume-D.-T.**, Gaveaux, Pierre (comp).

Suite des solitaires de Normandie, La, **Piis, Chevalier P.-A.-A. de.**, Barré, Pierre-Y.

Sultan généreux, Le, **Dorvigny, Louis-A.**

Supercherie par amour, La, ou Le Fils supposé, **Loeillard d'Arvigny, Charles J.**, Berton, Henri-M. (comp).

Suppléants, Les, **Legros.**

Suprises, Les, ou Les Rencontres imprévues, **Lebailly, Antoine-F.**

Surprise de l'amour, La, **Marivaux, Pierre-C. de C. de.**

Suspects, Les, **Picard, Louis-B.**

Sylvain, **Marmontel, Jean F.**, Grétry, André-E.-M. (comp).

Tabagie, La, **Boullault, Mathurin-J.**

Tableau parlant, Le, **Anseaume, Louis.**, Duni, Egidio-R. (comp).

Talismans, Les, **Plancher de Valcour, dit Aristide.**

Tambour nocturne, Le, ou Le Mari devin, **Destouches, Philippe-N.**

Tambourin de province, Le, ou L'Heureuse incertitude, **Monnet, Jean.**

Tancrède, **Voltaire, F.-M. Arouet, dit Arouet de.**

C.

Trois cousins, Les, **Lévrier de Champ-Rion, Guillaume-D.-T.**, Gaveaux, Pierre (comp).

Trois déesses rivales, Les, ou Le Double jugement de Pâris, **Piis, Chevalier-P.-A.-A. de.**, Barré, Pierre-Y.

Trois espiègles, Les, ou Les Arts et la folie, **La Martelière, Jean-H.-F.**

Trois fermiers, Les, **Boutet de Monvel, Jacques-M.**, Dalayrac, Nicolas (comp).

Trois frères, Les, **Berthe, F.-L.**

Trois frères rivaux, Les, **Lafont, Joseph de.**, Gilliers, Jean-C. (comp).

Trois gascons, Les, **Boindin, Nicolas.**, Grandval, Nicolas-R. de (comp).

Trois héritiers, Les, **Dorvo, Hyacinthe.**

Trois Horaces, Les, **Landrin.**

Trois jumeaux vénitiens, Les, **Marcouville, Pierre-A. Lefèvre de.**

Trois Léandres, Les, ou Les Noms changés, **Sedaine de Sarcy, Jean-F.**

Trois mariages, Les, **Du Buisson, Paul-U.**, Anfossi, Pasquale (comp).

Trois noces, Les, **Dezède, Nicolas.**

Trois rivaux, Les, **Laus de Boissy, Louis de.**

Trois voisins, Les, **Picard, Louis-B.**

Troqueurs, Les, **Vadé, Jean-J.**

Troubadours, Les, **Le Prévost d'Iray, Vicomte Chrétien.**, Gresnick, Antoine (comp).

Troubadours en voyage, Les, **Chazet, René-A.-P. de.**

Trousseau d'Agnès, Le, ou La Veuve à marier, **Beaunoir, Alexandre-L.-B. Robineau, dit.**

Turcaret, **Lesage, Alain-R.**

Turelure ou Le Cahos perpétuel, **Mayeur de St.-Paul, François-M.**

Turlututu, empereur de l'île verte, **Beffroy de Reigny, Louis-A.**

Tuteur, Le, **Dancourt, Florent C.**

Tuteur avare, Le, **Gabiot de Salins, Jean-L.**

Tuteur célibataire, Le, **Desforges, Pierre-J.-B. Choudard de.**, Jadin, Louis-E. (comp).

Tuteur dupé, Le, **"Monsieur de B."**

Tuteur dupé, Le, ou La Maison a deux portes, **Cailhava de L'Estendoux, Jean-F.**

Tuteur trompé, Le, **Laroche.**, Guillemain, Charles-J.

Un rien ou L'Habit des noces, **Beffroy de Reigny, Louis-A.**

Una Cosa rara, o Sia bellezza ed onesta, **Ponte, Lorenzo.**, Martin y Soler, Vincente (comp).

Union villageoise, L', **Desfontaines, François-G. Fouques, dit.**, Dalayrac, Nicolas (comp).

Urbélise et Lanval ou La Journée aux aventures, **Bourlin, Antoine-J.**, Pseud. Dumaniant.

Urgande et Merlin, **Boutet de Monvel, Jacques-M.**, Dalayrac, Nicolas (comp).

Usurier gentilhomme, L', **Legrand, Marc-A.**, Biancolelli, Pierre-F., dit Dominique.

Vacances, Les, **Dancourt, Florent C.**

Vadé à la grenouillère, **Duval, Georges-L.-J.**, Gouffé, Armand Alexandre Duval.

Val de vivre, Le, ou Le Berceau du vaudeville, **Duval, Georges-L.-J.**, Gouffé, Armand Alexandre Duval.

Valet de deux maîtres, Le, **Roger.**

Valet favorable, Le, ou Le Mariage par enlèvement, **Crêton de Villeneuve.**

Valet mal servi, Le, **Patrat, Joseph.**, Trial, Armand-E. (comp).

Valet rival et confident, Le, **Hippolite.**, Paisiello, Giovanni (comp).

Valet rusé, Le, ou Arlequin muet, **Valigny, P. de.**

Vallée de Montmorency, La, ou Jean-Jacques Rousseau à l'hermitage, **Piis, Chevalier P.-A.-A. de.**, Barré, Pierre-Y.

Veille des noces, La, ou L'Après souper de misanthropie et repentir, **Dorvo, Hyacinthe.**

Venceslas, **Rotrou, Jean.**

Vendange, La, ou Silvain et Lucette, **Joigny.**, Trial, Armand-E. (comp).

Vendanges de la vigne d'amour, Les, **Beaunoir, Alexandre-L.-B. Robineau, dit.**

Vendanges de Suresne, Les, **Dancourt, Florent C.**

Vendangeurs, Les, ou Les Deux baillis,

L'Enlèvement des cloches, **Raffard-Brienne, J.S.**

Vous et le toi, Le, **Plancher de Valcour, dit Aristide.**

Voyage de Figaro esclave à Alger, Le, **Destival de Braban.**

Voyage interrompu, Le, **Picard, Louis-B.**

Voyages de Cadet Roussel, Les, **Bourlin, Antoine-J., Pseud. Dumaniant.**

Voyages de Rosine, Les, **Barré, Pierre-Y.**, Radet, Jean-B., Desfontaines, François-G. Fouques, dit.

Vraie bravoure, La, **Picard, Louis-B.**

Vrais amis, Les, ou Le Père interéssé, **Pellegrin, Abbé-S.-J.**

Vrais sans-culottes, Les, ou L'Hospitalité républicaine, **Rézicourt.**, Lemoyne, Jean-B. (comp).

Washington ou La Liberté du nouveau monde, **Billardon de Sauvigny, Louis-E.**

Wenzel ou Le Magistrat du peuple, **Pillet.**, Ladurner, Ignaz.-A. (comp).

Werther, **Cammaille-Saint-Aubin, M.-C.**

Werther et Charlotte, **Dejaure, Jean-E. Bédéno.**, Kreutzer, Rodolpho (comp).

Zaïre, **Voltaire, F.-M. Arouet, dit Arouet de.**

Zelia ou La Grille enchantée, **Du Buisson, Paul-U.**, Anfossi, Pasquale (comp).

Zelia, ou Le Mari à deux femmes, **Du Buisson, Paul-U.**, Anfossi, Pasquale (comp).

Zelmire, **Belloy, Pierre-L.B. de.**

Zémire et Azor, **Marmontel, Jean F.**, Grétry, André-E.-M. (comp).

Zénéide, **Cahusac, Louis de.**

Zéphire et Flore, **Riccoboni, Antoine-F.**, Goldoni, Carlo., Riccoboni, Marie-J.-L. de Mézières, Mme.

Zing-zing ou La Relique, **Beaunoir, Alexandre-L.-B. Robineau, dit.**

Ziste et zeste ou Les Importuns, **Cailhava de L'Estendoux, Jean-F.**

Zoraime et Zulnar, **Godard d'Aucourt de Saint-Just, Claude.**, Boïeldieu, François-A. (comp).

Zoroastre, **Cahusac, Louis de.**

Zozo ou Le Mal avisé, **Guilbert de Pixerécourt, René-C.**

Zuma, **Le Fèvre, Pierre-F.-A.**

14

Index of Authors and Composers

*Composers and additional authors are shown in **bold**.
Consult Chapter 11 for complete listing under the first
author's name, shown in Roman type.*

Aldey (comp): Le Roy.
Andrieux, François-G.-J.-S.: Guillard, Nicolas-F.
Anfossi, Pasquale (comp): Bulle; Du Buisson, Paul-U.; Hennequin, Louis.
Anfossi, Pasquale et Cambini, Giovanni-G. (comp): Bertati, Giovanni; Gabiot de Salins, Jean-L.; Livigni, F.
Année, Antoine: Gersin.
Anseaume, Louis: Vadé, Jean-J.; Favart, Charles-S.
Anson, Pierre-H.: Hérissant, Louis-T.
Arnould, Jean-F. Mussot, dit: Audinot, Nicolas-M.
Arquier, Joseph (comp): Prévost-Montfort, P.
Austin: Pilhes, André-F. de.
Bambini, Arnauldo (comp): Vadé, Jean-J.
Barral: Duchaume.
Barré, Pierre-Y.: Piis, Chevalier-P.-A.-A. de.; Léger, François-P.-A.; Radet, Jean-B.
Beaumesnil, Henriette.-A. (comp): La Salle d'Offremont, Adrien-N. P.
Beaupré: Rouhier-Deschamps, J.
Beck, Franz (comp): Aumale de Cor-

senville.
Bellement, André-P.: Moithey.
Benda, George (comp): Dubois, Jean-B.
Berton, Henri-M. (comp): Andrieux, François-G.-J.-S.; Berton, Henri-M.; Dejaure, Jean-E. Bédéno; Desforges, Pierre-J.-B. Choudard de; Favières, Edmond-G.-F. de; Fiévée, Joseph; Joigny; Lesur, Charles-L.; Loeillard d'Arvigny, Charles J.; Pujoulx, Jean-B.
Bianchi, Francesco (comp): Bertati, Giovanni.
Biancolleli, Pierre-F. dit Dominique: Legrand, Marc-A.
Bizet: Chaussier, Hector; Valienne.
Blaise, A.B. (comp): Favart, Charles-S.
Blasius, Mathieu-F. (comp): Bertin D'Antilly, Auguste-L.; Desriaux, Philippe.
Boïeldieu, François-A. (comp): Godard d'Aucourt de Saint-Just, Claude.
Boizard de Ponteau, Claude-F: Beaunoir, Alexandre-L.-B. Robineau dit.
Bonnay, Franco (comp): De Senne.
Bourgeuil: Barré, Pierre-Y.
Bréval, Jean-B. (comp): Gautier.

Bruni, Antonio-B. (comp): Bodard de Tézay, Nicolas-M.-F.; Deschamps, Jacques-M.; Patrat, Joseph; Pigault-Lebrun, Charles-A.P. de L'Epinoy, dit.; Ponteuil, Triboulet, J.B., dit.; Poultier d'Elmotte, François-M.; Pujoulx, Jean-B.; Sedaine de Sarcy, Jean-F.

Cambini, Giuseppe-M. (comp): Du Buisson, Paul-U.; Dubreuil, Alphonse-D.; Gabiot de Salins, Jean-L.; Lepitre, Jacques-F.

Cammaille-St.-Aubin, M.-C.: Destival de Braban.

Campra, André (comp): Regnard, Jean-F. Renard, dit.

Capelle, Pierre-A.: Villiers, Pierre-A.-B.

Carpentier (comp): Moline, Pierre-L.

Cazotte, Jacques: Sedaine, Michel-J.

Champein, Stanislas (comp): Boissel de Monville, Thomas-C.-G.; Fallet, Nicolas; Favières, Edmond-G.-F. de; Forgeot Nicolas-J.; Grenier; Laugier, Marie; Lebas; Mayeur de St.-Paul; Radet, Jean-B.; Rouget de Lisle, Claude J.; Saulnier, Guillaume.-N.-F.

Chapelle, Pierre-D.-A. (comp): Bertin D'Antilly, Auguste-L.; Favart, Charles-N.; Rauquil-Lieutaud; Sewrin, Charles-A. de Bassompierre, dit.

Chardiny, Louis-A. (comp): Demautort, Jacques-B.; Guillemain, Charles-J.; Maille de Marencour.

Charles de Livry: Brazier, Nicolas.

Charpentier (comp): Guichard, Jean-F.

Châteauvieux, Armand-F.-R.-C.-L.: Berthevin, Jules-J.

Chazet, René-A.-P. de: Du Mersan, T. Marion, Ps.-T. et Mme. Olympe; Sewrin, Charles-A. de Bassompierre, dit.

Chérubini, Luigi (comp): Jouy, Victor-J. Etienne, dit de; Desfaucherets, J.L.B.; Hoffman, François-B.; Loraux, Claude-F. Fillette, dit; Marmontel, Jean F.; Reveroni Saint-Cyr, Baron Jacques-A. de; Saint-Aignan, E.

Chevalier-Seguenot: Capinaud.

Chevalier: Favart, Marie-J.-B.D.

Chevillet de Champmeslé, Charles:

Lafontaine, Jean de.

Cimarosa, Domenico (comp): Diodati, G.-M.; Du Buisson, Paul-U.; Savin-Desplasses; Zini, Francesco-S.

Clairville, Nicolas dit: Rolland, J.J.

Corsange de la Plant, Jean-F.-J.: Hapdé, Jean-B.-A.

Coupartantoine-M.: Lesage, Alain-R.; Serrières.

Dabaytua, J.: Hapdé, Jean-B.-A.

Dalainval, Cavanas, dit: Moller, Heinrich-F.

Dalayrac, Nicolas (comp): Andrieux, François-G.-J.-S.; Boutet de Monvel, Jacques-M.; Desfontaines, François-G. Fouques, dit; Fallet, Nicolas; Favières, Edmond-G.-F. de; Hoffman, François-B.; Lachabeaussière, Auguste-E.-X. P. de.; Marsollier des Vivetières, Benoît-J.; Picard, Louis-B.; Radet, Jean-B.

Dancourt, L.-J.-H.: Dorvigny, Louis-A.

Darcis, François-J. (comp): Marsollier des Vivetières, Benoît-J.

Dauvergne (comp): Vadé, Jean-J.

De la Salle: Dupeuty, Charles.

Dejaure: Loeillard d'Arvigny, Charles J.

Della-Maria, Dominique (comp): Després, Jean-B.-D.; Duval, Alexandre-V.P.; Ségur, Alexander-J.-P.

Demautort, Jacques-B.: Ducray-Duminil, François-G.

Desaugiers, Marc-A. (comp): Dubreuil, Alphonse-D.

Desbrosses (comp): La Ribardière, de.

Desfontaines, François-G. Fouques, dit: Barré, Pierre-Y.; Piis, Chevalier-P.-A.-A. de.; Léger, François-P.-A.; Radet, Jean-B.

Desfougerais, P.F.Aubin, dit: Buhan, Joseph-M.-P.; Chazet, René-A.-P. de.

Deshayes, Prosper-D. (comp): Boutillier, Maximilien-J.; Du Buisson, Paul-U.; Durival; Duval, Alexandre-V.P.; Eyraud; Lepitre, Jacques-F.; Rouhier-Deschamps, J.

Desorméry, Leopold.-B. (comp): Dorvigny, Louis-A.

Desprez, Jean-B.-D.: Barré, Pierre-Y.; Deschamps, Jacques-M.; Ségur,

Edmond-G.-F. de; Fenouillot de Falbaire de Quingey, Charles-G.; Forgeot Nicolas-J.; Gardel, Maximilien; Grétry, André-J.; Guy, Jean-H.; Hèle, Thomas d'; Hoffman, François-B.; Lourdet de Santerre, Jean; Maréchal, Pierre-Sylvain; Marmontel, Jean F.; Masson de Pezay, Alexandre-F.-J.; Morel de Chédeville, Etienne; Patrat, Joseph; Sedaine, Michel-J.

Grétry, Lucile (comp): Beaunoir, Alexandre-L.-B. Robineau dit.

Guérin de Frémicourt: Favart, Charles-S.

Guglielmi, Pietro.-A. (comp): Palomba, Giuseppe; Zini, Francesco-S.

Guillemain, Charles-J.: Laroche.

Hapdé, Jean-B.-A.: Aude, Joseph; Chaussier, Hector; Corsange de la Plante, Jean-F.-J.; Cuvelier de Trie, Jean G.-A.

Harny de Guerville: Favart, Charles-S.

Haydn, Joseph (comp): Du Buisson, Paul-U.

Jadin, Louis-E. (comp): Bellement, André-P.; Bourlin, Antoine-J.; Cottereau; Delrieu, Etienne-J.-B.; Desforges, Pierre-J.-B. Choudard de; Desriaux, Philippe; Ducaire; Falaise de Verneuil; Favart, Charles-S.; Favières, Edmond-G.-F. de; Léger, François-P.-A.; Loeillard d'Arvigny, Charles J.; Philipon, Louis de la Madeleine; Picard, Louis-B.; Planterre, Barthélemy; Saulnier, Guillaume.-N.-F.; Sewrin, Charles-A. de Bassompierre, dit.

Jauffret, Louis-F.: Patrat, Joseph.

Kalkbrenner, Christian (comp): Guillard, Nicolas-F.

Kreutzer, Rodolpho (comp): Bertin D'Antilly, Auguste-L.; Dejaure, Jean-E. Bédéno; Desforges, Pierre-J.-B. Choudard de; Favières, Edmond-G.-F. de; Hoffman, François-B.; Tissot, Charles-L.

La Borde, Jean-B. de (comp): Desfontaines, François-G. Fouques, dit.

La Houssaye (comp): Parisau, Pierre-G.

Ladurner, Ignaz.-A. (comp): Pillet; Ségur, Alexander-J.-P.

Langle, Honoré-F.-M. (comp):

Bosquier-Gavaudan, Jean-S.-F.; Linière, Comte de.

Lapotre, le P. Arthur: Charrin, Pierre-J.

Le Sueur, Jean-F. (comp): Dercy, P.; Dubreuil, Alphonse-D.

Lebailly, Antoine-F.: Linière, Comte de.

Leblanc (comp): Beffroy de Reigny, Louis-A.

Leblanc de Guillet, Antonio Blanc, dit (comp): Eve, Antoine-F., dit Maillot; Gougibus, J.-T. Gougy, dit; Léger, François-P.-A. Lutaine.

Lebrun, Louis-S. (comp): Dancourt, L.-H.; Desfaucherets, J.L.B.; Hennequin, Louis; La Salle d'Offremont, Adrien-N. P.

Lefranc-Ponteuil, Nicolas: Sewrin, Charles-A. de Bassompierre, dit.

Léger, François-P.-A.: Barré, Pierre-Y.; Cailhava de L'Estendoux, Jean-F.; Chazet, René-A.-P. de; Rouhier-Deschamps, J.l Vadé, Jean-J.

Legouvé, Gabriel, M.-J.-B.: Loeillard d'Arvigny, Charles J.

Legrand, Marc-A.: Alain, Robert.

Lemière, Jean.-F.-A. de Corvey (comp): Duval, Alexandre-V.P.; Picard, Louis-B.

Lemoyne, Jean-B. (comp): Beffroy de Reigny, Louis-A.; Forgeot Nicolas-J.; Guillard, Nicolas-F.; Hoffman, François-B.; Rézicourt; Rochon de Chabannes, Marc.

Lesouppey de la Rosière, J.-R.: Barré, Pierre-Y.

Lesueur, Jean-F. (comp): Lebrun Tossa, Jean-A.

Levacher de Charnois, Jean-C.: Landrin.

Loise (comp): Planterre, Barthélemy.

Longchamps, Charles de: Jouy, Victor-J. Etienne, dit de.

Lourdet de Santerre, Jean: Favart, Marie-J.-B.D.

Madame Kennens: Radet, Jean-B.

Marcouville, P.A. Lefèbvre de: Anseaume, Louis.

Marmontel, Jean-F. et Longchamps: Dard D'Aucourt de Saint-Just, Claude.

Ferrières, A. de; Lemontey; Philipon, Louis de la Madeleine; Saugiers, Marc-A.

Porta, Bernado (comp): Daine; Sedaine, Michel-J.

Procope-Couteau, M. Cottelli dit: Lagrange, Nicolas.

Propriac, Catherine-J.-F.-G. de (comp): Piis, Chevalier-P.-A.-A. de.

Pseud. Decour: Laffillard, Eugène-H.

Pseud. Dumaniant: Bourlin, Antoine-J.

Pseud. L. de Saint-Hughes: Gassier, J.-M.

Quaisin, Adrian (comp): Hennequin, Louis; Joigny.

Quêtant, François-A.: Audinot, Nicolas-M.

Radet, Jean-B.: Barré, Pierre-Y.; Léger, François-P.-A.; Piis, Chevalier-P.-A.-A. de.

Rameau, Jean-P. (comp): Bernard, Pierre-J.; Cahusac, Louis de.

Raymond, B. (comp): Guillemain, Charles-J.; Raymond, B.-Louis.

Rebory: Dognon, Jean-F.

Regnault (comp): Biancolelli, Pierre-F.; Rouhier-Deschamps, J.

Renout, Jean-J.-C.: Beaunoir, Alexandre-L.-B. Robineau dit.

Rey, Jean-B. (comp): Fuzelier, Louis.

Ribié, César: Arnould, Jean-F. Mussot, dit; Cammaille-Saint-Aubin, M.-C.

Riccoboni, Antoine-F.: Biancolelli, Pierre-F.

Riccoboni, Marie-J.-L. de Mézières, Mme.: Riccoboni, Antoine-F.

Rigel, Henri-J. (comp): Boutillier, Maximilien-J.; Dancourt, L.-H.; Delvieu; Lourdet de Santerre, Jean.

Riou de Kesauln, François-M.-J.: Pain, Joseph-M.

Rivière-Dufresney, Charles: Regnard, Jean-F. Renard, dit.

Rochefort, Jean-B. (comp): Bré D'Olivet, A.; Gallet, Sébastien; Mittié, Jean-C.

Rodolphe, Jean-J. (comp): Noverre, Jean-G.

Romagnesi, Jean-A.: Biancolelli, Pierre-F.

Rouget de Lisle: Després, Jean-B.-D.

Sacchini, Antonio (comp): Framery,

Nicolas-E.; Guillard, Nicolas-F.; Le Boeuf, Jean-J.

Salieri, Antonio (comp): Beaumarchais, Pierre-A.C. de; Boursault, Edmonde; Casti, Giambattista; Guillard, Nicolas-F.

Sarti, Giuseppi (comp): Du Buisson, Paul-U.

Scio, Etienne (comp): Chaussard, Pierre-J.; Monnet, Jean.

Sewrin, Charles-A. de Bassompierre, dit: Duchaume.

Sodi, Charles (comp): Harny de Guerville; Favart, Charles-S.

Solié, Jean-P. (comp): Favières, Edmond-G.-F. de; Hoffman, François-B.; Sewrin, Charles-A. de Bassompierre, dit.

St. Amand, J.Gassier dit: Cordier de Saint-Firmin, Edmond.

St. Honorine: Laffillard, Eugène-H.

Tarchi, Angelo (comp): Duval, Alexandre-V.P.; Favart, Charles-S.; Ségur, Alexander-J.-P.

Tissot, Charles-L.: Aude, Joseph.

Trial, Armand-E. (comp): Joigny; Noël; Parisau, Pierre-G.; Patrat, Joseph.

Vachon, Pierre (comp): Quétant, Antoine-F.

Valcour, Aristide: Destival de Braban.

Valois D'orville, Adrien-J. de: Laffichard, Thomas.

Vandenbroeck, Othon (comp): Cuvelier de Trie, Jean G.-A.

Vieillard, Pierre-A.: Du Mersan, T. Marion, Ps.-T. et Mme. Olympe.

Villeneuve, Ferdinand Vallon de: Brazier, Nicolas.

Villeneuve, Mme.: Dupeuty, Charles.

Vogel, Johann-C. (comp): Desriaux, Philippe.

Voisenon: Favart, Marie-J.-B.D.

Weiss, Matthias: Patrat, Joseph.

Zingarelli, Nicolas-A. (comp): Marmontel, Jean F.

15

List of Operas

*List of operas sorted by author and title followed by anonymous
operas sorted by title. Consult Chapters 11 and 12 for complete listing.*

Andrieux, François-G.-J.-S., Berton, Henri-M. (comp). *Deux sen-
tinelles, Les* [*Opéra* in 1 act, Prem. on 27-3-1791, Pub. in 1788].
Beaumarchais, Pierre-A.C. de. *Tarare* [*Opéra* in 5 acts, Prem. on 8-6-1787,
Pub. in 1787].
Bertati, Giovanni. *Convitato di pietra, Il* [*Opéra* in 4 acts, Prem. on 5-2-1787,
Pub. in 1790].
_____. *Villanella rapita, La* [*Opéra* in 3 acts, Pub. in 1802].
_____. *Vendemmia, La, ou Les Vendanges* [*Opéra* in 2 acts, Prem. on 12-5-
1778, Pub. in 1791].
Bertin D'Antilly, Auguste-L., Philidor, François-A. Danican et Berton,
Henri-M. (comp). *Bélisaire* [*Opéra* in 3 acts, Pub. in 1796].
Boissel de Monville, Thomas-C.-G., Champein, Stanislas (comp).
Nouveau don Quichotte, Le [*Opéra* in 2 acts, Prem. on 25-5-1789, Pub.
in 1792].
Boissy, Louis de. *Maire de village, Le* [*Opéra*, Prem. on 22-2-1793, Pub. in
1793].
Bonnefoy de Bouyon, Abbé., Mengozzi, Bernardo (comp). *Aujourd'hui
ou Les Fous supposés* [*Opéra* in 3 acts, Prem. on 3-2-1791].
Boutet de Monvel, Jacques-M., Dalayrac, Nicolas (comp). *Agnès et
Olivier* [*Opéra* in 3 acts, Prem. on 10-10-1791].
Boutillier, Maximilien-J., Deshayes, Prosper-D. (comp). *Alix de Beau-
caire* [*Opéra* in 3 acts, Prem. on 10-11-1791, Pub. in 1791].
Carpani, Giuseppe., Paisiello, Giovanni (comp). *Nina, o sia la pazza
per amore, La* [*Opéra*].
Casti, Giambattista., Salieri, Antonio (comp). *Grotta di Trifonio, La*
[*Opéra*].
Cottereau., Jadin, Louis-E. (comp). *Amélie de Montfort* [*Opéra* in 3 acts,

Prem. on 13-2-1792].

Cuvelier de Trie, Jean G.-A. *Fille hermite, La* [*Opéra* in 1 act, Prem. on 21-9-1797, Pub. in 1796].

_____. *Quiproco nocturnes* [*Opéra*, Prem. on 13-12-1797, Pub. in 1798].

Da Ponte, Lorenzo., Martini, Vincente (comp). *Finto cieco, Il* [*Opéra* in 2 acts, Prem. on 20-12-1786].

Danzel de Malzéville., Méreaux, Nicolas-J. (comp). *Laurette* [*Opéra* in 1 act, Prem. on 23-7-1777, Pub. in 1777].

Demoustier, Charles-A., Devienne, François (comp). *Agnès et Felix ou Les Deux espiègles* [*Opéra* in 3 acts, Prem. on 22-8-1795].

_____., Devienne, François (comp). *Amour filial, L', ou Les Deux suisses* [*Opéra* in 1 act, Prem. on 6-3-1792, Pub. in 1794].

_____., Devienne, François (comp). *Apelle et Campaspe* [*Opéra* in 1 act, Prem. on 12-7-1798, Pub. in 1798].

_____., Devienne, François (comp). *Sic paria, Le, ou La Chaumière indienne* [*Opéra* in 2 acts, Prem. on 8-10-1792].

_____., Devienne, François (comp). *Sophronime ou La Reconnaisance* [*Opéra* in 1 act, Prem. on 13-2-1795, Pub. in 1795].

Dercy, P., Le Sueur, Jean-F. (comp). *Caverne, La* [*Opéra* in 3 acts, Prem. on 16-2-1793, Pub. in 1793].

_____., Le Sueur, Jean-F. (comp). *Télémaque dans l'îsle de Calypso ou Le Triomphe de la sagesse* [*Opéra* in 3 acts, Prem. on 10-5-1796, Pub. in 1796].

Desfaucherets, J.-L.-B., Lebrun, Louis-S. (comp). *Punition, La* [*Opéra* in 1 act, Prem. on 23-2-1799].

Desforges, Pierre-J.-B. Choudard de., Jadin, Louis-E. (comp). *Alisbelle ou Les Crimes de la féodalité* [*Opéra* in 3 acts, Prem. on 2-3-1794, Pub. in 1794].

_____., Jadin, Louis-E. (comp). *Deux vizirs, Les* [*Opéra* in 3 acts, Prem. on 10-3-1792].

_____., Jadin, Louis-E. (comp). *Grisélide ou La Vertu à l'épreuve* [*Opéra* in 3 acts, Prem. on 8-1-1791].

_____., Jadin, Louis-E. (comp). *Joconde, La* [*Opéra* in 3 acts, Prem. on 14-9-1790].

Desriaux, Philippe., Blasius, Mathieu-F. (comp). *Démophon* [*Opéra* in 3 acts, Prem. on 15-9-1789, Pub. in 1789].

Destival de Braban, Jean N., dit. *Gâteau des rois, Le* [*Opéra* in 1 act, Pub. in 1792].

Diodati, G.-M., Cimarosa, Domenico (comp). *Impresario en Angustie, L'* [*Opéra* in 2 acts, Prem. on 6-5-1789].

Dognon, Jean-F., Foignet, Charles-G. (comp)., Rebory. *Prisonniers français en Angleterre, Les* [*Opéra* in 2 acts, Prem. on 8-4-1798, Pub. in 1798].

Du Buisson, Paul-U., Anfossi, Pasquale (comp). *Curieux indiscret, Le* [*Opéra* in 3 acts, Pub. in 1778].

_____., Anfossi, Pasquale (comp). *Epoux mécontents, Les, ou Le Divorce* [*Opéra* in 4 acts, Pub. in 1793].

_____., Anfossi, Pasquale (comp). *Flora* [*Opéra* in 3 acts, Prem. on 4-2-1792].

_____., Anfossi, Pasquale (comp). *Laurette* [*Opéra* in 3 acts, Prem. in 1779].

_____., Anfossi, Pasquale (comp). *Maître généreux, Le* [*Opéra* in 1 act, Prem. in 1786, Pub. in 1788].

_____., Anfossi, Pasquale (comp). *Trois mariages, Les* [*Opéra*].

Du Roullet, François-L. Gand Lebland., Gluck, Christoph (comp). *Alceste* [*Opéra* in 3 acts, Prem. on 16-4-1776, Pub. in 1776].

Duchaume., Barral. *Hiver, L', ou Les Deux moulins* [*Opéra* in 1 act, Prem. on 27-3-1793, Pub. in 1793].

Duval, Alexandre-V.P., Deshayes, Prosper-D. (comp). *Bella ou La Femme à deux maris* [*Opéra* in 3 acts, Prem. on 15-6-1795, Pub. in 1795].

Espic, Chevalier de Lirou, Jean-F., Piccinni, Niccolò. *Diane et Endimion* [*Opéra* in 3 acts, Prem. on 7-9-1784, Pub. in 1784].

Falaise de Verneuil., Jadin, Louis-E. (comp). *Avare puni, L'* [*Opéra* in 1 act, Prem. on 4-8-1792].

Fallet, Nicolas., Dalayrac, Nicolas (comp). *Noces cauchoises, Les* [*Opéra* in 2 acts, Prem. on 11-8-1790].

Faur, Louis-F. *Fête de la cinquantaine, La* [*Opéra* in 2 acts, Prem. on 9-1-1796, Pub. in 1796].

_____. *Intrigant sans le vouloir, L'* [*Opéra* in 2 acts, Prem. on 4-4-1796].

_____. *Phanor et Angela* [*Opéra*, Prem. on 11-7-1798].

Favières, Edmond-G.-F. de., Berton, Henri-M. (comp). *Primerose* [*Opéra* in 3 acts, Prem. on 7-3-1799].

Fiévée, Joseph. *Nuit espagnole, La* [*Opéra* in 2 acts, Prem. on 14-6-1791].

Forgeot, Nicolas-J., Méhul, Etienne-N. (comp). *Caverne, La* [*Opéra* in 3 acts, Prem. on 5-12-1795, Pub. in 1793].

Framery, Nicolas-E., Sacchini, Antonio (comp). *Infante de Zamora, L'* [*Opéra* in 4 acts, Prem. in 1779, Pub. in 1781].

Fuzelier, Louis., Rey, Jean-B. (comp). *Apollon et Coronis* [*Opéra* in 1 act, Prem. on 3-5-1781, Pub. in 1781].

Godard d'Aucourt de Saint-Just, Claude., Boïeldieu, François-A. (comp). *Zoraime et Zulnar* [*Opéra* in 3 acts, Prem. on 10-5-1798, Pub. in 1798].

Goldoni, Carlo. *Buona figliola, La* [*Opéra*].

_____. *Nozze di Dorina, Delle* [*Opéra* in 2 acts].

Gossec, François-J. (comp). *Offrande à la Liberté, L'* [*Opéra*, Prem. on 3-7-1792, Pub. in 1792].

Gourbillon, C.-Joseph., Paisiello, Giovanni (comp). *Bon maître, Le, ou Les Esclaves par amour* [*Opéra* in 3 acts, Prem. in 1786].

Guilbert de Pixerécourt, René-C. *Forêt de Sicile, La* [*Opéra* in 2 acts, Prem. on 23-4-1798].

_____. *Léonidas ou Les Spartiates* [*Opéra* in 3 acts, Prem. on 15-8-1799].

_____. *Petits auvergnats, Les* [*Opéra*, Prem. on 24-11-1797].

Guillard, Nicolas-F., Sacchini, Antonio (comp). *Louis IX en Egypte* [*Opéra* in 3 acts, Prem. on 15-6-1790, Pub. in 1790].

Guy, Jean-H., Grétry, André-E.-M. (comp). *Anacréon chez Polycrate* [*Opéra* in 3 acts, Prem. on 17-1-1797, Pub. in 1797].

Hoffman, François-B. *Adrien empereur de Rome* [*Opéra* in 3 acts, Prem. on 4-6-1799, Pub. in 1798].

_____. *Ariodant* [*Opéra* in 3 acts, Prem. on 10-10-1799].

_____. *Callias ou Nature et patrie* [*Opéra* in 1 act, Prem. on 19-9-1794, Pub. in 1794].

_____. *Euphrosine et Coradin* [*Opéra* in 3 acts, Pub. in 1790].

_____. *Médée* [*Opéra* in 3 acts, Prem. on 13-3-1797].

Hus, Eugène., Gaveaux, Pierre (comp). *Lise et Colin ou La Surveillance inutile* [*Opéra* in 2 acts, Prem. on 4-8-1796].

La Salle d'Offremont, Adrien-N. P. *Ils ne savent pas lire* [*Opéra* in 1 act, Prem. on 21-6-1791].

_____. *Plaire c'est commander* [*Opéra* in 2 acts, Prem. on 12-5-1792, Pub. in 1792].

Laffillard, Eugène-H., Pseud. Decour., St. Honorine. *Amour au village, L'* [*Opéra* in 1 act, Pub. in 1804].

Lavallée, Joseph. *Femme qui sait se taire, La* [*Opéra* in 1 act, Prem. on 28-10-1793].

_____. *Roi et le pèlerin, Le* [*Opéra* in 2 acts, Prem. on 2-6-1792].

Le Boeuf, Jean-J. *Apothéose de Beaurepaire, L', ou La Patrie reconnaissante* [*Opéra* in 1 act, Prem. on 2-1-1793, Pub. in 1793].

Lebrun Tossa, Jean-A., Lesueur, Jean-F. (comp). *Mont Alphea, Le, ou Le Français jatabite* [*Opéra* in 3 acts, Prem. on 6-12-1792, Pub. in 1793].

_____., Lesueur, Jean-F. (comp). *Savoir faire, Le* [*Opéra* in 2 acts, Prem. on 4-4-1795, Pub. in 1795].

Léger, François-P.-A. *Heureuse ivresse, L', ou Le Mari de retour* [*Opéra*, Prem. on 30-6-1791].

Lemontey., Plantade, Charles-H. (comp). *Palma ou Le Voyage en Grèce* [*Opéra* in 2 acts, Prem. on 22-8-1798].

Lépidor, M.-J. Mathieu, dit., Paisiello, Giovanni (comp). *Orgon dans la lune ou Crédule trompé* [*Opéra* in 3 acts].

Lepitre, Jacques-F., Deshayes, Prosper-D. (comp). *Renouvellement du bail, Le* [*Opéra* in 1 act, Prem. on 29-3-1794, Pub. in 1794].

Lescène-Desmaisons, Jacques. *Retour aux isles des amis, Le, ou Le Capitaine Cook* [*Opéra* in 2 acts, Prem. on 30-11-1790].

Levigni, F., Paisiello, Giovanni (comp). *Frascatana, La* [*Opéra* in 3 acts, Pub. in 1774].

Loeillard d'Arvigny, Charles-J., Berton, Henri-M. (comp). *Doria* [*Opéra* in 3 acts, Prem. on 12-3-1795].

_____., Berton, Henri-M. (comp). *Eugène, ou La Piété filiale* [*Opéra* in 3 acts, Prem. on 11-3-1793].

Maréchal, Pierre-Sylvain., Grétry, André-E.-M. (comp). *Denys le tyran, maître d'école à Corinthe* [*Opéra* in 1 act, Prem. on 21-8-1794].

_____., Grétry, André-E.-M. (comp). *Rosière républicaine, La, ou La Fête de la vertu* [*Opéra* in 1 act, Prem. on 2-9-1794].

Marmontel, Jean F., Grétry, André-E.-M. (comp). *Antigone* [*Opéra* in 3 acts, Prem. on 30-4-1790, Pub. in 1790].

_____., Grétry, André-E.-M. (comp). *Démophoon* [*Opéra* in 3 acts, Prem. on 2-12-1789, Pub. in 1788].

_____., Grétry, André-E.-M. (comp). *Roland* [*Opéra* in 3 acts, Prem. on 17-1-1777].

Marsollier des Vivetières, Benoît-J., Dalayrac, Nicolas (comp). *Asgill ou Le Prisonnier de guerre* [*Opéra* in 1 act, Prem. on 2-5-1793].

_____., Dalayrac, Nicolas (comp). *Emma ou Le Soupçon* [*Opéra* in 3 acts, Prem. on 15-10-1799].

_____., Dalayrac, Nicolas (comp). *Fausse peur, La, ou Les Vendanges de Taverni* [*Opéra* in 1 act, Prem. on 18-6-1774, Pub. in 1774].

Martin, Marie-J.-D., dit Barouillet., Méreaux, Nicolas-J. (comp). *Fabius* [*Opéra* in 3 acts, Prem. on 9-8-1793, Pub. in 1792].

Metastasio, Pietro., Mengozzi, Bernardo (comp). *Isola disabitata, L'* [*Opéra*, Pub. in 1789].

Moline, Pierre-L., Carpentier (comp). *Ariane dans l'île de Naxos* [*Opéra* in 1 act, Prem. on 24-9-1782, Pub. in 1782].

_____., Carpentier (comp). *Enlèvement au sérail, L'* [*Opéra* in 3 acts, Pub in 1782].

Monnet, Jean. *Lisia* [*Opéra* in 1 act, Prem. on 8-7-1793, Pub. in 1794].

_____. *Lisidore et Monrose* [*Opéra* in 3 acts, Prem. on 26-4-1792].

_____. *Orage, L'* [*Opéra* in 1 act, Prem. on 31-5-1798, Pub. in 1798].

_____. *Rêve de Kamailliaka, Le* [*Opéra* in 2 acts, Prem. on 16-7-1791].

_____. *Tambourin de province, Le, ou L'Heureuse incertitude* [*Opéra* in 1 act, Prem. on 13-9-1793, Pub. in 1793].

Morel de Chédeville, Etienne., Grétry, André-E.-M. (comp). *Aspasie* [*Opéra* in 3 acts, Prem. on 17-3-1789, Pub. in 1789].

Palomba, Giuseppe., Guglielmi, Pietro.-A. (comp). *Due gemelle, Le* [*Opéra* in 3 acts, Prem. on 12-6-1786, Pub. in 1790].

_____., Guglielmi, Pietro.-A. (comp). *Molinarella, La, ou L'Amor contrasto* [*Opéra*, Prem. in 1788].

Parisau, Pierre-G., La Houssaye (comp). *Julien et Colette ou La Milice* [*Opéra* in 1 act, Prem. on 3-3-1788].

Patrat, Joseph., Trial, Armand-E. (comp). *Adélaïde et Mirval ou La Vengeance paternelle* [*Opéra* in 3 acts, Prem. on 6-6-1791].

_____., Trial, Armand-E. (comp). *Débat des muses, Le* [*Opéra* in 1 act, Prem. on 31-12-1791].

_____., Trial, Armand-E. (comp). *Officier de fortune, L', ou Les Deux militaires* [*Opéra* in 2 acts, Prem. on 24-9-1792].

_____., Trial, Armand-E. (comp). *Petite ruse, La* [*Opéra*-Vaudeville].

Picard, Louis-B. *Ecolier en vacances, L'* [*Opéra* in 1 act, Prem. on 13-10-1794, Pub. in 1794].

_____. *Rose et Aurèle* [*Opéra* in 1 act, Prem. on 8-8-1794].

Plancher de Valcour, dit Aristide. *Mariage du curé, Le* [*Opéra* in 2 acts, Prem. on 25-12-1791].

_____. *Piques, Les* [*Opéra* in 2 acts, Prem. on 7-3-1792].

Planterre, Barthélemy., Loise (comp). *Agnès de Châtillon ou Le Siège de Saint-Jean d'Acre* [*Opéra* in 3 acts, Prem. on 12-5-1792, Pub. in 1792].

_____., Loise (comp). *Deux hermites, Les* [*Opéra* in 1 act, Prem. on 20-4-1793].

_____., Loise (comp). *Midas au Parnasse* [*Opéra* in 1 act, Prem. on 7-1-1793, Pub. in 1793].

Pompigny, Maurin de. *Gascon tel qu'il est, Le* [*Opéra*, Prem. on 10-7-1797].

Ponte, Lorenzo., Martin y Soler, Vincente (comp). *Una Cosa rara, o*

Sia bellezza ed onesta [*Opéra*, Prem. on 17-5-1781].

Prevot d'Ivrai, Tardu (comp). *Aurore de Gusman, L'* [*Opéra* in 1 act, Prem. on 24-10-1799].

Pujoulx, Jean-B. *Rencontre en voyage, La* [*Opéra* in 1 act, Prem. on 28-4-1798, Pub. in 1797].

Regnard, Jean-F. Renard, dit., Rivière-Dufresney, Charles. *Carnaval de Venise, Le* [*Opéra* in 3 acts, Prem. in 1699, Pub. in 1699].

Reveroni Saint-Cyr, Baron Jacques-A. de. *Elisa ou Le Voyage aux glaciers du mont St.-Bernard* [*Opéra* in 2 acts, Pub. in 1795].

_____. *Hospice de village, L'* [*Opéra* in 1 act, Pub. in 1795].

Rochelle, J.H. Flacon, dit, Pseud. Philidor. *Bélisaire* [*Opéra* in 3 acts, Prem. on 3-10-1796, Pub. in 1796].

Rochon de Chabannes, Marc. *Ile des femmes, L'* [*Opéra* in 3 acts, Pub. in 1789].

Rolland, J.J. *Arlequin perruquier* [*Opéra* in 1 act, Pub. in 1795].

Rouget de Lisle, Claude J., Champein, Stanislas (comp). *Bayard dans bresse* [*Opéra* in 2 acts, Prem. on 21-2-1791, Pub. in 1791].

Rouhier-Deschamps, J., Renault (comp). *Fin du jour, La* [*Opéra* in 1 act, Prem. on 1-8-1793].

Rousseau, Jean-Jacques. *Pygmalion* [*Opéra* in 1 act, Prem. in 1770, Pub. in 1775].

Roussel, Pierre.-J.-A. *Encore un tuteur dupé* [*Opéra*, Prem. on 22-2-1798, Pub. in 1798].

Salieri, Antonio. *Scuola de gelosi, La* [*Opéra*, Prem. on 20-5-1791].

Sarti. *Gelosie villane, Delle* [*Opéra*, Prem. on 14-4-1790].

Saugiers, Marc-A., Plantade, Charles-H. (comp). *Romagnesi* [*Opéra*, Prem. on 3-9-1799].

Sedaine, Michel-J., Grétry, André-E.-M. (comp). *Guillaume Tell* [*Opéra* in 3 acts, Prem. on 9-4-1791, Pub. in 1794].

Ségur, Alexander-J.-P., Vte. de. *Roméo et Juliette* [*Opéra* in 3 acts, Prem. on 10-9-1794].

Ségur, Louis-Philippe, Cte. de., Devienne, François (comp). *Mariage clandestin, Le* [*Opéra* in 1 act, Prem. on 11-11-1790, Pub. in 1779].

Sewrin, Charles-A. de Bassompierre, dit. *Deux orphelines, Les* [*Opéra*, Prem. on 26-5-1798, Pub. in 1797].

Souriguière de Saint-Marc, J.-M. *Céliane* [*Opéra* in 1 act, Prem. on 31-12-1796].

Tonioli, G., Paisiello, Giovanni (comp). *Locandiera, La* [*Opéra*, Prem. on 29-1-1791].

Valadier., Méhul, Etienne-N. (comp). *Cora* [*Opéra* in 4 acts, Prem. on 15-2-1791].

Vigée, Louis-J.-B.-E. *Projet extravagant, Le* [*Opéra* in 2 acts, Prem. on 11-7-1792].

Villiers, Pierre-A.-B. *Bébée et jargon* [*Opéra*, Prem. on 27-3-1797, Pub. in 1797].

Zini, Francesco-S., Guglielmi, Pietro.-A. (comp). *Pastorella nobile, La* [*Opéra* in 2 acts, Prem. in 4-1788, Pub. in 1789].

Anonymous or Unattributed Operas

A Qui la faute? [*Opéra*, Prem. on 29-1-1799].
Adèle ou La Chaumière [*Opéra*, Prem. on 1-2-1798].
Alexis et Fanchette [*Opéra* in 2 acts, Prem. on 11-11-1790].
Amour dragon, L' [*Opéra* in 2 acts, Prem. on 25-6-1792].
Amour par ressemblance, L' [*Opéra* in 2 acts, Prem. on 27-4-1792].
Antipathie, L' [*Opéra*, Prem. on 11-12-1798].
Arbre de la liberté, L' [*Opéra* in 1 act, Prem. on 3-1-1793].
Arlequin marchand d'esprit [*Opéra*].
Babet et Paulin ou Le Paysan supposé [*Opéra* in 2 acts].
Bastien et Colette [*Opéra* in 1 act, Prem. on 16-6-1791].
Bouquet de Lucinde, Le [*Opéra* in 1 act].
Cécile ou La Suite de Zélia [*Opéra* in 3 acts, Prem. on 25-2-1792].
Charlatans, Les [*Opéra* in 1 act, Prem. on 15-9-1794].
Choeur de Marathon, Le [*Opéra*].
Clavecin, Le [*Opéra*-Vaudeville].
Colinette à la cour ou La Double épreuve [*Opéra*, Pub. in 1782].
Communauté de Copenhague, La [*Opéra* in 3 acts, Prem. on 13-12-1790].
Compère Luc ou Les dangers de l'ivrognerie [*Opéra* in 2 acts].
Constance ou La Journée bien employée [*Opéra*, Prem. on 9-10-1798].
Coutelier de Bagdad, Le, ou Les Trois bossus [*Opéra* in 1 act, Pub. in 1792].
Défi, Le [*Opéra*, Prem. on 27-5-1797].
Deux frères, Les [*Opéra* in 3 acts, Prem. on 10-1-1792, Pub. in 1792].
Deux morts vivants, Les [*Opéra* in 1 act].
Deux Nicodèmes, Les [*Opéra* in 2 acts, Prem. on 21-11-1791].
Deux noces, Les [*Opéra* in 2 acts, Prem. on 15-4-1793].
Encore un diable [*Opéra*, Prem. on 13-6-1799].
Enfant républicain, L' [*Opéra* in 1 act, Prem. on 1-6-1794].
Enfants dans les bois, Les, ou La Tourterelle [*Opéra*, Prem. on 2-8-1797].
Eponine et Sabinus [*Opéra* in 3 acts, Prem. on 25-1-1796].
Epoux de seize ans, L', ou Le Berceau [*Opéra*, Prem. on 18-7-1798].
Extravagance de la vieillesse, L' [*Opéra* in 2 acts, Prem. on 21-5-1796].
Financier amoureux, Le [*Opéra* in 2 acts, Prem. on 5-11-1791].
Fou malgré lui, Le [*Opéra*, Prem. on 24-11-1798].
Fourberies de Frontin, Les [*Opéra*].
Gages d'amour, Les [*Opéra*, Prem. on 20-1-1792].
Gageure du pèlerin, La [*Opéra* in 2 acts].
Gasconnade [*Opéra* in 1 act, Prem. on 10-10-1796].
Grégoire et ses filles ou L'Intendant puni [*Opéra* in 1 act, Prem. on 5-11-1789].
Guillaume tout coeur [*Opéra* in 2 acts, Prem. on 23-1-1792].
Habitants du Vaucluse, Les [*Opéra*, Prem. on 1-6-1799].
Hôtellerie de Fontainebleau, L' [*Opéra* in 3 acts, Prem. on 18-5-1793].
Hymne à la paix [*Opéra*].
Inconstance sans inconstance [*Opéra*, Prem. on 22-10-1798].
Jacobins du 9 thermidor, Les [*Opéra* in 1 act, Pub. in 1795].
Laure et Zulme [*Opéra* in 3 acts].

Liberté de la presse, La [*Opéra* in 1 act, Pub. in 1794].
Lise et Justin [*Opéra* in 2 acts].
Livia ou L'Italienne à Londres [*Opéra* in 3 acts, Prem. on 13-4-1790, Pub. in 1787].
Lucette et Gercourt [*Opéra* in 1 act].
Lucinde et Raimond [*Opéra* in 3 acts, Pub. in 1794].
Maître de danse supposé, Le [*Opéra* in 3 acts].
Marcel [*Opéra* in 1 act, Pub. in 1795].
Mari jaloux, Le [*Opéra* in 2 acts, Prem. on 4-6-1791].
Mariages persans, Les [*Opéra* in 3 acts, Prem. on 5-1-1792].
Marie Christine ou La Promenade militaire [*Opéra*, Prem. on 12-11-1793].
Matinée des petits pères, La [*Opéra* in 1 act, Prem. on 2-5-1794, Pub. in 1794].
Mélinde et Ferval [*Opéra* in 2 acts, Prem. on 20-2-1796].
Miroir de la vérité, Le [*Opéra*].
Mirtil et Licoris [*Opéra*, Prem. on 9-4-1791].
Moine généreux, Le [*Opéra* in 4 acts].
Nautilde et Dagobert [*Opéra* in 3 acts, Prem. on 1-10-1791].
Olivia [*Opéra* in 1 act, Prem. on 4-1-1796].
Pari de 24 heures, Le, ou La Nouvelle prise de Toulon [*Opéra* in 1 act, Pub. in 1794].
Pierre Dandin [*Opéra*, Prem. on 11-2-1792].
Premier mai, Le, ou Les Bons paysans [*Opéra* in 1 act].
Prix de l'hospitalité ou Le Chevalier [*Opéra* in 2 acts].
Roméo et Juliette [*Opéra* in 3 acts, Prem. on 10-9-1794].
Sans-culottes, Les, ou Le Dîner interrompu [*Opéra* in 1 act, Pub. in 1794].
Sopha [*Opéra*, Prem. on 26-8-1791].
Tracasseries inutiles, Les [*Opéra* in 2 acts].
Triomphe de l'amour, Le [*Opéra* in 3 acts].
Vengeances, Les [*Opéra* in 2 acts, Prem. on 10-10-1791].
Voyage aérien de Madame Angot dans le ballon, Le [*Opéra*].
Washington ou Le Règne des lois [*Opéra* in 3 acts, Prem. on 5-5-1796].

16

Statistical Overview and Tables

The preceding Repertory of French Revolutionary theater is drawn from a database of daily play performances compiled from several sources. For each performance, the database contains the date of that performance, the name of the theater, the genre, number of acts, authors and composers, complete title, and dates of publication and premiere of the play. The database contains information concerning 90,744 performances of 3,742 different plays at some 50 different theaters from the January 1, 1789, to November 9, 1799. In addition to the preceding Repertory, the database allows us to generate a number of statistical summaries outlining the characteristics of the Parisian stage. The following will present the most significant and helpful statistical summaries in prose and tabular fashion as warranted.

In compiling the database, we have attempted to identify authors and composers of individual plays from several bibliographic sources, as the listings found in the *Petites affiches* and the *Journal de Paris* frequently do not list the authors and composers. We have identified at least one author/composer for 1,552 (58.5 percent) of the plays. As expected, we were able to assign an author or composer to the more popular plays. Thus, attributed plays comprise 74,257 (81.8 percent) of all performances in the database. A secondary element of authorial attribution is attribution of one or more composers for performances of operas and other plays with an important musical component. We have found a composer for 515 (13.8 percent) of the individual titles in the repertory. Performances of works with a significant musical component are relatively more important, comprising almost a quarter of all performances (20,944 performances or 23.1% of all performances, and

28.2 percent of attributed performances).

The genre of works was also compiled from a number of standard bibliographic sources. We were able to assign a genre to 77 percent of all works and 91 percent of all performances. The following table indicates that comedy, opera, pantomime, comic opera, and vaudeville were the most popular genres, in terms of both the number of works and the number of performances, though in rather different proportions. Thus, while comedies make up a little more than a third (36.9 percent) of individual plays, they comprise almost half (49.2 percent) of all performances.

Table 1. Top 15 Genres by Number of Performances
with Number and Percentage of Genre in the Repertory

Genre	Performances	(%)	Repertory	(%)
1. Comédie	44630	(49.2)	1383	(36.9)
2. Unknown	7941	(8.7)	866	(23.1)
3. Pantomime	6428	(7.1)	210	(5.6)
4. Opéra	5008	(5.5)	227	(6.1)
5. Opéra-Comique	3405	(3.7)	149	(4.0)
6. Tragédie	3226	(3.5)	135	(3.6)
7. Vaudeville	3167	(3.5)	154	(4.1)
8. Drame	2851	(3.1)	112	(3.0)
9. Fait Historique	1944	(2.1)	86	(2.3)
10. Ballet	1778	(2.0)	57	(1.5)
11. Tableau-Patriotique	1239	(1.4)	71	(1.9)
12. Opéra-Bouffe	1194	(1.3)	30	(0.8)
13. Pièce	1069	(1.2)	36	(1.0)
14. Divertissement/parade	923	(1.0)	31	(0.8)
15. Comédie mêlée d'ariettes	889	(1.0)	10	(0.3)

The stage remained a vital element of Parisian cultural life through every phase of the Revolution with almost twenty-five performances a day during the entire Revolution. As indicated in Table 2, even the political, economic and military crises of 1793-1794 had only a minimal impact on the number of performances held at Parisian theaters. Indeed, 1793 ranks second only to 1796 in terms of the number of performances. The entire period is also marked by a relatively consistent increase in the number of active theaters, reflecting important changes in the legislation governing the Parisian stage.

Table 2. Number of Performances and Number of Different Theaters by Year, 1789-1799

Year	No. of Performances	No. of Theaters
1789	6043	9
1790	7171	11
1791	8682	27
1792	7602	17
1793	9359	20
1794	7506	21
1795	7653	23
1796	10427	29
1797	8907	32
1798	8816	31
1799	8559	33

The number of performances of plays that either premiered or were published before 1789, and thus might be considered part of the "traditional" or *ancien régime* repertory, declined over the ten years of the Revolution. Overall, a significant proportion of plays (1097 or 37.4 percent of plays assigned dates) and almost half of all performances (38,204 or 46.8 percent of plays with attributed dates) were drawn from the *ancien régime*. Plays drawn from the pre-Revolutionary repertory were, as might be expected of older "classics," had significantly longer runs. Plays from the *ancien régime* were performed 34.8 times each, while plays which premiered or were published during the Revolution were performed 24.4 times. The 811 plays (representing 9189 performances) for which no date has been assigned were performed 9.7 times each. The large majority of these undated plays are probably from the Revolutionary repertory.

Table 3. Performances of Plays Premiered or Published Before and After 1789, with Percentages (excluding undated plays) and with Number of Performances of Undated Plays

Year(s)	Ancien Régime		Revolution		Undated
1789:	4392	(74.4%)	1510	(25.6%)	141
1790:	4084	(59.1%)	2830	(40.9%)	257
1791:	4987	(60.0%)	3316	(40.0%)	379
1792:	4120	(56.5%)	3165	(43.5%)	317
1793:	3932	(45.7%)	4678	(54.3%)	749
1794:	2169	(30.9%)	4846	(69.1%)	491
1795:	3054	(45.8%)	3613	(54.2%)	986
1796:	4435	(50.8%)	4291	(49.2%)	1701
1797:	2868	(39.1%)	4470	(60.9%)	1569
1798:	2106	(28.2%)	5359	(71.8%)	1351
1799:	2057	(28.1%)	5254	(71.9%)	1248
1789-1799:	38204	(46.8%)	43332	(53.2%)	9199

Table 4. Top 50 Plays by Number of Performances, 1789-1799

1. Desforges, Pierre-J.-B. Choudard de. *Sourd, Le, ou L'Auberge pleine*, 463
2. Anseaume, Louis. *Deux chasseurs et la laitière, Les*, 355
3. Baurans, Pierre. *Servante maîtresse, La*, 335
4. Molière, Jean-B. Poquelin de. *Ecole des maris, L'*, 316
5. Beaumarchais, Pierre-A.C. de. *Barbier de Séville, Le, ou La Précaution inutile*, 313
6. Arnould, Jean-F. Mussot, dit. *Forêt noire, La, ou Le Fils naturel*, 311
7. Molière, Jean-B. Poquelin de. *Dépit amoureux, Le*, 307
8. Guillemain, Charles-J. *Enrôlement supposé, L'*, 303
9. Picard, Louis-B. *Visitandines, Les*, 286
10. Molière, Jean-B. Poquelin de. *Médecin malgré lui, Le*, 284
11. Regnard, Jean-F. Renard, dit. *Folies amoureuses, Les*, 280
12. Beffroy de Reigny, L.-A. *Nicodème dans la lune ou La Révolution pacifique*, 266
13. Rousseau, Jean-Jacques. *Devin du village, Le*, 264
14. Gardel, Pierre-G. *Psyché*, 243
15. Destouches, Philippe-N. *Fausse Agnès, La, ou Le Poète campagnard*, 240
16. Boutet de Monvel, J.-M. *Blaise et Babet ou La Suite des trois fermiers*, 239
17. Lazzari, Ange. *Cinquantaine infernale, La, ou La Baleine avalée par Arlequin*, 221
18. Desfontaines, François-G. Fouques, dit. *Dot, La*, 220
19. Marsollier des Vivetières, Benoît-J. *Deux petits savoyards, Les*, 218
20. Grenier. *Mélomanie, La*, 214
21. Dorvigny, Louis-A. *Désespoir de Jocrisse, Le*, 211
22. Guyot de Merville, Michel. *Consentement forcé, Le*, 207
23. Gardel, Pierre-G. *Télémaque dans l'île de Calypso*, 203
24. Boutet de Monvel, Jacques-M. *Philippe et Georgette*, 201
25. Brueys, David-A. de. *Avocat Patelin, L'*, 199
26. Guillard, Nicolas-F. *Oedipe à Colone*, 196
27. Bourlin, Antoine-J. *Ricco*, 195
28. Pompigny, Maurin de. *Héritage, L', ou L'Epreuve raisonnable*, 195
29. Demoustier, Charles-A. *Amour filial, L', ou Les Deux suisses*, 194
30. Gaullard de Saudray, Charles-E. *Capucins aux frontières, Les*, 193
31. Gardel, Maximilien. *Déserteur, Le*, 192
32. Voltaire, F.-M. Arouet, dit Arouet de. *Nanine*, 192
33. Andrieux, François-G.-J.-S. *Etourdis, Les, ou Le Mort supposé*, 186
34. Cuvelier de Trie, Jean G.-A. *Fille hussard, La, ou Le Sergent suédois*, 183
35. Barré, Pierre-Y. *Arlequin afficheur*, 181
36. Deschamps, Jacques-M. *Piron avec ses amis ou Les Moeurs du temps passé*, 179
37. Bourlin, Antoine-J. *Guerre ouverte ou Ruse contre ruse*, 176
38. Gossec, François-J. *Offrande à la liberté, L'*, 174
39. Boussenard de Soubreville. *Réveil du charbonnier, Le*, 173
40. Barthe, Nicolas-T. *Fausses infidélités, Les*, 171
41. Lazzari, Ange. *Ariston ou Le Pouvoir de la magie*, 169
42. Marivaux, Pierre-C. de C. de. *Jeu de l'amour et du hasard, Le*, 169
43. Arnould, Jean-F. Mussot, dit. *Bascule, La*, 167
44. Cuvelier de Trie, Jean G.-A. *Petit poucet, Le, ou L'Orphelin de la forêt*, 163
45. Guillemain, Charles-J. *Boniface pointu et sa famille*, 163
46. Arnould, Jean-F. Mussot, dit. *Maréchal des logis, Le*, 162
47. La Martelière, Jean-H.-F. *Robert, chef de brigands*, 160
48. Pompigny, Maurin de. *Artisan philosophe, L', ou L'Ecole des pères*, 160
49. Léger, François-P.-A. *Gageure inutile, La, ou Plus de peur que de mal*, 159
50. Ségur, Alexander-J.-P., Vte. de. *Roméo et Juliette*, 157

Table 5. Top 100 Authors by Number of Performances, 1789-1799

1. Beaunoir, A.-L.-B. Robineau dit: **1968**
2. Molière, Jean-B. Poquelin de: **1864**
3. Guillemain, Charles-J.: **1780**
4. Barré, Pierre-Y.: **1662**
5. Dorvigny, Louis-A.: **1528**
6. Radet, Jean-B.: **1271**
7. Arnould, Jean-F. Mussot, dit: **1244**
8. Cuvelier de Trie, Jean G.-A.: **1223**
9. Boutet de Monvel, Jacques-M.: **1206**
10. Bourlin, Antoine-J.: **1118**
11. Pigault-Lebrun, C. de L'Epinoy: **1118**
12. Patrat, Joseph: **1090**
13. Marsollier des Vivetières, Benoît-J.: **1013**
14. Picard, Louis-B.: **1004**
15. Desforges, P.-J.-B. Choudard de: **900**
16. Voltaire, F.-M. Arouet: **896**
17. Léger, François-P.-A.: **885**
18. Gabiot de Salins, Jean-L.: **871**
19. Hoffman, François-B.: **867**
20. Lazzari, Ange: **865**
21. Sedaine, Michel-J.: **852**
22. Anseaume, Louis: **834**
23. Desfontaines, F.-G. Fouques, dit: **834**
24. Pompigny, Maurin de: **818**
25. Beaumarchais, Pierre-A.C. de: **811**
26. Beffroy de Reigny, Louis-A.: **754**
27. Du Buisson, Paul-U.: **745**
28. Gardel, Maximilien: **656**
29. Deschamps, Jacques-M.: **649**
30. Regnard, Jean-F. Renard, dit: **624**
31. Destouches, Philippe-N.: **613**
32. Ségur, Alexander-J.-P.: **583**
33. Marivaux, Pierre-C. de C. de: **559**
34. Dancourt, Florent C.: **545**
35. Demoustier, Charles-A.: **505**
36. Florian, Jean-P.-C. de: **477**
37. Guillard, Nicolas-F.: **475**
38. Audinot, Nicolas-M.: **469**
39. Dejaure, Jean-E. Bédéno: **448**
40. Fabre d'Eglantine, P.-F.-N.: **447**
41. Gardel, Pierre-G.: **446**
42. Hapdé, Jean-B.-A.: **437**
43. Destival de Braban, Jean N., dit: **433**
44. Duval, Alexandre-V.P.: **410**
45. Favières, Edmond-G.-F. de: **402**
46. Rousseau, Jean-Jacques: **400**
47. Ribié, César: **394**
48. Sedaine de Sarcy, Jean-F.: **389**
49. Marmontel, Jean F.: **376**
50. Baurans, Pierre: **353**
51. Sewrin, C.-A. de Bassompierre, dit: **353**
52. Favart, Charles-S.: **351**
53. Legrand, Marc-A.: **350**
54. Lebrun Tossa, Jean-A.: **344**
55. Aude, Joseph: **317**
56. Fagan, Barthélemy-C.: **310**
57. Andrieux, François-G.-J.-S.: **304**
58. Boissy, Louis de: **304**
59. Lachabeaussière, A.-E.-X.P. de: **301**
60. Loaisel de Tréogate, Joseph-M.: **301**
61. Racine, Jean: **298**
62. Legros: **292**
63. Rochon de Chabannes, Marc: **292**
64. Eve, Antoine-F., dit Maillot: **291**
65. Hèle, Thomas d': **288**
66. Piis, Chevalier P.-A.-A. de: **286**
67. Mercier, Louis-S.: **284**
68. Planterre, Barthélemy: **284**
69. Chénier, Marie-J.: **283**
70. Poisson, Philippe: **279**
71. Forgeot, Nicolas-J.: **273**
72. La Harpe, Jean-F. de: **268**
73. Hauteroche, Noel de: **266**
74. Brueys, David-A. de: **262**
75. Guilbert de Pixerécourt, R.-C.: **260**
76. Mayeur de St.-Paul, F.-M.: **260**
77. Placide, Alex.-P.-Bussart, dit: **260**
78. Pujoulx, Jean-B.: **258**
79. Crêton de Villeneuve: **251**
80. Collé, Charles: **247**
81. Collin d'Harleville, Jean-F.: **247**
82. Charlemagne, Armand: **245**
83. Hennequin, Louis: **244**
84. Vadé, Jean-J.: **242**
85. Monnet, Jean: **228**
86. Lesage, Alain-R.: **221**
87. Plancher de Valcour, Aristide: **218**
88. Grenier: **217**
89. Dercy, P.: **209**
90. Favart, Marie-J.-B.D.: **208**
91. Guyot de Merville, Michel: **208**
92. Du Roullet, François-L.: **201**
93. Rivière-Dufresny, Charles: **200**
94. Legouvé, Gabriel-M.-J.-B.: **198**
95. Corneille, Pierre: **197**
96. Parisau, Pierre-G.: **197**
97. Moline, Pierre-L.: **194**
98. Gaullard de Saudray, Ch.-E.: **193**
99. Biancolelli, Pierre-F.: **189**
100. De Senne: **189**

Table 6. Top Ten Plays by Number of Performances by Year

1789

1. Dorvigny, Louis-A. *Père Duchesne, Le, ou La Mauvaise habitude*, 83
2. Du Buisson, Paul-U. *Philosophe imaginaire, Le*, 69
3. Marsollier des Vivetières, Benoît-J. *Deux petits savoyards, Les*, 65
4. Thiemet. *Comédien de société, Le*, 51
5. Gourbillon, Joseph-A. *Marquis de Tulipano, Le*, 49
6. Ribié, César. *Enfants du soleil, Les, ou Les Vestales du nouveau monde*, 43
7. Guillemain, Charles-J. *Mensonge excusable, Le*, 43
8. Du Boccage, Anne-M.-L. *Amazones, Les*, 43
9. Lepitre, Jacques-F. *Bon père, Le*, 40
10. Plaute, Marcus-A. *Captifs, Les*, 38

1790

1. Arnould, Jean-F. Mussot, dit. *Homme au masque de fer, L', ou Le Souterrain*, 56
2. Bourlin, Antoine-J. *Ricco*, 53
3. Guillemain, Charles-J. *Menuisier de Bagdad, Le*, 52
4. Desforges, Pierre-J.-B. Choudard de. *Sourd, Le, ou L'Auberge pleine*, 50
5. Mayeur de St.-Paul. *Déguisements amoureux, Les*, 44
6. Gabiot de Salins, Jean-L. *Paris sauvé ou La Conspiration manquée*, 44
7. Arnaud, François-T.-M. *Amants malheureux, Les, ou Le Comte de Comminges*, 43
8. Desfontaines, François-G. Fouques, dit. *Dot, La*, 42
9. Léger, François-P.-A. *Folle gageure, La*, 40
10. Bourlin, Antoine-J. *Soldat prussien, Le, ou Le Bon fils*, 40

1791

1. Beffroy de Reigny, Louis-A. *Nicodème dans la lune ou La Révolution pacifique*, 171
2. Baurans, Pierre. *Servante maîtresse, La*, 88
3. Desforges, Pierre-J.-B. Choudard de. *Sourd, Le, ou L'Auberge pleine*, 84
4. Anseaume, Louis. *Deux chasseurs et la laitière, Les*, 74
5. Rousseau, Jean-Jacques. *Devin du village, Le*, 60
6. Regnard, Jean-F. Renard, dit. *Folies amoureuses, Les*, 59
7. Molière, Jean-B. Poquelin de. *Médecin malgré lui, Le*, 55
8. Anseaume, Louis. *Mazet*, 54
9. Marivaux, Pierre-C. de C. de. *Jeu de l'amour et du hasard, Le*, 53
10. Arnould, Jean-F. Mussot, dit. *Forêt noire, La, ou Le Fils naturel*, 52

1792

1. Molière, Jean-B. Poquelin de. *Médecin malgré lui, Le*, 71
2. Anseaume, Louis. *Deux chasseurs et la laitière, Les*, 69
3. Molière, Jean-B. Poquelin de. *Ecole des maris, L'*, 67
4. Barré, Pierre-Y. *Arlequin afficheur*, 61
5. Destouches, Philippe-N. *Fausse Agnès, La, ou Le Poète campagnard*, 57
6. Demoustier, Charles-A. *Amour filial, L', ou Les Deux suisses*, 53
7. Brueys, David-A. de. *Avocat Patelin, L'*, 53
8. Baurans, Pierre. *Servante maîtresse, La*, 52
9. Arnould, Jean-F. Mussot, dit. *Forêt noire, La, ou Le Fils naturel*, 52
10. Vadé, Jean-J. *Nicaise*, 51

1793

1. Picard, Louis-B. *Visitandines, Les*, 78
2. Gaullard de Saudray, Charles-E. *Capucins aux frontières, Les*, 58
3. *Sauteurs, Les*, 57
4. Barré, Pierre-Y. *Heureuse décade, L'*, 57
5. Gossec, François-J. *Offrande à la liberté, L'*, 57
6. Radet, Jean-B. *Bonne aubaine, La*, 55
7. Léger, François-P.-A. *Nicaise, peintre*, 55

8. Barré, Pierre-Y. *Colombine mannequin,* **53**
9. Aude, Joseph. *Cadet Roussel ou Le Café des aveugles,* **51**
10. Candeille, Amélie-Julie. *Catherine ou La Belle fermière,* **49**

1794

1. Radet, Jean-B. *Au retour,* **87**
2. Beaupré. *Sabotiers, Les,* **71**
3. Pigault-Lebrun, Charles-A.P. de L'Epinoy, dit. *Dragons et les Bénédictines, Les,* **66**
4. Pigault-Lebrun, Charles-A.P. de L'Epinoy, dit. *Dragons en cantonnement, Les,* **64**
5. Gaullard de Saudray, Charles-E. *Capucins aux frontières, Les,* **61**
6. Barré, Pierre-Y. *Heureuse décade, L',* **61**
7. Arnould, Jean-F. Mussot, dit. *Maréchal des logis, Le,* **60**
8. Deschamps, Jacques-M. *Claudine ou Le Petit commissionnaire,* **52**
9. Gamas. *Michel Cervantes,* **50**
10. *Fête civique, La,* **48**

1795

1. Picard, Louis-B. *Suspects, Les,* **112**
2. Lazzari, Ange. *Cinquantaine infernale, La, ou La Baleine avalée par Arlequin,* **77**
3. Molière, Jean-B. Poquelin de. *Dépit amoureux, Le,* **68**
4. Baurans, Pierre. *Servante maîtresse, La,* **67**
5. Guillemain, Charles-J. *Enrôlement supposé, L',* **59**
6. Anseaume, Louis. *Deux chasseurs et la laitière, Les,* **58**
7. Deschamps, Jacques-M. *Claudine ou Le Petit commissionnaire,* **55**
8. Ducancel, Charles-P. *Intérieur des comités révolutionnaires,*
     L', ou Les Aristides modernes, **52**
9. Salm-Reifferscheid-Dyck, Constance-M. *Sapho,* **51**
10. Patrat, Joseph. *Heureux quiproquo, L', ou Le Présent,* **50**

1796

1. Cuvelier de Trie, Jean G.-A. *Fille hussard, La, ou Le Sergent suédois,* **65**
2. Boutet de Monvel, J.-M. *Blaise et Babet ou La Suite des trois fermiers,* **65**
3. Baurans, Pierre. *Servante maîtresse, La,* **65**
4. Beaumarchais, Pierre-A.C. de. *Barbier de Séville, Le, ou La Précaution inutile,* **64**
5. Molière, Jean-B. Poquelin de. *Dépit amoureux, Le,* **63**
6. Guillemain, Charles-J. *Enrôlement supposé, L',* **62**
7. Desforges, Pierre-J.-B. Choudard de. *Sourd, Le, ou L'Auberge pleine,* **62**
8. Andrieux, François-G.-J.-S. *Etourdis, Les, ou Le Mort supposé,* **62**
9. Gouffé, Armand Alexandre Duval. *Deux Jocrisses, Les, ou Le Commerce à l'eau,* **59**
10. Riccoboni, Antoine-F. *Zéphire et Flore,* **58**

1797

1. Cuvelier de Trie, Jean G.-A. *Enfant du malheur, L', ou Les Amants muets,* **87**
2. Desforges, Pierre-J.-B. Choudard de. *Sourd, Le, ou L'Auberge pleine,* **86**
3. Gabiot de Salins, Jean-L. *Enfant du bonheur, L',* **85**
4. Lazzari, Ange. *Ariston ou Le Pouvoir de la magie,* **84**
5. Eve, Antoine-F, dit Maillot. *Mariage de Nanon,*
     Le, ou La Suite de Madame Angot, **74**
6. Eve, Antoine-F, dit Maillot. *Madame Angot ou La Poissarde parvenue,* **70**
7. Mittié, Jean-C. *Paix, La, ou Les Amants réunis,* **54**
8. *Amant hermite, L',* **52**
9. Boussenard de Soubreville. *Réveil du charbonnier, Le,* **49**
10. Beaumarchais, Pierre-A.C. de. *Barbier de Séville, Le, ou La Précaution inutile,* **49**

1798

1. Cammaille-Saint-Aubin, M.-C. *Moine, Le,* **96**
2. Cuvelier de Trie, Jean G.-A. *Petit poucet, Le, ou L'Orphelin de la forêt,* **79**
3. Duval, Alexandre-V.P. *Prisonnier, Le, ou La Ressemblance,* **71**

4. Dorvigny, Louis-A. *Désespoir de Jocrisse, Le*, **70**
5. *Fin du monde, La, ou La Comète*, **68**
6. Henriquez, L.-M. *Chaudronnier de St.-Flour, Le*, **68**
7. Aude, Joseph. *Cadet Roussel barbier à la fontaine des innocents*, **68**
8. Cuvelier de Trie, Jean G.-A. *C'est le diable ou La Bohémienne*, **66**
9. Lazzari, Ange. *Ariston ou Le Pouvoir de la magie*, **65**
10. Guillemain, Charles-J. *Enrôlement supposé, L'*, **63**

1799
1. Rigaud, Antoine-F. *Inconnu, L', ou Misanthropie et repentir*, **93**
2. Cuvelier de Trie, Jean G.-A. *Petit poucet, Le, ou L'Orphelin de la forêt*, **84**
3. Marsollier des Vivetières, Benoît-J. *Adolphe et Clara ou Les Deux prisonniers*, **67**
4. *Marquis de Bièvre, Le*, **57**
5. Jouy, Victor-J. E., dit de. *Comment faire ou Les Epreuves de misanthropie et repentir*, **56**
6. Cuvelier de Trie, Jean G.-A. *Fille hussard, La, ou Le Sergent suédois*, **56**
7. Patrat, Joseph. *Amants protées, Les, ou Qui compte sans son hôte compte deux fois*, **55**
8. Pompigny, Maurin de. *Barogo ou La Suite du Ramoneur prince*, **51**
9. Gardel, Maximilien. *Déserteur, Le*, **51**
10. Cuvelier de Trie, J. G.-A. *Damoisel et la bergerette, La, ou La Femme vindicative*, **48**

**Table 7. Top 50 Plays by Number of Performances During
the Terror, September 5, 1793 - July 27, 1794**

1. Radet, Jean-B. *Au retour*, **86**
2. Barré, Pierre-Y. *Heureuse décade, L'*, **77**
3. Gaullard de Saudray, Charles-E. *Capucins aux frontières, Les*, **67**
4. Beaupré. *Sabotiers, Les*, **66**
5. Pigault-Lebrun, Charles-A.P. de L'Epinoy, dit. *Dragons et les Bénédictines, Les*, **52**
6. Arnould, Jean-F. Mussot, dit. *Maréchal des logis, Le*, **51**
7. Gossec, François-J. *Offrande à la liberté, L'*, **51**
8. Molière, Jean-B. Poquelin de. *Médecin malgré lui, Le*, **46**
9. Radet, Jean-B. *Faucon, Le*, **45**
10. *Fête civique, La*, **45**
11. Brazier, Nicolas. *Alain et Suzette ou Le Fils adoptif*, **45**
12. *Départ des patriotes, Le, ou La Loterie des filles*, **42**
13. Du Buisson, Paul-U. *Flora*, **41**
14. Ségur, Alexander-J.-P., Vte. de. *Roméo et Juliette*, **40**
15. *Adèle de Sacy ou Le Siège du Mont-Cenis*, **40**
16. *Pomme de Rambour, La*, **39**
17. *Apollon ou Le triomphe des arts utiles*, **39**
18. Arnould, Jean-F. Mussot, dit. *Bascule, La*, **39**
19. Pigault-Lebrun, Charles-A.P. de L'Epinoy, dit. *Dragons en cantonnement, Les*, **38**
20. *Nouveau calendrier, Le*, **38**
21. *Laure et Zulme*, **36**
22. Quinault, Philippe. *Armide*, **35**
23. Gardel, Maximilien. *Nid d'oiseau, Le, ou Colin et Colette*, **35**
24. Gallet, Sébastien. *Fête civique, La*, **35**
25. Sewrin, C.-A. de Bassompierre, dit. *Loups et les brebis, Les, ou La Nuit d'été*, **34**
26. Puységur, A.-M.-J. de Chastenet, M. de. *Intérieur d'un ménage républicain, L'*, **34**
27. Desforges, Pierre-J.-B. Choudard de. *Sourd, Le, ou L'Auberge pleine*, **34**
28. Arnould, Jean-F. Mussot, dit. *Forêt noire, La, ou Le Fils naturel*, **34**
29. Radet, Jean-B. *Noble roturier, Le*, **33**
30. Picard, Louis-B. *Visitandines, Les*, **33**
31. Gamas. *Michel Cervantes*, **33**
32. Quétant, Antoine-F. *Savetier et le financier, Le, ou Contentement passe richesse*, **32**
33. Grenier. *Mélomanie, La*, **32**
34. Florian, Jean-P.-C. de. *Bon père, Le, ou La Suite du bon ménage*, **32**
35. Sewrin, Charles-A. de Bassompierre, dit. *Ruse villageoise, La*, **31**
36. Guilbert de Pixerécourt, René-.C. *Selico ou Les Nègres généreux*, **31**
37. Gourgault, J.B. Henri Dugazon pseud. *Modéré, Le*, **31**
38. Guillard, Nicolas-F. *Miltiade à Marathon*, **30**
39. Deschamps, Jacques-M. *Claudine ou Le Petit commissionnaire*, **30**
40. Regnard, Jean-F. Renard, dit. *Folies amoureuses, Les*, **29**
41. Radet, Jean-B. *Fête de l'égalité, La*, **29**
42. Patrat, Joseph. *Deux grenadiers, Les, ou Les Quiproquos*, **29**
43. Plancher de Valcour, dit Aristide. *Vous et le toi, Le*, **28**
44. Piis, Chevalier P.-A.-A. de. *Nourrice républicaine, La*, **28**
45. *Houlans, Les, ou Les Effets de la liberté*, **28**
46. *Gâteau des tyrans, Le*, **28**
47. Beaunoir, Alexandre-L.-B. Robineau dit. *Diable boiteux, Le*, **28**
48. Dubreuil, Alphonse-D. *Paulin et Virginie*, **28**
49. Voisenon, Abbé-C.-H. de Fusée de. *Mariages assortis, Les*, **27**
50. Marsollier des Vivetières, Benoît-J. *Camille ou Le Souterrain*, **27**

**Table 8. Top 50 Plays by Number of Performances during the
Thermidorian Reaction, July 28, 1794 - October 26, 1795**

1. Picard, Louis-B. *Suspects, Les*, 112
2. Deschamps, Jacques-M. *Claudine ou Le Petit commissionnaire*, 72
3. Gardel, Pierre-G. *Télémaque dans l'île de Calypso*, 66
4. Molière, Jean-B. Poquelin de. *Dépit amoureux, Le*, 64
5. Lazzari, Ange. *Cinquantaine infernale, La, ou La Baleine avalée par Arlequin*, 64
6. Ducancel, C.-P. *Intérieur des comités révolutionnaires,
          L', ou Les Aristides modernes*, 52
7. Bernard, Pierre-J. *Castor et Pollux*, 51
8. Arnould, Jean-F. Mussot, dit. *Forêt noire, La, ou Le Fils naturel*, 51
9. Anseaume, Louis. *Deux chasseurs et la laitière, Les*, 51
10. Patrat, Joseph. *Heureux quiproquo, L', ou Le Présent*, 50
11. Baurans, Pierre. *Servante maîtresse, La*, 50
12. Salm-Reifferscheid-Dyck, Constance-M. *Sapho*, 49
13. Rousseau, Jean-Jacques. *Devin du village, Le*, 49
14. Du Buisson, Paul-U. *Zelia ou Le Mari à deux femmes*, 48
15. Arnould, Jean-F. Mussot, dit. *Hérolhe américaine, L'*, 48
16. Pigault-Lebrun, C.-A.P. de L'Epinoy, dit. *Dragons et les bénédictines, Les*, 44
17. Pigault-Lebrun, Charles-A.P. de L'Epinoy, dit. *Dragons en cantonnement, Les*, 44
18. Guillemain, Charles-J. *Enrôlement supposé, L'*, 43
19. Boutet de Monvel, J.-M. *Blaise et Babet ou La Suite des trois fermiers*, 42
20. Gaullard de Saudray, Charles-E. *Capucins aux frontières, Les*, 41
21. Rousseau, Jean-Jacques. *Pygmalion*, 39
22. Léger, François-P.-A. *Christophe Dubois*, 39
23. *Fermier bienfaisant, Le*, 38
24. Picard, Louis-B. *Visitandines, Les*, 37
25. Chamfort, Sébastien-R.-N. *Jeune indienne, La*, 37
26. Boutet de Monvel, Jacques-M. *Philippe et Georgette*, 37
27. Barthe, Nicolas-T. *Fausses infidélités, Les*, 36
28. Sedaine, Michel-J. *Guillaume Tell*, 35
29. Bourlin, Antoine-J. *Guerre ouverte ou Ruse contre Ruse*, 35
30. Sylvestre. *Deux fermiers, Les*, 33
31. Piis, Chevalier P.-A.-A. de. *Plaisirs de l'hospitalité, Les*, 33
32. Hennequin, Louis. *Emilie et Melcour ou La Leçon villageoise*, 32
33. Ségur, Alexander-J.-P., Vte. de. *Roméo et Juliette*, 31
34. Planterre, Barthélemy. *Famille indigente, La*, 30
35. Guyot de Merville, Michel. *Consentement forcé, Le*, 30
36. Guillard, Nicolas-F. *Oedipe à Colone*, 30
37. Guillard, Nicolas-F. *Iphigénie en Tauride*, 30
38. Gardel, Maximilien. *Déserteur, Le*, 30
39. Desfontaines, François-G. Fouques, dit. *Fille soldat, La*, 30
40. *Cange*, 29
41. Loraux, Claude-F. Fillette, dit. *Lodoiska*, 29
42. Desforges, Pierre-J.-B. Choudard de. *Sourd, Le, ou L'Auberge pleine*, 29
43. Chaussier, Hector. *Jacobins aux enfers, Les*, 29
44. Barré, Pierre-Y. *Abuzar ou La Famille extravagante*, 29
45. *Prisonniers français patriotes, Les*, 28
46. *Plaisirs du printemps, Les*, 28
47. Guillemain, Charles-J. *Auberge isolée, L'*, 28
48. François de Neufchâteau, Nicolas-L. *Paméla ou La Vertu récompensée*, 28
49. Desfontaines, François-G. Fouques, dit. *Divorce, Le*, 28
50. Demoustier, Charles-A. *Divorce, Le*, 28

Table 9. Top Twenty Theatres by
Number of Performances, 1789-1799

	Performances	Theater
1.	9023	Th. des Grands Danseurs (Gaîté)
2.	8875	Th. de l'Ambigu Comique
3.	7669	Th. des Italiens (Opéra-Comique)
4.	7395	Th. du Vaudeville
5.	5913	Th. du Feydeau (de Monsieur)
6.	5852	Th. de la Citoyenne Montansier
7.	4527	Th. Français (Richelieu) (République)
8.	4283	Th. des Jeunes Artistes
9.	3331	Th. du Palais (Cité)-Variétés
10.	3092	Th. de la Nation (Comédie Française)
11.	3057	Académie de la Musique (Opéra)
12.	2758	Th. Lyrique des amis de la Patrie
13.	2490	Th. de l'Emulation (Gaîté)
14.	2099	Th. des Variétés Amusantes, Comiques...
15.	1948	Th. du Palais Royal
16.	1696	Th. de la Cité
17.	1641	Th. de Molière
18.	1574	Th. des Beaujolais
19.	1566	Th. du Lycée des Arts
20.	1459	Th. du Marais

Table 10. Plays Performed at Fifteen or More
Theaters, with Number of Theaters

Andrieux, François-G.-J.-S. *Etourdis, Les, ou Le Mort supposé*, **20**
Anseaume, Louis. *Deux chasseurs et la laitière, Les*, **21**
Barthe, Nicolas-T. *Fausses infidélités, Les*, **26**
Baurans, Pierre. *Servante maîtresse, La*, **31**
Beaumarchais, Pierre-A.C. de. *Barbier de Séville, Le, ou La Précaution inutile*, **18**
Boursault, Edmonde. *Mercure galant, Le, ou La Comédie sans titre*, **17**
Brueys, David-A. de. *Avocat Patelin, L'*, **17**
Cérou, Chevalier de. *Amant auteur et valet, L'*, **19**
Collé, Charles. *Dupuis et Desronais*, **22**
Dancourt, Florent C. *Mari retrouvé, Le*, **16**
Desforges, Pierre-J.-B. Choudard de. *Sourd, Le, ou L'Auberge pleine*, **15**
Destouches, Philippe-N. *Fausse Agnès, La, ou Le Poète campagnard*, **20**
Diderot, Denis. *Père de famille, Le*, **19**
Dorat, Claude-J. *Feinte par amour, La*, **23**
Dorvigny, Louis-A. *Fête de campagne, La, ou L'Intendant comédien malgré lui*, **16**
Fagan, Barthélemy-C. *Pupille, La*, **19**
Guyot de Merville, Michel. *Consentement forcé, Le*, **15**
Hauteroche, Noel de. *Crispin médecin*, **16**
Lesage, Alain-R. *Crispin rival de son maître*, **15**
Marivaux, Pierre-C. de C. de. *Jeu de l'amour et du hasard, Le*, **22**
Molière, Jean-B. Poquelin de. *Dépit amoureux, Le*, **34**
Molière, Jean-B. Poquelin de. *Ecole des maris, L'*, **25**
Molière, Jean-B. Poquelin de. *Médecin malgré lui, Le*, **22**
Molière, Jean-B. Poquelin de. *Tartuffe*, **20**
Poisson, Philippe. *Impromptu de campagne, L'*, **17**
Pont-de-Veyle, A. de Feriol, Comte de. *Somnambule, Le*, **17**
Regnard, Jean-F. Renard, dit. *Folies amoureuses, Les*, **29**
Rivière-Dufresny, Charles. *Esprit de contradiction, L'*, **15**
Rousseau, Jean-Jacques. *Devin du village, Le*, **23**

Rousseau, Jean-Jacques. *Pygmalion*, **20**
Saurin, Bernard-J. *Beverley*, **18**
Sedaine, Michel-J. *Gageure imprévue, La*, **15**
Voltaire, F.-M. Arouet, dit Arouet de. *Brutus*, **17**
Voltaire, F.-M. Arouet, dit Arouet de. *Nanine*, **25**

Table 11. Attendance at the Comédie Italienne
(Opéra Comique) 1760-1785; 1789-1893

```
AVERAGE/YEAR   (1760-1785):    183,124
AVERAGE/DAY                :       601

AVERAGE/YEAR   (1789-1793):    212,698
AVERAGE/DAY                :       646
```

Source: Clarence D. Brenner, *The Theatre Italien: Its Repertory, 1716-1793*
Berkeley: University of California Press, 1961. The table above gives our
computations based on Brenner's daily attendance records. The period
1760-1785 is based on the years 1760, 1765, 1770, 1775, 1780, 1785; the
years 1789-1793 are inclusive. The table proves that in spite of the open competition among four or five times as many theatres as existed before the Le
Chapelier Law of 1791, the Theatre Italien held its own. One may resonably
conclude that theatre going was, as contemporaries thought, more frequent
than ever.

Table 12. List of Plays Censured by the Commission of
Public Instruction, April to July 1794

A. Rejected Plays

Nanine [Voltaire, 192 performances]
Beverley [Saurin, 65]
Le Glorieux [Destouches, 102]
Le Jeu d'amour et du hasard [Marivaux, 169]
Le Dissipateur [Destouches, 99]
Le Joueur [Regnard, 61]
L'Avocat patelin [Brueys, 199]
Plus all Molière's comedies and twenty additional comedies

B. Corrected Plays

Le Devin du village [Rousseau, 264]
Le Père de Famille [Diderot, 139]
La Métromanie [Piron, 108]
Guillaume Tell [Le Mierre, 50]
Les Sans-culottes suisses
Brutus [Voltaire, 107]
La Mort de César [Voltaire, 56]

Mahomet [Voltaire, 95]

C. Authorized Plays

Encore un curé
Plus de bâtards en France
La Papesse Jeanne [Leger, 72]
La Mort de Marat
L'Esprit de prêtres [Prévost-Montfort, 7]
Les Crimes de la noblesse

Source: Vivien 1844, 399: One hundred and fifty one plays were censured of which 33 were rejected and 25 required changes. Thus 38% of plays submitted for approval were censored in one way or another in the three months following the establishment of formal censorship by the law of 25 florial an II [April 1, 1794]. This represents a serious effort to control repertory. Particularly significant is the number of censured plays that appear on our list of the fifty most performed plays of the decade. Conversely none of the authorized plays appear on that list.

Endnotes

PREFACE

1. Emmet Kennedy, "Traitement informatique des répertoires théâtraux pendant la Révolution française," in *Traitements informatiques de textes du 18e siècle, Actes de la Table Ronde...VIe Congrès international des Lumières (Bruxelles, 24-31 juillet 1983)*, série URL "Lexicologie et textes politiques, Equipe '18ème et Révolution,'" *Textes et documents*," Centre National de la Recherche Scientifique, série VII (1984), 43-60; Emmet Kennedy, "L'Image de la Révolution dans le théâtre parisien (1790-1795)," in *L'Image de la Révolution française. Communications présentées lors du Congrès mondial pour le Bicentenaire de la Révolution française, Sorbonne, 6-12 juillet 1989*, vol. 3 (Oxford: Pergamon Press, 1989), 1923-1928; Emmet Kennedy, "Old Regime Drama Performed in French Revolutionary Theatres of Paris, 1789-1799," in *Transactions of the Eighth International Congress on the Enlightenment*, vol. 2 (Oxford: The Voltaire Foundation at the Taylor Institute, 1992), 1235-1238; Emmet Kennedy, *A Cultural History of the French Revolution* (New Haven: Yale University Press, 1989), pp. 168-185, appendices A and B; Emmet Kennedy, "Neues und Altes in der 'Massenliteratur' der Revolutionszeit," in *Die Französische Revolution als Bruch des gesellschaftlichen Bewusstseins*, ed. R. Koselleck et al. (Munich: R. Oldenbourg Verlag, 1988), pp. 305-310; 362-365.

2. M. L. Netter, "Le Théâtre pendant la Révolution française: Instrument et miroir du politique," in *Mentalités et représentations politiques* (Roubaix: Ed. Edires, 1988); M. L. Netter, "L'Intégration de nouvelles valeurs par le théâtre," in *Actes du Colloque Théâtre et Révolution*, vol. 15 of Collection du Bicentenaire de la Révolution française, eds. L. Garbagnati, M. M. Gilli (Annales littéraires de Besançon, No. 393), pp. 25-31.

CHAPTER 1

1. Tissier's repertory covers 41 months; ours 132 months. We have checked our author attributions and titles against Tissier's. Where discrepancies existed, we usually went by the bibliographical entries of the *Catalogue des imprimés* of the Bibliothèque Nationale. André Tissier, *Les Spectacles à Paris pendant la Révolution: Répertoire analytique et bibliographique de la réunion des Etats généraux à la chute de la royauté, 1789-1792* (Paris: Droz, 1992).
2. See L. H. Lecomte, *Histoire des théatres de Paris, les Variétés Amusantes* (Paris: H. Daragon, 1908), p. 200; Maurice Albert, *Les Théâtres des boulevards (1789-1848)* (Paris: Hachette, 1902), p. 87; C. Alasseur, *La Comédie Française au 18e siècle: Etude économique* (Paris: Mouton, 1967), p. 141; Clarence D. Brenner, *The Théâtre Italien. Its Repertory, 1716-1793* (Berkeley: Univ. of California Press, 1961), p. 19; Gabriel Vauthier, "Le Théâtre de l'Estrapade," *Revue historique de la Révolution* 10 (1922), 284-287; L. H. Lecomte, *Le Théâtre de la Cité 1792-1807* (Paris: H. Daragon, 1910), pp. 4-6; Henri Lagrave, *Le Théâtre et le public à Paris de 1715 à 1750* (Paris: Klincksieck, 1972), p. 86; Albert de Lasalle, *Les Treize salles de l'Opéra* (Paris: Sartorius, 1875), p. 181; L. H. Lecomte, *La Montansier, ses aventures, ses entreprises (1730-1830)* (Paris: Librairie F. Juven [1904?]), p. 122.

CHAPTER 2

1. This chapter as well as chapters 4, 6, 7, and parts of chapter 9 were translated from the French by Emmet Kennedy.

CHAPTER 3

1. Napoléon, *Mémorial de Sainte Hélène,* quoted in P. Trahard ed., *Paul et Virginie* (Paris: Garnier, 1964), pp. xxx-xxxi.

CHAPTER 5

1. The text of the August 2 decree can be found in the *Archives Parlementaires de 1787 à 1860, Recueil complet des débats législatifs et politiques des chambres françaises,* première série (1787 à 1799), eds. J. Mavidal and E. Laurent, 82 vols. (Paris: Librairie Dupont, 1867-1913), vol. 70, pp. 134-135. Couthon of the Committee of Public Safety proposed the decree to the Convention.
2. However, the lines: "Arrêter un Romain sur de simples soupçons,/C'est agir

en tyrans, nous qui les punissions" (*Brutus,* IV, vii), which could have been taken as an allusion to the "surveillance" of "suspects" during the Terror and so were changed, according to A. F. Villemain, to "Arrêter un Romain sur un simple soupçon,/Ne peut être permis qu'en révolution" (cf. *Brutus,* in *Oeuvres complètes de Voltaire,* vol. 1. (Paris: Garnier 1877), p. 371. I have found helpful the plot summaries of Henry Carrington Lancaster's *French Tragedy in the Time of Louis XV and Voltaire, 1715-1774,* vol. 1 (Baltimore: Johns Hopkins University Press 1950), p. 126, and his *French Tragedy in the Reign of Louis XVI and the Early Years of the French Revolution, 1774-1792* (Baltimore: Johns Hopkins University Press, 1953), pp. 115-116, for *Brutus* and *Caïus Gracchus.*

3. I express my gratitude to members of the Johns Hopkins Humanities Seminar for pointing this out when I presented a preliminary version of this work to them in April 1985.

4. Ridgway 1961, pp. 71-74; P. Gay 1959, Ch. 13 and appendix 2; Niklaus 1963, p. 1240; and Voltaire, "Idées républicaines par un membre d'un corps," in *Oeuvres* (Paris: Pleiade, 1971), p. 516: "Le plus tolérable de tous [les gouvernements] est sans doute le républicain, parce que c'est celui qui rapproche le plus des hommes de l'égalité naturelle."

CHAPTER 7

1. See Joannidès 1901; Brenner 1961; P. Brunel and S. Wolff, eds., *L'Opéra* (Paris, 1982).

2. As with the authors, see the biographies in Michaud and in Balteau et al.

CHAPTER 8

1. This seems to be the case in John Lough, *Paris Theatre Audiences in the Seventeenth and Eighteenth Centuries* (London, [1957]; 1972), Ch. 3; Maurice Descotes, *Le Public de théâtre et son histoire* (Paris: Presses Universitaires de France, 1964), Ch. 7. While Descotes devotes only one chapter to the theatre of the Revolution, it is one of the best pieces written on the subject. The popularization of audiences began before the Revolution. See Jean François de La Harpe, *Correspondance littéraire addressée à son Altesse Impériale...aujourd'hui Empereur de Russie* Vol 4. (Paris: Migneret, *an* IX [1801]-1807), pp. 74-75: "nos spectacles ne sont plus ce qui ils ont été, une assemblée choisie d'amateurs et d'hommes plus ou moins instruits: c'est le rendez-vous d'une foule désoeuvrée et ignorante, depuis que le peuple des petits spectacles n'a eu besoin pour envahir les grands, que de payer un peu plus cher un plaisir dont on lui a donné le goût, et qui n'était pas fait pour lui. La

Multitude des sots donne la loi du moment."

2. Pierre Trahard, *La Sensibilité révolutionnaire* (Paris: Boivin, 1936). On 22 Brumaire *an* II (November 12, 1793), the *Journal de Paris* reported a trial before the Tribunal Révolutionnaire. Several witnesses had falsely accused three elderly persons of "comments tending to the reestablishment of royal authority and the vilification of the constituted authorities." The Assembly, the *Journal* reported, "shuddered with horror." "The Revolutionary Tribunal ordered that the four witnesses be immediately imprisoned and arrested (*sic*); that an act of accusation (indictment) be drawn up against them....The citizen Mme Dethorre asked pardon for her calumniators. Here a touching scene took place. Tears fell, but the People who always manifest themselves good and just, demanded justice and applauded this judgment of the Tribunal crying 'Vive la République.'"

Wolfe Tone, lamenting the French edulcorating Shakespeare (*Othello*) for Parisian audiences comments in 1796: "I admire a Nation that will guillotine sixty people a day for months, men, women, and children, and cannot bear the catastrophe of a dramatic exhibition!" Quoted by Tone's biographer Marianne Elliott, *Wolfe Tone, Prophet of Irish Independence* (New Haven: Yale University Press, 1989), p. 283. On Shakespeare in the Revolution, see Matthew Ramsey, "Revolutionary Politics and Revolutionary Culture, Shakespeare in France, 1789-1815" in David G. Troyansky, Alfred Cismaru and Norwood Andrews, Jr., eds., *The French Revolution in Culture and Society* (Westport, Conn.: Greenwood Press, 1991), pp. 57-69.

3. Caron, vol. 1, p. 35. See Root-Bernstein, pt. 4 and Appendix, Table 5, which shows that "pre-revolutionary" or borrowed repertory prevailed in three of the six boulevard theatres studied (the Gaîté, the Théâtre Patriotique, the Délassements Comiques), whereas the Variétés Amusantes, the Théâtre Français Comique et Lyrique, and the Ambigu Comique had a prevalence of new (which was not necessarily "Revolutionary") repertory. Nicolet's Gaîté, possibly the largest and most notorious boulevard theatre, offered a decidedly traditional boulevard repertory throughout the Revolution.

4. The playwrights included Marsollier des Vivetières, Picard, Laya, Grétry, Cherubini, Devienne, Planterre, and many others who worked for the instruction and *délassement* of their fellow citizens.

5. *P. A.* 25 Germinal *an* III [April 14, 1794], p. 3627; cf. ibid., October 2, 1793, p. 4154; May 25, 1794, p. 7771; 11 Brumaire *an* II [November 1, 1793], p. 139.

6. Concerning patriotism on stage there exists a collection in the Library of Congress's Rare Book Room consisting of one hundred published plays of the Revolutionary period, cataloged as "Pièces de Théâtre: Littérature patriotique," (PQ 1213. P55, vols. 1-22). While almost half (42) of these plays was never performed according to our records, of those 58 that were, the average performance count was 39.4, considerably higher than the average performance

record of 24 for all other plays. A helpful reprint of 132 plays of the Revolution, *Le Théâtre de la Révolution et de l'Empire,"* was published by Marc Regaldo (Microeditions Hachette, n.d.)—a microfiche collection.

CHAPTER 9

1. This is the interpretation suggested by the historian R. R. Palmer (letter to Emmet Kennedy, ca. 1980).

References

Abbott, E. B. 1936. "Robineau, dit de Beaunoir, et les petits théâtres du XVIIIe siècle." *Revue d'Histoire Littéraire de France*, 43: 20-54, 161-180.

Alasseur, C. 1967. *La Comédie française au 18e siècle. Etude économique.* Paris and The Hague: Mouton.

Albert, M. 1902. *Les Théâtres des boulevards (1789-1848).* Paris: Société Française d'Imprimerie et de Librairie.

Allorge, H. 1921. "Charlot, Janot et Jocrisse." *Grande Revue,* 106: 611-633.

Bachaumont, L. P. de. 1777. *Mémoires pour servir à l'histoire de la République des lettres en France depuis 1762.* 36 vols. London: Adamson.

Balteau, J., M. Prévost, M. Barroux, and Roman d'Amat. 1933-. *Dictionnaire de biographie française,* 17 vols. to date. Paris: Librairie Letougey et Ané.

Barbier, Frédéric. 1979. *Trois cent ans de librairie et d'imprimerie Berger-Levrault, 1676-1830.* Geneva: Droz.

Beaulieu, H. 1905. *Les Théâtres du boulevard du crime de Nicolet à Déjazet, 1752-1862.* Paris: H. Daragon.

Bingham, A. J. 1939. *Marie Joseph Chénier. Early Political Life and Ideas (1789-1794).* New York: Privately printed.

Blanchard, E. 1980. *Saint-Just et Cie.: La Révolution et les mots.* Paris: Nizet.

Bonnassiès, J. 1875. *Les Spectacles forains et la Comédie française à Paris au XVIIe et XVIIIe siècles.* Paris: E. Dentu.

Bouet, M. 1934. "Le Palais Royal de 1784 à 1831." In *Les Oeuvres libres,* 153: 293-338.

Brazier, N. 1838. *Chroniques des petits théâtres de Paris.* 2 vols. Paris: Allardin.

Brenner, Clarence D. 1947. *A Bibliographical List of Plays in the French Language, 1700-1789.* Berkeley: Privately published.

_____. 1961. *The Théâtre Italien, Its Repertory 1716-1793*. Berkeley: University of California Press.

Brunet, Charles. 1914. *Table des pièces de théâtre décrites dans le Catalogue de la bibliothèque de M. de Soleinne*. Paris: Damascène Morgand.

Campardon, Emile. 1877. *Les spectacles de la foire*. 2 vols. Paris: Berger-Levrault.

Carlson, M. 1966. *The Theater of the French Revolution*. Ithaca, N.Y.: Cornell University Press.

Caron, P., ed. 1910-1978. *Paris pendant la Terreur: Rapports des agents secrets du ministre de l'Intérieur*. 7 vols. Paris: A. Picard.

Catalogue de la précieuse bibliothèque de M. G. Pixerécourt. n.p. n.d. [Paris: Bibliothèque du Sénat.]

Charlton, David. 1986. *Grétry and the Growth of Opéra-Comique*. Cambridge: University of Cambridge Press.

Cioranescu, Alexandre. 1969. *Bibliographie de la littérature française du 18e siècle*. 3 vols. Paris: Editions du CNRS (Centre Nationale de la Recherche Scientifique).

Cochin, A., ed. 1935. *Les Actes du gouvernement révolutionnaire (23 août 1793-27 juillet 1794)*. Vol. 3. Paris: A. Picard.

Darnton, Robert. 1968. "The Grub Street Style of Revolution: J. P. Brissot, Police Spy." *Journal of Modern History*, 40: 301-327.

_____ 1971. "The High Enlightenment and the Low-Life of Literature in Pre-Revolutionary France." *Past and Present*, 51: 81-115.

_____ 1973. "The *Encyclopédie* Wars of Pre-Revolutionary France." *American Historical Review*, 78: 1331-1352.

_____. 1982. *The Literary Underground of the Old Regime*. Cambridge, Mass.: Harvard University Press.

Descotes, Maurice. 1964. *Le Public de théâtre et son histoire*. Paris: Presses Universitaires de France.

Diderot, Denis. 1966. *Rameau's Nephew* [bound with *D'Alembert's Dream*]. Trans. Leonard Tancock. Hammondsworth: Penguin.

Estrée, P. d'. [Henri Quentin]. 1913. *Le Théâtre sous la Terreur*. Paris: Emile Paul Frères.

Etienne, C. G., and A. Martainville. An XI [1802]. *Histoire du théâtre français depuis le commencement de la Révolution jusqu'à la Réunion générale*. 4 vols. Paris: Barba.

Flandrin, Jean Louis. 1979. *Families in Former Times: Kinship, Household and Sexuality*. Cambridge: Cambridge University Press.

Furet, François. 1992. *Revolutionary France, 1770-1880*. Trans. Antonia Nevill. Oxford: Blackwell Publishers.

Gay, Peter. *Voltaire's Politics*. 1959; 2nd ed. 1988. New Haven: Yale University Press.

Grimm, F. M., et al. 1877-1882. *Correspondance littéraire, philosophique et critique*. Ed. Maurice Tourneux, vol. 10. Paris: Garnier Frères.

Grove, Sir George, and Stanley Sadie. 1980. *The New Grove Dictionary of Music and Musicians*. 20 vols. London: Macmillan.

Guilbert, Noëlle, and Jacqueline Razgonnikoff. 1989. *Le Journal de la Comédie française, 1789-1799: La Comédie aux trois couleurs*. Sides Empreintes.

Hamiche, D. 1973. *Le Théâtre et la Révolution. La Lutte des classes au théâtre en 1789 et en 1793*. Paris: Union Générale d'Editions.

Herbert, R. L. 1973. *David, Voltaire, Brutus and the French Revolution*. New York: Viking.

Hérissay, J. 1922. *Le Monde des théâtres pendant la Révolution, 1789-1800*. Paris: Perrin.

Hesse, C. 1991. *Publishing and Cultural Politics in Revolutionary Paris, 1789-1810*. Berkeley: University of California Press.

Holmes, Stephen. 1984. *Benjamin Constant and the Making of Modern Liberalism*. New Haven: Yale University Press.

Huet, M. H. 1982. *Rehearsing the Revolution: The Staging of Marat's Death, 1793-97*. Berkeley: University of California Press.

Hyslop, Beatrice. 1945. "The Theater During a Crisis: The Parisian Theater During the Reign of Terror." *Journal of Modern History*, 17: 332-335.

Jauffret, E. 1869. *Le Théâtre révolutionnaire, 1788-1799*. Paris: P. Furne, Jouvet.

Joannidès, A. 1901. *La Comédie Française de 1680 à 1900*. Paris: Plon Nourrit & Cie.

Kennedy, Emmet. 1984. Traitement informatique des répertoires théâtraux pendant la Révolution française." In *Traitements informatiques de textes du 18e siècle, Actes de la Table Ronde....VIe Congrès international des Lumières (Bruxelles, 24-31 juillet 1983)*, série URL "Lexicologie et textes politiques, Equipe 18e et Révolution." *Textes et documents*, série VII (1984), pp. 43-60.

———. 1989. "L'Image de la Révolution dans le théâtre parisien (1790-1795)." In *L'Image de la Révolution française. Communications présentées lors du Congrès mondial pour le Bicentenaire de la Révolution française, Sorbonne, 6-12 juillet 1989*. 4 vols. to date. Oxford: Pergamon Press. Vol. 3, pp. 1923-1928.

———. 1992. "Old Regime Drama Performed in French Revolutionary Theatres of Paris, 1789-1799." *Transactions of the Eighth International Congress on the Enlightenment*. Oxford: The Voltaire Foundation at the Taylor Institute. Vol. 2, pp. 1235-1238.

Lacroix, Sigismund. 1894-1914. *Actes de la Commune de Paris pendant la Révolution*. 16 vols. Paris: Le Cerf.

Lagrave, Henri. 1972. *Le Théâtre et le public à Paris de 1715 à 1750*. Paris: Klincksieck.

Lecomte, H. 1905. *La Montansier: Ses aventures, ses entreprises, 1720-1820*. Paris: Juven.

_____. 1908. *Histoire des théâtres de Paris. Les Variétés Amusantes*. Paris: L'Auteur.

_____. 1910. *Le Théâtre de la Cité, 1792-1807*. Paris: L'Auteur.

Lieby, A. 1903-1904. "La Presse révolutionnaire et la censure théâtrale sous la Terreur." *Révolution française*, 45 (1903): pp. 306-53, 447-470, 502-529; 46 (1904): pp. 13-28, 97-128.

Lintilhac, E. 1904-1911. *La Comédie au XVIIIe siècle*. Vol. 4, 5 of *Histoire générale du théâtre en France*. Paris: E. Flammarion.

McKee, Kenneth N. 1941. "Voltaire's *Brutus* During the French Revolution." *Modern Language Notes*, 56 (1941): 100-106.

Mercier, L. S. 1773. *Du Théâtre, ou Nouvel essai sur l'art dramatique*. Amsterdam: E. Van Harrevelt.

Michaud, J. F. ed. 1854-62. *Biographie universelle ancienne et moderne*. 45 vols. Paris: Desplaces.

Mili, M. 1989. "L'Ecole de la vertu: Fonction didactique du théâtre pendant la Révolution française. 1789-1799." In *Image de la Révolution française*, Ed. Michel Vovelle. Paris: Pergamon Press. Vol. 3, pp. 1917-1922.

Netter, Marie-Laurence. 1988. "Le théâtre pendant la Révolution française: Instrument et miroir du politique." In *Mentalités et représentations politiques*. Roubaix: Ed. Edires.

_____. 1989. "L'Intégration de nouvelles valeurs par le théâtre." In *Actes du Colloque Théâtre et Révolution*. Vol. 15 of Collection du Bicentennaire de la Révolution française, eds. L. Garbagnati, M. M. Gilli. Annales littéraires de Besançon, No. 393, pp. 25-31.

_____. 1991. "L'image cachée de Robespierre à travers le théâtre pré-Thermidorien." In *Robespierre saisi par le théâtre*. Arras: Centre Culturel Noroit.

_____. 1992. "De L. S. Mercier à Pixerécourt: Le Mélodrame nécessaire." In *Il Melodrammatico*. Ed. M. Mengoli. Bologna: Università di Bologna.

Niklaus, Robert. 1963. "La Propagande philosophique au siècle des lumières." *Studies on Voltaire and the Eighteenth Century*, 26: 1223-1261.

Parker, H. T. [1937] 1965. *The Cult of Antiquity and the French Revolutionaries*. New York: Octagon.

Pougin, A. 1891. *L'Opéra-comique pendant la Révolution de 1788 à 1801*. Paris: Savine.

_____. 1902. *La Comédie française et la Révolution: Scènes récits et notices*. Paris: Gaultier, Magnier.

_____. 1903. "Un théâtre révolutionnaire en 1791. Le Théâtre Molière." *Bulletin de la Société de l'Histoire du Théâtre*, 6: 4-26.

Radicchio, G., and M. S. D'Oria. 1990. *Les Théâtres de Paris pendant la Révolution.* Fasano, Italy: Elemond Periodici.

Ramsey, Matthew. "Revolutionary Politics and Revolutionary Culture, Shakespeare in France, 1789-1815." In *The French Revolution in Culture and Society,* pp. 57-69. Ed. David G. Troyansky, Alfred Cismaro, and Norwood Andrews, Jr. Westport, Conn.: Greenwood Press, 1991.

Regaldo, Marc. 1976. *Un milieu intellectuel: La Décade philosophique, 1794-1807.* 5 vols. Lille: Université Lille III, Atelier [des] Reproductions des Thèses. Vol. 3.

Ridgway, Ronald S. 1961. "La Propagande philosophique dans les tragédies de Voltaire." *Studies on Voltaire and the Eighteenth Century.* 15 vols. Oxford: The Voltaire Foundation.

Root-Bernstein. Michèle. 1984. *Boulevard Theater and Revolution in Eighteenth-Century Paris.* Ann Arbor, Mich.: UMI Research Press.

Sadie, Stanley, ed. 1992. *The New Grove Dictionary of Opera.* 4 vols. London: Macmillan.

Saint-Just, A. L. L. 1984. *Oeuvres complètes.* Ed. Michèle Duval. Paris: Editions Gerard Lebovic.

Sarcey, F. 1884. *Théâtre choisi de Dancourt.* New ed. Paris: Laplace, Sanchez et Cie.

Schlanger, J. 1979. *L'Enjeu et le débat. Les Passées intellectuelles.* Paris: Denoël/Gonthier.

Schmidt, A., ed. 1867-1870. *Tableaux de la Révolution française publiés sur les papiers inédits du département de la police secrète de Paris.* 3 vols. Leipzig: Veit.

Thomasseau, J. M. 1984. *Le Mélodrame.* Series "Que sais-je?" Paris: Presses Universitaires de France.

Tissier, André. 1992. *Les Spectacles à Paris pendant la Révolution: Répertoire analytique, chronologique et bibliographique. De la réunion des Etats généraux à la chute de la royauté. 1789-1792.* Geneva: Droz.

Tourneux, Maurice. 1890-1913. *Bibliographie de l'histoire de Paris pendant la Révolution française.* Paris: Imprimerie Nouvelle.

Traer, James F. 1980. *Marriage and the Family in Eighteenth Century France.* Ithaca, N.Y.: Cornell University Press.

Tuetey, Alexandre. 1890-1914. *Répertoire général des sources manuscrites de l'histoire de Paris pendant la Révolution française.* 11 vols. Paris: Imprimerie Nouvelle.

Vivien. 1844. "Etudes Administratives, III. *Les Théâtres, leur situation actuelle an Angleterre et en France.*" *Revue des Deux Mondes,* n.s. 14, 6: 377-439.

Voltaire. 1784-1789. *Oeuvres complètes*. Ed. Caron de Beaumarchais et al.
          70 vols. [Kehl, Germany]: Société Littéraire Typographique. Vols.
          1,2,7.
Welschinger, H. [1880]. 1968. *Le Théâtre de la Révolution, 1789-1799*.
          Paris and Geneva: Slatkine.

Index

About the Authors

EMMET KENNEDY is Professor of European History at the George Washington University. He is author of *A Cultural History of the French Revolution, A Philosophe in the Age of Revolution: Destutt de Tracy and the Origins of 'Ideology,'* and coeditor of *The Shaping of Modern France: Writings on French History Since 1715.*

MARIE-LAURENCE NETTER is researcher at the Centre de Recherches Historiques, Ecole des Hautes Etudes en Sciences Sociales in Paris. In addition to numerous articles on education, theatre, and the French Revolution, she is author of *La Révolution française n'est pas terminée.*

JAMES P. McGREGOR is senior policy officer at the Office of Policy, United States Information Agency. He is author of numerous articles on Eastern Europe, Slavic studies, and political science.

MARK V. OLSEN is assistant director of the ARTFL Project at the University of Chicago. He is author of numerous articles on French history and computer science.

ISBN 0-313-28960-3

9 780313 289606

EAN

90000>

HARDCOVER BAR CODE